CUBANS: AN EPIC JOURNEY
THE STRUGGLE OF EXILES FOR TRUTH AND FREEDOM

SAM VERDEJA
GUILLERMO MARTÍNEZ

Copyright © 2011, Facts About Cuban Exiles, Inc.
All rights reserved.

Facts About Cuban Exiles, Inc.
9521 SW 103 St.
Miami, FL 33176

Published in cooperation with
Reedy Press
PO Box 5131
St. Louis, MO 63139, USA

No part of this publication may be reproduced or transmitted in any form or by any means, electronic or mechanical, including photocopy, recording, or any information storage and retrieval system, without permission in writing from the publisher.

Permissions may be sought directly from Reedy Press at the above mailing address or via our website at www.reedypress.com.

Library of Congress Control Number: 2011945128

ISBN: 979-8324125172

Please visit our website at www.reedypress.com.

Cover Design: República, LLC Advertising and Communication Companies

Printed in the United States
11 12 13 14 15   5 4 3 2 1

This book is dedicated to the memory of thousands of Cubans victims of the Castro communist regime—from those that were executed after summary trials before firing squads to others that languished in political prisons for daring to express their opinions.

It is dedicated to those brave men and women that took up arms against their totalitarian oppressors as well as to those brave enough to face the waves and drowned escaping the island-prison.

Unfortunately, as of this writing this great national tragedy is still ongoing, and so this book must also be dedicated to those human rights activists that have recently given up their lives or their liberties in order to demand from the state their God-given rights.

It is also dedicated to those separated from their families forced to seek a life outside their beloved homeland, and those family members left behind to live without the comfort of having their loved ones at home with them.

Finally, this work is dedicated to the late Tere Zubizarreta and Luis Botifoll, two of the founding members of Facts About Cuban Exiles (FACE), instrumental in getting out the word about the life and work of those who chose freedom and rebuilt their lives while staying faithful to the democratic principles they brought with them into exile.

César Pizarro
Chairman of the Board
FACE

ACKNOWLEDGMENTS

We would like to thank our sponsors for their contribution helping us achieve the objectives of this project:

The John S. and James L. Knight Foundation

The Armando Codina Family

First Bank of Miami

Mr. Carlos Migoya

Riteway Properties

We would also like to thank these companies and individuals for their support and cooperation:

The *Miami Herald* for providing many of the photos.

Republica LLC for the design of the book cover.

Juan Walte for translations.

Thirty-one writers and editors selflessly gave up their time and effort into producing this comprehensive history of Cubans in exile. This book is the result of their work, their research, and their own personal experiences. All must be recognized.

Most of all we want to thank the government and the people of the United States for opening their arms and hearts to hundreds of thousands of exiles who had lost their homeland and for allowing them to enjoy the political and economic freedoms this great nation has to offer.

CONTENTS

Acknowledgments		iv
Preface	*by Francisco Rodríguez*	ix
Introduction	*by Carlos Alberto Montaner*	xiii

PART I: THE HISTORY

Chapter 1	Cuba: Before the Revolution *by Guillermo Martínez and Sam Verdeja*	5
Chapter 2	Miami Before the Revolution *by Howard Kleinberg*	20
Chapter 3	Batista Flees, Castro Takes Over *by Guillermo Martínez and Sam Verdeja*	30
Chapter 4	The First Exiles *by Guillermo Martínez and Sam Verdeja*	47
Chapter 5	Bay of Pigs: A Program of Covert Action *by Howard Kleinberg*	56
Chapter 6	Bay of Pigs: The Invasion *by Howard Kleinberg*	70
Chapter 7	Bay of Pigs: The Aftermath *by Howard Kleinberg*	85
Chapter 8	The Missile Crisis *by Guillermo Martínez and Sam Verdeja*	102
Chapter 9	Camarioca to the Diálogo *by Guillermo Martínez and Sam Verdeja*	122
Chapter 10	The Mariel Exodus *by Silvia M. Unzueta*	142

Chapter 11	Not My-Ami *by Silvia M. Unzueta and Guillermo Martínez*	159
Chapter 12	Balseros *by Guillermo Martínez, Francisco Rodríguez, and Sam Verdeja*	175
Chapter 13	Elián *by Guillermo Martínez and Sam Verdeja*	192
Chapter 14	Executions and Political Prisoners *by Juan Clark*	213
Chapter 15	The Defense of Human Rights by the Exiles *by Juan Clark*	238
Chapter 16	The Cuban Diaspora *by Leonardo Rodríguez*	247

PART II: THE EXILE EXPERIENCE

Introduction to Part II *by Louise O'Brien*	272

Business and Finance

Chapter 17	Cuban Exiles' Impact in Banking *by Francisco Rodríguez, Leonardo Rodríguez, and Sam Verdeja*	278
Chapter 18	Entrepreneurs: The Pioneers *by Francisco Rodríguez, Leonardo Rodríguez, and Sam Verdeja*	288
Chapter 19	Entrepreneurs: The New Generation *by Francisco Rodríguez, Leonardo Rodríguez, and Sam Verdeja*	312
Chapter 20	Leaders in Corporate America *by Francisco Rodríguez, Leonardo Rodríguez, and Sam Verdeja*	325

Arts, Entertainment, and Religion

Chapter 21	Cuba's Wandering Literature *by Olga Connor*	334
Chapter 22	Plastic Arts *by Olga I. Nodarse*	355
Chapter 23	Theater *by Francisco Rodríguez*	384
Chapter 24	Movies and Documentaries *by Alejandro Ríos*	398
Chapter 25	Popular Music *by Eloy Cepero and Sonia Frías*	417
Chapter 26	Classical Music and Ballet *by Eloy Cepero and Sonia Frías*	434
Chapter 27	Cuban Sports Before and After the Revolution *by Roly Martín*	443
Chapter 28	Religion *by Marcos Antonio Ramos*	467

Media and Advertising

Chapter 29	Print Media *by Armando González*	486
Chapter 30	Electronic Media *by Alberto Vilar, José Cancela, and Guillermo Martínez*	501
Chapter 31	Advertising and Public Relations *by Aida Levitán*	522

Professionals

Chapter 32	Medicine *by René F. Rodríguez*	550
Chapter 33	Engineering and Science *by José C. Irastorza*	567

Chapter 34	Architecture *by Raúl L. Rodríguez*	587
Chapter 35	Accountants in Exile *by Enrique Viciana and Leonardo Rodríguez*	596
Chapter 36	Education *by Federico R. Justiniani, Rogelio de la Torre, and Eduardo Zayas-Bazán*	606
Chapter 37	Lawyers and Judges *by René V. Murai*	636

Political, Civic, and Social Life

Chapter 38	Exiles in U.S. Politics *by Carlos Curbelo*	656
Chapter 39	Exile Civic and Social Organizations *by José R. Garrigó*	671
Epilogue	The Cuban Nation *by Raúl Chao*	695

Appendixes

Appendix I	Timeline of the History of Cuba A Chronology of Key Events, 1940-2011 *by Leonardo Rodríguez*	716
Appendix II	Cuba 1958: By the Numbers *by Leonardo Rodríguez*	725
Appendix III	Cuban-American Community in the United States: By the Numbers *by Leonardo Rodríguez*	731
Appendix IV	Human Rights Violations in Cuba *by Juan Clark*	734
Appendix V	The Cuban Diaspora: By the Numbers *by Leonardo Rodríguez*	749
Contributors		757
Index		765

PREFACE
BY FRANCISCO RODRIGUEZ

Cubans have been coming to the United States since the 1860s. Among the first large groups were the exiles who arrived before the turn of the century, during Cuba's war for independence from Spain. They came to raise money, launch expeditions, and procure weapons to aid the rebels back home.

These early immigrants settled mostly in the New York–Philadelphia area, and in Tampa and Key West, Florida, where they created a successful hand-rolled cigar industry. Everything they did was aimed at freeing their homeland from a foreign yoke. When Cuba became a republic in 1902—after the Americans intervened against Spain—most of the exiles returned to the island. However, some remained behind, keeping strong commercial and family ties to Cuba.

Throughout the 20th century, Cubans continued to come to the United States, sometimes in search of jobs, and sometimes fleeing the persecution of corrupt governments. The cities of New York, Key West, Tampa, and—beginning in the 1930s—Miami, received exiles from the regime of President Gerardo Machado, who became a dictator in 1929. After he was ousted in 1933, he too became an exile in Miami. In 1940, Cuba began twelve years of political stability following the adoption of a new constitution. The exile flow diminished, leaving small but prosperous Cuban-American communities where the children became acculturated to American life.

Things began to change in Cuba in 1952, when Fulgencio Batista ousted President Carlos Prío. From this point on—though Cubans continued to settle in New York, Tampa, and Key West—Miami became the undisputed capital for the exiles. It was close enough to Cuba for family visits, and easier to keep in touch with events back home. Once again, Cuban exiles used the U.S. as a base from which to plan and finance military expeditions against the government. They viewed it as a temporary refuge until Batista was overthrown. That day came on January 1, 1959, when Batista and many of his followers fled Cuba. They filled up the flights from Havana to Miami, as well as the Key West ferry, just as thousands of exiles began heading in the opposite direction.

The returning exiles looked forward to a life in their homeland without a dictator in power. They joined a jubilant population in celebrating what they hoped would be the rebirth of democracy in their beloved island. Their dreams would be short-lived.

Within weeks of taking power, Fidel Castro disavowed the democratic goals he had previously espoused. Over the following year he distanced himself from the United States and moved closer to the Soviet Union. And he made it clear that anyone who didn't agree with him was his enemy. All who dared to oppose him would be crushed.

Throughout 1959, Castro continued to deny he was a Communist, but many of his followers saw that he had no intention of returning Cuba to democracy. His brother Raúl and close colleague Ernesto "Che" Guevara were both avowed Communists, and their influence on Fidel became more apparent every day. First to face the firing squads were members of Batista's Cuban Armed Forces. They were sentenced in summary trials and executed within forty-eight hours. The next, larger wave of executions encompassed all opponents of the new regime, even some who had previously supported the "revolution."

Prior to Castro's rule, the death penalty had not existed in Cuba. Murder and torture were used by previous regimes, but surreptitiously. Now the firing squad became a public part of "revolutionary justice." Slowly at first, the government began to confiscate properties and businesses, initially positioning it as recuperating "the ill-gotten profits of Batista followers." Next in line were companies owned by foreign "monopolies"—mostly American. They were followed by Cuban-owned businesses. This was all carried out in the name of "social justice."

Some Cubans—particularly the educated and middle class—were dismayed to realize that Castro's promise of democracy had been nothing but propaganda to win over the Cuban population, and keep the United States at bay. And it had worked. Now that Castro was in control, it looked as though his authoritarian regime might be the worst yet in the history of the young republic. In time it would become clear that this early authoritarianism was the first step on the road to Stalinist totalitarianism.

Those with sufficient visibility to see what Castro was doing began to leave Cuba for the United States, from which they hoped to engineer the overthrow of yet another repressive regime. By early 1961, the trickle became a steady stream. Even when President Eisenhower broke off diplomatic relations with Cuba on January 3, 1961, in protest for Castro ordering a sharp cutback in personnel at the U.S. Embassy, the exodus continued.

These new arrivals continued to think of themselves as Cuban exiles rather than U.S. immigrants. They believed their sojourn here would be temporary, as it had always been in the past. For the U.S., Cuba was the first outpost in Latin America. Cubans—as well as many Americans—were convinced that the U.S. would never tolerate a communist regime ninety miles south of its shores.

For a while, they had good reason to hope. The CIA was recruiting young Cubans and sending them to training camps in Central America. Many Cubans in Miami learned this through the rumor mill, and they waited for the inevitable American-supported invasion to begin. It looked as though Castro's rule would be brief, and that they would soon be returning to their homeland to resume their lives.

The Bay of Pigs invasion took place on April 17, 1961. It was doomed by President Kennedy's fateful decision to cut-off American support in the middle of the invasion. Even after that disaster, the Cuban exiles kept the flame of freedom burning in their hearts while they waited for the triumphant return to their homeland. Castro opponents on the island still fought the regime in the underground and in guerrilla groups in the Escambray Mountains in central Cuba.

More than half a century passed.

This is the history of those Cuban exiles.

INTRODUCTION
BY CARLOS ALBERTO MONTANER

Cubans: An Epic Journey is a historical overview—from the 1950s to the present—of the relationship between the people and government of Cuba, and the people and government of the United States. It takes us down the Cubans' road into exile, dramatizing their struggle for freedom against Castro's totalitarianism, and the triumphs and tribulations of their diaspora.

The book highlights an important difference between Cubans and most other immigrant groups: Cubans are political exiles who have courageously opposed a Communist dictatorship. Many of them fought heroically in the underground, and the survivors went into exile in large numbers, or escaped under dramatic circumstances, often after many years in prison. From this exile group emerged the members of the expeditionary force of the Bay of Pigs—almost fifteen hundred young people—and back into exile they returned after serving almost two years in prison.

Because the Cuban exiles living in the United States, mainly in South Florida, represent 55 percent of the diaspora, they are the main focus of the book.[1] There are also brief overviews of the Cuban communities in places like Venezuela, Puerto Rico, Spain, Mexico—and even those who were left behind in the Eastern European countries as a result of Cuba's three-decade-long membership in the Soviet bloc.

Cubans: An Epic Journey is rich in data and offers reasonable interpretations of historic events. It provides multiple perspectives on one of the most successful ethnic groups incorporated into the American melting pot. American society tends to look carefully at each of the parts that make up the nation. This is a good thing, as it is always useful to know who you are and where you came from, and the idea of "Americans" is an abstraction too general to explain a great country. Focusing on the dozens of individual component ethnic groups can sharpen the view. While the objective of any republic is to merge ethnic groups into a legal melting pot through voluntary adherence to a common law, it remains important to understand the makeup of any country's ethnic map.

Going by numbers only, Cubans are a relatively small segment of Hispanic America. They are the third largest Hispanic grouping after Mexican-Americans, who make up 63 percent, and Puerto Ricans, who represent 9.2 percent. Cubans are only 3.5 percent of Hispanic Americans, and less than 1 percent (0.57 percent) of the U.S. population (even if we include the children and grandchildren born in the country that welcomed them) This represents about 1.8 million people, though the method of counting is imprecise since each individual decides whether or not to register his or her Cuban descent on the decennial census form.[2]

Cubans have adapted admirably to the United States, and they are a remarkably successful group of immigrants. Their income is close to that of the average white American, they are well-educated, and they have quickly learned the peculiar democratic game of the country. Cuban-Americans have elected three U.S. senators and six members of the U.S. House of Representatives, as well as dozens of mayors and other officials in several states. Two Cuban exiles who arrived in the United States as adolescents have served as secretaries in the presidential cabinet, and there are many Cuban-American judges, prosecutors, and ambassadors appointed by state or federal authorities.

Their success is even more remarkable considering that the largest concentration of Cubans is in Greater Miami or Miami-Dade County, an urban area with relatively low wages. If the majority of Cubans were located in Boston or New York, despite shivering in the cold—a bleak prospect for any Caribbean—their income would be higher. But success in Miami has allowed them to establish a kind of "parallel mainstream," where their large middle and upper class can sustain a refined culture—creating and preserving its own music, food, literature, theater, cinema, radio. and television.

A visit to the Book Fair or Film Festival at Miami Dade College illustrates this unique experiment in the United States. The Cubans have created, not a cultural underworld hidden in a ghetto, but their own comfortable and livable mainstream. The operas performed at the Adrienne Arsht Center translate the text into both English and Spanish because sophisticated Cubans love *bel canto*.

Does this emerging parallel culture in South Florida somehow threaten the unity of the United States, at least in this part of the country? Not at all. It enriches American culture. The country's most definitive feature is its ever-changing character. It has an admirable ability to metabolize all those seemingly strange ingredients. After some time, immigrants magically become "Americans," and the America that results from the assimilation is more attractive and complex.

Just like the German, Italian, Russian, and Polish immigrants of the nineteenth century, succeeding generations of Cuban-Americans will set aside the public use of their ancestors' language and relegate it to the home. But they will still preserve the rich cultural footprint left by their elders on the country's urban landscape. That is the richness of nuance that one finds in diverse American communities such as Japanese-Americans and Chinese-Americans in California, or Italian-Americans in New York.

Why have Cubans been able to integrate into American society so successfully and in such a short time? Because by the time Castro took power in 1959, Cuba had achieved a high level of economic and social development that prepared the Cuban urban population well for its upcoming years in exile.

Social and economic progress in Cuba started long before the establishment of the Republic in 1902. Its first university was founded in 1728. During the nineteenth century—called "Cuba's golden century" by historians—Havana was a remarkable city with one of the largest and best-designed theaters of its time, the Teatro Tacón, which hosted European theater and opera companies. In 1898, when Spain's dominion over Cuba ended, the island's literacy rate was higher than that of Spain itself.

There is no doubt that American influence—also going back to the nineteenth century—contributed to Cuba's leadership position among Latin American countries. At the time of the revolution, it was ranked among the first four across most measures of development. Many new technologies—including electricity, telephone, railroads and street cars, radio, aviation, cinema, and television—arrived early in Cuba due to U.S. influence and investment. For example, Cuba had railroads before Spain.

The production of sugar is a complex agro-industrial enterprise that calls for the kind of scientific knowledge usually acquired in universities, as well as technological innovation, the use of large-scale capital, language skills, and international business and financial contacts. Cuba became proficient in these areas because of its North American neighbor's insatiable appetite for sugar. Naturally, the Cuban sugar elite—known as the sacarocracia or sucrosecracy—closely identified itself with American business and society.

New developments in the United States were quickly reproduced and adapted by the Cubans, who had a high regard for the American way of life. And, judging by the continued migratory pattern of the Cubans, it would appear this regard remains intact. A substantial part of the Cuban population still wants to live in the United States.

American companies operating on the island generally paid higher wages than Cuban companies and offered better working conditions. Until the 1950s, workers in electricity and phone companies, oil refineries, and U.S. financial institutions were guaranteed job security, reasonable wages, and opportunities for promotion. The loyalty this generated between Cuban workers and American businesses continued after the Communist government had expropriated U.S. companies, and many of their Cuban employees had fled. Roberto Goizueta was an engineer and partner in a Coca Cola bottling company in Cuba. After going into exile, he continued to work for the same company, and he eventually became its chairman. Under Goizueta's leadership, the Coca Cola Company—a flagship of American capitalism—reached the highest market value in its history.

Will Cubans in American society continue to perform well? All indications are positive, although the exodus of Cubans to the United States is still underway, with 20,000 to 30,000 Cubans entering the United States every year. The number of arrivals from 1990 to 2010 exceeds those who arrived between 1959 and 1980. Is each wave of Cuban exiles different from the last? Of course. Their life experiences were shaped by different key circumstances. However, they share a fundamental trait: the desire to integrate into American society. It's an old relationship based on an admiration that has not been diminished by a half century of intense "anti-Yankee" propaganda in Cuba.

NOTES

1. "Latinos Become Largest Racial Group in Miami-Fort Lauderdale-Palm Beach Metro Area." The Higley 1000: http://higley1000.com/archives/241.
2. United States Census Bureau, "The Hispanic Population: 2010. Census Briefs, Table 1. 'Hispanics or Latin Origin Population by Type: 2000 and 2010.'" Issued May 2011, p. 3.

CUBANS: AN EPIC JOURNEY

PART 1
THE HISTORY

1

CUBA BEFORE THE REVOLUTION

BY GUILLERMO MARTINEZ AND SAM VERDEJA

For more than half a century, Cubans in exile have fought on two fronts—against the Communist regime imposed on their homeland by Fidel Castro, and against the many academics and media throughout the world who defend Castro's revolution because they accept his version of the truth.

When Castro assumed power in January 1959, people outside of Cuba knew little about the state of its economic development and constitutional rights. Castro announced to the world that Cuba was a third- or fourth-world nation with widespread poverty, abysmal illiteracy, and repression of basic human rights. And these claims were widely accepted.

In his 1960 *History of Latin America*, Hubert Herring parroted the Castro credo. "Reflecting upon the sorry state of Cuba in 1960, the onlooker could say that two things are reasonably clear: Cuba was indeed overdue for a revolution and revolutions are never mild and gentlemanly."[1]

Spanish historian Francisco Morales Padrón, in his *Manual de Historia Universal: Historia de America*, said this about Cuba: "Concessions to big landholders ('latifundistas') and big business, etc. were circumstances that kept the rich Caribbean Island as an under-developed nation, without freedom, and as an economic appendix of the United States. The people did not benefit from this corruption; the mass of the people lived and worked in horrendous conditions, working only four months a year. This is why a revolution was needed. The government had to be changed and it did not matter in which way."[2]

Academics such as Herring and Padrón undoubtedly believed they were interpreting history as it had played out, not being used as weapons in a war of propaganda. However, a closer reading of their subject might have provided an education. Fidel Castro was always a believer that propaganda was a vital weapon in revolutionary struggles.

If we step back from the hype surrounding Castro's revolution and examine the actual data, an entirely different picture emerges. In 1958, Cuba's economy was growing at a healthy rate, and the country produced 75 percent of its own food consumption. Three-quarters of Cuba's population could read and write. Cuba had 58 daily newspapers, 160 radio stations, and 23 TV stations—more than any other Latin American country.

It also had a large middle class, with one of the highest per capita income levels in the western hemisphere. Agricultural workers earned a higher hourly wage in Cuba than they did in France, Denmark, or Japan. Wages in the industrial sector exceeded those in Australia, the UK, or Germany. Infant mortality was the lowest in Latin America and thirteenth lowest in the world, and Cuba had more physicians per capita than the UK.[3]

Far from being a struggling underdeveloped nation, Cuba was thriving economically and poised to join the developed countries of the world. Though economic factors played a role in the revolution, at its core it was not about economic deprivation or inequality. The Swedish economist Ingvar Svennilson, invited to Cuba by Castro in 1960, said "Cuba is not by any means an under-developed nation." The technical knowledge he observed among teachers, craftsmen, and specialized workers was not what he would expect in an under-developed nation.[4]

José M. Illán, in his book *Cuba: Facts about an Economy in Ruins*, reports that between 1945 and 1951, Cuba's economy grew more than 8 percent annually, and from 1952 to 1958 the growth "decreased some as a consequence of Batista's coup, but it did not stop."[5]

There are five stages of economic growth for countries, according to American economist W. W. Rostow, who served as political advisor to presidents John F. Kennedy and Lyndon B. Johnson. In his book *The Stages of Economic Growth: A Non-Communist Manifesto*, Rostow lists them as the Traditional Society, Pre-conditions for Take-off, Take-off, Drive to Maturity, and Age of Mass Consumption.[6]

Illán places pre-Castro Cuba in the Take-off stage, citing several factors. New industries were being established at the same time that existing ones were expanding and modernizing. Technological innovation was transforming traditional agriculture in all but a few isolated sectors. Guaranteeing the right of permanence on land had encouraged agrarian reform. Finally, Cuba's labor legislation was ahead of that of most countries, and the labor movement was strong and growing.

Sugar remained Cuba's most important product, but 121 of the 161 sugar mills in the country (which produced 62 percent of the sugar) were owned by Cuban nationals. American corporations owned most of the rest, though often with significant Cuban investors. Prior to World War II, Cuba had used traditional sugar production methods. After the war, the industry introduced new techniques and equipment at larger farms. Cuban farmers extended these methods to other agricultural products; as a result, the productivity of agricultural crops on the island increased rapidly.[7]

Though some economists remained critical of Cuba's dependence on sugar, other agriculture had developed sufficiently to enable Cuba by 1957 to grow 75 percent of its own food. This is one of the most important aspects in determining the stage of development for a country. If a nation can satisfy the food demands of its own people, it can begin accumulating wealth for long-term capital investments. In addition, Cuba's food prices were lower than those of many other countries dependent on food imports. Cuban agricultural production increased steadily between 1940 and 1957, at an annual rate of 3.7 percent, according to the *Economic Study of Latin America*, published in 1957 by the United Nations. This growth outpaced the 2.3 percent annual growth in population.[8]

Economic thinking in Cuba had matured to the point of recognizing that foreign capital was important but should be targeted at specific needs. Cuba was not going back to the days where Spanish or American capital ruled the country's economy. Even by the strictest standards, economists concluded that "the economic pre-conditions in general in Cuba indicated that between 1945 and 1957 the island had definitely entered the 'take-off' stage in spite of the many negative factors, which perturbed it and sometimes made it stumble."[9]

By the mid-1940s, a large number of Cuban workers were unionized under collective agreements. In 1947, the Communists lost control of the Confederación de Trabajadores de Cuba CTC (Cuban Confederation of Workers), which they had captured in the 1930s. Their influence in the trade union movement continued to decline into the 1950s. Between 1952 to 1958, Batista's regime placed tremendous pressure on the labor movement, which caused some independent union leaders to resign from the CTC in protest.

Nonetheless, labor remained a powerful force in Cuban business and national politics. It was the largest organization in the country, with one million members across nearly all sectors of the economy. One half of the workers in Cuba belonged to the fifteen hundred private sector unions represented in the thirty-three federations under the CTC.[10] An indication of the maturity of the relationship between private business and organized labor were the more than five thousand collective bargaining agreements signed and filed with the Ministry of Labor. Additionally, there were thousands of *"actas de advenimiento,"* or acts of agreement, that were legal instruments used to end labor conflicts.[11]

Though wages in certain sectors in Cuba were quite high in the 1950s, the prosperity was not equally shared. Urban workers, especially in the stronger unions, often flourished, while rural workers did not. And unemployment and underemployment in Cuba remained a serious problem. In 1957, Cuba had a working age population of 4.1 million. There were 150,000 underemployed and 361,000 unemployed—a total of 12.5 percent of the population. "The facts were so dramatic that even the most outspoken proponents of the slogan 'without sugar there is no country' understood that sugar had reached its capacity to satisfy the Cuban economical demands and that alone it could not produce enough income to keep a growing population at a decent standard of living."[12]

At the same time, Cuban entrepreneurship had created 330,000 industrial jobs. These workers, along with tens of thousands of professionals, including 6,600 medical doctors, made up the growing Cuban middle class. Many of these became early exiles. Their strong skills and work ethic would make Cuban exiles the most economically successful immigrant group in the United States.

There is no question that Cuba in 1959 had not achieved the full potential of its economy. Too much of the labor force still depended on sugar, which meant many workers were employed just four months a year. However, economic conditions were far better than Castro's propaganda machine and many American study centers led people to believe. Theories that lament American imperialism tend to ignore how much of Cuba's economic success was due to its proximity to the United States. Not only did the U.S. sugar quota guarantee an economic baseline for the island, but American investment played a critical role in the development of mining and light industry. And, without American tourists, there would have been no modern Havana hotels or gambling casinos.

Though wealth distribution in Cuba was not optimal, a couple of indicators suggest prosperity reached deeper into society than Castro's propaganda claimed. Cuba had one of the highest levels of per capita consumption of consumer products in Latin America. It led the region with 23 TV stations compared to Mexico, which was second with just 12. Cuba was also highest in TV sets per capita—56 per thousand inhabitants in 1959, compared to next highest Venezuela, with 29. In the number of telephones, Cuba ranked third, with 2.62 per 100 inhabitants, and in terms of automobile ownership, with 32 cars per hundred people, Cuba ranked third behind Venezuela and Argentina.[13]

Another positive factor in the country's economic development was the Cuban Constitution of 1940—one of the most advanced documents of social legislation in the western hemisphere. It guaranteed many worker rights such as social security, workers' compensation, a forty-four-hour work week with pay for forty-eight, special summer working hours, one month paid vacation, and nine paid sick days per year. It also prohibited discrimination on the basis of race, gender, or region of origin. The Constitution, in a section dedicated to the rights of individuals (Article 20), specifically states that "discrimination due to sex, race, color, or class and any other that might attempt at human dignity is illegal and punishable."[14]

Though the Constitution of 1940 was not perfectly implemented, it vastly improved economic prosperity and the rights of Cuban labor—especially for the first twelve years following its adoption. The only ingredient missing for sustained economic development in Cuba was political stability. Unfortunately, corruption was rampant among elected officials, as it is in many countries. Violence was endorsed by both ends of the political spectrum, and gambling groups in the country, closely affiliated with American Mafia families, had too much influence on government officials.

Most middle-class Cubans just ignored politics. Believing it was a corrupt business, they abstained from participating in the nation's political process. This created a huge vacuum—one that would allow a fringe activist with limited support to take over the entire country and undo the progress achieved over the previous fifty years.

Those who governed the island from 1940 to 1952 were elected through a fair process, openly monitored by a combative free press. Fulgencio Batista's election to president in 1940 was legitimate, as were those of Ramón Grau San Martín in 1944 and Carlos Prío Socarrás in 1948. The latter was a contested election in which a significant group of politicians split from the governing *Partido Revolucionario Cubano* (*Partido Auténtico*) and created their own political party, the *Partido del Pueblo Cubano* (*Partido Ortodoxo*). The founder was the charismatic Eduardo Chibás, who committed suicide in 1951. Most of the institutional progress made in those years came to an abrupt halt on March 10, 1952, when Batista overthrew Prio's Government in a nearly bloodless coup, just months before the scheduled presidential elections.

Cuba's middle class, organized labor, and most of the entrepreneurs on the island generally accepted the new government, which allowed the island's economy to continue to grow. But many others protested publicly, and a few began to conspire secretly against Batista. They did not believe that he would allow free elections in the future as he had done in 1944, when he lost to the opposition. This time, they thought, he'd want to stay in power at any cost.

In his first few months, Batista allowed public debate and criticism and used force sparingly against his opponents. That phase ended on July 26, 1953, when Fidel Castro—a fiery young lawyer with a reputation for violence from his days at the University of Havana's Law School—organized an attack on a government garrison in Santiago de Cuba, in the eastern part of the island.

Castro and his brother Raúl led simultaneous raids on the Moncada barracks, as well as a hospital and several government installations in Santiago de Cuba and Bayamo, another city in Oriente Province. Part of the assault was successful, but its main thrust against the Moncada barracks failed when a guard realized that the attackers' uniforms were not those of the Cuban army.

Historian Hugh Thomas reported in his book *Cuba: The Pursuit of Freedom* that half of the original 160 who participated that day were captured, and most of those captured were killed.[15] According to Antonio Rafael de la Cova's book on the attack, sixty-one rebels died in it or shortly afterward, along with nineteen members of Batista's armed forces and nine civilians. And there were dozens wounded.[16]

Both Castro brothers surrendered. Raúl turned himself in to authorities outside Santiago. Fidel sought refuge with Monsignor Enrique Pérez Serantes, who negotiated with authorities to ensure he would be well treated. Batista showed surprising leniency to the brothers. They were tried publicly, and sentenced to fifteen years in jail. At the end of his trial, Fidel delivered a four-hour extemporaneous speech in which, among other things, he promised to restore the Constitution of 1940. And he ended by saying: "History will absolve me." His speech was smuggled out for publication and became his political manifesto.

In a bid for legitimacy, Batista resigned and appointed Andrés Domingo Morales del Castillo, one of his closest ministers, as president. This allowed Batista to run in the presidential elections in November 1954. Most of the opposition leaders abstained because they did not believe Batista would really cede power again as he had done a decade earlier. The electoral process itself was clean, but because of the abstentions, Batista won by a ten-to-one margin.

That was Cuba's last real chance at democracy. Batista's opponents became convinced that he would have to be ousted by force. Castro's Moncada attack had been the first step, and soon there would be more attempts to overthrow the government. Still pursuing the trust of the Cuban people, Batista granted a general amnesty to all political prisoners in May 1955. One of those freed was Fidel Castro, who had served less than two years of his fifteen-year sentence.

Newly released, Castro traveled the country freely, giving speeches and granting interviews to newspapers as well as radio and television stations. He declared himself the true leader of the opposition, and many conveniently forgot his days as a militant student leader at the University of Havana. Even Raúl Chibás, leader of the *Ortodoxo* Party and brother of the late Eduardo Chibás, gave Castro his support. After six weeks, Castro left Cuba for Mexico because he believed he could not organize an uprising against Batista from within Cuba.

Attempts by opposition leaders to negotiate new legitimate elections in 1956 failed. As a conciliatory gesture, Batista met with Cosme de la Torriente, a veteran of Cuba's wars of independence. But he insisted he was elected through 1958, and would not back down. Multiple political factions began to conspire against his government. In April of 1956, a group of young military officers led by Col. Ramón Barquín plotted against Batista. They were quickly discovered and jailed at the Isle of Pines.

Later that same month, a group led by Reynol García and composed of members of the *Organización Auténtica* (OA), the Triple A, and the *Ortodoxo* Party, attacked the Goicuría Barracks in the city of Matanzas. Someone leaked the planned uprising to the government, and this assault also failed, resulting in eleven deaths, including Garcia's.

Meanwhile, in Mexico, Castro was organizing an expeditionary force with the financial support of ex-President Prio. Groups aligned with him expected their leader to land in Oriente province in the last days of November 1956. Frank País, Celia Sánchez, and others prepared an uprising on November 30 to coincide with his arrival, but bad weather delayed Castro's landing, and Batista's military quickly crushed the revolt. País survived and continued to lead the underground movement in Santiago until he was caught and killed July 30, 1957.

The Castro brothers, aboard the Prio-Socarras–financed yacht *Granma*, finally landed in Cuba on December 2. Batista's army quickly killed most of them. Only a handful of rebels, with the help of some peasants, made it to the Sierra Maestra mountains alive. Among them were Fidel and Raúl Castro and Ernesto "Che" Guevara, an Argentine adventurer who had joined the expedition in Mexico.

For weeks, nobody knew if Fidel Castro was still alive. The government claimed the entire landing force had been destroyed and Castro was dead. When Fidel learned that the world had accepted the official government version, he decided it was time to talk to the international press.

Not only did he need to tell the world he was alive and still fighting, but Castro knew better than anyone the power of public relations.

The representative of the American media who came to interview Castro in Sierra Maestra was Herbert Matthews, a foreign correspondent and member of the *New York Times*' editorial board. This was an unusual combination in American journalism which, in Matthews' case, had previously led to charges of biased reporting by his colleagues.

Castro couldn't have asked for a better candidate to relay his message to the world. Earlier in his career, Matthews had been in the field covering Benito Mussolini's African campaigns and Spain's Civil War. He became an ardent defender of the Italian Fascist dictator, and an equally strong supporter of the leftist Spanish Republic. According to Anthony DePalma, author of *The Man Who Invented Fidel*, Matthews had a "self-confessed passion for underdogs, and for the causes about which he wrote" and was therefore "easily won over by those he covered, regardless of their politics."[17] DePalma's biography examines how Matthews' background made him the ideal journalist for Castro's purpose, and how the heartfelt but highly partisan reporting by this one correspondent altered the course of history.

In February 1957, Matthews was fifty-seven years old and no longer a field reporter. Now confined to a desk in New York, he found that the chance to cover another revolution up close and personal was too good to resist. He flew down to Cuba with his wife, on the pretext of a shared vacation. After making the long and uncomfortable secret journey to Oriente Province, he was kept waiting overnight by Fidel. The interview lasted three hours and, according to DePalma, "Castro controlled the setting, the timing, and to a large extent the content of the interview."[18]

There was "ample stage-directing at the encounter," much of it designed to convince Matthews that the rebels were a larger force than they were in reality:

In all, Matthews figured he had seen or heard roughly forty individuals, which

> *seemed to correspond to Castro's description of "groups of ten to 40" and suggested that they were part of a larger force. . . . Had he written that Castro was holed up in the mountains with no more than a dozen rebels . . . such a low estimate, though in fact closer to the truth than the hundreds some had assumed were with Castro, would also have been challenged by the American embassy and nearly all the Cubans Matthews had spoken to before heading to the Sierra.*[19]

Matthews wrote a series of three articles for the *New York Times*, and these stories had an enormous impact on events in Cuba (and eventually the United States). First, his interview proved to all doubters that Castro was still alive. Second, Matthews unwittingly overestimated the number of rebel soldiers Castro had under his command. And third, he painted a picture of Robin Hood fighting the rich to give to the poor. "It amounts to a new deal for Cuba," he wrote, describing Castro's vision as being "radical, democratic and therefore anti-Communist."[20]

The Matthews articles "did not create Fidel from nothing, but they did change his image from hotheaded loser to noble rogue with broad ideals, a characterization that appealed to a large spectrum of Cubans as well as Americans. He immediately became the leading figure in the opposition."[21]

The image of Fidel Castro that Matthews created had a long shelf life. Even today, some in the U.S. and other nations consider Castro a hero—the man who stood up to an imperialist United States and lived to see eleven different American presidents occupy the White House. "By stressing Castro's youth . . . and mentioning his beard, the long hair of his followers, and their audacious attempt to challenge the existing order, Matthews was identifying essential elements of Fidel's rebel character for Americans who would, soon enough, watch their own youth adopt some of the same features as they marched into the radical and rebellious 1960s."[22]

Though Matthews tagged Fidel "the flaming symbol of the

opposition" to the Batista regime, he was not the only alternative at the time for Cuba. There were other strong opposition leaders and groups. Former President Prío sponsored another expeditionary force directed from the United States by Aureliano Sánchez Arango, one of the leaders of the *Organización Autentica*. About thirty men on board the yacht *Corinthia* landed in the northern coast of Oriente Province on May 24, 1957. Batista's forces had been expecting them, and only six survived.[23]

On March 13, eighty university students, aligned with the *Directorio Universitario* and the *Organización Auténtica*, attacked the Presidential Palace with the intent of killing Batista. They took over the city's most important news station to proclaim that the president was dead. The group that attacked the palace, under the command of Menelao Mora, almost succeeded, but it was unable to reach the upper floors of the palace. Instead of killing the president, twenty-seven of the attackers as well as five soldiers and police officers died that day.[24]

Another student leader, José Antonio Echeverría, president of the Federation of University Students (FEU) and one of the most respected young anti-Batista leaders, broadcast the announcement that Batista was dead over a radio station. He died in a battle with police while he was seeking refuge at the University of Havana. In Echeverría's pocket was the telephone number of Senator Pelayo Cuervo. That night, Batista's forces arrested and killed Pelayo Cuervo, even though he had not been involved in the attack. His body was found the next morning in an area of Havana known as "*el laguito*."[25]

On September 5, 1957, Cuban Navy personnel based in the city of Cienfuegos on the southern coast of Cuba revolted against Batista's government. They were joined by local civilian members of the 26th of July Movement and other revolutionary groups. Though they were able to secure the city, they did not receive the expected backing of other navy and air force units in Havana and Santiago de Cuba. After heavy fighting by loyal government Army units, the uprising was crushed. Dozens died in the revolt. Regardless of the immediate outcome, the revolt represented the first serious indication that the Cuban armed forces were not solidly in support of the Batista regime.

On April 9, 1958, clandestine forces in cities throughout the country tried to launch a general strike against the Batista regime. It failed within days. Castro had to reorganize his underground forces to continue the spread of his armed insurrection.[26] Batista's police also killed several underground operatives. Among them were José Adolfo Macau and Juan Oscar Alvarado, son of a congressman.

Non-Castro groups were also engaged in guerrilla warfare. Eloy Gutiérrez Menoyo opened up a second battle front in the central Cuba province of Las Villas. His group was called *El Segundo Frente del Escambray* (named after the mountain range where they operated). It grew rapidly, forcing the government to divide its forces. One of those who joined Gutiérrez Menoyo in May 1958 was Oziel González. He rose to the rank of captain. Students from the *Directorio Estudiantil*—now led by Faure Chaumon and Rolando Cubela—also took up arms in the mountains of Las Villas.

By late 1958, violence had spread to the point where it paralyzed the whole island. The economy came to a standstill in several provinces. Fidel and Raúl Castro's forces continued to attract followers, and they fought battles in two different areas of Oriente Province. Castro also dispatched "Che" Guevara and Camilo Cienfuegos to Las Villas to establish a front in that province. Oziel González, of the Segundo Frente, recalls that those fighting in the Escambray Mountains since early 1958 didn't welcome the arrival of Guevara and Cienfuegos. "They were arrogant and acted as if they were the only force fighting Batista."[27]

Batista tried to hold off the rebels, but he suffered a severe blow when President Dwight Eisenhower halted the sale of arms to the Cuban government in March 1958. From that point on, his days were numbered, though he would stay in power until December 31, 1958. In the end, Batista's government collapsed from within rather than being decisively defeated by Castro.

Back in 1952, when Batista had overthrown the democratically elected government of Carlos Prío, he claimed to have two purposes: to eliminate political violence and to eradicate government corruption. He had failed miserably in both.

One of the most exaggerated pieces of propaganda created by the Cuban Revolution is how many people Batista had killed in his last term in office. Castro claimed the number was 20,000. Though it's impossible to know for sure how many died, all credible estimates fall well short of that figure. *Bohemia* magazine published a list of those who died during the Batista years, and their total was fewer than 1,000.[28] British historian Hugh Thomas believes the number, including people killed by Batista's opposition, totaled no more than 2,000, while Ramón M. Barquín estimated the number at 2,495.[29]

And in a 1996 article in Miami's *El Nuevo Herald, Américas*, General Francisco Tabernilla—the son of Batista's top military commander—wrote that between December 2, 1956, and December 31, 1958, 543 Cuban armed soldiers died in action, while more than 2,000 were wounded.[30]

These were just the first of what was to be many losses by the Cuban nation.

NOTES

1. Hubert Herring, *A History of Latin America* (New York: Alfred A. Knopf, 1962), 422.
2. Francisco Morales Padrón, *Manual de Historia Universal: Historia de América* (Madrid: Espasa-Calpe S.A., 1962), 586.
3. Cuban census 1953, other sources cited in Appendix II.
4. Svennilson quoted in José M. Illán, *Cuba: Datos Sobre una Economía en Ruinas* (Miami: Impreso En Beacin Blvd., 1963), 4.
5. Illán, *Cuba*, 12.
6. Rostow, W. W., *The Stages of Economic Growth: A Non-Communist Manifesto* (Cambridge: Cambridge University Press, 1960), Chapter 2, "The Five Stages of Growth—A Summary," 4-16.
7. Asociación Nacional de Hacendados de Cuba, *Cuba, Económica y Financiera—Habana Anuario Azucarero de Cuba*.
8. Illán, *Cuba*, 37.

9. J. Alvarez Díaz, A. Arredondo, R. M. Shelton, and J. Vizcaíno, *Cuba: Geopolítica y Pensamiento Económico* (Miami: Colegio de Economistas de Cuba en el Exilio, 1964), 426.
10. Karl O. Magnusen and Rodríguez Leonardo, "Cuba, Labor and Change," *Labor Studies Journal* 23, no. 2 (Summer 1998), 30. Author interview with Manuel Fernández September 17, 1996.
11. Efrén Córdova, *Clase Trabajadora y Movimiento Sindical en Cuba, 1819-1959*, vol. 1 (Miami: Center for Labor Research and Studies, Florida International University, Ediciones Universal, 1995), 348.
12. Díaz, et al., *Cuba,* 366-67.
13. *America in Figures, 1960* (Washington, D.C.: Pan American Union).
14. Cuban Constitution of 1940, Fundamental Rights, First Section—"Of the rights of individuals," Article 20.
15. Hugh Thomas, *The Pursuit of Freedom* (New York, Harper & Row, 1971), 838.
16. Antonio Rafael de la Cova, *The Moncada Attack* (Columbia: University of South Carolina Press), 265-69.
17. Anthony De Palma, *The Man Who Invented Fidel: Castro, Cuba and Herbert L. Matthews of the "New York Times"* (New York: Public Affairs, a member of the Perseus Book Group, 2006), 77.
18. Ibid., 80.
19. Ibid., 85.
20. Ibid., 87.
21. Ibid., 109.
22. Ibid., 81.
23. Foreign Service Dispatch, American Embassy, Havana, May 29, 1957, signed by Arthur Gardner, Ambassador.
24. Octavio R. Costa, *Imagen y Trayectoria del Cubano en la Historia*, vol. 2 (Miami: Ediciones Universal, 1998), 374.
25. Thomas, *Pursuit of Freedom*, 930.
26. Marcos Antonio Ramos, *La Cuba de Castro y Después* (Nashville: Grupo Nelson, 2007), 234.
27. Author interview with Oziel González, January 12, 2009.
28. "Más de veinte mil muertos arroja el trágico balance del régimen de Batista," *Bohemia*, January 11, 1959, 180.
29. Thomas, *Pursuit of Freedom*, 1044; Ramón M. Barquín, *El día que Fidel Castro se apoderó de Cuba* (San Juan: Editorial Rambar, 1978), 124.
30. Silito Tabernilla, "En defensa del ejército," *El Nuevo Herald,* April 27, 1996.

2

MIAMI BEFORE THE REVOLUTION

BY HOWARD KLEINBERG

Miami's history with Cubans goes back as far as its incorporation in 1896. The *Miami Metropolis*, the settlement's infant newspaper, published in May 1896, carried the story of Luis González, a Cuban cigar manufacturer who had started a small factory in Miami. "He is a very bright gentleman," the paper reported, "and has an estimable wife and bright son."[1]

Throughout Cuba's long fight for independence from Spain, Cuban exiles came to Key West, Tampa, and Miami to raise money for the nationalists. Though the U.S. government officially discouraged armed support, Miamians found profitable opportunities in gun-running. The *Miami Metropolis* protested the seizure of a vessel that ran between Miami and Key West, claiming the law allowed American ships "engaged in the passenger business have as much right to transport arms, ammunition, and passengers to those shores [Cuba] as they have to any other country."

"The arms, however, should be in the hold," it editorialized sardonically, "and the men in the cabin."[2] The editorial conveyed Miami's attitude about the situation in Cuba more than it clarified the reading of any statute.

A stern-wheeler passenger vessel serving Miami called *The City of Key West* (a.k.a. the *City of Richmond*) transported both guns and men in support of Cuban revolutionaries. It partnered with a steamer called *The*

Three Friends, which was commanded by Napoleon Broward—a man who later would be elected governor of Florida, and have a county carved out of Dade County named in his honor.

The City of Key West picked up weapons for a rendezvous with *The Three Friends* off Key Biscayne where it would transfer its cargo of 165 Cubans, 4,000 rifles, 100,000 cartridges, 2 Gatling guns, and 2 tons of dynamite. Despite being chased by a Spanish gunboat, *The Three Friends* successfully delivered its cargo to Cuban soil. The *Miami Metropolis* wrote: "This boat is earning a good reputation and her owners must be making money. Success to the cause."[3]

Miami's involvement in the 1898 Spanish-American War that eventually gave Cuba its long and bitterly sought independence from Spain was minimal. Troops from several Southern states—chiefly Alabama—camped in tents on grounds now occupied by huge downtown office buildings. There the all-white soldiers clashed violently with local black citizens who lived west of the railroad tracks in today's Overtown. So contentious were relations between the troops and the people of Miami that the encampment was abandoned almost as quickly as it began.

A merchant from upstate Bartow saw opportunity and began selling goods at the campsite. This man—named William Burdine—thought so much of the new community's future that he stayed and created the historic Burdines department store chain (bought out by Federated in 1956 and renamed Macy's in 2005.[4]

In 1905, Henry Flagler began to extend his railroad from Miami/Homestead to Key West, in the hope that tourists and businessmen headed for Havana would take the train and then sail the remaining ninety miles. The "Railroad That Went to Sea" was never very successful. It was destroyed by a hurricane in 1935, and eventually replaced with a highway—the current U.S. Route 1.

Miami was dubbed "The Magic City" by its boosters because of its overnight growth. But there has always been a question of for whom it was "magic." Segregation cast a shadow over the community from its earliest days. The white founders, mostly from the Northeast, restricted not only blacks but Jews from purchasing property and staying in certain hotels. Carl Fisher, who began developing Miami Beach in 1913, was afraid that the presence of Jews would keep away the WASP moneyed set that had created Palm Beach and that he wanted to attract to his new resort. Even Al Smith, the Catholic governor of New York and 1928 Democratic presidential candidate, found himself excluded from Miami Beach's Surf Club because of his religion.[5] Until recently, the role of discrimination was often obscured in official history books.

Starting in the 1920s, Miami and Miami Beach were heralded as "America's Playground." Trains, steamships, airplanes, and automobiles beat a wintertime path south to the warm climate of the Miami area. Not only were tourists arriving, but South Florida land was being sold at an incredible pace and incredible prices, and with incredible caveats that included incredible chicanery. It was not unusual for a piece of property to change ownership several times in a single day. There were more real estate advertisements in Miami newspapers than in those of any other city. At the peak of the real estate boom, an issue of the *Miami Daily News* ran more than five hundred pages—a record then for an American newspaper.[6]

The boom came at a price. Illegal gambling and crime, along with embedded discrimination, rode the waves to Miami. In 1913, Dade County voters approved alcohol prohibition—seven years before it became an article of the American Constitution.[7] This gave rum running and other booze-related criminal activity in Miami a head start on the rest of the nation.

Despite the notoriety, Miami and Miami Beach never lost their glamour. Among the elite, social activity rose to new heights. Hotels in Miami Beach seemed to appear almost overnight. Sunshine sold itself.

The boom continued unabated until a ship carrying building materials capsized in Biscayne Bay in early 1926, blocking the shipping channel for months. Then came the great hurricane of 1926 that took a monstrous toll on the community. The final blow was the stock market crash of 1929, which halted economic development in Miami as it did everywhere else. All hotel construction in Miami Beach stopped until the mid-1930s.

This period saw the arrival of a new wave of Cuban exiles in Miami. In 1931, while Gerardo Machado was president, one of his predecessors, Mario García Menocal, chose exile in Miami over prison in Cuba. Menocal first established residence in Miami, then in a house on Lincoln Road and Collins Avenue in Miami Beach. He became the leader of a small but passionate anti-Machado exile group in the Miami area.

When Machado was overthrown in 1933, the exiles, including Menocal, returned to Cuba with a cordial sendoff. "Miami was glad to extend her hospitality to the exiles," editorialized the *Miami Herald* on August 17, 1933, "and will be sorry to lose them, but appreciates their desire to bask again in Cuban sunshine and breezes, to stroll Havana's avenues, to sip sparkling wine in the cafes, to breathe the air of freedom beneath the palms." It concluded prophetically, "Miami's gates will ever remain open to Cubans, as well as to men and women from every country and clime and state."[8]

In 1932, Carlos Prío Socarrás, a Havana student leader, came to Miami for the first of his three exiles in the Magic City. His Directory of University Students (DEU), called the "Miami Cell," sought Machado's overthrow, but it opposed U.S. intervention in Cuban affairs. Unlike Menocal's, this group was not popular in Cuban Miami and raised little money. Years later, when Batista ousted Prío in a coup on March 10, 1952, Prío returned to Miami. And in 1960 he began his third exile—this one for the rest of his life—when he broke ranks with Castro's Revolution.[9]

In the mid-1930s, construction in Miami resumed. Though the country was still in a depression, hundreds of hotels, large and small, rose in Miami Beach. Along Ocean Drive and Collins Avenue, in South Beach, a series of small hotels were built. They represented affordability as well as a revolutionary kind of style, and they were designed by talented architects from what was later labeled the Art Deco movement. At the time of their construction, they appealed more to middle-class New

Yorkers than the moneyed set. Eventually these tourists from New York, most of whom were Jewish, retired to Miami and could sometimes be seen rocking on the same front porches of these Deco hotels on Ocean Drive, which came to be known as "God's waiting room."

For some in South Florida, by the late 1940s it was as if the hard times had never happened. Dollars might have been scarce among permanent residents, but winter tourists brought in plenty of cash. Miami was established primarily as a tourist community. Manufacturing played a minor role in its service-oriented economy.

Not only was Miami Beach a winter wonderland for visitors from the northern United States, it also became a playground for Cuban tourists in the summer. Hotels that previously had closed now found that staying open in the summer months could be profitable. In 1948, the director of publicity for the city of Miami estimated that Cuban visitors that summer were worth about $500,000 monthly to the city's economy, and Miami's police department began requiring recruits to take forty hours of Spanish lessons.[10]

After World War II, Cuban visitors began coming in winter months as well. "For the past two years," wrote the *Miami Herald* on February 20, 1949, "visitors from the south, particularly from Cuba, have thronged the area during the summer. But this is the first time they have come in large numbers at this time of year." The city news bureaus brought on Spanish-speaking staffers, and more and more retail outlets posted the sign in their front windows: "*Se Habla Español.*"

The postwar period brought significant, permanent change to Miami and South Florida. U.S. armed forces had used Miami as a major training ground during the war, which created the "Sand-In-Your-Shoes" phenomenon. Veterans—many from the Northeast—who had trained on the golf courses and beach sands and slept in Miami Beach hotels appropriated by the wartime government, returned after the war to raise their families in the South Florida warmth. And new construction boomed once more under the G.I. Bill. Planned neighborhoods with new schools and shopping centers were created in North Miami, West Miami, Hialeah, South Miami, unincorporated Dade County, and points in-between.

The underside of Miami's economic development was the increasing activity of the mob. Though Al Capone had bought a home on Miami Beach's Palm Island in the 1930s, his stay was brief and uneventful. Meyer Lansky, on the other hand, became a powerful mob figure who virtually controlled illegal gambling in South Florida. He owned the Colonial Inn, a thinly disguised gambling casino in Broward County. Officials turned a blind eye to the activity and often picked up part of the booty. As a result, mob-run gambling and prostitution flourished throughout the Greater Miami area.

Popular among Miami's working poor was a numbers game based on the Cuban lotto. Called *bolita*—Spanish for little ball—the racket was run by Tampa-based Santo Trafficante, another mob figure who eventually encroached on Cuba and was rumored to be complicit in the assassination of John F. Kennedy.

In the early 1950s, a subcommittee of the U.S. Senate, under the chairmanship of Sen. Estes Kefauver of Tennessee, came to town to investigate organized crime. Mob activity declined, and Meyer Lansky shifted his focus to Cuba, where he had already established a close relationship with government officials.

The cross-straits link that Henry Flagler had envisioned when he extended was finally realized—by air as well as sea. In 1951, National Airlines was running five daily round trips between Miami and Havana. The fifty-eight-minute propeller-driven flight cost thirty dollars round trip. There was even a special package that combined the short flight with a picturesque Greyhound bus trip from Miami to Key West.[11]

By 1958, Cuban-owned Aerovías Q Airways was selling ten-dollar one-way flights from Key West to Havana, and other regularly scheduled flights to and from the Palm Beaches, Fort Lauderdale, and the Isle of Pines. Pan American, Cubana de Aviación, and other airlines covered the route as well.[12]

So widespread was the Latin American presence becoming that the *Miami News* began printing a weekly page in Spanish. Headed by anchor columnist "Tano" Gomez, the page was a weekly digest of international, national, local, and social news *en español*.[13] Cuban culture gained another toehold in Miami in 1949 when a delegation of Cuban educators, headed by Minister of Education Dr. Ramon Riverón, presented a bust of Cuban patriot José Martí to Miami Senior High School, which already boasted a small enrollment of Cuban-born students. That bust, the first of many to eventually be placed in Miami, still stands in one of the school's patios.[14]

Wealthy Cubans participated in the investment boom in Miami. The December 29, 1947, issue of *Life* magazine featured a dozen pages about "Miami: Babylon, U.S.A." Across two pages of the cover feature was a photo of a twenty-fifth wedding anniversary party at the Sunset Isle home of Mr. and Mrs. Julio Sanchez. The 125 guests were identified as "wealthy Cuban planters, many of whom come to Miami Beach for the season."

Sanchez and his two brothers had inherited from their father a hundred-thousand-acre sugar plantation in Cuba, which at one time employed seven thousand men. In Miami, the brothers were called the Cuban Sugar Kings, a name that, years later, also would apply to the professional baseball franchise in Havana. Sanchez was an avid master fisherman and fished often with Ernest Hemingway in Cuba and in the Bahamas. He was one of eight founders of the Miami Beach Rod and Reel Club in 1929, and he invented the "fighting chair," seen so often aft on game fishing boats. He claimed it was inspired by a barber chair. When Castro came to power, he seized Sanchez's property in Cuba. Sanchez lived in Miami until his death in 1985.[15]

A controversial Cuban politician named José Manuel Alemán became a visible investor in Miami. Starting out as a two-hundred-dollar-a-month personnel director in Cuba's Ministry of Education, Alemán became within a few years minister of education under President Ramón Grau-San Martín. His fortune was estimated between $70 million and

$200 million. How he came into those riches remains one of the widely discussed cases of official Cuban corruption. There were vivid, though undocumented descriptions of Alemán and his cohorts backing up a truck to the Cuban Treasury and removing millions in cash. Alemán died before any formal charges could be placed against him.[16]

Alemán diverted most of that money to South Florida. In addition to purchasing land, apartment buildings, and small hotels, he bought the local baseball team and built a new stadium. With his second wife, Elena Santeiro García Alemán, he purchased the whole of Cape Florida on Key Biscayne in 1948 for $1.5 million.[17]

When Alemán died in 1950, his holdings were divided between his wife and his son from a previous marriage, José Braulio Alemán. The two didn't get along. His widow focused on developing the land they had purchased on Key Biscayne. She cleared the native landscape and bulldozed down to naked soil in an effort to interest commercial developers. There was talk of constructing a causeway from Miami south to Key Largo, which would run directly through her property, making it extremely valuable.[18]

But the mid-bay causeway proposal was ultimately rejected by both the media and the politicians. Bill Baggs, editor of the *Miami News*, intervened on behalf of preservationists and convinced Mrs. Santeiro García and the state of Florida to negotiate the land for a state park. The park was named after Bill Baggs.

Meanwhile, her stepson was making headlines for a different reason. After his father's death, young José Braulio took over the Miami Sun Sox and regularly occupied the owners' box at Miami Stadium. Among his favorite players was Gilberto Torres, an avowed Cuban nationalist who disapproved of America's influence on his native country. When Fidel Castro came into power, Torres returned to Cuba and coached the Cuban national baseball team. José Braulio was impressionable and, under Torres' influence, he began to support anti-Batista activity in the Santa Clara region.

Al Rubio, who ran the stadium for Alemán (and later became manager of the Orange Bowl Stadium), told interviewers that José Braulio's link with the Miami branch of pro-Castro supporters slowly bled him dry. "They would get $50,000 or $60,000 from him and load a bunch of boxes and say they were flying to Cuba, but they never did. They milked him like they were milking a goat. They used to tell me to mind my own business, so I didn't say nothing: I didn't want to get shot."[19]

José Braulio Alemán sold his baseball stadium to the city of Miami in 1955 for a mere nine hundred thousand dollars in order to fund arms for Castro. After Castro assumed power, José Braulio returned to Cuba, expecting a warm welcome. Instead, the Communist regime confiscated his Cuban properties and, for a short time, held him under house arrest in Havana. He eventually returned to Miami a broken man and worked at insignificant jobs—including that of an extra in a Lloyd Bridges movie filmed at Villa Vizcaya—to support his family. But the strain was too much. In 1983, José Braulio Alemán went berserk, killing his aunt with whom he lived and wounding three others. As the police moved in to contain him, he held his gun to his head and pulled the trigger. "The poor kid could have gone out a millionaire," Rubio theorized reflectively.[20]

Alemán was not the only Cuban exile in Miami solicited for financial support of the revolution. When Castro came to Miami in November 1955, he spoke at a movie theater at West Flagler Street and 3rd Avenue, and a Cuban social club on 27th Avenue. Neither of his speeches was reported in Miami's English-language dailies. It is unclear how much money he raised. Ellis Riera-Gómez, who came to Miami in 1936 and helped found Diario Las Américas, hosted Castro during his ninety-hour visit. "He spoke like he was José Martí," Riera-Gómez said. "He fooled the hell out of us."[21]

In 1957, two years before the start of the major Cuban exodus, Greater Miami's population was 935,000. Over the previous decade, Dade County bank clearings had jumped from $3 billion to $13 billion. Manufacturing firms had increased from 870 in 1950 to 2,570 in 1960, and there were now more than three thousand restaurants and fifty shopping centers—with six more under construction. Amusements receipts had tripled, and food and beverage sales doubled in the decade of the 1950s. And segregation was beginning to collapse, both through the courts and at Woolworth's lunch counter.[22]

Prewar and immediate postwar inhabitants had settled in areas of southwest Miami known as Shenandoah and Riverside. As their fortunes improved, they moved out to prosperous new housing developments in areas such as Westchester, vacating the lower-cost housing in old areas.

This was the awaiting cradle of Little Havana.

NOTES

1. *Miami Metropolis*, May 15, 1896.
2. *Miami Metropolis*, July 3, 1896.
3. Ibid.
4. *Miami Metropolis*, June 24, 1896.
5. Tape-recorded oral history of Alfred Barton by Polly Redford, May 12 and 18, 1967, University of Miami Library, Coral Gables, Florida.
6. *Miami Daily News*, July 26, 1925.
7. "Dade County Is Voted Dry," *Miami Metropolis*, October 30, 1913.
8. *Miami Herald*, August 17, 1933.
9. Francis Sicius, "The Miami-Havana Connection—the First Seventy-Five Years," *Tequesta, the Journal of the Historical Association of Southern Florida*, no. 58, 1998.
10. "Cubans Enliven Miami Season," *New York Times*, September 5, 1948.
11. Advertisement, *Miami Daily News*, February 4, 1951.
12. Airline timetable images, www.timetableimages.com.
13. "Si Ud. Habla Espanol," *Miami Sunday News*, February 4, 1951.
14. "Green Statue in Foyer is José Martí; Good Will Gift of Cuba," *Miami High School Times*, September 29, 1949.
15. *Memoir of Nat Saunders*, as cited in Ashley B. Saunders, "The History of Bimini," September 25, 1980; "Inventor of Fishing Chair Dies," *Miami Herald*, July 16, 1985.
16. Joan Gill Blank, *Key Biscayne* (Sarasota, Fl.: Pineapple Press, 1996), 166.
17. Ibid., 166-67.
18. Ibid., 167-71.
19. *White Elephant*, a documentary film of Miami Baseball Stadium, directed by Rolando Llanes, 2008.
20. Ibid.
21. "Forget It, Miami: Fidel Did *Not* Sleep in This House," *Miami Herald*, April 16, 1991.
22. "Economic Almanac of Dade and Broward Counties," Bureau of Business and Economic Research, University of Miami, January 1957.

3

BATISTA FLEES, CASTRO TAKES OVER

BY GUILLERMO MARTINEZ AND SAM VERDEJA

As 1958 was ending, people in Havana and Cuba's western provinces had no idea how precarious Batista's hold on power was. Many heard via the shortwave Radio Rebelde—the official voice of the Castro movement—about battles between rebel and government forces, but nobody could confirm them. There was no official news. Even the rebel forces, with their own lines of communications, did not know how close they were to victory.

The Batista regime had imposed a strict censorship on newspapers, radio, and television stations. From December 1, 1958, through December 15, 1958, the only news published on Cuba's political turmoil was a brief and vague government military report printed by *Diario de La Marina*, one of the leading newspapers on the island. By late December, even the official government reports had disappeared from the newspapers.

On the surface, life in Havana continued as usual. Cuba's winter baseball league was in full swing. Newspaper front pages were full of international stories. Society pages still carried descriptions and photos of parties and holiday celebrations. Stores advertised their Christmas sales, and the classified pages were full.

Few people in Havana went out to celebrate New Year's Eve because of the bombs set off each night by the rebels. Some knew that ground transportation to eastern Cuba had come to a complete halt. It was impossible to call or send a telegram to Oriente. Leonardo Rodríguez, now a Florida International University (FIU) accounting professor, recalled that in Camaguey the bus and train stations had stopped selling tickets to Oriente Province.[1]

In a dispatch sent to the U.S. State Department on March 23, 1959—almost three months after Batista had fallen—the American Embassy described those last days of the Batista regime:

By the end of December, 1958 the military situation of the Batista regime was on the point of collapse in the three eastern provinces of Oriente, Camaguey, and Las Villas. The Army had no reserve strength to reverse that trend. Transportation by land had been severed in Las Villas Province. The economy of those provinces was nearly paralyzed. Censorship and lack of communications and transportation prevented the public from knowing the situation. The revolutionary forces were better informed, but their communications were deficient and they were not aware of the magnitude of the victories within their grasp. Batista knew the situation and realized that his regime would soon collapse. He left rather than attempt a hopeless defense.[2]

People in Havana and throughout the island could sense that the end was near. But nobody, including Batista's closest associates and the rebels, knew that the president was about to flee. Batista decided to leave on December 31. He made a list of his closest government officials and family members who would leave with him and shared it with Gen. Francisco (Silito) Tabernilla. Shortly after making a midnight toast at his Camp Columbia party, Batista read an official statement of resignation. He named General Eulogio Cantillo head of the armed forces, and suggested that Carlos M. Piedra, a senior member of Cuba's Supreme Court, be sworn in as president.

Shortly after 2 A.M., five planes carrying Batista and his entourage took off from Camp Columbia. Three planes headed for the Dominican Republic with Batista on board one of them. The other two went to the

United States. Many Batista supporters fled the island throughout the next day, or sought political asylum in the Latin American embassies in Havana.

Slowly, word of Batista's departure began to spread throughout Havana and the rest of the island. By early morning, radio and television stations were broadcasting the news. Fidel Castro, in his headquarters outside Santiago de Cuba, flew into a rage. Faced with imminent victory, he had no intention of letting a deal between Batista and General Cantillo get in his way. Claiming Cantillo had betrayed a previous agreement and couldn't be trusted, he ordered Santiago de Cuba be taken by force, and Manuel Urrutia Lleó—a judge with close ties to the revolution—be appointed president.

Castro sent his brother Raúl to take control of Santiago and the Moncada Garrison. His two most trusted commanders—Camilo Cienfuegos and Ernesto "Ché" Guevara—marched on Havana. Cienfuegos was to take over control of Camp Columbia, and Guevara the fortress of La Cabaña.

Cantillo, realizing he didn't have Castro's confidence and hoping to keep the army as a moderating influence over the revolution, released Col. Ramón Barquín from prison, and he surrendered control of the armed forces to Barquín. Police and army officials throughout the island turned over their weapons, creating a power vacuum for the thousands of people who had thronged the streets to celebrate Batista's departure. Some of the celebrants began destroying the much-hated parking meters recently installed in Havana. Others went after the casinos and attacked Batista supporters, looting their homes. Some Batista security forces were killed in skirmishes with supporters of the revolution who were trying to arrest them.

In Miami, New Year's Eve celebrations were unaffected by the turmoil in Cuba. The Orange Bowl football game between the University of Oklahoma and Syracuse drew a big crowd. Local nightclubs featured stars such as Sophie Tucker, Pupi Campo, Polly Bergen, Don Rickles,

Tony Martin, Xavier Cugat, and Buddy Hackett. Revelers who couldn't afford the nightclubs went to see the movie *South Pacific* while the social elite attended exclusive parties where elegant ladies still wore imported Italian kid gloves (advertised that day by Burdines Department Store for $3.99, marked down from $7.00.)[3]

The *Miami Herald*—a morning daily—went to press before word of events in Cuba leaked. Its lead story the next day was the settlement of the Eastern Airlines strike. "Happy '59—EAL Strike Ends!" was emblazoned across the front page, along with "King Orange Is the Juiciest Yet; Silver Festival Lights Up Miami." On page two of the *Herald* was an Associated Press story from Havana, reporting that Fulgencio Batista's troops were preparing to pound Fidel Castro's rebel forces around Santa Clara and drive them eastward out of Las Villas Province.[4]

Shortly after midnight, as Miamians tooted horns and sipped champagne, rumors of Batista's fleeing began to circulate. At about 3:00 A.M., phones began to ring in the homes of *Miami News* reporters and editors. Something big was happening in Havana.

The *News* had already prepared a special edition for New Year's Day with color coverage of the Orange Bowl parade and the starting lineups of the Oklahoma and Syracuse teams. But, as an afternoon daily, the issue had not yet gone to print. Out came the football story, and a new front page was quickly assembled: BATISTA, AIDES FLEE CUBA, it shouted in bold capital letters. Miami was about to change forever.

In the chaos immediately following Batista's departure, panicked American tourists fled Havana, while exultant Cuban expatriates in Miami returned to the island. On January 3, the *New York Times* reported that five hundred "celebrating Cuban expatriates" sailed aboard the ferry boat *City of Havana* from Key West to Havana after delivering a comparable load of American tourists from Cuba. The ferry was expected to return from Havana the next day with more fleeing Americans.[5]

Cubana Airlines flew people to and from Havana, with five daily roundtrips scheduled between the Rancho Boyeros José Martí Airport in Havana and Miami International Airport. The *Times* reported that the flights were made with the approval of rebel leader Fidel Castro, "who assured safe conduct for all Americans."

"Cuba's revolution has had some strange side effects on Miami Beach," reported the *New York Times* on January 11. "Last weekend's flood of American tourist and Cuban political refugees from Havana swamped Miami International Airport. The refugees landed mostly at Key West, roared northward toward this city by plane, bus and automobile."

The paper continued, "The abrupt end to the Havana weekend package business is leaving travel agents with an unsalable product. A large travel agency can book as many as 7,000 short-term, weekend airplane excursions to Havana during the winter season. The annual total of such trips out of here is well over 100,000 visitors who forsake Miami Beach for a whirl at the Havana night clubs and gambling casinos."[6]

The terms *political refugees* and *exiles* began creeping into the lexicon of English-speaking Miami.

Miami's former mayor, Abe Aronovitz, was among those visiting Havana when the rebels took over. "This was the most courteous revolution I ever heard of," Aronovitz said at the time. "The rebels did everything they could to protect us and make us as comfortable as possible at the hotel."[7] The impression of friendliness didn't last long.

As Castro's forces marched into Santiago de Cuba, "rebels saw people hanging from balconies. The crowd packed the street so tightly that sometimes the caravan came to a complete halt. '¡Viva Fidel'! '¡Viva la Revolución'! '¡Viva! ¡Viva! ¡Viva! ¡Viva! ¡Viva'!"[8]

While Cienfuegos and Guevara marched on Havana, Castro called for a national strike that would empower his 26th of July forces throughout the island. On January 3, Cienfuegos and Guevara arrived in Havana. Guevara assumed control of the Cabaña Fortress, and Cienfuegos embraced Barquín at Camp Columbia. Both military garrisons surrendered peacefully. In Santiago de Cuba, Castro named a new cabinet with Manuel Urrutia Lleó as president and José Miró Cardona as prime minister. The cabinet was full of well-known and respected professionals and political figures, most with close ties to Castro's movement.[9] Within a few short weeks or months, many of them would switch to opposing the Castro regime.

Conspicuously absent from any position of power—military or political—were members of other anti-Batista organizations such as the Organización Auténtica of former President Carlos Prío; the Directorio Estudiantil, led by Faure Chaumón and Rolando Cubela; and the Segundo Frente del Escambray, led by Eloy Gutiérrez Menoyo and William Morgan. These leaders were alarmed to be excluded from the provisional government—especially since the new cabinet was now the law of the land, superseding even the Cuban Constitution of 1940.

On January 8, Castro arrived in Havana, flanked by Huber Matos and Camilo Cienfuegos. At Camp Columbia, he gave a speech that was crucial to consolidating his power over the revolutionary forces. It was directed toward the Directorio Estudiantil and the Segundo Frente del Escambray, whose forces still controlled the Presidential Palace, the University of Havana, and the San Antonio Air Force Base.

Castro promised the Cuban people he would hold free elections within eighteen months. It was a promise the revolution would never keep. The speech is remembered for the famous line: "Why do we need weapons?" (*¿Armas para qué?*), which was Castro's successful bid to disarm the Directorio and Segundo Frente forces. There was also an important image engrained in accounts of that day—the white dove, an international symbol of peace, that flew over Castro and settled on his shoulder.

On January 9, Cuban newspapers covered Castro's every move, pointing out the joy with which the great majority of Cuban's welcomed their new leader. *Diario de la Marina* published a front-page editorial on the white dove. "We see the white dove on Fidel Castro's right shoulder as a clear sign of the All Mighty and that the universal symbol of peace represents the desires and eternal hopes of all the Cuban people."[10]

Castro's government continued to move swiftly. By January 10, the cabinet decreed that criminal laws could be applied retroactively. Next it gave the government the right to confiscate private property, proclaimed the enactment of the death penalty, and invalidated all private university degrees and credits obtained while the University of Havana was closed as a result of the struggle against Batista.[11]

Many Castro allies in the struggle against Batista were assigned to menial posts. Oziel González was named head of the Havana Fire Department. Comandante William Morgan was put in charge of a frog farm. The number of executions increased, some after mock trials and others based on no trial at all. On January 12, in Santiago de Cuba, government forces used bulldozers to dig a ditch. They ordered seventy-one prisoners to stand in front of it, and then executed them by firing squad, or *paredón*.

The new regime had been executing Batista supporters since early January, but as news of the seventy-one killed in Santiago filtered throughout the island, supporters began to question Castro's intentions. Some wondered if Castro, his brother Raúl, or Guevara had close ties to international Communism, though they continued to deny it. With local and international journalists at Havana's Hotel Riviera in mid-January, Castro insisted: "I am not a communist."[12]

Castro's executions and setting aside of the constitution alienated the moderate elements of the government he had appointed. On February 16, José Miró Cardona resigned as prime minister, and Castro took over the job himself a day later. Fifteen months after resigning his post, Miró Cardona sought political asylum in the Argentine Embassy in Havana. He had seen others who tried to separate themselves from the revolution get arrested and sentenced to lengthy prison sentences.

On February 18, 1959, Jesús Sosa Blanco, a colonel in Batista's army, was tried for murder in the Havana Sports Palace, in front of seventeen thousand live spectators and a national television audience. It was a spectacle worthy of ancient Rome, as Sosa Blanco himself was heard to observe. The witnesses who were called to testify against him contradicted each other. Some could not even recognize the defendant or describe his alleged crimes. It made little difference that the trial was a sham. Sosa Blanco was sentenced to death and executed the same day by firing squad. The author Gabriel Garcia Marquez attended the trial and execution and used the incident as the basis for his 1975 novel, *The Autumn of the Patriarch*.

The Sosa Blanco trial made many Cubans question whether the revolution was truly carrying out justice or simply trying to engender fear. On March 1, a Revolutionary Tribunal acquitted fifty Air Force pilots who were accused of bombing innocent civilians while fighting Castro's forces in the hills. The court determined that some defendants had not been involved in the bombing and others had deliberately dropped their bombs off the coast so they would not hurt anyone. Castro declared the trial void and demanded they be tried again. The second time the pilots were convicted and sentenced to thirty years of hard labor.

In the early days of the revolution, most of the people leaving Cuba had been Batista supporters and their families. But over time, many Cubans grew increasingly concerned about the direction the revolution was taking, particularly about certain economic changes decreed by the new government. On March 3, the Cuban cabinet seized the assets of the Cuban Telephone Co. Before that, they had only expropriated properties owned by Batista supporters. This was different. This was a private enterprise owned by an American company. Concerns grew in both Cuba and the United States that the Cuban Revolution, if not an outright Communist movement, was at least being infiltrated by Communists.

Castro traveled to the United States in mid-April to try to dispel the notion that he was leading a Communist revolution. He met privately with members of President Eisenhower's administration, and appeared on the national television program *Meet the Press*. Meg Craig, a flamboyant journalist in a large hat, asked Castro directly if he was a Communist. Castro replied: "I am not a Communist nor do I agree with Communism."

The next day, the *New York Times* reported that "Dr. Castro denied also that either his brother Raúl, a leader in the anti-Batista revolt, or Raúl's wife Vilma, was a Communist. There have been reports to this effect. If there happen to be any Communists in his Government he said, 'their influence is nothing.'"[13]

Castro met privately with Vice President Richard Nixon for three and a half hours, during which Nixon advised him "that it was the responsibility of a leader not always to follow public opinion but to help to direct it in proper channels, not to give the people what they think they want at a time of emotional stress but to make them want what they ought to have."

In a private memo to Eisenhower, Nixon wrote, "It was apparent that while he paid lip service to such institutions as freedom of speech, press and religion that his primary concern was with developing program for economic progress." He also observed that Castro is "either incredibly naïve about Communism or is under Communist discipline."[14]

Upon his return to Cuba, Castro continued to disavow Communism, telling an enormous crowd in the Plaza de la Revolución on May 8 that the leadership of the revolution was not made up of Communists. His actions, however, increasingly contradicted his words. On May 17 Castro signed the Agrarian Reform Law expropriating all large landholdings in Cuba. He promised to pay the owners for their property with bonds, and distribute the land among the landless peasants. He did neither.

In June, the government nationalized all private schools. This made even more people, both in and out of government, uneasy. Some government officials resigned. Others were forced out of their jobs.

Fidel Castro created a national crisis on July 17 when he resigned his role as prime minister, as the crowds demanded President Manuel Urrutia to resign. "Urrutia went to a friend's house, spent some time under house arrest and then took refuge in the Embassy of Venezuela, being permitted afterwards to leave the country with difficulty."[15] Urrutia spent two years in the Venezuelan Embassy before he was allowed to leave in March 1963.

Osvaldo Dorticós, a longtime known Communist, replaced Urrutia as president. Castro waited a few days to complete his plan. At a massive rally organized by Cuba's Popular Socialist Party (PSP)—the official name of the Communist Party in Cuba—the crowded shouted for him to return. Castro accepted. The date was July 26, 1959.

Throughout the year, the Cuban Revolution had been expropriating the property of all people who—according to the government—had made their money illicitly. Some prominent supporters of the revolution began to express disagreement with Castro's policies. On October 19, Major Huber Matos, one of Castro's key military commanders, resigned his leadership of the province of Camaguey. Castro refused to accept his resignation and sent Major Camilo Cienfuegos to arrest him. Matos and thirty-eight of his officers were brought back to Havana and jailed at the Morro Castle. On December 15 Matos was sentenced to twenty years in prison.

Another public defection occurred when Pedro Luis Díaz Lanz, commander of Cuba's Revolutionary Air Force, fled into exile. On October 21, Díaz Lanz flew over Havana, dropping leaflets that explained he was resigning because the revolutionary movement every day drew closer to Communist principles.

Most shocking of all, on October 29, Cubans learned that Camilo Cienfuegos had mysteriously disappeared on a small plane. Among the revolutionary leaders, Cienfuegos was second only to Castro in popularity. Neither the plane nor Cienfuegos' body were ever recovered. Many of his lieutenants were quickly killed, jailed, or escaped to exile.

In the fall of 1959, Manuel Artime, a captain in the rebel army, attended a secret two-day meeting of the National Institute of Agrarian Reform in Havana. According to documents in the U.S. National Security Archive, Artime said that at the meeting, "Castro also decides that the State will take possession of all land holdings, eliminating private property. At this point the Cuba peasants (campesinos) will not be told of the plan." Artime stressed that the leadership intended to deceive the Cuban public about the future plans for the revolution.[16] Artime subsequently left the country clandestinely, instructing his lifelong friend, Dr. Lino Fernández, to "begin stockpiling weapons . . . and to create a network of internal security and intelligence."[17]

By the last week of November, the Ministry of Labor had established rules that allowed the government to intervene, confiscate, or take over any business or industry that closed either temporarily or permanently. And by December, all newspapers were informed that whenever they ran stories against government interests, the workers of that newspaper had the right to publish a note at the end of the story saying they disagreed with its content. These notes were called *"coletillas."*

By the end of 1960, more than fifty thousand Cubans had already left the island, and many others were secretly planning escape. The executions, expropriations, restrictions on individual liberties, and the visible presence of Communists in the government all contributed to fears about the future. Cuban students and some former members of the revolution undertook a range of subversive activities against the government. The rapidly deteriorating conditions in Cuba, and the activism of opposition groups, convinced departing Cubans that their exile would be brief—as it had always been for resistors to previous Cuban regimes.[18]

Shortly after the revolution, Castro had confiscated media properties owned or operated by close supporters of the Batista regime. By 1960, the rules were broadened to include the newspapers *Avance*, *El País*, *Excelsior*, *El Mundo*, *Diario de La Marina*, and *Prensa Libre*. By year end, the newspaper *Información* and all other dailies were in the hands of the government. Also confiscated were Cuba's largest magazines, *Vanidades*, *Carteles*, and *Bohemia*—one the most influential and advanced news magazines in Latin America. Owner/editor Miguel Angel Quevedo had initially given the revolution the full support of his magazine, but as he began to distance himself from Castro, his business was seized. Quevedo fled to Venezuela, where he published *Bohemia Libre*.

Cuba's radio and television networks were next on Castro's list. By the end of 1960, there was no longer any private media in Cuba. The regime had total control over all information. From that point on, the Cuban people would read, hear, and see only the government's views.

In the fall of 1959, Castro had reached out to the Soviet Union and other Communist countries in Eastern Europe. The USSR agreed to purchase 380,000 tons of sugar, paying cash for 20 percent and trading Soviet products for the rest.[19] In February 1960, Anastas Mikoyan, first deputy chairman of the USSR Council of Ministers and a member of the Central Committee of the Soviet Communist Party, visited Mexico. Despite the denials of Cuban officials, he made an important stopover in Havana, where he placed a wreath with the Soviet hammer and sickle before the statute of Cuban patriot José Martí in Central Park.

A group of Catholic, anticommunist students from the University of Havana and other schools arrived at the park with their own wreath. Manuel Salvat, one of the student protestors, explained why they were there: "we went to protest the presence in Cuba of the man (Mikoyan) who was responsible for the 1956 Soviet massacre in Hungary, and because of the danger we perceived as the Cuban Government becoming more Communist each day."[20]

Castro's police clashed violently with the students. An American photographer, Andrew St. George, took pictures of the incident. That week the cover of *Life* magazine's Latin American edition showed Cuban police beating the students with clubs.

On Mikoyan's visit, they opened an exposition of Soviet products and signed a commercial pact that would provide economic assistance to Cuba, which already had begun establishing commercial and diplomatic relations with several nations in the Soviet bloc. On May 7 Cuba and the Soviet Union formally re-established diplomatic relations for the first time since the start of the Cold War.[21]

While Cuba drew closer to the Soviet Union, its relationship to the United States was rapidly deteriorating. In addition to his growing intimacy with the Soviet Union, Castro often attacked the United States in his speeches. And there was the issue of property expropriations. On July 2, 1960, the *New York Times* reported that when the three largest foreign oil refineries in Cuba—Esso, Shell, and Texaco—refused to process oil imported from the Soviet Union, the Cuban government nationalized the companies.[22]

Response from the United States was swift. With the authority granted by the unanimous vote of the U.S. House of Representatives, Eisenhower reduced Cuba's sugar quota by 700,000 tons on July 6 (almost twice the amount that the Soviet Union had agreed to purchase). By law, the United States gave Cuban sugar preferential treatment by paying a two-cent premium per pound of sugar and setting an annual purchase quota in advance.[23] Cuba retaliated on July 21 by seizing two of the largest American-owned sugar mills in the island—the Chaparra and Delicias.[24]

The *New York Times* on August, 21, 1960, reported: "The biggest grab of all occurred just two weeks ago on August 6. American properties with an investment value of more than $750,000,000 were formally nationalized, passing completely into ownership of the Cuban Government." Among the properties seized were the Cuban Electric Company, the previously intervened Cuban Telephone Company, two million acres of sugar cane fields, and the Moa Bay Nickel Mining Company.[25]

Throughout summer and fall, the expropriations continued. In October, the Castro regime "announced the most sweeping nationalization measures ever taken by a Western Hemisphere regime; 382 Cuban and foreign-owned companies with an estimated value of $2 billion were seized."[26] In response, the U.S. government suspended an economic agreement with Cuba, banned the purchase of Cuban sugar, and officially canceled Cuba's sugar quota for the first trimester of 1961 on December 16.[27] Two months earlier, Eisenhower had also started to restrict American exports to the island, in what constituted a limited embargo. A total embargo (except for food and medicine) would come a year later under President John F. Kennedy.

The Law of Nationalization, announced by Castro in August, led to the confiscation of thousands of American private business enterprises. "U.S. nationals have filed 8,816 claims for a total asserted amount of $3,346,406,271.36 against the Cuban government. This sum not only represents more than the amount expropriated by all other Communist governments combined (USSR, Poland, Rumania, Czechoslovakia, Hungary, Yugoslavia, and Bulgaria) but also indicates the extent of direct U.S. involvement in the Cuban economy prior to the Cuban revolution."[28]

As Cuba and the United States escalated their economic battles throughout 1960, opposition to Castro's regime within Cuba also intensified. "Throughout the month of January [1960], sabotage and small bombing missions in Cuba increased in frequency."[29] These small bombings, as well as the number of anticommunist groups, increased as the year wore on and the government became more totalitarian each day. On May 8, the government expelled anticommunist students from the University of Havana. Workers who were identified as anticommunist were purged from the labor movement and lost their jobs.

There was no longer a middle ground in Cuba. People were either supporters of the revolution or its enemies. Fidel Castro made it clear: anyone who is anticommunist is a counterrevolutionary. And the government began persecuting anticommunists, jailing many based on the perception that they opposed the revolution. Porfirio Ramírez, the president of the Las Villas University's Student Council, was executed by a firing squad.

An incident that shook the government, occurred at the port of Havana when La Coubre, a French ship carrying arms and ammunitions for the Cuban Armed Forces, blew up. More than one hundred people died in the explosion and three hundred were wounded. "That day at funerals of the victims Fidel Castro accused the United States of responsibility for the action."[30] The case has never been solved.

The Cuban government also began to crack down on religious

activity. The Catholic Church, as the largest religious group in Cuba, bore the brunt of the early confrontation. In August, Cuba's Catholic hierarchy wrote a pastoral letter denouncing the spread of communism in Cuba.[31] Determined to suppress this open challenge, government militia forces broke into churches to stop priests from reading the pastoral letter from the pulpit.

Committees in Defense of the Revolution were a block-by-block group that encouraged Cubans to spy and inform on the activities of their neighbors. It gave "the people" the right to search any house in their neighborhood any time. They were urged to be vigilant of any suspicious activity by anyone thought to be opposed to the regime. These reports were used to determine who would be allowed to attend university, what status a person held at his place of employment, and sometimes even who ended up in jail. In Cuba, you could no longer trust neighbors or members of your own family not to turn you in for counter-revolutionary activities.[32]

On September 16, government militia moved into the three U.S.-owned banks as rumors spread in Havana that the government was going to "intervene" or seize the banks.[33] The rumors became fact the next morning. On October 14, the Urban Reform Law decreed that all private residential properties now belonged to the state. Cubans no longer legally owned their homes, and it was against the law to buy or sell any residential property. Even moving required government approval.[34]

Castro's government simultaneously carried out what the *New York Times* called "the most extensive nationalization program ever attempted in the Western Hemisphere." It added, "In twenty months of rule moved to nationalize or control much of the land, industry and even commerce in the island."[35]

By the start of 1961, government control over everyday life was virtually absolute. Cuba had become a totalitarian regime, and its population now broke down into three groups. The first was made up of people who still believed in the revolution, or at least became active supporters in order to survive.

A second group was committed to ousting the Castro government and preventing Cuba from becoming another Soviet satellite nation. Knowing they would be imprisoned or executed if they were caught, members of this group joined underground networks in the cities or joined those fighting the regime in the Escambray Mountains.

A third group wanted to leave Cuba.

NOTES

1. Interview with Leonardo Rodríguez, Florida International University, January 21, 2009.
2. Interview with Oziel González on January 12, 2009.
3. Advertisements, *Miami Herald*, January 1, 1959.
4. "Batista Troops Pounds Rebels from Province," *Miami Herald*, January 1, 1959.
5. "500 U.S. Refugees arrive in Florida," *New York Times*, January 3, 1959.
6. "Effects on Florida," *New York Times*, January 11, 1959.
7. "500 U.S. Refugees arrive in Florida."
8. John Dorschner and Roberto Fabricio, *Winds of December* (New York: Coward, McCann & Geoghegan, 1980), 453.
9. Hugh Thomas, *Cuba: The Pursuit of Freedom* (New York: Harper & Row, 1971), 1065-66.
10. *Diario La Marina*, January 9, 1959. ("No; en la paloma Blanca sobre la mano diestra de Fidel Castro vemos un claro designio del Altísimo, pues ese símbolo universal de la paz traduce e interpreta cabalmente el gran deseo, la voluntad entera, de todo el pueblo cubano.")
11. Emeterio S. Santovenia and Raúl M. Shelton, *Cuba y su Historia* (Miami: Rema Press, 1965), 308.
12. Herminio Portel Vilá, *Nueva Historia de la República de Cuba* (Miami: La Moderna Poesía, 1996), 729.
13. "Castro Rules Out Role as Neutral; Opposes the Reds," *New York Times*, April 20, 1959.
14. The National Security Archive: Bay of Pigs, Washington, D.C., 1-2.
15. Thomas, *Pursuit of Freedom*, 1233.
16. Manuel Artime Bueza, *¡Traición! Gritan 20,000 Tumbas Cubanas* (Mexico City: Editorial Jus, 1960), 3-16.
17. The National Security Archive: Bay of Pigs, 3.
18. Tracy S. Voorhees, *Report to the President of the United States on the Cuban Refugee Problem* (Washington, D.C.: Government Printing Office, January 18, 1961), 1; U.S. Bureau of the Census, *U.S. Census of Population: 1960*, vol. 1.
19. "Russians purchase more Cuban Sugar," *New York Times*, October 2, 1959.
20. Interview with Manuel Salvat, May 29, 2010.

21. Tad Szulc, "Cuba is Exchanging Envoys with Soviet," *New York Times*, May 8, 1960.
22. Tad Szulc, "Last 2 Refineries Seized by Castro: Oil Supplies Low," *New York Times*, July 2, 1960.
23. "Castro Forces Carry Out Seizure of U.S. Properties," *New York Times*, August 8, 1960.
24. Hart R. Phillips, "2 U.S. Sugar Mills Seized by Cubans," *New York Times*, July 22, 1960.
25. Richard Rutter, "U.S. Investment in Cuba Shrinks," *New York* Times, August 21, 1960.
26. "The Week in Review," *New York Times*, October 30, 1960.
27. *New York Times*, December 17, 1960.
28. Lynn Darrell Bender, *The Politics of Hostility: Castro's Revolution and United States Policy* (Hato Rey, Puerto Rico: Inter American University Press, 1975), 101.
29. National Security Archive: The Bay of Pigs, 4.
30. National Security Archive: The Bay of Pigs, 6.
31. Joseph Holbrook, *The Church in Cuba: Ambivalence between Regime and Revolution 1952-1962* (Miami: Florida International University, 2009).
32. "History of the (CDR) Committees to Defend the Revolution" (*Comités de Defensa de la Revolución*), *Prensa Latina*, September 28, 2005.
33. Hart R. Phillips, "Cuba Opens Move on U.S. Banks," *New York Times*, September 17, 1960.
34. Hart R. Phillips, "Castro's Cuba Takes Long Step to Left," *New York Times*, October 16, 1960.
35. Ibid.

4

THE FIRST EXILES

BY GUILLERMO MARTINEZ AND SAM VERDEJA

The Cubans who chose to leave their homeland had certain things in common. Some had been jailed previously and knew they would be arrested again if they stayed. Others knew they had already been identified as antirevolutionaries and could expect economic deprivation or even imprisonment. Many of those included in these groups were professionals, for whom opportunities had narrowed greatly since the revolution. And still others just wanted to protect their children.

As private schools were taken over by the Communist regime, parents who opposed the system transferred their children to other private schools, or schooled them at home. Castro announced a literacy campaign through which adolescents would be sent to serve as teachers in the countryside, far from their families. They would live in barracks with poor sanitation and no checks on promiscuity, undergo political indoctrination, and be exposed to physical peril.

The literacy manuals handed out to peasants were full of propaganda. For example, to teach vowels it used "*OEA, Organization of American States, an imperialist organization against Cuba.*" Years later Castro established an organization for children called Pioneers of the Revolution. These are the children that still today wear a red kerchief around their neck and shout, "Let us be like Ché (Guevara)."

This was not the life middle-class Cuban parents had dreamed of for their children. But if they resisted the government, they would lose their jobs or end up in jail. The situation was akin to a fire in a building, and many parents felt they had to get their children out first.

It was not easy for adults to leave. They needed visas from a foreign country, as well as government permission to leave Cuba. But those who requested exit permits automatically lost their jobs if they worked for the government—and the government was well on its way to becoming the country's only employer. In addition, inspectors from the Committee for the Defense of the Revolution would show up at would-be exiles' houses to inventory all their belongings, down to every picture frame. Once the government had a list of all property, including automobiles, adult Cubans couldn't sell, give away, or barter anything they had once owned.

Cubans who were allowed to leave were forced to turn over their properties to the government. They arrived at their destination with no money and just the clothes they could carry in a suitcase. The American government, under Eisenhower, created the Cuban Refugee Emergency Center in 1960. The *Refugio*, as Cuban exiles called it, gave those arriving in the United States cash, clothes, food, medical assistance, and access to adult education centers. The arriving exiles were also given airplane tickets to other parts of the country where religious or social organizations could help them get re-established. Those with relatives or friends in Miami could remain in the area.

On January 18, 1961, two days before the end of his term as president, Eisenhower received a report from Tracy Voorhees, his personal representative, on the growing Cuban refugee population in the United States and their impact on South Florida. Voorhees noted that, although some of the arriving refugees had resettled in New York and Newark and a smaller number in other cities throughout the country, "the majority remain in the Miami area. The ever-mounting Cuban population quite obviously has overrun the community's capacity to cope with it. The problem is now a national one." According to Voorhees, by the end of 1960 there were about 50,000 Cubans in the U.S., "most of whom, whether they are called tourists or refugees, are in reality exiles."[1] (However, the 1960 Census showed that in 1960 there were 124,000 Cubans in the United States).

On February 3, 1961, the recently inaugurated president John F. Kennedy agreed that the Cuban exiles needed more help from the Federal Government. Along with Secretary of Health, Education, and Welfare Abraham Ribicoff, Kennedy issued the following guidelines:

1. Provide all possible assistance to voluntary relief agencies in providing daily necessities for many of the refugees, for resettling as many of them as possible, and for securing jobs for them.

2. Obtain the assistance of both private and governmental agencies to provide useful employment opportunities for displaced Cubans, consistent with the overall employment situation prevailing in Florida.

3. Provide supplemental funds for the resettlement of refugees in other areas, including transportation and adjustment costs to the new communities and for their eventual return to Miami for repatriation to their homeland as soon as that is again possible.

4. Furnish financial assistance to meet basic maintenance requirements of needy Cuban refugee families in the Miami area are [also] required in communities of resettlement administered through federal, state, and local channels and based on standards used in the community involved.

5. Provide for essential health services through the financial assistance program supplemented by child health, public health services, and other arrangements as needed.

6. Furnish federal assistance for local public school operating costs related to the unforeseen impact of Cuban refugee children on local teaching facilities.

7. Initiate needed measures to augment training and educational opportunities for Cuban refugees including physicians, teachers, and those with other professional backgrounds.

8. Provide financial aid for the care and protection of unaccompanied children—the most defenseless and troubled group among the refugee population.

9. Undertake a surplus food distribution program to be administered by the county welfare department with surplus foods distributed by public and voluntary agencies to needy refugees.

In the White House statement accompanying Kennedy's recommendations, the president said, "Secretary Ribicoff paid tribute to the refugees as a proud and resourceful people, whose courage and fortitude in the face of tragic disruption of their lives is magnificent."

The president added he was particularly interested in Secretary Ribicoff's proposal to make effective use of the faculty of the University of Havana, three-fourths of which are reported to be in south Florida at the present time. I have asked Secretary Ribicoff to examine how this community of scholars could be most effectively used to keep alive the cultural and liberal traditions for which this faculty has been justly noted. It represents a great inter-American asset for their own people, for this country and for the entire hemisphere.[2]

In Cuba, many married couples had one spouse in prison or in hiding, while others were thinking about leaving, but could not for personal or family reasons. Whatever the reason, many families wanted to get their children out of Cuba.

James Baker, the headmaster of Havana's bilingual Ruston Academy, and Msgr. Bryan Walsh of the Archdiocese of Miami and head of Catholic Charities, helped establish a visa waivers program that allowed unaccompanied minors to travel to the U.S. where the federal government and private organizations would find homes for the children.

In Cuba, Polita Grau Alsina and her brother Ramón—the niece and nephew of former Cuban president Dr. Ramón Grau San Martín—with a group of society ladies began to spread the word that the American government would take care of unaccompanied children once they arrived in Miami. Monsignor Walsh was in charge of receiving the children and placing them in camps named Kendall, Matecumbe, Florida City, Jesuit's Boys Home, and St. Raphael to await assignment to foster homes and orphanages. If relatives volunteered to take them, these children would be entrusted in their care.

Polita was arrested and spent the next fourteen years in prison for an alleged conspiracy with the CIA, which included her role in this operation. Ramón and Albertina O'Farrill, one of the organizers, were also jailed. When the U.S. severed relations with Cuba, Penny Powers, a British nurse experienced in evacuating Jewish children from Germany, took over in Havana along with staff from many European embassies. Hebrew and Protestant congregations also handed out visa waivers. Sometimes passports were falsified to evacuate male youths of military age.

Francisco and Nieves Rodríguez, ages twelve and fourteen, were at their Havana home one summer day in 1961 when their parents asked them if they would go to the U.S. alone. They explained the difficult political situation in Cuba, and that they believed things would get worse before they would get better. They told their children they could go to school in the United States and return to Cuba when Communism had been brought down.

Their mother, Christina, worked at the University Hospital, where she had been singled out as an opponent of the regime. She wanted to leave with her children, but her parents were old and infirm, and the couple needed to stay in Cuba to take care of them until "the storm" was over. Francisco and Nieves agreed to go. Because they didn't want to attend a Communist school, they took English lessons all summer long until the day of their flight, August 4, 1961.

The Rodríguez children became part of Operación Pedro Pan (a name applied years later by the Miami media), which enabled 14,048 children[3] to leave Cuba between December 1960 to October 1962,[4] bound for American foster homes or orphanages.

In the memoir he wrote many years later, Francisco remembered arriving with his sister at the home of plumber James Hammond in Libby, Montana—population two thousand, and just ninety miles from the Canadian border. They thought they would never see their parents or Cuba again. One year later they were reunited with their parents and grandparents in Miami, though they have never returned to their beloved island. When asked if he has ever been back to Cuba, Francisco replies, "I never left."[5]

Though Francisco and Nieves for the most part had a good experience, they did suffer culture shock, nostalgia, and loneliness in the snow-capped Rocky Mountains with their below-zero temperatures. All the Pedro Pans, as they are affectionately called, suffered to one degree or another. Some of the worst stories were publicized by Castro's regime. When Cuban exiles debate the issue they ask themselves: given the same circumstances, what would they do? Opinions are divided, but all agree that the Pedro Pans have enjoyed tremendous success in American society. From developer Armando Codina to singer Willy Chirino, from U.S. Senator Mel Martínez to businessman Carlos Saladrigas, Pedro Pans have attained the highest levels of achievement. They share a bond similar to that of veterans, a bond of gratitude both to their parents and to the nation that took them in.

Codina looks back on his experience and recalls the hard times away from his family. But now, as a father and grandfather himself, he understands what his own parents endured. "To me this is the story of the sacrifice of Cuban parents to save their children from Communism. They are the true heroes of this story."[6]

Children were not the only ones fleeing Cuba. As the repression and human rights abuses in Cuba continued, the Cuban exodus encompassed people of all ages. The exiles settled in Spain, Puerto Rico, Venezuela, and a number of other Latin American countries, in addition to the United States. For a number of reasons, Spain became a preferred destination for Cuban exiles fleeing the revolution.

The foreigners most affected by Castro's expropriations and nationalizations were not Americans, but the Spaniards who owned much of the wholesale and retail trade sector in Cuba. In addition, Cuba was very Spanish—with tens of thousands of families on the island having Hispanic roots. Many of these chose to return in the early 1960s. How many joined in that first exodus? An estimate is about 125,000 to 200,000, of which 80,000 eventually went on to the United States. It's difficult to establish with certainty because some of those who emigrated already had Spanish citizenship, and for others Spain was merely a way-station on their journey.[7]

When the Cuban exodus began, Luis Muñoz Marín, then the governor of Puerto Rico, generously welcomed his Caribbean neighbors fleeing the Communist dictatorship. Throughout the first half of the 1960s, a wave of intellectuals, artists, and businessmen arrived who quickly integrated into their new adopted country. The Cuban community in Puerto Rico peaked at more than thirty thousand people and left a positive mark in business, industry, and the arts.[8] Given the close cultural and ethnic ties between the two islands, children and grandchildren of the exiles very often married Puerto Ricans creating a mix affectionately called *cubarriqueños*. Something similar had occurred in Cuba in the early twentieth century, when the Republic was established, and between twenty and twenty-five thousand Puerto Ricans were fully integrated into Cuban society.

The best estimate of the number of Cuban exiles in Venezuela, called *venecubanos*, is between forty and fifty thousand. Rómulo Betancourt, president of Venezuela in 1960, had lived in exile in Cuba in the 1940s and early 1950s, and he was convinced that from the beginning Castro intended to establish a Soviet-style Communist dictatorship in Cuba. So, like Muñoz Marín in Puerto Rico, he welcomed Cubans who were fleeing. The fate of Cuban exiles in Venezuela was similar to their fate in the United States and Puerto Rico. Though most arrived penniless, within a few years, they were leaders in television, radio, advertising, sugar processing, and other businesses. When Hugo Chavez came to power, many of these families fled Venezuela, generally for the United States.

About eighty thousand Cuban exiles obtained visas to settle in Mexico, with many subsequently moving on to the United States.[9] In Chile there are an estimated twenty thousand Cubans. Ecuador and the Dominican Republic also received exiles from the Cuban Revolution, with their Cuban communities growing substantially from later migrations up to the present time. However, the majority of Cuban exiles came to Miami and stayed. This was closest to home, and most believed their stay would be brief.

In South Florida some Cubans struggled to find work and lived in crowded small apartments. Others quickly joined exile groups—often supported by the CIA—and began training in the Everglades. By March 1960, "The CIA begins training 300 guerrillas, initially in the U.S. and the [Panama] Canal Zone. Following an agreement with Guatemalan President [Manuel] Ydigoras [Fuentes] in June, training shifts to Guatemala." Simultaneously, "the CIA begins work to install a powerful radio station on Greater Swan Island, ninety seven miles off the coast of Honduras."[10]

In May, five anti-Castro groups held an organization meeting in the United States to create an umbrella group called the Frente Revolucionario Democrático (FRD). They were: Manuel Artime's MRR; Rescate Revolucionario, headed by Tony Varona; the Christian Democratic Movement, led by José Ignacio Rasco; the Asociación Montecristi, led by Justo Carrillo; and Aureliano Sánchez Arango's Frente Nacional Triple A. The groups joined forces officially and issued their first manifesto in Mexico City in June of 1960.[11]

The interest of Cuban exiles to oust Castro increasingly coincided with American interests. U.S. officials believed that the strategy they had successfully used a few years earlier to remove the leftist regime of Jacobo Arbenz in Guatemala could be used against Castro.

On September 20, 1960, Castro attended a meeting of the United

Nations General Assembly in New York and ratified Cuba's dependency and ties with the Soviet Union. This was after a much publicized stay at the Hotel Theresa in Harlem, where he met with Malcom X, a militant African American leader; Jawaharlal Nehru, the prime minister of India; and Nikita S. Khrushchev, the premier of the Soviet Union.[12]

The Cuban delegation was delighted with the attention the Soviet premier had given them. The *New York Times* quoted Castro, explaining that he had chosen the "predominantly Negro hotel" as "a further example of the bond he felt with American Negroes and with Africa."[13]

By the end of 1960, the Cuban government had executed 1,062[14] of its citizens, jailed more than 3,300,[15] and lost thousands to other countries.

NOTES

1. Tracy S. Voorhees, *Report to the President of the United States on the Cuban Refugee Problem* (Washington, D.C.: Government Printing Office, January 18, 1961), 1.
2. Ibid. 11.
3. Yvonne M. Conde, *Operation Pedro Pan: The Untold Exodus of the 14,048 Cuban Children* (New York, Routledge Press, 1999), xii.
4. www.pedropan.org.
5. Francisco Rodríguez interview on February 23, 2010.
6. Armando Codina interview on September 18, 2009.
7. Pilar González Yanci and José Aguilera Arilla, *La Inmigración Cubana en España. Razones Políticas y de Sangre en la Elección de Destino.* UNED. Espacio. Tiempo y Forma Serie VI, Geografía, t. 15, 2002. p. 14-15.
8. José A. Cobas and Jorge Duany, *Cubans in Puerto Rico: Ethnic Economy and Cultural Identity* (Gainesville: University Press of Florida, 1997), 41.
9. Migration Policy Institute Data Hub, *Migration Facts, State, and Maps. Country and Comparative Data.* http://www. Migration information.org (datahub/country data/data.cfm.
10. National Security Archive, The Bay of Pigs, 5.
11. Calixto C. Masó, *Historia de Cuba* (Miami: Ediciones Universal, 1975), 683.
12. Christopher Gray, "Castro Slept Here," *New York Times*, May 3, 2009.
13. Max Frankel, "Cuban Delegation Is Pleased by Attention from Russia," *New York Times*, September 21, 1960.
14. Esteban M. Beruvides, *Cuba y sus Mártires* (Miami: 12th Avenue Graphics, 1993), 83–188.
15. Esteban M. Beruvides, *Cuba y su Presidio Político* (Miami: 12th Avenue Graphics, 1994), 207–267.

5

BAY OF PIGS: A PROGRAM OF COVERT ACTION

BY HOWARD KLEINBERG

During the fourth televised presidential debate on October 22, 1960, Democratic candidate John Kennedy infuriated Vice President Richard Nixon by suggesting that the Eisenhower Administration was not doing enough to address the Castro threat.[1] Aware that Kennedy had been briefed on Cuba by CIA Director Allen Dulles, Nixon assumed that his opponent knew the full extent of the current administration's "operational" plans for Cuba, and that he was trying to take credit for a strategy that was not his own.

Determined to protect the confidentiality of the project, he attacked Kennedy for "probably the most dangerously irresponsible recommendation" of the campaign. Yet, according to Arthur Schlesinger, Jr., author of the Kennedy Administration memoir *A Thousand Days*, Kennedy didn't learn until November 17 that troops were already training in Guatemala for a Cuban invasion.[2]

Keeping Kennedy and his campaign in the dark had seemed necessary in order to maintain a secrecy which was already unraveling. On October 30, a Guatemalan newspaper, *La Hora*, reported that training was underway on a coffee plantation in the mountains. In November, the *Hispanic American Report* editorialized that while people in the U.S. did not know what was going on in Guatemala, Fidel Castro did. By December, *The Nation*, the *Los Angeles Mirror*, and the *St. Louis Post-Dispatch* were speaking of the secret camps, and on January 10 the *New York Times* even published a map of the Guatemalan base.[3]

Two days before the fourth Kennedy-Nixon debate, Eisenhower had announced an embargo on all U.S. goods shipped to Cuba, except food and medicine.[4] When the president had first considered a blockade of Cuba in January 1960, his advisors warned that it would punish the Cuban people more than their government. But Eisenhower was concerned about Castro's growing ties with the Soviet Union, as well as his execution of political opponents, and his escalating rhetoric against the United States. The president asked Dulles to develop a strategy to deal with Castro, and Dulles turned to Richard Bissell, his deputy director for plans.

Bissell controlled the "operations" half of the CIA budget, which included "black operations." In addition to spearheading an operational strategy for Cuba, he was already involved in clandestine operations in Laos and the Congo. Bissell developed a top secret policy paper entitled "A Program of Covert Action against the Castro Regime." Its purpose was to "bring about the replacement of the Castro regime with one more devoted to the true interests of the Cuban people and more acceptable to the U.S. in such manner as to avoid any appearance of U.S intervention."[5]

By his own admission, Bissell was the "hands-on" architect of both the Eisenhower and Kennedy plans for invading Cuba. According to his autobiography *Reflections of a Cold Warrior*, published posthumously in 1996, "Successful operations in Iran and Guatemala, where unfriendly governments were destabilized and replaced with regimes compatible with U.S. interests, had provided the agency with enough experience and confidence to believe that Cuba would offer another suitable and manageable target."

He and Dulles presented their plan—code-named Operation Pluto—to Eisenhower and his team in March 1960:

Following presentation and discussion of the concept, the president said he knew of no better plan. As always, he also demonstrated his desire for security and plausible deniability . . . [he said] Everyone must be "prepared to swear that he has not heard of [the plan]." . . . [W]e estimated that a covert action and intelligence organization, or a guerilla movement, could probably be created within sixty days. We left with Eisenhower's approval to carry it forward.[6]

The original idea was to provide support for the underground resistance that had been fighting Castro since the beginning of 1959. By the end of that year, thousands of peasants had rejected the government's agrarian reforms and taken up arms in the same Escambray Mountains where they had fought the Batista regime. Eloy Gutiérrez Menoyo, the leader of the *Segundo Frente del Escambray* and one of the most important military figures in the struggle against Batista, fled Cuba for Key West. Like others in the underground, Menoyo had become convinced that military resistance would be necessary to regain what they had fought for in the revolution, and then lost to Communism.

In Miami, anti-Castro activity had been on the rise ever since the first exiles fled the revolution. A shadowy figure named Frank Bender was busy recruiting on behalf of the CIA. Bender, a German-born CIA agent whose real name was Gerry Droller, had participated in the CIA-led overthrow of Guatemala's elected but leftist president Jacobo Arbenz in 1954. One of his early Cuban recruits was Manuel Artime, head of the Movement for the Recovery of the Revolution, who had previously fought on the side of the anti-Batista rebels and ran an area of Castro's Agrarian Reform Institute. After publicly resigning from Castro's administration in protest over its Communist direction, Artime had been spirited out of Cuba in December 1959.[7]

Based in a house on Miami's SW 27th Avenue, Artime began recruiting exiles to train for a military overthrow of Castro. Among his recruits were sixteen-year-old Humberto Martínez Llano and his older brother Eduardo. Their odyssey would take them to Guatemala, Nicaragua, and eventually the Bay of Pigs.[8] Nineteen-year-old Ricardo Sánchez, who arrived in Miami with only five dollars in his pocket, also signed on with Artime. "I was looking for ways to return but not under a Castro dictatorship," he recalled. "There was a house across the street from the old Omni hotel where you could enlist to fight Castro. I went there first and was told to report to a little house near the Orange Bowl." He and thirty others boarded an unmarked bus for Opa-locka airport, where they were flown on to Guatemala.[9]

According to Schlesinger, by the end of 1959, Miami was alive with anti-Castro political activity that Schlesinger described as "unorganized and feckless." He observed sarcastically that "every time two or three refugees gathered together a new union or Movimiento was likely to emerge."[10] Bissell and the CIA agents on the ground had their hands full trying to organize Cuban exiles in Miami into a coalescent force.

In June 1960, the five leading exile groups formed the *Frente Revolucionario Democratico*. Three of the groups represented prerevolutionary Batista Cuba, while two were led by men who had briefly served Castro's revolutionary government. These parties all had different perspectives and objectives in their resistance to Castro, making consensus challenging. It was this internecine rivalry that Bissell claimed "prevented them from playing a more active and authoritative role in organizing, training, and directing the operation and meant that it had to be conducted by an American-run enterprise. Moreover, not every leader of the exile community was persona grata to the men in the training camps."[11]

As early as August 1960, journalists were sniffing around the Florida Everglades trying to monitor exile activities. According to future Second Battalion Commander Hugo Sueiro, he and other exiled graduates from Cuba's Cadet School "started going out to the Everglades to shoot and do light training. . . . With the support of wealthy Cubans in Miami, we bought equipment and guns."[12]

The CIA was finding it difficult to make contact with the guerilla insurgents in Cuba, and CIA personnel feared these groups had been infiltrated by Castro agents. This is where the organizational structure and politics of the CIA came into play. Schlesinger wrote that "it appeared only later that the intelligence branch of the CIA had never been officially apprised of the Cuban expedition. . . . [T]he men on the Cuban desk who received the daily flow of information from the island were never asked to comment on the feasibility of the venture."[13]

The exile leaders in Miami would later make the same point to Schlesinger: those who had the most knowledge of and connections with the internal resistance were neither informed of the plan nor given the opportunity to come up with a better one. So the focus shifted to the invasion force being trained in Guatemala. Sometime between the American presidential election and the transition from Eisenhower to Kennedy, Bissell claimed his original plan underwent a metamorphosis. "It was during the transition period," Bissell wrote, "that the concept of Brigade 2506 began to take its final form."[14]

With the cooperation of Guatemalan president Manuel Ydígoras, the CIA secured a training site high in the mountains, on land owned by the family of the Guatemalan ambassador to the U.S.[15] The group at Base Trax, originally consisting of 28 men including 10 former Cuban military officers, had grown to 160 members by September. The CIA appointed José Perez (Pepe) San Román as commander, and assigned Brigade members identification numbers beginning with 2500—so everyone would think there were more people involved.[16] The brigade was named after one of its members—Carlos Rodríguez Santana: Number 2506—who was killed in an accident.

The Alabama Air Guard, under the command of General Reid Doster, played a pivotal role in planning the invasion. The CIA had "purchased" twenty surplus B-26 bombers from the U.S. Air Force "graveyard" in Arizona and recruited Alabama Air Guard pilots to train the Cuban exile pilots because it had been the last military organization to fly B-26 bombers in combat.[17]

New Year's Day, 1961, marked the second anniversary of the Cuban

Revolution. On January 3, Castro ordered the American Embassy in Havana to reduce their diplomatic personnel to just eleven officials. The next day, Washington broke off diplomatic relations with Cuba.[18] Eisenhower's anxiety escalated, and "he was prepared to 'move against Castro' before Kennedy's inauguration . . . if a 'really good excuse' was provided by Castro," Bissell wrote. "'Failing that,' he said, 'perhaps we could think of manufacturing something that would be generally acceptable.'"[19]

On January 20, John F. Kennedy was sworn in as president. A week later he reviewed the existing plans for Cuba and expressed concern about both the probability of success and the "plausible deniability" of the United States. But the team he inherited pushed hard to keep the planned invasion on course. Schlesinger described the situation:

> *Both Dulles and Bissell were at a disadvantage in having to persuade a skeptical new administration about the virtues of a proposal nurtured in the hospitable bosom of a previous government—a proposal on which they had personally worked for a long time and in which their organization had a heavy vested interest. This cast them in the role less of analysts than of advocates, and it led them to accept progressive modifications so long as the expedition in some form remained; perhaps they too subconsciously supposed that once the operation began to unfold, it would not be permitted to fail. . . . [T]he determination to keep the scheme alive sprang in part, I believe, from the embarrassment of calling it off.*[20]

One of the most convincing arguments for Kennedy was what Dulles called the "disposal problem." As Kennedy told Schlesinger after the meeting, "if we have to take these men out of Guatemala, we will have to transfer them to the United States, and we can't have them wandering around the country telling everyone what they have been doing."[21]

For an invasion site, the CIA had selected Trinidad, on Cuba's southern coast. It was close to the Escambray Mountains, remote from Castro's main army, and it had a decent harbor and beaches that could be defended as a beachhead. However, the landing strip was not long enough to land B-26 bombers, and Kennedy felt an invasion there would be "too spectacular." He suggested they find an alternative site for a quiet night landing. The Joint Chiefs of Staff then recommended an area one hundred miles west of Trinidad, near Cienaga de Zapata. The *Bahia de Cochinos*, or Bay of Pigs, had an acceptable landing strip as well as swamps to provide a natural defense for the invaders. Kennedy agreed to move forward in planning the Bay of Pigs invasion, with the stipulation that U.S. forces would not be used. He also reserved the right to call off the operation at any point, even "as late as twenty-four hours before D-day."[22]

Training in Guatemala was not going as well as Kennedy's progress reports indicated. In January the discontent escalated to mutiny. According to Schlesinger, "almost half the now more than 500 Cubans in the camp resigned and refused to accept [San Román as their military leader.] . . . In one of the unhappier passages in this unhappy story, the CIA operatives arrested a dozen of the ringleaders and held them prisoner under stark conditions deep in the jungles of northern Guatemala."[23]

For two and a half months, Humberto and Eduardo Martínez trained with Americans "in the M-1 rifle, bazooka, machine gun and carbine."[24] Ricardo Sánchez completed basic military training at Base Trax, and then became a paratrooper. He'd never before jumped from a plane. "We started off by jumping from 50-gallon oil drums to get the feel of a landing," he recalled. After two weeks of training—and five real jumps—he and his group would fly to Puerto Cabezas to prepare for the assault.[25]

On March 21, Cuban exile leaders created a new umbrella group of anti-Castro organizations—the Cuban Revolutionary Council (CRC) to replace the *Frente Revolucionario Democratico*. The new group was headed by former Castro Prime Minister José Miró Cardona, included most of the *Frente* organization, and added Manuel Ray's *Movimiento Revolucionario del Pueblo*. The CRC appointed Manuel Artime as its political liaison with the invading force being trained in Guatemala.

President Kennedy flew to his Palm Beach compound on March 29, accompanied by U.S. Senator William Fulbright, a powerful member of the Senate Foreign Relations Committee. Fulbright used the opportunity to try to dissuade Kennedy from going forward with the invasion. He gave Kennedy a memorandum that said: "To give this activity even covert support is of a piece with the hypocrisy and cynicism for which the United States is constantly denouncing the Soviet Union in the United Nations and elsewhere. This point will not be lost on the rest of the world—nor on our own consciences."[26] Schlesinger also wrote a memo to Kennedy opposing the invasion, but their voices were drowned out by the rest of his advisors.

Kennedy sent Schlesinger and three other staffers to meet with Miró Cardona in Miami and persuade him to beef up the social and economic sides of the Council's program. "Miró threw his hands in the air, heartily agreed, and said that we must understand the situation in Miami; whenever he delivered a speech about social justice, half the audience went away convinced that he was a communist."

They used this opening to suggest the Council move their headquarters to New York, and "away from the feverish atmosphere of Miami dominated by Cubans of the right." Schlesinger was relieved when Miró acquiesced again, but began to think about "the humiliating lot of the exile who wished above all to maintain his political group and the sources of its income and who therefore must permit himself to be buffeted about by all those in a position to open a purse, whether wealthy refugees, CIA spooks or now Washington officials."[27]

On April 8, Ted Szulc of the *New York Times* described Miami as

> *a city of open secrets and rampaging rumors for the legions of exiled Cubans who plot the downfall of Premier Fidel Castro and his regime. Men come and go quietly on their secret missions of sabotage and gun-running into Cuba, while others assemble at staging points here to be flown at night to military camps in Guatemala and Louisiana. Families and friends gather to bid farewell to the soldiers. . . . The men are given khaki uniforms, then put aboard*

trucks to be driven to abandoned Florida airfields where unmarked aircraft are waiting to fly them to Central America.[28]

At a press conference on April 12, Kennedy stated: "There will not be, under any circumstances, an intervention in Cuba by the United States Armed Forces. . . . The basic issue in Cuba is not one between the United States and Cuba. It is between the Cubans themselves. I intend to see that we adhere to that principle and as I understand it this administration's attitude is so understood and shared by the anti-Castro exiles from Cuba in this country."[29]

The president's words could not have been clearer. Unfortunately, no one except Kennedy himself believed them—not the exile leadership, nor the brigade, nor even Kennedy's own staff.

The day after the press conference, Kennedy sent Schlesinger to New York to meet again with Miró Cardona and make sure that he and the Council fully understood the U.S. position. But Miró "waved the President's news conference disclaimer aside as an understandable piece of psychological warfare and kept pressing us to say how far the administration meant to go."[30] When Schlesinger reported back that he felt Miró still didn't believe they wouldn't be getting armed support from the United States, the president telephoned Bissell and told him to make sure Miró understood that "either he agrees to proceed on the basis of no United States military intervention or else the whole expedition would be called off. Bissell sent Tracy Barnes to New York that day to stress the point. Though Barnes got a formal assent, he too returned to Washington doubtful whether Miró really believed him."[31]

At Base Trax, where troops had begun boarding trucks on April 10 for the journey to the Puerto Cabezas docks in Nicaragua, Humberto Martínez recalled being issued new equipment. Once aboard the command ship *Houston*, "they gave us maps and things like that. We fully expected U.S. support. When you see the U.S. Navy next to you, you assume you are supported."[32]

Even some of Kennedy's own team continued to assume that his opposition to overt U.S. intervention was just public relations—or at the very least that the president would change his mind when it became clear that U.S. military support was crucial to avoiding disaster (as Eisenhower had done in Guatemala in 1954). Schlesinger suggests that both the Joint Chiefs of Staff and the CIA leadership might have continued to advocate the plan, despite their own misgivings, in the hope of forcing the president to take decisive action against Castro.

On April 13, 1961, a speedboat manned by Cuban exiles shelled the Texaco refinery in Santiago de Cuba. The underground resistance set fire to sugar-cane fields and Cuba's famous high-end department store El Encanto, as well as planting bombs throughout the island. Five days later, the government rounded up the opposition leaders, including Rogelio González Corso (Francisco) and Humberto Sori Marín, a lawyer who had fought alongside Castro in the Sierra Maestra and was a member of his first cabinet.

D-Day had originally been set for April 5, but it was pushed back to April 10, then April 17. Right up until the end the president seemed uncertain about proceeding. However, a few factors persuaded him to move forward. The first, according to Schlesinger, was that "the massed and caparisoned authority of his senior officials in the realm of foreign policy and defense was unanimous for going ahead."[33] Second, the president kept coming back to the "disposal problem," telling Schlesinger that "if we have to get rid of these 800 men, it is much better to dump them in Cuba than in the United States, especially if that is where they want to go."[34]

Finally, Kennedy received an unambiguously confident evaluation of the Brigade's readiness from a marine colonel who was with the troops in Guatemala. "The message reached the White House on April 14 shortly before the hour of what is known in Pentagonese as the 'no-go' decision on preliminary operations. The fervent testimonial confirmed the President in his intention to let the expedition go ahead."[35]

At the same time, so anxious was the Kennedy Administration to disguise U.S. complicity in the seaborne invasion that on April 13, Chairman of Joint Chiefs of Staff Admiral Lemnitzer sent a telegram to Admiral Robert Dennison, Commander in Chief of Atlantic Naval Forces, with the following instructions:

> *Original concept for U.S. naval support . . . was to ensure that when once embarked this operation must not fail. Concept . . . modified by the later plan which provides that cancellation possible until landing phase actually starts. Concept further modified by provision in rules of engagement that if intervention by U.S. military element is required and actually takes place while Cuban Expeditionary Force en route to transport area then operation must abort. . . . Actual engagement of Castro ships or aircraft should be withheld until last possible moment and action taken only after it becomes clear that otherwise total destruction of friendly ships may be imminent.*[36]

On April 14, Kennedy also gave Bissell

> *a fairly ambiguous instruction. He wanted to play down the magnitude of the invasion in the public eye and therefore did not want a full-strength strike but a more limited one. As far as I know, he made this decision without consulting with the Joint Chiefs or the Secretary of Defense. I was simply directed to reduce the scale and make it "minimal." He left it to me to determine exactly what that meant, and I responded by cutting the planned sixteen aircraft to eight.*[37]

The uncontestable truth about the invasion floats in a dissonant sea as ragged as the reefs near Playa Girón. The initial and subsequent recollections are as diverse as the people providing them. U.S. bureaucrats and military officers remember events differently from the Revolutionary Council or the men who actually made the landings. And Fidel Castro has his own version. What is clear is that "plausible deniability" ruled the day. The additional constraints imposed by the president undoubtedly hampered the Brigade's mission, which had a meager chance of success to begin with.

At dawn on the morning of April 15, the scaled-back air attack took place. The B-26 bombers had been painted to resemble Cuban Air Force planes. Of the seventeen available bombers at Puerto Cabezas, only eight took off for Cuba; a ninth made a beeline for the coast of Florida. This was all part of the "plausible deniability" scheme to make it look like rogue Cuban Air Force pilots were leading the raids.[38]

The air attack inflicted only modest damage to the airfields at Campo Libertad, Maceo Airport at Santiago de Cuba, and at San Antonio de los Baños. Anti-aircraft fire caused one of the planes to ditch at sea, killing the crew. The B-26 that landed at Miami International Airport exhibited bullet holes in its fuselage to support the story that it was a Cuban Air Force defector that had been struck in combat.

Cuba's foreign minister Dr. Raoul Roa appeared before the United Nations in an emergency session and made formal charges of U.S. involvement. Adlai Stevenson, U.S. ambassador to the UN, read a prepared speech he'd been given with orders not to change a single word. He reiterated the CIA cover story—even reporting that the aircraft that had landed in Florida were defectors from Castro's Air Force—and asserted "No U.S. personnel participated."[39]

At first, the U.S. press fell for the story, but they quickly figured out the ruse, reporting that the damage to the plane was inflicted while the plane was still on the ground in Nicaragua and that its wing guns had never been fired. The pilot, Mario Zuñiga, was hustled back to Nicaragua the following day.

When Stevenson learned the truth, he was furious that he'd been hung out to dry. Schlesinger had participated in briefing Stevenson, but admits "our briefing, which was probably unduly vague, left Stevenson with the impression that no action would take place during the UN discussion of the Cuban item."[40]

The collapse of the cover story convinced Secretary of State Dean

Rusk that a second air strike from Nicaragua would put Stevenson and the United States in "an untenable position internationally." He and McGeorge Bundy called the president at his Virginia retreat and, "After a long conversation, the President directed that the strike be cancelled."[41]

Meanwhile, the expeditionary force was gathering off the *Bahia de Cochinos*. The assault was to begin at 1:00 A.M. on April 17 and continue into the daylight hours, with additional air strikes against Cuban Air Force bases.

About this time, Bundy notified the CIA that "we could not be permitted to launch air strikes the next morning until they could be conducted from a strip within the beachhead. Any further consultation regarding this matter should be with the Secretary of State." This instruction then was passed on to General Maxwell Taylor, in charge of U.S. military operations.[42]

Alarmed for the success of the mission, Bissell and his CIA team argued with Rusk against this latest curtailment. Though Rusk held firm, he offered Bissell an opportunity to plead his case directly with the president. But Bissell decided the die had been cast. "Today I view this decision as a major mistake," he wrote in his memoir. "For the record, we should have spoken with the President and made as strong a case as possible on behalf of the operation and the welfare of the brigade."[43]

NOTES

1. "Kennedy Asks Aid for Castro Rebels to Defeat Castro," *New York Times*, October 21, 1960.
2. Arthur M. Schlesinger, Jr., *A Thousand Days* (Boston: Houghton Mifflin Company, 1965), 212-13.
3. Hugh Thomas, *Cuba: Pursuit of Freedom* (New York: Harper and Row, Publishers, 1971), 1304-5. [Citation: "U.S. Helps Train an Anti-Castro Force At Secret Guatemalan Air-Ground Base," *New York Times*, January 10, 1961.]
4. "U.S. Puts Embargo on Goods to Cuba; Curbs Ship Deals," *New York Times*, October 20, 1980.
5. Department of State, *Foreign Relations of the United States 1958-1960*, vol. 6, *Cuba*.
6. Richard M. Bissell, *Reflections of a Cold Warrior* (New Haven: Yale University Press,

1996), 152-53. [Citation: Andrew J. Goodpaster, Memorandum of Conference with the President, 18 March 1960, Intelligence Matters (14), Box 15, Subject Series, Alpha Subseries; "A Program of Covert Action against the Castro Regime," 16 March 1960, CIA Policy Paper Re: Cuba, Box 4, International Series.]
7. Howard Jones, *The Bay of Pigs* (New York: Oxford University Press), 74; Haynes Johnson, *The Bay of Pigs: The Leaders' Story of Brigade 2506* (New York: W.W. Norton & Co., 1964), 23-31.
8. Author interview with Humberto Martínez Llano, Miami, Fl., June 30, 2009.
9. Author interview with Ricardo Sánchez, September 9, 2009.
10. Schlesinger, *A Thousand Days*, 213
11. Bissell, *Reflections*, 156.
12. Victor Andres Triay, *Bay of Pigs: An Oral History of Brigade 2506* (Gainesville: University Press of Florida, 2001), 22.
13. Schlesinger, *A Thousand Days*, 233.
14. Triay, *Bay of Pigs*, 156.
15. Johnson, *The Bay of Pigs*, 42-45.
16. Ibid., 24-29.
17. Warren Trest and Don Dodd, *Wings of Denial, the Alabama Air National Guard's Covert Role in the Bay of Pigs* (Montgomery, Ala.: New South Books, 2001), 17.
18. National Security Archive, "Bay of Pigs 40 years after."
19. Bissell, *Reflections*, 161
20. Schlesinger, *A Thousand Days*, 227.
21. Ibid., 227.
22. Ibid., 242-43.
23. Ibid., 236-37.
24. Martínez interview.
25. Sanchez interview.
26. Schlesinger, *A Thousand Days*, 251.
27. Ibid., 260.
28. Tad Szulc, "Cuban Intrigue Boiling in Miami As Castro Foes Step Up Efforts," *New York Times*, April 8, 1961.
29. Schlesinger, *A Thousand Days*, 245.
30. Ibid., 247.
31. Ibid., 264-65.
32. Martínez interview.
33. Schlesinger, *A Thousand Days*, 242.
34. Ibid., 241.
35. Ibid., 267-69.
36. U.S. Department of State, Office of the Historian, *Foreign Relations of the United States, 1961-1963*, vol. 10, *Cuba, January 1961-September 1962*, Document 96.
37. Bissell, *Reflections*, 143.
38. Jones, *The Bay of Pigs*, 75-77.
39. Porter McKeever, *Adlai Stevenson* (New York: William Morrow & Company, 1989), 487-88.
40. Schlesinger, *A Thousand Days,* 254.
41. Ibid., 255.
42. Office of the Historian, Document 108.
43. Bissell, *Reflections*, 184.

6

BAY OF PIGS: THE INVASION

BY HOWARD KLEINBERG

Long before the first Brigade members disembarked at Playa Girón, the deck was stacked against them. The team who devised Operation Zapata—as the reconfigured plan was called—lacked firsthand knowledge of everything from the logistics of amphibious landings and the Cuban coastline to the organization of Cuba's underground resistance. They relied on incomplete and inaccurate intelligence on Castro's Air Force and ground capabilities. Under any scenario, the Brigade would be massively outnumbered by Castro's forces, and there had been no real coordination with resistance leaders. The exile force was undertrained, insufficiently armed, and mostly lacking in military experience. The air strike, which had been cut in half, deprived them of the element of surprise and failed to achieve its objective. And most important of all, the U.S. government had no intention of backing them up.

Brigade 2506's situation would only worsen as the invasion proceeded.

Just after midnight on April 17, the landing craft *Blagar* and *Barbara J* entered the Bay of Pigs, 150 kilometers (km) southeast of Havana. Each ship carried a CIA operations officer and an underwater demolition team of frogmen. Behind them were the transport ships (*Houston, Rio Escondido, Caribe, Lake Charles,* and *Atlantico*) carrying about fourteen hundred ground troops. The battlefield command ship *Blagar* directed the landing at Playa Girón—the first of three embarkation points. Cuban coast watchers immediately sounded the alarm, forcing the troops to hurry their disembarkation. While Cuban B-26 bombers began to strafe the beach, some of the transport ships ran aground on coral reefs they had not expected to encounter.

At daybreak, Castro's counterattack intensified. The Cuban Air Force, which the pre-invasion raids were supposed to wipe out, was alive and well. Aboard the *Houston*, Humberto Martínez was preparing to disembark 35 km further northwest at Playa Larga when Castro planes attacked his battalion. Stuck in the middle of the bay, the *Houston* made an easy target. As it began to sink, Captain Luis Morse managed to beach it on a sandbar. Martínez and his surviving colleagues swam to shore where they planned to wait out the day before returning to the still-burning *Houston* to retrieve their weapons.[1]

The loss of the *Houston*, which carried most of the Brigade's munitions and equipment, can be directly attributed to the lack of air cover. In a secret memorandum, dated May 9, 1961, and only recently released from the files at the Kennedy Library, CIA Deputy Director General Charles Cabell said, "Failure to neutralize the Cuban Air Force very early on D-Day [meant] no fighter cover was being provided. . . . The beachhead could thus be overwhelmed by the superior surface attack and . . . the planned air strikes against Cuban airfields, a harbor, and a radio broadcasting station, could not be permitted."[2]

Pepe Hernandez of the Second Battalion reached Playa Larga on one of the first boats that went ashore. Castro forces fired at them from the beach, and the boat landed on the rocks. Hernandez jumped overboard with all of his equipment. He and forty other *Brigadistas* defeated Castro's troops and moved up the road toward a rendezvous with paratroops at the Australia sugar mill.[3]

Rafael Montalvo also landed at Playa Larga with the Second Battalion:

I was flat as I could be, the firing was continuous and incredible. The enemy was really close in front of us. We had no trenches, nothing. . . . Later we went back to the beach. It was just daylight, and it was very quiet. You could see a lot of dead militiamen. A little while later [Hugo] Sueiro came over and ordered a retreat. We couldn't believe it because we had beaten the shit out of those people. . . . Everyone got on trucks and went on to Girón.[4]

Ricardo Sánchez, along with nineteen other paratroopers, was dropped at Yaguaramas. "We got on the planes in Nicaragua between eleven and midnight and we flew for five or six hours." Sánchez recalled further that their equipment was not ready for combat. Though trained on a specific .57mm recoilless rifle, they were issued a different model just before the flight to Cuba. "I also never received the telescopic sight. Besides that, the .57 came only with antipersonnel rounds and no antitank ones, even though it had that capacity. We ran out of ammunition and more was sent to us by parachute. The ammunition was the right size, the clips they came in were wrong. We had to take the ammo and reload it into used clips."[5] At about 9:30 A.M. on the first day of the invasion, Sanchez and the other paratroopers began engaging Castro forces and were quickly surrounded. They kept fighting until rescued in the late afternoon.

Tulio Díaz Suárez, a twenty-five-year-old who had only trained in Guatemala for a few weeks before the invasion, was on a landing craft with 150 others from the Sixth Battalion. He watched as Castro's Hawker Sea Fury fighters shattered the *Río Escondido.*

When I disembarked, I went underwater with all the rockets, an M-3, a pistol, and three boxes of bullets. I was finally able to jump atop the coral and swim toward shore. . . . In front of me, I saw a Sea Fury coming towards us. The landing craft departed, and I was caught between the beach and the woods. I found the darkest spot on the grass, and I lay down and opened fire on the plane when it came over me. It was a difficult moment, but I felt good because he didn't hit me. I acted like a man, and that filled me with spirit.[6]

News of the invasion spread quickly in Miami, causing both apprehension and jubilation among Cuban exiles. Before noon on April 17, the *Miami News* was out on the street with a bold headline proclaiming "Rebel Invasion of Cuba!" The paper reported that information coming out of the island was both sketchy and contradictory. There were rumors that Fidel Castro had already ordered a jet to be ready for a quick exit, that Santiago de Cuba had fallen to the rebels, and that the Isle of Pines had been shelled from the air and sea. None were true.

The same issue of the *Miami News* reported that between five hundred and eight hundred young exiles had jammed a recruiting station at 427 SW 4th Avenue. "It took about three minutes to enlist a man—who then was hurried to a back room, stripped down and given a spot physical check." At least three other recruiting stations had been opened in the city for exiles wishing to join the fight.[7]

As beleaguered Brigade troops looked from the beach to the skies for assistance, Castro's security forces were arresting anyone suspected of government opposition. To detain the large number of prisoners—reported by Schlesinger to reach 200,000[8]—they set up temporary camps in rural areas and locations such as Cuba's Sports Palace.

As retaliation for the invasion, Castro began to carry out executions of political prisoners. Tomas Fernandez-Travieso was eighteen years old, a student, and one of eight resistance members who were tried and condemned on the same day the invasion began. "The trial took only twenty minutes," he said. "It was interrupted several times by the noise of the army tanks leaving La Cabaña fortress racing toward Playa Girón."[9]

Tomas, the youngest, was sentenced to thirty years in prison. He was the only one of the eight spared the *paredón*—death by firing squad. One at a time, the young men were removed from the chapel at La Cabaña. The first called was Carlos Rodríguez Cabo. Tomas embraced him one last time through the prison bars, and took Carlos's ring to give to his daughter. Then he and those still waiting their turn listened for the "coup de grace" pistol shot signaling their friend's death. Efrén Rodríguez

Lopez, laughing and saying he could not leave "Carlitos" to die alone, was called second.

Law student Virgilio Campanería Angel wrote to his "fellow students and to the people of Cuba" that "[m]y death will be another step backwards for those who think that they can drown in blood the yearning for liberty of the Cuban people...."[10] The third to face execution, he shouted "¡*Viva Cuba Libre!*" and required three pistol shots to die.

Alberto Tapia Ruano—"Tapita"—was an architecture student who led the Revolutionary Student Directorate. In a final letter to his parents, he wrote, "I can assure you that I have never had such a spiritual calm as I have now...."[11] He prayed to the Virgin he'd be called next and he was.

Filiberto Rodríguez Ravelo was nicknamed "the Martian" because he told his captors he was an alien. Before walking to his death he joked, "Not even the Martians can save me from the *paredón* now." Lázaro Reyes Benitez, José Calderín, and Carlitos Calvo Martínez were the last three to die.

Left alone in his cell, Tomas remembers thinking, "I could no longer share their jokes and singing. I became the repository of their memories, their link with life. I would bear witness to their sacrifice."[12]

It was the beginning of a long line of executions.

DAY TWO

Early in the morning of April 18, Sánchez and his fellow paratroopers moved to a point halfway to San Blas, where they joined about sixty other paratroopers who had been dropped at Covadonga and San Blas. Again they were surrounded by Castro troops, but they were rescued around noon by Battalion 4. Once they all reached San Blas, they were subjected to heavy artillery fire for more than twelve hours before retreating four hundred yards from town to wait out the second night.[13]

By midday, it was apparent to all observers that the invasion was in disarray. The air support that Cuban exiles believed was promised by the U.S. never arrived. U.S. General Gordon Gray reported a dozen Castro tanks on Playa Larga in a wire to Admiral Robert Dennison, Commander in Chief of Atlantic Forces: "We need data on situation ASAP. . . . Use officer observers with amphibious experience if quickly practicable, to give us judgment of situation. There may be Castro MIGs in area. . . . Take all possible precautions to avoid having operations identified as U.S."[14]

A telegram from CIA headquarters to agency personnel in Nicaragua reflected the weakness of U.S. resolve. "American contract crews can be used for B-26 strikes in beachhead area and approaches only. Cannot attach sufficient importance to fact American crews must not fall into hands of enemy. In event this happens despite all precautions crews must state hired mercenaries, fighting communism, etc.; U.S. will deny any knowledge."[15]

At 4:42 P.M. task force commander Admiral John Clark forwarded to Dennison a series of intercepted messages from Brigade commanders:

Blue Beach [Playa Girón] must have jet air support in next few hours or will be wiped out. Under heavy attacks by MIG jets and heavy tanks.

Have no ammo left for tanks and very little left for troops. Enemy just launched heavy land attack supported by tanks. Cannot hold for long.

Under heavy attack supported by 12 tanks. Need air support immediately. Red Beach [Playa Larga] wiped out. Request air strikes immediately.[16]

By the second day euphoria in Miami had given way to despair. As discouraging news kept trickling in, the exile community turned to prayer, radio, and the cafes—hoping for a deliverance that was not to come. Reactions elsewhere in the United States—particularly in academic circles—were very different. College students staged campus demonstrations to protest the invasion itself—not its failure. Sentiment was high against interfering with the Castro regime, on the assumption this could drive Castro into the Soviet camp. Protesters picketed the White House accusing the supposedly liberal Kennedy Administration of turning militaristic. Attacks came from the right as well as the left, but for very different reasons.

Schlesinger described Day Two of the invasion as "long and grim," though clearly not as long or as grim as it was for the men fighting at the Bay of Pigs. President Kennedy, in office only ninety days, knew there was no way the invasion could succeed without the support of U.S. troops. But he steadfastly refused to give the order, fearing both Russia's reaction and world opinion. After a series of meetings throughout the day and into the evening, Kennedy called a middle-of-the-night Oval Office session and told Schlesinger and diplomat Adolf Berle to leave immediately for Miami, where they were to meet with the members of the Cuban Revolutionary Council and convey the futility of the situation.

Humberto Martínez and his colleagues, with no weapons, spent the second day in hiding. At nightfall, they swam back to the *Houston*, retrieved rubber rafts and arms, and headed back to the swamp to fight.[17] Making radio contact with other Brigadistas, they learned the assault had failed, and that the others were just trying to get out. Martínez recalled, "We had broken up into groups of ten or fifteen. It was difficult trying to cross the swamp, my feet were cut, my shoes wet. We heard about a submarine in the bay picking up troops at night. We went inland to try to go south and, later, fell asleep within three hundred to four hundred feet of the shore. One of our men fell in a foxhole; it made noise and, suddenly, we were surrounded—and captured."[18]

Just before midnight, the Americans received a message from Brigade Commander José (Pepe) San Román. "Do you people realize how desperate the situation is? Do you back us up or quit? All we want is low jet cover close support. . . . I need it badly or cannot survive. Please don't desert us. Am out of tank and bazooka ammo. . . . I will not be evacuated. Will fight to the end if we have to. Need medical supplies urgently."[19]

DAY THREE

In the early hours of April 19, Admiral Dennison messaged Admiral Clark, "As you must realize I am groping in the dark and any info you can supply . . . would be of great help. . . . We may be called upon for evacuation of wounded. This might involve helicopters and stop off in [aircraft carrier U.S.S.] *Essex* prior to transfer to yet undetermined destination."[20]

Thirty minutes later, Dennison informed Admiral Arleigh Burke, Chief of Naval Operations, that the U.S. evacuation of wounded was out of the question "unless I am permitted to put sufficient force ashore, with air and gunfire support from the sea, to provide a beach head [*sic*]."[21]

Finally recognizing the unfolding catastrophe, the Joint Chiefs of Staff directed Dennison to fly air cover. "This means active air-to-air combat against any aircraft in the area. . . . No attack against ground forces authorized."[22] For the first time since the invasion began, the CIA now allowed the Alabama Air National Guardsmen who had trained Brigade pilots to join the Cuban crews and support the evacuation. If captured, the American pilots were to state they were mercenaries, not U.S. military.[23]

Around 7:00 A.M., Frank Bender, a mysterious CIA operative, met Schlesinger and Berle in Miami. They drove for a while, then stopped at a hamburger stand to meet a second car. "One began to feel like a character out of a Hitchcock film," Schlesinger wrote. At the deserted airbase of Opa-Locka, an old hangar was serving as a CIA base of operations. They went to "a nondescript frame house deep in the encampment [where] young American GIs, their revolvers conspicuous in holsters were patrolling the grounds.... [A]s we stumbled onto the sun porch, a young man lying asleep on a cot stirred uneasily and got up. It was ... Manuel Ray."[24]

All the Council members were there: Miró Cardona, Tony Varona, Antonio Maceo, Justo Carrillo, Carlos Hevia, and Manuel Ray. According to Schlesinger, Miró Cardona looked ten years older than he had just a week before. The president's men explained Kennedy's position on the invasion, why he felt he couldn't directly intercede, and how much he admired the cause and the courage of the Brigade fighters.

One by one, the members of the Council responded, often in fiery terms. Miró Cardona spoke first, urging that it was not too late to "turn the tide" if they could send in more contract flyers. He closed by begging that the Revolutionary Council members be allowed to die with their comrades in the invasion. Varona angrily critiqued each step of the way the CIA had handled things, and suggested the president dispatch the marines. Maceo pointed out that the struggle in Cuba was not between two groups but "two ways of life; failure on the beaches would mean a worldwide defeat for democracy."

Ray was the most vociferous:

We have been brought here without any knowledge of the operations. We thought we might have the opportunity to discuss strategy. We have found no one who will discuss it with us. We are not allowed to communicate with anybody. We have the feeling of being in a vacuum; nothing we can do is being coordinated with anything else.... The Council has no power. Action is taken in our name without our control, without our clearance and even without our knowledge.

Carlos Hevia, a graduate of Annapolis and once provisional president of Cuba said that "this combination of accountability without authority makes us feel that, if these boys are to be wiped out on the beachhead, our place is to die there with them." They closed by saying they felt more like prisoners than allies, and intended to leave the house immediately and hold a press conference.[25]

Schlesinger and Berle couldn't allow the Council members to go public with their story. When Washington told them it was too late to send them to Nicaragua to join the fight, they decided to fly the Council members to Washington to meet with the president. Kennedy received the group immediately. He was gracious and apologetic, and indicated he was "prepared to run more risks to take the men off the beaches than to put them there." Schlesinger described the exile leaders as "deeply moved." They agreed to issue a statement giving the U.S. plausible deniability.[26]

That same day, the Castro regime executed by firing squad two Americans and one Cuban underground leader who had been arrested a week before the landings. Forty-one-year-old Howard Anderson owned a string of service stations in Cuba, and he was accused of being a CIA agent. Twenty-five-year-old Angus McNair had been arrested after landing a boatload of arms near Havana.[27] And Joaquin del Cueto was head of the anti-Communist Acción Cívica.

After his capture, Humberto Martínez was herded into the back of a truck with 150 other Brigadistas. Commander Osmani Cienfuegos (the brother of the deceased rebel commander Camilo Cienfuegos) said, "If they die in there, that's fine; that way we'll save on bullets."[28]

Those who survived the ensuing journey described it as a rolling dungeon of death:

We had no food or water on the truck. The drive to Havana started around 10 a.m. and was to last about nine hours. . . . [N]ine prisoners died in the metal truck. It was so hot and humid inside, and we were so overheated that it actually rained inside the truck. There were wounded aboard and as we rode on, their screams became terrible. . . . One of us used his belt buckle to bore a hole through the metal chassis where we could gasp at small amounts of air. No one tried to treat the wounded. When we arrived at the Sports Palace in

Havana, my legs were gone; I simply fell out of the truck. I must have fainted for a while. Afterward, I looked back into the truck and saw the bodies. It was an atrocity.[29]

Jorge Silveira of Battalion 3 was on the truck with Martínez. He too accused Cienfuegos of extreme cruelty:

During the trip . . . they stopped at different places and we screamed. I have no doubt they knew what was happening back there. It was all premeditated. . . . Cienfuegos gave the order directly, and I personally hold him responsible—as well as his superiors for never punishing him. . . . They dropped us off at the Sports Palace. . . . Those of us who were injured were thrown in front of the doors, and the rest were taken to stadium seats. Doctors came to see the injured and some were taken to the hospital. The doctor who saw me—he was not Cuban—mentioned that perhaps I had gangrene in my legs. One of the Brigade doctors who was with us looked at me and told me I had nothing and that I should get out of there lest they amputate one of my legs. . . . That night some companions massaged my legs, and I was walking the next day—with difficulty, but I was walking. It was simply a lack of circulation.[30]

Martínez and other survivors later filed a human rights abuse lawsuit in Spain against Osmani Cienfuegos, who went on to become a leading member of the Castro regime.

As Martínez, Silveira, and their comrades were being taken on their infamous journey, Ricardo Sanchez and his fellow paratroopers were holding their position outside San Blas when two Brigade tanks from Battalion 3, along with support units from Battalion 4, moved into the town with Covadonga in their sights. According to Sánchez, the momentum in the April 19 battles swung back and forth throughout the day.

At about 11, our advancing forces retreated without reaching Covadonga due to lack of ammunition. . . . That afternoon we engaged a long convoy of

Castro tanks coming from San Blas. We needed to retreat and one of our bazooka teams put a halt to the tank column, allowing us a way out. We reached Girón about 5 p.m. The town was empty except for one person, but we came under fire from a Castro plane. We found an abandoned truck full of our wounded and started towards Cienfuegos where we were told our remaining forces had retreated to. While others continued toward Cienfuegos, we stayed in the woods that night with the wounded.[31]

It was to be their last night of freedom. Early in the morning of April 20,

one of us went to the road to see if we could see anybody. Some time passed, and all of a sudden we started hearing gunfire. So Julio [Alonso, Richard Nodarse] and I got off the truck with our handguns. When we came out of the bushes, every miliciano and every Castro soldier [you] can imagine was there, all over the highway. We were captured. Castro was less than a block away, with a whole bunch of newspaper people. He came and stood right in front of us and asked, "Where are the rest of your people?" We told him, "We are alone, with a truck full of wounded." He asked, "How many of you are in this thing?" We told him, "Just a few, around a thousand." He asked, "What about the Americans?" He was not hearing what he wanted to hear, he didn't want the press to hear it.[32]

After his capture, Ricardo's hands were tied behind his back and he was taken to a garage where he came face to face with his cousin, Augusto Martínez Sánchez, who was one of Castro's officers:

(Augusto) said, "What the hell are you doing here?" I told him, "All I want—let's not get into an argument—is for you to go and tell my parents that I'm alive." My father had been responsible for Augusto going to the university, as his father died when he was very young. My mother had gotten him his first job. He shoved me and said, "You don't deserve the parents you have."

He really loved my parents. From there, he sent somebody over to put them in prison. I think he realized I could damage him politically, so he needed to do something not to be associated with us.[33]

As Castro forces were rounding Brigade members, the Joint Chiefs of Staff directed Admiral Dennison that his ships were "to take personnel off the beach and from (the) water to (the) limit of their ability. We are anxious to save people as long as you can do so."[34]

A little more than an hour later, the commander of the U.S. Special Task Force off the coast wired Dennison "that Blue Beach [*Playa Girón*] was lost and no troops were [left on the beach]. Men fled into the woods. . . . Report that nothing left to salvage on the beach and Castro is waiting on the beach."[35]

Another hour passed, and the Joint Chiefs again wired Dennison that "Based on report from [Cuban Expeditionary Force] Commander ashore that he was destroying communications CIA has assumed he has taken to the woods. . . . CIA has ordered their shipping to disperse and proceed to various ports. . . . Request you assume operational control . . . and take action as feasible to salvage ships and cargo."[36]

Twenty-two men who landed at Playa Girón managed to escape capture aboard a small ship named *Celia*. After a horrific ordeal of sixteen days at sea, they were eventually rescued by a U.S. cargo ship near New Orleans.

The procession of vehicles bringing captured prisoners to the Sports Palace continued unabated. Humberto Martínez, finally off the sealed truck, was given something to drink and a T-shirt. "Ché and Fidel were there," Martínez recalled. "Interrogators kept trying to get us to incriminate the U.S. government. They asked who trained us, what language they spoke. We received no further physical abuse at the time."[37]

Four days later, on April 25, the White House issued a press release: "President Kennedy has stated from the beginning that as President he bears sole responsibility. . . . He has stated it on all occasions and he restates it now.... The President is strongly opposed to anyone within the administration attempting to shift the responsibility."[38]

Richard Bissell, the architect of *Bahia de Cochinos*, was less apologetic when interviewed by *Newsweek* in 1977: "Some people say if it had not been for Kennedy calling off a particular air strike, it would have succeeded. Others say it was doomed no matter what. I disagree with both. I think it would have had a chance of success—only a chance—if the President had taken a strong stand. There were a lot of reasons why it failed, but I think we gave it a good college try."[39]

NOTES

1. Author interview with Humberto Martínez, June 30, 2009.
2. Kennedy Library, National Security Files, Countries Series, Cuba, Subject, Taylor Report, Secret. Document 108.
3. Victor Andres Triay, *Bay of Pigs: An Oral History of Brigade 2506* (Gainesville: University Press of Florida, 2001), 99.
4. Ibid., 102-3.
5. Author interview with Richard Bissell, September 9, 2009; Triay, *Bay of Pigs*, 93-95.
6. Triay, *Bay of Pigs*, 91-92.
7. "Refugees Swarm to Volunteer for Fight," *Miami News*, April 17, 1961.
8. Arthur M. Schlesinger, Jr., *A Thousand Days* (Boston: Houghton Mifflin Company, 1965), 257.
9. Tomás Fernández Travieso, *Fifty Years Ago*, unpublished manuscript given to author May 26, 2011.
10. Juan M. Clark, *Cuba: Mito y Realidad*, 2d ed. (Miami-Caracas: SAETA Ediciones, Second Edition, 1992), 154.
11. Ibid.
12. Fernández Travieso, "Fifty Years Ago."
13. Author interview with Ricardo Sánchez, September 9, 2009.
14. Office of Historian, Document 122.
15. Office of Historian, Document 120.
16. Office of Historian, Document 125.
17. Martínez interview.
18. Martínez interview.
19. Office of Historian, Document 135.
20. Office of Historian, Document 137.
21. Office of Historian, Document 138.
22. Office of Historian, Document 147.
23. Warren Trest, "Wings of Denial: The Alabama National Guard in the Bay of Pigs," *Alabama Heritage*, January 1, 2005; Triay, *Bay of Pigs*, 110.

24. Schlesinger, *A Thousand Days*, 261.
25. Ibid., 262-64.
26. Ibid., 266.
27. "Two U.S. Citizens Executed in Cuba," *New York Times*, April 20, 1961.
28. "A Little Known Tragedy Revisited," *Miami Herald*, November 6, 2006.
29. Martínez interview.
30. Oral interview of Jorge Silveira cited in Triay, *Bay of Pigs*, 138-39.
31. Author interview with Ricardo Sánchez, August 9, 2009.
32. Triay, *Bay of Pigs*, 97.
33. Ibid., 97.
33. Office of Historian, Document 151.
34. Office of Historian, Document 153.
35. Office of Historian, Document 154.
36. Martínez interview.
37. Schlesinger, *A Thousand Days*, 290.
38. "Brigade 2506," *Newsweek*, December 12, 1977, 20.

7

BAY OF PIGS: THE AFTERMATH

BY HOWARD KLEINBERG

The "good college try" was not good enough for underground leader Rogelio González Corso (Francisco), Humberto Sorí-Marín, and ten other members of the underground resistance shot by Castro firing squads on April 21. It was an ironic end for Sorí-Marín, whom *Time* magazine had labeled Castro's "Scolding Hero" in a February 1959 profile. A former minister of agriculture and Castro's adjutant general, he'd served on a three-man military panel that handed out death sentences to former members of Batista's armed forces and operatives.[1]

Those and other executions caused the *New York Times* to write that the anti-Castro rebels had suffered crippling blows: "Although new anti-Castro operations are planned, it was believed here that the underground in Cuba needed some time to become reorganized after the events of the week."[2]

This was later corroborated by Javier Souto, who had been infiltrated to help González Corso communicate with the invasion planners. Souto said the arrest and subsequent executions of the top underground leaders "left Cuba's clandestine forces without any local leadership for months. And those who came in to replace them were never as effective."[3]

Brigade members Humberto Martínez and Ricardo Sánchez slept on the floor at Havana's Sports Palace for three nights before being taken to the Naval Hospital. It was the same Sports Palace where Fidel Castro had staged trials for Batista supporters two years earlier. Martínez said, "There were twenty of us in a room—all on the floor. They kept us there for four or five weeks, doing nothing. All they really did was to treat me for cuts on my foot from the mangroves near the beachhead."[4]

From the Naval Hospital, the men were taken to the Castillo del Príncipe, an icon of Havana's colonial past. Pepe San Román said he, Manuel Artime, and Erneido Oliva were first put into separate cells at El Príncipe. They were dark and filled with rats and cockroaches. "I thought that only a pig could live there," Pepe said. Later they were moved to a larger cell area—Las Leoneras—where they were reunited with other members of the Brigade."[5]

Ricardo Sánchez recalled:

At the Naval Hospital, Fidel Castro would visit while he was trying to establish a prisoner committee to negotiate with the U.S. for our release [and] our families were allowed to bring us food. At El Príncipe, the food was . . . one piece of bread and coffee. At noon, we got soup, which was not much more than water and chick peas. . . . I contracted hepatitis. . . . 40-50 of us became ill. . . . The epidemic lasted about three months. When we got better, we were returned to the general population.[6]

Jorge Silveira also came down with hepatitis.

We had so little food that when we would lie down, we sometimes could not get up because we were so dizzy. There were times when they gave us only eight or ten boiled pieces of macaroni three times a day. We were physically debilitated. . . . Things took a turn for the worse when the negotiations in the United States broke down. That's when the rumors began about a trial and possible selective executions. During one of my family visits, we arranged that an aunt of mine in Cuba and the mothers of two other men would dress in black and stand on a street corner we could see from the prison if they heard that the rumors about the trial were true. On the agreed upon day, they were there, not only dressed in black, but they also had black umbrellas, black shoes and black socks.[7]

After his victory at the Bay of Pigs, Castro was on top of his game. The timing of the ill-fated invasion—so close to May Day, when countries around the world celebrate Labor Day—was perfect for him. In Communist countries, it is the day when they celebrate the struggle of the proletariat against capitalism. On that May Day, Castro addressed a crowd of 500,000 in Havana's Plaza Cívica and declared Cuba to be a Socialist nation. He also suspended any future elections, and he announced a pending law to bar foreign clergymen from Cuba.[8]

As the *Miami Herald* reported, "Attacking the United States for its role in the recent invasion against his regime, Castro said, 'If Mr. Kennedy does not like socialism, we don't like imperialism, we don't like capitalism.'"[9]

In a televised address two weeks later, Castro offered to exchange the captured Brigade members for five hundred bulldozers and tractors. The alternative was to place the prisoners in forced labor gangs.[10]

President Kennedy seized upon the offer, but he met resistance from Republicans in Congress. He turned to the American public, appointing a committee to raise private funds for "Tractors for Freedom." Chairing the committee were three prominent public figures: former United Nations ambassador Eleanor Roosevelt, auto union chief Walter Reuther, and Milton Eisenhower, president of Johns Hopkins University and brother of the former U.S. president.

The Miami community was sharply divided, with the majority of exiles supporting the exchange which could free their sons and fathers, while non-Cubans did not. The city's two daily newspapers took opposite sides. The *Miami News* urged its readers to send money to the newspaper as part of a "Buy a Life" program, while the *Miami Herald* called Castro's proposal "blackmail from Havana."

Cuba "paroled" ten Brigade prisoners to come to the United States to participate in negotiations.[11] The prisoners arrived in Miami on May 21. After a brief interrogation, they changed from prison fatigues to casual clothing and left for the DuPont Plaza Hotel in downtown Miami. There, the hotel manager requested that "a Negro male among the prisoners," Felix Perez Tamayo, be removed from the premises because of hotel policy. When someone pointed out that this could be exploited by the Communist press, he responded, "I only work here."[12]

The next day, attired in their crisp khaki Brigade uniforms with a jaunty shoulder patch, the prisoners flew to Washington. Accompanying them in an Immigration Service plane were José Miró Cardona and Manuel Antonio de Varona. Ulises Carbó, acting spokesman for the group, was optimistic about success. "You must remember," he said, "that we have the responsibility for 1,200 men. We cannot talk carelessly."[13]

The negotiations quickly broke down over the issue of indemnification. The U.S. and Brigade team saw this as a simple trade of tractors for prisoners. Castro, however, insisted that the tractors were "indemnification for material damage." As the two sides couldn't agree on language, and criticism within the U.S. mounted, the tractor committee threw up its hands and disbanded on June 23.

Castro claimed the committee had "paralyzed the negotiations with its insolent and ill-intentioned attitude."[14] Nonetheless, he sent the same team of prisoners back to Key West on June 24. Mrs. Roosevelt fought back in her syndicated column:

> *When he [Castro] changed his wordage to calling the monetary value of the tractors "indemnification," he ruled out the possibility of any private individual or individuals in the U.S. being able to negotiate.... Castro's return of the prisoners here when he knew the committee was out of existence was a trick that must be deeply resented. We would certainly have liked to have freed the prisoners, but, as U.S. citizens, we cannot mandate matters that are beyond our mandate.*[15]

John Hooker, Jr., the executive secretary of the disbanded committee, flew to Key West to meet with the prisoners and listen to whatever new terms Castro was proposing. Though he didn't report publicly on the initial meetings, the committee announced on June 30 it would not re-form and resume negotiations due to the recurring issue of "indemnification." Hooker told the prisoners that "in the name of honor the committee finds it cannot send Dr. Castro tractors, money, or credit for indemnity—not $28,000,000 or $28."[16]

On July 5, the twelfth day of Castro's fifteen-day limit on their stay in the U.S., the prisoners announced they were forming a new committee, made up of their friends and relatives, to raise funds for the exchange. The group would be called the Families Committee for the Freedom of Cuban Prisoners of War, and headquartered at 276 Northeast 25th Street in Miami.

The new committee immediately requested support from President Kennedy and the disbanded Tractors Committee, as well as the sixty-five thousand letters that had been received in response to the original committee's fundraising appeal.[17] Rather than forward the unopened letters to the Families Committee, the four officers of the disbanded Tractors for Freedom Committee announced on July 8 that all letters were being returned, still unopened, to the donors, if there was a return address, and sent to the dead letter office if not.

U.S. officials gave the prisoners thirty days from July 1 to raise the funds themselves. Though there is no indication that Castro acquiesced to the deal, the prisoners were on their own until July 31, when they had to return to Cuba. At the end of the month, two of the ten prisoners—Mirto Collazo and Pico Román—defected, claiming with no hope of an exchange the result for the prisoners would be "bullets." Luis Morse accused the "cowards" of breaking their word, not only to Castro, but to their comrades.[18]

More than five hundred cheering exiles came to see the eight returning prisoners off on the morning of July 31. Three members of the Families Committee—Ernesto Freyre, Alvaro Sánchez, and Virginia Betancourt—accompanied them back to Havana to rescue sixteen hospitalized Brigade prisoners. If that effort succeeded, Freyre said, they would take their fundraising drive national.[19] However, Castro refused to meet with the committee members, and they returned to Miami a month later.

After the Bay of Pigs, Castro had decreed that any Brigade prisoner who had been part of the Batista regime and "committed crimes" before the invasion would be tried for those crimes rather than for the invasion. On September 8, twenty-four former Batista officials and police among the Brigade prisoners were tried in Santa Clara. Five were sentenced to death and nineteen others to thirty years in jail. Trial, verdict, sentencing, appeal, and execution all took place within a period of nine hours.[20] These executions were a small part of the hundreds of executions carried out in Cuba for alleged antigovernment activity.

On August 7, 1961, Cubans were asked to exchange their old pesos for a new currency, signed *Che,* for the new head of the National Bank of Cuba. The law had been suddenly announced over the previous weekend. Citizens were allowed to exchange two-hundred-dollar old pesos for two-hundred-dollar new pesos, and they could deposit the rest in an account with the government. On August 9, the rules changed. Those who had ten thousand dollars or less could withdraw up to one hundred dollars a month. But anyone who had deposited more than ten thousand dollars had all their funds confiscated to help pay the national debt.[21]

The government also cracked down on organized religion. On September 8, the day Cubans honor their patron saint, Our Lady of Charity (*Caridad del Cobre*), the government banned all religious processions. Thousands of people protested outside of the Iglesia de la Caridad in Havana, chanting "Long Live Christ the King" and "Down with Communism." Castro's security forces opened fire on the crowd, killing one young Catholic. Three days later the government arrested Auxiliary Bishop Eduardo Boza Masvidal and expelled hundreds of priests and nuns. Cuba's only cardinal, Manuel Arteaga, was forced to seek refuge in the Vatican's embassy in Cuba. In a televised speech later that month, Castro reiterated the prohibition on religious processions.

In mid-October, Raúl Castro swore in fifteen thousand Cuban children as Pioneers of the Revolution. This alarmed many parents who decided to leave Cuba with their families, if possible, or send their children out of the country alone. In November, opposition leader Jorge Fundora Fernandez was captured in Matanzas Province and executed. Castro formalized what had been the practice for two years: any counterrevolutionary who was captured would be tried and executed secretly within forty-eight hours of their arrest.

In December, the Families Committee announced that negotiations with Castro were continuing, and they advertised in the *New York Times* the day after Christmas seeking $2 to $3 million as a down payment for the tractors. Rebuffed by both Kennedy and the Tractors Committee, their campaign was arduous and frustrating.

On March 30, 1962, Castro put 1,182 Brigade prisoners on trial in the outdoor courtyard of Castillo del Príncipe. Presiding over the five-man tribunal was Major Augusto Martínez Sánchez, first cousin of prisoner Ricardo Sánchez. "My God, his mother and my father were brother and sister," Ricardo lamented.[22] Denying prisoner requests for their own attorneys, the court appointed University of Havana professor Dr. Antonio Cejas to represent all of them.

No reporters from non-Communist countries were allowed at the trial, and civilian police surrounded the fortress to keep relatives, friends, and onlookers away. All the defendants wore white shirts and dark denim trousers. Havana newspapers reported that the men admitted their guilt by the second day of the trial. In a photo distributed by the Cuban government, Ulises Carbó, spokesman for the U.S. prisoner delegation, is shown at the microphone.

Prisoners recall a different version of the trial. Jorge Marquet of Battalion 5 said:

A companion of mine called Juan Torres Mena had a problem during the trial. The guard insulted his mother, and Juan hit the guard. He was hit with a bayonet. Chaos broke out, people went after the guards, and there was swinging and punching. Erneido Oliva screamed, '¡Brigada, Atención!' Everyone stopped. Oliva spoke to the troops, saying "Gentlemen we did not come here for this: We came to die, to liberate Cuba. We must give an example of dignity.'[23]

Rafael Montalvo of Battalion 2 described a lighter moment:

The first day of the trial, they asked us to testify. They went to the first guy in the first row, and he said, "I have nothing to say; I refuse to defend myself." The second one said the same. They kept asking, and they were puzzled because they thought people wanted to testify. In the back, Luis González Lalondry raised his hand. The judge said, "You—what is it that you have to say?" Luis said, "I request permission to pee." The place went wild. The guards freaked out, and we had a riot. The judges ran and locked themselves up. They took us back to our cells, and we spent all night singing, "Tu ves yo no lloro" [You see, I don't cry].[24]

By the fourth day of the trial, the UPI wire service reduced the number of reported Brigade defendants by three, without explanation. Five days later, the tribunal found all 1,179 defendants guilty of treason and sentenced them to thirty years each in prison. But there was a surprising caveat: the prisoners could be ransomed individually for varying amounts based on the social grading of the defendants.

The highest ransom—$500,000—was assigned to the three leaders of the invasion: Artime, San Roman, and Oliva. Landowners, well-to-do, and former military were assigned $100,000; office workers, students, and members of the middle class were set at $50,000; lumpen [a multilingual pejorative expression used to refer to lower classes of society], and farm workers at $25,000. Humberto Martínez' ransom was set at

$100,000 because they claimed he was a land owner though he denies he was. Ricardo Sánchez was assigned the student category. All the individual ransoms added up to $62 million—nearly triple what Castro had originally demanded in the tractor exchange.

A 1981 issue of the Cuban *Bohemia* magazine, recounting the Bay of Pigs invasion, broke down the "social composition" of Brigade prisoners:

100 large land holders, 24 large property owners, 67 multiple home owners, 112 multiple business owners, 184 ex-military, 179 well-off, 37 industrial magnates, 112 lumpens and others. . . . It also said the tribunal sought to recover by these convictions: "27,556 caballerías [a specific measure of land], 9,666 apartment buildings and houses, 70 industries, 10 sugar mills, three banks, five mines and 12 cabarets, bars and many other properties.'[25]

Following their sentencing, prisoners with a $100,000 or higher price on their heads were transferred to the *Presidio Modelo* on the Isle of Pines (later renamed Isle of Youth). Ironically, that was where Fidel Castro had served time after his failed attack on the Moncada Barracks in 1953. Among the Brigade prisoners sent to the Isle of Pines was Humberto Martínez. He shared one and a half toilets with more than two hundred other prisoners. Tulio Díaz Suárez of the Sixth Battalion described conditions there:

Life was monotonous, and they did not let us into the yard except for two times. There came a time when they would give us spoiled food, and some people got dysentery. Our water was in very short supply. The worst part of being in the place was the screams of the people in the punishment cells. In cold weather, the guards would throw buckets of water and feces on the prisoners every hour or so; in turn, the prisoners moaned and swore at the guards who were punishing them.[26]

Plagued with hepatitis, Ricardo Sánchez remained at El Príncipe in La Enfermeria, where he was harassed by a political officer and attempted an unsuccessful jail break. Sánchez explained that the prisoners communicated with people on the outside using sign language that could be seen through small openings in the prison walls. That was how they learned about the Cuban Missile Crisis.[27]

Berta Barreto de los Heros, the Cuba liaison for the Families Committee and the mother of prisoner Pablo Pérez-Cisneros, was worried about the outcome of the trial and frustrated at the lack of progress in negotiations. On April 6, she took matters into her own hands; she began calling the mothers of other prisoners, as well as people with connections to Castro and Ernesto Freyre, the leader of the Families Committee in Washington.[28]

Berta's persistence paid off when she got through to Conchita Fernández, Fidel Castro's personal secretary and a friend of Berta's husband before the revolution. Conchita connected her with Celia Sánchez, Castro's revolutionary companion and close advisor, who asked Berta for details of what the Families Committee wanted and what they were offering. Berta told her the U.S. committee had raised $28 million, which was an exaggeration, though when she contacted Freyre for confirmation, he insisted the committee had pledges of $26 to $28 million.[29]

Berta's plea made an impression on Castro because of his history with her late husband, Guy Pérez-Cisneros. Many years previously, while serving as Cuba's ambassador to an OAS meeting in Bogota, Perez Cisneros had arranged transportation back to Havana for two young firebrands who had gotten into political trouble in Colombia. One of them was Fidel Castro.

At 5:00 A.M. on April 8, Berta's home phone rang. Celia Sánchez was on the line and said, "Fidel wants to talk to you." Castro interrogated her on political matters, including the whereabouts of her three sons. He reminisced for a while about her late husband and then said: "Berta, call the Families Committee and tell them they can come. This time I'm going to receive them. For convenience sake, they should stay at your house. Let Celia know when they will arrive."[30]

With the groundwork laid, Berta informed the committee. On April 10—the day after the Brigade prisoners were sentenced—Freyre, Alvaro Sánchez, Enríque Llaca, and Mrs. Virginia Betancourt de Rodríguez flew to Havana and went directly to Berta Barreto's home. Castro, in uniform and carrying a .45-caliber pistol at his side, arrived an hour later.

"The Americans offered me five hundred ridiculous little toy tractors worth a little over three million dollars," Castro complained to the committee. "They chose to have no faith in my offer. As a result, eleven months have gone by." He then stunned everyone by declaring he would release the most seriously wounded prisoners to return to the U.S., as soon as the committee had collected their ransoms and deposited the cash in the Royal Bank of Canada. In an even more astounding move, Castro arranged for the prisoner representatives in Príncipe prison to have dinner at Berta's house that night. "For the first time in two years, counting the training camps," recalled Erneido Oliva, "I sat at a table with a tablecloth and silverware."[31]

Freyre and the committee members remained in Havana negotiating the release of fifty-four wounded prisoners—all in the twenty-five thousand dollar ransom category. Six more ill prisoners were released at the last minute to fill all seats on the plane. Their departure from Havana was delayed because the released men at first refused to leave their comrades behind.

On April 14, 1962—almost one year after their capture—sixty Brigade members flew to Miami, where they were greeted by crowds waving hankies, crying, and swaying to the sounds of the patriotic anthem from the movie *Bridge on the River Kwai*. The *New York Times* that day reported a crowd of five thousand, but reliable estimates were closer to twenty thousand.

Last to leave the plane was Enrique Ruiz-Williams, called Harry, who had been second in command of his battalion and received over seventy combat wounds. In recognition of his heroism, he moved up the invisible ladder of Brigade leadership in Príncipe. Along with Alvaro Sánchez, Jr., he released a statement which read: "We shall consider ourselves prisoners until the last one of our companions is at liberty. The Brigade 2506 is one and indivisible. We are one in morale, in our convictions and in history. Should our companions not be set free, we would voluntarily return to the Castillo del Príncipe in Havana."[32]

The men were taken to Mercy Hospital in Miami for medical observation; twenty-five were detained for further evaluation and/or surgery. Ruiz-Williams flew on to Washington, D.C., to consult with Attorney General Robert Kennedy on organizing a fundraising drive to free the remaining prisoners.[33]

Following Robert Kennedy's advice, Ruiz-Williams and the other returned prisoners traveled the country, speaking to companies, veterans' organizations, and any group that might help in their search for funds. After two months, they were still far short of their goal, and Ruiz-Williams went back to the attorney general. Kennedy told him he needed someone who could deal directly with Castro and work out more favorable terms. He recommended James B. Donovan, a New York attorney and a Democrat, who was in the midst of a Senate race against popular liberal Republican Jacob Javits.

During World War II, Donovan had served as legal advisor to William "Wild Bill" Donovan (no relation) who headed the Office of Strategic Services, forerunner of the CIA. He had defended accused Russian spy Rudolf Abel and negotiated the release of U-2 spy pilot Gary Francis Powers from the Soviet Union.[34] A tough and crafty negotiator, Donovan was just the man to take on Castro. With the urging of friends such as Princess Lee Radziwill (Jackie Kennedy's sister), and Richard Cardinal Cushing, not to mention the support of the Kennedys, Donovan accepted the pro bono role.[35]

In late August, Donovan flew to Havana. Castro now demanded hospital equipment, mechanical parts, and food in addition to the original request for tractors. By early October, Donovan had made eleven trips to Cuba, and *Time* magazine called him "Kennedy's Man in Havana," (from the 1958 popular Graham Greene mystery novel). Release of the prisoners was just days away when the Cuban Missile Crisis changed everything.

On September 4, 1962, President Kennedy had announced they had information from a "variety of sources which establishes without doubt that the Soviets have provided the Cuban Government with a number of anti-aircraft defensive missiles with a slant range of twenty-five miles." Initial reports were understated, and U-2 over flights ultimately confirmed the worst fears: the Soviets had placed nuclear-tipped missiles in Cuba. On October 18, President Kennedy sent a squadron of jets to the Boca Chica Naval Air Station outside Key West.[36]

In El Príncipe, Ricardo Sánchez recalled drastic changes taking place. The political commissioner told the men about the situation, though "we already knew through our sign language with people on the outside. . . . Although we knew what was happening, we didn't know the details."[37]

On October 22, Kennedy imposed a naval blockade of Cuba and said that any nuclear attack from Cuba would be regarded as an attack by the Soviet Union on the United States. The bitter standoff between Kennedy and Khrushchev was resolved on October 28, when Khrushchev reversed missile-laden ships bound for Cuba and agreed to dismantle the sites already in place. In turn, Kennedy promised not to invade Cuba. While this was considered a victory for the U.S., Cuban exiles now feared their homeland was lost forever.

As the Missile Crisis wound down, prisoner negotiations resumed. On December 15, Donovan reported that a deal was near completion for the delivery of drugs and food to Cuba in exchange for the prisoners. It was later revealed that Gen. Lucius Clay and Robert Kennedy had raised almost $3 million in one week to meet Castro's "good faith" demands, and Richard Cardinal Cushing of Boston was responsible for raising $1 million. The Cuban Families Committee arranged with the

Pharmaceutical Manufacturers Association to donate medicines, and the American Red Cross began collecting food, medicine, and supplies.[38] Two days later, the freighter *African Pilot* sailed from Baltimore for Port Everglades to load the supplies for Cuba.

On December 19, Castro lifted the ban on relatives sending food and clothing to the prisoners. One mother said she was sending twenty boxes of clothing to the Isle of Pines prison.[39] As the U.S., Soviet Union, and Cuba continued to haggle about the Missile Crisis before the United Nations, James Donovan completed his work in Havana on December 21, getting Castro's commitment that the prisoners would be released before Christmas. He also secured the exodus of an additional eighty-five hundred Cubans, including many relatives of the prisoners, as well as three CIA agents and twenty-seven other imprisoned Americans.

At 6:00 P.M. on December 23, a plane carrying 107 of the 1,113 prisoners landed at Homestead Air Force base south of Miami. Due to the tight security—Homestead was a Strategic Air Command base at the time—the greeting crowd was small. Over the next couple of days, about a dozen more flights from Cuba brought the rest of the freed captives. The arrivals were transported to Dinner Key Auditorium, in the Coconut Grove section of Miami, where boisterous relatives rejoiced and shed tears.

At the same time, the *African Pilot* docked in Havana with a reported $11 million in food and drugs as down payment on the negotiated deal. There, American Red Cross volunteers assisted in unloading the cargo.[40] The Bay of Pigs prisoners were exchanged for $53 million, paid in baby food and medicine.[41]

The Bay of Pigs chapter in Cuban exile history was almost over, and a new one was beginning. Speaking to the throngs assembled December 24 at Dinner Key, Brigade leader Manuel Artime set the tone for future relations between the exile community and the Castro regime: "We are not here to receive honors, not to cry over our failures.... We have come to call you with the voices of the number of our dead to war again in the name of the mothers who gave their sons. Today we want no tears. We call everybody to war."[42]

On December 27, as the *African Pilot* prepared to transport the prisoners' relatives back to Port Everglades, Castro demanded they turn in the keys to their houses and vehicles and provide proof that all their bills in Cuba had been paid. Some passengers had to get off, surrender their places, and wait for another ship.[43] Later that day, the *African Pilot* arrived with 922 Cuban passengers, ranging in ages from twenty-two months to eighty-nine years. They were transported to Dinner Key Auditorium to be reunited with the returned prisoners.

Coincidentally, or not, President Kennedy spent Christmas at his family compound in Palm Beach. The prisoner leadership met with him there to hear his explanations and apologies, and Kennedy accepted their invitation to meet the Brigade at Miami's Orange Bowl Stadium on December 29.

Some members of the Brigade, disgusted at the way the Kennedy Administration had let them and their country down, boycotted the event.

Almost forty thousand people gathered to cheer as President Kennedy and his popular Spanish-speaking wife Jacqueline, drove onto the field in a white convertible. While bands played the U.S. and Cuban national anthems, Kennedy went down the line of Brigade members, greeting them and shaking hands.

Rolando Novoa, a wounded member of the Brigade on crutches, handed the Brigade flag to Erneido Oliva who, in turn, presented it to President Kennedy.[44] The president turned toward Pepe San Román and José Miró Cardona and uttered the words that would come to haunt the Kennedy legacy forever: "Commander, Doctor, I want to express my great appreciation to the Brigade for making the United States the custodian of this flag. I can assure you that this flag will be returned to this Brigade in a free Havana."

The response from the Brigade was loud and swift: *"¡Guerra! ¡Guerra!,"* they shouted. *"¡Libertad! ¡Libertad!"*

Juan Sordo, a physician and member of the Brigade, reflected years later about the day Kennedy came to the Orange Bowl. "I was at the head of the medical corps. Kennedy . . . stopped and shook my hand. I shook his hand and all that, but under my breath I muttered, 'son of a bitch.'"[45]

NOTES

1. "Cuba: The Scolding Hero," *Time*, February 2, 1959.
2. "Rebels Hopeful," *New York Times*, April 21, 1961.
3. Author interview with Javier Souto, June 10, 2010.
4. Author interview with Humberto Martínez, June 30, 2009.
5. Haynes Johnson, *The Bay of Pigs: The Leaders' Story of Brigade* 2506 (New York: Norton, 1964), 249.
6. Author interview with Ricardo Sánchez, September 9, 2009.
7. Victor Andres Triay, *The Bay of Pigs: An Oral History of Brigade 2506* (Gainesville: University Press of Florida, 2001). 140.
8. "Castro Rules Out Elections in Cuba," *New York Times*, May 2, 1961.
9. "Castro Puts End to Free Elections," *Miami Herald*, May 2, 1961.
10. "Castro Proposes 'Deal' on Captives," *New York Times*, May 18, 1961.
11. They were later identified as Ulises Carbó, Mitro Collazo, Luis Morse, Felix Pérez Tamayo, Juan J. Peruyero, Waldo Castroverde, Hugo Sueiro, Severino Álvarez Castellón, Gustavo García Montes, and Reynaldo Pico. "Cuban Prisoners in Florida Again," *New York Times*, June 26, 1961.
12. Memo from Lt. Frank Chapel, Supervisor, Criminal Intelligence, to Thomas J. Kelly, Metropolitan Sheriff, May 22, 1961, Dade County OCB file #153; Cuban Information Archives, Document 0031.
13. "Confidence is Expressed," *New York Times*, May 22, 1961.
14. "Cubans Prisoners in Florida Again," *New York Times*, June 25, 1961.
15. "My Day," Eleanor Roosevelt, June 28, 1961.
16. "Tractor Unit Says Exchange is Dead," *New York Times*, July 1, 1961.
17. The *New York Times* reported that the new committee's eleven members "included José Ignacio de la Cámara, former president of the clearing house for banks in Cuba; Julio Lobo, once called 'sugar king' of Cuba; Enrique Godoy Zayán, a former insurance broker and banker; and Caridad Rosales, president of the Cuban Catholic Association." The article added that "[o]ther members, who have sons or other relatives among the prisoners, include Manuel Arca, Virginia Betancourt de Rodríguez, Carlos M. Falla, Ernesto Freyre, Marcelo Hernández, Enrique Llaca and Alvaro Sánchez, Jr." "Prisoners Renew Tractor Effort," *New York Times*, July 6, 1961.

18. "Cuba Unit Offers Prisoner Deal," *New York Times*, July 31, 1961.
19. "8 Rebel Prisoners Return to Cuba," *New York Times*, August 1, 1961.
20. "Cubans Execute 5 April Invaders," *New York Times*, September 9, 1961. Among the executed were Ramón Calviño, George King Yun, Emilio Soler Puig, Roberto Pérez Cruzata, and Antonio Valentín Padrón Cárdenas—all accused of capital crimes during the Batista regime.
21. Leovigildo Ruiz, *Diario de una Traición—Cuba 1961* (Miami: Lorié Book Stores, 1972), entry of February 12, 2010, 138 and 143.
22. Author interview Sánchez. Other members of the tribunal were Juan Almeida, Sergio del Valle, Manuel Piñeiro, and Guillermo García, all majors.
23. Triay, *The Bay of Pigs*, 152.
24. Triay, *The Bay of Pigs*, 152.
25. *Bohemia*, April 17, 1981.
26. Triay, *The Bay of Pigs*, 153.
27. Interview with Sánchez.
28. Pablo Pérez-Cisneros, John B. Donovan, and Jeff Koenreich, *After the Bay of Pigs* (Miami: Alexandria Library Incorporated, 2007) 41-43.
29. Johnson, *The Bay of Pigs*, 279-80.
30. Pérez-Cisneros, Donovan, and Koenreich, *After the Bay of Pigs*, 45-48.
31. Johnson, *The Bay of Pigs*, 281-82.
32. "60 Ill or Wounded Cuban Prisoners Greeted in Miami," United Press International, April 13, 1962; *New York Times*, April 14, 1962.
33. Johnson, *The Bay of Pigs*, 289-92.
34. "Kennedy's Man in Havana," *Time*, October 19, 1962.
35. Johnson, *The Bay of Pigs*, 305-6.
36. "Squadron of Jets Sent to Florida In Reply to Cuba," *New York Times*, October 19, 1962.
37. Interview with Sánchez.
38. "Cuban prisoners may be released before holidays," *New York Times*, December 15, 1962.
39. Associated Press, December 19, 1962.
40. Associated Press, December 23, 1962.
41. Pérez-Cisneros, Donovan, and Koenreich, *After the Bay of Pigs*, 170.
42. United Press International, December 25, 1962.
43. Ibid.
44. After Kennedy's assassination, the Brigade requested that the flag—its promise unfulfilled—be returned to them. Finally on April 14, 1976, it was removed from its crate at the Kennedy Library in Massachusetts and returned to the Brigade in Miami.
45. Triay, *The Bay of Pigs*, 155.

8

THE MISSILE CRISIS

BY GUILLERMO MARTINEZ AND SAM VERDEJA

The Bay of Pigs not only exacerbated tensions between the United States and Cuba, it also introduced a powerful third party into the equation. Though Castro's relationship with the Soviet Union began shortly after he took power in Cuba, the partnership had deepened over time. In a February 1961 interview with an Italian Communist newspaper, Castro put an end to the speculation about his ideological beliefs. "It is . . . true that at first the Communists distrusted me and us rebels. It was a justified distrust, an absolutely correct position . . . because we of the Sierra . . . were still full of *petit bourgeois* prejudices and defects, despite Marxist reading. . . . Then we came together, we understood each other and began to collaborate."[1]

After the Bay of Pigs invasion, the Cuban-Soviet partnership took a deadly turn that brought the world closer to nuclear war than at any other time in history. Castro's increased paranoia about the United States undoubtedly played a role in this shift, but so did the loss of face that John F. Kennedy had suffered in the eyes of his own people and the world.

When Kennedy met Soviet Premier Nikita Khrushchev in Vienna in June 1961, the Soviet leader made no effort to disguise his contempt. In an interview with James Reston of the *New York Times*, Kennedy said that the Soviet premier had scolded him like a "little boy—lecturing him on American misdeeds, threatening to take over West Berlin, and boasting about the inevitable triumph of communism."[2]

Just how bad was the meeting between the two heads of state? In his book *One Minute to Midnight*, Michael Dobb quotes several observers. Vice President Lyndon Johnson said, "Khrushchev scared the poor little fellow dead." British Prime Minister Harold Macmillan compared the meeting to "Neville Chamberlain trying to hold a conversation with Herr Hitler." And Kennedy himself admitted that "[h]e just beat the hell out of me" and assumed that "I'm inexperienced . . . stupid. Maybe, most important, he thinks that I had no guts."[3]

Coming after the Bay of Pigs, the disastrous Vienna meeting further emboldened the Soviet leader to test America's resolve. Throughout the entire missile crisis, Kennedy's thoughts would keep returning to that meeting with Khrushchev. To prevent a nuclear war, he would have to walk a fine line to overcome the perception of weakness without setting off the volatile Russian leader.

Following the Bay of Pigs, Kennedy's inner circle—particularly his brother Bobby—made Castro's downfall a personal mission. Ernest May and Philip Zelikow, in their 1997 book *The Kennedy Tapes*, said that this was why the Kennedy Administration organized a new set of covert operations named Mongoose—to stir up trouble in Cuba and "if opportunity offered, to bring down Castro. Some looked to the assassination of Castro. . . . [T]he United States would help the people of Cuba overthrow the Communist regime from within Cuba and institute a new government with which the United States can live at peace."[4] However, Operation Mongoose was never fully implemented. According to National Security documents, in February 1962 the project scope was reduced to an "intelligence gathering operation only."[5]

By the summer of 1962, few could dispute that Cuba had become the Soviet Union's closest ally in the Western Hemisphere, and the most dangerous enemy of its democratic neighbor only ninety miles away. On July 27, Castro announced that he was taking measures that would make an American attack on Cuba the equivalent of world war. The reference to his strong alliance with the Soviet Union was clearly intended as a threat.

Both Cuban underground operatives and the exiles leaving the island began reporting suspicious military activities involving Soviet personnel and possibly arms. Yet for some reason, these early warnings were ignored. In a post-mortem study of the October missile crisis, American officials admitted they didn't pay as much attention as they should have. They believed the reports were either false, or the observers couldn't differentiate between defensive and offensive missile deployment.

Attorney General Robert Kennedy wrote in his memoirs that several of the early reports turned out to be accurate,

> *one from a former employee at the Hilton Hotel in Havana . . . and another from someone who overheard Premier Fidel Castro's pilot talking in a boastful and intoxicated way one evening about the nuclear missiles that were going to be furnished Cuba by Russia. But before these reports were given substance, they had to be checked and rechecked. They were not even considered substantial enough to pass on to the President or other high officials within the government. In retrospect, this was perhaps a mistake.*[6]

Papers from the Kennedy Library indicate that throughout 1962, "the movement of Soviet personnel and equipment to Cuba had aroused suspicions in the American intelligence community. In response U.S. ships and planes began photographing every Cuba-bound Soviet vessel, and U-2 spy planes began regular reconnaissance flights over the island."[7] By August 1962, Maxwell Taylor, chairman of the Joint Chiefs of Staff and head of a special group in charge of the Cuba operation, told President Kennedy that he saw "no likelihood that the Castro government can be overthrown without direct military intervention." His group recommended "a more aggressive Operation Mongoose," which the president authorized with the stipulation that it could not include overt U.S. military involvement.[8]

CIA Director John McCone (who had replaced Dulles in the aftermath of the Bay of Pigs) was the first to issue an official warning. According to British historian Lawrence Freedman, McCone believed that the most likely explanation for the activity observed by reconnaissance planes was nuclear missiles. He assumed the Soviet Union would not let Cuba fail, and therefore at some point they would go beyond conventional military aid to sending ballistic missiles to Cuba. On August 10, McCone sent a memo to the White House suggesting that medium range ballistic missiles (MRBM's) would soon be deployed in Cuba, if they were not already. However, no one took McCone's assessment very seriously. Freedman said, "His own estimators concurred with senior policy makers that Khrushchev would not be so bold."[9]

About this time, Soviet troops arriving at the Cuban port of Mariel, just a few miles west of Havana, were accompanied by large open-bed trucks suspiciously draped in tarpaulins. "The first evidence of the arrival in Cuba of surface-to-air missiles, missile-equipped torpedo boats for coastal defense, and large number[s] of Soviet military personnel came in photographs taken in late August."[10] Finally, Kennedy and his team paid attention. In September, the president warned Khrushchev about building so-called "defensive" Soviet missile bases in Cuba.

U.S. Secretary of the Interior Stewart Udall was on a goodwill visit to the Soviet Union when he received a surprise invitation to meet with Khrushchev on September 5. Since it was unusual for a head of state to meet with an interior secretary who had no involvement in foreign affairs, the White House assumed this was Khrushchev's way of sending a message. Udall flew to Sochi on the Black Sea, where he was met by the gruff Soviet premier. After a short discussion of the situation in Berlin, Khrushchev startled Udall by launching into a bully-boy tirade. "It's been a long time since you could spank us like a little boy," he told Udall, "now we can swat your ass."[11] Of course, Udall at the time had no idea what he was talking about.

On September 11, Soviet Foreign Minister Andrei Gromyko warned the United States that an attack on Cuba would mean war with the U.S.S.R. Kennedy responded with a prime-time speech on September 13, in which he went public with the evidence of Soviet nuclear arms in Cuba, and warned: "If at any time the Communist build-up in Cuba were to endanger or interfere with our security in any way . . . or if Cuba should ever . . . become an offensive military base of significant capacity for the Soviet Union, then this country will do whatever must be done to protect its own security and that of its allies."[12]

The American media didn't understand the gravity of what was happening in Cuba. On the day after Kennedy's speech, the *New York Times* editorialized that "the time has not come for a military invasion or any other drastic, unilateral action by the United States against Cuba," and that even though "the Soviet Union has greatly extended its military as well as economic aid to Cuba . . . this aid has not reached the point where it gives Cuba an offensive power or permits her to be a direct threat to the security of the United States."[13]

They were echoing the official Soviet position. In his memoirs, Robert Kennedy recalled that Soviet Ambassador Anatoly Dobrynin had assured him, on more than one occasion, that the Soviet Union had no intention of placing offensive weapons in Cuba. Knowing otherwise, the attorney general warned him that the United States was watching the buildup carefully, and "it would be of the gravest consequence if the Soviet Union placed missiles in Cuba. That would never happen, he assured me, and left."[14]

Though political tensions between the three countries remained high throughout September and October, the crisis didn't begin until the United States received indisputable evidence that the Soviet Union was placing missiles in Cuba that were capable of hitting targets in the United States. After Congress approved in late September a joint resolution backing President Kennedy on any action that he might have to take in Cuba, Kennedy ordered additional U-2 reconnaissance flights on October 9, which were delayed several days by bad weather.

On October 16, Robert Kennedy was summoned to the White House, where the president "told me that a U-2 had just finished a photographic mission and that the Intelligence Community had become convinced that Russia was placing missiles and atomic weapons in Cuba."[15] President Kennedy wanted to keep this latest intelligence secret until he decided what to do. He created a group of top advisors, later dubbed the "Ex Comm," that included Secretary of State Dean Rusk, Secretary of Defense Robert McNamara, National Security Advisor McGeorge Bundy, and CIA Director John McCone, among several others.[16]

At the first meeting, Robert Kennedy recalled that a majority of the group wanted to launch an air strike against the missile sites. McNamara argued a quarantine or blockade would provide more flexibility and give Khrushchev the opportunity to reconsider his actions without losing face with the hard-liners at the Kremlin. The rest of the group pointed out that a blockade would not remove the missiles from Cuba and wouldn't stop the work currently underway. They also feared a blockade would force confrontation with the Soviet Union when the United States should be concentrated on Cuba and Castro. As the day wore on, new intelligence revealed that the missile-launching sites in Cuba "were being directed at certain American cities, the estimate was that within a few minutes of their being fired eighty-million Americans would be dead."[17]

On October 17, Soviet Foreign Minister Andrei Gromyko formally requested that the United States stop threatening Cuba, while continuing to assure President Kennedy that any arms assistance to Cuba was for purely defensive purposes. Kennedy was not ready to show his hand yet, but he reminded Gromyko that "serious consequences . . . would arise if the Soviet Union placed missiles or offensive weapons within Cuba."[18]

While keeping all options open, Kennedy was informed on October 18 "that the necessary planes, men and ammunition were being deployed and that we could be ready to move with the necessary air bombardments on Tuesday, October 23."[19] McGeorge Bundy even prepared an "air attack" speech—locked away in the Kennedy files for four decades—in which President Kennedy "with a heavy heart" would have announced military action against Cuba in order to remove "this intolerable communist nuclear intrusion into the Americas" and minimize "the loss of life on all sides."[20]

After hearing final arguments among the Ex-Comm, the president decided in favor of a blockade on Saturday, October 20. According to Robert Kennedy, when the chief of the Tactical Air Command told the president that even a major surprise air attack could not be certain of destroying all the missile sites and nuclear weapons in Cuba "that ended the small lingering doubt that might still have remained in his mind. It had worried him (President Kennedy) that a blockade would not remove the missiles—now it was clear that an attack could not accomplish that task completely, either."[21]

The administration dispatched envoys to convince the governments of Europe and the members of NATO that the U.S. was acting in self-defense, and that the missiles in Cuba represented a threat not just against the United States but to its allies as well. Diplomats worked hard to get consensus among the Organization of American States (OAS) and the United Nations. At the same time, Kennedy ordered troops deployed to Florida and American military forces throughout the world to be placed on high alert.

Gaining the support of Congress was his most challenging task, according to Robert Kennedy. "Many Congressional leaders . . . felt that the President should take more forceful action, a military attack or invasion, and that the blockade was far too weak a response. . . . Others said they were skeptical but would remain publically silent, only because it was such a dangerous hour for the country."[22]

Early on Monday, October 22, Kennedy wrote Khrushchev:

> *In our discussions . . . the one thing that has most concerned me has been the possibility that your Government would not correctly understand the will and determination of the United States . . . since I have not assumed that you or*

any sane man would, in this nuclear age, deliberately plunge the world into war which it is . . . crystal clear no country could win and which could only result in catastrophic consequences to the whole world, including the aggressor.

He closed the letter by saying, "I hope that your Government will refrain from any action which would widen or deepen the already grave crisis and that we can agree to resume the path of peaceful negotiations."[23]

The same day, the president sent marine reinforcements to Guantánamo and ordered the military to go to "DEFCON 3" (defense readiness condition) alert status. At 7 P.M. that evening, he addressed the nation on television, revealing that the U.S. had proof that the Soviet Union was installing medium- and intermediate-range missiles in Cuba. "To halt this offensive build-up, a strict quarantine on all offensive military equipment under shipment to Cuba is being initiated. . . . We are not at this time, however, denying the necessities of life as the Soviets attempted to do in their Berlin blockade of 1948." He also asked the Soviets to remove from the island all missiles and the aircraft capable of carrying them.[24]

When Khrushchev learned of Kennedy's planned address a few hours beforehand, he told his son Sergei: "They have probably discovered our missiles. They're defenseless. Everything can be destroyed from the air in one swipe." At an emergency meeting of the Soviet Presidium, Soviet Defense Minister Rodion Malinovsky suggested that the American reaction was "a pre-electoral trick. If they were going to declare an invasion of Cuba, they would need several days to get prepared." Khrushchev didn't agree with Malinovsky, fearing that "if they were to use all means without exception, which would include the [medium-range] missiles . . . [i]t would be the start of a thermonuclear war. How can we imagine such a thing?"[25]

Khrushchev struggled to reconcile President Kennedy's indecisiveness during the Bay of Pigs with his actions now. Reminding his advisors how the Soviet Union had crushed the October 1956 uprising in Hungary, he wondered how they could expect the Americans to do any less with Cuba. That was the way superpowers behaved. "Stopping a new American invasion of Cuba had been the principal motivation for [the Cuban operation]," Khrushchev said. "We didn't want to unleash a war; we just wanted to frighten them, to restrain the United States in regard to Cuba."[26]

When the Soviets had begun planning to arm Cuba in early May, they knew there was a risk that the regular U.S. reconnaissance missions might identify the missile installations before they were all operational.[27] Now that fear had been realized. Khrushchev told the Soviet Presidium that the R-12 medium-range missiles had been deployed, but most were not yet operational, and that the intermediate-range R-14s were aboard a dozen Soviet ships still on the high seas. What Washington didn't know was that the Soviets had already placed on the island dozens of short-range nuclear-armed missiles that were capable of destroying any invasion force. "The tragic thing," Khrushchev said, "is that they can attack us, and we still respond. This could all end up in a big war."[28]

Although records from this crucial meeting of the Soviet Presidium are fragmentary and confused, in his book *One Minute to Midnight* Dobbs concludes that Khrushchev clearly believed an invasion of Cuba was imminent, and "he was prepared to authorize the use of tactical nuclear weapons against American troops."[29] Ironically, the hawkish Malinovsky convinced Khrushchev that American naval forces in the Caribbean were insufficient for a lightning strike at Cuba. Therefore, "a premature move by the Kremlin would do more harm than good. It might even provide an excuse for a U.S. nuclear strike." Though both Khrushchev and Kennedy had initially reacted to each other's steps with wounded pride and grim determination not to give in, according to Dobbs, neither could conceal their fear over what had been unleashed.[30]

In Cuba, people were shocked by Kennedy's October 22 speech. War preparations had become part of daily life on the island, and most assumed that the rumor of an American invasion was just Castro rhetoric.

Those who secretly opposed the regime hoped an American invasion would oust Castro. At the same time, they feared more government arrests and executions of perceived resisters, as had happened during the Bay of Pigs invasion. Even Castro supporters had mixed feelings. The most militant were ready to fight the hated imperialists for every inch of their land. Others worried about what might happen to them if Americans took over Cuba. Yet even the people right in the middle of the missile crisis had no idea how close the world was to a nuclear confrontation.

On October 23, the U.S. Navy blockaded all traffic to and from Cuba, while the OAS unanimously approved a resolution recommending the use of force if necessary to get nuclear arms out of Cuba. The same day, Khrushchev replied to Kennedy's letter and speech in strong terms, claiming the United States had violated the UN Charter, which prohibits one nation from inspecting the ships of another in international waters. "And naturally neither can we recognize the right of the United States to establish control over armaments which are necessary for the Republic of Cuba to strengthen its defense capability."[31]

The next day, on October 24, Khrushchev learned that William Knox, the president of Westinghouse Electric, was in Moscow on business. He invited him to the Kremlin, confirmed the presence of missiles in Cuba, and said "if Kennedy really wanted to know what kind of weapons the Soviet Union had deployed to Cuba, all he had to do was order an invasion, and he would find out very quickly. The Guantánamo Naval Base would "disappear the first day." Khrushchev ended the meeting with a warning for Knox to convey to Kennedy. "I'm not interested in the destruction of the world, but if you want us to meet in Hell, it's up to you."[32]

Following that meeting, Khrushchev wrote to Kennedy that the Soviet government considered the blockade a violation of the freedom to use international waters and "an act of aggression which pushes mankind toward the abyss of a world nuclear-missile war." He said that

Soviet vessels bound for Cuba would not observe the American blockade, and, "if the American side violates these rules, it must realize what responsibility will rest upon it. . . . [W]e will then be forced . . . to take the measures we consider necessary and adequate in order to protect our rights. We have everything necessary to do so."[33]

When Kennedy received Khrushchev's letter, he ordered the military to DEFCON 2 status—for the first and only time in history—then went to sleep before drafting a response.

In the morning, he wrote:

In early September I indicated very plainly that the United States would regard any shipment of offensive weapons as presenting the gravest issues. After that time, this Government received the most explicit assurances from your Government and its representatives both publicly and privately, that no offensive weapons were being sent to Cuba. . . . In reliance on these solemn assurances I urged restraint upon those in this country that were urging action. . . . And then I learned that all those public assurances were false and that your military people had set out recently establish a set of missile bases in Cuba. I ask you to recognize clearly, Mr. Chairman, that it was not I who issued the first challenge in this case, and that in the light of this record these activities in Cuba required the responses I have announced.[34]

As the White House waited for Khrushchev's reply, they continued to get briefings from the CIA Robert Kennedy recalled that "reports came in that a greater number of Russian personnel were working to expedite the construction of the missile sites and to assemble the IL-28s."[35]

In Key West, radar and antiaircraft equipment was set up on George Smathers Beach, and the celebrated Casa Marina Hotel became an army barracks.[36] Preparing for the worst in Miami, Dade County manager Irving McNayre issued emergency orders:

Ignore rumors; keep informed through the media; do not travel unnecessarily; lay in a two-week supply of food and water, and provide for cooking and eating utensils and equipment; Get shelter from radioactive fallout; first warning will become radio, TV, other media; The ALERT will be a 3-to-5 minute steady blast of warning sirens throughout the area; the TAKE COVER signal will be a 3-minute warbling tone or series of short blasts over the warning sirens. It means to take cover in the best available shelter.[37]

Similar defensive measures were under way nationwide. Claude Sitton, reporting from Atlanta for the *New York Times*, wrote: "Residents of the 8-state region stretching from Raleigh, N.C. to New Orleans and from Memphis to Key West are aware that they are within easy range of Soviet missiles poised on Cuban launching pads." Overnight, South Florida became an armed camp. Trains carrying troops and equipment—including missiles—were pouring down the state's peninsula, bound for Miami. Troop encampments and hospital services were set up at the old Naval Air Station in Opa-Locka. The entire southeast United States was on alert. In Miami, consumers loaded up on batteries, water, and other essentials normally reserved for hurricane warnings. The Federal Aviation Authority placed commercial aircraft in South Florida under strict limitations.[38]

Cuban exiles in Miami watched these preparations and hoped once again that their deliverance was at hand. They were not concerned about a nuclear holocaust, because at the time no one knew how close the Kennedy-Khrushchev confrontation came to that outcome.

Meanwhile, Fidel Castro had become convinced that an American invasion was imminent. He ordered his brother Raúl to mobilize forces in Oriente Province, near the U.S. Naval Base in Guantánamo, and sent Ché Guevara to the western province of Pinar del Río.[39]

At 7:00 A.M. on October 26, the U.S. Navy stopped and boarded a ship registered in Lebanon and bound for Cuba under a Soviet charter. When no armaments were found on board the ship, it was allowed to continue its journey to Cuba. The Russians didn't retaliate because it was not a Soviet ship.

That afternoon, Khrushchev replied to Kennedy's last message in a long and somewhat incoherent message that nonetheless contained a glimmer of hope. "We, for our part will declare that our ships, bound for Cuba will not carry any kind of armaments. You would declare that the United States will not support any sorts of forces which might intend to carry out an invasion of Cuba. Then the necessity for the presence of our military specialists in Cuba would disappear."[40]

Khrushchev didn't rely just on his letter to get his point across. In a highly unusual maneuver, an official at the Soviet Embassy in Washington approached John Scali, an ABC correspondent, with a message for the U.S. government. According to Robert Kennedy, the official told Scali that "the Soviet Union would remove the missiles under United Nations supervision and inspection and the U.S. would lift the blockade and give a pledge not to invade Cuba as its part of the understanding."[41]

By Saturday, October 27, the quarantine was in full effect, but the Soviet ships continued their journeys, and additional U-2 flights showed accelerated construction of missiles sites in Cuba. Robert Kennedy wrote, "This was the moment we had prepared for, which we hoped would never come.... Comparisons with the pictures of a few days earlier made clear that the work on those sites was proceeding and within a few days several of the launching pads would be ready for war." Around 10:00 A.M., McNamara reported that two Russian ships were approaching the quarantine barrier and would be intercepted before noon. Even more disturbing, a Russian submarine had moved into position between the two ships. The U.S. aircraft carrier *Essex* had been dispatched to "signal the submarine by sonar to surface and identify itself. If it refused, depth charges with a small explosive would be used until the submarine surfaced."[42]

Robert Kennedy recalled that these few minutes were the time of greatest concern for the president: "Was the world on the brink of holocaust? Was it our error? A mistake? Was there something further that should have been done? Or not done? His hand went up to his face and covered his mouth. He opened and closed his fist. His face seemed drawn, his eyes pained almost gray. We stared at each other across the table. For a few fleeting seconds, it was almost as though no one else was there and he was no longer President."[43]

Though Kennedy had put things in motion, he no longer was in control. Robert Kennedy said that "the minutes in the Cabinet Room ticked slowly by." Finally, at 10:25 A.M., CIA Director McCone reported that "some of the Russian ships have stopped dead in the water."[44]

The crisis was not over. A second and more formal letter arrived from Khrushchev, with a different message from the one received the previous day. Now Khrushchev offered to remove the missiles from Cuba in exchange for the U.S. disarming its bases in Turkey.[45]

Kennedy didn't want to withdraw the missiles from Turkey under Soviet pressure. As his team debated the best way to respond, they learned that "Major Rudolf Anderson Jr. . . . one of the two Air Force pilots who had uncovered the presence of missiles in Cuba . . . had been hit by a SAM missile . . . crashed in Cuba and . . . had been killed."[46]

Kennedy's advisors clamored for an attack to destroy the S.A.M. sites that had brought down Major Anderson. The president, anticipating Soviet reactions down the line, kept a cooler head. He decided not to attack in retaliation for Anderson's death, and that he would reply to Khrushchev's first letter, rather than his second. With the help of his brother and Ted Sorenson, Kennedy carefully crafted a response. He suggested that the Soviet Union remove all weapons systems from Cuba "under appropriate United Nations observation and supervision, and undertake, with suitable safeguard, to halt the further introduction of such weapons systems into Cuba." In return, the U.S. agreed to "remove promptly the quarantine measures now in effect, and . . . give assurances against an invasion of Cuba."[47]

Kennedy added that the United States was willing to address Turkey, but in a separate forum with the participation of NATO allies. The attorney general reassured Ambassador Dobrynin that the president "had been anxious to remove those missiles from Turkey and . . . had ordered their removal. . . . [W]ithin a short time after the crisis was over, those missiles would be gone."[48]

Both the president and the attorney general believed the United States had gone as far as it could to avoid a confrontation with the Soviet Union. "The President was not optimistic nor was I," recalled Robert Kennedy. "He ordered twenty-four troop-carrier squadrons of the Air Force Reserve to active duty. They would be necessary for an invasion. He had not abandoned hope, but what hope there was now rested with Khrushchev's revising his course within the next few hours. It was a hope, not an expectation. The expectation was a military confrontation by Tuesday and possibly tomorrow."[49]

Kennedy also sent a message to Fidel Castro, using the left-leaning president of Brazil, João Goulart, as an intermediary. If the missiles were not gone within forty-eight hours, Goulart told Castro, the U.S. would destroy them.[50] Castro was so agitated that he couldn't get his thoughts together in order to write a letter to Khrushchev. He went to the apartment of Soviet Ambassador Alekseev to seek help. There he wrote: "If . . . the imperialists invade Cuba with the goal of occupying it . . ., the danger that the aggressive policy poses for humanity is so great that following that event the Soviet Union must never allow the circumstances in which the imperialists could launch the first nuclear strike against it."[51]

Records at the Soviet Ministry of Foreign Affairs report the following conversation between Castro and Alekseev:

Alekseev: "*Do you wish to say that that we should be first to launch a nuclear strike on the enemy?*"

Castro: "*No, I don't want to say that directly, but under certain circumstances, we must not wait to experience the perfidy of the imperialists letting them initiate the first strike and deciding that Cuba should be wiped off the face of the earth.'*[52]

The Soviet ambassador reported to the Kremlin that Castro believed a U.S. attack "was almost inevitable and would occur in the next 24-72 hours."[53]

On Sunday morning, October 28, Robert Kennedy was with his daughters at a horse show at the Washington Armory. He got a call from Secretary Rusk around 10:00 A.M. "He said he had just received word from the Russians that they had agreed to withdraw the missiles from Cuba." He rushed to the White House where the president confirmed the news.[54] Khrushchev was planning to read his letter to Kennedy that day on Radio Moscow—in order to discourage any disgruntled third party from trying to disrupt the peace agreement.

In Moscow, Premier Khrushchev sent instructions to his troops in Cuba not to use any missiles, and to ground all Soviet jets in order "to avoid a clash with U.S. reconnaissance planes."[55] He also had to decide what to do about Castro, whom he felt "had lost all sense of proportion and was advocating nuclear suicide."[56] Khrushchev put together a hurried letter telling Castro not to start hostilities by firing on any American aircraft, warning that the "militants in Washington would seize upon any opportunity to wreck the diplomatic agreement with Kennedy."[57]

One hour before Khrushchev's Radio Moscow broadcast, Defense Minister Malinovsky ordered the dismantling of the missile sites.[58]

Castro immediately vowed not to accept the agreement, which had been reached between the two superpowers without his involvement. In the October 29 issue of the party newspaper *Revolution*, he listed his own conditions for any agreement: The U.S. must lift its economic embargo, put to an end what he called "pirate attacks" from bases outside Cuba, stop supporting subversive operations on the island, leave Guantánamo, and cease all flights over Cuban air space.[59]

On November 2, President Kennedy spoke briefly to the nation to announce that the Soviet Union had begun to dismantle the missiles in Cuba. Three days later, the Soviet ship *Aleksandrovsk* departed Cuba with most of the nuclear warheads onboard.[60] Their return voyage was closely monitored by U.S. war planes and ships.

On November 20, Khrushchev informed Kennedy that the Soviet Union would remove the IL-28s from Cuba, the last remaining point of disagreement between the two nations. The same day, Kennedy again went on television to tell the nation that the Soviet Union had agreed to withdraw all offensive weapons from Cuba.

Two casualties of the missile crisis received little attention at that time. The most important one was the agreement that the United States guaranteed the Soviet Union that it would not invade Cuba and that it would impede Cuban exiles from launching attacks against the islands. Years later, that became known in exile circles as the "Kennedy-Khrushchev Agreement."

The second casualty was that of two Cuban exile CIA operatives. Michael Dobbs, in his book *One Minute to Midnight,* finally told the story of Miguel Orozco and Pedro Vera, who were infiltrated into Cuba on October 19 to sabotage the Matahambre copper mines in Pinar del Río. Both had been soldiers in Batista's army and participated in the Bay of Pigs invasion. Orozco had trained many of the infiltration teams sent to Cuba during the failed invasion, and Vera was parachuted into the fray and managed to avoid capture, surviving a week at sea aboard a raft before he was rescued. The CIA recruited them in the early days of the missile crisis as part of the re-activated Operation Mongoose and prepared them for a sabotage mission considered to have an excellent chance of success.

The two heavily armed men carried with them food and water to last a week, and the explosives to bomb the mine. Orozco and Vera made it to the copper mines and planted the bombs before heading back to the coast to wait for the team that would take them out of Cuba between October 28 and October 30. Hidden in the hills, they heard explosions in the distance and assumed their mission had succeeded. What they did not know is that these were controlled explosions carried out by Cuban military forces, and that their sabotage mission had failed.

Once Khrushchev agreed to withdraw the missiles, according to documents in the National Security Archives, "all operation by Task Force W, the CIA's action arm for Operation Mongoose activities, are called to an immediate halt." However, three of ten sabotage teams had already been dispatched to Cuba, including Orozco and Vera.[61]

While they waited to be rescued, the Kennedy Administration decided that bringing them out of Cuba during the missile crisis presented too great a risk. Considered "expendable" by the U.S. government, Orozco and Vera were captured on November 12 and spent the next seventeen years in Castro's prisons, before they were released and allowed to return to the United States.[62]

NOTES

1. *L'Unitá*, February 1, 1961, as cited in Hugh Thomas, *Cuba* (Cambridge, Mass.: Da Capo Press, 1988), 1313.
2. Michael Dobbs, *One Minute to Midnight* (New York: Vintage Books, 2008), 6.
3. Dobbs, *One Minute to Midnight*, 7.
4. Ernest R. May and Philip D. Zelikow, *The Kennedy Tapes* (Cambridge, Mass.: Belknap Press of Harvard University Press, 1997), 26.
5. National Security Archives, Bay of Pigs, "Guidelines for Operation Mongoose 3/14/62," 77.
6. Robert F. Kennedy, *Thirteen Days: A Memoir of the Cuban Missile Crisis, 1969* (New York: W. W. Norton & Company Inc., 1971), 23-24.
7. Kennedy papers.
8. National Security Archives, Bay of Pigs, "Guidelines," 80.
9. Lawrence Freedman, *Kennedy's Wars: Berlin, Cuba, Laos, and Vietnam* (New York: Oxford University Press, 2000), 163-64.
10. Kennedy papers.
11. Aleksandr Fursenko and Timothy Naftali, *One Hell of a Gamble: Khrushchev, Castro, and Kennedy, 1958-1964: The Secret History of the Cuban Missile Crisis* (New York: W.W. Norton & Co., 1997), 209.
12. Kennedy papers.
13. *New York Times*, September 14, 1962.
14. Kennedy, *Thirteen Days*, 21-22.
15. Ibid., 19.

16. Other members were Secretary of the Treasury Douglas Dillon, Presidential Counsel Ted Sorensen, Under Secretary of State George Ball, Deputy Secretary of State U. Alexis Johnson, Chairman of the Joint Chiefs of Staff General Maxwell Taylor; Assistant Secretary of State for Latin America Edward Martin, advisor on Russian Affairs Llewellyn Thompson, Deputy Secretary of Defense Roswell Gilpatric, Assistant Secretary of Defense Paul Nitze, and, intermittently, Vice President Lyndon B. Johnson, Ambassador to the United Nations Adlai Stevenson, Special Assistant to the President Ken O'Donnell, and Deputy Director of the United States Information Agency Don Wilson.
17. Kennedy, *Thirteen Days,* 27-28.
18. Ibid., 31-32.
19. Ibid., 29.
20. Dobbs, *One Minute to Midnight*, 31.
21. Kennedy, *Thirteen Days*, 38-39.
22. Ibid., 42.
23. Letter from President Kennedy to Chairman Khrushchev, October 22, 1962, John Fitzgerald Kennedy Presidential Library & Museum, "The World on the Brink: John F. Kennedy and the Cuban Missile Crisis—Kennedy Khrushchev Exchanges during the '13 Days.'" These texts are from versions published in *Foreign Relations of the United States, 1961-1963*, vol. 6, *Kennedy-Khrushchev Exchanges* (Washington, D.C.: U.S. Department of State, 1996).
24. "The World on the Brink: John F. Kennedy and the Cuban Missile Crisis—Radio and Television Report to the American People on the Soviet Arms Buildup in Cuba, President John F. Kennedy. The White House October 22, 1962."
25. Dobbs, *One Minute to Midnight*, 32-33.
26. Dobbs, *One Minute to Midnight*, 33-34.
27. Fursenko and Naftali, *One Hell of a Gamble*, 191.
28. Dobbs, *One Minute to Midnight*, 34.
29. Ibid., 34.
30. Ibid., 34-35.
31. Letter from Chairman Khrushchev to President Kennedy, October 23, 1962, John Fitzgerald Kennedy Presidential Library & Museum, "The World on the Brink: John F. Kennedy and the Cuban Missile Crisis—Kennedy Khrushchev Exchanges during the '13 Days.'" These texts are from versions published in *Foreign Relations of the United States, 1961-1963:* vol. 6, *Kennedy-Khrushchev Exchanges* (Washington, D.C.: U.S. Department of State, 1996).
32. Dobbs, *One Minute to Midnight*, 85.
33. Letter from Chairman Khrushchev to President Kennedy, October 24, 1962, John Fitzgerald Kennedy Presidential Library & Museum, "The World on the Brink: John F. Kennedy and the Cuban Missile Crisis—Kennedy Khrushchev Exchanges during the '13 Days.'" These texts are from versions published in *Foreign Relations of the United States, 1961-1963:* vol. 6, *Kennedy-Khrushchev Exchanges* (Washington, D.C.: U.S. Department of State, 1996).
34. Letter from President Kennedy to Chairman Khrushchev, October 25, John Fitzgerald Kennedy Presidential Library & Museum, "The World on the Brink: John F. Kennedy and the Cuban Missile Crisis—Kennedy Khrushchev Exchanges during the '13 Days.'" These texts are from versions published in *Foreign Relations of the United States, 1961-1963:* vol. 6, *Kennedy-Khrushchev Exchanges* (Washington,

D.C.: U.S. Department of State, 1996).
35. Kennedy, *Thirteen Days*, 63.
36. "Life Goes On, But It's Not the Same," *Miami News*, October 25, 1962.
37. "What You Should Do In an Emergency," *Miami News*, October 28, 1962.
38. "Measures Taken in Civil Defense," *New York Times*, October 26, 1962.
39. Fursenko and Naftali, *One Hell of a Gamble*, 268.
40. Department of State Telegram Transmitting Letter from Chairman Khrushchev to President Kennedy, October 26, 1962, John Fitzgerald Kennedy Presidential Library & Museum, "The World on the Brink: John F. Kennedy and the Cuban Missile Crisis—Kennedy Khrushchev Exchanges during the '13 Days.'" These texts are from versions published in *Foreign Relations of the United States, 1961-1963*: vol. 6, *Kennedy-Khrushchev Exchanges* (Washington. D.C.: U.S. Department of State 1996).
41. Kennedy, *Thirteen Days*, 69.
42. Ibid., 53.
43. Ibid., 53-54.
44. Ibid., 54-55.
45. Letters from Chairman Khrushchev to President Kennedy October 27, 1962, John Fitzgerald Kennedy Presidential Library & Museum, "The World on the Brink: John F. Kennedy and the Cuban Missile Crisis—Kennedy Khrushchev Exchanges during the '13 Days.'" These texts are from versions published in *Foreign Relations of the United States, 1961-1963*: vol. 6, *Kennedy-Khrushchev Exchanges* (Washington, D.C.: U.S. Department of State, 1996).
46. Kennedy, *Thirteen Days*, 73.
47. Telegram of President Kennedy's Reply to Chairman Khrushchev's Letter of October 26, John Fitzgerald Kennedy Presidential Library & Museum, "The World on the Brink: John F. Kennedy and the Cuban Missile Crisis—Kennedy Khrushchev Exchanges during the '13 Days.'" These texts are from versions published in *Foreign Relations of the United States, 1961-1963*: vol. 6, *Kennedy-Khrushchev Exchanges* (Washington, D.C.: U.S. Department of State, 1996).
48. Kennedy, *Thirteen Days*, 83
49. Kennedy, *Thirteen Days*, 83.
50. James G. Hershberg, "JFK's Secret Attempt to Defuse the Missile Crisis with the Help of Brazil," *Journal of Cold War Studies*, 6, nos. 2 and 3 (Spring and Summer, 2004), and Gamble, 272.
51. Fursenko and Naftali, *One Hell of a Gamble*, 272.
52. Fursenko and Naftali, *One Hell of a Gamble*, 272-73, citing Soviet Ministry of Foreign Affairs, October 27, 1962, Folio 3, List 65, File 905, 144-52.
53. Fursenko and Naftali, *One Hell of a Gamble*, 272-73.
54. Kennedy, *Thirteen Days*, 84.
55. Fursenko and Naftali, *One Hell of a Gamble*, 286.
56. Ibid.
57. Ibid., 285-86.
58. Ibid., 287.
59. Ibid., 293.
60. Ibid., 311.
61. National Security Archives, Bay of Pigs, "Alleged Assassination Plots Involving Foreign Leaders 11/20/75, 147-48.
62. Dobbs, *One Minute to Midnight*, 114-16, 152, 213-14.

9

CAMARIOCA TO THE DIALOGO

BY GUILLERMO MARTINEZ AND SAM VERDEJA

Even after the Bay of Pigs and the Missile Crisis, Cuban exiles continued to hope they would soon be returning to a free Cuba. These years were known as *la maleta*—for the suitcase that many Cuban families kept always packed, ready to go home at a moment's notice.

In October 1962, the Castro regime halted direct commercial flights to the U.S., making it virtually impossible for exiles to return even to visit a sick parent. Telephone calls were difficult to place, and letters sent via third countries could take three or four months to reach the recipient. Over the next three years, the two communities grew apart, each developing its own stereotyped view of how the other side lived. Many in Cuba believed Castro's propaganda, which claimed that life in exile was harder than in Cuba. The exiles faced numerous adjustments in their new country, but they invariably felt their freedom was worth the price.

The last sizable waves of exiles arrived in the United States in 1963, aboard the ships *Shirley Lakes* in January and *American Surveyor* in April. The *Shirley Lakes* carried 1,170 refugees—most of them relatives of the Bay of Pigs veterans whose release James Donovan had negotiated just before Christmas 1962. On the *American Surveyor* were 675 exiles who had sought asylum in Havana embassies.

The armed struggle against Castro continued, both within the island

and from exiles seeking to return. Most exile groups were funded by personal resources, and they used homemade bombs and their own boats. In March 1963, a group called Commandos L shelled a Soviet freighter docked in the Port of Caibarién. Several days later, American authorities captured a forty-foot yacht named *Alisan*, which had two homemade bombs and twenty-millimeter cannon onboard. The boat's owner, Dr. Santiago Alvarez, Sr., a member of a traditional Cuban political family, said he did not know who was using his boat.[1]

Despite their agreement with Khrushchev, President Kennedy and his brother Robert never stopped funding anti-Castro commando groups. One of the most prominent was Manuel Artime's Movimiento de Recuperación Revolucionaria (MRR). Artime, one of the leaders of the Bay of Pigs invasion, remained a CIA favorite and enjoyed a close personal relationship with Bobby Kennedy. His group trained infiltration teams in the jungles of Costa Rica and maintained operations in Monkey Point, Nicaragua, and Haina, in the Dominican Republic.

When the United States closed down the Cuban units training in Fort Jackson and Fort Benning in mid-1963, many of those men joined Artime's group, which had the best and most modern weapons in the U.S. military arsenal. Jim Nickless, an NBC cameraman, spent months with the MRR documenting several of its raids for his network. He says that the anti-Castro commandos had "swift boats and M-16s" even before the American forces fighting in Vietnam.[2]

On November 23, 1963, President Kennedy was assassinated in Dallas, Texas. Theories immediately sprang up suggesting Castro was behind it—that the assassin, Lee Harvey Oswald, had met with Cuban diplomats in Mexico. However, the official investigation concluded that Oswald acted alone.

The president's death didn't stop American support for Cuban exile guerilla groups. In an interview with the authors, Jim Nickless said that as long as Robert Kennedy was attorney general, the MRR had all the financial assistance they needed. Santiago Alvarez, Jr., the captain of MRR

Swift boat *La Gitana*, concurred.[3]

When Alvarez's boat arrived at Monkey Point, it had only one fifty-caliber gun on board. To prepare the vessel for raids, he needed soldering equipment so they could make aluminum-base weapons compatible with *La Gitana's* aluminum shell. Though this equipment was very expensive, "within a week a man came back with the equipment we needed and told me it came from the highest levels of the U.S. government. He added the attorney general wished us good luck." *La Gitana* ended up with seven fifty-caliber guns on board.[4]

Cuban historian Enrique Ros, in his book *Años Críticos: Del Camino de la Acción al Camino del Entendimiento*, gave details of a daring MRR raid against the Pilón sugar mill in May 1964, as well as an August attack on a Cuban radar installation manned by Soviet military personnel.[5] In September 1964, MRR commandos attacked a Spanish cargo ship—the *Sierra Aranzazu*—believing it was a Cuban cargo vessel of the same size and shape. The captain and two crew members were killed.[6]

The attack on a civilian vessel in international waters attracted adverse publicity, making it difficult for the MRR to continue its raids on Cuba. Still, they completed three more missions that year. First, they dropped an infiltration team near La Coloma in Pinar del Río, then they went to the Dominican Republic for a few days before returning to Cuba to shell oil tanks at the Port of Casilda in southern Las Villas. Emilio Palomo was one of the gunners on *La Gitana* and remembers the Casilda attack well. "The tanks must have been empty because they did not explode," he told us. But Castro's forces still responded with a hail of bullets as tracers lit up the night sky.[7]

In January 1965, *La Gitana* and *Monty* returned to Pinar del Río to pick up the infiltration team they had dropped off earlier. The *La Gitana* crew exchanged messages with the infiltration team that didn't match what they were supposed to say, according to the plan. Palomo said, "[W]e suspected that the Cuban government was preparing a trap for us." As the exile boats approached La Coloma, two Cuban speedboats appeared and began shelling the exile vessels. They repelled the attack but were discovered by a Cuban Air Force spotter plane as they were returning to Nicaragua. After watching from afar for several hours, the Cuban plane dropped bombs that failed to hit their target. "We thought the Cuban plane had radioed for help," Palomo said, "and soon MiG planes would attack us, but fortunately for us they never came and we were able to reach our base."[8]

Palomo returned to Miami in February 1965 to attend a funeral mass on the first anniversary of his father's death. As he prepared to return to his exile group at Monkey Point, he learned that the camps were being closed and there would be no more American government assistance for Artime's MRR.[9] Following Lyndon Johnson's inauguration to his own elected term as president, the support for Cuban exile guerrillas diminished.

The MRR was not the only exile group attacking Castro's regime. In December 1964, a bazooka had been fired against the United Nations building in New York City while Ché Guevara was speaking. The Movimiento Nacionalista Cubano took credit for the attack. Eloy Gutiérrez Menoyo, who had fought Batista as a leader of the Segundo Frente Nacional del Escambray and served on the Cuban Revolutionary Council during the Bay of Pigs, formed the small band of guerrillas called Commandos L. In December 1964, he had landed near Baracoa in Oriente Province and spent a month trying to bolster internal forces fighting Castro. On January 25, his group was captured and jailed. Menoyo would spend the next twenty-two years in Castro's prisons.[10]

Castro continued to wage a public relations war with the United States throughout the early 1960s, exhorting his Latin American neighbors to stage revolutions against American imperialism. He suffered a setback in February 1964 when the Organization of American States (OAS) censured Cuba for sending weapons to Venezuela to arm a guerrilla movement against the democratic government of President Romulo Betancourt. The OAS slapped Castro again in July, urging its members to break off diplomatic relations with Cuba. Mexico was the only holdout to this resolution. An even greater embarrassment for Castro was the defection of his sister Juanita in June 1964. Accusing her brother of betraying the revolution, Juanita Castro fled to Mexico and later moved to the United States, where she became a visible critic of the Castro regime.

The Cold War confrontation in Africa gave Castro another path to pursue his agenda against the United States. In the early 1960s, the Congo, newly independent from Belgium, held enormous mineral riches that were important to both the Soviet Union and the United States. The Soviet Union deployed Cuban forces, led by Ché Guevara, to support Congolese leader Patrice Lubumba. To protect its interests in the region, the United States had recruited and trained a team to fly missions against the Communist-aligned forces in the Congo. Because they wanted "plausible deniability," U.S. leaders chose Cuban exiles to fight their battles in the Congo. Many of those who went to the Congo had participated in the Bay of Pigs invasion, and they continued working for the CIA afterwards.

In his book *Cold War in the Congo*, Frank R. Villafaña wrote, "The fact that Congo became an East versus West battlefield during the first half of the decade of the 1960s is unquestionable. Literature on these hostilities is abundant, yet mention of the participation of Cuban exiles in Congo is scant."[11]

In the beginning, the CIA-sponsored Cuban exile forces didn't know they were facing Cuban government troops. But when they discovered Cuban government credentials on the body of a soldier killed in battle, and learned that Ché Guevara was heading the Cuban contingent, they dedicated themselves to destroying his supply lines. The Cuban exiles pursued Guevara, and several times they came close to capturing him. Though he escaped, he had failed in his mission and returned to Cuba.[12]

By lowering the draft registration age to sixteen in 1964, the Cuban government gave families a tough choice. They could either leave their military-age children behind, or stay and wait until all could leave together. So it was a major surprise when Castro announced, on September 28, 1965, that any Cubans who wanted to leave the country were free to do so as of October 10. He opened the Port of Camarioca, in Matanzas Province, for exiles in the U.S. to come pick up their relatives.

President Johnson quickly accepted Castro's challenge, authorizing Cuban exiles to travel only to Camarioca while at the same time asking Congress for $12 million to relocate the new arrivals throughout the United States. Yet Johnson hoped to negotiate a more orderly system for the departures, and to persuade Cuba to give preference to family members of U.S.-based exiles.

Cuban exiles in South Florida didn't wait for a resolution to the negotiations, or even the October 10 date set by Castro. By October 5, exile vessels were streaming toward Camarioca. Some of the flotilla encountered problems navigating the treacherous Florida Straits and had to be rescued. A quick and efficient response by the U.S. Coast Guard meant that few died on this journey.

Sandra Jarro was a teenager living in Miami with her older brother, Miguel Angel. Her parents had stayed behind in Cuba because they wouldn't leave without her other brother Carlos, who was a political prisoner. Miguel Angel had arrived in Miami in 1961 and served in the U.S. Armed Forces as part of a troop trained to fight in Cuba. The force was disbanded before it went into action, and Miguel Angel subsequently married and had a son.

As the news about Camarioca began spreading throughout the Cuban exile community, Miguel Angel heard that Cuban guards could be bribed to release political prisoners. "He left South Florida in a boat named *Jane*," Sandra told the authors, "with the hope of being able to bring my brother and both of my parents."

Sandra never heard from her brother again. Family and friends in Miami began a massive search. Her parents went to the Cuban authorities and wrote to the U.S. Interest Section in Havana. But Miguel Angel was never found. "There are people who said they saw him in Camarioca escorted by a group of militia," Sandra says. "My family . . . throughout the years has speculated as to what really happened. Was he imprisoned, was he killed by the *milicianos* because they saw his 'dog tags' from the U.S. Armed Forces that he always carried in his wallet? Or, did he drown in the Florida Straits?"

Sandy and her family were able to get her brother Carlos and her parents out of Cuba. Sandy Gonzalez Levy went on to become a senior vice president at Florida International University, and an influential member of the Cuban community in Miami. But she has never been able to forget what happened during Camarioca. "My biggest regret," she says, "is that my parents both died not knowing what happened to their son [Miguel Angel] and that his son grew up without his father—an incredible and sensitive human being."[13]

Bad weather on November 3 stranded many exile-manned vessels at Camarioca, and the U.S. offered air transportation for anyone leaving Cuba who had relatives in the United States. This was the beginning of the Freedom Flights, which would last through 1973. Eventually, close to 270,000 Cubans came to the U.S. on these flights. Tomás Regalado, mayor of Miami, was a young journalist for Cuban radio in 1965, and he had the job of reading the names of those who arrived on the flights each day. Anyone with relatives in South Florida who could support them could remain in the area. The others were relocated by the Cuban Refugee Center and several social and religious agencies to homes, parishes, and towns all over the United States.[14]

As the number of Cuban exiles in the United States grew, the existing process for attaining residency proved cumbersome. In order to change their status from refugee to legal resident, Cubans needed to travel outside the country, and few could comply with that requirement. The Cuban Adjustment Act, passed in 1966, gave Cubans fleeing Communism preferential status, similar to that given a decade earlier to Hungarian refugees. Under this law, the United States welcomed hundreds of thousands of Cubans, who were now able to emigrate for all kinds of reasons, not just political.

Life in Cuba got tougher for those who stayed but didn't support Castro's regime. In November 1965, the government established the UMAP (Unidades Militares de Ayuda a la Producción) in Camaguey Province. These prisons were originally designed to detain young men of military age who the government believed opposed the regime and therefore should not be trained for the military. Soon, however, the program grew to include all dissidents and anyone considered "undesirable." This included Jehovah's Witnesses, Catholics, and practitioners of Santeria, as well as homosexuals, people with no visible employment, and owners of confiscated businesses. All it took was for someone linked to the government to accuse a person of being opposed to the revolution. There were no trials. The U.M.A.P. prisons were forced labor camps, surrounded by barbed-wire fences, with unacceptable hygiene, inedible food, and wooden slabs for beds. Conditions were so bad that international pressure forced the government to cancel U.M.A.P. within a couple of years, yet most prisoners remained in jail under similar programs given different names.

Cuba also harassed anyone who wanted to leave the island. As soon as Cubans applied for an official exit permit, they were fired from their jobs and sent to a rural labor camp. The rules applied equally to men and women. Conditions in the agricultural camps were terrible. Though the detainees were allowed weekend family visits, most of the time the distance was too great for this to occur.

Throughout 1963 and 1964, opposition forces based in the Escambray mountains had continued to attack the government. Enrique Encinosa, in his book *Unvanquished: Cuba's Resistance to Fidel Castro*, wrote that "[i]n the summer of 1964, thirty Cuban insurgents, including Mario Borges and Julio Emilio Carretero . . . fell into a state security trap as they attempted to leave the mountains and reach exile in the United States. Twelve guerrillas and several supporters were executed with dozens more imprisoned. The executed, including Carretero and Borges, died singing the Cuban National Anthem."[15]

José Luis Fernández, who fought with the Escambray guerillas until he was captured, described the struggle in Jacobo Machover's book *El Libro Negro del Castrismo*. He estimates that at one point there were more than a thousand men fighting the regime, with little or no assistance from outside Cuba. Most of the Escambray guerrillas survived through 1965, and some into late 1966, because of the help they received from peasants in the area.[16] One of the best-known and longest-lasting guerrilla leaders in Escambray was Luis Santana Gallardo, alias Luis Vargas. He fought the regime from late 1959 through December of 1965, when he was captured and quickly executed.

Sabotage against the government increased during the summer of 1966. In one incident, an airplane dropped bombs over the city of Nuevitas in Camaguey Province. In October 1966, the government captured José Reboso—the last guerrilla of Luis Vargas's Escambray group. This was a crushing blow for the resistance.[17]

One of the most significant events of 1967 for Cuban exiles happened neither in Cuba nor the U.S., but in the jungles of Bolivia. Ché Guevara had left Cuba with a small cadre of followers in 1965, when Fidel Castro chose Soviet Communism over the Chinese model, which Guevara supported. Determined to replicate the Cuban Revolution's success in other countries, Ché went to Bolivia, where both Castro and Communists in Argentina and Bolivia had promised help. None of the support ever materialized.

The CIA recruited Felix Rodríguez, later author of the book *Shadow Warrior*, to work closely with the Bolivian armed forces in tracking and capturing Guevara. He received specific orders in Washington that if Guevara was captured alive, "no resources would be spared by the U.S. to get him back to Panama alive for debriefing."[18] He and another Cuban working for the CIA, who was known by his *nom de guerre* Eduardo, arrived in Bolivia in August 1967.

According to Rodríguez, Guevara's team had grown over time to fifty-three armed guerrillas, "thirty were Bolivian, seventeen Cubans, three Peruvians, one Argentine, one East German, and one whose *nom de guerre* Danton was the French communist writer Regis Debray."[19] Debray had been captured by Bolivian forces on April 20, 1967. He was mistreated by his captors until a Cuban-born CIA agent known as Gabriel García García (his real name was Julio), who was the intelligence advisor to the Bolivian minister of the interior and public security, arrived. Rodríguez says that "after Julio showed up, Debray was treated with humanity and respect."[20]

Debray provided information that, according to Rodríguez, enabled them to track down Guevara's guerrilla group. On October 8, Bolivian armed forces notified the headquarters in Vallegrande that Guevara had been captured and was wounded. That night, while celebrating Guevara's capture, Bolivian Colonel Joaquín Zenteno Anaya asked Rodríguez to accompany him to La Higuera the next day to verify Guevara's identity and question him.

The next day, Rodríguez answered a radio call. The message was "you are authorized by the Superior Command to conduct Operation Five Hundred and Six Hundred."[21] Operation Five Hundred was the code name for Guevara. Operation Six Hundred was the code for dead. He asked the Bolivian Superior Command to verify the orders, and they sent a confirmation.

Rodríguez told no one at the camp about the instructions until Colonel Zenteno returned from his command post. Rodríguez stressed to Colonel Zenteno that the United States government wanted Guevara taken "alive under any circumstances." Zenteno replied, "[I]f I don't comply with my orders to execute Ché, I will be disobeying my own President and I'll risk a dishonorable discharge."[22]

On October 9, 1967, Bolivian soldiers shot and killed Ché Guevara.

Exiled Cubans celebrated Ché Guevara's death. To them, he was one of the most reviled symbols of the Cuban Revolution, who had personally ordered hundreds to face the firing squads, many without a trial. It seemed fitting that Guevara had died the same way.

Rebellion against the Castro regime continued, despite more limited resources and increased government control over all aspects of life on the island. In August 1967, a small group of anti-Castro commandos landed in Cuba's Pinar del Río Province, but they were quickly captured and executed. Among them were José Roig Rodríguez, Roberto Lauzurica, and Federico Avila Azcuy. In late December, an American pilot named Everett D. Jackson was shot down, captured, and jailed while trying to parachute weapons into Las Villas Province.

One of the military leaders of Alpha 66, Vicente Méndez, attempted to infiltrate a small group of commandos into Cuba in January 1970. However, a storm blew their small vessel off course, and they landed at the U.S. military base in Guantánamo. American officials arrested them and sent them back to the United States for breaking U.S. neutrality laws. Before he could be tried, Méndez set out again for Cuba, landing in April near the northern Oriente city of Baracoa, where he was killed in combat by Cuban government troops.[23]

In May, another group of exiles led by Antonio Mosquera landed in Oriente Province. They, too, were quickly captured and jailed. In September, eight exile commandos led by Colonel José Rodríguez Pérez landed near Boca de Samá in Oriente Province and harassed government forces for four days before being defeated by Cuban troops. Only two of the commandos survived. Rodríguez Pérez died of wounds suffered in combat.[24]

When Socialist Salvador Allende was elected president of Chile in November 1970, Chile became the first Latin American country to break the diplomatic isolation of Cuba. Allende sent Jorge Edwards, a well-known writer and diplomat, to Cuba as ambassador. Years later Edwards wrote a book, *Persona Non-grata*, in which he criticized Fidel Castro and the Cuban Revolution.

In March 1971, Cuban poet Heberto Padilla, who had been awarded the Julián del Casal poetry prize in 1968, was imprisoned after being forced to confess that he was a CIA agent. Though he was only in jail for five days, the resulting controversy soured intellectuals throughout the world on the Cuban Revolution.

In October 1971, a commando group from a recently created exile organization called the Plan Torriente—headed by José Elías de la Torriente—destroyed a Cuban military barracks near Boca de Sama in Oriente. Two Castro Cubans were killed and four others wounded in the attack. The commando attack was successful, but American officials confiscated the boat and returned it to the United States. The Plan Torriente developed a two-pronged plan. The military strategy called for commando raids on Cuba, and the diplomatic strategy aimed to further isolate the Castro regime from other Latin American countries.

By this time, the United States government had stopped providing assistance to anti-Castro groups. As a result, exile militants began targeting Cuban offices and officials outside the island, as well as people believed to be Castro sympathizers. Assassination attempts were also made against anti-Castro leaders in the United States, presumably by the Cuban government. American authorities believed that some of the funding for these activities came from the drug trade. It was all part of the violence that shook up the Cuban exile community in the 1970s.

In his book *Unvanquished*, Enrique Encinosa said that exiles targeted Cuban government commercial offices in Montreal in April 1972. "Juan Felipe de la Cruz arrives in Montreal with a suitcase full of plastic explosives. A radio announcer and community figure in the Miami area, he had fought as a teenager in the DRE's underground forces (in Cuba). The day after reaching Montreal, De la Cruz placed an explosive charge on the roof of the Cuban Commerce Affairs Building. The explosion killed Cuban diplomat Sergio López. Shrapnel wounded seven other members of the Cuban diplomatic corps."[25]

On June 7, 1972, five men broke into the Watergate offices of the Democratic National Committee in Washington, D.C., and were arrested. The incident triggered the largest political scandal in the history of the United States and led to the resignation two years later of President Richard M. Nixon. Four of the burglars—Bernardo Barker, Virgilio González, Rolando Eugenio Martínez, and Frank Sturgis—were anti-Castro activists recruited in Miami by CIA agent E. Howard Hunt.

In December 1972, several Caribbean countries re-established diplomatic relations with Cuba. Among them were Trinidad-Tobago, Grenada, Jamaica, and Guyana. Grenada, in particular, became a close ally of Cuba and allowed the presence of Cuban troops on the island. As 1973 began, several American airplanes were hijacked to Cuba. The two countries signed an antihijacking agreement in February.

After eight years, the Cuban government unilaterally ended the Freedom Flights on April 6, 1973. This began another long period of isolation between Cuban exiles and their homeland. Cubans who wanted to flee the regime could either risk their lives on small vessels to cross the dangerous Florida Straits or seek visas to travel to a third country.

Only those Cubans living abroad who sympathized with the revolution were allowed to travel to and from Cuba. Some made yearly journeys to work in agricultural camps, providing an excellent propaganda tool for the government. Among those were the Antonio Maceo Brigade and Areíto.

Fulgencio Batista y Zaldívar, once Cuba's strongman, died in Málaga, Spain, on August 6, 1973.

Meanwhile in Chile, the Cuban Revolution lost a close ally when on September 4, 1973, General Augusto Pinochet ousted Salvador Allende's socialist regime in a coup d'état. Allende was killed while resisting the military forces attacking Chile's Palacio de la Moneda (the Presidential Palace). Chile's military said they ousted Allende because he wanted to impose a Cuban-style regime in Chile. Many of his closest security guards were Cuban. Some were killed in the attack, while others were apprehended.

A year later, Pinochet offered to exchange jailed Cuban security guards for political prisoners serving time in Castro's prisons. He specifically asked for the release of former Cuban rebel leader Huber Matos. Cuba never replied to Chile's offer.

Casualties in the Cuban exile community mounted as the 1970s wore on. In March 1974, Arturo Rodríguez Vives, of the exile group Christian Democratic Movement, was gunned down in New York City. On April 12, anti-Castro leader José Elías de la Torriente was killed in his Coral Gables living room on Good Friday. Two years earlier, Torriente's organization had been responsible for the last successful anti-Castro raid in Cuba. A Cuban government radio broadcast after the raid "rated a full-length Castro speech at the time, vowing to take the offensive against exiles."[26] Torriente's killer was never caught. Some believed Cuban government agents were responsible, and others whispered that he'd been killed by another anti-Castro group. Neither theory has ever been proven.

A year later, Luciano Nieves was gunned down as he left Miami Children's Hospital. Militant exile groups had accused Nieves of being a Castro government agent. Years later, in 1979, a street in Havana was named after him. Rolando Masferrer, a controversial figure in Cuban politics from his days as a University of Havana student, was blown up by a bomb on October 31, 1975, in Miami. In Cuba, Masferrer had organized a private pro-Batista force that actively fought Castro in the Sierra Maestra Mountains. His group was known as los Tigres de Masferrer (Masferrer's Tigers).

Several bombs exploded in federal government buildings in Miami on December 3 and 4, 1975. Federal authorities charged anti-Castro militant Rolando Otero with the bombing.[27]

April 1976 was a violent month. On the 13th, Ramón Donésteves, a proponent of rapprochement with the Cuban government, was assassinated in Miami. On the 22nd, a bomb exploded at the site of Cuba's Embassy in Lisbon, Portugal, killing two people. And on the 30th, a bomb was detonated underneath the parked car of Cuban exile radio commentator Emilio Milián in Miami. Milián, who was a harsh critic of terrorist activities among the Cuban exile community, survived but lost both his legs.

Chief Lt. Thomas Lyons, of the Strategic Investigation Section of Dade County's Organized Crime Bureau, described the challenges of solving these mysterious bombings and assassinations to Edna Buchanan of the *Miami Herald*. "Death lists with 15 to 30 people each," he said, "[a]ll from different organizations, some claiming to be the same organizations with different names. There's a contract on so and so—he's a communist. There's a contract on so and so—by the communists. There's a contract by so and so—he's a dope dealer."[28]

In his book, Encinosa wrote: "More than fifty bombings occurred in Miami during the mid-seventies, most aimed at businesses that mailed packages to Cuba. Publicly the exile groups argued that Fidel Castro's Government was raking in millions of dollars from the package trade. The FBI intensified its campaign against the exile groups, deploying scores of agents; but arrests were infrequent."[29]

On July 9, anti-Castro militants placed a bomb on a Cubana Airlines plane in Kingston, Jamaica. It did not explode. On the 23rd of the month, exile militants also tried to kidnap Cuba's consul in Mérida, Mexico. His bodyguard died in the attack. Former Chilean Minister Orlando Letelier and his companion Ronni Moffett were killed by a car bomb in Washington, D.C., on September 21, 1976. Letelier had served Chilean Socialist president Salvador Allende, a Castro ally. A group of Cuban exiles, most linked to Cuban Nationalist Movement (M.N.C. in Spanish), were accused of participating in the plot along with Chilean intelligence services known as DINA, under the government of Augusto Pinochet. Among the Cubans were brothers Guillermo and Ignacio Novo, José Dionisio Suárez, Virgilio Paz, Alvin Ross, and several other M.N.C. members.[30]

On October 6, a Cubana de Aviación airplane, Flight 455, en route from Caracas to Havana, exploded as it took off from Barbados. Venezuelan authorities accused two anti-Castro fighters, Dr. Orlando

Bosch and Luis Posada Carriles, of masterminding the bombing. Seventy-three people aboard the airline died, including Cuba's fencing team. Bosch spent eleven years in jail while he was being tried by Venezuelan authorities. Three times they put him on trial, and three times Venezuelan courts acquitted him.[31] Bosch was released from prison in Venezuela in early August 1987, and shortly thereafter entered the United States. Posada Carriles, who Venezuelan authorities said had links to the CIA, escaped from a Venezuelan jail in September of 1985.

In his book *Unvanquished*, Encinosa claimed that the Barbados bombing ended exile violence because the resulting tragedy had discredited "any tactic that remotely resembled it."[32]

The inauguration of Jimmy Carter as president in January 1977 brought a different kind of dialogue between Cuba and the United States. Officials started discussing a fishing agreement, and Secretary of State Cyrus Vance announced there would be no preconditions to begin talks on other topics. Carter even suspended American spy flights over the island.

In September, the two countries established Interests Sections. In Washington, Cuba's diplomats would work under the auspices of Czechoslovakia, and in Havana, the United States would operate under the Swiss flag. Each country could have up to ten personnel in their Interest Section, headed by a chargé d'affaires, a rank underneath full ambassador. This was the biggest step toward re-establishing relations since the United States broke them off in January of 1961.

A formal agreement in December of 1977 defined "a maritime boundary between the two countries. The pact . . . was the first treaty between the United States and Cuba since 1960."[33] In early January, the Treasury Department authorized Cuban-Americans to send up to five hundred dollars to any single close relative in Cuba to assist the recipient in emigrating from Cuba.

Cuba and the United States began to allow artists and athletes to travel to each other's country for artistic presentation or athletic competitions, and several members of Congress and American businessmen visited Cuba in an attempt to pressure the Carter Administration to lift the embargo. But Carter stopped short of this goal, reiterating the U.S. position that in order to lift the economic embargo, the Cuban government would have to respect human rights, release political prisoners, permit the reunification of Cubans on both sides of the Florida Straits, and withdraw its troops from Africa.

Cuba's extensive involvement in Africa was a major impediment to improved relations between the countries. In November 1975, President Agostinho Neto, head of the Movement for the Liberation of Angola, had asked Cuba for troops to fight the anti-Communist rebel forces led by Jonas Savimbi. Castro's commitment had grown since then. Cuban historian Marcos Antonio Ramos wrote that "tens of thousands of Cubans went to Angola in what became known as Operation Carlota. Thousands of Cubans died or were wounded in these battles, but their presence in the African continent served as an impediment to groups backed by the United States and South Africa winning the war."[34]

By 1977, Cuba had become a surrogate army for Soviet ambitions in Africa. Cuba provided soldiers, doctors, and teachers to help pro-Soviet Communist governments in the region fight off their anti-Communist opponents, and the Soviet Union paid handsomely for these services. By1978, Moscow's annual subsidy of its Caribbean ally had grown to over $2 billion annually.

While he negotiated with the Carter Administration, Castro started a parallel communication channel with the Cuban exile community. In August of 1977, Cuban government officials had told a Cuban exile living in Panamá that they wanted to meet with Bernardo Benes, a prominent exile banker in Miami with excellent contacts in the Carter Administration. Benes and his partner Carlos Dascal went to Cuba to meet with Fidel Castro. As a result of these meetings, Castro invited American journalists to a press conference in Cuba in September of 1978. There he announced he was willing to release Cuban political prisoners and to permit Cuban exiles to travel back to the island to visit their relatives.

Castro asked Benes to coordinate a meeting between the Cuban government and a group of what he called "moderate exiles," which would exclude anyone who had resisted Castro's regime. This group became known as *El Comité de los 75* (for the number of exiles that participated in the talks) and met with Castro at his offices in the Palace of the Revolution in November and December of 1978. Many, though not all, were members of pro-Castro exile groups, like the ones who published the magazine *Areíto*, and the Antonio Maceo Brigade. Other participants—like Rosa Rivas de Izaguirre—joined the group to beg Castro to release family members. In Rosa's case, Castro heard the mother's plea and released her son, Alfredo Izaguirre.

In October, American and Cuban-American journalists had been allowed to interview political prisoners at El Combinado del Este, Cuba's largest prison. Benes went with them, and he returned to the United States with the first forty-six freed prisoners. Mirta Ojito, in her book *Finding Mañana*, said that among those who traveled with Benes back to Miami were "Tony Cuesta, who had lost an arm and his eyesight when a bomb exploded in his face during a 1966 undercover operation that Benes had helped finance. Cuesta had been in jail ever since."[35]

These conversations between the Committee of 75 and Fidel Castro became known as *"el diálogo"* (the dialogue). They induced Castro to free more than thirty-six hundred political prisoners, though some—such as Roberto Martín Pérez and Andrés Vargas Gómez—remained incarcerated in Cuban jails. As a result of *el diálogo*, Cuba invited exiles living abroad to return to the island to visit relatives.

The *diálogo*, and the exile visits it brought about, created controversy within the Miami exile community. Some welcomed the opportunity to visit family, while others opposed even this indirect support for the Cuban government. Despite the debate, in less than a year, more than 100,000 exiles made the pilgrimage back to their homeland.

In his book *Secret Mission to Cuba*, Robert M. Levine said that Castro told Benes he wanted Cyrus Vance to visit Cuba to continue negotiations, but the process stopped as soon as the prisoners were released. "President Carter's goal—normalization of relations with Cuba based on Cuba's acceptance of the Helsinki agreement on human rights and other reforms—remained unfulfilled. Cuba and the United States remained too far apart."[36]

In October of 1979, Castro finally released Huber Matos, one of his old revolutionary allies, who had spent the past twenty years in jail.

After almost two decades of limited communication between Cuban exiles and those who remained behind, no one was prepared for the effects of the increased contact. Cubans on the island had been living under the influence of the Soviet Union, and they knew little about life in the United States. Now visiting exiles brought precious gifts of clothing, food, medicines, and candy—things rarely seen in Cuba. Some of the exiles exaggerated their financial success, leading Cubans to believe that U.S. streets were paved with gold. Though most settled for a few gifts from relatives, some within the island began to dream of greater economic opportunity and freedom.

Soon they would have an opportunity to make these dreams come true.

NOTES

1. Dom Bonafede, "Determined Exile Groups to Press Campaign Against Castro," *Miami Herald*, April 8, 1963.
2. Author interview with Jim Nickless, November 27, 2009.
3. Separate author interviews with Santiago Alvarez, Jr., November 15, 2009, and with Jim Nickless, November 27, 2009.
4. Author interview with Santiago Alvarez, Jr., November 11, 2009.
5. Enrique Ros, *Años Críticos: Del Camino de la Acción al Camino del Entendimiento* (Miami: Ediciones Universal, 1996), 182-83.
6. Separate author interviews with Alvarezand with Nickless.
7. Author interview with Emilio Palomo, November 15, 2010.
8. Ibid.

9. Ibid.
10. George Volsky, "Castro's Gulag," *New York Times*, October 18, 1987.
11. Frank R. Villafaña, *Cold War in the Congo: The Confrontation of Cuban Military Forces, 1960-1967* (New Brunswick, N.J.: Transaction Publishers, 2009), ix.
12. Enrique Encinosa, *Unvanquished: Cuba's Resistance to Fidel Castro* (San Francisco: Pureplay Press, 2004), 88-90.
13. Author Interview with Sandy González Levy, February 26, 2010.
14. The *Miami Herald* compiled a list of all Cubans who arrived on the Freedom Flights. These names have been published on the web at: Miami Herald database of freedom flight passengers, http://www.miamiherald.com/flights/.
15. Enrique Encinosa, *Unvanquished: Cuba's Resistance to Fidel Castro* (San Francisco: Pureplay Press, 2004), 91.
16. Jacobo Machover, *El Libro Negro del Castrismo* (Miami: Ediciones Universal, 2009), 71.
17. Calixto Masó, *Historia de Cuba,* Tercera Edición (Miami: Ediciones Universal, 1968), 706-7.
18. Félix Rodríguez and John Weisman, *Shadow Warrior* (New York: Simon & Schuster, 1989), 136.
19. Ibid., 135.
20. Ibid.
21. Ibid., 163.
22. Ibid., 163-64.
23. Encinosa, *Unvanquished*, 98-99.
24. Ibid., 99.
25. Ibid., 112.
26. Hilda Inclán, "'We're going to blow you up,' Cuban liberationists warned," *Miami News*, April 16, 1974.
27. Edna Buchanan, "Murder in Exile," *Miami Herald*, April 18, 1976, 1D.
28. Ibid.
29. Encinosa, *Unvanquished*, 122.
30. Ibid., 122-23.
31. James LeMoyne, "Grizzled Castro-Fighter Still Man with a Mission," *New York Times*, August 1, 1990.
32. Encinosa, *Unvanquished*, 126.
33. David Bender, "U.S. and Cuba Prepare to Draft a Maritime Agreement; A Two-Year Period for Ratification Reparations Issue Stalls Relations," *New York Times*, January 15, 1978.
34. Marcos Antonio Ramos, *La Cuba de Castro y Después . . . Entre la Historia y la Biografía* (Nashville: Grupo Nelson, 2007), 274.
35. *Finding Mañana*—Op. Cit. pp. 52
36. Robert M. Levine, *Secret Missions to Cuba* (New York: Palgrave, 2001), 109-10.

10

THE MARIEL EXODUS

BY SILVIA M. UNZUETA

On April 1, 1980, Héctor Sanyustiz crashed a bus through the gates of the Peruvian Embassy in the Miramar section of Havana. The Cuban guards opened fire, injuring two of the bus occupants and killing one of their own guards in the crossfire. Sanyustiz was an unemployed bus driver who had planned the embassy event with a few friends, in the hope of obtaining political asylum.[1] Even though there had been similar episodes during the previous year, Sanyustiz's bus became the spark that lit a long smoldering fire.

The exiles who had returned to Cuba as a result of the *Diálogo* painted a picture of life outside Cuba that stirred both envy and anger among island residents. The journalist Gustavo Godoy had traveled to Cuba in August 1979 to cover the first visit of Cuban-Americans since they had left their homeland as exiles. As a busload of exiles from Miami arrived at the Habana Libre Hotel, he overheard a woman in militia uniform muttering to herself *"¡Le ronca!"* ("This sucks!"). Godoy spoke with Maribel, a mulatto woman, who was furious that her country was allowing these *gusanos* ("worms," as those who left Cuba after the revolution were called) to stay in a hotel where a party loyalist like her was not allowed to set foot. Maribel complained that she had cut sugar cane in the fields and sacrificed comfort for the ideals of the revolution. And now the *gusanos* reaped the rewards of her labors. To

Godoy, Maribel symbolized a growing discontent with the revolution.[2]

Tension mounted to the point that anyone who publicly admitted they wanted to leave the island was attacked by both government officials and supporters. Alina Fernández, the daughter of Fidel Castro and Nati Revuelta, was studying diplomacy at the University of Havana in early 1980. She remembers a mother coming to the university to request her daughter be officially discharged so that she could leave the country. "A man slapped her across the face," Alina told the author, "as the masses screamed: *¡Escoria! ¡Escoria!* ('Scum! Scum!') Frightened, the two women ran . . . and the mob followed them."

Fernández says that these incidents—known as *Actos de Repudio* ("Acts of Repudiation")—were common at the time. Her neighbor, Alfredo Berenguer, was a former government official who wanted to leave Cuba. "People congregated in front of his house . . . screaming and shouting insults. . . . Witnessing these incidents was a turning point in my own life. I decided then that I would leave my country."[3]

During his assault on the Peruvian Embassy, Hector Sanyustiz was shot in the leg and buttocks. Embassy workers rushed him and one of his comrades, who had suffered superficial wounds, to a Havana hospital. Outside his window, Castro loyalists shouted that he should face a firing squad.[4]

Fidel Castro demanded that Perú turn over the six Cubans on the bus that had rammed the embassy gates. The Peruvian charge d'affaires and highest-ranking official in Cuba, Ernesto Pinto Basurto, refused.[5] On April 4, Castro ordered the Cuban guards who had been protecting the embassy to abandon their posts. Still believing he was in control, he declared on the front page of the Communist Party newspaper *Granma* that the Cuban government would no longer protect embassies "which do not cooperate in their own protection."[6]

As the early trickle of asylum seekers turned into a flood, Castro realized his mistake and reinstated the guards outside the embassy. But it was too late. By April 6—Easter Sunday—10,834 Cubans were crammed into the grounds of the Peruvian Embassy. The incident made news around the world and became a source of international embarrassment for the Cuban government.[7] Castro tried to negotiate his way out of the crisis by sending Pinto Basurto back to Lima with a personal message for Peruvian President Francisco Morales Bermúdez.[8]

The international media flocked to cover the rapidly escalating crisis. Despite Cuba's efforts to keep journalists away from the embassy, newspapers ran front-page photographs of people crowded in trees and on the roof, and they reported that people inside the embassy lacked water, food, and basic necessities. The *Miami Herald* quoted Peruvian foreign minister Arturo García, who said, "Peru cannot feed the refugees at the embassy because the Cuban food is purchased with ration cards."[9]

Miami mayor Maurice Ferré issued an early statement that the refugees camped out in the Peruvian Embassy would be welcome in Miami. On April 10, the *Miami News* published on their front page the results of a call-in survey they had conducted that showed local residents opposed following through on Ferré's invitation by a ratio of three to one. A dozen local leaders who were interviewed agreed that "despite generally good relations between Latins and non-Latins here, there is an unspoken undercurrent of resentment and reserve on both sides."[10]

Cuban-Americans in the U.S. and other countries staged public demonstrations in support of the people in the Peruvian Embassy. In Miami, thirty-two Cuban exiles went on a hunger strike. "Spontaneous marches, some several miles long, have been forming and reforming," reported Jo Thomas of the *New York Times* from Miami on April 14. "Horn-honking has been so popular that at one point the Hialeah Police Department was getting about two complaints a minute and 300 in eight hours."[11]

After a two-week standoff, Castro finally agreed to allow the departure of those barricaded in the embassy. President Carter declared the U.S. would admit up to thirty-five hundred, and Peru, Spain, and Costa Rica all agreed to accept some of the refugees.[12] On April 16, two Costa Rican airliners transported the first two hundred émigrés to San José and then returned to Havana for more. One of the passengers on the first flight, Juan Alberto Rodríguez, had cuts on his face and a bloody knee. When he arrived in San José he told the Associated Press that he "had been beaten as he boarded the plane in Havana." Others reported their buses were stoned on the way to the airport. Rodríguez said: "I came alive today. I was dead. I was like a robot, but now I am a man again."[13]

Jo Thomas interviewed thirty-two-year-old Mario Leyva about his experiences in the Peruvian Embassy. "We ate a cat," he admitted to her. "Someone found two dogs. We ate the black one but the white one hid. A papaya tree was eaten from the leaves to the trunk and then we pulled the roots out of the ground."

Frank Gallardo had lost thirty-two pounds in his eight days in the embassy without food. Gallardo was one of those to whom Castro had granted safe passage from the embassy back to his home, where he was supposed to await a flight out. "When we went back . . . they threw rocks at our house," he told Thomas. "They told our children to leave us—that they were the children of the country; our neighbors. We lived for 20 years in the same house. Our neighbors did it out of fear."[14]

In Costa Rica, international officials sent about seven hundred of the arriving refugees on to Perú, since that's where they had originally sought asylum. There they were housed at the Tupac Amaru Park, in Lima, where some would later stage a hunger strike in an unsuccessful bid to be allowed into the United States. Many ended up living in the park for years.

On April 18, Castro surprised the world by canceling the airlift. Journalists covering the crisis cynically suggested he did this while there were still refugees in the Peruvian Embassy so that he would have a worldwide audience of journalists to witness his annual Bay of Pigs commemorative parade, scheduled for April 20.

Some in the State Department believed that Castro had provoked a quarrel with Perú and the other Latin American countries to demonstrate that these countries, while upholding the right of asylum for

Cubans who had taken refuge in their Havana embassies, were unwilling to accept many Cubans for resettlement. However, when President Carter declared his support for the embassy refugees, Castro saw an opportunity to shift the focus from a multilateral conflict among Cuba and Latin American nations to a bilateral confrontation with the United States—his longtime nemesis.

To win the propaganda battle, he couldn't let it be known that Cuba's best citizens were eager to leave, and had flocked to the Peruvian Embassy. He needed to control who left, and an orderly system of departures, which the U.S. government was requesting, would not serve his purpose. He had to convince his own people, and the world, that the only people who wanted to leave Cuba were the *"lumpen proletariat"*—the degenerates and social undesirables who were incapable of self-sacrifice for the revolution. So Castro fell back on the same strategy that had worked so well for him with Camarioca in 1965. He changed course mid-crisis, turning a diplomatic defeat into a propaganda victory. Once again the Cuban exile community would take matters into their own hands when diplomatic initiatives failed.

Back on March 8, 1980, he had even warned the U.S. of what they could expect: "We hope they will adopt measures so they will not encourage the illegal departures from the country, because we might also have to take our own measures. . . . We were forced to take measures in this regard once. We have also warned them of this. . . . We once had to open Camarioca port. . . . We feel it is proof of the lack of maturity of the U.S. government to again create similar situations."[15]

On Sunday, April 21, two boats—*Dos Hermanos* and *Blanchie III*—piloted by Cuban exiles Napoleon Vilaboa and Félix Díaz, left Key West for the port of Mariel, approximately twent-five miles from Havana. They returned to Key West in the early hours of April 22 with about forty refugees. This was the beginning of what would become known as the Mariel Boatlift. After Vilaboa's trip, other small boats made the journey to Mariel to pick up friends and relatives. U.S. officials were caught off-guard. It's "unlawful and unhelpful," a U.S. State Department spokesman complained. "All this does is complicate things."[16]

Vilaboa had long been suspected by the exile community of being a Castro collaborator. Years after Mariel, in a 1989 interview with *Miami Herald* reporter Liz Balmaseda, he claimed to be the instigator of the boatlift. Vilaboa told Balmaseda he had formed a relationship with a Castro official, Rene Rodríguez, during his time in prison after participating in the Bay of Pigs invasion. He said Rodríguez had invited him to Havana in 1980 to meet with Castro about the refugees in the embassy, and in the meeting he suggested a boatlift similar to Camarioca that brought between three thousand and five thousand refugees to the U.S. According to Balmeseda's interview, Vilaboa then returned to Miami and met with Hialeah preacher Manuel Espinosa—another suspected and later-admitted Castro agent—who put him in touch with the Cuban envoy to the United Nations. When he was told that Cuba had authorized the boatlift, Vilaboa took to the Spanish-language airwaves to urge exiles to join the flotilla to Mariel.

At one time called the "father of the freedom flotilla," Vilaboa was later condemned by the exile community for his Castro connections. After Mariel, he spent eight years in Costa Rica before returning to Florida under an assumed name.[17] On the thirtieth anniversary of the boatlift, in 2010, Vilaboa resurfaced in an interview with Juan Tamayo of *El Nuevo Herald*. Denying he had ever been a Castro agent, he said he had only been trying to help refugees, even claiming that he had once plotted to overthrow the Cuban dictator.[18]

Miami prepared to receive most of the refugees from the Peruvian Embassy. On April 21, Tony Ojeda, Metro-Miami (Dade County) assistant manager, said finding shelter for the embassy refugees would not be a problem. Aida Levitan, director of Metro's Office of Latin Affairs, reported that housing would be available for 750 refugees for as long as a month. Ojeda also urged relatives of the refugees to remain calm and not to cause traffic jams with their celebrations. He asked the media not to stir things up further, to let the situation resolve itself.[19]

This was asking a lot. Radio stations in Miami, particularly those that broadcast in Spanish, were fixated on the unfolding Mariel story. Herb Levin, the general manager of Spanish-language station WQBA and Jorge Luis Hernández, his news director, met with Vilaboa, who told them that Castro was going to allow a boatlift from Mariel. In an on-air interview, Vilaboa told listeners that Castro would welcome exiles who went to pick up their relatives.

South Florida's public sector mobilized overnight. Silvia Unzueta, a young manager with Miami-Dade County government, got a call early in the afternoon of April 21, from Sergio Pereira, assistant county manager. He asked her to report immediately to the Manuel Artime Community Center in the heart of Little Havana, but he didn't tell her anything more. When she got there, the streets were packed with vehicles. Though the magnitude of the crisis was not yet known, the urgency was palpable. The city and county were about to undertake the largest domestic relief operation in the history of the U.S. This mass migration of extraordinary proportions would start a whole new chapter for life in South Florida.

In Miami, the initial processing and housing of refugees was considered the top priority, and tools were immediately put in place to handle the crisis. Coordinated by the Metropolitan Dade County government and the support of the state of Florida and the city of Miami, the hands-on effort was delegated to a few local, state, and federal officials. The staff at Tamiami Park improvised with donations of desks—where the refugees were interviewed—and food and staples that were dispensed to the refugees. The FBI, the CIA, and the INS (Immigration and Naturalization Service) shared the space where the refugees were fed, fingerprinted, X-rayed, checked by volunteer physicians, and—if requirements were met—released to anxiously waiting family, friends, and others who offered to serve as sponsors.

Tearful reunions took place as hundreds of Miami exiles greeted the new arrivals through the barbed wire at Tamiami Park. A white "X" sticker on a person's clothing indicated those who had already been processed. Names were called through a bullhorn for those with the sticker who were ready to leave the park for their new homes.[20]

By April 23, the Straits of Florida had turned into a two-way sea lane with dozens of boats headed for Mariel. WQBA kept its audience informed by broadcasting the names of those boats arriving daily in Key West.[21] The rush to rescue people from Cuba was on. Marine supply stores on the lower southeast coast of Florida were inundated with people buying supplies and food. Those who did not have boats were getting boats. "We're selling anything that floats," one marine supply owner told the *Miami News*. "People are buying lifesavers, lamps, ropes—anything just as long as they need it on a trip to Cuba."[22] Fleets of lobster boats were being fueled at the Two Friends Fish Company on Stock Island, immediately north of Key West. "Let's go! Let's go!" a woman shouted. "We've just bought a boat for 35,000 pesos. We're going to Cuba."[23]

Though many South Floridians lent a helping hand, some tried to profit by offering boats at usurious pricing. José Alvado, a Cuban-American who came down from New Jersey to rescue family members, told the *Miami News* that a man offered to get him a boat the following day, but wouldn't tell him how much it cost. "I have $2,000," Alvado said, "I can't possibly pay these prices—up to $30,000 these people want. . . . I'm giving up [and] going back to New Jersey."[24] The *New York Times* reported that some boat owners were charging five thousand dollars for each person they brought out of Cuba. Others offered boats for charter at between thirty thousand and forty thousand dollars.[25]

It soon became evident that some of the Mariel refugees were neither family of Cuban-Americans nor participants in the Peruvian Embassy incident. Horacio Unzueta sailed to Cuba in his twenty-five-foot yacht, expecting to come back with his relatives. "Instead," he says, "at the Port of Mariel, the Cuban government filled my boat with thirteen total strangers."

Unzueta described deplorable conditions at the port. "Passion and determination brought them to Mariel to find and bring their relatives to freedom. Unfortunately, greatly due to tremendous storms, lack of sailing skills, basic navigational equipment and supplies, some suffered greatly and others even paid with their own lives."[26]

On April 26, as the exodus accelerated, Florida governor Bob Graham declared a state of emergency in Miami-Dade and Monroe counties. That day, the head of the Federal Emergency Management Agency (FEMA) finally arrived in Miami to manage the crisis. Unlike the municipal government, the federal government had been slow to mobilize for the Mariel refugees. In the aftermath of a blown hostage rescue in Iran and the subsequent crisis at the State Department, the question of Cuban refugees—albeit thousands of them—was on the rearmost of back burners.

At first, the Mariel refugees were considered economic refugees, and therefore eligible for limited benefits. One of the complications for federal policy makers was the simultaneous flow of illegal Haitians who arrived in rickety crafts, hoping the U.S. would admit them on the same terms as the Cubans. In time, the policies were revised, and the White House announced that Jack Watson would coordinate these issues with Victor Palmieri, ambassador at-large and U.S. coordinator for refugee affairs in the United States Department of State.

Secretary of State Cyrus Vance called a meeting for April 26 in Washington with top national experts in Cuban affairs as well as with a large group of exile community leaders. Vance became embroiled in disagreement with President Carter on the ill-fated Iran rescue attempt and delegated the meeting to Undersecretary of State Warren Christopher. His resignation was rumored for days in the media, though he didn't actually resign until April 28.

The Washington meeting was attended by the political and civic leadership from Dade County and included Raúl Martínez, future mayor of Hialeah, and Maurice Ferré, mayor of Miami, as well as representatives from Miami-Dade County government and a group of community leaders from around the country. Members of the press included Guillermo Martínez Márquez, a prominent exile journalist; Herb Levin of WQBA; and Tomás García Fusté, a radio commentator from the New York-New Jersey area.[27]

In an unpublished 1983 manuscript titled "Act of War: The Inside Story of the 1980 Mariel Boatlift," Palmieri described the meeting as contentious. The South Florida delegation was incensed that neither Vance nor Vice President Walter Mondale attended. Warren Christopher tried to convince the Miami group to help slow if not stop the boatlift, suggesting fines and sanctions for people bringing unauthorized refugees into the country.

"It would be difficult to imagine a less receptive audience," wrote Palmieri. "Many were hardline militants who had come to demand that the United States grasp the opportunity to overthrow Castro. When Jack Watson tried to talk about 'long term strategy for dealing with Castro,' he was shouted down. . . ."

Palmieri said that Miami mayor Maurice Ferré pointed out the naiveté of asking the Cuban-Americans to issue a statement condemning the boatlift as illegal. "How in the world," Ferré asked, "did they expect any Cuban to make a statement like that? Even if they believed it, they wouldn't say it because they had to come back and live in the community."[28]

On April 27, a "mini hurricane" thundered through the Florida Straits with winds of more than sixty knots. Rescuing flotilla boats became a matter of life and death. The Coast Guard cutters *Ingham* and *Diligence* were inundated with frantic calls for assistance. At one time, the *Ingham* had five ships under tow and many passengers rescued from swamped boats. The *Diligence* was towing six, and it carried twenty-three additional passengers from a foundering boatlift ship. The Coast Guard warned the Cuban government not to allow overloading of the ships at Mariel.[29]

Florida congressman Dante Fascell appeared on CBS news that

weekend, supporting family reunification and demanding that the federal government assume responsibility in the handling of the crisis. South Florida alone, he said, could not absorb hundreds of thousands of refugees. On April 29, Presidential Assistant Eugene Eidenberg arrived in Miami to review the developing crisis.

About this time, rumors began to circulate that Castro had taken prisoners from jails and forced them to leave the country. On April 28, Immigration and Naturalization Service (INS) officer Kent Wheeler had complained that Castro "is sending his incorrigibles." That same day a new arrival named Félix Juster González told WQBA that he was a paroled convict and that Cuban guards had come to his home to tell him he must either leave for the U.S. or face a firing squad. He said the guards told him to lie to U.S. officials and claim he had been at the Peruvian Embassy. The reaction from Miami-Dade mayor Steve Clark was, "For every person who has a relative here, Castro is sending four more, from what background we don't know."[30]

On April 29, the *Miami Herald* reported that thirty-two hundred Cubans had arrived to date, and there were fifteen hundred boats still waiting in Mariel Harbor to pick up more refugees. An editorial in that issue said: "Local resources—particularly housing—already are exhausted, and a potentially ugly backlash is building among non-Hispanics."[31]

Miami News photographer Bill Reinke returned to Key West from a week in Havana on May 1, accompanied by eighty-one others aboard the *Nature Boy*. Of his fellow passengers, he said: "Many of them were criminals. They told us so. They told us somebody took them out of jail and put them in the boat."[32] On the same day, the *Miami Herald* reported that President Carter had ordered the Navy to assist the flotilla as "Castro uncorked a storm tide of refugees from Mariel, increasing the exodus so much—and salting the refugee rosters so heavily with criminals—that federal officials said they would open a military base within 24 hours as a processing and detention center capable of handling 15,000 to 20,000 refugees."[33] The following day, the *New York Times'* Joseph Treaster wrote: "Immigration officers said that, in screening the refugees, they had identified 55 who they believed were common criminals."[34]

By May 4, the flow of refugees arriving in South Florida had reached three thousand a day. The following day, President Carter declared: "We will continue to provide an open heart and open arms to refugees seeking freedom from Communist domination." Though his extemporaneous comment was widely interpreted as encouragement for the refugees to keep coming, it didn't translate into any policy directive for the Coast Guard or the INS.[35]

On May 5, the U.S. government suspended legal immigration from Cuba. According to the *Miami Herald*, that meant that "the only route from Cuba to the United States is aboard the illegal sealift which already has brought 13,055 refugees to South Florida." David Passage, a State Department spokesman, said it was impossible "to conduct normal relations with a country which apparently officially sanctions an unwarranted and unprovoked attack on people lined up outside the United States Interests Section seeking permission to leave Cuba."[36]

The Florida Congressional Delegation persuaded the president on May 6 to issue a declaration of emergency, retroactive to May 1, and approve $10 million in federal funds to reimburse voluntary agencies for processing and resettlement of refugees. U.S. Marines were deployed to Key West to assist with processing the escalating number of daily arrivals.

The Cuban-American community pitched in enthusiastically, with the Cuban Patriotic Junta providing forty dollars to each new arrival, while other local Cubans donated forty tons of clothing. Silvia Unzueta, working as a coordinator at Tamiami Park, told *Time* magazine, "We have enough Pampers for every child in the world."[37] Arturo Cobo's family spearheaded *El Hogar de Tránsito* ("The Transitional Home") for Mariel arrivals in Key West.

A new record for arrivals was set on May 11, when 4,588 refugees arrived in Key West. "When will it end?" federal relief coordinator William

Traugh asked aloud. "I see no prospect . . . any time soon. If we get two days in a row like today we're really going to be under a terrific strain."[38]

Though most coverage remained focused on the boatlift successes, the media was increasingly highlighting the "criminal" issue and the local backlash against the *marielitos*, as the refugees were being called. On May 11, Edward Schumacher of the *New York Times* reported that two hundred common criminals and people of "mental retardation" were headed to Key West aboard the catamaran *America*, and the fishing boat *Valley Chief*.[39]

Inside the same issue of the paper, Joseph Treaster quoted federal officials who estimated only about 1 percent of the three hundred suspected felons and psychiatric patients among the first boatlift arrivals might be considered dangerous. "More than 20 percent of refugees," reported Treaster, "have been let out of jail in the past few days . . . but an overwhelming majority of them have been imprisoned for so-called 'anti-social' and 'anti-revolutionary' offenses such as attempting to flee Cuba, refusing to work and criticizing or actively opposing the Castro regime."[40]

The disclaimer was lost on many non-Cuban Miamians, who now looked at every new arrival as a potential criminal. The front page of the *Miami Herald* on May 11 trumpeted: *'Dade Fears Refugee Wave, Poll Shows."* The article called Dade County "the land of the free and the home of the scared." Citing a poll in which seven out of ten non-Latin whites, and more than half of blacks, believed the area would be better off without the new Cuban and Haitian refugees, the paper said, "While there was sentiment that Cuban refugees who arrived in the 1960s and '70s helped Dade County, the overwhelming majority believe these new refugees will mean . . . a tighter local housing market . . . more unemployment . . . [and] trouble in the schools."[41]

In areas like South Beach and East Little Havana, criminal incidents involving *marielitos* began surfacing.[42] Many non-Cuban residents were concerned about how the influx would affect the community both financially and physically. The "Anglo backlash" grew as neighborhood groups in Miami argued to keep the refugees out of their backyards.[43] Refugees were held at the Krome North and South missile bases and the Homestead Armory, but even these were not large enough to keep pace. When the city of Miami was forced to open the historic Orange Bowl Stadium, it became obvious that South Florida needed help. Local officials appealed to the White House for relief, forcing the federal government to open military bases throughout the country to receive and process the new arrivals. Many localities were less hospitable than Miami-Dade. For example, an attempt to open a base in Bainbridge, Maryland, failed due to local opposition.

On May 1, Eglin Air Force Base in the Florida Panhandle began receiving refugees. In just nine days, it was filled to capacity with ninety-seven hundred Cubans. Fort Chaffee in Arkansas opened on May 8; Fort Indiantown in Gap, Pennsylvania, on May 17; and Fort McCoy, Wisconsin, on May 29.[44]

One of those held at Eglin was César García Hernández, who had entered the Peruvian Embassy grounds on April 4. Like Frank Gallardo, he was granted safe passage to his home to wait for clearance to leave Cuba. García left the Peruvian Embassy for a relative's home to take a shower and eat something after spending days without food. When he returned that evening to the embassy, he showed Cuban officials his *salvoconducto*. The same guard who had given him the *salvoconducto* that morning now tore it up and threw it away. "After they destroyed my safe passage, I was immediately arrested and taken to the 7th Police Station in Marianao, Cuba, where I spent that night. From there I was taken to the Combinado del Este Prison to a cell with 15 beds, housing approximately 90 inmates."[45]

After forty days in jail, government officials escorted him to "El Mosquito," a holding place at the Port of Mariel. From there he was allowed to board the boat that would take him to the U.S. As he clambered eagerly aboard, he slipped and lost his shoes. He had concealed the name and phone numbers of his U.S. relatives at the bottom of his shoes. That small accident landed him at Eglin Air Force Base for weeks, until a dedicated church volunteer researched and finally was able to help him find his Miami relatives who immediately took him in.[46]

On May 14, less than ten days after President Carter issued his "open heart invitation," he ordered a halt to the boatlift, calling on Castro to negotiate a more orderly process. But the flotilla boats already waited in Mariel Harbor, and Castro had no intention of changing his agenda.

One day after the U.S. Coast Guard set up a two-hundred-mile-long patrol zone to prevent boats leaving for Mariel (but not yet stopping those that already were on their way back), tragedy struck.[47] On May 17, the *Olo Yumi*, a thirty-six-foot cabin cruiser overloaded with fifty-two refugees and crew, went down in bad weather just twenty-five miles from Cuba. Coast Guard helicopters rescued survivors, but fourteen of the refugees perished. The U.S. blamed Cuba for putting too many people on ships leaving Mariel.[48]

The face of thirteen-year-old Ibis Guerrero as she stared at the cadavers of her parents and two sisters in the makeshift morgue in Key West would remain forever in the memory of those who witnessed her grief. Her father, Ricardo Guerrero de la Torre, was an ex-political prisoner who had planned to leave Cuba for Spain, along with his wife, Olga, his mother, and his three young daughters. Unexpectedly, Cuban officials showed up at the Guerrero home and offered them the opportunity to sail straight to America aboard the *Olo Yumi*. When the vessel split in two and sank, Ibis Guerrero lost her mother, father, grandmother, and two sisters. The Cobo family in Key West opened their hearts to Ibis, who eventually married and now lives in Miami with two children of her own.[49]

NOTES

1. Fabiola Santiago, "The Cuban Who Sparked the Exodus Breaks His Silence," *Miami Herald*, September 6, 1998.
2. Author interview with Gustavo Godoy, October 20, 2009.
3. Author interview with Alina Fernández, April 17, 2009.
4. Santiago, "The Cuban Who Sparked the Exodus Breaks His Silence."
5. Chauncey Mabe, "Marielito and Proud: Journalist offers perspective on Boatlift," *Sun Sentinel*, April 11, 2005.
6. Jo Thomas, "2,000 Who Want to Leave Cuba Crowd Peru's Embassy in Havana," *New York Times*, April 6, 1980.
7. *Mariel 25*, video produced by Channel 23 in Miami; Helga Silva, producer and vice president, 2005.
8. Thomas, "2,000 Who Want to Leave Cuba Crowd Peru's Embassy in Havana."
9. Guillermo Martínez, "Thousands Jam Embassy in Attempt to Flee Cuba," *Miami Herald*, April 7, 1980.
10. *Miami News*, April 10, 1980, p. 1.
11. Thomas, "2,000 Who want to leave Cuba crowd Peru's Embassy in Havana", *New York Times*.
12. In doing so, the U.S. said it already had admitted 15,000 Cubans to the country in the previous eighteen months and that there were now 800,000 Cubans in the country since the advent of the Castro regime. Graham Hovey, "U.S. Agrees to Admit up to 3,500 Cubans from Peru Embassy," *New York Times*, April 15, 1980.
13. Associated Press, "200 Cuban Refugees Arrive in Costa Rica," as published in the *New York Times*, April 17, 1980.
14. Ibid.
15. U.S. House of Representatives Permanent Select Committee on Intelligence, *The Cuban Emigrés: Was There a U.S. Intelligence Failure?*, 3.
16. Janet Battaile, "Cuban Exiles' Boats Pick Up 40 Refugees," *New York Times*, April 22, 1980.
17. Liz Balmaseda, "Exile: I Was Mastermind of Mariel," *Miami Herald*, July 31, 1989.
18. Juan Tamayo, "Napoleon Vilaboa, Father of Mariel Boatlift, Speaks," *El Nuevo Herald*, May 15, 2010.
19. Morton Lucoff, "Play It Cool As 1st Exiles Land, Hispanics Told," *Miami News*, April 21, 1980.
20. Patrice Gaines-Carter and Lesley Valdés, "Freedom's Road Begins at Dade's Tamiami Park," *Miami News*, April 24, 1980.
21. Author interview with Herb Levin, former owner of WQBA, March 2010.
22. Ana Veciana, "Any Boat That Will Make it to Cuba Will Do," *Miami News*, April 23, 1980.
23. Larry Wippman, "Cuban Boatlift Rushes to Keys," *Miami News*, April 23, 1980.
24. Heather Dewar, "Cashing in on Cuban Exodus," *Miami News*, April 28, 1980.
25. "3 Refugee Boats Are Seized by U.S.," *New York Times*, April 29, 1980. The majority of vessels that joined the freedom flotilla were simply recreation and fishing boats owned and piloted by Cuban exiles who took it upon themselves to make the journey.
26. Author interview with Horacio Unzueta, July 15, 2009.

27. Author interview with Herb Levin, general manager of WQBA, July 2009.
28. Victor Palmieri and Guillermo Martínez, "An Act of War: The Inside Story of the 1980 Mariel Boatlift," unpublished manuscript, 1983-84.
29. Undated account of Mariel operations, United States Coast Guard, Historian's Office, Vice Admiral Benedict L. Stabile, USC retired; Dr. Robert Scheina.
30. Heather Dewar and Ana Veciana, "Even Bigger Wave of Refugees Awaited," *Miami News*, April 29, 1980.
31. *Miami Herald*, April 29, 1980.
32. Heather Dewar, "Miami News Photographer Held in Cuba a Week," *Miami News*, May 1, 1980.
33. *Miami Herald*, May 1, 1980.
34. Joseph Treaster, "Refugees Pour In; Second Processing Center Slated," *New York Times*, May 2, 1980.
35. Robert Pear, "As Castro Zigged and Zagged on the Refugees so Did Carter," *New York Times*, May 18, 1980.
36. Guillermo Martínez and Richard Morin, "Legal Cuban Immigration Halted," *Miami Herald*, May 5, 1980.
37. "Nation: Open Heart, Open Arms," *Time*, May 18, 1980.
38. Heather Dewar, "Despite 'Terrific Strain,' Sealift Goes On," *Miami News*, May 12, 1980.
39. "Retarded People and Criminals Are Included in Cuban Exodus," *New York Times*, May 11, 1980.
40. Joseph Treaster, "Screening Finds 1% of Refugees May Be Felons," *New York Times*, May 11, 1980.
41. "Dade Fears Refugee Wave, Poll Shows," *Miami Herald*, May 11, 1980.
42. Martínez and Palmieri, "An Act of War."
43. Bob Murphy and Mort Lucoff, "Sealift Total Hits 21,000," *Miami News*, May 7, 1980.
44. National Archives, records of the Cuban-Haitian Task Force, Record Group 220.
45. Author interview with Cesar Garcia Hernandez, August 23, 2009.
46. Ibid.
47. Joseph Treaster, "Coast Guard Vessels and Aircraft Deployed to Cut Off Boats to Cuba," *New York Times*, May 18, 1980.
48. Joseph Treaster, "As Survivors Reach Florida Shore, U.S. Blames Cuba in Death of 14," *New York Times*, May 19, 1980.
49. *Mariel 25*.

11

NOT MY-AMI

BY SILVIA M. UNZUETA AND GUILLERMO MARTINEZ

The year 1980 marked a turning point in Miami's history. Prior to Mariel, there were already more than 400,000 Cuban exiles in the greater metropolitan area—prompting some longtime residents to lament the changes in their city. But adding 125,000 new Cuban refugees, along with another 25,000 Haitians in just a few months, pushed a city already on the edge into crisis.

The impact this wave of refugees had on the economic and institutional framework of the Miami-Dade County community cannot be overstated. The size and suddenness of the boatlift placed enormous burdens on municipal infrastructure and support services, creating multiple points of stress for community residents. Lines at the Immigration and Naturalization Service (INS) offices began forming early in the morning and got longer every day. Demand for care by county hospitals and community mental health centers overwhelmed their capacity. Governmental services such as social security, driver licenses, and food stamp offices were flooded.[1]

Compounding the frenzy of the boatlift was a growing rift among Miami's existing population, specifically the divide between black and white. In the early morning hours of December 17, 1979, Miami police pursued a thirty-three-year-old black man on a motorcycle through the Liberty City neighborhood. Arthur McDuffie had accumulated traffic citations and was driving on a suspended license, which perhaps explains why he attempted to run away from the police after allegedly running a red light. He had no criminal record and was unarmed.

Four city of Miami police officers finally caught up with him, handcuffed him, and beat him. McDuffie was taken to the hospital, where he died four days later from multiple skull fractures. The police officers were charged with manslaughter and fabricating evidence. Charges against one officer were later elevated to second-degree murder. The trial venue was moved from Miami to Tampa, where an all-white male jury acquitted the four officers on May 17, 1980.

The McDuffie verdict followed the trial of the first African-American superintendent of schools for Dade County, Johnny Jones, who was accused of spending school money on personal projects. On April 30, Jones had been convicted by another all-white jury—five black jurors had been excused on preemptory challenges by the prosecution. His conviction was reversed in 1985.[2]

Miami's black community was outraged by these two verdicts, widely seen as unfair and discriminatory. Florida International University professor Marvin Dunn, an African-American, said after the McDuffie acquittal: "If we couldn't get justice in this case, we can't get justice in any."[3] Black neighborhoods in Miami exploded in three days of riots that left fourteen dead, many wounded, and $100 million in property damage.[4]

According to Alejandro Portes and Alex Stepick, authors of *City on the Edge*, the McDuffie riot was "different from similar urban uprisings in three ways: first it was isolated rather than part of a national trend; second, it was unusually violent; third it took place with at least the tacit approval of many Black leaders, who under other circumstances could have been trusted to oppose it."[5]

After days devoted to the mayhem of the McDuffie riots, the Cuban refugees grabbed the headline of the *Miami Herald* on May 25: "Eglin Wait Boils over into Rioting." At Eglin Air Force Base in northern

Florida, hundreds (among thousands) of Cuban refugees threw stones and scuffled with military police. They rushed the main gate of what was called Camp Liberty, shouting *"¡Libertad! ¡Libertad!"* Both guards and refugees were injured in the riot, and seventeen refugees were arrested.[6]

Life in a camp, where Cuban arrivals were held until a family member or sponsor could be found, was not what the refugees had envisioned in coming to the U.S. The camp's criminal element preyed upon the weakest of the refugees. Physical and psychological abuse was not uncommon, and it sometimes escalated to beatings or rape. The Mariel exiles had expected freedom, and instead they found themselves caged by barbed wire and wrapped in the red tape of government bureaucracy.

Two days after the Eglin riot, more than two hundred refugees escaped from Fort Chaffee, Arkansas, adjacent to Fort Smith. A spokesman for the local sheriff's office said, "We've got Cubans all over the countryside." Governor Bill Clinton alerted the state police and National Guard, who captured about fifty of the escapees and continued to search for others.[7]

The local communities didn't want the refugees in their neighborhood to begin with, and the riots heightened their resentments. In Fort Smith, locals were facing high unemployment and worried the refugees would take their jobs. In early May, they had picketed the camp, chanting for the refugees to go home. One unemployed local, Lenor Grandon, told the *New York Times* he felt compassion for the Cubans, "but there's children here who need food and men and women needing jobs, and Arkansas doesn't have them."[8]

On June 2, the headline in the *Miami Herald* read, "Cubans Rampage in Arkansas." Angry refugees pelted law enforcement and military personnel with stones as they stormed the main gate. Forty people were injured and four buildings burned to the ground. Governor Clinton sent in three hundred Army troops to quell the riot.[9]

The agitators were confined to the base stockade. A Miami delegation visiting the camp that day observed that the refugees were in "enemy territory." Miami assistant city manager Cesar Odio called Fort Chaffee "a powder keg," suggesting that the refugees had been baited by the locals, though acknowledging "it doesn't take much to get them going because they are frustrated. You can sense it—they're mad."[10]

Jo Thomas, an old hand at reporting from Havana, Mariel, and Central America for the *New York Times*, described the tedium and confinement that was so frustrating the refugees, saying, "Nearly everyone inside and outside Fort Chaffee seems to agree it would be safest at the moment to keep the Cubans and the local residents apart; the biggest risk seems to be misunderstanding."[11]

"Frustration at Ft. Chaffee resulted from their inability to see light at the end of the tunnel," Siro del Castillo told the authors on July 9, 2011. "The experiences at Chaffee marked me deeply. Working with the Mariel exodus, I came to understand them and myself better. They deserved a chance for a new start, and they got it."

In addition to a concentration camp atmosphere, refugees had to cope with an increase in the number of broken sponsorships. Those whose sponsorships, for one reason or another, had not worked out, needed additional housing and other services. But perhaps the most serious problem faced by some refugees was the lack of attachment to family and friends outside of Cuba. Without a support system, the resettlement process was much harder for both the refugees and the responsible American agencies.

A study co-authored by Juan Clark, a Miami-Dade college professor, estimated that 50,000 men in the boatlift came without their families. As part of the migration process, almost 20,000 of these men had been forcibly separated from their spouses by the Cuban government—in clear violation of their human rights.[12] Mariel also brought 6,855 children to the United States, of which more than 5,000 were younger than four, and another 1,400 between five and twelve years old.[13] Dr. José Szapocznik, director of the Cuban-American Adolescent Management Program (CAMP), operated by the University of Miami Department of

Psychiatry, provided services to the children, some of whom were unaccompanied minors.[14]

On June 4, the Mariel arrivals set a new daily record. To improve the refugee resettlement process, Cuban-born Sergio Pereira—assistant to Dade County manager Merrett Steirheim—was loaned to the federal government and a special consultant to the White House. Pereira had been in charge of local coordination of the arrival of thousands of Cubans into Dade County since September 1978.[15]

Twenty-six thousand more Cuban refugees arrived in the month of June—bringing the cumulative total for the boatlift to almost 115,000. Miami had reached the limit of its capacity to cope with the human tide flowing across the Florida Straits. The front page of the June 19 *Miami Herald* proclaimed, "Lack of Aid may build a Cuban ghetto," and reported that "hundreds of hungry, homeless, and jobless Cuban refugees who sleep in Miami streets prompted several city leaders Wednesday to warn that the city faces a new social crisis unless it gets immediate federal help."[16]

By July, the federal efforts to curtail the refugee flow began to work, and only 2,629 new Mariel arrivals entered the U.S. The number of Haitians, however, who left their homeland in overcrowded vessels to come to Miami more than doubled, from 2,267 in June to 4,670 in July.

On July 6, Cuban government forces sank a hijacked excursion boat near the Canimar River in Matanzas Bay. Fifty-six adults and four children were killed—and the massacre didn't become public until 1985, when Radio Martí, a U.S. government radio station that broadcast to Cuba, reported on it. According to official records of the Revolutionary Tribunal of La Cabana Fortress and testimony of family members of the victims, the river excursion boat *XX Anniversario* was hijacked by three young men fleeing Cuba: Ramón Calveiro León, fifteen years old, and brothers Silvio and Sergio Aguila Yanes, eighteen and nineteen. Sergio was a sergeant in the Cuban Armed Forces.

When the hijackers shouted "To Miami!" most of the one hundred surprised passengers aboard cheered. A guard resisted and was shot, then put on a small craft along with one other passenger who didn't want to go to the United States. They alerted Cuban authorities, who dispatched the Cuban Navy with orders to stop the excursion boat from leaving Cuba—even if that meant sinking it. The navy boats opened fire, and the hijackers fired back. A Cuban Air Force plane strafed the excursion boat, covering the deck with the blood of the wounded and the dead. As the excursion boat approached international waters, government forces sank it.

The victims were not allowed funerals in Cuba, and the government ordered the survivors to keep silent about the massacre. For several years, government agents monitored their activities and offered victims, relatives, and survivors gifts of televisions, refrigerators, and other appliances usually reserved for high government officials. The final toll of the disaster was eleven bodies recovered and forty missing at sea.[17]

The Truth Recovery Archive on Cuba says:

There are conflicting reports about the fate of Sergio Aguila Yanes. The Cuban government claims he committed suicide with his pistol. Others report that Sergio was taken from the water by the crew of the Cuban Navy patrol boats. . . . Silvio Aguila Yanes serves a 30-year prison sentence at Combinado del Este prison in Havana. Witnesses to his imprisonment report he has been subjected to psychiatric torture, receiving large doses of psychotropic drugs. 15-year-old Roberto Calveiro served time in prison but reportedly was released and lives in Spain. Other witnesses have made it into exile.[18]

On July 15, 1980, President Carter formally established the Cuban-Haitian Task Force to coordinate the resettlement of Cuban and Haitian refugees, with representation from the INS, State Department, Department of Justice, Federal Emergency Management Authority (FEMA), Department of Education, and Department of Agriculture.

Between July and September, press coverage both inside and outside of Miami increasingly focused on the criminal element among Mariel refugees. In late July, the *Miami Herald* ran a two-day series that reported a 34 percent increase in Miami Beach crimes since the arrival of the Mariel refugees (many of whom were housed in the rundown old Art Deco hotels along Ocean Drive and Collins). On September 18, a *Miami Herald* front-page article "reports a crime wave in Little Havana, the perpetrators being Mariel criminals: 775 percent more robberies than in 1979; 284 percent more car thefts; 191 percent more burglaries; 110 percent more assaults."[19]

This focus on crime would have a long-lasting effect on Miami's Cuban community, as well as the city's image throughout the world. Despite all the hype, the facts—which took some time to fully emerge—suggest that criminals were a small if visible part of the Mariel exodus. It was estimated that less than 10 percent of the refugees had been in prison in Cuba. Of these, the City of Miami Police Department estimated the number of hardcore criminals to be at about 1 percent. Many of the prisoners who came as part of the exodus were ex-political prisoners, while others were incarcerated for minor infractions.

Originally, the Immigration and Naturalization Service had 1,761, or 1.4 percent, in custody, charged with committing felonies and other serious crimes in Cuba. Later, the number of deportable Mariel refugees in various U.S. jails was raised to approximately 2,500.[20]

Margarita Esquiroz, who served as a lower court judge in Miami-Dade County during the Mariel Boatlift and handled some refugee cases, said:

> *It was clear then, and even more so almost three decades later, that Castro manipulated the mix of persons coming by releasing criminals and mental cases. The end result of that mix accounted for the initial negative perception given not only to Mariel refugees, but also the Cuban American community in Miami Dade county and elsewhere. Time has given credence to the fact that the number of undesirables who came was small and the final assessment of their presence is a positive one.*[21]

On September 26, 1980, the Mariel Boatlift ended as abruptly as it had started. Castro sent back the boats waiting in Mariel Harbor empty. The exodus had brought 125,266 Cuban men, women, and children to the United States. At the end of September, in final negotiations with the U.S. government, Cuba advised the Interest Section in Havana of an additional 600 Cubans stranded by the abrupt closure of Mariel, and requested they be cleared for admission into the United States. These were the final entrants granted full "refugee status."

The last refugee boat, the *Hedonist*, arrived at Key West on September 27. Hundreds more who wanted to emigrate remained stranded in the port of Mariel in a camp known as *El Mosquito*. Among those aboard the *Hedonist* was Orlando Martínez, who said, "We are so fortunate. We were lucky." His wife, Arabia, reflected on those left behind: "Those poor people, they must be desperate; they must be feeling someone has put a knife to their hearts. . . . [T]he Cuban people have become submissive since Fidel. I cry for them."[22]

However, the end of the boatlift was not the end of Mariel's impact on Miami. Sergio Pereira, assistant Dade County manager and special consultant to the White House, eloquently summarized how profoundly Mariel changed Miami, specifically the relationship between Latins and non-Latins. In an interview with the authors, he said:

Before Mariel, the Cuban diaspora in Greater Miami collectively believed itself to be very well and fully integrated into South Florida's mainstream business, social and political institutions. Life was relatively good and calm. Cuban-Americans were proud to be fair-share contributors to a vibrant tapestry. Sure, there were many challenges, but we understood that the challenges did not discriminate, that the community faced its share of challenges together, for the common good. Mariel ripped that pretty picture to shreds.

The tiny, fringe component of extreme Mariel refugees who did not ever, ever belong in American society literally sucked to the surface a latent . . .

"uneasiness" by many non-Cubans . . . felt apparently for a very long time and never before expressed by so many.

Today we call it "pushback." Back then it was raw . . . and it was shocking to the Cuban community. Daily life was transformed. 'Mariel' seemed to have given license to so many people to vent literally decades of pent-up frustrations, anger and, frankly, bigotry. Everyone walked on eggshells, on both sides of what became a palpable divide. Cuban-Americans who had spent so many years flourishing in what they truly believed to be the "land of equal opportunity" were . . . simply crushed, emotionally and spiritually.'[23]

According to journalist Gustavo Godoy:

Mariel was the first referendum in the twenty-year history since the inception of Castro's revolution. It brought out the best from the Cuban American exiled community. Exiles offered their total support to the new arrivals. Yet, the influx of Cubans covered with tattoos worried the Cubans already in the United States. They were afraid the mix sent by Castro would negatively affect the solid image established by years of hard work.

Encountering the Mariel arrivals made Cuban Americans realize how much they had changed; how Americanized they had become. This great divide at the time blurred the many good attributes of the arrivals and the fact that they too were yearning to be free.[24]

Mariel became one of several burdens that President Carter carried into the November 1980 elections. Americans faced with double-digit inflation, the Iranian hostage crisis, and the Mariel Boatlift were in no mood to re-elect a president also weakened by a challenge from his own party. Ronald Reagan, a conservative Republican, won the 1980 election easily.

Reagan's election brought new hope to Cuban exiles. He was

a staunch anti-Communist who believed in standing up to the Soviet Union's aggressive international policies. He also thought that President Carter's soft approach toward Cuba's Communist regime had to be changed. Wrote María Cristina Garcia, "For the first time in many years, Americans had elected a president whose views on communism (and Cuba) were compatible with those of the *émigrés*."[25]

However, Mariel created a serious image problem for the previously extolled Cuban exile community. Before Mariel, Cubans were often cited as one of the most successful immigrant groups in the United States. Ninteen eighty destroyed that pristine image. As a result of the boatlift, race and ethnic relations in Miami-Dade County deteriorated significantly.

Portes and Stepick argue that a grassroots movement of native whites was organized in Miami "as a direct outgrowth of Mariel." This movement saw the growing bilingual nature of Miami as a threat, and by the election of November 1980, it had enough followers to put the language issue up for a vote. "The Cuban community was still unorganized in local affairs and the 'antibilingual' referendum passed overwhelmingly. . . . The referendum victory marked the high point of the Anglo-centered effort to hang on to hegemony."[26]

Years later, the "antibilingual" referendum was overturned.

Though more and more Cuban exiles had become citizens and started to vote during the 1970s, their political focus had remained the liberation of Cuba. In 1980, the backlash against Mariel—particularly the antibilingual referendum—came as a sharp slap in the face. The fact that the slap was administered by their adopted home town, a city to which Cuban exiles had made enormous economic and cultural contributions, motivated them to pay more attention to local politics. A group of Cuban community leaders got together to develop a plan. They had learned their lesson and intended to be more proactive and assertive going forward. Rather than waiting for federal or local government to take the lead, they would propose practical solutions.

The Cuban community leaders met with Jewish lobbying groups to better understand how they had organized themselves to influence congressional campaign races and fight defamation. Two organizations were created in 1981 that would begin to build Cuban-Americans into a strong political constituency in Miami-Dade and the United States: the National Coalition for a Free Cuba (a Political Action Committee, or PAC) and the Cuban American National Foundation (CANF).

Jorge Mas Canosa, who became CANF chairman, developed a personal relationship with President Reagan, and he invited him to address the group in Miami. Reagan commended the group and vowed to work for a free Cuba. His support and participation in Cuban-American politics rallied the community and encouraged exiles to register and to vote in big numbers. This was how being Republican became a part of the predominant Cuban exile culture. Though many Cubans have more liberal social views than traditional American conservatives, the strong anti-Communist credentials of Reagan and other leading Republicans were important to their cause. The bad experiences with Democratic presidents from John Kennedy to Jimmy Carter also contributed to the mass migration to the GOP.

An important item on CANF's agenda was the creation of a Cuban radio station modeled after Radio Free Europe. To promote this goal, CANF members and its PAC began making political contributions and cultivating personal relationships with both Republican and Democratic candidates in congressional campaigns throughout the United States. The fight to launch Radio Martí, named after the Cuban patriot, was long and difficult. When Radio Martí made its first broadcast to Cuba on May 20, 1985, the exile community celebrated.[27]

If anything hit Miami harder than the boatlift itself, it was *Time* magazine's cover story on November 23, 1981, titled "South Florida: Paradise Lost." The article reported that "an epidemic of violent crime, a plague of illicit drugs and a tidal wave of refugees have slammed into South Florida with the destructive power of a hurricane . . . and threaten to turn one of the nation's most prosperous, congenial and naturally gorgeous regions into a paradise lost."[28]

About the same time, Brian DePalma's remake of the classic movie *Scarface* was released. Starring Al Pacino as a Mariel drug dealer, the film provided a frightening view of modern Miami and another unflattering characterization of Cuban refugees. In response to this kind of adverse publicity, in August of 1982 Cuban exiles created Facts About Cuban Exiles (FACE), an organization dedicated to combating all forms of bigotry and discrimination against persons of Cuban origin.

Cubans were learning that they did not need to forsake their struggle to free Cuba in order to be good Americans. CANF and FACE became the new image of the Cuban exile community. "We must have influence at the highest levels of government instead of shouting and yelling on SW Eighth Street," said Luis Botifoll, a prominent banker who sat on the boards of both CANF and FACE. "We must learn how to act in the same manner as the groups that represent the different ethnic groups in this country."[29]

Thus was the persona of the "new" Miami stamped: for Cuban-Americans, it was a sleepy southern town awakened by a Latin beat; for African-Americans, it was "Your-Ami, not My-Ami"; and as long-established, self-designated white Miamians left South Florida, they asked for the last one to leave to please bring the flag with them.

* * * *

When Cuba and the United States finally reached an immigration agreement in 1984, the U.S. still held more than twenty-five hundred Mariel Cubans in prisons. Some had never been released because authorities had determined they were a danger to society. Others had been freed and incarcerated again for crimes they committed in the United States. In exchange for returning these "excludable aliens," the U.S. agreed to accept three thousand Cuban political prisoners and up to twenty thousand regular immigrants a year.

The agreement didn't last long. In May 1985, Fidel Castro suspended the immigration accord in response to Ronald Reagan's approval of Radio Martí. During the year that the agreement was in effect, the United States deported back to Cuba 201 of the Mariel Cubans detained in American prisons. Seventy-three of them were immediately put behind bars.

On November 20, 1987, the State Department announced a new agreement with Cuba that included the return of about 2,500 of the 125,000 refugees who came to this country in the Mariel Boatlift. In a federal detention center in Oakdale, Louisiana, more than 1,000 refugee inmates fearing deportation rioted. Most of them had already completed their sentence for the crimes they committed in the United States, but still they were subject to deportation because they had committed crimes. Bearing knives, pipes, and other makeshift weapons, they took twenty-eight prison staff members hostage.[30]

To quell the riots, the U.S. government offered a moratorium on deportations. Not only did this fail to calm things down, but a group of Mariel prisoners in Atlanta began rioting—starting fires and taking seventy-five hostages. Outside the prison, relatives of both prisoners and hostages stood vigil. "This prison has been a time bomb set to go off," commented Georgia congressman John Lewis.[31]

The Atlanta riot went on for eleven days. Numerous negotiations resulted in a stalemate. The Mariel inmates said they would release the hostages only when they talked to auxiliary bishop of Miami-Dade County, Msgr. Agustín Román. But the Justice Department did not want any "outsiders" to get involved in the negotiations. As the days dragged on, FACE held an emergency meeting in which Miami city manager César Odio, a FACE director, suggested they get the assistance of Leon Kellner, the U.S. attorney in South Florida. It was Kellner who convinced Justice Department officials in Washington to allow Msgr. Román, also a member of FACE, to participate in the negotiations.

The Justice Department asked Roman to attend a meeting in

Washington the following morning. As there were no commercial flights available that would get the group to Washington on time for the meeting, FACE chairman Carlos Arboleya put up ten thousand dollars to charter the plane. (The organization later repaid him.) Msgr. Román, Arboleya, Kellner, and Rafael Peñalver, Msgr. Roman's close advisor, met with Attorney General Edwin Meese; Michael Quinlan, director of the Federal Bureau of Prisons; and other Justice Department officials. Msgr. Román suggested that the government draft a fair hearing process for the inmates, and the officials agreed. "That in itself is a huge step forward and an unprecedented one," said Odio.[32]

The formal release of the inmates took several days and two trips by Msgr. Román, first to the Oakdale prison and a few days later to Atlanta. At the Oakdale prison, Msgr. Román first addressed the inmates over a loudspeaker from the bed of a flatbed truck that traveled on a perimeter road around the prison. He urged them to lay down their arms and release the hostages. "Within minutes, inmates walked to the center of the yard, laid down their homemade spears, machetes and other weapons and covered them with sleeping bags," the *Miami Herald* reported.[33]

The Atlanta prisoners demanded that Msgr. Román be present at their signing ceremony. All hostages were released, and the government announced an unspecified moratorium on deportations as well as amnesty for most of those involved in the riot, paroles for those eligible, and individual case reviews of the inmates. Accompanying Msgr. Román were Peñalver and FACE chairman Carlos Arboleya.[34]

"To think that a person would rather live in prison in another country than return to their country of birth," Msgr. Román said. "That says something and I hope that those who did not understand that before this moment, understand that now."[35]

If seven years earlier, the Cuban-American community's actions had contributed to the Mariel crisis, in the fall of 1987 its leaders were part of the solution. Many felt that the Cuban-American community came of age during those two weeks.

But Mariel still was not over. Thousands of Cubans had been resettled under less than ideal conditions in Perú, Spain, and other countries. In 1987, the Cuban American National Foundation, led by Jorge Mas Canosa, negotiated with Reagan Administration officials to let them fund and administer a program to bring many of these Cubans to the United States. The program was named the Cuban Exodus Relief Fund (FUND). It reunited more than ten thousand Cuban exiles who had been resettled in other countries in 1979 and 1980 with their relatives in the United States. Lourdes Zayas Bazán, the coordinator of the program sponsored by the U.S. State Department, the INS, and FUND, called it "the first private sector refugee resettlement program in U.S. history."[36]

NOTES

1. Silvia M. Unzueta, Special Projects Administrator for Refugee Affairs, Miami-Dade County Government, "A Year in Retrospect," Miami-Dade County Official Report, 1981.
2. Marvin Dunn, *Black Miami in the Twentieth Century* (Gainesville: University Press of Florida, 1997).
3. "Community Leaders Express Dismay, Urge Peace for City," *Miami News*, May 19, 1980.
4. "Guard Troops Withdraw," *Miami News*, May 21, 1980.
5. Alejandro Portes and Alex Stepick, *City on the Edge* (Berkeley: University of California Press, 1993), 48.
6. "Cubans Protest 3-week Detention, Fight Police at Tent City in Florida," Associated Press, May 25, 1980.
7. "200 Cubans Flee Arkansas Camp," Associated Press, May 27, 1980.
8. William Stevens, "Pickets Add to Problems for Refugees in Arkansas," *New York Times*, May 11, 1980.
9. "Cubans Rampage in Arkansas," *Miami Herald*, June 2, 1980.
10. Jack Knar, "In Enemy Territory," *Miami News*, June 3, 1980.
11. Jo Thomas, "Refugees at Ft. Chaffee Wait in Boredom and Uncertainty," *New York Times*, June 6, 1980.
12. Juan Clark; José I. Lasaga, and Rose S. Reque, *The 1980 Mariel Exodus: An Assessment and Prospect* (Washington, D.C.: Council for Inter American Security, 1981).
13. *Mariel 25*, video produced by Channel 23 in Miami; Helga Silva, producer and vice president, 2005.
14. José Szapocnik, Raquel Cohen, and Roberto E. Hernández, *Coping with Adolescent Refugees: The Mariel Boatlift* (New York: Greenwood Publishing Group, 1985).
15. "Pereira Is Refugee Consultant," *Miami News*, June 6, 1980.

16. Guillermo Martínez, "Lack of Aid May Build a Cuban Ghetto," *Miami Herald*, June 19, 1980.
17. Sources cited by the Truth Recovery Archive on Cuba: Official records of the Revolutionary Tribunal of La Cabana Fortress and from the records of the Provincial court of Matanzas, published by Dr. Alberto Fibla, "Barbarie-Hundimiento del Remolcador 13 de Marzo," Rodes Printing, 1996; "Cuba reportedly sank hijacked excursion boat in 1980," Associated Press, December 8, 1985; Joseph B. Treaster, *New York Times*, September 8, 1985; José Perez-Marat, *La Masacre del Canimar, Miami*, undated book. Sources: Records of the provincial court of Matanzas (reproduced in *Bibla*, 1996, 256); Testimony of Maria Julia Hernandez, niece of victim Vicente Fleites Cabrera; Norberto Fuentes, edited by Modesto Arocha; *Children of the Enemy* (The International Republican Institute, October 1996).
18. Ibid.
19. "Crime in Little Havana," *Miami Herald*, September 18, 1980.
20. Unzueta, "A Year in Retrospect."
21. Written statement of Judge Margarita Esquiroz given to author August 24, 2009.
22. Marilyn Moore, "Last Arrivals: 'We Were Lucky,'" *Miami News*, November 27, 1980.
23. Author interview with Sergio Pereira, August 2009.
24. Author interview with Gustavo Godoy, October 20, 2009.
25. María Cristina Garcia, *Havana USA* (Berkley: University of California Press, 1996), 146.
26. Portes and Stepick, *City on the Edge*, 34.
27. Author Interview with Raúl Masvidal, October 2010, and Mario Elgarresta, December 2010.
28. "South Florida: Paradise Lost," *Time*, November 23, 1981.
29. Guillermo Martínez, "Cubans Come of Age in America," *Miami Herald*, September 30, 1982.
30. Ronald Smother, "Cuban Inmates Riot in Louisiana Over New Threat of Deportation," *New York Times*, November 23, 1987.
31. Fred Grimm, Christopher Marquis, and Martin Merzer, "Cuban Inmates Riot in Atlanta," *Miami Herald*, November 24, 1987.
32. Tina Montalvo, "Maneuvering in Miami Brought Bishop into Act," *Miami Herald*, November 28, 1987.
33. Carlos Harrison, Christopher Marquis, and Martin Merzer, "Oakdale Prison Siege ends: Miami Bishop Issues Appeal," *Miami Herald*, November 30, 1987.
34. Fred Grimm, Mirta Ojito, and Martin Merzer, "Inmates End Siege," *Miami Herald*, December 4, 1987.
35. Harrison, Marquis, and Merzer, "Oakdale Prison."
36. Author interview with Lourdes Zayas-Bazán, February 3, 2011.

12

BALSEROS

BY GUILLERMO MARTINEZ, FRANCISCO RODRIGUEZ, AND SAM VERDEJA

During the 1980s, five influential world leaders came to power who together changed the course of world history. These leaders were Ronald Reagan, Margaret Thatcher, Pope John Paul II, Mikhail Gorbachev, and Lech Walesa. All of them contributed in a unique way to the rising democracy movement in Eastern Europe—which answered the question, for once and for all, of whether socialism or democracy provided a better way of life. With the fall of the Berlin Wall in November 1989, the verdict was in—and the direction chosen for Cuba by Fidel Castro was the loser.

The changes began in 1978 with the surprising election of Polish Cardinal Karol Jozef Wojtyla to Pope of the Roman Catholic Church. Wojtyla, the first non-Italian Pontiff in over four centuries, took the name of Pope John Paul II. He made it his mission to shatter the Communist rule in his native country. Millions of Poles turned out to greet him on his first visit to Poland in 1979. While publicly blessing his flock, he worked behind the scenes with labor leader Lech Walesa to create and legitimatize an anti-Communist labor movement. By 1980, Walesa's Solidarity Movement was strong enough to force Poland's Communist government to officially recognize it, though the following year, under pressure from Soviet authorities, they arrested Solidarity leaders, forcing the movement to go underground.

Meanwhile, across the Atlantic, Republican Ronald Reagan defeated incumbent Democratic President Jimmy Carter. Reagan was sworn in as president of the United States in January 1981. From that point on, Pope John Paul II and Lech Walesa had a powerful ally in the United States. In 1979, the British had elected a Conservative government, led by Prime Minister Margaret Thatcher—known as the "Iron Lady" because she adhered so strongly to her principles. Thatcher and Reagan became close friends and allies, sharing a staunchly anti-Communist philosophy and the goal to bring down the Soviet system.

In 1985, Mikhail Gorbachev became general secretary of the Communist Party of the Soviet Union. Gorbachev immediately began to democratize his country's political system and decentralize its economy. On June 12, 1987, in a famous televised speech delivered to a huge crowd near the Berlin Wall, Reagan asked whether Gorbachev's reforms were the "beginnings of profound changes in the Soviet State? Or are they token gestures, intended to raise false hopes in the West, or to strengthen the Soviet system without changing it?" There was one sign; he said that would "advance dramatically the cause of freedom and peace."[1] And President Reagan issued his historic personal challenge to Gorbachev: "General Secretary Gorbachev, if you seek peace, if you seek prosperity for the Soviet Union and Eastern Europe, if you seek liberalization: Come here to this gate! Mr. Gorbachev, open this gate! Mr. Gorbachev, tear down this wall!"[2]

Reagan's words became the rallying cry for pro-democracy movements throughout Eastern Europe, and they signaled the beginning of the collapse of Communism in the Soviet Union and throughout the world.

In June 1989, the Polish people elected a new government headed by a non-Communist prime minister and including many opposed to the Communist regime. Hungary quickly followed and weakened the Communist bloc by opening its borders to Austria and allowing thousands of East Germans to flee to the west. On November 9, 1989, a few short weeks after the German Democratic Republic (East Germany) celebrated its fortieth anniversary in power, the Berlin Wall fell and Germany was reunited. The symbolic significance of this cannot be overstated.

Bulgaria's government was ousted the very next day, in another peaceful revolution. In Romania, Dictator Nicolae Ceasescu retaliated with armed force against the protestors, but Romanian soldiers refused to obey the government's orders. Instead, they joined the protest movement. Ceasescu was executed on Christmas Day 1989.

The changes were not confined to Europe. In Nicaragua, the pro-Communist Sandinista regime held elections in April of 1990. Though pollsters predicted that President Daniel Ortega would be re-elected easily, the Nicaraguans ousted the pro-Cuba Sandinista government. Violeta Chamorro, an anti-Communist, was elected president.

After Albania and Yugoslavia also moved away from Communism in 1991, the Soviet Union itself collapsed in December of 1991, breaking into the fifteen separate countries that had been previously conquered by the Russian Communist regime. "Its collapse was hailed by the West as a victory for freedom, a triumph of democracy over totalitarianism, and evidence of the superiority of capitalism over socialism . . . thereby ending the Cold War. . . . Indeed, the breakup of the Soviet Union transformed the entire world's political situation, leading a complete reformulation of political, economic and military alliances all over the world."[3]

These were heady times for Cuban-Americans in South Florida. As Communist regimes fell like dominos, delirious exiles believed the liberation of Cuba was imminent. A hit song by Cuban performer Willy Chirino celebrated the end of Communism, and Cuban exiles all knew the words to *Nuestro Día—Ya Viene Llegando* ("Our Day is Coming"). When Chirino shouted out the name of each liberated country at the end of the song, the audience cried out at the top of their voices, "*Libre*" ("Free").[4]

While the Soviet Union's demise was good news for Cubans in exile, it increased the economic deprivation of Cubans still living on the island.

The Soviet Union had begun to cut back on its subsidies to Cuba in 1989. Life under Castro had never been easy, but without the influx of Soviet cash, life for ordinary Cubans became hell. Electricity blackouts became an everyday occurrence. Food was scarcer than ever. The quality of services declined substantially. As the country's economy collapsed, Castro feared he could face the same fate as other Communist regimes around the world. In August of 1990, he called on Cubans to make extreme sacrifices, enduring a "special period in times of peace" so the socialist revolution could survive.

Ironically, during this harsh economic period, Cuba became even more dependent on visits by Cuban exiles. To draw more tourists, the government began opening up its economy to mixed enterprises with foreign hotel chains and allowing U.S. dollars to circulate. Cubans could now rent rooms and open small restaurants in their homes to visitors. These new restaurants, called "*paladares*," were open only to foreigners.

Despite these changes, the economy remained so bad that more people sought to flee the island on whatever boats were available—even homemade rafts. Of course, Cubans had been seeking freedom on the open seas since January 1, 1959. Not counting the 125,000 that came on the Mariel Boatlift in 1980, more than 63,000 Cubans fled the island by sea in hopes of reaching the United States between 1959 and 1994. Thousands more washed up in the Bahamas, Mexico, Jamaica, or in the Cayman Islands. These asylum-seekers came to be known as rafters—or *balseros*—because they would use anything that could float to leave the country. Some experts estimate that at least 16,000 *balseros* did not survive the crossing.[5]

Juan Manuel Cao, anchor at Channel 41 América Teve in Miami, covered many dramatic stories of *balseros*. In 1993, he reported on a nine-year-old boy that rowed across to the Bahamas for days while his mother, Raísa Santana, lay dying on the floor of their boat. A journalist got Raísa flown to Jackson Memorial Hospital in Miami, where she died from drinking seawater. She had saved the fresh water for her son.[6]

While in Cancún in 1994, Cao interviewed a young girl who had been lost in the Gulf of Mexico for several days, during which she kissed and rocked her dead two-year-old daughter as if she were still alive.

Cao tells another story of seven *balseros* buried in Mexico, each in a tomb bearing his or her name and a cross. On July 31, 1993, a group of fifteen Cubans set out from Cienfuegos on a rustic launch, aiming for the Cayman Islands. A storm knocked them off course, wrecking their boat a short distance from the Mexican coast at Punta Herrero, on the Yucatán Peninsula. Of the four men, four women, five teenagers, and two children who had been on board, only eight survived. They were immediately deported back to Cuba. Cao filmed the group being forced into an airplane. "Please, don't send us back, not there!" the refugees begged. The unfortunate group had to be forced into an airplane.

Press stories like these angered Cuban-Americans, who began to demonstrate in New York, San Juan, and Miami. The three Cuban-American congressional representatives from South Florida announced that they would not vote for the approval of the North America Free Trade Agreement (NAFTA) between the U.S., Canada, and Mexico. And the political pressure seemed to work. The eight survivors of the ill-fated July voyage were allowed to return to Cancún, where Cao interviewed them. It was hard for them to talk about the shipwreck and the loss of their friends. Hilda Pérez Sánchez, forty-three, had been one of those screaming as she was forced to board the airplane. "Why is it that nobody feels our pain?" she asked Cao. "Nobody wants to believe that that place is a hell, right?"

The Cuban American National Foundation (CANF) obtained U.S. visas for the survivors. Ninoska Pérez Castellón, a prominent Cuban-American radio talk show hostess in Miami, and Clara María del Valle, a member of CANF's board of directors, worked to have the bodies of those buried in Mexico exhumed, and CANF brought them to Miami for burial. The funeral procession was ten thousand strong. That afternoon, *Miami Herald* reporters Ana Santiago and Cynthia Corso discovered among the crowd Juanita Castro, sister of Fidel and Raúl Castro. Hilda Pérez Sánchez spoke at the cemetery. "The people (in Cuba) know of the unity here," she said. "They know we are one people, ready to struggle."[7]

In July 1994, Eduardo Suárez Esquivel, a computer engineer who had already attempted unsuccessfully to flee Cuba on several occasions, decided to try again. He convinced his brother-in-law, Fidencio Ramel Prieto, who was in charge of operations at the Port of Havana and served as one of its Communist Party secretaries, to act as skipper aboard the tugboat *13 de Marzo*. Raúl Muñoz, a friend and former harbor pilot of the *13 de Marzo*, was recruited to pilot the tugboat during the escape.

The plan included numerous family members and close friends. Only Ramel had the entire list of the approximately fifty-two passengers who were to go. The organizers were divided into groups, and each had a leader in charge of getting his group to the pier. They chose three different dates, and they ended up aborting the escape when insiders working at the port announced unexpected security measures. They finally settled on July 13, and the group of men, women, and children boarded the recently renovated tugboat, unaware that they would be sailing into a trap set by government authorities who had been receiving information on their plans all along.

Even if they had known they should be caught, they would have expected imprisonment but not death. Because information in Cuba is tightly controlled and all media is owned by the government, the outcome of two previous incidents was unknown on the island. Earlier that year, on April 28, the tugboat *Polar 12* had been commandeered in Havana Harbor and taken to Key West, Florida, with sixty-eight on board. And on June 17 another tugboat, the *Mar Azul*, had also been taken to Florida with seventy-four on board. Reportedly, both tugboats had been pursued by the Cuban Coast Guard, rammed by its vessels in international waters, and attacked with machine guns, even though they carried women and children as passengers.

At 3:15 in the morning of July 13, the *13 de Marzo* left Havana Harbor and was immediately pursued by another tugboat. The pursuing vessel first tried to drive the *13 de Marzo* into a dock, then rammed it. The *13 de Marzo* avoided the attacks and kept sailing forward.[8]

People at nearby piers and at the Malecón, Havana's seawall promenade, witnessed the attack and yelled at the government vessel to let them go. Just as the *13 de Marzo* cleared the harbor; two other tugboats waiting in the dark joined the chase with their water cannons spraying high-pressure jets. The wooden *13 de Marzo* was now being hounded by tugboats made of steel—the *Polargo 2, Polargo 3*, and *Polargo 5*.

As the *13 de Marzo* kept on going, the pursuing tugboats continued to spray the high-pressure water and tried to intercept it. About seven miles out to sea, the government boats began ramming the *13 de Marzo*, which now stopped and signaled its willingness to surrender. The pilot attempted an S.O.S., but the pounding water had damaged the electrical equipment. A Cuban Coast Guard cutter arrived on the scene, but stayed back, observing.

The adults brought the children out on deck, thinking to deter the jet streams and collisions. Parents held their children up in the air and pleaded for their lives, while the attackers continued to bombard them, scattering people all over the deck, ripping clothing off, and tearing children from their parent's arms to be swept into the ocean.

In a frantic attempt to find safety, some passengers went below deck. But the *13 de Marzo* was now taking in water from the incessant ramming. The *Polargo 5* rammed it decisively one last time, and it began to sink. The passengers pinned below decks desperately pounded on the walls and ceilings as the children wailed in horror. Muñoz, the pilot, tried frantically to open the trap door on deck but couldn't get it to budge with all the water. Silence soon replaced the desperate cries as those trapped below drowned. The *13 de Marzo* sank at 4:50 A.M., seven miles northeast of Havana Harbor.

The survivors floated atop a large refrigeration box, hung onto anything else that floated by, or simply treaded water. The three government boats circled them, creating wave turbulence for around forty-five minutes.[9] All of a sudden, the attackers stopped, and their crews told survivors to swim toward the Cuban Coast Guard ships on the scene. Once onboard, some noticed a merchant ship with a Greek flag close by approaching Havana Harbor. Survivors believe this is the only reason the attackers allowed them to live.

After returning to Cuba, the thirty-one survivors were imprisoned and given psychotropic drugs in an effort to persuade them to say it had all been an accident. Thirty-seven passengers were confirmed missing by their grieving families, and four more may have perished but were never identified. Despite the intimidation and harassment, many survivors immediately denounced the premeditated ramming of the *13 de Marzo* and the deliberate aggression against unarmed citizens.

When the story of the *13 de Marzo* massacre reached the outside world, Rafael Dausá, the head of the Cuban Interests Section in Washington, called it "science fiction" and blamed the incident on the "thieves who stole the boat."[10] *Granma* published an official version of the events, stating that the pursuing vessels "had attempted to intercept and that the maneuvers undertaken to that effect had resulted in a regrettable accident that had made the boat sink."[11]

Some survivors ended up in Guantánamo and were later summoned to testify before the U.S. Congress. According to survivor María Victoria García, who came to the U.S. in 1999, many more than thirty-one would have survived the incident if the government boats had taken different actions. Mrs. García, whose ten-year-old son, husband, and other close family members died in the incident, stated: "After nearly an hour of battling in the open sea, the boat circled round the survivors, creating a whirlpool so that we would drown. Many disappeared into the seas.... We asked them to save us, but they just laughed."[12]

On July 26, just two weeks after the *13 de Marzo* was sunk, the ferry *Baraguá* was hijacked from Havana Harbor, intercepted by the U.S. Coast

Guard, and returned to Cuba. On August 3, yet another ferry, *La Coubre*, was hijacked bound for the U.S. Nothing seemed to deter those who wanted to leave. On August 5, protestors began gathering in the Havana seaside boulevard known as El Malecón, and staged what became one of the largest ever protests against the Castro regime. People came from all over the city, waving their arms in the air and chanting "*Libertad*" (Liberty). From the colonial promenade Alameda de Paula the protest extended four kilometers to the General Maceo Park and beyond.

Jorge del Río told *El Nuevo Herald*: "There were many in the streets throwing Molotov cocktails at the police, garbage cans were burned, and I saw at least three patrol cars burning. There was complete cooperation from the people to protect us in their homes; everyone knew what was going on." Fourteen days after this interview, del Río was on a raft heading north.

By the time Fidel Castro showed up that evening with a heavy military escort, the demonstrations had been squelched. Fifteen years later *Granma* would report these protests for the first time, claiming a victory for the revolution. Not mentioned in this article were the actions of the Rapid Response Brigades, karate-trained security personnel in civilian clothes who beat up the demonstrators with steel pipes.

Three days later, on August 8, 1994, Roberto Aguiar Reyes, a lieutenant commander in the Cuban Army, was killed when an army conscript named Leonel Macías González commandeered a boat to leave Cuba. The ship was picked up by the U.S. Coast Guard with twenty-six others on board who were granted asylum in the U.S.[13] In 1995, the U.S. government decided not to prosecute Macías.[14]

Aguiar Reyes' body was found on August 10, and the government staged a huge funeral for him in the Port of Mariel. Right after the funeral, seven hundred mourners took control of the tanker *Jussara*, as it was offloading oil, and attempted to flee the country. Their escape was thwarted by the authorities.[15]

The negative publicity generated by recent government actions forced Castro to open up the safety valve, for the third time in his history, to allow dissidents to leave rather than stay and cause trouble. On August 12, 1994, he announced that people would be allowed to leave the island unhindered, in whatever vessel they could construct. It was the beginning of the largest mass migration after the Mariel exodus of 1980.

Thousands of Cubans put truck tires together and built rafts to cross the Florida Straits for the United States. "It was crazy, people going from here to there," Antonia Falcón, of Cabañas, recalled in an interview. "People were selling water, food, rope, compasses. It was a bonanza: people were exchanging motorcycles, cars and houses for a boat. Barrels, tractor tires, nets, polyurethane sheets, anything that could be of use to cross the 90 miles that separate the island from the U.S was being sold. Some boats were but nutshells."[16]

Washington ordered U.S. Coast Guard vessels to guard the Florida Straits and detain refugees before they touched U.S. soil. On August 19, 1994, President Clinton announced that the *balseros* would not be allowed to land in Florida, and that those captured at sea would be shipped to the U.S. Naval Base in Guantánamo. His policy would become known as "Operation Able Vigil."

About seventy-six hundred Cubans were first sent to U.S. bases in Panamá to later unite with the rest of the rafters at Guantánamo. There they remained until Clinton's policy changed to finally allow them into the United States in 1995. One of these *balseros*, Luis Arias, who left Cuba on August 16, 1994, provided this account to the authors:

> *I found myself at the age of 28 in Cuba, just like any other regular Cuban, born and raised within the Communist system, barred from any contact or information from the outside world. Although I was never a part of the system as such, I always considered myself a dissident, by the grace of God and the upbringing of my maternal grandmother, who from the start was one of the many made to suffer by the arbitrary nature of a cruel and ruthless system.*

Many, many books would not suffice to relate the opprobrium, desperation, and frustration that a human being feels upon deciding to abandon his own country, his relatives, and a five-year-old son, to enter into an adventure that entails climbing aboard a raft and launching it into the Straits of Florida, where the odds of survival are stacked against you.

While living in the township of Regla, a State Security agent showed up accompanying the inert body of Luis Quevedo, stating that Quevedo had been surprised in the midst of trying to "illegally" exit the country. Why it is illegal for citizens to leave their own country is an issue that only comes up in police states. Even more important, why should an individual lose his or her life over this? These questions kept haunting me. Once the agent had left the funeral home, the family went in to see the body, finding that it had been savagely beaten. Quevedo's body showed signs of an AK47 rifle butt on the face, and a bullet wound in his private parts. The regime's border patrol had taken his life. This finding caused a big commotion in the town, one that lasted for three days, giving State Security the opportunity to show off their cruel nature. With my own eyes I was able to see how the Communists struck down and jailed people for the simple act of protesting.

On August 5, 1994, at Havana's seawall boulevard, The Malecón, things were quiet among passersby when a young man appeared, jokingly talking about how he was getting ready to leave the country. A policeman jumped on him right away and began to beat him up, bringing on the protest of the crowd, which began to walk around the narrow streets of Old Havana shouting "Freedom!"

In my case, only my faith in Christ gave me the strength and courage that I needed at that very moment to go out into the waters for such an unpredictable journey. Only the mercifulness of God and his infinite love for his creatures can deliver one out of such a hopeless situation.

When I was finally rescued on August 21, 1994, almost dehydrated and unable to stand up on account of my physical condition, I was taken to Guantánamo Bay, where I was to remain as a refugee for 1 year, 2 months, and 10 days.

It was a very sad experience for me, as we had to endure the political games played between the Communists on the one hand, and the government of Bill Clinton—at the time the president of the most powerful country in the world— who was yet unable to find a solution to our dilemma, as we were literally between the devil and the deep blue sea. As a result of this macabre game I witnessed suicide attempts by many Cubans that lacked the strength of character or the faith to sustain them throughout these so very difficult times."

During the day [at the Guantánamo Naval Base camp] there was an unbearable heat, while at night it was as cold as in the desert. Those defeatists among us would tell us every day that we would remain in Guantánamo for an indefinite amount of time, staying in tents. They would spread rumors that we would never be returned to Cuba, and that we would be relocated in third countries, but never in the United States of America. On the other hand, the Cuban government on the radio was calling us "ill-informed brethren," encouraging us to go back home or to rebel against the American Marines that were guarding us. That was the state of mind of around 33,000 Cubans who were going through this harrowing experience.[17]

Eric Schmitt reported in the *New York Times* on January 23, 1995, that thirty-one Cubans had tried to hang themselves or overdose on prescription drugs in the past six weeks, equaling suicide attempts among refugees in the first thirteen weeks of the Panama operation—another camp for seventy-six hundred Cuban refugees. The vast majority of the suicide attempts were by single men, sixteen to thirty years old, who had no relatives in the camps or in the U.S., and who had little chance of legally making it to the United States under the Clinton Administration's initial policy.[18]

In the Guantánamo refugee camp, single men went to one area while families with children were housed in another. The refugees were resourceful in using cardboard to construct furniture and organizing social activities. Eventually English classes were held, and the refugees were allowed to go swimming at the beach.

According to Guarioné Díaz, who headed up services for the *balseros* in Miami, this group of rafters

> *constituted the most diverse group of Cuban Americans émigrés ever. They included a mix of children and elderly, Black and White, teachers and other professionals, health workers, manual laborers, unemployed youth, scientists, and members of Cuba's military. Cuban rafters interned in Guantánamo, more than past defectors, represented different geographic areas in Cuba. They included a large number of high school graduates but just a few individuals proficient in English.*[19]

On September 9, 1994, the U.S. and Cuba signed a migration agreement stating that Cuban security forces would prevent the departure of more rafts, and in turn, the U.S. would allow at least twenty thousand additional Cubans to enter the country (not counting those who had family members in the United States). This agreement led to the *bombo*—or lottery—in Cuba that determined which applicants would be chosen for interview at the U.S. Interests Section in Havana.[20] A total of 38,560 Cubans were interdicted at sea during Operation Able Manner.[21]

In May 1995 U.S. policy regarding Cuban refugees changed once again. The United States and Cuba reached a new immigration agreement in which the U.S. agreed that Cubans intercepted at sea, without setting foot on American territory, would be returned to Cuba; Cuba, in turn, agreed to accept them without reprisals. This agreement paved the way for the Clinton Administration to begin to slowly admit the Cubans being held in legal limbo in Guantánamo and Panama. Cuba agreed that a percentage of those allowed to enter the United States would come from the twenty thousand annual visas agreed to by the two governments in September of 1994. This policy became known as "the Wet Foot-Dry Foot" and was written into law as an amendment to the 1966 Cuban Adjustment Act.[22]

After this abrupt change in policy, Attorney General Janet Reno referred to the *balseros* as illegal aliens. Despite the longstanding assumption that Cuban immigrants were victims of Communism, now they needed to be stopped.

The Cuban Adjustment Act of 1966 gave Cubans the right to become legal resident aliens of the United States a year and a day after their entry date to this country, and this benefit remains in effect for all Cubans who enter the United States legally. It also applies to the rafters; to people smuggled ashore on fast boats; to those who win the annual immigration lottery; and even to the increasing number of Cubans who take the long way to the United States: Cuba to islands off the coast of Honduras or Mexico, then to Mexico, crossing the U.S. border on foot. All qualify under the Cuban Adjustment Act and are eligible for its privileges.

Even after the Wet Foot-Dry Foot policy was in place, Cubans continued to take to the sea in rickety rafts. Brothers to the Rescue (BTTR), a Miami-based group of volunteer pilots founded in 1991, would take to the air to notify the Coast Guard of rafters who needed assistance to survive. They would also throw the rafters cell phones, water, and food. In the midst of these flights it was hard to resist the temptation of flying over Havana and dropping antigovernment leaflets. They had been successful several times, but they were unaware that a Cuban secret agent had infiltrated their organization.

On February 24, 1996, two Cuban Air Force MiG-29s shot down two BTTR planes over international waters. Killed in action were pilots Carlos Costa, Armando Alejandre, Jr., Mario de la Peña—all U.S.

citizens—and Pablo Morales, a U.S. resident. A third plane, flown by the group's founder, José Basulto, escaped. On the plane piloted by Basulto were three other exiles: Sylvia and Andrés Iriondo and Arnaldo Iglesias.[23]

Details of the incident emerged from a partial transcript of communications between the Cuban MiGs and ground control, in which it was clear that the MiGs were "authorized to destroy" the BTTR planes, and ground control congratulated the pilots on their successful strike. Secretary of State Madeleine Albright was able to get a rare UN declaration against the Cuban regime for shooting down the planes. She told the Security Council that Cuba's action was a sign of cowardice.

In response to the criminal attack, the Clinton Administration and Congress enacted on March 12, 1996, the Helms Burton Act, which tightened commercial restrictions on commerce with Cuba. Still, no effort was made to prevent travel between the exile community and friends and relatives on the island. Americans needed special permission from the government to travel to the island, but those born in Cuba, or their children, could do so legally merely by asking, provided the Cuban government allowed them entrance.

Since then, although Cubans have continued to escape by boat, there has been no organized effort to assist them in crossing the seas. Cubans try to evade interdiction so they can be "dry foot" and not be returned to Cuba; in response, a thriving business of rapid boats has developed. These Miami-based boats land in Cuba, where they are apparently assisted by the government in loading up passengers for money. Additionally, thousands of Cubans gain visas to third countries and make their way into the U.S. where they surrender to the authorities and can adjust their status to resident in one year and one day.

Article 216 of Cuba's Penal Code still forbids citizens from leaving the island without prior government authorization. Attempting to do so is punishable by up to ten years of imprisonment. Thousands of Cubans have paid for foiled escape attempts with jail time, sometimes with long prison sentences. Even more tragically, many have paid with their lives.

In October 1996, the Inter-American Commission on Human Rights of the Organization of American States (OAS) released a special report declaring that the Cuban state was responsible for premeditated murder in the cases of those killed while trying to escape on the *13 de Marzo* tugboat. Over time, as more survivors and witnesses left the island and their accounts were pieced together, it became apparent that the Cuban government had planned the murder of those who had hoped to escape.

In 1997, Amnesty International reported that there was sufficient evidence to indicate that it had been an official operation and that, if events occurred in the way described by several of the survivors, those who died were victims of extrajudicial execution.

On November 23, 1997, Jorge Mas Canosa, the main political figure in the Cuban American National Foundation (CANF), died after a short illness. His funeral cortege from St. Michael's Church was followed by thousands of exiles to Woodland Memorial Cemetery on Little Havana's Calle Ocho.

In January 1998, Pope John Paul II visited Cuba and conducted masses in several provincial capitals from Havana east to Santiago de Cuba. He met with Castro and called for Cuba to "open to the world and for the world to open to Cuba." Though expectations were high that the visit would bring reforms, very little changed in Cuba. The desire of many Cubans to leave the island remained just as high as before.

NOTES

1. President Ronald Reagan's speech given in front of the Berlin Wall on June 12, 1987.
2. Ibid.
3. The Cold War Museum, http://www.coldwar.org.
4. Gustavo Pérez Firmat, *Next Year in Cuba: A Cubano's Coming-of-Age in America* (New York: Anchor Books-Doubleday, 2006), 4.
5. See http://balseros.miami.edu/Mainnavigation.htm, Overview and Definition. See also Guarioné Díaz, *The Cuban American Experience* (St. Louis: Reedy Press, 2007), 41.
6. *El Nuevo Herald*, December 26, 1993.

7. Reuters, September 15, 1993.
8. Free Society Project, Inc., March 2007, Cuba Archive/Free Society Project.
9. Ibid.
10. Ibid.
11. Ibid.
12. Maria C. Werlau, "Cuba: The Tugboat Massacre of July 13, 1994," PDF, available at http://cubaarchive.org.
13. *New York Times,* August 11, 1994.
14. *Miami Herald,* September 20, 2000.
15. Associated Press, August 17, 1994
16. Isabel Sánchez, Agence France Press, August 15, 2009.
17. Author interview with Luis Arias, August 18, 2010.
18. Eric Schmidt, "Suicide Attempts on the Rise among Cuban Refugees," *New York Times*, January 23, 1995.
19. Díaz, *Cuban American Experience*, 40.
20. Mark P. Sullivan, Issues for the 111th Congress, March 31, 2009.
21. Testimony by Capt. Anthony S. Tangerman of the U.S. Coast Guard at the Judiciary Committee of the U.S. House of Representatives on May 18, 1999. See http://judiciary.house.gov/legacy/tang0518.htm.
22. Jefferson Morley, "US-Cuba Migration Policy," *Washington Post*, July 27, 2007.
23. Statements of Arnaldo Iglesias, passenger on Basulto's plane, found in "Excerpts of the Conversation Between Brothers to the Rescue Pilots and Cuban Air Traffic Controllers," http:/www.fiu.edu/~fcf/shootdown.html.

13

ELIAN

BY GUILLERMO MARTINEZ AND SAM VERDEJA

On Thanksgiving Day 1999, five-year-old Elián González was rescued off the Florida coast just hours after witnessing his mother's death. The two had fled Cuba five days earlier in a twenty-foot aluminum boat with a dozen others. Lázaro Rafael Munero García, Elián's stepfather, had organized the departure from Cárdenas, a city 110 miles east of Havana. When a storm hit, their motor stalled, overturning the boat. The passengers clung to inner tubes for almost three days. Arianne Horta and her boyfriend, Nivaldo Fernández Ferrán, drifted ashore at Crandon Park. All the others except Elián drowned at sea. His mother, Elizabet Brotons, had made the ultimate sacrifice so her son could have a better life.

From Jackson Memorial Hospital, Horta told the *Miami Herald* she didn't know if it was hours or days since their boat had capsized. She remembered calling out to other boats for help, but none heard or saw them. She said one of the women from their group watched her two sons drown and let go of the raft, because without them she had no will to live.[1] Finally, two men on a fishing trip from Fort Lauderdale rescued Elián, severely dehydrated and clinging to an inner tube.

The family of Elián's father brought the boy to live with them in Miami. He was a happy, outgoing, and handsome boy, and he appeared to enjoy life in his new home. The Cuban exile community followed the story avidly. Elián was a symbol of the ultimate sacrifice of a mother for freedom.

A story by Elaine del Valle in the *Miami Herald* on December 13, 1999, pieced together the background of the ill-fated journey that brought Elián to the United States. Lázaro Munero García, the boyfriend of Elián's mother, had first come to South Florida eighteen months earlier. Border Patrol agents apprehended him and three other Cubans in the Florida Keys the night of June 29, 1998. They were then sent to the Krome detention center in South Dade and released to relatives the next day.

Munero's family told del Valle that he was not happy at having left other family members behind in Cuba. "From the beginning he would cry for his parents, his (common-law) wife and the boy (Elián)," Munero's uncle said. He worked at a car wash from morning to night and sent most of what he earned back to his family in Cuba. But he could not stay in South Florida without Brotons and Elián, whom he loved as if he were his own son.

In October, Lázaro Munero made it safely back to Cuba aboard an inflatable raft with a motor attached. Cuban authorities jailed him for sixty-two days. As soon as he was released, Munero began to plan a new trip, this time with his family.[2] The group of thirteen left Cuba on Sunday, November 21, with high hopes. A few days later, all but three of them were dead.

If Elián was an important symbol to the Cuban exile community, he was equally important to the Cuban government. They mounted a formidable legal, diplomatic, and public relations campaign to reunite the young boy with his father, Juan Miguel González, in Cuba. Five-year-old Elián became the epicenter of an international dispute between Cuban authorities and the U.S. government.

At first U.S. authorities argued that Elián should remain with his extended family in Miami. But they soon changed their mind and indicated a willingness to return the boy to Cuba. The Cuban exile community protested that the child would be better off in the United States than in Cuba, where he'd face economic deprivation and loss of personal freedom.[3] The legal, political, and moral dilemma faced by American authorities was outlined by a *New York Times* editorial:

> *The effort to win new life here costs lives, and creates dilemmas to test the wisdom of Solomon. . . . Whatever happens, the American system must now accord Elián González the same care and protection that any child would receive in a custody case. That could mean having a family court consider the child's wishes, once he has had time to recover from the shock of losing his mother and also to determine the best home environment for him. His father has a right to press his claim, and American authorities have an obligation to make an apolitical judgment that serves the boy's interest rather than any political interest.*[4]

Events in the story unfolded rapidly. On November 27, Juan Miguel González appealed to the Cuban government to help secure Elián's return. Three days later, U.S. immigration authorities gave Elián legal permission to stay in the country. On December 10, Lázaro González, the boy's great-uncle, filed a request for Elián to be granted political asylum in the United States.

On January 10, 2000, a family court in Miami granted Elián's uncle temporary custody of the boy. Two days later, Attorney General Janet Reno decided the case should be heard in a federal court. On January 27, the Immigration and Naturalization Service (INS), an agency under Reno's jurisdiction, asked a federal court in Miami to reject the asylum request, giving the parental bond precedence over political considerations. Elián's father still insisted that his son be returned to Cuba, but on February 22, the United States Supreme Court rejected a petition for Elián's return to Cuba.[5]

In March, Juan Miguel González hired one of President Clinton's former impeachment lawyers—Washington insider Gregory B. Craig—to represent him in the battle to regain custody of his son. The *Miami*

Herald reported that neither the Cuban government nor the Clinton Administration had anything to do with González hiring Craig, but that this added "another tantalizing layer to the already tangled web of legal and political strategy surrounding the case." Up to that point, González had insisted that he did not need to travel to the United States because the U.S. attorney general had already ruled that his son should be returned to him in Cuba. But things were getting more complicated, and Craig informed the Justice Department that "Juan Miguel González is prepared to come to the United States to take custody of his son . . . if necessary at the earliest possible moment."[6]

A federal judge again denied an asylum hearing for Elián on March 21, deferring to Reno's ruling. Juan Miguel González arrived from Cuba on April 6 and went directly to Washington, D.C., to begin the U.S. legal process to reclaim his son and return with him to Cuba.[7] On April 12, Reno set a deadline for 2:00 P.M. the next day for Elián's relatives to turn the boy over to U.S. officials at an airport outside Miami. When the family refused, the Justice Department said it would not enforce the handover until an appeals court could review the Miami family's request to keep Elián at their house, at least temporarily.[8]

The house where Elián lived in the middle of Little Havana became a pilgrimage site for the exile community. Cuban women from all walks of life gathered daily to say the rosary. The *Miami Herald* described the scene at the house of Lázaro González: "The crowd of protesters . . . mushroomed from a few dozen in recent days into thousands Thursday (April 13). Spanish language commentators continually primed the pump. Singer Gloria Estefan, actor Andy García and many other Cuban-American celebrities arrived to lend their support."[9]

"Why are they pressuring the family to betray the trust of a child and not pressuring the father, who is in this country, to come here?" Estefan asked in an impassioned speech that questioned the federal government's position and brought cheers from the exile crowd. "We want no violence," she said. "We're asking all Cuban-Americans to continue protesting as they have done so far, in a respectful manner, and not be carried away into violence or civil disobedience."

García added: "He won't have any freedom in Cuba."[10]

The U.S. government had shifted sides, and it was now supporting the position of Cuba and Elián's father, though they maintained a dialogue with Elián's Miami family and the Cuban exile community. These discussions continued into the early hours of April 22. While still talking on the phone with friends of the families and representatives of the exile community, Reno gave the order to seize Elián.

At 5:15 A.M., a group of INS agents broke into the house of Elián González's great-uncle. The *New York Times* described the scene in the morning edition:

> *About twenty agents of the Immigration and Naturalization Service leaped from the vans and tore through a chain-link gate. Eight broke through the front door and displaying automatic weapons stormed through the tiny house in search of Elián. . . . The boy was hiding in a closet in the arms of Donato Dalrymple, one of the two fishermen who rescued Elián from the Atlantic Ocean and who had been a constant presence at the house. An agent in helmet and body armor, holding an automatic rifle, pulled the boy from Mr. Dalrymple's arms. The agent, Mr. Dalrymple said, pointed the rifle at him as Elián cried "No! No! No!"*[41]

An Associated Press photographer (Alan Díaz) won a Pulitzer Prize for the dramatic picture that showed the gun close to Elián's face.

> *Elián's eyes were wide open. He cried and seemed terrified as all around him people screamed, cursed and fought against a line of federal agents who formed a wall with shields and automatic weapons as a cloud of tear gas and pepper spray wafted down the street. . . . A few protesters tried to form a human chain to block the front of the house and keep the agents from taking the boy. Ramón Saúl Sánchez, an exile in Miami . . . said he was struck by an agent's*

gun butt. He bled from an ear as a young man held him upright.[12]

Elián was bundled onto an airplane and flown to Washington to be reunited with his father the same day. His fate was still up to the courts, but in the meantime Elián would live with his father. Two months later, the U.S. Supreme Court refused to block Elián's departure from the United States, ruling that the boy belonged with his father. On June 28, a private jet flew the six-year-old boy and his father from Washington to Havana.[13]

To Cuban exiles, the violent INS raid felt like something that would happen in Communist Cuba, not the United States. They felt betrayed by the Clinton Administration and the Democratic Party. The peaceful prayer sessions outside Elián's house in Little Havana turned into loud protests. Throngs of Cuban exiles marched down the streets shouting, "In November, we'll remember."

Elián's story was covered extensively by the national media, which had criticized the Cuban exiles' role in the Elián case long before Reno ordered INS agents to seize the child. In an op-ed piece in the *New York Times* three weeks earlier, David Rieff did not mince words: "Miami has once more demonstrated its excessive influence over United States national politics; it remains in political terms, an out-of-control banana republic within the American body politic. This is bad for the city and bad for the United States."[14]

Many Americans sympathized with a father's desire to get his son back, though the photos of INS agents aiming automatic rifles at innocent people felt like "overkill." A *Miami Herald* story evaluated the impact of the negative publicity on both the Cuban-American community and the tourist economy of South Florida: "For decades, the world has watched as Greater Miami weathered riots, hurricanes, cocaine cowboys, tourist murders, political scandals and waves of refugees. The Elián González saga once again has turned the spotlight on Miami, and it hasn't been kind."[15]

They interviewed Tom Pinko, a New York business consultant, who said, "Looking at this in business terms, this is a stock—the Cuban-American community—that is plummeting. Business is based on stability and continuity and you don't want things to get crazy." Stuart Blumberg, president of the Greater Miami and the Beaches Hotel Association, disagreed. "This is a very resilient community and industry that will take this one in stride and keep moving forward."[16]

Prominent members of the Cuban-American community tried to set the record straight. Pedro Freyre, chairman of Facts About Cuban Exiles (FACE), wrote an editorial for the *Miami Herald*. "The Cuban-American community," he wrote,

> *as loyal an immigrant group as has ever reached our shores, learned that while America, its beloved adopted land, is a magnificent country, its politicians, oftentimes are incapable of delivering fairness and justice. In three violent minutes, the Clinton administration and Attorney General Janet Reno broke faith with Cuban Americans from all walks of life. . . . There are vast chasms in the way an ethnic group perceives itself and the way it is perceived by its neighbors.*[17]

Tom Fiedler, editor of the *Miami Herald* Editorial Board, wrote a column in which he quoted letters from local residents such as Jeffrey R. Roth, who described himself as a native Anglo Miamian. Roth wrote, "As long as some members of the Cuban community consider themselves exiles, we are not a community of immigrants. They lack the emotional acceptance that the United States is their permanent home. That is the glue that holds us." Fiedler's response was that "exiles don't behave like immigrants."[18]

People like Jeffrey Roth, along with much of the media, overlooked a couple of important points. The first was that though American law generally upheld the rights of natural parents, this was not the only consideration in custody cases, which placed the overall well-being of the child above all else. The second was that Cuban exiles had a perspective on Elián's future well-being that the average American, and even American courts, lacked. Cuban-Americans had experienced life under Castro. They knew firsthand that Elián would not only enjoy greater economic opportunity if he stayed in the United States, but he'd have the freedom to make up his own mind. They fought hard to keep the child in the United States because they believed passionately in the American system. The will to fight sprang not from the insularity of a narrow ethnic community, but from a broad and deep patriotism toward their adopted country.

THE AFTERMATH

Relations between the Clinton Administration and Cuba improved after Castro's victory in the Elián incident. For many years, American agricultural and pharmaceutical companies had lobbied to allow them to sell to Cuba, and in October of 2000, Congress granted their wish.[19]

On November 7, 2000, in one of the closest and most-fiercely fought electoral battles ever, Republican presidential candidate George W. Bush defeated Al Gore, Clinton's vice president. Florida, which gave their twenty-five electoral votes to Bush, was the swing state. After Gore challenged the vote count in court, a hand count of absentee ballots gave Bush an edge of 537 votes.

According to the *Miami Herald*, the Elián factor played an important role. They quoted pollster Sergio Bendixen, who said "of the 400,000 Cuban-Americans in the state, 27 percent to 30 percent voted for Bill Clinton in 1996. This year, about 20 percent voted for Gore. That's a swing of 30,000 to 50,000 votes." Rob Schroth, another pollster who specialized in Hispanic voting, said, "I don't think there's any doubt that the boy could be the reason for George W. Bush's victory."[20] Though

Gore initially had argued in favor of Elián being allowed to remain in the United States, he was the one who paid the price for the Clinton Administration's handling of Elián González.

Just as the exile community had feared, Elián González became a prized propaganda object for Castro upon his return to Cuba. His father, a restaurant employee, was elected to Parliament, and the country celebrated his birthday every year with parades. Elián did all the things expected of a loyal young Cuban Communist, including joining the Young Communist Union in 2008. Two years later, Cuba released a picture of the young man "wearing an olive-green military school uniform and attending a Young Communist Union congress."[21]

When George W. Bush became president, he paid his debt to the Cuban-American community by reversing Clinton's position on Cuba. In May 2001, he hosted a White House celebration of Cuban Independence Day, and announced, "My administration will oppose any attempt to weaken sanctions against Cuba's government—and I will fight such attempt—until it frees its political prisoners, holds democratic free elections and allows free speech."[22]

On September 11, 2001, nineteen al Qaeda terrorists hijacked four jetliners, crashing two of them into the World Trade Center towers in New York and one into the Pentagon. The fourth plane was brought down in a Pennsylvania field by passengers who overcame the hijackers. Nearly three thousand Americans died that day, and the country declared war on international terrorism.

In May 2002, Under Secretary of State John Bolton added Cuba, along with Libya and Syria, to the "axis of evil countries"—originally comprised of North Korea, Iran, and Iraq. "Cuba has at least a limited offensive biological warfare research and development effort," Bolton said, "(and has) provided dual-use technology to other rogue states."[23]

Former president Jimmy Carter visited Cuba that month (the first president or former president to ever do so) and toured scientific centers. He claimed they were medical facilities, and that there was no evidence of weapon building. Carter took the opportunity to lecture Cuba on human rights and urge the United States to lift the embargo on Cuba.[24]

Relations between the two countries continued to sour. James Cason, who had been appointed head of the U.S. Interests Section in Havana in September 2002, began to invite dissidents to his home and to U.S. diplomatic functions. This infuriated Castro. A year later, he aimed the fury mostly at the dissidents, arresting seventy-five in March 2003 and sentencing some to serve an unprecedented twenty-seven years behind bars. Among those sentenced, after single-day trials, were independent journalists Raúl Rivero and Omar Rodríguez Saludes, dissident Héctor Palacios, economist Martha Beatriz Roque, Dr. Oscar Elías Biscet, and Oscar Espinosa Chepe, who wrote critical articles about the Cuban economy for Internet sites run by exile groups in Miami. The roundup ended a decade of tolerance by the Cuban government, in which small opposition groups grew from having a few dozen members to hundreds of supporters throughout the island. This had international repercussions. The events soon became known as Cuba's Black Spring. (*Primavera Negra* in Spanish).[25]

Dagoberto Rodríguez, head of Cuba's diplomatic mission in Washington, blamed the United States, pointing to Cason's interactions with local "independent" journalists, economists, and librarians. In a three-hour press conference in Havana, Cuban Foreign Minister Felipe Pérez Roque accused the Bush Administration of ordering the Interests Section "to be turned into a 'headquarters of internal subversion' in Cuba."[26]

The 2003 Black Spring badly damaged Cuban relations not only with the United States but with the European Union, which pulled back from its historically conciliatory policy toward the Castro regime. The changes in EU policy "had an enormous impact within the dissident community in Cuba."[27]

Wayne Smith, head of the U.S. Interests Section in Havana under President Jimmy Carter and a frequent critic of American policies towards

Castro, argued that the crackdown in Cuba was a direct result of Bush's change in policy. "Cuban officials are alarmed by talk of 'regime change,' the new buzz-word in official Washington circles," he said. "They (Cuba) may be next so they are battening down the hatches." Other Cuba analysts disagreed, citing "more Machiavellian motives, such as Castro's record of picking fights with the United States to distract attention from domestic problems such as energy shortages and food rationing."[28]

In a three-hour speech on April 25, Castro announced the execution of three young black Cubans, who had attempted to escape to the United States. Castro "claimed that a conspiracy between the U.S. government and Cuban exiles in Miami was to blame for his dissident crackdown and the execution of the three hijackers."[29]

"Following the arrests of scores of government opponents across the island," the United States had announced new rules for travel to Cuba on March 24, 2003. In June, it denied travel permission to organizers of the U.S. Food and Agribusiness Exhibition in Havana.[30]

President Bush also imposed limits on cash transfers that exiles could send their relatives in Cuba, approved a forceful new information campaign, and created the Commission for Assistance to a Free Cuba. In October, senior Bush diplomat Roger Noriega told attendees at a conference at the University of Miami's Institute for Cuba and Cuban-American Studies that the president was "wholly committed to the cause of Cuban freedom" and ending Castro's government. At the same conference, Mikhail Gorbachev pleaded for a more conciliatory approach. "It would be a great thing if the United States, as the only remaining superpower, would take the first step and lift the embargo. . . . I think it would have far-reaching consequences." Raising his voice, Gorbachev pleaded, "Lift the embargo."

The three Cuban-American congressional representatives from South Florida—Ileana Ros-Lehtinen and brothers Lincoln and Mario Díaz-Balart—called Gorbachev "a former KGB guy who can only be considered a reformer with a small 'r'."[31]

FIDEL STEPS BACK

On July 31, 2006, a short Cuban television announcement shocked Cubans on both sides of the Florida Straits. President Fidel Castro had suffered "an intestinal crisis with sustained bleeding" and was temporarily turning over control of Cuba's government and his title as president to his brother Raúl. The rumor was that Castro was very sick, though this had long been treated as a state secret in Cuba. It seemed as though the man who had ruled Cuba with an iron fist for forty-seven years might be dying. In its coverage of this momentous event, the *Miami Herald* described South Florida Cuban-Americans as jubilant. "My heart is thumping so hard you can see it," said Angelina Adrian of Westchester.[32]

The *New York Times* reported that rumors were rampant in Havana. "Some people pointed to the fact that Mr. Castro's message had been written on a computer as evidence that his health was much worse that the government had led on. 'People are very disoriented,' one history professor said in a telephone interview speaking on condition of anonymity because he feared arrest. 'Dissidents are worried and fear that at any moment there could be a wave of detentions.'"[33]

CNN described the glee in Miami as "the streets of Miami were filled with Cuban exiles honking their car horns and shouting 'Cuba Libre'" as well as the somber mood in Havana as residents tried to carry on with their daily lives, without being able to "obviously avoid a sense of concern."[34]

In February 2008, the transfer of power from Fidel to Raúl Castro became official. Fidel had not been seen in public since 2006, appearing only in official photographs and videos. His voice had continued to be heard, through the "dense essays" known as "*Reflecciones*," published in Cuba's official newspaper. Most of them focused on international themes rather than local politics, which he left to his brother.[35]

The changes in Cuba raised expectations abroad for a more open economy. The European Union, apparently forgetting the jailed dissidents, began to improve relations with Cuba. In October 2009, Spain announced that when it took over the presidency of the twenty-seven-country European Union it would, as the *Miami Herald* syndicated columnist Andrés Oppenheimer said, "seek a major improvement in European ties with Cuba." They even urged other European nations with embassies in Cuba to stop inviting dissidents to diplomatic functions.[36]

When Democratic senator Barack Obama was sworn into office as president in January 2009, American policy toward Cuba also underwent change. During the campaign, Obama had said he wanted a new beginning with Cuba. In April 2009, the Obama Administration, claiming the measures had only punished the Cuban people, lifted the restrictions on exile visits and the amount of money they could spend or send as remittances.[37]

That same month, in the first shakeup since Fidel's resignation, the Cuban government removed two of its most important young leaders—Cabinet Secretary Carlos Lage and Foreign Minister Felipe Pérez Roque—from their posts. Both men publicly admitted their "errors," and Cuban television broadcast a video that showed them speaking disrespectfully about Vice President José Ramón Machado Ventura, whom they called "the man with the hairpiece." Machado Ventura was one of the original revolutionary leaders, and the ouster of the younger leaders showed that Raúl didn't intend to step aside any time soon for a new generation.[38]

In June 2009, Cuba won an important diplomatic victory when the Organization of American States (OAS) rescinded the 1962 ban on Cuba's membership. But, after publicly celebrating the decision, the Cuban government announced it wouldn't rejoin the OAS because it was a lackey of U.S. foreign policy.[39]

Cuban dissidents remained outspoken even after the 2003 Black Spring. A group of women dressed in white—the wives, mothers, sisters, and daughters of those arrested—staged peaceful protests every

Sunday in Havana's Santa Rita Catholic Church. Quickly they became known as the Ladies in White *("Las Damas de Blanco")* "After Mass, they would walk 10 blocks to a nearby park . . . each woman carrying a pink gladiolus flower and wearing a button with her loved one's picture that says 'prisoner of conscience.' They demand the prisoners' release."[40] The *Miami Herald* reported that "most of their marches are harassed by government-run mobs that hurl insults at them . . . and sometimes hit them on their backs, pinch their arms and stomp on their feet. . . . Security forces broke up the protests by dragging them into busses and driving them away."[41]

The Internet transformed protests in Cuba, as it did around the world. In April 2007, Yoani Sánchez, began a blog called "Generación Y." Sneaking into hotels to surreptitiously access their Internet connections, Sánchez tried to present the views of Cubans born in the 1970s and 1980s, under the influence of the Soviet Union (when many were given first names starting with the letter Y). Her poignant postings gained her worldwide recognition and several international awards, including the Principe de Asturias Award from Spain in 2008. Cuba wouldn't allow her to travel to receive any of the awards.[42]

On February 23, 2010, Orlando Zapata Tamayo, a forty-two-year-old mason and a prisoner of conscience, died after an eighty-three-day hunger strike to protest "repeated beating by guards and many other abuses." His was the first death from a hunger strike in Cuba since Pedro Luis Boitel was allowed to die in prison in 1972. The Zapata Tamayo hunger strike led to protests inside and outside of Cuba. "Zapata's case sparked street protests by government critics, earlier this month, including one during which police in Camaguey detained some 35 people for several hours . . . some of them beaten during the roundups. His death also unleashed a string of protests among Florida's congressional delegation with Republican Rep. Mario Díaz-Balart calling on the Obama Administration 'to stand in solidarity with the Cuban people and stop appeasing the Cuban regime.'"[43]

A month later, "tens of thousands" of Cuban exiles "wearing white and carrying gladioluses and flags marched for blocks along Calle Ocho (in Little Havana) with singer Gloria Estefan in support of Cuba's Damas de Blanco (Ladies in White), the peaceful dissidents who last week were attacked by government security forces in Havana."[44]

In April 2010, seventy-three-year-old Cardinal Jaime Ortega, who had previously been reluctant to criticize the Cuban government, said the country was "in one of its worst crises in recent times with its people demanding political and economic changes sooner rather than later." He asked the United States to lift the embargo, while urging his own government to do a better job of protecting the lives of dissidents and political prisoners.[45]

The Catholic Church and the Spanish government began lobbying Cuban authorities to free the fifty-three dissidents from the 2003 Black Spring who were still in jail. Paul Webster, former British ambassador to Cuba, said that "the church's assertiveness followed EU and international outrage and showed what many suspected—that the church has long underused its potential for political influence."[46] Most of the released prisoners went to Spain, though some refused to leave Cuba. Dr. Oscar Elías Biscet—the last of the prisoners arrested in the 2003—was freed in March 2011.[47]

As more and more former government officials defect from Cuba, the world is learning about the full extent of Cuba's involvement, over the past half-century, in political subversion and promoting revolution. At various points in its history, Cuba tried to oust a democratic government in Venezuela, trained guerrilla forces in Nicaragua and El Salvador, and provided military support to terrorist organizations in several African countries.

One of the former Cuban officials who defected, Juan F. Benemellis, has written several books detailing Cuba's involvement in worldwide subversion. In an article written for *El Nuevo Herald*, Benemellis compared Cuba's espionage competence to the ruthless East German Secret Police known as the Stasi. He quotes historian Andrew Conteh, who said "no other country of Cuba's size and resources can even come close to the worldwide impact of Cuba's foreign policy."[48]

For decades, Cuban exiles had known that Castro's spies had infiltrated even the most militant exile organizations in South Florida and Washington, but no one outside the Cuban community really believed the stories. The only documented case was Juan Pablo Roque, who betrayed the Brothers to the Rescue and fled to Cuba the day before their planes were shot down by Cuban MiGs. It turned out Roque was a double-agent, who had been paid by the FBI to inform on drug dealers and anti-Castro militants while spying for the Cuban government.[49]

Juan Tamayo reported the names and stories of Cuban spies in a June 2009 article in the *Miami Herald*. The first group, called "Red Avispa" (the Wasp Network) was apprehended in 1998. Of the ten members arrested, five cooperated and received short prison sentences; the other five did not and were sentenced to much longer terms. In February 2000, Mariano Faget, a Cuban-born exile who worked for the Immigration and Naturalization Service, was arrested and sentenced to five years in jail.

The 2001 arrest and conviction of Ana Belén Montes, a Puerto Rican who worked for the Pentagon's Defense Intelligence Agency, shook up Washington insiders. Montes, who had access to top-secret American documents at the Defense Department and provided input to American policy toward Cuba and Latin America, was the top Cuban spy ever arrested. She was convicted and sentenced to twenty-five years in jail.

In January 2006, two professors at Florida International University, Carlos Alvarez and his wife, Elsa Prieto, were identified and pleaded guilty to working for the Cuban government.[50] Later that year, Walter Kendall Myers, a seventy-two-year-old State Department employee, and his wife, Gwendolyn Steingraber Myers, were convicted of spying for Cuba. Myers was sentenced to life without parole, but he cooperated in exchange for a lighter prison sentence for his wife.[51]

Cuban authorities arrested a U.S. contractor named Alan Gross in

January 2010, accusing the sixty-year-old social worker of being a spy. The United States government said Gross had gone to Cuba to provide communication equipment to Jewish nonprofit organizations.[52] Cuba held Gross for more than a year without putting him on trial, attempting to negotiate an exchange for the five members of the Red Avispa whom the Cuban government considers heroes. Finally, on March 11, 2011, Gross was convicted of being a U.S. spy and sentenced to fifteen years in jail.[53]

The world economic crisis of 2008 did not spare Cuba. The Cuban people had already undergone the "Special Period" in the early 1990s after the fall of the Soviet Union, when feeding one's family became a daily challenge. By 2009, electricity blackouts plagued the island again. The *Miami Herald* published a story about how Cuba had resorted to using oxen in agriculture again.[54] The government announced it would scrap its ration books, in effect since 1962, because Cuba could not afford them anymore.[55]

In May 2011, the Communist Party released new economic guidelines. Among other changes, the government was considering letting Cubans travel abroad as tourists. The *Miami Herald* reported that

> since taking over from his brother in 2008, Cuban President Raúl Castro has championed a limited but significant shift to the free market. Last year he announced that Cubans would be allowed to go into business for themselves in 178 approved enterprises, hire employees and rent out cars and homes. Castro has also promised to fire half a million unnecessary state workers and has warned his countrymen that the government can no longer afford the deep subsidies it gives workers in return for wages that average $20 a month.[56]

In Cuba, mass layoffs were easier said than done. Andy Gómez of the University of Miami wrote in the *Miami Herald* that "the government's own bureaucracy has not been able to process the dismissal papers of approximately one million workers fired from their government jobs."[57]

Increased economic deprivation once again fired the desire of large numbers of Cubans to leave the island. Some departed legally on planes, while others continued to flee by boat or cross the border on foot from Mexico. In December 2007, the *Miami Herald* published a study done by the Institute for Cuban and Cuban-American Studies of the University of Miami that showed a record number of Cubans had arrived since the new millennium:

> *A decade later [after the rafters crisis] and largely without the high-seas drama of that crisis, from approximately October 2005 through September 2007, nearly 77,000 Cubans are known to have reached U.S. territory—more than twice the total of the 1994 Balsero refugees.*

> *U.S. Homeland Security data on new legal permanent residents by country of origin reveals that emigration from the island into the U.S. has reached levels not seen since the peak years of the late 1960s and early 1970s.... Moreover, the trend appears to be escalating.*

> *Tacitly if not overtly, the Castro regime once again appears to be turning to mass migration as its policy of choice to both deflate mounting dissatisfaction at home and arguably set the stage for more favorable negotiating terms in its relations with Washington.*[58]

Another study by the same organization published in 2009 concluded "in the past nine years alone the U.S. has welcomed more than 235,000 new Cuban immigrants, a rate of migration which rivals that of the historic mass exodus during the Cold War years of the late 1960s and early 1970s."[59]

More than fifty years after the revolution came into power, Cubans in the island were worse off than they were before Castro. "As best as we can tell, current income is well below its pre-revolutionary peak suggesting that despite possible accomplishments elsewhere, the revolution permanently reduced Cuban income per capita." This was the conclusion from a paper titled "The Road Not Taken: Pre-Revolutionary Cuban Living Standards in Comparative Perspective."[60]

Still, Cuba and Castro always held a trump card—the use of legal and illegal migration as an escape valve. The Cuban government alone dictated how many Cubans could leave the island. It mattered little that the United States tried to limit those allowed to enter the country legally. It approved a lottery of 20,000 visas established by the Clinton Administration in 1995, and it continued granting visas to those claimed by their relatives in the United States. But other Cubans kept migrating. Clinton enacted the Wet-Foot, Dry-Foot policy establishing that Cubans who reached U.S. soil would be allowed to stay, while those intercepted at sea would be forced to return.[61]

The exodus of Cubans continues to this day.

NOTES

1. Lisa Arthur, Bruce Taylor Seeman and Elaine del Valle, "5-Year-Old Survivor Clung to Inner Tube, Two More Rafters Rescued, but 11 Other Cubans May Have Died at Sea," *Miami Herald*, November 26, 1999.
2. Elaine del Valle, "The Deadly Voyage: How it Happened," *Miami Herald*, December 13, 1999.
3. David González, "Cuban Government Enters Fight for Boy," *New York Times*, November 30, 1999.
4. "The Future of Elián González," *New York Times*, November 30, 1999. The editorial in essence predicted the difficult events and decisions that were to come in the weeks and months ahead.
5. "The Elián González Chronology: Custody Tug of War over Cuban Boy," *New York Times*, April 14, 2000.
6. Andrés Viglucci, "Elián's Dad Hires ex-Clinton Attorney," *Miami Herald*, March 10, 2000.
7. Randall C. Archibald, "2 Who Rescued Elián Try to Talk With Father," *Miami Herald*, April 9, 2000.
8. Viglucci, "Elián's Dad."
9. "Throng Outside House Swells to Thousands Emotions Run High; Reach 'Crisis Mode,'" *Miami Herald*, April 14, 2000.
10. Ibid.
11. Rick Bragg, "The Elián González Case: The Overview; Cuban Boy Seized by U.S. Agents and Reunited with His Father," *New York Times*, April 23, 2000.

12. Ibid.
13. Andrés Viglucci and Jay Weaver, "Elián's Odyssey Ends," *Miami Herald*, June 29, 2000.
14. David Rieff, "The Exiles' Last Hurrah," *New York Times*, April 2, 2000.
15. Mimi Whitefield, "Miami's Seesaw Image Suffering in Spotlight Experts Weigh the Impact of Turmoil," *Miami Herald*, April 29, 2000.
16. Ibid.
17. Pedro Freyre, "What Might Have Been," *Miami Herald*, May 3, 2000.
18. Tom Fiedler, "Can We Long for the Past While Living for the Future?" *Miami Herald*, May 7, 2000.
19. Cal Thomas, "Profiting from Elián González," *Jewish World Review*, May 8, 2000.
20. John Dorschner, "Historic Turning Point Any of Many Twists May Shape Outcome Factors Range from Rowdy Republicans to Ballot Design," *Miami Herald*, December 5, 2000.
21. Associated Press, "Elián González Shown at a Cuban Youth Meeting," November 16, 2010.
22. Frank Davies, "President Backs Aid for Cuba's Dissidents Tough Talk Marks Independence Day," *Miami Herald,* May 19, 2001.
23. *BBC News Americas*, May 6, 2002, and Douglas Jehl, "Ex-Officials Say Bolton Inflated Syrian Danger," *New York Times*, April 26, 2005.
24. Jimmy Carter, "President Carter's Trip to Cuba," May 21, 2002, The Carter Center.
25. Nancy San Martín, "Cuba attacks dissent with prison," *Miami Herald*, April 8, 2003.
26. David Adams, "Crackdown on dissent a Cuban question mark," *St. Petersburg Times*, April 20, 2003.
27. José Ribeiro Castro, 'Bilateral Relations Between the EU and Cuba (2003-2008): 5 Years, Little Progress," Cubalog.EU, Overcoming Information Blockade-Cuba.
28. Adams, "Crackdown."
29. Anita Snow (Associated Press), "Fidel Castro Blames Dissident Crackdown and Executions on Conspiracy," April 26, 2003.
30. Nancy San Martin, "U.S. Pulls Plug on Cuba Expo," *Miami Herald*, June 23, 2003
31. Nancy San Martín, "Stances on Cuba Collide," *Miami Herald*, October 5, 2003.
32. Elaine del Valle, Frances Robles, and Martin Merzer, "Castro's Health Crisis Could Transform Island and U.S. Exiles," *Miami Herald*, August 1, 2006.
33. "Castro 'Stable,' But His Illness Presents Puzzle," *New York Times*, August 2, 2006.
34. "Raúl Castro Replaces Fidel in Cuba," *CNN International*, August 1, 2006.
35. Anita Snow (Associated Press), "Fidel Castro Resigns Cuban Presidency After Nearly Half-Century in Power," February 22, 2008.
36. Andrés Oppenheimer, "Spain Nudging EU to Ease Cuba Stand," *Miami Herald,* October 22, 2009.
37. Sheryl Gay Stolberg and Damien Cave, "Obama Opens Door to Cuba, but Only a Crack," *New York Times,* April 14, 2009.
38. Wilfredo Cancio Isla, "Video Shows Why Two Men Were Ousted," *Miami Herald*, May 23, 2009.
39. Alex Leff, "Cuba Refuses OAS Offer to Rejoin," *Tico Times*, San José, Costa Rica, and *McClatchy-Tribune Regional News*, June 9, 2009.
40. Carlos Lauría, Monica Campbell, and María Salazar, "Cuba's Long Black Spring," Committee to Protect Journalists (CPJ), March 18, 2008.
41. Juan Tamayo, "United by Pain, Icons Vow to Keep Marching," *Miami Herald*, April 25, 2010.

42. See http://www.desdecuba.com/generaciony/.
43. Juan Tamayo, "Cuban Activist Dies on Hunger Strike," *Miami Herald*, February 24, 2010.
44. Luisa Yánez, José Cassola, Jennifer Lebovich, and Fabiola Santiago, "Marchers Send Message," *Miami Herald*, March 26, 2010.
45. Associated Press, "Catholic Cardinal Ortega Says Country Is in Crisis," *Miami Herald*, April 20, 2010.
46. Paul Webster Hare, "It Took More than Dialogue to Free Them," *Miami Herald*, July 18, 2010.
47. Juan Carlos Chávez, "Oscar Elías Biscet Says Cuban Dissidents Are Willing to Discuss Transitional Government," *Miami Herald*, April 11, 2011.
48. Juan F. Benemelis, "Cuba: Centro y Motor de la Subversión Mundial," *El Nuevo Herald*, December 26, 2008.
49. Pazdera Torriero, "FBI Admits Paying Cuban to Spy, Inform—On Exiles," *Fort Lauderdale Sun-Sentinel*, February 29, 1996.
50. Juan Tamayo, "Cuban Espionage: A Deadly Game," *Miami Herald*, June 14, 2009.
51. Lesley Clark, "U.S. Agent for Cuba Gets Life in Prison," *Miami Herald*, November 21, 2009.
52. Ginger Thompson and Marc Lacey, "Contractor Jailed in Cuba Was Aiding Religious Groups, U.S. Says," *New York Times*, January 12, 2010.
53. Lesley Clark, "U.S. Rejects Conviction of Contractor by Cuba, Demands His Release," *Miami Herald*, March 12, 2011.
54. Juan Tamayo "Cuba Uses Oxen to Tackle Crisis," *Miami Herald*, August 26, 2009.
55. *Miami Herald* wire services, "Ration Book Could Be Scrapped," October 10, 2009.
56. Paul Haven (Associated Press), "Cuba Publishes Awaited Details of Economic Changes," *Miami Herald*, May 9, 2011.
57. Andy Gómez, Last Congress for Cuba's Old Guard," *Miami Herald*, April 12, 2011.
58. "Another Exodus from Cuba Is Now Under Way," *Miami Herald*, December 1, 2007 (article covering the findings reported in "Coming to America: The New Cuban Migration Crisis: A Recent Staff Report from Institute for Cuban and Cuban-American Studies of the University of Miami").
59. "Cuban Migration to South Florida: Impact and Implications—The Politics of Contemporary Cuban Immigration, 1994-2008," *Focus on Cuba*, no. 114, October 9, 2009, an information service of the Cuba Transition Project, Institute for Cuban and Cuban American Studies, University of Miami.
60. Marianne Ward and John Devereux, "The Road Not Taken: Pre-Revolutionary Cuban Living Standards in Comparative Perspective," *Journal of Economic History*, Cambridge, England.
61. Jefferson Morley, "US-Cuba Migration Policy," *Washington Post*, July 27, 2007.

14

EXECUTIONS AND POLITICAL PRISONERS

BY JUAN CLARK

EXECUTIONS

Prior to 1959, the Cuban constitutions prescribed the death penalty only under the most extreme circumstances—such as prosecuting spies during war. When Fidel Castro assumed power, the firing squad became a part of the revolution. Under the current Communist regime, thousands of "counter revolutionaries" have been imprisoned for long periods, and an estimated five thousand to six thousand people have been executed—without due process—for political reasons.[1]

The role that political prisoners and executions have played in the Castro regime has its roots in his psychological history. Throughout his life, Fidel Castro relied on physical intimidation to eliminate real or perceived competitors. As a child he picked fights with his fellow students without provocation. At Belén Jesuit High School in Havana, Castro was highly competitive and the best athlete in his class. But he showed early signs of violence, and he had a pistol that teachers had to confiscate.[2]

At the University of Havana, Castro aspired to the presidency of the Federacion Estudiantil Universitaria (FEU)—in English, the Federation of University Students—which included all the university student government associations. It was considered an important stepping stone for national politics. When Leonel Gómez, a student leader from the

Instituto de La Habana (High School), was about to enter the University of Havana, Castro believed he would be a rival and talked to his friends about "eliminating" Gómez. He actually shot at Gómez from a distance, but hit another student and somehow managed to avoid prosecution for attempted murder.[3]

Though Fidel didn't pull the trigger, he planned and participated in the murder of the distinguished university student leader and former FEU president Manolo Castro (no kin to him). Then he and a friend shot a university police sergeant, Oscar Fernández Caral, who said Fidel Castro had been involved in planning Manolo Castro's murder. Fernández Caral did not die immediately, and he reportedly named Fidel as his killer. Yet Castro again managed to manipulate the system and evade justice.[4]

Long before the Moncada barracks attack, in which dozens of people died, Castro planned other violent events. In Mexico, while preparing for his Granma expedition, he had more than one of his crew killed on suspicion of being a spy. He shot one trainee himself in front of many others.[5]

The use of firing squads, generally after a mock trial, was formalized in the Sierra Maestra struggle. Executions were sometimes carried out for relatively minor infractions. To teach a lesson to the other guerrillas, Castro tried a teenage peasant rebel soldier for misconduct and executed him, despite the disapproval of many followers.[6] These early stories foreshadowed what would become a pattern once Castro assumed power.

Castro's first public victims were police or military personnel who had served the Batista regime. They were accused of murder, war crimes, or torture; sentenced at mock trials; and executed. Catholic priests were often called to administer the last rites, and sometimes the media was allowed to film or photograph the execution. *Bohemia* magazine published gruesome pictures of some of the executed, like Col. Cornelio Rojas and Lt. Ernesto Despaingne, to intimidate the population and eliminate potential enemies. Involving religion and the media in the executions served to both spread the news and inspire terror. These initial executions demonstrated what opponents of the revolution could expect. Some of the media, particularly *Bohemia*, a popular and influential weekly magazine that had practically deified Castro, published uncorroborated stories of murders and torture under Batista that convinced many Cubans the executions were justified.

In addition to the liberal use of firing squads, Castro relied on mysterious "suicides" and "accidents" to take out his enemies. Felix Lutgerio Pena, the rebel comandante who had presided over a trial that acquitted Air Force pilots and mechanics charged with genocide, was found dead in his car, shot through the heart in March of 1959. Castro had been infuriated at the acquittal, and he ordered a retrial. The official version of Pena's death was suicide, despite the fact that the direction of the bullet indicated Pena had been shot from his left side, outside the car, though he was right-handed.[7]

Political executions waned by mid-1959, but they began to ramp up again in the mid-1960s when Castro deployed 100,000 militia troops to put down uprisings in the Escambray Mountains. Some of Castro's original guerilla leaders were executed during this period, including Comandantes Humberto Sorí Marín (who was very close to Castro), William Morgan, and Jesus Carreras. No compassion was shown, even to those with a "revolutionary record," such as Captain Ricardo Olmedo, who had been handicapped from an injury in the attack on Batista's presidential palace.[8]

There was no press coverage or religious assistance in this new wave of executions, just a brief announcement by the government. Families were not given the corpses for burial, being told only the location of the unmarked graves. Many of the victims bravely faced the firing squad shouting "Down with Communism!" or "Long Live Christ the King!" Then they began to gag the condemned to prevent the defiant expressions. All members of the firing squad would shoot a real bullet, eliminating the tradition of having a rifle loaded with a blank cartridge. Spectators invited to witness the executions became de facto collaborators. Some witnesses reported that this "special" crowd often made fun of those about to be executed.[9]

A particularly barbaric aspect of Castro's executions was the practice of exsanguination—extracting as much blood as possible while still keeping the condemned alive. Castro defended the practice, which he learned from Eastern Europe, saying that "the blood of these counter-revolutionaries will not be wasted, since it will be used to save the lives of the soldiers defending the fatherland."[10]

THE "HISTORICAL" POLITICAL PRISON

Resistance fighters who were caught and escaped the firing squad faced long prison sentences. According to some estimates, the number of political prisoners peaked at 60,000 in the 1960s.[11] Amnesty International reported about 20,000 prisoners released in the 1970s.[12] In a country the size of the United States, that would be equivalent to the existence of 466,000 to 1,410,000 political prisoners between the 1960s and 1970s. In fact, Communist Cuba had the highest per capita incidence of political prisoners in the world, even higher than the former Soviet Union.[13]

This was a departure from Cuban history, including the colonial period. During the nearly fifty-seven years since independence, Cuba had few political prisoners except during the dictatorships of Machado and Batista.[14] Even during these periods, the number of political prisoners was small compared to Castro's regime: about five thousand under Machado and five hundred under Batista. Though both leaders sometimes had political opponents assassinated by the police after arrest, those who made it to prison were briefly incarcerated and not mistreated.[15] Detainees could count on a hearing before a judge and independent legal defense, and they were kept separate from criminal prisoners. Political prisoners under Machado and Batista were not forced to do labor; they had access to the communications media, which were often watchdogs against mistreatment; and family connections or friendship often saved them.

It was not uncommon for a "revolutionary" to go into exile thanks to a safe-conduct pass obtained for him by a government politician granting a personal favor.

The social background of the prisoners before and after 1959 was another important difference. Before 1959, most political prisoners were middle-class whites: military personnel, professionals, students, or labor union leaders. After 1959, the mix shifted lower in the socioeconomic scale. Research conducted with political prisoners who were released by 1976 and went to the United States and Venezuela shows that the vast majority of Castro's political prisoners were of peasant and working-class origin, with the remainder made up of students.[16] In addition, the current regime has imprisoned more blacks for political reasons than under previous dictatorships.

An interesting comparison in the treatment of political prisoners before and after Castro is the Communist leader's own experience following the attack upon the Moncada and Bayamo garrisons on July 26, 1953. Fidel Castro received a real trial, at which he was sentenced to fifteen years, the longest of any participant. Yet Castro and the other *moncadistas* served only about twenty months, thanks to a general amnesty Batista granted in May 1955. In his half-century rule, Castro has never granted any general amnesty.

While in prison, the *moncadistas* were allowed many privileges, including conjugal visits, a private library, radio and newspapers, volleyball and Ping-Pong, civilian clothing, and even prison personnel to clean their areas. They were separated from the common prisoners kept in the *circulares*, where the population density was much higher and overall living conditions worse. The two women nurses in the Moncada attack were sentenced to less than a year, and they were housed at the Guanajay female prison in Pinar del Rio Province. Here they had a special section redesigned for them with separate sleeping, cooking, eating, and bathing quarters.

Once Castro came to power, these conditions would never again be replicated for political prisoners.

THE REHABILITATION AND PROGRESSIVE PLANS

In 1962, penal authorities established a "Rehabilitation Plan," by which political prisoners could obtain freedom if they performed labor, wore a uniform similar to common criminals, and publicly disavowed their political beliefs. During the early 1960s, few prisoners accepted the "Rehabilitation Plan." In 1967, more than a thousand political prisoners refused to wear the blue common prisoners' uniforms, preferring the alternative of staying in their underwear.[17] The traditional khaki uniform in use since 1959 was re-established for political prisoners in 1968, and most of them accepted this. About a hundred inmates still remained in their underwear, and they were isolated from the rest. The holdouts were labeled *plantados*.[18]

In 1970, the regime adopted a "Progressive Plan" that allowed the release of the political prisoners through work, without requiring political indoctrination. Most of those who had rejected the Rehabilitation Plan accepted the Progressive Plan. In May 1983, a group of young men who had entered prison after 1979 formed the "New Political *Plantados* Prisoners" (to distinguish themselves from the earlier group that had set the example for them, referred to as "historical").[19] The *plantados* have always been secluded in areas of greater security in the prisons. They have been often held in isolation, and some have had to endure the cruellest forms of psychological and physical punishment.[20]

Poor-quality food and inadequate medical treatment have been part of the disciplinary strategy against political prisoners. Inmates at the Isle of Pines often fainted when they had to stand up during *recuentos* (recount). At the Boniato prison, inmates would swell up due to the lack of vitamins and malnutrition, and several died from these causes.

Political prisoners have been kept in overcrowded cells that are stifling in summer and freezing in winter, and lack adequate sanitary facilities. The privilege enjoyed in the pre-Castro era of keeping their choice of books was abolished. Only books approved by the government were allowed.[21]

In 1961, the prison complex at the Isle of Pines was planted with dynamite so it could be blown up if there was an attempt to free the prisoners. The explosives were left in place until after the 1962 Missile Crisis. Among the political prisoners was an expert in the use of explosives, and they were able to deactivate the detonation system in such a way as to fool the government's explosives experts.[22]

The Boniato prison near Santiago de Cuba was also planted with dynamite before the Missile Crisis, according to a former 26 of July Movement leader who was imprisoned there at the time.[23]

ASSASSINATIONS, BEATINGS, AND SUICIDES

A partial list prepared in 1987 of political prisoners killed in captivity indicated that forty-four died as a result of shootings, beatings, hunger strikes, or accidents as they were performing forced labor.[24] Eight committed suicide. The majority of the others died as a result of inadequate medical treatment. Hundreds of political prisoners have been physically crippled or psychologically impaired. Julio Tang, a young militant of the JOC (Juventud Obrera Católica—Young Catholic Workers) and former lieutenant in the Rebel Army, died on September 3, 1966, from a bayonet wound inflicted by a guard while he was doing forced labor at the Isle of Pines.[25]

One of the bloodiest events in Castro's prisons, known as the "Boniato Prison Massacre," took place in 1975. One person was assassinated and dozens wounded. Armando Valladares's account in his book, *Contra Toda Esperanza (Against All Hope)* writes:

> *The soldiers then entered the galley of the tapiadas [sealed cells] and began to open the doors. As the prisoners came out they were steered, under a shower of blows and kicks, all the way to the end of the galley.*

There were only five or six more cells left to open. The beaten prisoners hesitated. The shower of blows with sticks, bayonets, chains, did not stop; but, suddenly, as if to protect them, a skeletal man wedged himself between them and their aggressors. White haired, with smoldering eyes, he opened his arms to form a cross, lifting his head to the invisible sky . . .

"Forgive them, Lord, for they know not what they do . . . !"

The Brother of the Faith [Gerardo González] nearly didn't get to finish the phrase because Lt. Raúl Pérez ordered the guards to stand back and shot him with his AK submachine gun. The gust of fire travelled up the Brother of the Faith's chest to his neck, which was left almost disconnected, as if it had been cut through by a brutal ax. He died instantly.

Then real carnage was unleashed, organized, and systematic. Lieutenant Carranza, of the Political Police, fired his rifle and others followed suit (some 20 fell wounded). . . .

Those that were still left in the cells got machacados [minced]. Not a single prisoner was left untouched by his quota of blows in that orgy of blood and horror.[26]

Many prisoners have died under mysterious circumstances. Rafael Del Pino Siero, a Cuban-born American citizen and World War II veteran, had been a close colleague of Castro's until he turned against him in Mexico in 1956. He was later captured in a trap while flying back into Cuba to rescue some of Castro's foes in 1959. As a result of an injury, his urinary system became impaired, but he was still not released with other American citizens. The regime later claimed that he committed suicide, though witnesses dispute that.

General José Abrantes, Cuban interior minister until 1989, knew more than anyone about Castro's involvement in drug trafficking and other illegal activities. He was arrested in 1991, in excellent health at the time, but reportedly died shortly after of a heart attack.[27]

In the 1960s, Cuban penal authorities relied heavily on physical punishment. Since then, they have developed more refined and selective methods for undermining psychological balance. International humanitarian organizations have denounced the physical and psychological experiments performed on prisoners, and the lack of confidentiality of psychiatric treatment received by the population.[28]

Inmates at the Boniato prison and Kilo 7 in the early 1980s suffered particularly bad conditions. One prisoner described his experience:

[I]n July 1979, right at the time when that whole business about the "dialogue" with the "Cuban Community Abroad" was going on . . . many of us thought we were going to be pardoned (indultado) just as promised, and as was the case for some of our compañeros. But, instead, we began having problems with food and . . . discipline. . . .

They took away our visits, walled up our cells and prevented us from sunning ourselves. We went hungry. They . . . imposed the blue uniform of the common prisoner. Once again, we found ourselves clad in underpants. They then refused us medical assistance. A 33-day hunger strike was imposed on us. . . . And everything was much worse later, in November 1983, when we got thrown into Boniatico. . . . There we were totally isolated not only from the world but from the rest of the prisoners. They raised walls that went as far up as the building's roof and on top they installed an iron mesh through which not even the tiniest birds could pass. . . . The garrison was a special one from the State Security (DSE). The requisas (searches of belongings) were a daily matter, the provocations constant. No visits, no correspondence, no medical assistance, water withdrawn. It was enough to drive anyone insane.[29]

Family members of political prisoners are often harassed and used by State Security as pawns to promote the rehabilitation of their jailed relatives.[30] Prison guards routinely confiscated items brought under great sacrifice to loved ones. Political prisoners routinely were housed hundreds of miles away from their own homes making it very difficult to visit the prisoners. Female family members were subjected to humiliating body searches.

Political prisoners who completed their sentences, but refused to accept either the Rehabilitation Plan or the Progressive Plan, were "re-sentenced until total rehabilitation" without a new trial. In most cases the resentenced were jailed alongside common criminals to make their new imprisonment even more painful. They would be freed only after accepting one of the plans.[31] These additional sentences were handed down arbitrarily, based on a subjective judgment concerning the prisoner's *peligrosidad posdelictiva* (latent potential to do harm).

Castro's regime has accepted ransom payments for inmates whose families abroad had the required resources, and he used political prisoners as hostages in order to obtain political or economic benefits.[32] He did this in 1962 after the Bay of Pigs with captured members of the 2506 Brigade, and again in 1979 when the *diálogo* with a group of Cuban exiles resulted in a partial *indulto* (pardon) for 3,600 political prisoners who were allowed to emigrate mostly to the United States.[33]

The liberation of political prisoners has been used as a "gift" to please heads of state, celebrities, or institutions, such as the U.S. Catholic Church. In 1982, Castro released the poet Armando Valladares upon the request of French President François Mitterand. In 1984, to please black leader Jesse Jackson, he freed twenty-six prisoners who had completed their twenty-year sentences but were still in prison. One of them was Andrés Vargas Gómez, the grandson of Máximo Gómez, one of the leaders of Cuba's independence war against Spain. Vargas Gómez and his wife were infiltrated into Cuba five days before the Bay of Pigs Invasion, captured, and served twenty-two years in Castro's jails, most of the time as a *plantado*. In 1985, Castro took advantage of the visit by French oceanographer Jacques Cousteau to liberate other prisoners. And in 1987, he "granted" to the president of Spain the release of former Comandante Eloy Gutiérrez Menoyo.[34]

HUNGER STRIKES

Cuban political prisoners have periodically resorted to hunger strikes—a risky strategy when the government controls the media and can keep the news of the strike inside the prison walls. Pedro Luis Boitel was a former university leader and Castro supporter in 1959 who died in May 1972 after fifty-three days on hunger strike. He was refused medical assistance. His case attracted little international attention except from Cuban exiles. After his death, no funeral was allowed, and his mother was told only later where her son had been buried.[35]

Orlando Zapata Tamayo was an uneducated black masonry worker who had been involved in the defense of human rights. He died in February 2010 after eighty-five days of hunger strike, fifteen of which he'd been denied water. Unlike Boitel's many years earlier, Zapata's death caused a worldwide uproar, especially after Guillermo Fariñas, a black psychologist and dissenter, started a hunger strike.

Cuba was in a severe economic crisis, and the country desperately needed international economic assistance. Zapata's death cast Raúl Castro's regime in a negative light, and it opened the doors for the release of political prisoners that began a few months later. To satisfy international pressures without losing face, Raúl Castro asked the Catholic Church to serve as mediator. Cuban Cardinal Jaime Ortega made the announcement of the prisoners' release, sparing the government from recognition of the opposition. The potential troublemakers were then immediately deported to Spain.

FEMALE POLITICAL PRISONERS

Castro built a separate system for female political prisoners that was unprecedented in both Cuban and world history. It began in 1959 and lasted until about 1979.[36] Cuba had no female political prisoners in colonial times, and only a few during Machado's dictatorship.[37] Under Batista, only two women connected with the 1953 assault on the Moncada barracks were incarcerated, and they received a seven-month sentence.[38]

It has been impossible to accurately determine the total number of women incarcerated by Castro for political reasons. This is because some have been sent to regular prisons or prison camps (known as *granjas*). Estimates range from one thousand to five thousand.[39] All social classes have been represented among female political prisoners, who ranged in age from minors to over seventy and included housewives, shopkeepers, and peasant farmers as well as professionals.

Like their male counterparts, female political prisoners were initially segregated from common prisoners. Since the 1960s, when the government realized segregation united the political prisoners, women convicted of "counterrevolutionary" crimes have been housed with common criminals, making it harder for international human rights organizations to monitor their conditions. In fact, little was known about their predicament either within the island or abroad, and this lack of support made incarceration even more difficult, as it did for male political prisoners.

They have also been subject to overcrowding, malnutrition, poor or no medical attention, solitary confinement, beatings, violent searches, and other types of physical and psychological abuse. In prisons such as the Reclusorio Nacional de Mujeres de Guanajay in Havana, cells designed to hold one prisoner sometimes held as many as eight women. There have been many documented cases of abuse of women prisoners during both detention and incarceration.[40]

On Mother's Day in 1961, the Guanabacoa prison, just east of Havana harbor, was the site of a brutal, large-scale beating of female political prisoners.

Another major beating incident occurred in 1963 when prisoners were returning to Guanajay prison from Baracoa prison (female prisoners seem to have been transferred often, which kept them psychologically off guard.) In recent years, the penal authorities have used regular inmates to carry out beatings of political prisoners, though there have also been cases of common prisoners helping the political ones.

At the time, the Castro government limited family visits and confiscated the *jaba* (bags) they brought with medication, food, and hygiene items. Women were required to submit to a re-education plan, sometimes writing a political autobiography and confessing their errors. They had to list all their accomplices, and this had to include someone still out on the street.[41] As with the male political prisoners, those who refused to submit to re-education were known as *plantadas,* and they experienced the harshest treatment in prison.

Lydia Pérez was in the early stage of pregnancy when she and her husband were sent to prison in 1961. She died a few months later while giving birth. The death was attributed to malnutrition and inadequate medical attention in the Reclusorio Nacional in Guanajay. By the time the guards responded to her fellow inmates' cries for help and took her to the military hospital, it was too late. Neither Lydia nor her child could be saved.[42] In December of that same year, Julia González, also housed in the Reclusorio Nacional in Guanajay, died of septicemia caused by an abscessed tooth for which she was never treated.[43]

Aida Pérez López was a former nun of the Daughters of the Charity. She left her congregation in the early 1960s due to a serious heart condition. Charged with an anti-Castro political activity, she received a long prison sentence which aggravated her poor health. She died alone in the military hospital, and her family was not even allowed to bury her.[44]

The female political prison system formally ended in 1979, though women continued to be incarcerated for "economic crimes"—generally, black-market dealing.

THE CURRENT SYSTEM FOR POLITICAL PRISONERS

The Castro regime claims that there are no political prisoners in Cuba. What that means is that those categorized as "counter-revolutionaries" are housed with common criminals, making it easier for the government to control them.[45] This puts political prisoners at the mercy of the common criminals who often are encouraged by penal authorities to beat them or steal their belongings.[46] Occasionally common prisoners help the political ones, out of respect. Because political prisoners are not housed as a unit, estimates of their number are imprecise.

The practice of putting political prisoners together with common criminals was introduced in 1974 in the Morón and Kilo 7 prisons. A group of eleven political prisoners in the Morón prison were sent to live among highly dangerous common prisoners in a galley where the windows and doors were welded shut with steel plates. It was part of a psycho-sociological experiment planned by the Cuban government.

It should be pointed out that the treatment of common prisoners in Cuba is generally worse. Prison denies them their most basic rights, and the contempt for life was demonstrated by the deaths of more than thirty-five prisoners in the short span of one year at the Morón and Kilo 7 prisons.[47] According to a 1997 Amnesty International report, in a period of less than two months there were thirteen suicide attempts in the Kilo 7 and Kilo 8 prisons. The principal causes were "the harshness, the psychiatric torture, malnutrition, and the brutal treatment by the authorities." The method of suicide most commonly utilized has been cutting one's veins, along with hanging and poisoning.[48] The report also documented that both food and medicine had been denied to certain prisoners as a form of punishment.[49]

The government now tries as much as possible to avoid convicting dissidents for clearly defined political offenses. Instead, they press charges for economic crimes that would likely apply to most citizens struggling to get along in Cuba's Communist system. Many of the new political prisoners are convicted for vague crimes such as "contempt of authority," "spreading enemy propaganda," "consorting with the foreign media," and "actions against the sovereignty and independence of the national territory."

Although the "politically convicted" are more dispersed throughout Cuba, they have higher visibility due to the increased attention paid to Cuba's human rights record since the fall of the Soviet bloc.[50] This made it necessary for Cuba to improve relations with the United States and the European Union. As Castro began to court Western investors, they tolerated to some extent the growth of human rights organizations and the operation of independent journalists.[51] Through this partial "opening," the world has learned more about abuse of political prisoners. A former prisoner who spent six years in the "new system" shared his perspective: "[T]he foreign exposure that the earlier system did not have . . . enables us to communicate with the outside world and protects us. . . . This stimulates [the political prisoner] and it makes him feel like he is not alone, although he may be so physically. . . . Before, a prisoner suffered and no one knew about it. . . . Now there are international denunciations, and that is not convenient for them [the government]. The political price is very high."[52]

Because political prisoners are no longer consolidated, it's hard to know exactly how many there are in Cuba. Estimates range from five thousand in 1996,[53] to about two hundred by 2010.[54] The higher figure could be explained by the fact that many are convicted of nonpolitical offenses that are actually political in nature.[55] The current total number of prisoners in Cuban jails is somewhere between 100,000 and 200,000, distributed among 294 prisons and correctional camps throughout the island.[56]

In 1994, the family of prominent imprisoned dissident Sebastián Arcos Bergnes reported that common prisoners housed in his cell beat Arcos while trying to steal the bag of food he had tied to his hands while he slept. Arcos had been sentenced to four years and five months in 1991 for "enemy propaganda" for leading the Cuban Pro-Human Rights Committee, directed by his brother Gustavo, who had fought alongside Castro in the Moncada attack. Gustavo was seriously injured there, while another brother, Luis, who came in the Granma expedition, was killed after the landing.[57] Sebastián had been offered freedom if he agreed to leave the country, but he refused.

INTERNATIONAL CONDEMNATION AND THE PROSPECTS FOR CHANGE

According to Amnesty International, the Cuban political prison can be considered "one of the longest running in the world in terms of prisoners serving long sentences."[58] This explains why Cuban authorities have refused to allow international human rights organizations—even the Red Cross—to inspect the political prison system, interview the inmates, or investigate accusations of abuse. In late 1988, the Castro government allowed a few visits by the United Nations Human Rights Commission and other organizations to certain political prisons. They had made efforts to improve the conditions of these prisons in advance of the visits, particularly the solitary confinement cells.[59]

During the UN visit, the government arrested dozens of citizens who tried to talk to commission delegates or presented denunciations. After the visit, the government cracked down on dissidents, aiming to eliminate their leadership by mid-1989.[60] The repressive measures became more severe after the crisis involving the ministries of the Armed Forces and of Interior (MININT), which began in June of 1989 and led to the unprecedented execution of Division General and "hero of the Republic of Cuba" Arnaldo Ochoa, and three other high-ranking officials, as well as the imprisonment of the minister of interior, General José Abrantes, and various other high-ranking Army and MININT officials.[61]

Because of the problems that the 1988 UN visit caused the Cuban government, the Human Rights Commission has not been invited back. The UN and other international organizations like the Inter American Commission on Human Rights of the Organization of American States have produced reports condemning the prison situation based on the testimony of exiles who have experienced it. All of these reports emphasize the quantity and quality of food, describing it as "unfit for human consumption." They reference "the alarming lack of medical care for prisoners, most of whom are ill from the food and hygienic conditions," and they describe political prisoners who "are constantly denied medical care" with the result sometimes being death. They also report regular beatings of prisoners with the goal of either punishment or intimidation.[62]

One of the most dramatic descriptions of Cuba's political prisons was part of the 1996 United Nations report on La Manga prison, in the eastern Granma Province.

> *They placed us with highly dangerous criminals; people who suffer from personality as well as psychiatric disorders. In many cases State Security (S.S.), aware of these situations and the low moral values they have, utilize them to offend our dignity. Many are utilized by the S.S. as informants, promising them benefits if they can provide information about what we are talking about. They are also authorized to beat us if we talk badly about the President of the Republic. On another level, the penal authorities have created a system in which certain common prisoners are placed in charge of the discipline of other prisoners in exchange for certain privileges. They are highly dangerous, violent people with no scruples who employ excessive harshness.*
>
> *For any little disciplinary detail that is found, the prisoner is humiliated with*

denigrating and offensive words; and often the prisoner is savagely beaten. . . . We are taken in for grueling interrogations due to the false information that the common prisoners give, and our lives are also threatened. . . . The food is badly prepared. Many times the fish given to us is rotten. . . . They threaten to accuse those of us, who are Christian, of common crimes for doing what the authorities refer to as "proselytizing work;" we are also denied religious services because they say that we utilize those times for political ends. . . .[63]

In the early 1990s, in an effort to improve Cuba's international image, Castro relaxed some of the religious restrictions on prisoners.[64] Some political and common prisoners were liberated in 1998 upon petition by Pope John Paul II on his visit to the island that year. The majority of the former were forced to leave the country, with many going to Canada.[65]

Conditions for Cuban political prisoners did not change throughout the 2000s, nor did the number of total prisoners.[66] The Castro regime, now with brother Raúl in command, does not appear inclined to end imprisonment for political dissent. The threat of political imprisonment continues to loom over the Cuban people, like the Sword of Damocles. If anything, the pendulum has swung back toward longer sentences. In 2003, seventy-five human rights activists, opposition leaders, independent journalists, and independent librarians were sentenced up to twenty-eight years, in contrast with the 1990s, when sentences rarely exceeded ten years. Many in this group were affected by some type of illness resulting from the deplorable conditions of prisons, and the Castro government has begun releasing some of them on medical parole in the last few years. The arrest of these dissidents gained worldwide attention and their imprisonment became known internationally as the Black Spring.

As a result of the hunger strikes described previously and the death of Orlando Zapata Tamayo on February 23, 2010, the prison doors were opened partially. By mid-2011, all seventy-five dissidents detained in March and April 2003 (known internationally as Cuba's "Black Spring") had been released on condition they leave for Spain immediately, without even seeing their families.

It is clear that the Castro regime is trying to improve its international image while maintaining tight control over Cuban society. Unfortunately for the Cuban people, political incarceration will continue to exist as long as the island is ruled by a totalitarian dictatorship.

By August of 2011, General Raúl Castro's government once again began using repressive techniques against an ever-growing number of dissidents all over the island.

NOTES

1. Maria C. Werlau, based on data provided by the Cuban Commission on Human Rights and Reconciliation and recorded in the Truth Recovery Archives on Cuba, part of the Free Society Project, November 2004.
2. Author interview with Fr. Amando Llorente, S.J., May 2008. Fr. Llorente was one of Castro's former teachers at Belen School and very close to him during those years. Castro once told Fr. Llorente that he and the other teachers at Belen School "are the only family I ever had."
3. Author interviews with Santiago Touriño and other of Castro's contemporary university students, August 1997. Touriño, a lawyer, was a former law schoolmate of Castro's at the University of Havana.
4. Author interview on March 15, 1999, with Enrique Ovares, who served as FEU president around that time, and on September 9, 1999, with Gustavo Alemán, a student at the UH with knowledge of the events.
5. Author interview with Miguel A. Sanchez (*el coreano*), Castro's primary military trainer in Mexico and a firsthand witness.
6. See Dariel Alarcón Ramírez (Benigno), *Memorias de un Soldado Cubano* (Barcelona, Spain: Tusquet Editores S.A., 1997), 48-49.
7. Author interview with Guillermo Estévez in 1998. He was one of the pilots tried, who researched Pena's death after his liberation in 1979. Estévez spoke with the forensic doctor who worked on the case and was living in the U.S. The author also interviewed Comandante Antonio Michel Yabor, another member of the initial "Revolutionary Court" that acquitted the pilots.
8. See Juan Clark, *Cuba: Mito y Realidad*, 2d. ed. (Miami-Caracas: Saeta Ediciones, 1992), 151, based on the testimony of a person who shared the prison cell with Olmedo in the Cabaña Fortress.
9. Ibid., 153-54.
10. It was also used in the Iraq-Iran War. In China, with thousands executed every year, the procedure was more gruesome, since in many instances the internal organs were "harvested," taking advantage of the "clean" killing method: one bullet in the

back of the head. Some of the organs were then sold for great profit.
11. See an analysis of the political prison under Castro by Frank Calzón, *Castro's Gulag: The Politics of Terror* (Washington, D.C.: Council for Inter-American Security, 1979), 9-11. Journalists Frank Greve and Miguel Pérez estimate that Castro held up to 100,000 political prisoners up to the year 1976. See Greve and Pérez, "Castro's Jails: Still Bulging 17 Years Later," *Miami Herald*, May 23, 1976.
12. Amnesty International Report, 1978 (London, 1979). The report mentions that as of September 1977, "20,000 people have been freed upon completing their sentences."
13. Calzón, *Castro's Gulag*, 10.
14. Based on author interviews with Dr. Justo Carrillo (July 7, 1988) and Dr. Manuel Antonio de Varona (September 14, 1988). Both were leaders in the student revolutionary movement against Machado, and they were imprisoned under his regime. They also opposed Batista and Fidel Castro's totalitarian regime.
15. Before 1959, political prisoners were normally confined in one of the circulars (or in other buildings) of the Modelo prison of the Isle of Pines, built under Machado's presidency, with capacity for some twenty-five hundred inmates; in Castro's time, the total penal population would be tripled. Another important center for confining political prisoners was the Castillo del Príncipe—a military fortress from the colonial period in the Vedado area of Havana. A section of La Cabaña Fortress, built in the second half of the eighteenth century to protect Havana Bay, occasionally served as jail, particularly for military personnel and later for Castro's political prisoners. In some cases, political prisoners remained in jails located in the provinces where they resided, some dating from colonial times or built during the Republic.
16. Interviews with former political prisoners revealed that individuals from peasant and working-class background made up approximately 80 to 90 percent of the prison population.
17. Only Fidel Castro's regime has imposed a uniform on political prisoners, who prior to his rule dressed in civilian clothes of their choice.
18. The name *plantado* for Cuban political prisoners was coined at the Isle of Pines in 1964, when several prisoners refused to work in the Camilo Cienfuegos Plan of forced labor in 1964. It was said that they had "stood up the work." In time, the term was used to refer to those prisoners who had stood up for their beliefs and not accepted any kind of rehabilitation, re-education, forced labor, or common prisoner uniforms.
19. Based on "Nuevo presidio político plantado, El Diario de la 'Sección 5 de Abril, 1870'" (manuscript).
20. For an account of the mistreatment endured by a *plantado*, see the historical novel by Hilda Perera, *Plantado* (Barcelona: Editorial Planeta, 1981). Luisa Pérez and Lesbia O. Varona produced a remarkable study of the literature a group of *plantado* prisoners. See their "Cuba: Realities of a Hidden Segment—'Plantado' Political Prisoners in Boniato Prison," in *Latin American Masses and Minorities: Their Images and Realities: Papers of the 30th Annual Meeting of the Seminar on the Acquisition of Latin American Library Materials* (Princeton, N.J.: June 19-23, 1985), 74-107. See also ICOSOCV, *El Presidio Político*, 293-96.
21. To learn how Castro was able to read whatever he pleased in his own political prison (1953-1955)—including Marx's *Das Kapital*—see Carlos Franqui, *Diario de*

la revolución cubana (R. Torres, 1976), 85-89, 92, 93, 97, 111. He also specifically mentions (p. 97) Lenin's work *State and Revolution*. For an account of the difficulties in getting books inside the Isle of Pines prison during the Castro regime, see *El Presidio Político en Cuba Comunista* (Caracas: Ediciones ICOSOCV, 1982), 275-76.
22. For a detailed account of this procedure, see *El Presidio Político*, 217-33.
23. Enrique Canto Bory, *Mi Vida* (San Juan: Ramallo Bros. Printing, Inc. 1993), 363.
24. The partial list of prisoners who died in prison was prepared by former Cuban political prisoners in Miami in 1987 and sent to several international institutions working on behalf of human rights. The list contains cause of death, prison, and date of death. See also Ernesto Díaz, *Rehenes de Castro* (Miami: Linden Lane Press, 1995), 104-6, where a detailed listing is offered of twenty-eight political prisoners who died in captivity, with their dates and causes of death, and Angel Pardo, *Memorias de un Prisionero Político* (Miami: Ahora Printing, 1992), 104, 164, 190, 257, 275.
25. *El Presidio Político*, 361, 362 (testimony of Florentino Rodríguez). About this incident, see also Pardo, *Memorias*, 65.
26. See Armondo Valladares, *Contra Toda Esperanza* (Plaza & Janes Editories, 1985), 342-345. For an early account of the "Boniato Massacre," see Frank Greve and Miguel Pérez, "'Boniato Massacre': What really happened?" *Miami Herald*, May 24, 1976. Dr. Humberto Medrano's articles, in his regular column in the *Diario Las Américas*, are also a good source of information concerning brutality against political prisoners. For other, more recent sources on the "Boniato Massacre," see Pardo, *Memorias de un Prisionero Político*, 216-17, and Ernesto Díaz Rodríguez and Rehenes de Castro, *Testimonio del Presidio Político de Cuba* (Miami: Linden Lane Press, 1995), 291.
27. If there was a person that Castro would have wanted dead in prison, it was Abrantes. He had been a typical case of a very subservient official, extremely close to Castro and very cognizant of all his dealings. Persons close to Abrantes believe that a heart attack was induced in this case. Medical treatment was conspicuously delayed when the attack took place, probably to ensure its negative outcome.
28. See Calzón, *Castro's Gulag*, 43, quoting Fifth Report on the Situation of Human Rights in Cuba (June 1976). See also "Denuncian Torturas Psicológicas Bajo Castro," *El Miami Herald*, February 2, 1978, and "Siquiatras Cubanos Denuncian Torturas Sistematizadas," *Diario Las Américas*, February 16, 1978. A total of twenty-four Cuban psiquiatristas in exile denounced the systematic psychological torture inflicted upon the population, especially upon political prisoners. Of more recent publication, see Frank Calzón, "La Siquiatría Como Castigo en Cuba," *El Nuevo Herald*, February 23, 1989, and Pablo Alfonso, "Cubano Narra Abuso Siquiátrico," *El Nuevo Herald*, October 25, 1989.
29. Testimony by the former political prisoner Angel De Fana of September 15, 1984, 15. Another former prisoner who remained four years in one of these sealed, or walled-in cells at Boniatico told us how several of these military personnel members of Seguridad del Estado and the Special Brigades who kept them under custody requested to be taken out of there "because torture was not their task. . . . The cook took off his uniform right then and there, saying that he had not struggled against Batista for that." Author interview with Luis M. Zúñiga, a former political prisoner, December 15, 1988.
30. A good description of pressures imposed upon families and even of blackmail

used against them is illustrated in the case of Roberto Quintairos, who was told he could attend his mother's funeral if he would put on the uniform meant for the common criminals. This approach was used also in cases when the parent was still dying. See *El presidio político*, 424-27. See also Bárbara Gutiérrez, "Revela A. Valladares Las Torturas Mentales que Aplicaron a su Madre," *El Miami Herald*, December 13, 1982.
31. See Interamerican Commission on Human Rights, *Sexto Informe Sobre la Situación de los Presos Políticos en Cuba* (Washington, D.C.: Organización de Estados Americanos, 1980), 39-42. See also Nerin Sánchez, *Mis 6440 Días de Prisión en Cuba Roja* (Miami, 1981), 72. The cases of twenty-four persons were documented here.
32. See "Los Recondenados por Castro," *Revista Ideal*, June 1978, 12. A political prisoner wrote a letter on this matter of March 21, 1978, and smuggled it out of the Combinado del Este. Researchers have verified its authenticity. A list of eight cases involving this type of ransom was obtained. That publication does not include the names of persons who were ransomed, but the original document was given to us to examine. Later, the arrival of the liberated prisoners confirmed their reliability.
33. The Cuban government on that occasion left some six hundred political prisoners in jail (most of them the *plantados*) and said that they would not be pardoned because they had been "war criminals" (in reference to military personnel from Batista's regime, in prison since 1959) or because it was claimed they had "terrorist links." What is certain is that Castro appears to have wanted to keep several hundred prisoners to be used as future pawns for exchange and negotiation. In most cases, the excuse given to deny the pardon was false.
34. The list of prisoners who were released as a result of direct orders from Fidel Castro answering petitions from international agencies or celebrities is more extensive. Among them is the case of Roberto Martín Pérez, in 1987, thanks to the intercession of the Panamanian President General Manuel Noriega; those of Ricardo Montero and Ramón Conte in 1986, the last remaining prisoners of the 2506 Brigade, liberated thanks to the intercession of Sen. Edward Kennedy; engineer Andrés Solares, in 1988, also arranged for by Sen. Kennedy and his colleague Robert Dole in conjunction with Amnesty International; and engineer José Pujals, released in August 1988, thanks to American legislators. In 1987 and 1988 the Bishops' Catholic Conference of the United States, with New York Archbishop Cardinal John O'Connor, in particular, and with representatives from other American Protestant churches, were also able to obtain the release of more than two hundred political prisoners, who, significantly, were to travel directly from prison to the United States. It should be pointed out that, also in the 1960s and 1970s, important personalities and institutions petitioned Fidel Castro for the liberation of all political prisoners, or for that of particular individuals; on those opportunities no releases were obtained. During all those years of greatest rigor in Cuba's political prisons, exiled Cubans and other advocates of freedom and human rights—some not so well known—continued to denounce the horrors that Castro's regime was committing against Cuban political prisoners. It is mostly through them that institutions and personalities abroad were able to learn about conditions inside those jails. This motivated them to ask Castro to free certain prisoners while taking advantage of the international pressures that those denunciations have generated against his regime. Valladares' book (cited and quoted above) has been of considerable importance in getting that information

Executions and Political Prisoners 235

out to a wider public, as has been the documentary film by Jorge Ulla and Néstor Almendros, *Nobody Listened*, first released in February 1988. See the last section of this chapter for more detail on this process.

35. See the documentary *Nobody Listened*, where Boitel's mother is interviewed in the U.S. on the details of her son's case. See also J. A. Albertini, *Cuba y Castrismo: Huelgas de Hambre en el Presidio Politico* (Miami: Instituto de la Memoria Histórica contra el Totalitarismo, 2007).
36. It was when the vast majority of the women who were initially sentenced for political reasons and were kept together until their release.
37. From testimony given to the author by Dr. Gustavo León, a student of this subject, interviewed on May 7, 1998.
38. This was in sharp contrast with Castro's prison system as shown earlier. See Mario Mencía, *La Prisión Fecunda* (Havana: Editora Politica, 1980), 5, 93, 97. They were even allowed to distribute toys to the children of common prisoners on January 6, 1957, the Three Kings celebration, the traditional day to give presents to children in Cuba.
39. From various testimonies collected for this study from former female political prisoners currently residing in Miami. See also Jesús Díaz, "Una Docena de Mujeres Siguen en las Cárceles Castristas por Motivos Políticos," ABC, Madrid, May 11, 1998, and *Informe Sobre la Violación de Derechos Humanos en Cuba*.
40. One of these women, Ana Lázara Rodríguez, sentenced to thirty years in prison, served nineteen years before she was released. She provides vibrant testimony in her book *Diary of a Survivor, Nineteen Years in a Cuban Woman's Prison*, written with Glenn Garvin (New York: St. Martin's Press, 1995).
41. According to interviews with several female political prisoners.
42. Testimony of Luisa Pérez, April 4, 1998.
43. Ibid.
44. According to the 1988 testimony of Cristina Cabezas, a former political prisoner. This is a regular practice in the cases of those executed.
45. See Ana Veciana Suárez, "Groups Renew Appeals for Cuban Prisoners," *Miami Herald*, May 15, 1982.
46. Human Rights Watch, *Cuba's Repressive Machinery. Human Rights Forty Years after the Revolution* (New York: Human Rights Watch Report, 1999), 89.
47. *El Presidio Político Histórico Cubano, 50 Testimonios Urgentes* (Miami: Ediciones Universal, 1987), 35, 36 (testimony of Pablo Alfonso).
48. See Raúl Rivero, "13 Reclusos Intentan Suicidarse, Dice Informe," *El Nuevo Herald*, May 10, 1997.
49. See Pablo Alfonso, "Amnistía Pide Atención Médica Para Presos," *El Nuevo Herald*, July 20, 1997.
50. The United Nations Human Rights Commission has condemned the Castro regime for its violation of human rights from 1991 to 2003, excluding 1998. Swedish ambassador Carl-Johan Groth was named in 1991 a special rapporteur or observer for this question.
51. See Siro del Castillo, Mercedes Grandío, Andrés Hernández, and Amaya Altuna, "Lista de Organizaciones Disidentes, Opositoras y de Derechos Humanos," in *Informe sobre la Violación de los Derechos Humanos en Cuba, Enero-Diciembre 1997* (Miami: Commission on Human Rights of the Cuban Christian Democratic Party, 1998). This publication lists the names and other available information for 376

organizations.
52. Author interview with Omar del Pozo, medical doctor and former political prisoner, July 7, 1998. He was released that year and forced to go into exile.
53. See the report by Pax Christi Holland, *Cuba, la Realidad tras el Símbolo*, March 1996, 17.
54. See Castillo, Grandío, Hernández, and Altuna, *Informe Sobre la Violación de los Derechos Humanos en Cuba, Enero-Diciembre 1997*, March 1998. In this extensive work, the names, cases, and sentences of 544 persons—496 men and 48 women—are listed. By 2011, the number of persons incarcerated for politically related reasons was about one hundred. See EFE, "En Cuba Hay aún un Centenar de Presos Políticos, Según una Commision Opositora." *Diario Las Américas*, January 28, 2011.
55. See Giancarlo Summa, "An interview with Elizardo Sánchez Santa Cruz," *L'Unita* (Rome: January 22, 1997), 16.
56. See UN Commission on Human Rights, *Report on the Situation of Human Rights in Cuba* (Geneva: January 1997), 24.
57. *El Presidio Político Histórico Cubano, 50 Testimonios Urgentes* (Miami: Ediciones Universal, 1987), 35, 36 (testimony of Pablo Alfonso).
58. Amnesty International Report, 1978. This pattern has continued through the present time.
59. The prisoners called these "cosmetic" improvements as *"Plan Valladares,"* referring to the fact that they were carried out as a result of the denunciations of human rights violations in Cuba spearheaded by former political prisoner Armando Valladares, then United States ambassador to the United Nations Human Rights Commission. See Ariel Remos, "Preso Político Llegado de Cuba Relata la Golpiza a Reos y 'Mejoras' de Prisiones," *Diario Las Américas*, June 23, 1998; Pablo Alfonso, "Renuevan prisión," *El Nuevo Herald*, July 14, 1988; Ariel Remos "Exhibe Valladares en Washington Fotos que Delatan Arreglos de Castro en las Cárceles," *Diario Las Américas*, August 11, 1988; and Luciano García, "Cuba Remoza Cárceles, Dicen Presos," *El Nuevo Herald*, September 3, 1988. See also Comisión de Derechos Humanos, *Estudio del Informe*, paragraphs 67-77, pp. 24, 25.
60. See "Diezmando Movimiento Disidente Cubano," *El Nuevo Herald*, October 4, 1989.
61. See "Cuba Arrests General, Cites Corruption," *El Nuevo Herald*, June 15, 1989; "Detenido por Corrupción Otro Alto Jefe Militar Cubano," *Diario Las Américas*, June 15, 1989; "Presos en Cuba Varios Jefes Militares," *El Nuevo Herald*, June 16, 1989; "Dice Del Pino que el Grupo de Militares Arrestados fue por Apoyar la Perestroika," *Diario Las Américas*, June 17, 1989; "Ochoa al Paredón, Dicen Diplomáticos," *El Nuevo Herald*, June 20, 1989; "Cubans Disclose a Drug Network," *New York Times*, June 24, 1989; "General Facing Cuban Drug Tribunal," *New York Times*, June 25, 1989; "Comienza Juicio Contra Ochoa," *El Nuevo Herald*, June 25, 1989; "Cuba Orders Officer Tried for Treason; Execution Possible," *Miami Herald*, June 28, 1989; "Cuba Replaces Top Security Officer," *New York Times*, June 30, 1989; "Cuba Tries General, 13 Others as Scandal Widens," *Miami Herald*, July 1, 1989; "Cuba Pide Paredón Para 7," *El Nuevo Herald*, July 6, 1989; "4 Cuban Officers Sentenced to Die for Drug Trafficking," *New York Times*, July 8, 1989; "Del Pino Vincula Juicios de Ochoa en Cuba con Una 'purga política'," *Diario Las Américas*, July 12, 1989; "Dimiten 7 Generales en Purga Cubana," *El Nuevo Herald*, July 15, 1989; "Crisis Cubana se Agudiza," *El Nuevo Herald*, August 1, 1989; "Abrantes: 20 Años," *El Nuevo Herald*, September 2, 1989. For a thorough

analysis of Ochoa and Abrantes' cases, see the book of a firsthand witness who was in Cuba at that time, Norberto Fuentes, *Narcotrafico y Tareas Revolucionarias. El Concepto Cubano* (Miami: Ediciones Universal, 2002). Fuentes published this book in exile.
62. United Nations, *Report on the Situation of Human Rights in Cuba*, prepared by Ambassador Carl-Johan Groth, November 19, 1992, 17-18.
63. See United Nations Commission on Human Rights, *Informe Sobre la Situación de los Derechos Humanos en Cuba* (Geneva, February 7, 1996), 24-25.
64. Author interview with Dr. Omar del Pozo, July 7, 1998. See also AFP, "Revista Dice Impiden Actos Religiosos a los Presos," *El Nuevo Herald*, April 19, 1998. This article cites the Archdiocese of Havana's magazine *Palabra Nueva*, where the obstacles to religious services were denounced.
65. See Olance Nogueras, "Ex Presos Inician Nueva Vida en Canadá," *El Nuevo Herald*, April, 11, 1998.
66. See Comisión Cubana de Derechos Humanos y Reconciliación Nacional, "Lista Parcial de Sancionados o Procesados por Motivos Políticos o pPolítico-Sociales," Havana, July 1, 1998, which affirms that 381 convicted prisoners are awaiting trial. On the other hand, see "EE.UU. Pide Liberación de Cuatro Opositores," *El Nuevo Herald*, July 18, 1998, which presents figures that estimate around 1,000, according to the Directorio Revolucionario Cubano, and 600, according to Amnesty International.

15

THE DEFENSE OF HUMAN RIGHTS BY THE EXILES

BY JUAN CLARK

Throughout the years, Castro's revolution has been praised for its achievements in education and health. It also has been denounced for the violation of human rights. Accusations against Castro's government have focused on the deplorable living conditions of the thousands who have spent time in political prisons in Cuba. To this day, there are many still incarcerated for political reasons. Yet, in contrast to the early 1960s, political prisoners are now denied that status and are housed with common prisoners. (Details of Human Rights Violations in Cuba are in Appendix IV.)

Cuban exiles have been the most vigilant critics of the Castro regime. Their efforts to achieve worldwide awareness of the human rights abuses in their native land have done more than anything else to help political prisoners in Cuba. Though many exiles have expended great effort on behalf of this cause, a number of individuals and organizations deserve special credit. We are aware that the following account is not exhaustive and we apologize for any omissions.

An early pillar in the defense of human rights in Cuba was the distinguished journalist Humberto Medrano. In Cuba, he'd been an outspoken advocate for a free press at *Prensa Libre*, a popular daily newspaper that was confiscated by the government in May 1960. From then on, he continued his work in Miami, defending the same principles in *Diario Las Américas*.

His initial focus was the rights of political prisoners of the early 1960s. Gathering information from letters and relatives as well as other sources in Cuba, he denounced the mistreatment of the politically incarcerated in Castro's prisons. He highlighted the forced labor, inadequate nutrition, medical assistance, and living conditions, as well as the beatings and killings that were taking place, particularly at the "Model Prison" in the Isle of Pines.

In 1961, the late Luis V. Manrara founded the organization The Truth about Cuba Committee (TTCC). Manrara, a successful accountant, devoted his life in exile to informing the English-speaking public of the abusive conditions Cubans were experiencing. The TTCC produced a number of publications, and due to his excellent English, Manrara was able to make hundreds of presentations throughout the United States.

TTCC's most important contribution was the 1971 documentary *Breaking Point*, which vividly presented for the first time the desperation of the *balseros* fleeing their "workers' paradise" in makeshift rafts.[1] The work of the TTCC, which continued through the mid-1970s, was made possible by Manrara's leadership, the work of dedicated volunteers, and the donations of many exiles.

In 1974, a coalition of Cuban students, intellectuals, and civic leaders in Washington, D.C., under the leadership of the late Dr. Elena Mederos, gathered detailed information about the conditions of Cuba's political captives and distributed it to opinion leaders throughout the world. They visited newspapers, members of Congress, bishops, and labor and human rights leaders. In addition to press conferences, they published an English-language newsletter named after their organization, Of Human Rights (OHR).

Dr. Mederos was its first chairperson. In her long life (1900-1984) she campaigned for the right of Cuban women to vote, and for a return to constitutional rule in the mid-1950s. In 1959, she was named to the first revolutionary cabinet as minister of social welfare, along with a number of other respectable leaders. This was part of Castro's tactic of initially inspiring confidence in him while consolidating power. When Mederos realized Castro's true intentions, she resigned and went into exile. Upon her retirement, she moved to Washington and dedicated the rest of her life to campaigning for the release of Cuban political prisoners.

Based in a tiny room at Georgetown University, OHR became the voice in Washington for the defense of human rights in Cuba. Among other leaders of the organization were: Bishop Eduardo Boza Masvidal, who had been expelled from Cuba in 1961; Professors Carlos Ripoll of Queens College, Luis Aguilar León of Georgetown University; Juan Clark of Miami-Dade College; Filiberto Agusti, Esq.; Gerardo Mora Adelit, its first treasurer; Uva Clavijo; Dr. Claudio Benedí; Carlos Alberto Montaner; Bishop Agustín Román; Oilda del Castillo; and Frank Calzón, its executive secretary. It also included a number of non-Cubans, including British Historian Hugh Thomas, former Filipino foreign minister Raúl Manglapus, and Professor Jeane Kirkpatrick, who later served as U.S. ambassador to the UN.

Just like Amnesty International, OHR "adopted" cases and concentrated on them until the prisoner was released. Among the first cases pursued were former rebel Comandante Húber Matos, poet Armando Valladares (who later served as U.S. ambassador to the UN), and writer Heberto Padilla. The organization was non-partisan on all issues other than human rights in Cuba. Its funding campaigns asked for both contributions and the names and addresses of others interested in Cuba who might also donate to the cause. It sponsored raffles, concerts, lectures, and poetry recitals.

Frank Calzón became the executive secretary of OHR and continued to provide leadership for human rights in other organizations.[2] He has extensive media contacts, writes articles, and testifies before the U.S. Congress. In 2004, after testifying before the UN Commission on Human Rights in Geneva, Calzón was attacked by a member of the

Castro delegation and knocked unconscious.

Another important organization, the CEDEHU (Center for Human Rights) was formed in Miami in 1974. Initially operating under the aegis of the Christian Democratic Movement of Cuba (MDC), the CEDEHU has been led by Jesús Permuy along with former political prisoner Alcides Martínez Calzadilla and former labor leader Rafael Naranjo. They collected information from direct contacts with human rights activists within the island as well as recent arrivals, documented violations of human rights, and presented to the UN Commission for Human Rights in 1976. As a non-governmental organization, they were granted a seat at the annual meeting of the forum, where they confronted the Castro delegation face to face. For more than a decade, the expenses of sending the CEDEHU's delegation to Geneva were raised through radio marathons in Miami.

Father Miguel A. Loredo was a member of CEDEHU's delegation to Geneva. He had served ten years out of a fifteen-year sentence for a crime he did not commit.[3] His participation enabled the documentation of human rights violations for political prisoners, with special focus on the type of religious persecution he had suffered.

Armando Valladares, poet and writer, was a political prisoner for twenty-two years. His nutritional deficiencies due to hunger strikes put him in a wheelchair. Thanks to the mediation of French President Francois Mitterand, Armando was freed in 1982. He organized in Paris a "trial" on the performance of Castro's government concerning the violation of human rights and wrote *Against All Hope*, which described the appalling prison conditions in Cuba. It was a worldwide bestseller and was translated into sixteen languages.

His book was so powerful that President Ronald Reagan named Valladares ambassador to the UN Commission of Human Rights in 1987. While in that post, he sent a commission to Cuba to investigate firsthand the situation of human rights. The commission confirmed that practically all the thirty articles of the 1948 Declaration were being violated. Valladares earned the second highest award for civilians in the U.S.—the Citizens' Presidential Medal, and the State Department's Superior Award. After leaving his ambassadorial position, he organized support committees in thirteen countries to promote the cause of human rights in Cuba.

The northeast region contains the second largest concentration of Cuban exiles in the U.S. In 1988, Guillermo Estevez, who served twenty years in a Cuban jail,[4] organized a collective, multi-city hunger strike demonstration for former political prisoners throughout the Northeast, as well as Washington, D.C., Miami, Tampa, Los Angeles, and New Orleans. The biggest demonstration took place in New York, in front of UN Headquarters. This attracted considerable media attention and UN secretary general Javier Pérez de Cuellar promised to take action. Later that year, a UN commission went to Cuba.

The Foundation for Human Rights in Cuba (FHRC) was created by the Cuban American National Foundation in 1992 to educate governments and international human rights organizations on Cuban human rights violations. The FHRC collects evidence and disseminates it to the media, universities, and international organizations. They have participated in UN forums in Geneva thanks to the Nicaraguan government, which allowed the foundation's representative a seat as part of their delegation. They maintain a website and provide technical assistance and material support to organizations in Cuba that promote human rights.

The FHRC developed the "Quilt of Fidel Castro's Genocide," as a memorial to his victims. It consists of eight-by-ten-inch panels sewn together with the names of the executed, along with date and manner of death. The quilt contains 11,000 documented cases of deaths under Castro's totalitarian dictatorship. The FHRC also created a replica of the punishment cells for political prisoners. Luis Zuñiga Rey, a former political prisoner who managed to escape from Cuba, founded FHRC and was succeeded by Omar López Montenegro, a Cuban intellectual and human rights activist who later became an exile.

MAR (Mothers and Women Against Repression) is an organization of women who are related to political prisoners or victims of executions. It was founded in 1994 and has participated in many national and international events, as well as in the UN Commission for Human Rights annual meeting in Geneva, the European Union Parliament, the Ibero-American Summits, and the OAS (Organization of American States) annual meeting, among others.

MAR's sole funding source is private donations from the organization's directors and members, as well as the broader exile community. Silvia Iriondo has led MAR for many years. She was in one of the three spotting planes from Brothers to the Rescue (BTTR) that were attacked by Castro's MiG fighters on February 24, 1996. MAR denounced the action of the Cuban military in downing two of the planes and killing four members of Brothers to the Rescue.[5]

The Cuban Committee for Human Rights (CCPDH) was founded by Gustavo Arcos Bergnes and Ricardo Bofill, while in prison during the early 1980s. Before becoming a vocal dissident, Arcos had been involved with Castro's revolution since 1953. Bofill was forced to leave Cuba in 1988 due to the harassment of State Security. In exile he continued the work of the committee with the help of other exiles such as Eddy López Castillo. The CCPDH publishes the periodical *Siglo XXI*, which is now disseminated through the Internet. Bofill directs a daily program on Radio Martí.

Dr. Martha Frayde, another founder of the CCPDH, publishes a bulletin in Spain three times a year. It is aimed at Spanish citizens but also other Spanish-speaking countries. The CCPDH of Venezuela, led by Dr. Silvia Meso Pérez de Corcho, published *Cuba ¿Derechos Humanos?*, a 481-page book that was the result of the 1991 International Conference on human rights in Cuba. It also published a brief report on the July 1994 sinking of the tugboat *13 de Marzo* called *Un Crimen Sin Castigo*.

The Cuban Municipalities in Exile represents most of the municipalities that existed in the pre-Castro era. They created the National

Commission of Human Rights to develop a consciousness both abroad and within the island in the respective municipalities of the nature of human rights and how they are violated by Castro's government. The leaders of the Cuban Municipalities in Exile were the late educator Dr. Moravia Capó and the Rev. Miguel Tudela.

The Directorio Democrático Cubano was founded in 1990 with the mission of providing a bridge between human rights activists in Cuba and the international organizations that track violations worldwide. The *Directorio* participates in meetings of the UN Commission on Human Rights, as well as that of the Organization of American States (OEA) and Latin American and European parliaments. They have made presentations to the national parliaments of Europe and Latin America and facilitated the participation in those forums of victims of human rights violations who have managed to flee the island.

Every year, the *Directorio* publishes a detailed list of violations and special reports about political imprisonment. In 2009 the *Directorio* also published a special report on torture in Cuba that was presented to the OAS. In 2005 they published the book *Boitel Vive* (Boitel Lives),[6] written in prison by Jorge Luis García Pérez (Antunez).

The Coalition of Cuban-American Women (CC-AW), established in Miami in 1996, has the motto "For the Love of Homeland and Humanity." In addition to ongoing support for human rights in Cuba, its special focus is the plight of women and children affected by political imprisonment and executions. The coalition has an active Internet presence and a juvenile chapter called Ismaelillos, made up of children of numerous nationalities. It tries to instill in children the importance of a free society, of civic duty in a democracy, and the value of human solidarity. CC-AW is led by Laida Carro, Lucrecia Rodríguez, Isolina González, and María Luisa Abreu.

The Committee for the Human Rights of Children is a non-profit educational organization founded in Miami in 1999. It has been led by child psychiatrist Dr. Lidia Usátegui, M.D.,[7] and founders included physicians, educators, and human rights activists. They produced a documentary titled *Made in Cuba: Children of Paradise*. Completely financed with their own resources, the film provides an inside look at the lives of children under Castro and highlights why rafters—many of whom are young—risk their lives at sea to reach freedom. It premiered in February 2001 at the Miami International Film Festival, and has been viewed by over six million people worldwide. In May 2003 it was selected for distribution to all 374 educational U.S. public PBS TV stations.

There have been many books written on the conditions of political prisoners in Cuba, and its violations of the Universal Declaration. Some of the best include:

Human Rights in Cuba: An Experiential Perspective (as well as its Spanish version *Los Derechos Humanos en Cuba: Una perspectiva Vivencial*), by Juan Clark, Angel de Fana, and Amaya Sánchez (Coral Gables: Research Institute for Cuban Studies, North/South Center, University of Miami, Saeta Ediciones, 1991). This was the first major work analyzing the application of the thirty articles of the UN Declaration, based on firsthand testimony. Also by the same authors *Los Derechos Humanos en Cuba: Una Perspectiva Vivencial* (Caracas-Miami: Saeta Ediciones, 1988).

Human Rights. The Theme of Our Times, by Dr. Claudio Benedí, 2d ed. (St. Paul, Min.: Paragon House, 1998), presents a historical perspective on human rights in Cuba and introduces the concept of the institutional violation of those rights.

Prof. Carlos Ripoll, who died in 2011, presented a comprehensive analysis to the U.S. House of Representatives: *Human Rights in Cuba*. He deals in-depth with freedom of expression, using the cases of dissidents Ariel Hidalgo and Ricardo Bofill. Dr. Ripoll has also written numerous articles and monographs dealing with the subject of human rights in Cuba.

NOTES

1. Ariel Remos, "'Breaking Point', el Documental que Ilustraría a la Opinión Publica Americana Sobre la Tragedia de Cuba," *Diario Las Americas*, October 23, 1971, p. 1B.
2. These have been the Cuban American National Foundation, Freedom House, and the Center for a Free Cuba.
3. For further details, see Juan Clark, *Cuba: Mito y Realidad*, 2d ed. (Miami-Caracas: Saeta Ediciones, 1992), 339-341.
4. Estevez, a former military pilot with the deposed regime, was sentenced early in 1959 to thirty years imprisonment after being acquitted by a Revolutionary Court, together with other pilots and mechanics. Castro disliked that verdict and ordered another trial, violating a basic legal principle as well as human rights. It is said that Castro wanted the death penalty for the pilots. Estevez was freed in 1979 and came to the U.S., becoming a great activist in the cause of human rights. For more details see Clark, *Cuba*, 68-69.
5. Four Cuban-Americans perished in this sort of "extra-judicial" killing. The two Cuban MiG fighters went unchallenged by nearby American fighter planes stationed in Key West.
6. Pedro Luis Boitel was a University of Havana student leader who initially was a strong Castro supporter, and after realizing the magnitude of his betrayal of his own promises of democratic restoration, turned against him and was sentenced to thirty years imprisonment. He died in 1972 after a hunger strike of fifty-two days after being denied proper medical assistance.
7. Dr. Usátegui was very involved in the Elián González case. This case gave Dr. Usátegui great insight about the conditions of children in Cuba.

16

THE CUBAN DIASPORA

BY LEONARDO RODRIGUEZ

Fidel Castro's rule transformed Cuba from an immigrant nation to an emigrant one. The exodus of over a million people represents about 15 percent of the population who have chosen to abandon the country they love for greater freedom in another nation.

In surveys of recent arrivals from Cuba, a majority cite human rights violations as their primary motivation for fleeing their homeland.[1] Given that Cuba was one of the original architects of the 1948 UN Human Rights Declaration, it is ironic that the current government has been condemned for the violation of those rights before the UN Commission of Human Rights in Geneva.

They are fleeing a country very different from what it once was. Castro's totalitarian regime has ruined the economy. Once ranking near the top of Latin American countries in most important economic indicators, Cuba has fallen to the bottom. Formerly the world's largest exporter of sugar, the island now has to import it. It went from producing 80 percent of its own food to 20 percent, even turning to the United States in recent years in order to feed its people. The deteriorating infrastructure in Havana and other cities further contributes to an appallingly low standard of living, which has also motivated Cubans to seek exile.

Today, more than fifty years after the inception of the Cuban Revolution, Cubans in exile can be found in many different countries.

The Cuban diaspora has not only changed the face of its native land, but of the many destinations that the exiles found.

THE UNITED STATES

Exiles living in the United States, mainly in South Florida, represent 55 percent of the diaspora. Cubans have been coming to the United States since the nineteenth century, usually due to temporary changes in political and economic circumstances. But the early emigrations were relatively small in numbers, and in most cases the exiles returned to Cuba when the government changed hands. A combination of geographical proximity, history, existing commercial relationships, and, above all, the open-arms reception made the United States the ideal place for exiles from the Cuban Revolution to go.

The first large wave left on regular commercial flights until the 1962 Missile Crisis when those were stopped. After 1965, many left through the Freedom Flights—a program of twice daily flights sponsored by President Lyndon Johnson. These lasted until 1973, bringing 265,000 new political refugees to the U.S. In 1980, the Mariel Boatlift added another 125,000 Cubans to the United States. In 1994, over 38,000 Cubans were allowed to flee the island in makeshift rafts during a period of three months. This exodus followed in the tradition of thousands of rafters who had illegally attempted that avenue since the early 1960s, often using inner tubes as floating devices. It is estimated that only one in three made it.[2]

A 1984 agreement between the U.S. and Cuba stipulated that up to twenty thousand Cubans would be admitted annually. Between the late 1980s and early 1990s, the United States admitted an average of only twenty-five hundred per year. As social pressures mounted in their homeland, Cubans began to bypass official channels and attempt to reach the U.S. shores by whatever means were available. In 1994, U.S.

authorities intercepted 36,791 rafters.[3]

As shown in Appendix V: The Cuban Diaspora by the Numbers, the number of Cubans in the U.S. has continued to increase throughout the last fifty years. According to the 2010 U.S. Census, Cubans represent approximately 3.5 percent of the Hispanics in this country.

From the very beginning of the Cuban diaspora, Miami-Dade County, and the city of Miami in particular, was the preferred destination. 228,805 Cuban refugees registered at the Cuban Refugee Emergency Center in Miami between 1961 and 1966. Of these, 134,945 refugees were resettled to other parts of the United States, though many of these eventually decided to return and make Miami-Dade their home.[4] Table II in Appendix V shows the gradual "Cubanization" of Miami-Dade over the years.

Bergen and Hudson counties in New Jersey—and particularly the town of Union City—became a magnet for Cuban exiles. The first Cubans who arrived in Union City, N.J., in the decades of the 1940s and 1950s came mostly from New York City. According to Yolanda Prieto's book *The Cubans of Union City Immigrants and Exiles in a New Jersey Community*, these first Cuban arrivals originally were from small towns and rural areas from the province of Santa Clara in the center of Cuba.

The arrival of more exiles in the 1960s gave Union City its Cuban profile. Even before the arrival of Mariel refugees, the Cuban population of Union City was 18,000.[5]

Union City is one of twelve municipalities in Hudson County, N.J., all of which became home to Cuban exiles. During the decades of the 1990s and the 2000s, however, the Cuban population started to decline, as shown in Tables III, IV, and V of Appendix V.

PUERTO RICO

Shortly after the beginning of the exodus, many Cubans decided to move to Puerto Rico. At that time, Gov. Luis Muñoz Marín—who very generously opened his arms to Puerto Rico's Caribbean neighbors fleeing the Communist dictatorship—governed the island. In the first half of the 1960s, a wave of intellectuals, artists, and businessmen arrived in Puerto Rico and quickly integrated in their new adopted country.

At its peak, the Cuban presence in Puerto Rico reached more than thirty thousand people who left a positive mark in business, industry, and the arts.[6] Given the close cultural and ethnic ties between the two islands, children and grandchildren of the exiles often married Puerto Ricans, and this led to what are affectionately known as *cubarriqueños*.

It was the reverse of what had occurred in Cuba in the early twentieth century, when the Republic was established, and between twenty thousand and twenty-five thousand Puerto Ricans were fully integrated into Cuban society.

According to José A Coba and Jorge Duany's book *Cubans in Puerto Rico: Ethnic Economy and Cultural Identity*, there was a rapid increase in migration followed by a gradual decline in the Cuban population. Five hundred thirty-eight Cubans emigrated in 1960, 26,000 in 1970, and 30,410 in 1971.[7] The 1980 Census identified 22,811 Cuban-born residents in 1980 and 19,736 in 1990.[8]

Table VI in Appendix V details the corresponding numbers for the 2000 Census as well as the 2005 Estimate of the General Demographic Characteristics for Puerto Rico by the American Community Survey.

SPAIN

The close relationship between Cuba and Spain is the result of history, culture, language, and family. Between the second half of the nineteenth century and the first half of the twentieth, there was considerable emigration of Spaniards to Cuba. In 1899, there were 125,000 Spaniards on the island. Between 1910 and 1925, Cuba absorbed one third of all Spanish immigrants to Latin America—almost 100,000 in 1920 alone. By 1930, there were 257,596 Spaniards in the island. Between 1946 and 1958 the immigration of Spaniards to Cuba decreased to less than 20,000.[9]

The start of the Cuban Revolution in 1959 signaled the practical end of the immigration from Spain to Cuba. It is often forgotten that the foreigners most affected by the expropriations and nationalizations were not Americans, but the Spaniards who owned much of the wholesale and retail trade sector in Cuba. In the early 1960s, Cuban citizens born in Spain began to return. By 1970, only 74,026 Spaniards remained. The number fell further to 60,000 by 1980 and only 1,184 by 1994.[10]

Tracking the Cuban diaspora in Spain since 1959 is tricky because many Cubans went to Spain first, on their way to the United States. The estimated number of Cubans who arrived in Spain during the 1960s ranges from 125,000 to 200,000—but at least 80,000 of them subsequently went on to the United States.[11] These were the original exiles, one of three clearly defined groups differentiated by ideology and time.[12]

By the mid-1970s, the next group of *Hispanocubanos*, the "children of the revolution," started to arrive. This group typically chose to come to Spain or Europe rather than the United States for political reasons, according to Mette Louise Berg.[13] Finally, after the collapse of the Soviet Union and the resulting economic crisis in Cuba, the third group—economic immigrants—began to arrive in Spain. Six thousand ninety-seven arrived in 1995 and 27,323 in 2003, according to Pilar González Yanci and José Aguilera Arilla in their research paper, "La Immigración Cubana en España. Razones Políticas y de Sangre en la Elección del Destino."

The *Padrón Municipal de Habitantes,* published by the Instituto Nacional de Estadística (INE), reports 10,000 Cubans emigrated to Spain in 2007, and the Cuban community in Spain reached 91,886 by January 2008.[14]

In the future, the number of Cubans emigrating to Spain will likely increase due to a 2007 Spanish law which allows the descendants of those who went into exile after the 1936-1939 Spanish Civil War to apply for Spanish citizenship.

Most recently, in an interview with the Spanish news service *EFE*, the undersecretary of Spain's Ministry of Fomento (Development), Jesús Miranda, cited a figure of 104,000 Cubans living in Spain. This interview appeared on June 28, 2011, in *El Nuevo Herald* in Miami.

VENEZUELA

Estimates of *venecubanos* range from forty thousand to fifty thousand. At the time of the Cuban Revolution, Rómulo Betancourt was the president of Venezuela. For a time during the late 1940s and early 1950s, Betancourt had lived in exile in Cuba. He did not like Castro, being convinced that Fidel wanted to establish a Soviet-style Communist dictatorship in Cuba.

As in the United States, the Cuban exiles in Venezuela became prominent in television, radio, advertising, sugar processing, and commercial activities of various kinds. In just a few years, most of the exiles—even though they arrived penniless in Venezuela—were among the middle and upper social classes of the country and showed a remarkable level of integration. When Hugo Chavez came to power, many of these families fled the country, almost always for the United States.

OTHER COUNTRIES

There are large Cuban communities in several other nations. In Mexico, some 80,000 Cubans obtained visas to settle in that country, though many then moved on to the United States. Recent reports indicate that 6,647 Cubans live in Mexico.[15] In Chile, there are an estimated 20,000 Cubans. In the case of Ecuador, the news agency *Agence France Presse* (AFP) has reported that since 2006 some 64,310 Cubans have arrived in that country and that about 56,180 subsequently went elsewhere.[16]

There are an estimated 15,000 Cubans in the Dominican Republic. There is even a small Cuban community in Moscow—what remains of the thousands of students who experienced the end of Communism, and decided not to return to Cuba. At one time they were called in Cuba the "red worms."

According to a variety of sources,[17] the other leading destinations for the Cuban diaspora, with the year estimated where available, are:

Italy 15,883 (2008)
Canada 14,110 (2006)
Germany 8,383 (2002)
Argentina 2,377
Sweden 1,549 (2001)
United Kingdom 1,083
France 880 (1999)
Brazil 761
Australia 493 (2006)
Denmark 271 (2003)
Finland 180 (2001)
Greece 125 (2001)
Ireland 100 (2002)

The sad truth is that Cubans are willing to emigrate en masse to anyplace that will open its doors to them. Such was not the case before the revolution of the Castro brothers.

NOTES

1. Juan Clark, *Cuba: Mito y Realidad*, 2d ed. (Miami-Caracas: Saeta Ediciones, 1992), 31-36.
2. *U.S. History Encyclopedia*, "Cuban Americans," http://w.w.w.Answers.com/topic/cuban-americans.
3. Ibid.
4. The Research Institute for Cuba and the Caribbean Center for Advanced International Studies University of Miami, Coral Gables, Florida. *The Cuban Immigration 1959-1966 and Its Impact on Miami-Dade County, Florida*. A Study for the Department of Health, Education and Welfare United States Government. Contract: HEW WA-66-05, July 10, 1967. Appendix B. Table 3 Cubans in Dade County, 1960-1966.
5. Yolanda Prieto, *The Cubans of Union City Immigrants and Exiles in a New Jersey Community* (Philadelphia: Temple University Press, 2009), 26.
6. José A. Cobas, Jorge Duany. *Cubans in Puerto Rico: Ethnic Economy and Cultural Identity*. (Gainesville: University Press of Florida, 1997), 41.
7. Ibid., 41.
8. Ibid., 41-42.
9. Pilar González Yanci and José Aguilera Arilla, *La Inmigración Cubana en España: Razones Políticas y de Sangre en la Elección de Destino* (UNED. Espacio, Tiempo y Forma Serie VI, Geografía, t.15, 2002), 14-15.
10. Ibid., 16.
11. Mette Louise Berg, "Cubans in Spain: Memory, Politics and Diaspora," in *Cuba: Idea of a Nation Displaced*, ed. Andrea O'Reilly Herrera (Albany: State University of New York Press, 2007), 18-26.
12. Ibid., 18-26.
13. Ibid., 21.
14. Michel Suarez, "Casi Diez Mil Cubanos se Instalaron en España el Año Pasado," http://www.cubaencuentro.com, Madrid, September 23, 2008.
15. Migration Policy Institute Data Hub, Migration Facts, Stats, and Maps: Country and Comparative data, http://www.migrationinformation.org/datahub/countrydata/data.cfm.
16. *El Nuevo Herald*, September 9, 2010, *Agence France Presse*.
17. Migration Policy Institute Data Hub, Migration Facts, Stats, and Maps: Country and Comparative data, http://www.information.org/datahub/countrydata/data.cfm.

Fig. 1. View of Old Havana. From left to right: *Capitolio Nacional*, *Centro Gallego* and *Inglaterra* Hotel.

Fig. 2. Corner of Galiano and San Rafael streets, downtown Havana, 1950s.

Fig. 3. Batista inside Columbia Barracks in midst of coup d'etat, Havana, March 10, 1952. (*Revista Bohemia*, 1959)

Fig. 4. Fidel Castro with Ernesto "Ché" Guevara in August 2, 1961, Havana, Cuba. (UPI Photo)

Fig. 5. Father Domingo Lorenzo, January 17, 1959, Matanzas, Cuba. José Cipriano Rodríguez holds a crucifix as he kneels before the priest a short while before Rodríguez was executed. He was found guilty by a military tribunal in a summary trial for the deaths of two. (Corbis Image)

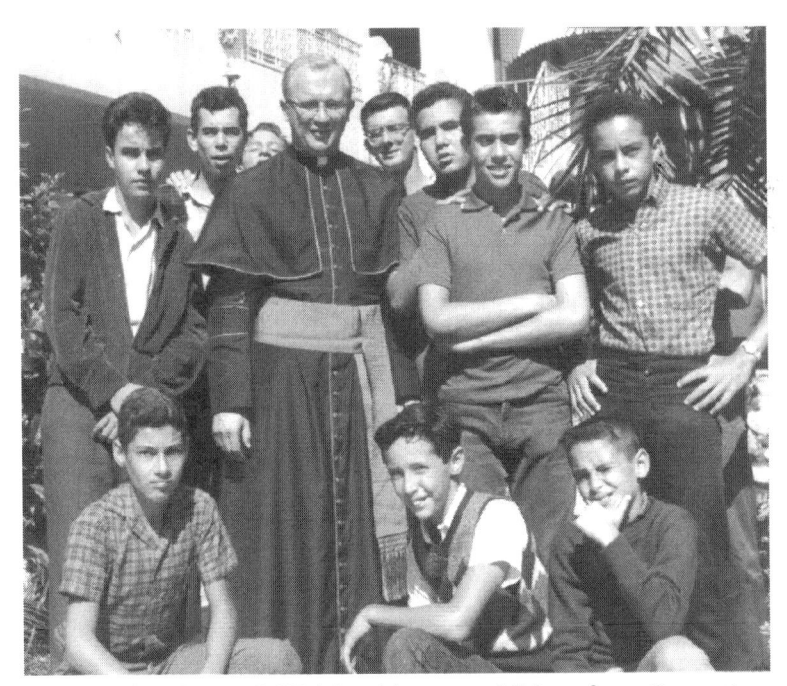

Fig. 6. Father Bryan O. Walsh with some children from Operation Pedro Pan. (Photo courtesy of Barry University Archives)

258   Cubans: An Epic Journey

Fig. 7. President John F. Kennedy receiving the 2506 Brigade flag from Erneido Oliva and Manuel Artime at Orange Bowl Stadium. Miami, December 29. 1962. (*Miami Herald*)

Fig. 8. Soviet freighter (top), loaded with nuclear missiles removed from Cuban soil by U.S. demands, being escorted by American destroyer outside Cuban waters during the 1962 Missile Crisis. (Getty Images)

Fig. 9. Cuban exile raids on Cuba after the Bay of Pigs from gunboats based in Monkey Point Bay, Nicaragua. (Photo courtesy of Jim Nickless)

Fig. 10. Camarioca Exodus from Cuban port of Camarioca, 1965. (U.S. Coast Guard)

Fig. 11. Cuban refugees disembarking at Miami International Airport from a chartered DC8. More than 270,000 Cubans were airlifted out of Cuba from 1965 to 1973 in Operation Freedom Flights. (*Miami Herald*)

Fig. 12. Peruvian Embassy in Havana is crammed to full capacity by 10,800 freedom-seeking Cubans in April 1980. (latinamericanstudies.org)

Fig. 13. The Mariel Boatlift brought 125,000 Cubans to the U.S. in 1980, following the incident at the Peruvian Embassy in Havana. (*Miami Herald*)

Fig. 14. Mario Chanes de Armas (1927-2007), a former ally of Fidel Castro in the Moncada Barracks attack became one of the longest political prisoners in history after thirty years of harsh imprisonment. (Delio Regueral)

Fig. 15. Three Cuban rafters beg to be rescued during 1994 mass exodus. The U.S. Coast Guard took around 34,000 to Guantánamo Bay awaiting decision on what to do with them. Eventually, President Clinton allowed all to come to the U.S. (latinamericanstudies.org)

Fig. 16. Elián González is taken away by U.S. agents from the arms of Donato Dalrymple, one of the pair of fishermen that had rescued him from the ocean after Elián's mother drowned trying to get her son to liberty in the United States. Miami, April 22, 2000. (Alan Díaz, AP)

Fig. 17. Ladies in White (*Damas de Blanco*) opposition movement by wives and female relatives of jailed dissidents protest attending mass and silently walking the streets. They received from the European Parliament the 2005 Sakharov Prize for Freedom of Thought.

Fig. 18. Cuban exile Jorge Mas Canosa (1939-1997) built the Cuban American National Foundation, the most effective lobbying group in Washington against the Cuban Communist regime. He was considered the leading figure in the Cuban exile community. In the back: "Pepe" Hernández, a CANF director. (*Miami Herald*)

Fig. 19. Roberto Goizueta (1931-1997) was chairman, director, and CEO of the Coca-Cola Company from 1981 until his death. He is credited with invigorating the company with a global vision. (University of Miami, Cuba Heritage Collection)

Fig. 20. Benjamín León, Jr., emigrated to U.S. with his family in 1961. In 1964, his father founded the first pre-paid medical center in Miami. Under León, Jr., Leon Medical Centers is a leading health provider for Medicare recipients. (Leon Medical Center)

Fig. 21. Armando Codina is a Cuban-American self-made millionaire. A prominent figure in real estate and Miami civic and community activities, Codina sits on the board of a number of corporations, companies, and organizations. He is chairman and chief executive officer of Codina Partners, LLC, a firm based in Coral Gables. (armandocodina.org)

Fig. 22. Carlos Gutiérrez's family flew to U.S. in 1960 when he was six years old. Gutiérrez currently serves as vice chairman of Citigroup's Institutional Clients Group. He was the 35th U.S. Secretary of Commerce (2005-2009). Gutiérrez is a former chairman of the Board and CEO of the Kellogg Company. (Official U.S. Photo)

Fig. 23. Saxofonist, clarinetist, and composer Paquito D'Rivera was a child prodigy in Cuba. He was a founding member of the band Irakere. Paquito sought assylum in the American Embassy in Madrid in 1981. His first GRAMMY came in 1996. He received two nominations for Jazz-ClaZZ. (paquitodrivera.com)

Fig. 24. Renowned Cuban exile singer Celia Cruz (1925-2003), "The Queen of Salsa," earned twenty-three gold albums. Her music is prohibited in Cuba. Singer Willy Chirino came to the U.S. in "Operation Pedro Pan." His "Ya viene llegando" or "The Day is Coming" has become an anthem for Cuban exiles hoping to see a free Cuba. (*Miami Herald*)

Fig. 25. Gloria Estefan is a Cuban singer with over 100 million albums sold worldwide. She has won seven Grammy Awards. Her husband Emilio Estefan, Jr., is a Cuban musician who founded the Miami Sound Machine band and is the producer of many famous singers. (*Miami Herald*)

Fig. 26. Andy García is a Cuban actor. He appeared in *The Godfather: Part III*, *The Untouchables*, *Internal Affairs*, *When a Man Loves a Woman*, *Ocean's Eleven*, and its sequels, and *The Lost City*. García was nominated for the Academy Award for Best Supporting Actor for his role as Vincent Mancini in *The Godfather: Part III*. (*Miami Herald*)

Fig. 27. Olga Guillot (1922-2010) was a Cuban singer known as "The "Queen of Bolero." Guillot opposed Fidel Castro's regime early on. In 1961, she began exile in Mexico City. Her music is prohibited in Cuba. (*Miami Herald*)

Fig. 28. Cundo Bermúdez (1914-2008) was a Cuban painter. His works are exhibited in museums all around the world. In 1994, Sothebys honored him on his eightieth birthday. In 2000, the Cuban American Endowment for the Arts published "Cundo Bermudez," a formidable full-color book published at a cost of approximately $250,000. (Delio Regueral)

Fig. 29. Trumpet virtuoso Arturo Sandoval was granted political asylum in the U.S. in 1990. A protégé of the legendary master Dizzy Gillespie, he evolved into one of the world's most acknowledged guardians of the jazz trumpet. Sandoval has been awarded four Grammy Awards, six Billboard Awards, and an Emmy Award. (Delio Regueral)

Fig. 30. Hall of Famer Atanasio (Tony) Pérez, is a former Major League Baseball player. Pérez was a key member of Cincinnati's "Big Red Machine," and also played for the Montreal Expos, the Boston Red Sox, and the Philadelphia Phillies. After retiring, Pérez went on to manage the Reds and Florida Marlins. The Reds retired his #24.

Fig. 31. Guillermo Cabrera Infante "Cain" (1929-2005) was a Cuban writer who went into exile in London in 1965. He is best known for his novel *Tres Tristes Tigres*, compared favorably to James Joyce's *Ulysses*. In 1997, he received the Premio Cervantes, presented to him by King Juan Carlos of Spain.

Fig. 32. Mgsr. Agustín Román (1928-2012). Ordained in 1959 and expelled from Cuba in 1961 along with another 130 priests. From 1962 to 1966, he was spiritual director and professor at the Institute of Humanities in Temuco, Chile. In 1979, he was named by Pope John Paul II as the auxiliary bishop of the Archdiocese of Miami. (*Miami Herald*)

Fig. 33. Modesto Maidique, a graduate of MIT was the president of Florida International University for twenty-three years. During his tenure, the Colleges of Law and Engineering and the Schools of Architecture and Medicine were founded. (FIU)

Fig. 34. Eduardo Padrón arrived in the U.S. as a refugee at age fifteen. Since 1995, he has served as president of Miami Dade College. He is widely recognized as one of the top educational leaders in the world, often invited to participate in educational policy forums in the U.S. and abroad. (MDC)

Fig. 35. Goar Mestre (1912-1993) studied at Yale University. A radio and television entrepreneur he built Radiocentro, a Radio City-style complex in Havana. In 1960, his properties were confiscated and Mestre exiled in Buenos Aires, where he pioneered television in Argentina.

Fig. 36. Mario Díaz-Balart, Ileana Ros-Lehtinen, and Lincoln Díaz-Balart from Miami, were all at one time U.S. representatives from Florida. Conservatives on foreign and economic policy, they support continued sanctions against the Castro regime. (*Miami Herald*)

Fig. 37. Cuban-American David Rivera was born in New York City and moved to Florida in 1974. He earned a bachelor of arts degree with honors in Political Science from Florida International University in 1986 and an MPA in 1994. Rivera was elected U.S. representative from Florida in 2010. (rivera.house.com)

Fig. 38. Mel Martínez served as chairman of the Republican Party (2006-2007). He served as secretary of housing and urban development under President George W. Bush. He was the first Cuban to serve in the U.S. Senate. Martinez resigned from the Senate in 2008. (Official U.S. photo)

Fig. 39. Bob Menéndez was elected to the U.S. Senate in 2006. Previously, he was a member of the U.S. House of Representatives, from New Jersey, mayor of Union City (1986–1992), and member of the New Jersey General Assembly and the New Jersey Senate. (Official U.S. photo)

Fig. 40. Born to Cuban exile parents, Marco Rubio earned his law degree from the University of Miami. In the 1990s, he served as a city commissioner in West Miami and later as speaker of the Florida House of Representatives becoming a U.S. Senator in 2010. (Official U.S. Photo)

Fig. 41. Born in the Cuban town of Bejucal, Albio Sires grew up in the waning years of pre-Communist Cuba. His family fled to U.S. in January 1962 with the help of relatives in America. He served as mayor of West New York, New Jersey, from 1995 to 2006. He has been a U.S. representative from New Jersey since 2006. (*Miami Herald*)

Fig. 42. A native of Cuba, Ray Rodríguez worked as entertainer's Julio Iglesias' worldwide manager and CEO. He joined Univision in 1990 as vice president, spending twnety years helping to lead the company. He was president of Univision when he retired in 2009. (knightfoundation.org)

Fig. 43. Paul L. Cejas, a native of Cuba who arrived to U.S. in 1960, is chairman and chief executive officer of PLC Investments, Inc. He also served as ambassador to Belgium under U.S. President Bill Clinton. Cejas was listed among the "100 most powerful people in southern Florida" by *South Florida CEO* magazine. (nndb.com)

PART 2
THE EXILE EXPERIENCE

INTRODUCTION

BY LOUISE O'BRIEN

The epic journey didn't end when the Cuban exiles made it safely to American shores. Most arrived here with little more than the shirts on their backs. And they were not welcomed with open arms. Many remember signs posted around Miami in the 1960s that said: "No Jews, No Cubans, No Dogs."

Families who had left comfortable homes and lifestyles moved into the deteriorating neighborhoods of Miami and other cities. Packed by the dozen into tiny houses, they often had to sleep in shifts because there weren't enough beds or couches to go around. Yet, no matter how scarce money or space was, exile households made room for the entire family—and for Cubans this often included loyal employees.

It can be difficult to get Cuban exiles to talk about those early days—not because they don't remember, or are in any way ashamed of what they went through. But they don't like to talk about past struggles. Resilience and toughness are admired in the Cuban culture; whining is *verboten*. Most exiles say they just did what they had to do. Usually, that meant finding whatever jobs they could in order to feed their families. Many of the inspirational stories in the following chapters start out at the very bottom of the economic ladder.

According to Dr. Raúl Moncarz, of Florida International University:

"For professionals, it was difficult to practice or work in the academic disciplines they were working in back in Cuba, and the variables affecting their professional adaptation remained the same over the years: (1) the age effect (the inverse relationship between age and the ability to incorporate into your academic discipline as well as the ability to learn a new language), (2) the recognition effect (firms and employers acquired confidence in the abilities

> *of Cubans only after employing the first Cuban . . . [who] proves to be a "hard worker. . . ." The recognition effect is of tremendous importance in all professional categories because of the lack of knowledge (real or imaginary) manifested by the different National Associations, State Boards of Professional Practice, and employers regarding the educational experience, background and legal status of Cubans.*[1]

Doctors who had previously trained at America's best hospitals still had to re-qualify to practice in the United States. Prominent attorneys from Cuba had to learn American law and pass their state bar exams. In academia and media, the exiles were disadvantaged by language or subject to unfounded cultural prejudice. Businessmen generally fared better because their results could be measured objectively. The free market is a meritocracy, and Cuban entrepreneurs have proved over and over again that they have the "Midas touch." Cuban-Americans represent only 3.5 percent of the total Hispanic population in the U.S.,[2] but own 11 percent of the companies, employ 13 percent of the total employees, and generate 15 percent of the revenues and annual payroll.[3] Yet, even in business, some opportunities were off-limits to the pioneering exiles. Selling insurance, for example, required U.S. citizenship, which took a minimum of five years to establish.

Despite all the barriers, Cuban exiles were determined to recreate both the economic prosperity and the cultural freedom they had experienced in Cuba. Fifty years later, their accomplishments in many fields place them among the most successful immigrants in American history. Even more extraordinary is the comparison between the lifestyle that Cuban exiles have achieved in the U.S. and other nations and the stagnant standard of living in Castro's Cuba. The contrast is so dramatic one can't help wonder, did the Communist revolution cause a "brain drain" of Cuba's most talented and productive citizens? Or is the success of the exiles simply due to superior opportunities in the U.S. and elsewhere?

The answer is probably yes to both questions. Since Castro's regime actively suppressed individual initiative, every time he has opened the door for emigration, ambitious and individualistic citizens in Cuba have flooded out. The United States, on the other hand, has a free-market economy and an open culture. Most professional fields reward the very same personal attributes that get a person in trouble in Cuba.

There is also clearly something about the experience of exile that seems to increase an individual's odds of success in just about any endeavor. In the forthcoming chapters, many Cuban-Americans tell their personal and professional stories. Some of their careers and companies took off immediately, while others labored for many years to achieve success. Some of the individuals have become household names, at least within their local communities, while others are sharing their stories publicly for the first time. But what cuts across all of the examples is the struggle that preceded success. Prominent Cuban-Americans exhibit an extraordinary level of desire and energy, which they bring not only to their professional careers, but to the protection of their families and the improvement of their communities.

Psychological and neurological research increasingly shows that suffering or hardship of any kind not only strengthens the human spirit, it actually changes the structure of our brains. There is no question that Cuban-Americans were changed by the trauma of forced exile from their homeland. As Armando Codina said, "After Pedro Pan, what else could be as hard as that?" He was referring to the program that brought more than fourteen thousand unaccompanied children to the United States. Many of the exiles echoed Codina's sentiment.

They will also point out, with some pride, that their life in pre-Castro Cuba was good preparation for success in the U.S. It was a country with a sophisticated, worldly culture and a competitive multinational business community. Many of the Cubans who subsequently built their own successful companies in the U.S. or climbed to the top of the ladder in multinational corporations had experience working for American companies in Cuba. The educators, artists, and artisans who were trained in

Cuba had much to teach their colleagues and audiences in the United States.

Cuba before Castro was more advanced in many fields than those outside the country knew. By the late 1950s, Cuba was the envy of Latin America when it came to its broadcasting industry. A colorful example of its ingenuity and technological prowess was the televising of the 1954 World Series. Goar Mestre, founder of CMQ Radio/Television, flew a DC-3 between Havana and Miami during the games so that Cubans were able to watch live as Willy Mays made his sensational running catch in Game One of the Series.[4]

Another common element in many exile success stories is how much they depended on their own community to get their start. Early support came from friends, families, and neighbors. More than most immigrant groups in the U.S., Cubans have taken care of, and patronized, their own. In the Internet age, this is known as an "incubator"—a protected environment in which fledgling businesses, or artistic careers, are nurtured until they are strong enough to compete on a larger scale.

The early exiles in Miami re-created organizations that had fostered professional development in Cuba, such as the Asociacion Interamericana de Hombres de Empresa (AIHE). This group of Cuban-American businessmen would meet regularly at the Horn and Hardart Automat, because they couldn't afford a meal in a real restaurant. Most of them owned just a single suit, but they always wore that suit to the meetings. Here and at the American Club (another Havana institution that was transplanted to Miami), deals were done that put many Cuban entrepreneurs on the track to great success.

Manuel Salvat, who opened his bookstore in the 1960s and published facsimile editions of Cuban classics, would give the books to customers and tell them to "pay me when you can." His store thrived, which is a tribute to both the exile culture of honor and how highly the Cuban-Americans value literature and reading. The chapter on banking describes the "character loans" that were a key tool to the early success of Cuban exile bankers. Eschewing FICO scores, Cuban lenders looked at what they knew about a candidate. They took the long-term view, and it paid off for everyone involved. The fact that these business models based on *personal* relationships worked so well for the Cuban-American pioneers is interesting in light of the recent global credit crisis, which has its roots in the *depersonalization* of the banking industry. If all banking transactions were still done with a handshake while looking someone in the eye—subprime loans and credit default swaps couldn't have done the damage that is blamed on them.

As the following chapters demonstrate, though many successful Cuban-Americans started out in the "incubator" of the close exile community, few were content to stay there. Cuban careers and Cuban companies have grown beyond the confines of Little Havana and Miami to establish themselves on a statewide, national, or even international level. In each chapter, the author has tried to select representative success stories—some now famous but many not. The good news for the exile community is that the number of accomplished individuals in each field far outstrips the capacity of one book to adequately tell their stories.

NOTES

1. Interview with Professor Raúl Moncarz, December 12, 2010.
2. 2010 Census Briefs of the U.S. Census Bureau, issued May 2011.
3. U.S. Census Bureau, 2007 Survey of Business Owners: Hispanics, published on October 1, 2010.
4. Mike V. Salwen, *Radio and Television in Cuba* (Ames: Iowa State University Press, 1994), 59.

BUSINESS AND FINANCE

17

CUBAN EXILES' IMPACT IN BANKING

BY FRANCISCO RODRIGUEZ, LEONARDO RODRIGUEZ, AND SAM VERDEJA

Banking played a critical role in the success of Cuban exiles in Miami, which is not surprising given how important the banking system had been to Cuba's economic growth in the decade before the Castro takeover.

The Cuban Constitution of 1940 outlined the ways in which Cuba's government was expected to grow the economy. It chartered the Banco Nacional de Cuba, similar to the U.S. Federal Reserve, as well as six other important banks.[1] The success of these institutions helped fuel Cuba's economic boom during the so-called Decade of Progress of the 1950s. In addition to public development banks and funds, Cuba enjoyed a healthy private banking system with around forty Cuban-owned banks.[2]

Additionally, many American and Canadian banks operated branches in Cuba, along with the Banco Franco-Cubano (Société Générale) and the Bank of China.[3] The strong presence of Cuban-owned and international banks supported the value of the Cuban peso on parity with the U.S. dollar. Soon after Castro took over, on September 17, 1960, foreign banks, such as National City Bank of New York, Chase, and the Bank of Boston were confiscated. And on October 13, 1960, all Cuban private banks were also confiscated. The Bank of Nova Scotia and the Royal Bank of Canada were the only remaining banks to receive any kind of compensation; they were allowed to continue in operation in order to maintain commercial ties with Canada.

The nationalization of the banking industry in Cuba undoubtedly drove many of its leading bankers into exile in 1960, with most choosing Miami, New York, or San Juan as destinations offering the greatest opportunities.[4] In the 1950s, Miami already had some prominent Cuban bankers, such as Matías Vildóstegui, employed by the Florida National Bank.

Bankers and other businessmen such as accountants, people dealing mostly with numbers, found work in their chosen professions much more easily than others in other occupations. Yet, many newly arrived bankers got the cold shoulder in the U.S. regardless of their prior experience, and in spite of their willingness to start at levels far below what they had achieved in Cuba. The lack of welcome was mostly due to a fear of the unknown, such as the concern that hiring exiles might cause information to leak back to the Castro regime. On the other hand, some Americans still romanticized Castro and his revolution and questioned the motivation of those who were abandoning Cuba.

Most Cuban bankers arrived in the U.S. with little or no money, and they had to take menial or clerical jobs in hotels, factories, and restaurants. But, over time, their proven abilities and work ethic were recognized and American banks began to offer them jobs lending to other Cubans. As the years passed, the demonstrable results achieved by Cuban banking pioneers put them on the fast track for promotions, eventually leading some to become presidents and CEOs of the same institutions they had joined as clerks and tellers.

The first Cuban exile to become president of a bank was Carlos Arboleya, followed by Arístides Sastre, Rafael Corona, and Antonio Infante.

When Arboleya came to Miami in 1960, he took a job as an inventory clerk in a shoe factory and soon after found a job in the bank handling the factory's business. Shortly after, he was hired by Boulevard

National Bank as an operations officer. Cubans with no credit began to show up asking for money to finance their fledging operations or their new "shoestring" businesses. Banking officers such as Arboleya knew that the people across the desk from them had either owned a similar business in Cuba or knew of their character and work ethic, that these were people who would provide the know-how and the sweat capital needed for a new enterprise to take root and survive in Miami—and for the bank to get its money back, plus interest.[5]

And so these exiles were granted "character loans," loans based on the reputation and/or personal credit history of a borrower, rather than collateral. For these exiles the loans were granted more on trust than on a balance sheet or credit rating (and they undoubtedly would have been assigned a low FICO score today!). Arboleya either knew them personally or knew others who knew them personally.

In 1966, Arboleya was approached by executives from the failing Fidelity National Bank of South Miami. "They said to me, 'If you pull the bank out of this mess we'll give you the presidency when you become a citizen.' To make a long story short, I got sworn in as a citizen at 10:00 one morning and I became president of the bank at 2:00 the same day."[6]

Arboleya spent seven years at Fidelity before starting his own bank with a partner. They eventually sold it, and he joined Barnett Bank, which in 1975 had only two branches in Miami and no significant name recognition, especially among the burgeoning Hispanic population. His first day at Barnett he ran into Luis López in the lobby. López was the founder of Camilo Furniture in Miami:

> *He was fuming. He said, "I'm going to leave this bank because I've asked for $50,000 for three weeks now, and I can't get a straight answer!" That was a lot of money back then. I said, "Luis, I just got here today. I don't even know where the bathroom is. Please give me a chance and come back tomorrow and you'll get your money." I knew Camilo Muebles [funiture], I knew their story*

in Cuba, I knew they were hard-working people and I knew I couldn't go wrong. . . . And those were the kind of character loans that we made.[7]

Arboleya eventually became president and vice chairman of Barnett Bank of Miami, retiring as vice chairman of Bank of America when it bought Barnett Bank.

Slowly but surely, other pioneering Cuban exile bankers, such as Aristides Sastre at Republic Bank, had also convinced their senior officers that character loans were good business. It was a return to an old-fashioned way of lending. These loans were all incremental new business for the banks—and targeted a highly attractive customer segment of solid individuals who considered it a matter of honor to repay their loans fully and on time.

"Sastre has helped make a few millionaires," wrote the *Miami Herald,* "like Fernando Rodríguez, who with a fourth-grade education and $500 set up a tiny grocery store. He later borrowed $2000 from the bank to expand and now owns Varadero Supermarkets, a seven-store chain grossing $25 million a year."[8]

Sastre had gone to New York out of Cuba and would later come to work for the First National Bank of Miami developing private banking clients in Central and South America. He then went on to play a critical role at Republic National Bank, bought by Alberto Díaz Masvidal and others as a community-oriented bank. Later, Luis Botifoll, as the bank's chairman, became the face of Republic as it became the largest minority-owned bank in the U.S. by lending to the Cuban exile community. As head of the loan committee in 1971, he had a "parade of penniless" through his office. Years later, Botifoll was very involved with Cuban heritage, founding the publishing house *Editorial Cubana* that is dedicated to rescuing vital historical documents.

"Across from the banker would sit a desperate, dignified man, holding out a brooch, a gold locket, a pair of pearl earrings, a diamond," the *Miami Herald* wrote. "'Tome estos,' the man would say. 'Take these. They are my wife's jewels. They are all I have, the only things of value we could take from Cuba. I need a loan. . . .' 'Keep the jewels' Botifoll would say, 'a handshake will do.'"[9]

Also at Republic National Bank were its president Oscar Bustillo and Angel Medina, Jr., group president and area executive of Regions Bank's Southeast Florida market. (Regions was born out of mergers with AmSouth Bankcorporation and Union Planters Corp.)

Another early pioneer was José Ramón Garrigó, hired by the Metropolitan Bank of Miami in November 1960 as an assistant in the International Division. By 1963, he had become the youngest assistant cashier in Miami. He describes the typical character loan applicant as someone with $125 in the bank, a car on which he was making payments, some jewelry he had overvalued, and a hole-in-the-wall business in Miami which he had also overvalued. With this profile, the applicant would get a loan of between $500 and $5,000, with a term of ninety days, or perhaps $100 a quarter. Yet, Garrigó slept well, knowing he would be paid back. Throughout the entire decade of the 1960s, all but two of his loans were paid back. Garrigó eventually became president of Pan American Bank and his wife, Victoria, rose to the position of senior vice president and regional manager for Florida at HSBC Private Bank Americas.[10]

One of Garrigó's first character loans was to Benjamín León, Sr., who launched a medical clinic business as he had done in Cuba. He also financed a number of Cuban used car dealers who made installment loans for Cubans to get their first car—usually called a "transportation," because they were nothing more than jalopies.

As Cuban bankers became increasingly successful, they not only presided over local banks, but began to create new banking institutions with their own capital or by becoming magnets for Latin American funds. Amaury Betancourt, a vice president at Coconut Grove Bank, became president and chairman of Total Bank, one of Miami's Cuban-owned banks with fifteen branches. It had been founded in 1974 under the name Americas Bank in a mobile trailer on Coral Way at 27th Avenue. By the time Betancourt retired in 1982, the bank's branches covered all of Miami.[11]

They also took on community leadership roles such as the presidency of the bankers associations in Florida and chairmanship of chambers of commerce, and they were invited to join corporate boards of directors for both local and *Fortune 500* companies. Alberto Valdés, president of the International Bank of Miami (after moving to Miami for Citizens & Southern Bank of Atlanta), served as president of the Florida International Bankers Association from 2002 to 2003. Fernando Capablanca presided over FIBA from 1995 to 1996, while he was the general manager of Banco Crédito e Inversiones (Chile) in Miami. He later went on to become president of Union Bank.

A very helpful banker was Alberto Guernica, vice president of the First National Bank of Hialeah and for a long time at Republic National Bank. He was instrumental in the creation of the Club Bancario Nacional in Havana, a seaside club for all Cuban bankers, from bank clerks to bank presidents. The building would be personally taken over by Fidel Castro.

Other Cubans who started banks include Anthony "Tony" Infante, who was the controlling stockholder of Trade National Bank, later sold to Total Bank, and Raúl Masvidal, who was resident vice president of Citibank in Puerto Rico and Madrid. He later moved to Miami to head up the Royal Trust Bank. In 1977, he became chairman and principal stockholder of Biscayne Bank, now Espirito Santo Bank of Florida. In 1983, he became chairman of the board and controlling stockholder of Miami Savings and Loans Bank, and he later opened M Bank, a commercial bank.

Another to rise through the ranks was Adolfo Henriques, who left the Bank of Nova Scotia ending up as chairman of Regions Bank for the U.S. Southeast after being a top Miami executive for Bank of America. He was also chairman, president, and CEO of railroad and real estate company Florida East Coast Industries before it was sold to Fortress Investment Group, LLC.

Among the many Cubans in banking was José Concepción, who presided over Ocean Bank, and Orlando Baró, who in the 1970s was president of Popular Bank of Hialeah, a subsidiary of Popular Bancshares until it and the Bank of Miami were acquired by Southeast Bank. Meanwhile, Abel Holtz established Capital National Bank in 1974, and Nancy Márquez was an executive at Colonial Bank and also at Barnett Bank, while Ivonne Santamaría was at Ponce de Leon Savings and Loans.

One of the great Cuban success stories is developer and plumbing supplies entrepreneur Sergio Pino (Century Homebuilders), who founded U.S. Century Bank with Ramón Rasco as chairman and Octavio Hernández as president. Another board member is Sedano's Supermarkets CEO Manuel Herrán.

Many Cubans became presidents of banks. Carlos Migoya, former city manager of Miami and current president of Jackson Memorial Hospital, was president of First Union for the South Florida region and CEO for the Atlantic Region for Wachovia Bank while Ramiro Ortiz was regional president at SunTrust Bank and senior vice president at BankUnited.

Other prominent Cuban bankers include Raúl R. García, executive committee chairman at First Bank of Miami, whose president is Jorge Triay. And in 2007, Alvaro G. de Molina joined GMAC Financial Services as chief operating officer (COO) after having a similar title at Bank of America.

Perhaps one of the Cuban bankers to hold the highest position in U.S. banking is Carlos Palomares. He was president of Citibank Federal Savings Bank from 1992 to 1997 and then COO-Latin America Consumer until 2000, working on great consumer issues in Latin America. When he left Citigroup in New York, he became COO of Capital One Federal Savings Bank to work on the credit card system of Mexico until 2006, when he became president and CEO of SMC Resources. He is also currently a member of the board of directors of the Pan American Life Insurance Co. and of Coral Gables Trust.[12]

Cuban-American bankers helped transform the city of Miami into a financial mecca known today as the "Gateway to Latin America" and one of the three main financial centers in the U.S., along with New York and San Francisco. By 1982, the Florida International Bankers Association had seventy-two member banks comprised of twenty domestic banks, twenty-seven Edge Act Corporations, and twenty-five foreign banks. Eventually Miami had thirty-two Edge Act Corporations—one more than New York City—and the highest number in the country.

The recognition of Miami as a finance center was acknowledged in an article in the *Financial Times* of Britain in October 1983 that proclaimed Miami "the newest frontier town in international banking." The article added, "Miami bankers stress that this is the logical financial center for this part of the world over the long term."[13]

The Cuban-American banking community has energized and facilitated the international trade that flows through Miami. "The original cadre of banker practitioners that came to these shores in the first years of the exodus from Cuba had brought with them management and administrative knowledge and experience, as well as the integrity that characterized their unique type of work in an island that had a first-class banking system," the Florida International Bankers Association noted.[14]

After five decades, by virtue of their presence in and acquired knowledge of the U.S. market and that of Latin America, the original Cuban banking pioneers and their succeeding generations of new Cuban-American bankers, educated in the best American universities, are recognized as having contributed mightily toward the economic development of the county and city that welcomed them with open arms when they were destitute refugees.

PARTIAL LIST OF OTHER IMPORTANT CUBAN-AMERICAN BANKERS

Eduardo Aguirre, president, International Private Banking for Bank of America (before becoming U.S. ambassador to Spain); vice chairman and COO, U.S. Export-Import Bank. Eduardo Benet, president, International Division, Sun Bank. Brígida Benítez, Head Office of Institutional Integrity (a division that investigates bank fraud) Inter-American Development Bank. José Manuel Casanova, executive vice president, Inter-American Development Bank. Amadeo López Castro, founder of Westchester Bank (became part of International Finance Bank); president, Intercontinental Bank. Simón Cruz, CEO, Bank of Coral Gables. Juan del Busto, director, Miami Federal Reserve Bank. Manuel Fernández, founder, Security National Bank. Calixto García, founder, First Bank of Florida. Joe García, president, Popular Bank of Tampa, a subsidiary of Popular Bancshares. José Miguel Morales Gómez, Boulevard National Bank. Joseph Guerra, president, Unibank. Octavio Hernández, president, U.S. Century Bank. Marcos A. Kerbel, Pan American Bank of Miami, and general manager of Israel Discount Bank in Miami. Justo Legido, president, Bank of Miami. Miriam López, president, Transatlantic Bank; president, Marquis Bank; president, Florida Bankers Association. Jorge Martínez, president, Continental Bank. Eduardo Masferrer, founder, Hamilton Bank. Sergio Masvidal, president, American Express Bank International in Miami. Víctor Pedroso, founder, Banco Pedroso. Félix Reyler, first president, Florida International Bankers Association; president, International Division Pan American Bank. Carlos Salman, chairman, Terra Bank. Alex Sánchez, president and CEO, Florida Bankers Association. Ricardo Sánchez, president, Terra Bank. Enrique Senior, managing director, Allen & Co. José Valle and Felipe Solarana, associated with Intercontinental Bank (and later with the banks of Amadeo López Castro. Angel Fernández

Varela, chairman, Consolidated Bank in Miami. Carlos García Vélez, vice president, First Federal Savings & Loan Association of Miami. Francisco "Pancho" Blanco and Manuel "Manolo" Vergara, Total Bank (now part of Grupo Banco Popular Español).

NOTES

1. The other banks were Banco de Fomento Agrícola e Industrial de Cuba, BANFAIC, which facilitated the development of the agricultural and cattle industry; Fondo de Seguros de Depósitos Bancarios (similar to the U.S. FDIC); Financiera Nacional (National Finance Agency), a development bank providing long-term loans and advice; Fondo de Hipotecas Aseguradas, FHA (Mortgage Insurance Fund, similar to the U.S. FHA); Banco Cubano del Comercio Exterior (a Cuban Ex-Im Bank); and Banco de Desarrollo Económico y Social, BANDES (Economic and Social Development Bank). See *Cuba: Past, Present and Future of Its Banking and Financial System* (Miami: Cuban Banking Study Group, Inc., 1995), 44.
2. Among them were the Trust Co. of Cuba (which controlled 20 percent of Cuba's deposits), Banco Nuñez, Banco Continental, Banco Agrícola e Industrial, Banco Gelats, Banco de los Colonos, Banco Pujol, Banco Pedroso, Banco Godoy y Sayán, Banco Garrigó, Banco Financiero, Banco Hispano Cubano, and Banco Agrícola y Mercantil.
3. The largest foreign banks in Cuba were the Royal Bank of Canada; the National City Bank, today Citibank; the First National Bank of Boston; the Chase National Bank; the Bank of Nova Scotia; Canadian Bank of Commerce; and even the Federal Reserve Banks of Atlanta and Boston opened agencies in Cuba.
3. *Cuba: Past, Present and Future of Its Banking and Financial System,* 28.
4. Ibid., 49.
5. Interviews with Carlos Arboleya, January 2010.
6. William Plasencia, *South Florida CEO* magazine, October 2004.
7. Ibid.
8. Patricia Duarte, *Miami Herald,* January 26, 1987.
9. Andrés Viglucci, *Miami Herald,* September 22, 1985.
10. Interviews with José Ramón Garrigó, April 2010.
11. George Gilder, *The Spirit of Enterprise* (New York: Simon and Schuster, 1984), 100.
12. nacdfl.org/Portals/0/PalomaresBio.pdf.
13. *The Financial Times of Britain,* October 1983.
14. *Leading the Way: A Comprehensive History of International Banking in Florida* (Miami: Florida International Bankers Association, October 22, 2004), 22.

18

ENTREPRENEURS: THE PIONEERS

BY FRANCISCO RODRIGUEZ, LEONARDO RODRIGUEZ, AND SAM VERDEJA

The Cuban entrepreneurial spirit survived the demise of a free-market economy on the island and thrived everywhere it was replanted—from the U.S. to Puerto Rico, Venezuela, and Spain. Cubans brought valuable experience in traditional Cuban industries such as tobacco, sugar, and rum. They also quickly adapted to the changing market needs of the countries they chose.

Starting in 1959, thousands of Cuban industrialists, managers, professionals, small merchants, farmers, and former landowners arrived in the U.S. in successive waves of exiles. The process of creating new businesses began immediately. Through blood, sweat, and tears, they transformed Miami-Dade County into Cuba's Taiwan.

In 2010, Dr. Jorge Salazar Carrillo, economics professor at FIU, summarized the local impact of the Cuban exiles: "Cubans represent a third of the economy of Miami-Dade, generating approximately $40 billion in yearly revenue," he said. "Cuban businesses account for more than 10 percent of Hispanic enterprises in the U.S., moving forward on what had been started back in Cuba, the rapid economic development of the 1950s"[1]

The 2007 U.S. Economic Census analyzed the distribution by sector of the 251,070 Cuban-owned firms. Fifteen percent are in construction;

14 percent in repair and maintenance, or personal and laundry services; 12 percent in administrative or waste management and remediation services; 11.0 percent in health care and social assistance; 11 percent in transportation and warehousing; 11 percent in professional, scientific and technical services; and 28 percent in all other industries.[2]

Neither academic research nor media articles can fully capture the anguish of those who lost everything to a government that took businesses, homes, and freedom, forcing its victims to leave their own country to regain these things. The extraordinary drive of the Cuban exiles has been well-documented. What is not always understood, however, is that it had as much to do with self-worth and love of country as it did with economic survival.

Benjamín León, Sr., and his family were part of the mass exodus to Miami in 1961. Recognizing that the influx of refugees was placing an unprecedented demand on an ill-prepared community and that many immigrants were experiencing significant gaps in medical care due to language barriers and an overburdened health-care delivery system, Leon and his partner, Moisés Liber, decided to do something about it. In 1964, they introduced the concept of the prepaid medical clinic (something available in Cuba since the 1800s) to the Miami Hispanic community, opening Clínica Cubana, Miami's first Cuban medical clinic.

Most of the physicians at the clinic had been professors of medicine at the University of Havana, including Dr. Armando Fernández, Dr. Rodolfo Sotolongo, and Dr. Costales-Latatud. Benjamin León, Jr., joined his father as the first director of member services at Clínica Cubana, which quickly became one of the largest, most respected medical service providers in the county.

By 1970, the Leóns had founded Clínica Asociación Cubana (CAC) and become central figures in the development of the original Health Management Organization (HMO) Act of October 1, 1972. On March 6, 1973, the company was granted the state's first HMO (HMO-73-1) license, becoming a pioneer in the HMO movement in Florida.

León, Jr., later established Leon Medical Centers, Inc. (LMC) in 1996, and Leon Medical Centers Health Plans, Inc., an HMO with a Medicare Advantage contract in May 2005. LMC Health Plans was sold to HealthSpring, a national HMO based in Nashville for $355 million in cash in 2007. Leon Medical Centers went on to add two new state-of-the-art facilities for its patients, while retaining ownership and leadership.[3]

Under León, Jr.'s leadership, LMC and LMC Health Plans became models for health care nationally. LMC is allied with Miami-Dade's most prominent hospitals, and it was featured as one of the four best healthcare institutions in the nation in an article entitled "American Medical Home Runs" by Arnold Milstein, M.D., in *Health Affairs*.[4]

In 2009, León, Jr., and his family donated $10 million to Florida International University for its nascent medical school, which received matching state funds to establish a geriatric research center. This made Leon Medical Centers the first institution of its kind to become an academic center and teaching institution. With more than two thousand health-care professionals serving thirty-seven thousand Medicare recipients, Leon Medical Centers and Leon Medical Centers Health Plans are redefining the status quo in the health-care industry. Their goal, as stated by Leon, Jr., is to extend "beyond the boundaries of Miami-Dade County and mak[e] it the solution for national Medicare reform and reconciliation."

The story of Benjamín León, Jr., and of his father—now continued with Benjamín León III and other family members—is similar to many entrepreneurs who started a business because nobody else would hire them. Most exiles didn't speak English well, and they had no money socked away in Miami. In many ways, though, they were the cream of the crop of Cuban society. Education had always been serious business in Cuba, and Cuban society was very open to business. It had always been a "modern society," well informed, and now, in exile, very motivated to survive.

The first wave of exiles—still thinking they were going home soon—nonetheless began to take root in the swampy South Florida soil.

Many businesses started out by catering to the exile community, though the most successful soon branched out to the rest of Florida, the U.S., and the world. This expansion helped make Miami the international city it is today. In a land where all who want to work have an opportunity to succeed, Cuban immigrants carved out their own piece of the American Dream. At the time, most exiles thought only of survival. Few could have predicted the success they would achieve.

A myth about the Cuban exile community is that they were a bunch of rich émigrés who arrived in the U.S. with their wealth intact. The fact is that most Cuban businessmen of the 1950s reinvested all of their profits in Cuba, and therefore lost their hard assets and cash to Communist unpaid confiscation.

An example of this was Julio Lobo, Cuba's richest man (his confiscated collection of Napoleon artifacts is today housed in Havana's *Napoleonic Museum* at Orestes Ferrara's Florentine palazzo). He arrived in the U.S. with about $5 million of his original $200 million fortune, but he owed almost $7 million, making his net worth less than zero.[5]

Lobo was a master trader who had controlled three of the six million tons of sugar that pre-Castro Cuba produced. (Cuba, once the sugar bowl of the world, now rations sugar to consumers and even imports sugar. Today, half a century later, three million tons of sugar would be thrice the amount produced by the state-controlled Cuban sugar industry whose latest harvest produced just over a million tons, equivalent to the output in 1905.) He set about rebuilding his fortune at age sixty-three, "trading sugar from his office at 79 Pine Street in New York—much as he had from the Galbán Lobo office on O'Reilly Street in Havana."[6]

In his article "Cuba's Builders of Wealth Prior to 1959," Oscar A. Echevarría highlights the small and medium firms such as the 147,772 independent cattlemen and the 62,000 sugar cane growers, which were to the socio-economic fabric "what the small veins and arteries are to the human body: suppress them and decay ensues."

One family that was able to bring money out of Cuba was the Fanjul brothers, Alfonso "Alfy," José "Pepe," Alexander, and Andrés. Today, they own the brands *Domino Sugar* and *Florida Crystals*. Their parents had created a conglomerate of sugar mills, refineries, distilleries, and real estate. In 1960, Alfonso, Sr., bought four hundred acres near Lake Okeechobee, as well as sugar mills in Louisiana. By 2007, the company owned 400,000 acres. The family also bought up the assets of Gulf & Western, developers of the resort La Casa de Campo in the Dominican Republic.[7]

Norberto Azqueta, of Trucane Sugar, married Lian Fanjul, sister of Alfonso and Pepe. His father Jesús Azqueta had a sugar mill in Venezuela. Today, the area of West Palm Beach and Clewiston, Florida, look like Cuba because of the sugarcane fields and mills owned by Cubans and the Cuban bodegas. Diego Suárez, an anti-Castro activist and founder of the Cuban Liberty Council, developed a complete line of equipment for the sugarcane industry at Inter-American Transportation Equipment Co. (Vanguard).

In the southern rural area of Miami-Dade County, around Goulds, the Redlands, and Homestead, Cuban farmers kept Cuban roots alive literally with fields of malanga root (similar to arrowroot) and many other vegetables that make up the Cuban diet. Other Cuban farmers also established roots in Venezuela, the Dominican Republic, and Central America. Viriato Gutiérrez, who studied agricultural engineering at the University of Havana, sought political asylum at the Peruvian Embassy in Havana. He later started a meat processing plant in Honduras, and then purchased Arrocera Centroamericana, a rice-growing enterprise, which he managed until retirement in 1966.

One of the few Cuban enterprises already international in scope in the 1950s was Bacardí, founded in 1862 in Santiago de Cuba by Don Facundo Bacardí Massó, who revolutionized the spirits industry by creating the world's first light-bodied rum. By the time Castro took over, Bacardí was already diversified internationally with plants in Mexico and Puerto Rico, so it was able to defend its trademark name—and signature bat logo—from the Communist takeover. Its president at the time, José

"Pepín" Bosh, became very much involved in the struggle to liberate his homeland, following the example of Emilio Bacardí, who was twice imprisoned and deported during colonial times, and "Emilito," who became a colonel in the Cuban Liberation Army under General Antonio Maceo.

Bacardí, the world's largest distiller, producing more than 240 million bottles in 170 countries, is headed by chairman of the Board Facundo Bacardí, a direct descendant and namesake of the company's founder. Bacardí Limited is one of the largest spirits companies in the world, with more than 200 brands and labels of rum, vodka, whisky, gin, vermouth, and tequila products, among others, most of which are sold on a global basis, including Grey Goose, Dewar's, Bombay Sapphire, Eristoff, Cazadores, and Martini. The company had most of its assets in Cuba, but it was able to fight off Castro's army of international lawyers to maintain its brand and to save the Havana Club brand name, which it bought from Arechabala Distillers.

Another great Cuban rum is Matusalem, now produced in the Dominican Republic by the fifth generation of the family under Claudio R. Alvarez. It has partnered with Camacho Cigars, a leading Cuban cigar manufacturer from Miami, to market its rum in the U.S.

Ramón Cifuentes is the man behind Partagas cigars. Soon after Castro took control, he seized all cigar factories, locking Cifuentes out while offering him the job as head of the nation's cigar industry. Cifuentes refused and fled the country in 1961. His wife got a job with Bloomingdale's, and Cifuentes went to Connecticut to work for General Cigar Co, which later sent him to Jamaica to instruct workers in the art of cigar making. In 1974, the Cifuentes family made a deal with General Cigar to produce Partagas cigars in Jamaica. General paid the family a fee and agreed to pay a royalty for every Partagas cigar it made.

The first non-Cuban Partagas cigars hit the market in 1977. The brand, now made in the Dominican Republic, is among the best-selling premium cigars in the U.S., with more than twelve million cigars sold each year. Ramon Cifuentes died in 2010.[8]

In 1916, Don Santiago Toraño emigrated from Spain to Cuba, where he fell in love with the tobacco leaf and became a broker. He had three sons, Jaime, José, and Carlos, who helped transition the business from broker to one of the largest growers of the Cuban tobacco leaf. By 1959, the family was supplying most of the great cigar factories in Cuba, and exporting large quantities of tobacco leaf to factories around the world. When the Cuban regime expropriated their seventeen farms, Carlos went to the Dominican Republic. Today, growers there credit him with being one of the driving forces of the Dominican cigar industry by introducing Cuban seed and teaching farmers how to grow what is known as "Piloto Cubano."

When Carlos died, his son Carlos continued his father's legacy and expanded the Toraño family business into Nicaragua, Mexico, and Ecuador. Today, they make cigars in Nicaragua and Honduras under the direction of Carlos' son, called Charlie.[9]

Founded in 1961 by Simón Camacho, Camacho Cigars was acquired by the Eiroa family in 1995 and is now part of the Oettinger Davidoff Group. Camacho Cigars is one of the key players in the international cigar market. The flagship Camacho brand is produced in Honduras.

Calle Ocho in Miami is also stocked with many cigar makers, such as La Gloria Cubana as well as Padrón Cigars using Cuban-seed tobacco cultivated in Nicaragua. Miami is today the new Tampa, with many famed brands such as Cohiba being disputed on both sides of the Florida Straits.

Oscar Boruchin's father and mother were born in Russia, and came to Cuba with the intention of going on to the U.S. quickly. But they felt the Cuban people were so nice that they decided to stay (a common sentiment among Eastern European immigrants). Oscar fled Cuba after the family business was nationalized in 1960, and he began driving a cab in Miami. When a Cuban exile fresh off the plane paid his fare with cigars—the only possession of value Castro had allowed him to take out—Boruchin decided to sell the cigars. He now owns several popular brands such as Licenciados and the 8-9-8 Collection. Boruchin built the brands after leaving General Cigar Co. to become a part owner of Mike's Cigars. Later, he became the sole proprietor of the business, which includes a large wholesale and mail-order operation in Bal Harbor, Florida.[10]

Like rum, cigars, and sugar, coffee was one of Cuba's leading products. Cubans brought to Miami the traditions of *café con leche* (espresso coffee with milk), *cortadito*, (demi tasse of espresso coffee with cream . . . or evaporated milk for an extra twenty-five cents!), *cafecito* (demi tasse of espresso), and the *colada* (the full percolation to take back to the office for the *americanos aplatanados*). Early Cuban exiles filled their Italian-made espresso coffeemakers with Café Bustelo (founded in the Bronx in the 1920s by Spaniard Gregorio Bustelo), since using a coffee "sock" to filter was too time consuming in the fast pace of America.

José "Pepe" Souto and his father came to Florida in 1960 after Castro had confiscated Café Souto, their successful coffee business launched in 1865. They established a roaster in Miami to replicate the family's unique blend, and he and his wife, Haydeé, started selling Cuban-style coffee door-to-door from an old Volkswagen. As each son reached driving age, they would outfit him with an old Beetle to help with the deliveries. In 1967, Souto bought the Café Pilón brand from Rowland, establishing a Hialeah roasting plant with three employees. Café Pilón had begun in the 1860s in the eastern province of Oriente where the mountain shade provided ideal conditions for growing coffee. In 1975, they opened a New Jersey distribution center. As soon as the vacuum-packed, "brick" technology became available in 1982, the Souto family adopted it.

In 2000, the Souto's bought Rowland Coffee Roasters of Miami, by then the owner of Café Bustelo. Other brands marketed by Rowland include Café Oquendo, Café El Pico, Café Estrella, Café Ideal, Medaglia d'Oro, and Moka d'Oro. In 2011, after more than 146 years in the coffee business, the Souto family sold Rowland to J.M. Smucker Co. for $360 million.[11]

Café La Llave also began to compete for the taste of the newcomers. Café La Llave was started by José Gaviña's family. His three sons and a daughter continued the legacy in the U.S. since 1967. In addition to La Llave, another strong brand is Don Francisco Gourmet Coffee. Gaviña Gourmet Coffee has yearly sales of $110 million dollars with 270 employees producing close to 40 million pounds of roasted coffee a year.

The top beer in Cuba was Hatuey, brewed by Bacardí, which has relaunched it in the U.S., while La Tropical beer was launched by the Blanco Herrera family in Havana in 1888. Small at first, the brand reached beyond the island to win awards in Europe and the U.S. By 1958, La Tropical was Cuba's largest brewer, producing 58 percent of the island's annual beer production with brands such as La Tropical, Cristal, Tropical 50, and Maltina. La Tropical Brewery's Gardens were a replica of the Alhambra de Granada in Spain, and it became a popular site for parties during the 1950s. Everything came to an end when in 1960 the Communist Revolution confiscated La Tropical.

In 1998, Manuel J. Portuondo, a Cuban-American with experience marketing beer for companies such as Anheuser-Busch and Brahma, helped Ramón Blanco Herrera, the great-grandson of La Tropical's founder, re-launch the brand under the guidance of Julio Fernández Selles, who had served as brew master and plant manager of Cervecería La Tropical in Cuba from 1939 to 1960.[12]

In 1986, Juan Galán and Alfonso Cueto started together in business as the Miller Beer distributor for Miami-Dade and Monroe counties from Miami to Key West. They sold Gato Distributors in 1994.

Though Coke and Pepsi were popular in pre-Castro Cuba, they shared the market with several local soft drinks such as Salutaris and Jupiña, a pineapple drink produced by Cawy Bottling since 1948. In 1962, Vicente Cossio relaunched the Cawy brands in the U.S. with Cawy Lemon Lime, eventually expanding its offerings to include other fruit-flavored drinks (pineapple-flavored Jupiña, Cawy's biggest seller) and herbal drinks such Materva, a yerba mate soda.[13]

In 1937, in the midst of the worldwide Great Depression, Sixto C. Ferro and his brothers in Pinar del Rio, Cuba, decided to make their own guava paste. Slathered on inexpensive Cuban bread (affectionately referred to as "*pan con timba*"), it helped fill a hungry stomach. During World War II, the U.S. government, in need of canned food and juices for troops, provided financial assistance to the Ferros to build a modern factory. At the end of the war, they expanded this factory to process many different products, including California peaches and rock lobster and tuna fished from their own boats.

Fidel Castro's regime nationalized Industrias Ferro, S.A., and the Cuban government has operated the confiscated factory ever since under the usurped company brand Conchita. But by 1964, the Ferro family had Conchita up and running again in Miami, albeit on a small scale. Thanks to them, the Cuban exiles could find a little taste of home at their local "*bodegas*." Today, under the guidance of the second and third generation of Ferros, Conchita Foods' product line has grown to over 150 items.[14]

Elpidio Nuñez came to the U.S. from Cuba in 1960, becoming a leading importer and exporter of meat products in 1961 in Miami, specifically beef, pork, poultry, and seafood. In addition to traditional meat and seafood, *Northwestern Meat* distributes exotic foods such as cuttlefish, frog legs, octopus, ostrich, pheasant, and sea cucumber. Northwestern Meat serves customers throughout the U.S., Latin America, and the Caribbean through facilities in Florida and Puerto Rico.

Domingo A. Moreira was the chicken king in Cuba with twenty-five El Caporal restaurants, something akin to KFC in the U.S., though frog legs were also in the menu at El Caporal. Domingo revolutionized the chicken business in Guatemala, where he transplanted El Caporal in 1957. Today, his son Domingo R. Moreira runs an operation that's one of the biggest players in producing, distributing, and marketing shrimp from Central and South America, Ladex Foods.

Quirch Foods was started by Guillermo Quirch, Sr., and his two sons, Eduardo and Guillermo, Jr. The Quirch family's involvement in the food industry dates back to the early twentieth century when Guillermo, Sr., managed a meat packing and distribution company in Havana. Forced into exile by the revolution of 1959, the family founded a meat distribution company, Oriente Comercial, in Puerto Rico, and then E&G Trading in Miami. The company was re-incorporated as Quirch Foods Co. in 1999, and it is now managed by Guillermo Jr.'s three sons, Guillermo III, Ignacio, and Mauricio.

What began as a small family outfit with five employees has become a major wholesale distributor with four distribution centers in the U.S. and Puerto Rico, and over four hundred employees. The company's product line has grown from a few staple meat and seafood items to thousands of different products in all of the major perishable food categories: meat, poultry, seafood, processed meats, dairy, and frozen foods.

Walter Vázquez, Sr., is another exile who launched a successful food distribution business in the highly competitive arena of fresh produce: Freedom Fresh Produce. His company serves retail supermarkets, gourmet stores, wholesalers, and the cruise ship industry. Their Services Division provides storage and handling for third-party produce importers. Today, the second generation of the family—Walter, Jr., and Jorge—run the business with a state-of-the-art warehouse that can accommodate over seven hundred different products.[15]

Carlos Pérez left Cuba in 1960 at age twenty-eight with twenty-seven dollars in his pocket, and no English in his vocabulary. Despite these handicaps, he succeeded in establishing a wholesale produce business that by 1984 was grossing nearly $40 million a year. His company, National Foods, sells a commercially packaged fried plantain chip—under the brand Mariquitas—that competes with those cooked at home by Latin American families in Miami or area restaurants. The Small Business Administration appointed him a member of the agency's National Advisory Council and chairman of its committee on minority business, and President Reagan used Pérez in a speech as a shining example of the "spirit of enterprise."[16] Others who made it one plantain chip at a time were Julio Borges and Isidoro Rodríguez.

Badía Spices is another well-known brand in the Miami area and nationwide. With 250 employees and sales of $25 million, it is yet another impressive example of exile entrepreneurship. In 1960, looking for new opportunities, José Badía left Spain for Santiago de Las Vegas, Cuba, where he opened a hardware store, Badía y Garrigó. In 1963, fleeing Communism, he moved to Puerto Rico and entered the world of spices. In 1967, the company relocated to Miami and began to sell to Sedano's Supermarkets. José, Azucena, and his son Joseph would hand-pack the spices in the evening and wake at dawn to distribute orders to more than thirty small stores across Miami Beach. Beginning in 1979, their spices have been available in many U.S. cities and other countries.[17]

José "Pepe" Ortega, known to his friends as "El Gallego," was born in Havana in 1929. His father died when he was very young, and he went to work for F. Bonet y Cía., a food distribution business. Before long, he applied his natural entrepreneurial talent to launching his own business. "Though he was very young, he had a lot of creativity for business," his son José Antonio said. "He founded the first automobile air-conditioning business in Cuba and soon had a broad clientele."

Pepe left Cuba with his wife and two children in 1960. After a brief stay in Colombia, he moved to Puerto Rico in 1963 and started a successful spice business that eventually became Sazón Goya, in partnership with the Unanue family, owners of Goya Foods. In 1976, Pepe moved to Miami, where he continued to lead his company until his death in 2009.[18]

The first Sedano's was built in Hialeah by René Sedano. Armando Guerra, who arrived from Cuba as an exile, saw the value of a market for Cuban food in Hialeah and bought the store in 1961, keeping the popular name. Guerra grew Sedano's to become one of the top Hispanic businesses in the U.S. In 1971, he brought in Manuel Herrán, a Spaniard who had fled Cuba and had married his niece, to help in the daily operations. The chain grew to twenty-eight supermarkets, becoming the largest member of Associated Grocers of Florida. Only Winn Dixie and Publix (including Sabor, its Latin-style offering) still compete with Sedano's. Both these giants have had to adapt to Latin tastes in order to match the specialized services provided by Sedano's, where Cuban families can order their pigs to roast for *Noche Buena* (Christmas Eve). Now they sell La Caja China, invented by Roberto Guerra, which roasts a pig inside a metal box using heat from above rather than below. It has become all the rage among famous U.S. chefs, including Bobby Flay.

Fernando Rodríguez opened Varadero Supermarket and Liquor Store on Miami's Coral Way. The aqua walls were painted to re-create his native Varadero Beach in Cuba. A mural depicted the rowboat he used to escape. Although he later sold the Coral Way store to Winn Dixie, Varadero is still in business as a supermarket and liquor store.

Felipe Valls and his family own many Cuban or Cuban-Spanish restaurants in the Miami area, including eight locations of La Carreta restaurants, Café Versailles (perhaps the most famous Cuban restaurant in the world), and the elegant Casa Juancho. The Valls Group now has twenty-four hundred employees.[19] Café Versailles, which opened on June 11, 1971, at Calle Ocho and 35th Avenue, is the epicenter of Cuban Miami. Whenever a news story breaks, the news vans for both English and Spanish TV stations congregate there. All major networks have rented space in and around Versailles for the fateful day when Fidel Castro dies.

Cuban culture has made a number of contributions to the American food scene, particularly in Miami. For many years at the Versailles or the Latin American Cafeteria, you could find the *lonchero* (derived from the English word lunch)—a guy wearing black pants and a white shirt with a knife in one hand and a fork in the other, making Cuban sandwiches from a raised podium behind glass. This is losing ground, along with the *pan con lechón*, as healthy-minded new generations try to avoid the greasy pork sandwiches. Still, the *lonchero*—the catering trucks that visit the *factorías* of Hialeah—continue to thrive in their business of providing good Cuban sandwiches and *café con leche* to workers for a reasonable price.

Another Cuban Miami culinary institution is the *Palacio de los Jugos*, a roof without walls housing different kiosks where people pay separately for food to go or to stay to enjoy their fruit juices that give it its name, "Juice Palace." As the Chinese population of Havana fled Communism, signs of "Comida China" began popping up in New York and Miami. Pekín Restaurant was the mainstay of early Cuban exiles at Calle Ocho and 8th Avenue, where for $1.25 Rafael and Federico would give you *arroz chino, mariposa, y ensalada* (fried rice, wonton, and salad).

Cuban bakers are also renowned for delicacies such as *pasteles de guayaba*. Among the early bakeries were La Gran Vía, which adapted its jingle to its new phone number in Miami, "call Franklin 9-8-5-2-3, for La Gran Vía" (there was also one in Puerto Rico) and Los Pinos Nuevos (makers of *turrón,* a seasonal Spanish nougat pastry for Christmas). Like many businesses launched by exiles, the bakeries first targeted Cuban-born clientele before broadening their appeal to "americanos aplatanados"—those who enjoy the Cuban side of Miami.

George Feldenkreis fled to Miami in 1961 at age twenty-five, accompanied by his pregnant wife and one-year-old son. Unable to practice law in his new country, Feldenkreis used his Russian father's overseas contacts to import such diverse products as motorcycle parts from Asia and window glass from Portugal. He began traveling to Japan and other Asian countries, importing school uniforms for Puerto Rico and, eventually, *guayaberas*—the Cuban shirt that replaces a jacket in tropical countries.

In 1967, he and his brother created Supreme International for their burgeoning clothing business. In addition to importing on a commission basis, George began to manufacture his own goods. In 1978, he bought out his brother's interest, and in 1993 he went public. Supreme International purchased Perry Ellis in 1999. By 2011, Perry Ellis had achieved sales of one billion dollars and employed two thousand workers in the U.S. and three hundred throughout Asia. George still serves as chairman and CEO. His son Oscar is president and COO, and his daughter Fanny is the treasurer. His advice to young people starting out in business is that "there is no shame in starting from the bottom, that way you know very well what it is you are doing."[20]

While Perry Ellis is the best-known clothing empire owned by a Cuban and inventor of the Cubavera brand, La Casa de las Guayaberas by the late Ramón Puig is the leading manufacturer/retailer of the original Cuban shirt. One of his competitors is Miami Cool Wear.

La Época, founded in Havana in 1885, began operations as a small fabric store. In 1927, Angel Alonso and his younger brother Diego, both immigrants from Spain, took over the store and expanded rapidly from its original location. In 1955, after the completion of a new building on the corner of Galiano and Neptuno streets, *La Epoca* became the third largest department store in Havana, employing four hundred people and spanning five floors on half a city block. In 1960, the Castro government forcibly confiscated the store as part of its campaign to end private enterprise in Cuba. The Alonsos relocated to Miami to start all over again.

In 1965, *La Epoca* opened its doors in downtown Miami as a small corner store in the Alfred I. DuPont Building. Diego Alonso, along with his sons Tony and Pepe, was determined to build one of Miami's best retail businesses. With Angel, Sr., serving as consultant until he retired in 1970, the department store quickly expanded to nearly the entire ground floor of the building, including an upscale boutique for women and its own electronics store. In 1992, the Alonso family purchased the six-floor, fifty-thousand-square-foot Art Deco Walgreen's building, built in 1936.

The store survived some hard times in the wake of Hurricane Andrew, and it has enjoyed new life since moving into the former Walgreen's building in December 2005.

As a profile in the *Miami Herald* said, "This is definitely no longer the La Epoca where *abuelita* used to shop. All that remains from the past are a small rack of polyester women's blouses and two-piece suits."[21]

Sofia Horenstein came to Cuba from Russia at the age of nine and began working as a seamstress almost immediately. She saw a future in zippers, and she started *Factoría Onlat* with her savings, eventually employing 175 people in Cuba. In Miami, after saving her money once again, she founded Scott Notion in 1970, catering to garment, shoe, and luggage manufacturers. Sophia was active in her business until age ninety-one. She once visited her old factory in Cuba only to find it abandoned.[22]

Many small jewelers from Cuba re-opened their businesses in Little Havana's Calle Ocho. They catered to Cuban tastes, often pawning articles from Cuban refugees. Gedalio "Gerry" Grinberg began selling alarm clocks in Havana in 1946, and he moved up to luxury watches. He decided to leave Cuba after the Castro police interrogated him following his meeting with an American citizen. After briefly selling meat in Miami, he went to New York to distribute Piaget watches, "the most expensive watches in the world." He built Piaget from $165,000 in revenue to $30 million through savvy marketing and aggressive salesmanship. He bought Concord in 1969 and transformed it with quartz technology. In 1983, he was finally able to acquire Movado, designers of the Bauhaus-inspired "Museum watch," and repositioned the brand for a younger clientele. The entire business is now known as the Movado Group; it reported revenues of $382 million in January 2011. The Movado Group also includes Concord, Ebel, and ESQ along with Coach, HUGO BOSS, Juicy Couture, Lacoste, and Tommy Hilfiger-licensed watch brands.[23]

José Navarro, Sr., founded Farmacias Navarro in Cuba in 1940. After Castro confiscated the Navarro stores, forcing the family to flee to the U.S., Navarro cashed in an insurance policy and used the four thousand dollars to open a pharmacy on Calle Ocho and 13th Avenue—what would become the heart of Miami's Little Havana. By 2008, Navarro Discount Pharmacies had a 17 percent market share, ahead of both Walgreen's and CVS. It employed two thousand people, and generated $320 million in revenues in 2009 from its thirty-one stores throughout Dade and Broward counties (including the recent acquisition of Sedano's pharmacies). In 2007, Navarro's heirs sold 60 percent of their shares to MBF Healthcare Partners, headed by Mike Fernández. In 2011, Navarro announced the launch its own Vida Mia branded products.[24]

The León family was not the only successful medical clinic founded by Cuban exiles. Pasteur Medical Center, started by Dr. Ismael Hernández, now has several clinics in Miami-Dade, and many others provide culturally relevant health care to Cubans and Hispanics in general.

The late Ricardo Mayo founded Doral Pharmamedics, a wholesaler of drugs, cosmetics, and toiletries, which is now run by his son Rick. Mayo, Sr., had started Rimaco in Puerto Rico before starting the operation in Miami.

Cuban exiles brought with them their traditional funeral practices, such as the wake or "*velorio*," which lasted all night, requiring heavy doses of Cuban coffee available at the funeral home. Though some of these traditions are gradually yielding to American practices, the exiles have tended to patronize Cuban funeral homes that did things the Cuban way. Funeraria Caballero was established in Havana in 1857, and reopened in Miami in the 1960s on Calle Ocho. In 1990, Caballero merged with Woodlawn Park Cemeteries and Funeral Home, and in 1993, they acquired Rivero Funeral Homes (established in 1946 in Havana)—the largest funeral home business in Florida. The name of the combined entity was changed to Caballero Rivero Woodlawn Funeral Homes. It now runs Woodland Cemetery, where many famous Cubans are buried, such as former presidents Gerardo Machado and Carlos Prío; Manuel Artime, civilian leader of the Bay of Pigs invasion; and Jorge Mas Canosa, founder of the Cuban American National Foundation. Other Cuban institutions in Miami include Bernardo García Brake as well as the funeral homes Mas Pons and La Nacional.

Leslie Pantín, Sr., and Víctor Pantín were introduced to the insurance business by their father, who ran Cuba's second largest insurance company. A year after Castro came to power, the Pantíns left Cuba with three suitcases, expecting to return within six months. The law banned non-U.S. citizens from brokering insurance, so the Pantín brothers worked for another agency for one hundred dollars per month, soliciting their exile friends as customers. But many insurance companies refused to insure the Cuban exiles. "They said Cubans were a bad risk, they didn't speak good English, they couldn't read traffic signs, they were bad drivers," Leslie Pantín, Sr., told the *Miami Herald*. "It was the bias that's normal when there's a new immigration to a country."[25]

By 1966, Pantín became a U.S. citizen and Pantín Insurance prospered, becoming (under the name AmerInsurance) one of the largest Hispanic-owned property and casualty insurance agencies in Florida. Pantín, Sr., became a bridge builder between the new Cuban community and the Miami business establishment, and he was the first Cuban on the Orange Bowl Committee.

Tony Sierra is founder and chairman of BMI. Sierra leads a company that lists $5.5 billion in policies and 200,000 customers in Latin America, Asia, and Europe. The second-generation Anthony and David now work in the operation as well.

Mike Carricarte is chairman and CEO of Amedex. The company employs two hundred people in the claim center. In addition, the Amedex front line boasts three thousand sales agents in Latin America and twenty-six outside sales agencies.

Soon after establishing themselves in a job or business and getting U.S. residency, Cuban exiles began to travel with a Reentry Permit, the white passport that allowed them to go to Europe and Latin America, their two favorite destinations. Mena Travel, founded in Havana in 1943, was one of the first to cater to exile travelers in the U.S. Mena Travel is now a fourth-generation business, run by siblings Carlos and Hilda María Mena. It is a full-service agency offering everything from tours featuring Spanish-speaking guides to wholesale travel services. Carlos and Hilda even serve as guides themselves.

Brothers Teófilo (Omar), Santiago, and Lincoln Babun were three Bay of Pigs veterans whose family owned Maderera Babun (sawmills and timberlands), Cementos Nacionales (cement manufacturing), Constructora Diamante (infrastructure construction and marine projects), and Babun Lines (maritime fleet) in Santiago de Cuba. They brought their shipping expertise to Miami, founding Antillean Marine Shipping Corp. in 1963 on the Miami River with a single break-bulk ship. Today their firm handles over a million tons of cargo a year, with a fleet of eleven multipurpose cargo vessels that travel between South Florida and the Caribbean. José Babun, the current chairman, is the younger brother of the founders.[26]

In 1960, the owners of Pieles Moisés Egozi, Moisés and David Egozi, fled Cuba after Castro seized power. Their manager, Alberto Barrocas, remained behind to handle their leather-shoe business, but he provoked Castro's ire when he refused to relinquish the business when it was confiscated.[27] Settling in Miami, chairman and CEO David Egozi and President Eugenio Ramos founded Suave Shoes. Ramos had sold the Keds sneaker brand in Cuba. By the 1970s, their business was part of a successful Jewish Cuban enclave in Hialeah for the manufacturing of sneakers. When competition from the Far East began to undercut manufacturing costs in Hialeah in the 1980s, the company expanded with recognizable licensed characters and brands including Superman and Batman. Today, they are a leading manufacturer of tennis, boat, basketball, aerobics, fitness, and track shoes with fabric, leather, or vinyl uppers in a variety of colors and sizes.[28]

After Alberto Barrocas fled Cuba with little more than his contacts in the shoe business, he became a sales manager for Apex Tire and Rubber. In 1964, he helped found Injection Footwear with the Egozi family. In 1977, Barrocas bought out the Egozi family and ran the business with his sons until selling it in 1999. By the 1980s, Injection Footwear Corp. employed twelve hundred people and produced ten million pairs of shoes, sneakers, and sandals each year. "They were really the pioneers of the shoe industry, and they were selling not just to the local market, they were selling to the whole world," said banker Abel Holtz.[29]

Guillermo Miranda, Sr., a fellow refugee and president of Miami's Gator Industries, sold raw materials such as vinyl to Barrocas for many years. Though Gator later became a direct competitor with its Gator

Shoes Co., the two remained good friends. "Every time I walked into his office, it was a learning experience," Miranda said. He was joined in his business by sons Guillermo Miranda, Jr., and José Miranda.[30]

Orlando A. Gómez was only twenty when he took over Fundición de Gómez Hermanos y Cia after the death of his father in 1940 in Jovellanos, Matanzas, Cuba. Their main product was grinding rollers for sugar mills. In 1962 he left Cuba for Puerto Rico, working as a manager at Porto Rico Iron Works. Moving to Miami in 1974, he opened Everglades Steel Co., and served as CEO until his death in 2010. With thirty employees and over $30 million in annual revenue, they provide steel products to sugar mills, mining, ship builders, power plants, bridge construction, metal fabrication, and cement companies, domestically and abroad. Orlando García, Orlando's grandson, is now the CEO of the company.[31]

Alberto Badía developed Montura Ranch Estates, one of the largest development projects started by Cubans in the area of Clewiston, Florida, where parcels were sold for building ranches for horse enthusiasts. *Montura*, which means "saddle," became very popular with Miami and Latin American residents.

The late Jorge Mas Canosa became a Miami branch manager for Iglesias y Torres Co. of Puerto Rico after being a milkman in Miami on his arrival from Cuba. Mas Canosa met E. B. McKinney, Southern Bell's general manager for South Florida. This began a business relationship that would continue for decades. In 1969, Mas Canosa renamed the company Church and Tower; he bought out the business in 1971. He formed MasTec, which lays telephone cable, in 1994. Today, MasTec is one of the leading Hispanic-owned businesses in the U.S., run by his son, Jorge Mas Santos (who also heads the Cuban American National Foundation, as his father did).

Jerónimo Esteve-Abril, born in Santiago de Cuba in 1929, inherited from his father Jerónimo Esteve Marsan an entrepreneurial spirit and a love of business. Soon after completing junior college in Massachusetts,

Jerónimo returned to Havana in 1950 and started his first independent business: a retail seller of home appliances. Within a few years, he became a factory representative and distributor of coin operated *vitrolas* (juke boxes). In 1960, Jerónimo liquidated all loans and accounts and left for Puerto Rico with his wife, son, and fifteen dollars in his pocket to manage a "*vitrola*" distribution business.

A year later, Jerónimo started Esteve International with small capital contributions from family and friends. He partnered with Juan José Bellapart, the Honda Motor representative in the Dominican Republic, to establish Bella International, initially a distributor of Honda motorcycles in Puerto Rico. Ten years later, the Honda Civic that revolutionized the automobile business because of its extraordinary fuel economy would make them millionaires. Esteve was a founding member and president of the Asociación Interamericana de Hombres de Empresa.

Jerónimo Miguel Esteve joined his father's company in 1984, selling the complete line of Honda products. In 1986, they added luxury Acura vehicles. In the 1990s, Esteve, Jr., purchased Miami Rainbow Group, and turned it into a Toyota dealership. In Puerto Rico, the company diversified its car dealerships by adding Chrysler, Dodge, Jeep, and Daewoo. In Miami, Esteve, Jr., became the first Hispanic Lexus dealer in 1993, and he opened Headquarter Lincoln-Mercury in 1996.

Car dealerships have been a lucrative path for a number of Cuban exiles. Charles Dascal was the first Cuban-American awarded a Ford franchise dealership in the U.S. Since then his South Motors Automotive Group has grown into one of the region's most recognizable and respected automotive retailers of several other car makers, such as Infiniti, BMW, and Honda. Gus Machado, who came from Cuba in 1957, owns Gus Machado Ford dealerships in Hialeah and Kendall, and Manuel Villamañán owns Midway Ford Isuzu, part of South Motors.

The plant nursery business is another that has attracted many exile entrepreneurs. Carlos Barceló came from Cuba in 1962 and started his palm tree business in 1972 in Southern California. Barcelo Enterprises (his second business, founded in 1998) recorded sales of $22 million in 2011, down from a high of $30 million. He employs three hundred workers and has five hundred acres under cultivation in California and Arizona. The company has 2.5 million square feet of soil in greenhouses and is run by the founder with his wife, Rosa, and his three children, Rosa, Antonio, and Roberto, in California and cousin Roberto Barceló in Arizona. Carlos attributes his success to *"trabajar como un mulo"*—loosely translated as "working like a mule," with determination, passion, and willingness to learn, as well as a commitment treating your customers right.[32]

Driving down the Florida Turnpike Extension are extensive fields of royal palms, palmettos, sabal palm, Bismarck palms, and coconut trees owned by Manuel Díaz Farms, founded by Manuel Díaz. Tony Costa started Costa Nursery Farms, which owns large-scale fields in southern Miami-Dade, and Manuel Arencibia owns Manuel Arencibia Farms, Inc., in the palm business near the Florida City-Homestead area of Miami-Dade County.

In the 1920s, Simón Capó traded farm products for used furniture which he would restore and sell in Pinar del Río, Cuba. By the 1950s, Casa Capó (still in business now in Calle Ocho run by another branch of the family) was a large manufacturer and retail enterprise managed by Simón's son Manuel Capó. Soon after their business was confiscated without payment, Manuel fled Cuba in 1966 with sons Carlos and Luis aboard a small sailboat named *El Dorado*. They ended up in Mexico, but they moved to Miami where they opened their first El Dorado store in 1967.[33] With 2009 sales of $300 million and eight hundred employees, El Dorado Furniture recently capped its expansion with the Boulevard, a huge store in Little Havana's Calle Ocho that resembles a small town with streets, buildings, and cafés.

Several other prominent furniture stores were launched in Little Havana, such as Lavín Baby Center, La Canastilla Cubana for baby furniture, and La Ideal. All of these filled niches in the furniture tastes of the new arrivals. The López brothers Camilo, Luis, José, and some of their children operate Camilo Office Furniture, which today competes with major national chains.

Manuel Salvat, known as "El Gordo Salvat," opened a small bookstore in Calle Ocho in 1965. Exiles would gather there to seek out books in Spanish, news from Cuba, or just to "shoot the breeze." Gradually, Salvat's small Librería Universal became Ediciones Universal—a powerhouse that has published more than a thousand books containing the combined talents of three exile generations and preserving the heritage of Cuba.

Other bookstores that played an important part in Calle Ocho history were Librería Cervantes and La Moderna Poesía—both now closed—and Librería Impacto, still in operation. La Moderna Poesía in Cuba was part of Ediciones Cultural, a leading textbook publisher in Cuba. Many Cubans ended up as editors in leading U.S. publishers, as the mantle of textbook publishing passed on to Editorial Playor, begun by Carlos Alberto Montaner, a leading publisher of textbooks in Puerto Rico and Spain.

The seeds of exile success in business were sown by the early pioneers in the 1960s. By the start of the next decade, a second wave of Cuban entrepreneurs picked up the baton to carry existing businesses to new heights and to launch new businesses in areas the pioneers could not have imagined. They were either children of the original founders, or younger exiles who, armed with a U.S. education as well as the example of their parents, were ready to achieve the American Dream. Cuban exiles were already being recognized for their unusual business acumen and outstanding work ethic.

NOTES

1. Interview with Dr. Jorge Salazar Carrillo, professor of economics, Florida International University, Miami, 2010.
2. http://www.census.gov/econ/sbo/get07sof.html?11. Survey of Business Owners-Hispanic-Owned Firms: 2007. Summary of Findings.

3. Interview with Benjamín León, Jr., June 2, 2010.
4. Arnold Milstein, M.D., "American Medical Home Runs," *Health Affairs*, September/October 2009.
5. John Paul Rathbone, *The Sugar King of Havana: The Rise and Fall of Julio Lobo, Cuba's Last Tycoon* (New York: Penguin, 2010), 230.
6. Ibid., 235.
7. sun-sentinel.com/sfl-powfanjulsjun30.
8. cigaraficionado.com/Cigar/CA_Archives/CA_Show_Article/0,2322,279,00.html.
9. http://www.torano.com/downloads/ToranoHistory_Web.2009.pdf.
10. cigaraficionado.com/Cigar/CA_Profiles/Cigar_Stars_Profile/0,2547,119,00.html.
11. Elaine Walker, "Smucker Buys Café Pilon, Café Bustelo for $360 Million," *Miami Herald*, May 17, 2011.
12. http://www.cervezatropical.com/id1.html.
13. Carli Teproff, "Cuban Immigrant Started Cawy Bottling in Miami," *Miami Herald*, March 19, 2011.
14. conchita-foods.com/pages/conchita-aboutus.html.
15. Interview with Walter Vazquez, May 2011.
16. http://www.newsmax.com/US/Immigration-Carlos-Perez-Cuba/2010/01/11/id/345997.
17. http://www.badia-spices.com/business/history.cfm.
18. miamiherald.com/2009/09/20/1242161/jose-antonio-ortega-bonet-founder.html#ixzz0pLZ8m2gG.
19. Fabiola Santiago, "Versailles: 40 Years Serving Food with a Side of Politics," *Miami Herald,* July 11, 2011.
20. Interview with George Feldenkreis, August 17, 2001.
21. Interview with Angel Alonso, Jr., June 16, 2011, and Elaine Walker, "La Epoca Store Updates Itself for a New Downtown," *Miami Herald*, August 9, 2007.
22. *Miami Herald*, February 8, 2009.
23. http://www.movadogroupinc.com.
24. Melissa Sanchez, "Navarro Set to Launch Own Line of Products," *Miami Herald*, June 7, 2011.
25. Luis Feldstein Soto, *Miami Herald*, February 6, 1988.
26. Interview with Teo Babun, February 12, 2011.
27. Carol Marbin Miller, "Alberto Barrocas, 82, Cuban Exile Led Miami to Top of Shoe Industry," *Miami Herald*, November 27, 2004.
28. http://www.business.com/directory/retail_and_consumer_services/apparel_and_accessories/shoes.
29. Carol Marbin Miller, "Alberto Barrocas," *Miami Herald*.
30. Ibid.
31. Interview with the Gómez and García families, July 26, 2011.
32. Interview with Carlos Barcelo, August 15, 2011.
33. Business Network, http://resources.bnet.com/topic/el+dorado+furniture+corp.html.

19

ENTREPRENEURS: THE NEW GENERATION

BY FRANCISCO RODRIGUEZ, LEONARDO RODRIGUEZ, AND SAM VERDEJA

One difference between the first wave of immigrant-entrepreneurs and later waves was the support and backing of their fellow Cubans. Though Cubans have always tried to help each other, by the 1970s and 1980s, the exile community had substantially greater resources at their disposal. In addition to a ready-made Cuban-American customer base, the later entrepreneurs found both an investor base and valuable community contacts among the pioneering generation.

Armando Codina, the son of a past president of the Cuban Senate, arrived in Miami at age fourteen, one of fourteen thousand children in Operation Pedro Pan. Codina was sent to an orphanage in New Jersey, and then rotated through three different foster homes. The orphanage felt more like juvenile hall. "I didn't really go through a lot of pain until my first night at the orphanage, when I went to sleep crying, thinking to myself, 'Why am I here? I didn't belong in an orphanage,'" he says. "However, Pedro Pan was all about parents making the ultimate sacrifice." He knew that his mother would one day join him in the U.S. "even if she had to swim over."[1] He believes the level of stress Cuban parents must have felt at placing their children on an airplane headed for an uncertain future in the U.S. was worse than anything he experienced.

Early in his career, Codina had a great idea for a business. He knew medical doctors were coping with increasingly complex paperwork for Medicare reimbursements. Armando took a job with a computer company—"to get the other pieces of the puzzle I was missing"—and then borrowed $18,000 from the Small Business Administration to start Professional Automated Services, a medical billing company. It grew from a one-man, home-based operation to a company with two hundred employees and more than $10 million in annual revenues. Codina sold his company in 1978 for more than $4 million.

After devoting himself for several years to civic activities, the young millionaire started a development company, where future Florida Governor Jeb Bush worked in 1979. He merged his company with Flagler Development (established by Henry Flagler when he brought his railroad to Miami) in 2006, forming the Flagler Development Group, the real estate development subsidiary of Florida East Coast Industries, Inc. FECI was sold to a private equity firm for $3.5 billion. Armando Codina stepped down as chief executive of Flagler, remaining as chairman. In 2009, he started Codina Partners, a boutique real estate development company.

Codina is lead director of American Airlines parent AMR Corp. and is on the board of Home Depot. He sat on the boards of GM and Merrill Lynch during the tough economic times that began in 2008. Prior to that, he also served on the boards of Quaker Oats, FPL, and American Bankers. He was the lead director while serving on the board of BellSouth.

When asked who his mentors were, he said that in business it was Frank W. Sherman, a banker in Jacksonville, who taught him that he was indeed ready to take on the challenges to be successful in business. In civic matters he takes after his very close friend, the late Alvah Chapman, the South Florida leader who was the chairman of Knight Ridder.

"How did I start a business without even a college degree?" Codina asks. "Well, after Pedro Pan what else would be as hard as that?" His appreciation for what he has achieved in the United States is demonstrated by the name of his boat: *What a Country*.[2]

Developer Jorge Pérez was born in Argentina to Cuban parents, and he lived in Colombia prior to moving to Miami in 1968. He decided to get into real estate development while serving as the city of Miami's economic development director. In 1979, he founded the Related Group with New York builder Stephen M. Ross. They first found success building low-income, multi-family apartments and then branched into rental apartments before becoming one of the most prolific high-rise condo builders in the Southern U.S. Pérez has owned fifty condo towers in various stages of completion in South Florida and South and Central America. The Related Group of Florida had $2.1 billion in revenue in 2004. They scaled back during the financial crisis of 2007-10, but Pérez is now back to doing new projects.

Manny Medina left Cuba in 1965 when he was thirteen. He graduated from Florida Atlantic University with a degree in accounting, his ticket to credibility in the business world. After working for PriceWaterhouse's Latin American Division, he went out on his own. In 1980, he formed Terremark, which focused on commercial and high-rise real estate development in Florida and the Middle East. In the 1990s, he started building infrastructure for telecommunication companies, including the Network Access Point (NAP), a 750,000-square-feet data center in downtown Miami that is the hub for telephony in the Americas. In 2011, Medina sold Terremark to Verizon for almost $2 billion.[3]

Ramón Oyarzún is another entrepreneur trained in accounting. After ten years in public accounting for a firm in Coral Gables, in 1984 he joined Silver Eagle Distributors, a beer distributor of Anheuser-Busch. Two years later, he acquired Silver Eagle Distributors, Ltd.—the exclusive distributorship for Anheuser-Busch, which he sold in 2006.[4]

Carlos Manuel de la Cruz, chairman of Eagle Brands, an Anheuser-Busch wholesaler in Miami-Dade County, had an estimated $100 million in annual sales. Born in Havana, de la Cruz attended the University of

Pennsylvania's prestigious Wharton School, receiving a BS in 1962 and an MBA in finance in 1963. After graduation, he worked as a securities analyst, a mutual fund portfolio manager, and a partner in a bank. After several years in Spain, he and his family returned to Miami, where he received a law degree from the University of Miami in 1979. In addition to leading Eagle Brands and Anheuser-Busch, de la Cruz is chairman of the Coca-Cola bottler in Puerto Rico and several South Florida automobile dealerships.

Omar Rodríguez and Manuel Marín opened their first Presidente Supermarket in Miami in 1990, at the corner of 5th Street and Biscayne Boulevard. A second store followed in 1992, and today Presidente Supermarkets-Tropical Supermarket have one thousand employees and operate twenty stores from Miami-Dade County to the city of Lake Worth in Palm Beach County. They also operate other stores under the Tropical name.

Antonio and Nilda Vilariño came to South Florida in the Mariel Boatlift in the 1980s. Four years later, they opened their first Las Vegas restaurant in Hollywood, Florida, and Cuban dining hasn't been the same since. The Vilariños and their five daughters now operate six Las Vegas sites—five in Broward and one in Miami Beach, plus their new flagship restaurant in Doral with huge banquet areas.

Chef Douglas Rodríguez, nicknamed the "Godfather of Nuevo Latino Cuisine," is the son of Cuban immigrants. He grew up in Miami with the sights, smells, and tastes of Cuban-American cuisine, and he developed a passion for food early on. At fourteen, he landed his first restaurant job as a summer apprentice at the Four Ambassadors Hotel in Miami, before attending culinary school at Johnson and Wales University in Providence, R.I.

In 1989, Rodríguez opened Yuca, an upscale Cuban-style restaurant in Coral Gables. Yuca was a success, and at age twenty-four, Chef Rodríguez was a celebrated Miami chef, winning the "Chef of the Year, Miami" award from the Chefs of America and receiving his first and second "Rising Chef of the Year" nominations by the James Beard Foundation. In 1994, Rodríguez opened Patria in New York City, a laboratory for his cooking which he labeled "Nuevo Latino." Patria received rave reviews, and Rodríguez followed up with Chicama—a Peruvian Ceviche bar, and Pipa, a Tapas bar.

In 2004, Rodríguez headed back to Miami Beach and opened OLA, followed by De Rodríguez Cuba at the Astor Hotel in December 2009. The most recent addition to De Rodríguez' restaurant empire is De Rodríguez Ocean, located at the Hilton Bentley on Ocean Drive in Miami Beach. *Newsweek* selected Rodríguez as one of the one hundred Americans who will influence the coming millennium.[5]

In 1986, Leopoldo Fernández Pujals started *Telepizza* in Spain, a pioneer in American-style pizza home delivery, which became the second largest fast food restaurant in Spain after McDonald's. Arturo G. Torres opened his first grocery store at age eighteen in Cuba. After Castro began to seize his holdings, Torres joined the resistance and escaped Cuba disguised as a Catholic priest. As an exile, he went from washing dishes in Miami Beach, to owning numerous Pizza Hut and Taco Bell franchises across the U.S., Caribbean, and Europe.[6]

Bakeries were among the first businesses started by Cuban entrepreneurs because the exiles craved cakes made of *nata* (cream) and other delicate tastes stored in their memories from the island. Two popular Cuban bakeries are Gilbert's, owned by the Salgado family, and Ricky's, owned by Ricky Alvarez. Housewife Edda Martínez launched Cakes by Design in her family kitchen in 1978. Over the past thirty years, Edda's Cake Designs has grown to four stores in South Florida. Edda and her cakes have been featured in prominent publications, such as *Martha Stewart Weddings, In Style, Ocean Drive Magazine,* and the *Miami Herald.* Master baker Lucila Jiménez started Sweet Art by Lucila, which now sells at Publix and Sedano's Supermarkets.

The first sign that Mike Fernández was destined to become an entrepreneur came when fourteen-year-old Fernández worked at the souvenir kiosk of the American Museum of Natural History in New York. Noticing there were no replicas of a brontosaurus for sale, Fernández bought a box of one hundred of the plastic dinosaurs and sold them in two hours. He was promptly fired. In the 1970s, he moved to Miami after three years with the 82nd Airborne, and he began to sell employee life insurance to small companies. He later sold this business for $3.5 million.

In 1993, Fernández founded a Tampa-based HMO, Physicians Healthcare Plans. He sold that company in 2002 for $181 million. The remainder of the company became CarePlus Health Plans, sold to Humana in 2004. Together, the two companies grossed $607 million. He and his co-investors in CarePlus gave $28 million of their take to employees to reward them for their contribution to CarePlus' success.

As soon as Fernández cashed out of CarePlus, he formed a $240-million private equity firm, MBF Partners, with two executives he had known for years, Marcio Cabrera and Jorge Rico. They invested in Navarro Discount Pharmacies, the largest Hispanic-owned drugstore chain in the U.S. In 2010, MBF purchased Total Health Choice, and folded it into new umbrella company Simply Healthcare Plans that will expand beyond Florida.[7]

Many of the second generation of Cuban entrepreneurs focused on opportunities in health care. Paul Cejas founded CareFlorida Health Systems, the largest Hispanic-owned health-care company in the U.S. until it merged in 1994 with Foundation Health of California for stock worth $90 million. A graduate of the University of Miami, Cejas was listed among the "100 most powerful people in southern Florida" by *South Florida CEO* magazine. President Clinton appointed Cejas ambassador to Belgium.

Given that the health-care field is rife with fraud, it's not surprising that some exile businesses have gotten caught up in it. Pharmed Group was founded by Carlos and Jorge de Céspedes, Pedro Pan brothers who built their South Florida medical supply firm into one of the country's largest Hispanic-owned businesses before it collapsed in 2007 when both admitted to cheating on their taxes and billing Kendall Regional Medical Center for $5.4 million worth of surgical supplies that Pharmed never delivered.

Miguel G. Recarey, Jr., built the successful International Medical Centers empire during the 1980s, before being indicted for bribery and embezzlement. He skipped bail and escaped the country after receiving a $2.2 million refund from the IRS. Recarey fled to Spain, where judges refused to extradite him.[8]

Twelve-year-old Carlos Saladrigas arrived in Miami in 1961 as a Pedro Pan child, with three dollars in cash, six changes of clothing, five bottles of rum, and a box of cigars. In one year, he saved four hundred dollars mowing lawns, delivering papers, and waxing cars. A high school dropout, he went on to earn a degree in accounting at night, a bachelor's degree in business administration *cum laude* from the University of Miami, and an MBA with honors from Harvard University.

Saladrigas co-founded the Vincam Group, a Miami-based professional employer organization, in 1984. He took it public in 1996, and in 1998, with revenues exceeding $1 billion, Vincam was named the largest Hispanic-owned company in the U.S. by *Hispanic Business* magazine. In March 1999, Vincam merged with Automatic Data Processing Inc. (NYSE: ADP), and Saladrigas retired in 2002 as CEO of ADP TotalSource.

Since 1976, Avanti Press, owned by Joe Arriola and Pepe Sánchez, has grown sixty-fold, achieving revenues of $140 million per year and reaching 1,500 employees. In 1993, it acquired Case-Hoyt. Avanti's specialty became printing high-quality catalogs for companies like Royal Caribbean Cruise Lines. Avanti was sold to St. Ives Group in 2001.

From 2003 to 2006, Joe Arriola went on to become city manager of Miami for a salary of one dollar year, and in 2007 he was hired as a consultant to Pullman Tours, by then part of Royal Caribbean Cruise Lines, to structure their catalog business in Madrid.

Fatherless from a young age, José S. Suquet recalls how his mother imbued him with love of country and his native language, and she convinced him that hard work pays off in the USA. As a young man in Manhattan, he worked for Chock-Full-O'Nuts, becoming a restaurant manager before turning to selling insurance. Suquet graduated from Fordham University with a BS, and he holds an MBA from the University of Miami. He joined AXA Financial and rose to senior executive, vice president, and chief distribution officer. During his six-year tenure at corporate headquarters, revenues increased from $5.5 billion to more than $13 billion.

Suquet joined Pan-American Life Insurance in November 2004 as president and CEO, and he led it through the devastation of Hurricane Katrina in August 2005, with an emergency recovery plan that would become an industry case study. He is now chairman of the board, president, and CEO of Pan-American Life Insurance Group. Suquet likes to recount how he is the only insurance executive to actually have his offices destroyed by two different hurricanes—the first by Hurricane Andrew in 1992 in Miami while he worked for AXA, and the second when Katrina destroyed his fifth-floor office in New Orleans.[9]

Frank del Río came to the U.S. in 1961 at age seven, with a single suitcase—because his parents, like all the other exiles, assumed they wouldn't be staying long. He earned a degree in accounting from the University of Florida and worked for Peat Marwick for three years before joining Certified Vacations, where he became executive vice president of sales and marketing. He then joined Renaissance Cruises and became co-CEO of the luxury cruise provider, which went bankrupt after 9/11.

In 2002, Del Río launched Oceania Cruises with one used ship, and by 2010 they had three. In 2011, the new ship *Marina* was delivered; *Riviera* will follow in 2012. Oceania takes cruisers off the beaten path. It has 275 employees on shore and around 2,000 at sea. In 2008, his group bought Regent Seven Seas Cruises, and consolidated the companies under Prestige Cruise Holdings. Del Río, who serves as chairman and CEO, says he learned two important lessons from the Renaissance bankruptcy.

"One is not to discount the importance of travel agents . . . the second is to innovate or evaporate."[10]

Félix Sabatés was the oldest of seven children in a family that owned an import-export business, jewelry and optical stores, insurance, sugar, cattle, service stations, and pharmacies. He arrived in Boston at age sixteen with twenty-five dollars and two boxes of cigars, and he found work at the local hospital washing pots and pans. Later, he resettled in Lexington, North Carolina, where he worked twelve-hour shifts at a furniture factory, before persuading a Chevrolet dealer to give him a shot at selling cars. He convinced the dealer by offering to work for free.

A businessman read about his record sales achievements in the local newspaper, and he offered him a manufacturer's representative job. Again, Sabatés broke the sales records, and in 1974, at the age of thirty-two, Sabatés bought the company Top Sales, which sold the Atari products Pong and Pac Man, and Teddy Ruxpin, the talking Teddy Bear. When the popular bear became a "gotta-have-it" gift for Christmas, Sabatés chartered a Boeing 747, removed the seats, and filled the aircraft with Teddy Ruxpins.

Next, he began to sell Nintendo's Super Mario Bros. game. His core distribution business included products from Black and Decker, Emerson Electronics, and Uniden. When Compaq Computer wanted to sell PCs to consumers and small businesses, Top Sales helped establish their brand name almost overnight. Sabatés surprised many by selling his company in 2001 to his employees, reportedly for less than he could have gotten on the open market.

In 1988, he founded SABCO Racing, and a new NASCAR Winston Cup competitor entered the scene. He hired driver Kyle Petty in 1989. In 1992, Sabatés' team branched out into the Busch Series. Petty found his groove in the Winston Cup circuit, finishing in the top five in the final point standings for the season. The team fielded both cars in the Winston Cup circuit the following year, and Petty again finished top five in total points. In 1988, as one of the original owners of the New Orleans

Hornets basketball team, Sabatés played an intregal part negotiating with the NBA to grant franchise rights to Charlotte. After starting the first professional indoor soccer league in the 1980s, he was one of the first investors in the World Football League. In 2000, he bought Trinity Yachts.[11]

Sabatés' advice to future entrepreneurs is, "Don't quit. If you get a 'no' answer it means that you need to ask again to get a 'yes.'"[12]

One of the most successful Cuban entrepreneurs was a housewife, mother, and full-time student when she arrived in Miami as an exile. Remedio Díaz-Oliver had hoped to become a college professor, but the Communist regime undercut her plans. In the United States, she went to work for American International Container and rose to the position of president. She resigned from her employer in 1991 to found her own company, All American Containers, with a client list that includes Coca-Cola, McCormick, Schering, and PepsiCo. Half of the company's revenues come from South America and the Caribbean. Today, hers is among the wealthiest Hispanic families in the U.S. Díaz-Oliver is a global entrepreneur: despite the name, All American Containers distributes in fifty-two countries.

David Hernández attended Palm Beach Atlantic University and obtained an MBA in finance and marketing from New York University in 1999. He went to work for Enron as a finance manager and was laid off in 2001. With another Cuban exile, Alberto Daire, Hernández started Liberty Power, an independent retail electric provider, in December 2001. Aptly named because of his Cuban origins, Liberty was the only national, minority-owned energy provider in the U.S. By 2006, it had grown to $120 million in revenue.[13]

Several new entrepreneurs went into the building supply business. Among them were:

- Osvaldo "Ovi" Vento who founded Everglades lumber and Building Supplies, one of the largest suppliers of building material in South Florida.

- Ignacio Pérez who brought his family from Cuba in 1972. His company Gancedo Lumber produces millwork and reinforcement bar (rebar). Three generations have been in the business for four decades.
- Carlos Nachón established Nachón Lumber in 1973, and he is one of the main lumber suppliers in Hialeah, Florida.
- Israel García came to Miami when he was nine years old during the 1980 Mariel Boatlift. After quitting school at sixteen to work in the construction business, he founded Heights Roofing Inc. and Value Metal Corp. in 1999.

After only nine years as a dealership owner, Frank Rodríguez was elected president of Ford Motor's National Dealer Council. He built Greenway Ford (Orlando) into one of the country's largest Hispanic businesses, consistently ranked among Ford's top twenty dealerships. He and business partner, Carl Atkinson, are among the first U.S. car dealers venturing into the Chinese market by opening a dealership in China, Greenway Shanghai Motors. In addition to Greenway Ford, Rodríguez owns Greenway Chrysler-Dodge-Jeep, the Kia Store in Orlando, and a Ford dealership in Tampa.[14]

Many Cuban exiles have established highly successful auto dealerships. Lombardo Pérez, Sr., opened Metro Ford in July 1983. After many years at the same location, it recently inaugurated a new multi-million-dollar showroom. Pérez also acquired Miami Lincoln Mercury and moved that operation to his previous location. The next step was the modernization of Metro Ford Lincoln Mercury Service and Parts Departments to accommodate the influx of Lincoln Mercury customers. His son Lombardo Pérez, Jr., helps run the operation.[15]

Mario Murgado turned around several auto dealerships before establishing Brickell Motors in the heart of Miami's Little Havana neighborhood. Gregorio Santiesteban started Sanfer Sports Car Inc. in 1973, serving international clientele as well as the local Miami area. Gregorio's son, Carlos Santiesteban, now runs the $23 million company along with his son Carlos, Jr.

Iván Motta and Carlos Domenech founded Automotores Zona Franca Automotive Group, a full-service international automobile trading company in Miami. Since 1993, it has been selling and exporting premium brand-new vehicles to foreign companies and individuals worldwide, with a large portfolio of automobiles and trucks for immediate delivery.

Néstor Fernández fled to the U.S. in 1961 at the age of nineteen, accompanied by his wife, Nancy, and a younger brother, sister, and cousin. In Miami, he washed dishes and took machine shop courses at night. The family moved to Dayton, Ohio, and Néstor began working in a tool shop. He and Nancy founded Digitron in 1976 with four thousand dollars—by 2003 they had reached $43 million in annual sales. The company is a manufacturer and distributor of tools and dies, special machines, and industrial supplies. Serving the automotive and aerospace industries, it has such clients as General Electric, Ford, General Motors, Rockwell International, and Pratt & Whitney.

When a GM engineer suggested Digitron could qualify as a minority supplier, they received a $120,000 loan in 1977 from Motor Enterprises, GM's minority enterprise small business investment company. "We paid it back ahead of schedule," says Néstor, pointing out that such programs only give minority businesses an opportunity to bid on a contract. "Customers will drop you if you don't deliver the goods."

They offer good advice for anyone launching their own businesses. "Be cheap," Néstor answers when asked the formula for success. "So many people who start a small business live beyond their means as soon as they become successful. If you have a small business and want to grow, you can't start reaping the harvest. You have to put it right back into the business."

The Fernándezes, who live modestly, pay some of their employees more than they pay themselves. "You have to invest in your people," explains Néstor. Nancy adds that sometimes you need to discipline your urge to grow. She acknowledges Néstor might have grown the company faster, but she reined him in. "Growing is nice," she says, "but you don't always have the backup to do it. In the economic position we are in, you have to have time to regroup."[16]

FURTHER READING

For a complete overview of the statistics of the Cuban entrepreneurial miracle in the U.S., see Appendix III—Cuban-American community in the United States: By the Numbers.

NOTES

1. Interview with the author, March 11, 2011.
2. Ibid.
3. *Miami Herald*, October 26, 2009; manny-medina-ceo-of-terremark-part-1.
4. Interview with the author, May 5, 2010.
5. http://www.olamiami.com/about-the-chef.
6. http://havanajournal.com/cuban_americans/entry/arturo-torres-a-cuban-american-success-story.
7. *Miami Herald*, April 14, 2010.
8. http://www.faqs.org/abstracts/Law/Businessman-ABCs-20-20-has-jaundiced-eye-a-Miami-jury-is-hearing-a-libel-case-brought-by-a-local-rea.html#ixzz0ybdlLydF
9. Interview with the author, November 3, 2010.
10. Patricia R. Olsen, "Out of Cuba with a suitcase," *New York Times*, June 11, 2011.
11. Cruising Victory Lane, www.greatercharlottebiz.com/article.asp?id=149.
12. December 2, 2009, http://video.forbes.com/fvn/bestplaces/rebuilding-detroit-manufacturing-and-technology?partner=playlist.
13. http://investing.businessweek.com/research/stocks/private/person.asp?personId=25744807&privcapId=7925185.
14. http://wardsdealer.com/ar/auto_dealer_move_started.
15. www.metroford.com/ou/miami-ford/console. do? page=a_history.
16. Sharon Nelton, *Nations Business*, January 1984.

20

LEADERS IN CORPORATE AMERICA

BY FRANCISCO RODRIGUEZ, LEONARDO RODRIGUEZ, AND SAM VERDEJA

In addition to the entrepreneurs who started their own businesses, many Cuban exiles have thrived in established American and multinational companies, where they have quickly scaled the corporate ladder and made it to the very highest levels in the leadership pyramid.

Their success is remarkable for the speed in which it was achieved. As Professor Raúl Moncarz of Florida International University (FIU) says, "Most of the Cubans adapted rapidly to a competitive and individualistic market pattern . . . [due to] a vigorous tendency to display personal initiative and to assume responsibility for one's own future. Cubans have blended into the local, national and international economy in a relatively short interval without the need for any major adjustments."[1]

One Cuban refugee who truly embodied the American Dream was Roberto C. Goizueta, chairman of the board and CEO of the Coca-Cola Company from 1981 until his death in 1997. Goizueta was born in Cuba in 1931, attended the Colegio de Belén in Havana, and then went to Connecticut to the Cheshire Academy to learn English. He graduated from Yale in 1953 with a degree in chemical engineering. A year later, he joined the Coca-Cola Company in Havana. He left Cuba with his wife and children in 1960 and headed for Miami. The exile experience changed his life and outlook forever.

"My story boils down to a single, inspiring reality," Goizueta said. "That a young immigrant could come to this country, be given a chance to work hard and apply his skills, and ultimately earn the opportunity to lead not only a large corporation, but an institution that actually symbolizes the very essence of America and American ideals."[2]

Twenty years later, Goizueta was chosen to lead the iconic Coca-Cola Company. During his sixteen years as chairman and CEO, the company's market value increased from $4 billion to $145 billion. The year he died, *Fortune* named Coca-Cola "America's Most Admired Corporation" for the second consecutive year.[3]

Like many leading Cuban-American businessmen, Goizueta and his family have done a great deal for charity. In 1992, he established the Goizueta Foundation, which supports the Cuban Heritage Collection of the University of Miami Libraries, among other causes. In 1999, the Goizueta Foundation, led by Roberto's wife, Olga, made a challenge grant of $2.5 million to the University of Miami toward the building of a new home for the Cuban Heritage Collection. With additional support from the Elena Díaz-Versón Amos and the Fanjul family, the Cuban Heritage Collection's Roberto C. Goizueta Pavilion was completed in the fall of 2002. It was dedicated on January 28, 2003, to commemorate the 150th anniversary of the birth of José Martí.

Roberto's son Javier followed in his father's footsteps in joining Coca-Cola; he now serves as president of the Global McDonald's Division, responsible for the alliance with one of Coke's largest business partners.

Cuban-Americans have also played important roles at Coke's competitor corporation, PepsiCo. Dr. Néstor Carbonell Cortina, a Bay of Pigs veteran, ran Pepsi's operations in the Americas and Europe as senior vice president of Pepsi-Cola International. Throughout his career with Pepsi, he continued to work for the end of the Castro regime. Abelardo E. Bru joined Pepsi in 1976, and in 1999 he became chairman & CEO of Frito-Lay, PepsiCo's largest and most profitable operating division, known for attracting and developing outstanding talent. After leading Frito-Lay through one of its most successful periods, Bru retired in 2005 as vice chairman of PepsiCo.[4]

Another prominent Cuban exile in corporate America is Carlos M. Gutiérrez, former CEO of Kellogg, who served as the thirty-fifth secretary of commerce of the U.S. under President George W. Bush. Gutiérrez was born in Havana, the son of a successful businessman who was considered an enemy of the state by Fidel Castro. After his father was arrested and the family plantation expropriated, they fled to the United States and eventually settled in Mexico.

Gutiérrez started working for Kellogg at the age of twenty, "driving a cereal truck around the seedier parts of Mexico City, selling *Zucaritas* (Frosted Flakes) to small mom-and-pop stores. By 30 he had worked his way up to general manager of Kellogg's troubled Mexican operations."[5] He was appointed CEO of Kellogg in 1999—the youngest in the company's hundred-year history, and at the time the only Latin CEO of a *Fortune 500* company. In 2004, *Fortune* magazine dubbed Gutiérrez "The Man Who Fixed Kellogg":

> *Since becoming CEO of the cereal giant five years ago, the 50-year-old Cuba native has transformed a lumbering, insular, volume-obsessed company into an innovative, profit-focused powerhouse admired by Wall Street and Wal-Mart alike. He has breathed new life into brands like Frosted Flakes and Special K, regaining the top spot in the $9 billion U.S. cereal market . . . and put some snap, crackle, and pop into Kellogg's stock, which is up 26% over the past year and has dramatically outperformed its peers for three years running.*[6]

In November 2004, President Bush appointed Gutiérrez secretary of commerce, saying, "He understands the world of business, from the first rung on the ladder to the very top. He knows exactly what it takes to help American businesses grow and to create jobs."[7]

Ralph de la Vega, president and CEO of AT&T Worldwide, left

Cuba by himself at the age of nine. His family was stopped at the airport from leaving with him, and they chose to send him on to freedom alone, though it would be four years before they would be reunited. He started as a management assistant at BellSouth (then Southern Bell) in 1974 and rose to become president of BellSouth Latin America before joining Cingular Wireless as CEO in 2004. After the close of the AT&T-BellSouth merger, which consolidated ownership of Cingular, he was appointed president and CEO of AT&T Mobility in 2007. He has written a book entitled *Obstacles Welcome,* about which former UN Ambassador Andrew Young said, "De la Vega's leadership principles are a great example of public purpose capitalism—a profit model guided by integrity, a genuine concern for workers, and a commitment to providing a product that improves a community."[8]

Another prominent Cuban-American at AT&T is Dr. Alicia Abella, daughter of Cuban refugees and executive director of the Human Computer Interface Services Research Department. She joined AT&T in 1995 after earning a doctorate in computer science from Columbia University, New York.[9] Abella is also the executive vice president for AT&T's Young Science Achievers program, which aims to bring more minorities into the science field and boost their overall awareness of college.

Dr. Ralph de la Torre, who trained as a heart surgeon, now heads Steward Health Care System in Massachusetts—a for-profit company with eight acute care centers. In 2008, he took over the failing Caritas Christi Catholic Hospitals, turning them into a profitable operation. His mission is to build a large network of lower-cost, high-quality community hospitals—what some have branded a "Southwest Airlines" approach to medicine—that could be replicated in other parts of the country. De la Torre believes community hospitals have a critical role to play in reducing health care costs and improving their quality throughout the United States. In 2011, they made an unsuccessful bid to acquire Jackson Memorial Hospital in Miami.

According to an in-depth profile in the *Boston Globe*:

The de la Torre family story bears the markings of the classic immigrant overachiever narrative. Ralph's father, Angel, was an internist in Cuba who fled his homeland for political reasons in 1960. He arrived in Florida with no money and no English. When he started over his medical training, he chose cardiology. His oldest son, Ralph, was born during his training. Angel was a demanding dad. When Ralph would proudly present a test grade of 97, his father would ask, 'Did anyone in the class score a 100?' When the reporter asked his colleagues to rate Ralph de la Torre's drive on a scale of 1 to 10, 'they reliably responded '11.'"[10]

The fast food industry has proven to be fertile territory for Cuban-American business leaders. Ralph Alvarez retired in 2009 as head of operations, the number two job in McDonald's Corporation. Before that, he had been president of McDonald's North America. And José Armario is group president for Canada, Latin America, and International Franchising at McDonald's. Julio Ramírez, a second-generation Cuban-American, received a BS in economics from Georgia State University and an MBA from the University of Georgia. After working for Xerox, Southern Bell, and AT&T Information Systems, he joined Burger King in 1984, served as president for the Latin American region, and in 2007 was appointed executive vice president, global operations, reporting to the CEO.

Finance is another business sector that has attracted many talented Cuban-Americans. After earning a BS in operations research from Columbia University and an MBA from the Stanford Graduate School of Business, Leopoldo E. Guzmán joined Lazard Freres in 1976. He moved to mergers and acquisitions at Chase Manhattan Bank in 1980, and he became chief investment officer of Gulf Investment Co. in Kuwait in 1982. Guzmán founded his own investment banking and institutional brokerage firm in Coral Gables, Florida, in 1987, which in 2009 was ranked in the top ten in the country for trading efficiency on both the NYSE and NASDAQ exchanges. In 2005, Guzmán was appointed by

President George W. Bush to the advisory committee of the Pension Benefit Guaranty Corporation.

George Reyes earned a BA degree in accounting from the University of South Florida and an MBA from Santa Clara University before spending thirteen years at Sun Microsystems in a variety of jobs, including vice president and corporate controller from 1994 to 1999, and then vice president and treasurer from 1999 to 2001. George later went on to become chief financial officer at Google, until his retirement in 2007, and he served on Symantec's Board of Directors.

Alvaro G. de Molina began his career in 1979 with PriceWaterhouse, before leading the emerging markets business at J.P. Morgan. He then joined Bank of America, where he worked for seventeen years, rising to the position of chief financial officer. In 2007, he became CEO of GMAC Financial Services, and transformed GMAC into a bank holding company—a move that was approved by the U.S. Federal Reserve in 2008.[11]

Alberto Vilar founded Amerindo Investment Advisors in 1979, and he had made his first million by 1981. Amerindo's primary investment focus was technology—a sector that was severely impacted by the bursting of the dotcom bubble in 2000. Vilar became a prominent philanthropist, sponsoring many musical events, particularly opera. In November 2008, he was found guilty of fraud charges and sentenced to nine years in prison.[12]

Leonard Simkovitz left Cuba in 1960 with the dream of flying airplanes. He not only achieved his goal, but also began leasing airplanes. In 2000, he opened Airline Capital Leasing, which leases planes in Latin America, the Middle East, Africa, and Russia. And Zoé Cruz capped a successful career on male-dominated Wall Street by becoming co-president of Morgan Stanley and the highest paid woman on Wall Street in 2007.[13]

Rafael Montalvo, a Bay of Pigs veteran, founded Nortek, an airplane parts and repair business, now known as AvBorne. In 1997, he sold the business. AvBorne has a huge presence around Miami International Airport where it provides maintenance to thousands of airplanes a year. For many years Montalvo was a top Eastern Airlines executive.

Outside of these industries, Cuban-American senior executives can be found across many diverse companies. Oscar Suris is an executive vice president in charge of Corporate Communications at Wells Fargo. María A. Sastre is vice president and total guest director for Royal Caribbean International. Laurene Gandolfo is executive vice president for Macy's Home Private Brand, responsible for the development of all brands owned by Macy's: Bloomindale's, Hudson Park, and Sky Textiles. Raquel "Rocky" Egusquiza is vice president of Multicultural Markets for the American Association of Retired Persons (AARP).

Luis Manuel Ramírez, whose father fought with and then against Fidel Castro, leads the Industrial Solutions Group at General Electric—a $3 billion division in charge of fifteen thousand employees in sixty factories around the world. Jorge Piñón was president and CEO of Transworld Oil US, before becoming president of Amoco Oil de México and Amoco Oil Latin America, based in Mexico City, in 1994. After the 1999 merger between Amoco and BP, Piñón managed BP Europe's western Mediterranean petroleum supply. He retired from BP in 2003.

José Fernández, an accountant by training, helped form Legal Applications Holding Corp., which later purchased Client Profile, a legal case management software company. He became the COO and CFO for the company, which eventually partnered with Microsoft's Quantum Leap program creating the CRM4Legal software product.

Ricardo Coro, who came from Cuba as a child, is senior vice president and chief information officer at Advance Auto Parts, Inc., a leading after-market retailer.

Antonio "Tony" Navarro, a Castro supporter who became an anti-Castro resistance fighter with the nickname "Tocayo," obtained a chemical engineering degree from Georgia Tech and worked for Shell Chemical before joining Julio Lobo's Galbán Trading Co., one of Cuba's biggest sugar exporters. In 1961, his communications helped guide airdropped shipments of food and weapons to resistance fighters who were to support the Bay of Pigs invasion. Navarro spent twelve years in Peru as general manager for W.R. Grace and Co.'s extensive sugar, chemicals, and diversified industries. He then moved to New York as assistant to the CEO, subsequently holding a series of executive positions before leading Radio and TV Martí in the early 1990s.

Francisco Codina came to the U.S. at age thirteen. He joined Ford Motor in 1977 as zone manager for New Orleans, and he finished his career in 2007 as group vice president for North America Marketing, Sales, and Service. In an interview with *Hispanic Business*, Codina says, "I wanted to be in the automotive industry, as a whole, but Ford had that iconic brand—the fabric of America. When I walked in there thirty years ago, from day one, I knew it was where I belonged. I literally walked in and started answering phones."[14]

NOTES

1. Interview with Professor Raul Moncarz, December 12, 2010.
2. Roberto Goizueta speech at Independence Day ceremonies, Monticello, Virginia, 1995.
3. *Fortune*, March 1998.
4. www.people.forbes.com.
5. Matthew Boyle, "The Man Who Fixed Kellogg," *Fortune*, September 6, 2004.
6. Ibid.
7. November 10, 2008, georgewbush-whitehouse.archives.gov.
8. www.Obstacleswelcome.com.
9. *Hispanic Business*, April 2010.
10. *Boston Globe*, February 6, 2011.
11. *Wall Street Journal*, Top Executives Bios.
12. Alberto Vilar: 1940–: Investor, Philanthropist - A Frustrated Music-lover - Fund, Business, Amerindo, Internet, Investment, and Washington. http://biography.jrank.org/pages/3489/Vilar-Alberto-1940-Investor-Philanthropist-Frustrated-Music-Lover.html#ixzz1SUPeXvdW.
13. *El Nuevo Herald*, December 2, 2007.
14. *Hispanic Business*, November 2007.

ARTS, ENTERTAINMENT, AND RELIGION

21

CUBA'S WANDERING LITERATURE

BY OLGA CONNOR

Much of the literature of the Cuban exile does not begin in 1959, the year in which the longest-ruling dictator in recorded world history came to power. Cubans have suffered a terrible fate: They are the most desirous of freedom, and yet the most constrained to reach it. This has been the case ever since they aspired to become independent, first from the Spanish since 1868, then from the United States after 1898, and later on after the dreadful alliance with Russia that could have led to a nuclear holocaust in 1962. Ultimately, the Cubans who today hold power have betrayed the hopes and ideals of a people who have not been able to free themselves from that burden, because they have had neither the understanding nor the support of foreign nations.

That same lack of understanding for the Cuban exile community has led many contemporary writers to suffer twice the absence of a homeland, unlike previous exiles during the Spanish Colonial era. Since then, a large part of our literary production has been generated outside the island so that somehow we have a culture wandering or roaming between the two Cubas: One inside the island, and the other universal—but spiritually Cuban—although it is not based on our soil.

In the first stage, that of the colonial era, José María Heredia (1803-39) was one of the poets who began to define Cuba's nationality. He was a totally accomplished poet who wrote one of the most sublime of romantic poems, *Oda al Niágara*. If he didn't suffer from the rejection, he certainly did so because of the anguish of having to learn English when, in 1823, at the age of twenty, he had to flee the island for the United States. He then moved to Mexico, where he devoted himself to the legal profession and journalism. He wrote another sublime poem, *En el teocalli de Cholula*. Heredia was the first poet condemned to exile because of the ideal of freedom in Cuba.

Félix Varela (1788-1853) was another exile who wrote of his work in the United States but who, nevertheless, was an encouragement to the conscience of the emerging national sentiment. As a member of the lower house of the Spanish Cortes (the legislature in Spain) in 1821, he defended Cuba's freedom and the abolition of slavery so that when the Cortes dissolved itself, he was sentenced to death for his ideas. This forced him to escape to Gibraltar and from there to New York in 1823. The following year, while living in Philadelphia, he began publishing *El Habanero*, a newspaper that stated that the island should be both "in politics as it is in nature." In 1835, he published his *Cartas a Elpidio* (Letters to Elpidio).

But the most prominent Cuban exile in the late nineteenth century was José Martí (1853-95), who promoted the idea of national independence with a revolutionary ideal that included national and individual freedoms. Martí also produced an extensive journalistic body of work, and he was a translator and precursor of modernism with his poems and stories, especially his famous children's journal *La Edad de Oro* (The Golden Age), which he practically produced by himself and which never stopped being up-to-date because it became required reading in Cuban schools. Martí not only had a political ideal, but a literary one as well. He sought beauty with his words, and that is why he is considered the pioneer of the new world style in the Americas. He was recognized as such throughout the continent, being one of the first Cubans to reach the status of a universal paragon. The great Nicaraguan poet Rubén Darío describes him as such in his book, *Los Raros*. José Martí, the most Cuban among Cubans, produced most of his literature outside Cuba, mostly in New York, from where he communicated to newspapers all over Latin America his vision of the great northern continent as well as his vision for Cuba. "The best man of our race," is how Gabriela Mistral described him. His books of poetry were few—*Ismaelillo* (1882), *Versos Sencillos* (1891), and *Versos Libres* (posthumously).

Nationalism as a focal point in the Cuban literature of exile is a kind of destiny. Even in times when the creators have tried to separate themselves from political issues by seeking art for art's sake, there has been a fervor—sort of a pendulum that goes from the identification with the island to linking it with other countries in an effort to build bridges across the horizon and, at the same time, to help it take root in the soil. That which was most stylistic was also Cuban. But it is the joining with a universal literature that keeps the authors within the stream of Western consciousness.

The interesting thing is precisely the fact that much of our literature was written in exile, unlike what happened in Spain—where few authors and artists could stand to be outside of the country for a long time, even during the Franco era.

The Cuban literary work abroad after the island's independence continued with examples like those of thinker Jorge Mañach (1898-1961), the author of outstanding essays on the definition of Cubanness such as *La Crisis de Alta Cultura en Cuba* (1925), *La Indagación del Choteo* (1928), and *Martí, el Apóstol*, in the 1940s. In 1927, he founded *Avance*, an avant-garde journal, and in 1931 he was part of ABC, an underground group dedicated to overthrowing dictator Gerardo Machado. In 1934, after being secretary of education for a short time, he left for the United States amid a turbulent time on the island. He returned in 1939 since he had been appointed as ABC's delegate to the Constitutional Assembly. His second exile began in 1960, when he became disillusioned with the revolution. Much of his intellectual work took place outside of Cuba as a student at

Harvard University, then at the Sorbonne in Paris, and finally as an exile for the second time in Puerto Rico, where he wrote *Teoría de la Frontera*, which was published posthumously. He was a professor at the University of Havana and professor emeritus at Columbia University in New York and the University of Puerto Rico.

When writers started to go into exile because of the dictatorial policies of Fidel Castro and his government's covenant with the international Left, the image of the Cuban exile became negative for intellectuals and writers. While many received academic support at U.S. universities, or were welcomed in Rome, Paris, and London, or Buenos Aires and Caracas, all underwent a difficult task in trying to convince their hosts of the horrible nightmare endured by Cuba. Even today there are memories of those injustices exemplified by the mere fact that Guillermo Cabrera Infante (1929-2005)—who ironically would receive the Cervantes Prize in 1997—could not remain in exile in Spain when he decided to leave the island in 1964 and settled in London.

Another case was that of the poet Heberto Padilla, whose wife at the time in the late 1970s, Belkis Cuza Male, poet, artist, and director of the magazine *Linden Lane*, decided to move to Princeton University in New Jersey. By her own testimony, neither she nor her husband was invited to participate in university life.

The definition of what is great in literary work is very peculiar; it is socially determined, since it depends on acceptance among peers and critics. The canon of literature highlights certain authors and not others, so even if one could mention many writers who made the Cuban literature in exile a vast country without a home, only a few have come to be recognized as examples and models, despite the Cuban propaganda against them. Still, since the early 1960s, Cuban literature in exile has had to face the rejection of university groups, critics, and journalists in all countries where it flourished.

The illusion of the "Cuban Revolution" was in vogue worldwide, especially in intellectual circles, usually Left leaning or "liberal" as this general tendency is called in the United States. It was emotionally difficult to abandon the idea that the revolution was socially just. During the 1960s and 1970s, being a Cuban exile on an American university campus was almost synonymous to having the plague.

THE DECADES OF THE 1960S AND 1970S

To name some of the first writers who went into exile in 1959 and during the decade of the 1960s, one must include the poet Gastón Baquero, the playwright and critic Matías Montes Huidobro, and the poets Orlando Rodríguez Sardiñas "Rossardi," Isel Rivero, and Mercedes Cortázar. They were followed by the novelists Luis Ricardo Alonso, who was the revolutionary government's ambassador in London where he went into exile, and Guillermo Cabrera Infante, who, after winning the *Biblioteca Breve* Award with *Tres Tristes Tigres* (1964), decided to part company with the Castro regime.

Cabrera Infante was not just a writer of high stature, but also a political activist against the Castro regime and all Communist dictatorships. Because of this, he suffered on many levels. On the other hand, his love for Havana was such that *Tres Tristes Tigres* is a tribute to his city as well as a musical and poetic world lost forever. Among his other novels are *Vista del Amanecer en el Trópico* (1974-75), *La Habana Para un Infante Difunto* (1979), and—among his books of critiques—*Mea Cuba* (1993 and 1999), *Un Oficio del Siglo XX*, *Arcadia Todas las Noches* (1995), and *Holy Smoke* (1985). He has also been a scriptwriter under the name Guillermo Caín, which was a pseudonym he used as a film critic for the Havana magazine *Cartele*s. He also used that name in the cult film *Vanishing Point*, and the screenplay with his real name of *La Ciudad Perdida/Lost City*, the story of what happened in Cuba with the coming of the revolution. The movie was directed by Andy García.

Others among the early writers include Ramón Ferreira, a playwright who settled in Puerto Rico, and Lino Novás Calvo, one of Cuba's best short-story writers who lived in New York since he went into exile in 1959. Early on in her years in exile, New York was also the home of a future writer, Uva de Aragón, who came to the United States with her parents Carlos Márquez Sterling and Uva Hernández Catá.

The lyrics are not like the plastic arts or the movies. They move more easily on paper and in a book, so that soon we saw the works of other poets and writers outside Cuba in the 1960s, the first of our evolution in the post-revolutionary diaspora. The result of this endeavor is evident in a book published by *Ediciones Universal* in 1970, *Poesía en Exodo* (*El Exilio Cubano en su Poesía*, 1959-60), which was chosen and prologued by Ana Rosa Núñez, poet and librarian at the University of Miami. She dedicated the book thus: "In Cuba, the first verse in exile; to my mother, one more verse in exile."

The persons mentioned in the acknowledgments were the first codifiers of everything Cuban: Juan Manuel Salvat, editor par excellence of the exile; José Sánchez Boudy, who began collecting witty Cuban proverbs and jokes, such as *Lilayando*; Rosa Abella and Lesbia Orta de Varona; librarians of things Cubans such as Ana Rosa Núñez, Mercedes de Villiers, and Alberto Baeza Flores. Baeza Flores was a Chilean poet and essayist who helped many Cuban poets in those early years, including Teresa María Rojas.

This book is an invaluable tool in helping to understand these early efforts because it depicts the poetry for each year of the 1960s, including covers of published books, and has—at the end—an index of all poets that would be impossible to reproduce here. It also contains some surprises. For example, there are some verses of Angel Cuadra, imprisoned in Cuba in 1968; the reproduction of the poster of the *Primera Exposición Simultánea de Arte y Poesía Miami 1966*, which took place December 27-30 of that year and was sponsored by the *Asociación Fraternal Latinoamericana*; and an extensive section on underground poetry illegal in Cuba. The list of "Cuban literary magazines published in exile" is impressive. The first is *Protesta*, which only had one issue that came out in 1962. Artist Zilia Sánchez did the cover, and the magazine included the works of Mercedes Cortázar, Wiliam Busch, Jack Micheline, Isel Rivero, and René Ariza. Mauricio Fernández is the poet who appears as director of most of these publications in the 1960s, including *Exilio: Revista de Humanidades,* published in New York by Victor Batista Falla, and *La Nueva Sangre,* with Rolando Campins, Dolores Prida, and others. It was founded in 1968. The magazines were used to collect single poems and essays, and thus there is no doubt that this was very important for impoverished poets.

Among the poets mentioned in this book many names are repeated in the *Bibliografía Crítica de la Poesía Cubana: Exilio 1959-1971* (Plaza Mayor, Spain, 1973). Yara González Montes and Matías Montes Huidobro, two faithful reporters of Cuban literary events, wrote it and confirmed that there were many poets in exile in full creative work. Some of them were especially and greatly appreciated, such as Mercedes García Tudurí de Coya, always an admired poet from Cuba; Rafael Esténger and Paul Le Riverend, also of that generation; and other younger ones like Norma (Niurka) Acevedo, niece of actress Miriam Acevedo, and Rita Geada.

If Ana Rosa Núñez from Miami had emphasized only the poets of the exile, Rossardi—working from Spain—considered that all poets were part of the same literature, as seen in his anthology *La Ultima Poesía Cubana* (Hispanova, 1973). Included in this anthology were José Mario and Antón Arrufat, Martha Padilla and Carlos M. Luis, Cintio Vitier and Gastón Baquero. These last two are relevant as Catholic poets: Baquero, exiled in Spain for having belonged to the era of Fulgencio Batista; Vitier, a Catholic and theoretician of the new Cuban regime. The anthology also introduced Eugenio Florit, an outstanding poet who settled in New York, and Nicolás Guillén, another relevant poet who was a Communist standard-bearer on the island. There is also the distinguished Pura del Prado from Miami, and the voice of Pablo Armando Fernández in Havana. And, of course, he published Heberto Padilla, who had not left Cuba but had already passed through his notorious prosecution because of his book *Fuera de Juego*.

Two other writers of that generation are Concepción Alzola and Gladys Zaldívar. The first is an ethno-linguist and author of puppet theater, and the second is a poet of fine creations. Both are deceased. Amelia del Castillo has many published books of poetry, and she is still a pillar of the *Pen Club de Escritores Cubanos en el Exilio*.

Matías Montes Huidobro, who has written *La Narrativa Cubana Entre la Memoria y el Olvido* (The Cuban Narrative between Memory and Oblivion), speaks of these names from the first decade of the exile when referring to the Cuban novel: Salvador Díaz Versón, Emilio Fernández Camus, Manuel Cobo Sausa, Eugenio Sánchez Torrentó, Orlando Núñez Pérez, René Landa, Raoul Fowler, and Peter A. López. All of these wrote political novels. And there is also Bernardo Viera Trejo, who is the most important one of this group. Other novels were written in different styles by Manuel Linares, Alvaro de Villa, and Pedro Entenza.

Severo Sarduy worked with Montes Huidobro and Cabrera Infante at the magazine *Lunes de Revolución* in the early 1960s. And like both of them, he left Cuba soon and became successful in Paris, where he studied at the *Ecole du Louvre* and higher studies in *La Sorbonne*. While in Paris, Sarduy became an important part of the *Tel Quel* group, led by the structuralist critic Roland Barthes. His first work was *Gestos,* which was widely accepted, but it was his second novel that made him famous, *De Dónde Son los Cantantes* (1967).

During the 1970s came significant novels by Carlos Alberto Montaner, Juan Arcocha, Celedonio González, José Sánchez Boudy, and Fausto Masó. The last published in Venezuela *Desnudo en Caracas* (In Caracas in the Nude, 1970). Many other novelists also published their works, including, most prominently, Arturo A. Fox, Rosario Rexach, Anita Arroyo, and Nivaria Tejera, all led by Hilda Perera.

Among the playwrights who left Cuba in the early years of the exile the roster is smaller and includes José Cid; Ramón Ferreira; Leopoldo

Hernández; Raúl de Cárdenas—who would not write again until penning *Las Carbonell de la Calle Obispo* in the 1980s; Julio Matas; Fermín Borges; Eduardo Manet, who lives in Paris and is the author of *Las Monjas*; and Montes Huidobro, who in 1979 wrote *Ojos Para no Ver*. At the end of the 1970s, other playwrights left Cuba, including José Triana, author of *La Noche de los Asesinos*, and former political prisoner René Ariza. Triana goes to Paris and Ariza to California, but Ariza presented his work several times at residences in Miami.

There is also the *insilio*; in other words, an internal exile within the country. While in prison in Cuba, José Fernández Travieso and Jorge Vals write two important plays. Virgilio Piñera continued writing without leaving the island, but he was not appreciated there until long after his death. For seventeen years Antón Arrufat could not publish anything and ceased doing theater work. He was censured for his work *Siete Contra Tebas*; this happened from 1969 to 1971, at the same time as the Padilla case.

In 1979, a theatrical phenomenon appeared in New York: Ivan Acosta opened *El Super*, which later became a cult film. He also debuted other works, including the short film *Rosa and the Executioner of the Fiend*.

THE DECADE OF THE 1980S: *MARIEL*

During the 1980s, a large contingent of writers arrived in Miami. Among them was Reinaldo Arenas, a storyteller already well known by literary critics outside Cuba. Arenas served as the moving force and the cohesive center at meetings of literary and visual artists. This was confirmed by fellow writers such as the Abreu brothers (José, Juan, and Nicolás), Luis de la Paz, and Reinaldo García Ramos. Together, they founded the magazine *Mariel*, which was important not only because it launched a new creative movement, but also because it paid tribute to other great writers who worked while in exile, such as José

Martí, and internal exiles, such as José Lezama Lima. Carlos Victoria also published his first writings in this magazine—writings that were never published in Cuba, though he wrote *Halloween*, which was included in the book *Las Sombras en la Playa* (1992), in Miami. The same is the case with *La Travesía Secreta*, a novel translated into French, which won the Best Book of the Month Award in France. In Miami, he won the Letras de Oro Award for his novel *Puente en la Oscuridad*.

Lydia Cabrera, an ethnographer and extraordinary writer of fiction and author of anthropological studies of Afro-Cuban mythology, was one of the most important writers in Miami who supported this influx of writings and the arts. There were also the important writers Enrique Labrador Ruiz and Carlos Montenegro, who were highlighted in the magazine *Mariel*, having met with that group in the gatherings at Nancy Pérez Crespo's library and gallery, SIBI. Pérez Crespo was a great supporter of the writers of this exodus, editing their books and showing their works of art. In New York, Octavio Armand, with the magazine *Escandalar*, helped rescue one of the *"origenistas,"* Lorenzo García Vega, who lived in Miami and whose work was also published in one of the editions of *Mariel*. The term *"origenista"* came from the magazine *Orígenes*, founded by José Lezama Lima in Cuba.

Pedro Yánez, Carlos Ripoll, Giulio V. Blanc, and Florencio García Cisneros, with the magazine *Notas de Artes*, were other important supporters of this new generation, which settled mostly in New York. In Miami were the poets Esteban Luis Cárdenas and Néstor Díaz de Villegas, who left Cuba earlier but were considered part of this generation. Carlos Valero settled in Washington, D.C.

Reinaldo García Ramos became the heir to Arenas in organizing these writers when he re-edited a commemorative edition of *Mariel* in 2003 with the influence of the group that arrived with the Mariel Boatlift, which gave a big boost to the Cuban exile culture.

The best known of this group is Reinaldo Arenas (1943-1990), who made possible the 2000 Julian Schnabel film *Antes que Anochezca/*

Before Night Falls. It starred Oscar-winning Spanish actor Javier Bardem in the role of Arenas, and it is based on his posthumous autobiography. The book was on the *New York Times* list of the ten best books of the year in 1993. Despite his short life, Arenas had a remarkable body of work, and he began to be published abroad while still in Cuba, where he was very much persecuted by the revolutionary authorities. The book that first made him well known in the Spanish-speaking world was *El Mundo Alucinante* in 1966. It was translated into English in 2001 with the title *Hallucinations*. It engendered more praise outside Cuba, even by the Mexican writer Carlos Fuentes, and it was soon translated into many other languages. Other Arenas novels are *El Palacio de las Blanquísimas Mofetas* (1982) (The Palace of the White Skunks, 1990), and *Celestino Antes del Alba* (Singing from the Well, 1987). Many of his novels, such as *Otra Vez el Mar* and *El Color del Verano*, translated as *Farewell to Sea* and *The Color of Summer* respectively, were published once he left Cuba. Arenas also published other works, among them *El Central, Termina el Desfile*, and *Arturo la Estrella Más Brillante*. These dealt with the infamous forced labor camps of the UMAPs (*Unidades Militares para la Ayuda de Producción*, or Military Units to Aid Production). These novels showed that Arenas' works were always a fierce criticism of the dictatorship in Cuba that led to the suppression of individual rights. Many of his works were translated, which explains why he was the best-known author, among the writers of that time, by U.S. college students and those of many other countries.

Also in the 1980s, two Miami-based poets appeared on the scene. Angel Cuadra was a former political prisoner and founder and leader of the Pen Club de Escritores Cubanos en el Exilio, while Orlando González Esteva—who came to the Florida city as a child—represented two generational points of view. Both are prolific authors. The former cannot escape the constraints of several years of prison life, and devotes all his efforts to writing essays and being active in exile organizations to fight the dictatorship. González Esteva, sponsored by the great Mexican poet and Nobel laureate Octavio Paz, could not forget the place where he was born, and his poetry is one of nostalgia and remembrance. He is also a singer and radio journalist who has made it his mission to rescue Cuban music and history. Cuadra's work includes *Poemas en Correspondencia* (1979), *Esa Tristeza que nos Inunda* (1985), *Fantasía Para el Viernes* (1985), *Las Señales y los Sueños* (Teruel Award, Spain), *La Voz Inevitable* (1994), *De los Resúmenes y el Tiempo* (2003), and several books of essays, such as *Jose Martí, Análisis y Conclusiones,* and *Las Motivaciones de Pedro Luis Boitell*. González Esteva has published the essay *Cuerpos en Bandeja: Frutas y Erotismo en Cuba*/A Carnal Platter: Fruit and Eroticism in Cuba, *Libros de la Espiral*/Books of the Spiral, and *Concierto en La Habana*. He also published books of poems, including *Elogio del Garabato* and *Fosa Común*.

TEACHERS AND CRITICISM

Cuban literary critics are almost all established scholars in the "publish or perish" world of universities, which has driven a large critical literature. Yara González Montes, one of these important professors, likes to emphasize "that one of the most important areas to address is the intensive work done by Cuban professors at universities in this country. This allowed us also to make known our literature, to get in direct contact with American professors in our respective fields of expertise." She and her husband, Matías Montes Huidobro, started the publishing house *Persona* and the magazine *Caribe* in Hawaii, where both were university professors and where they published many critical works. It should be noted that there is one work that is a must-read to learn about the Cuban drama theater. It is titled *Persona Vida y Máscara en el Teatro Cubano* (1973), which dealt with the 1950s and 1960s. This was the work of Montes Huidobro, and many more would follow in recent years. Those books took up again the theme of drama writing to the present time—works such as the four-volume *Cuba Detrás del Telón*. Her most creative work includes many more creations, all written outside of

Cuba. That includes *Exilio*, which premiered at the Cuban Museum in Miami.

"We must remember that we, for example, began to teach in the mid-1960s. Being university professors opened for us the doors to national and international conferences where we got in touch with scholars and writers from around the world," explains González Montes. "As part of literary panels we could discuss amicably with international and academic left, and even with the left that came from Cuba itself. This way, they were forced to listen to us with respect, even though they did not share our ideas and the audience was exposed to different points of view."

Georgina Sabat de Rives is fondly remembered as she dedicated her life to the criticism of the work of Mexican poet Sor Juana Inés de la Cruz. But she also directed many doctoral theses, including that of Madeline Cámara, who also teaches and has studied the works of Cuban writers in exile, such as María Elena Cruz Varela.

We should also remember many others, including Estrella Busto Ogden, from Villanova University, whose expertise was Chilean and Cuban literature; Arturo Fox, who wrote a storybook and several critical works about Spanish literature while at Carlyle; and the poet Roberto Lima, from Penn State University. José Olivio Jiménez, author of several anthologies, and Humberto Piñera Llera at the University of New York; poet Jesús Barquet, at the University of New Mexico, who edited *Ediciones El Puente* in 2011, making it mandatory academic material; and Luís González Cruz in Pittsburgh, author of the serial novel *Olorún* and also of anthologies of theatrical plays and books of poems. Julio Matas is also a playwright whose works *La Crónica* and *El Suceso* (written in Cuba) and *El Extravío* (1987-88), set in exile, are considered part of our heritage. Matas has also written several critical works, including *La Cuestión del Género Literario* (1979). All are excellent representations of their fellow Cubans and of the history of Cuban literature.

WRITERS IN EUROPE

Most of the Cuban writers sought exile in the United States, but many also went to Spain, England, and France. The editorial firms that published them were mainly in Spain. A few were in other countries. *Seix Barral* is one example, but soon there arose in exile a number of publishers who joined Juan Manuel Salvat's *Ediciones Universal*. Felipe Lázaro, who started *Betania* in 1986, provided his list of publishers and writers in Spain.

Poets in Madrid: Isel Rivero (of the *El Puente* generation; he went into exile early), Jorge Luis Arco (who in 1998 was still editor of the magazine *Unión* of the *Unión de Escritores y Artistas de Cuba* (Union of Writers and Artists of Cuba—UNEAC, for its initials in Spanish); Pío Serrano; Alberto Lauro; David Lago; Roberto Cazorla; Orlando Fondevila, editor-in-chief of the magazine *Revista Hispano Cubana* in Madrid and a contributor to Radio Martí; and Felipe Lázaro himself. Poets who left via Spain: León de la Hoz, who was director of *La Gaceta de Cuba* and who won several poetry awards from UNEAC, chairs the *Asociación Cultural Gastón Baquero*, and contributes to *Otro Lunes* on the Web. Cuban professor, linguist, and philologist Humberto López Morales excels in Madrid. He is secretary of the *Real Academia de la Lengua Española* for the Americas, and he is a renowned linguist, author, and editor of several books about the Spanish language in the Americas, including the United States, and of the *Diccionario de Americanismos* (Dictionary of Americanisms), which he developed before his academic life in Puerto Rico.

"The connection with Spanish colleagues depended on the dates: During the decades of the 1960s, 1970s, and even in the 1980s, it was very difficult," says Felipe Lázaro. "Being an exiled Cuban writer at that time was like being the devil and they were rejected just for being anti-Castro, with few opportunities for access to publishers (that's why exile-based publishing houses were founded) or to publish articles in the Spanish press. From the decade of the 1990s to the present, there is much more interest in the work of exiles who publish in *Tusquets, Alfaguara, Planet*, etc. And some even have access to the national press articles, such as Zoé Valdés in *El Mundo*, César Leante (*El Mundo*), Carlos Alberto Montaner (*ABC*) and Rafael Rojas (*El País*)."

"The Cuban cultural exile in Spain has a quantitative and qualitative importance, with several dozens of poets and writers, cultural journals, with publishers, painters and sculptors, musicians and journalists, as well as professionals (doctors, architects) and important businessmen," according to Lázaro. "In this sense, the Cuban cultural exile in Spain has enlarged or widened that 'plural geography,' as Baquero called it, along with exiled Cuban intellectuals residing in such other European nations as France, Sweden, Italy, Germany, England; and in Mexico, Puerto Rico, or in the USA. In other words, the current Cuban culture has transcended its own borders and—though it is one—it complements with that practiced both on the island and in exile. To be sure, never, ever, in these many years of Castroism was there or existed a cultural exile as strong, representative and important as the one today."

Lázaro adds that "perhaps the most important exiled Cuban intellectual (poet, journalist, and essayist) who has been in Spain is Gastón Baquero, from 1959 to 1997. Currently, the poets of the 1950s generation in the Canary Islands, Manuel Díaz Martínez; César Leante, novelist and journalist of the time of *Lunes de Revolución*; and the novelist Daniel Iglesias Kennedy. And more recently: Jorge Luis Arco and Raúl Rivero. In Barcelona, Iván de la Nuez, of the group that came out in the 1990s, and Juan Abreu, of the Mariel group, and Fernando and Miñuca Villaverde. There were also the novelist and playwright Abilio Estévez and the poets Rolando Sánchez Mejías, Ramón Fernández Larrea and Rodolfo Häsler." And to those one has to keep adding Antonio José Ponte—who was editor of the magazine *Encuentro*—and who is now the Web-based deputy director of the *Diario de Cuba*. And the essayist Ernesto Hernández Busto, who publishes *Penúltimos Días* on the Web.

PUBLISHERS AND LITERARY PUBLICATIONS

The importance of Cuban publications and publishers are obvious. There is no writing if it's not published. In Madrid, those who have excelled include Playor of Carlos Alberto Montaner, Pliegos of Caesar Leante, Verbum of Pio Serrano, Colibrí of Victor Batista, Trópico of Mario Parajón, Hispano Cubana of the HC Foundation, and Betania of Felipe Lázaro. Outside Madrid, there is Aduana Vieja of Fabio Murrieta.

Spain was home to magazines such as *El Puente* and *La Gota de Agua*, founded by José Mario in the 1970s. And following the 1990s, there were the magazines *Revista Hispano Cubana* (directed by Javier Martínez Corbalán); *Encuentro de la Cultura Cubana*, started by Jesús Díaz, who—after his death—was succeeded as co-directors by the poet Manuel Díaz Martínez in the Canaries and essayist Rafael Rojas in Mexico, and then by Antonio José Ponte until its closure; and, finally, the *Boletín del Comité Cubano Pro Derechos Humanos,* whose founder and director was Martha Frayde. In Miami, *Alacrán Azul* (1971), designed by the great artist Mijares and jointly directed by Fernando Palenzuela and Juan Arcocha, in *Ediciones Universal*, with only two editions; *Catálago de Letras*, founded by Soren Triff; *Ujule*, of Lorenzo García Vega, Carlos Díaz, and Octavio Armand. *Linen Lane* is a magazine that has endured the longest in terms of years; it has been published for about thirty consecutive years by the poet Belkis Cuza Male, who founded it in Princeton in 1982, without funds of any kind—neither from the government nor from private sources. It is now being edited in Miami, where she lives.

Miami was the home of previously mentioned Juan Manual Salvat's *Ediciones Universal*; Nancy Pérez Crespo's SIBI; Carlos Díaz's *La Torre de Papel*, as well was *Editorial Cubana*, which publishes classics of Cuban literature started by Luis Botifoll. He was succeeded by José Ignacio Rasco, and it is now managed by Armando Cobelo. The new publishing houses are many, including: *Baquíana, Bluebird, Entre Ríos, Silueta,* etc.

On the Web there is a vast body of work by Cubans: *La Gota de Agua*, of Rolando Morelli, based on the publishing house started by José Mario in Spain; *La Zorra y el Cuervo,* of George Riverón; *La Habana Elegante*, of Francisco Morán; *La Peregrina Magazine,* which includes many authors such as Juan Cueto, Germán Guerra, Ena Columbié, and Felix Luis Viera; *Baquiana* itself, of Maricel Mayor Marsán, who writes poetry and theater. There are others, including some that have been discontinued, such as *Decir del Agua* of Reinalo García Ramos, and *El Ateje* of Luis de la Paz. One that has excelled is *Teatro de Miami*, directed by playwright Ernesto García and which has become an excellent digital magazine about the theater scene of that city.

THE NEW GENERATIONS FROM THE 1990S TO THE PRESENT

Alejandro Ríos, who made Cuban literature and cinema popular through his work at Miami Dade College, mentions a group of Cuban writers who went into exile during the decade of the 1990s and after the year 2000: German Guerra, Félix Lizárraga, Rosi Inguanzo, Teresa Dovelpage, Claribel Terré Morell, Yanitzia Canetti, and Juan Manuel Cao; Karla Suárez in Rome; Elena Cruz Varela, Carmen Duarte, and Carmen Díaz in Miami; Roberto Urías, Roberto Madrigal, and "Lichy" Diego in Mexico; and Reinaldo Bragado Bretaña, defender and founder of the campaign of *Derechos Humanos en Cuba*, whose books were published in Miami during the 1990s. His first novel was *La Estación Equivocada*; it was followed by *La Muerte sin Remitente, La Noche Vigilada*, and *La Ciudad Hechizada*. The Russian-Cuban writer José Manuel Prieto is an academic who lives between Mexico and New York. But Prieto is a special case; his novels are all about the situation in Russia after the fall of the Soviet Union. They include a trilogy: *Enciclopedia de una Vida en Rusia, Livadia,* and *Rex*. He is better known abroad than he is among Cubans themselves because of the translations of his work into several languages, especially Russian.

Among other storytellers, one who first lived in Colombia is the novelist Antonio Orlando Rodríguez, who was also a theater critic and who won the prestigious Alfaguara Award for novelists for his novel *Chiquita*. He has had international renown as has Daína Chaviano, who was already known in Cuba for her writing of magic, science, and religion, but who has now emerged as a novelist with her works dealing with Cuban issues. She won the Azorín Award in 1998 for her novel *El Hombre, la Hembra y el Hambre*. Other works of this trilogy have also been very successful, especially *La Isla de los Amores Infinitos*, which was translated into twenty-five languages. However, magic and fantasy are still the main foundations of her stories.

William Navarrete, based in Paris and Madrid, has published several books, among them an anthology of Cuban poets in Paris, *Insulas al Pairo* (2004). And he has undertaken the task of an organizer, when he created a society and literary bulletins in anticipation of the *Centenario de la República de Cuba* in 2002. He was also involved with another organization that would continue this work, the *Asociación por la Tercera República Cubana* (Association pour la Troisieme Republique Cubaine). In 2005, he published his poems in the book *Edad de Miedo al Frío* in Cadiz, Spain. And several other works by him on music and Cuban art have also been published.

"It is pleasing to see how the most important Latin American (and Spanish) publishing houses are now dealing with Cuban literature, which is alive and functioning—both those inside Cuba (Pedro Juan Gutiérrez, with *El Rey de La Habana*, for example, and when Antonio José Ponte still lived there, with *Cuentos de Todas Partes del Imperio* and *Un Arte Nuevo de Hacer Ruinas*) and those outside the island's soil. Previously, they only had eyes for certain writers who were 'committed to the system' (Miguel Barnet, Pablo Armando Fernández, etc.) in disgraceful deals," said Alejandro Ríos. "It took a while to regard Reinaldo Arenas as the great author he is, for example."

Zoe Valdés deserves a special place for the extraordinary work she did from Paris, the bias in favor of the Cuban revolutionary government that always existed in French culture. But she is highly valued because of the literary success, most importantly, of her significant novel *La Nada Cotidiana* (finalist of the Planeta Award in 1995), which gave her international recognition as it was published in numerous languages. The Planeta publishing house supported her unconditionally and her creative ardor makes it possible to publish ever more books of narratives and essays. A short list includes: *La Ficción Fidel* (2008), *La eternidad del Instante* (2004), *Lobas del Mar* (2003), *Querido Primo Novio* (1999), *Café Nostalgia* (1997), *Te dí la Vida Entera* (1996), and among her books of poems, *Todo Para Una Sombra* (1986).

CUBAN LITERATURE IN ENGLISH

But it's also necessary to mention the authors who write in English. Nilo Cruz is one of the great playwrights who has done outstanding work, as he won the Pulitzer Prize in 2003 for his work *Ana en el Trópico/Anna in the Tropics*. Carolina Hospital compiled in anthologies her work as well as that of other authors of the 1980s who began to excel in English-language poetry and narratives, but with flashes of the Spanish of their childhood and with the same feeling of nostalgia and anti-Communism of their parents. The work published included *Cuban American Writers: Los Atrevidos*, Ediciones Ellas, 1988; *A Century of Cuban Writers in Florida: Selected Prose and Poetry*, Pineapple Press, 1996; and *The Child of Exile: A Poetry Memoir*, Arte Público Press, 2004.

This was also the case of Ricardo Pau Llosa, the author of several books of poetry including: *Parable Hunter* (2008), *The Mastery Impulse* (2003), *Vereda Tropica* (1999), *Cuba* (1993) [all published by Carnegie Mellon Press], and *Bread of the Imagined* (Bilingual Press, 1991), as well as books and critical essays about Latin American painters.

Writings that have been successful and were translated into Spanish were those of Gustavo Pérez Firmat, who wrote *Next Year in Cuba: A Cubano's Coming-of-age in America,* and he created the concept of *La Vida en el Guión/Life on the Hyphen.* In 2010 he published *The Havana Habit,* about the Americans' obsession with Havana. Pérez Firmat is currently the David Feinson Professor of Humanities at Columbia University. *Life on the Hyphen* was awarded the Eugene M. Kayden University Press National Book Award in 1994; his memoir *Next Year in Cuba* (1995, 2000) was nominated for a Pulitzer Prize in non-fiction.

Another Cuban-American and son of immigrants, who won the 1990 Pulitzer Prize for Literature, is Oscar Hijuelos for his novel *The Mambo Kings Play Songs of Love* (1989). It was made into a movie starring, among others, Celia Cruz and Antonio Banderas. Hijuelos has continued writing about Cuba with such works as *A Simple Havana Melody* (2002) about the Cuban Moisés Simons and his songs. And more recently, he wrote *Beautiful Maria of My Soul* (2010).

One author, who excelled after many years as a professor of religion at Yale University, was Carlos Eire with the book *Waiting for Snow in Havana: Confessions of a Cuban Boy* (2003). He himself said this work brought him countless fulfillments on the world stage. Eire won the 2003 National Book Award in Nonfiction. He is the T. Lawrason Riggs Professor of History and Religious Studies at Yale University.

To all of these, one has to add the writer of detective stories Carolina García Aguilera. Her books about detective Lupe (Guadalupe) Solano are a reflection of the Cuban exile community in Florida and its generational struggles vis-à-vis Fidel Castro and Cuba. The first in the series was *Bloody Waters* (1996). There is also Cristina García, the author of *Dreaming in Cuban*. She later wrote *The Agüero Sisters, Monkey Hunting* (2003) and *A Handbook to Love* (2007). García began as a reporter for *Time* magazine.

Another reporter, Achy Obejas of the *Chicago Tribune*, is now writing novels and has published the best work about the current situation in

Cuba, *Ruins*. She also just translated *Cien Botellas en la Pared* by Ena Lucía Portela, a writer from Havana who lives in internal exile, the same as Lezama Lima did in the past.

In the area of children's books, Alma Flor Ada is the author of an extensive bibliography in Spanish and English. Her tale *Gold Coin* has been included in textbooks all across the United States. Another example of the English-language literature is the book of stories and anecdotes by this journalist and professor called *Parables of Women*, which was translated into Spanish as *Palabras de Mujer*, and published by Betania as a bilingual work in 2006.

EPILOGUE

This is just a brief history of Cuban literature in exile, an example of all the details yet to be written to add the great accomplishments of the expatriates to the history of that torn island. They have not given up in providing testimony as to their creative strength and courage—faced with all kinds of obstacles—to make known their voice, their expression, and their art while in exile. At the same time, they have borne witness that even though many are shackled in today's Cuba, there are still persons who dare to think and create, but who—after all is said and done—have had to flee the island to be able to breathe at great length so that they can make their work known everywhere.

22

PLASTIC ARTS

BY OLGA I. NODARSE

"Light defines itself—and darkness."
—*Spinoza*

". . . a surrealist painter is the same as a poet . . ."
—*José Lezama Lima, letter to Jorge Camacho, 1969*

"Suicide is the sole, and of course definitive, Cuban ideology."
—*Guillermo Cabrera Infante*

ON LOOKING:

CONVERSATIONS AND REFLECTIONS ON CUBAN ART

Here is the first definition of Cuban art: it is not so much Cuban art as art made by Cuban artists. (As the great Guido Llinás once said, "I've never seen a tube of paint that is labeled *Cuban paint*.") Cuban art really stops in the middle part of the twentieth century, perhaps with the passing of the first and second wave of *Vanguardia* painters (1927-1950), and certainly with the beginning of the long exile of 1959. From 1959 until the present, there is beautiful, horrifying, show-stopping, classical, funny, dramatic, erotic, sad, profound, banal, very bad, very good contemporary art—made by all kinds of Cubans. Whether it is just contemporary art, art made by Cubans, or Cuban art is moot, as quite a bit of it is truly breathtaking.

I: HISTORY

The nineteenth century saw the formative years that led to the development of the Cuban nation, inspired and encouraged by the thought, writings, and action of such men and women as Félix Varela, Domingo del Monte, José de la Luz y Caballero, Carlos Manuel de Céspedes, José Antonio Saco, Miguel de Aldama, and Gertrudis Gómez de Avellaneda in the first part of the century, and José Martí, Antonio Maceo, and others later on. A distinct identity as a nation developed slowly and very organically for artists painting in Cuba for close to a century. The art produced at first followed classical canons of Europe or the United States—the Hudson School of landscapes, or the Barbizon School. The same academic and classical techniques were applied to local landscapes, and sometimes to folkloric figures. Notable exponents of Cuban painting at this time are the three brothers Chartrand from Limonar, in the province of Matanzas. Of course, Matanzas was known as the Athens of Cuba, an important cultural center in the island. Matanzas was part of the nascent sugar industry, so it is not strange that Esteban, Philippe, and Augusto Chartrand—members of a cultured and wealthy landed family—painted the scions of the most important families in the province as well as romantic, spectacularly beautiful, even haunting landscapes of their environs and properties.

Four paintings now lost to the Cuban memory: *El Río Canimar, El Cementerio del Ingenio Santa Bárbara, El Ingenio Santa Bárbara*, and a portrait of William Davis, were commissioned by Davis, an American from Philadelphia who married Isabel Kugler y Sardiñas, daughter of Mariana

Sardiñas, owner of the Santa Bárbara sugar mill. The *Canimar* painting was a large, horizontal composition on canvas; the one of the cemetery is a vertical composition showing the family cemetery surrounded by a simple ironwork; and the magnificent painting of the sugar mill, another horizontal composition but larger than the *Canimar*. The portrait of *William Davis* is that of a handsome man with reddish blonde hair, moustache, and laughing.

Other earlier colonial painters of note were José Nicolás de la Escalera (1734-1804) and Vicente Escobar (1757-1854). Both trained in local formal traditions, i.e., European canons, and both followed European tendencies and styles long before the foundation of the San Alejandro Academy in 1818.

At the end of the nineteenth century and beginning of the twentieth century, two Cuban painters stand out: Leopoldo Romañach and Armando Menocal, portraitists and landscapists in the manner of the great Spanish painter Joaquín Sorolla (1863-1923); they painted landscapes, seascapes, some Cuban characters, and scenes from the War of Independence and the *Mambises*. Both painters are associated in important ways with the San Alejandro Academy; Romañach, for example, taught Amelia Peláez and other *vanguardistas*.[1]

Nineteenth-century "Cuban" academic painting disappeared (actually, it continued but had no effect on the modern culture) with the first avant-garde movement, the *Vanguardia*, an extraordinary group of artists emerging around 1927 (with the first important exhibition of the group in Havana) who were quite relevant until the early 1950s. Professor Juan Martínez writes, in his *Cuban Art and National Identity: The Vanguardia Painters, 1927-1950*: "Born around the turn of the century, these artists grew up in the turmoil of constructing a new nation . . . and reached maturity when Cubans were engaged in discovering and inventing a national identity."[2] The most important first-generation modernists with early and significant stylistic breakthroughs were Carlos Enríquez, Eduardo Abela, Jorge Arche, Wifredo Lam, Victor Manuel García,

Marcelo Pogolotti, Antonio Gattorno, Amelia Peláez, and Fidelio Ponce de León. Most of these painters attended San Alejandro in the early 1920s. A second generation of Cuban painters, a continuation of the *Vanguardia* painters—among them, Mario Carreño, Mariano Rodríguez, Cundo Bermúdez, and René Portocarrero, together with the early *vanguardistas*—were invited to participate in an epochal exhibition organized by New York's Museum of Modern Art (MoMA) director Alfred H. Barr, Jr., in 1944, with the help of the critic/curator José Gómez Sicre and the art patron María Luisa Gómez Mena. Wifredo Lam was very much part of the *Vanguardia*, although Lam declined to participate in the MoMA show; the others accepted. Other international group shows followed, cementing these painters' fame. Carlos Franqui poetically wrote about some of them in his text for a 1979 Camacho book:

> *"When does this Cuban light, this color, filter through into our painting?*
> *In the expressionist whites of Ponce.*
> *In the horses and mulatto girls of Carlos Enriquez.*
> *In the tropical gypsy girls of Victor Manuel.*
> *In the cubist objects and stained glass windows of Amelia Peláez.*
> *Light filters."*[8]

This was a period of enormous creative freedom, innovation, and the production of colorful and strong paintings; this was also a period when these painters were developing the concept of a Cuban identity, of a Cuban nation, through their rich palette and their themes. Applying the new freedom from academia to their art and using very Cuban landscapes and figures as their protagonists, some of these artists of the *Vanguardia* created the first truly modern Cuban art. Some—like Carlos Enriquez, Victor Manuel, Amelia Peláez, and Cundo Bermúdez—exhibited Cuban landscapes and characters in their paintings; some, like Fidelio Ponce, painted compositions that were truly not very "Cuban" at all, showing that quality of contemporary art as precursor of the total freedom of abstract expressionism, with its unbound brushstrokes, heavy textures, and absolutely unexpected use of colors—or lack thereof. There are no palm trees, *guajiros,* or landscapes in Ponce's work. In the years just before his death in 1949, Ponce visited the *Academia de Artes Plásticas de Matanzas* frequently, and a few collectors bought his paintings for truly small sums. The Academy of San Alejandro, in Havana, as the one in Matanzas, were superb forges of truly great artists, teaching them the classical canons of art. Ponce attended but did not graduate from San Alejandro; the other *Vanguardia* painters graduated, while rejecting its traditional teachings in their works.

In the 1950s, some important Cuban art reflected international tendencies, especially abstract expressionism (*Los Once*) and geometric abstraction (*Diez Pintores Concretos*). *Los Once,* whose number actually varied, had as its strongest talents Guido Llinás, Hugo Consuegra, and Agustín Cárdenas, as well as Antonio Vidal, Raúl Milián, Antonia Eiriz, Gay García, and others, who inserted themselves in the European and American tendencies of the times. Paraphrasing Cintio Vitier and Carlos Luis, *en las transmutaciones de lo cubano a favor de una inserción en un lenguaje universal.* The *Diez Pintores Concretos,* a group formed around 1958 and of short duration, was initiated by Carmen Herrera, and it had among its ranks Salvador Corratgé Ferrera, Loló Soldevilla, Rafael Soriano, Mario Carreño, and Mijares. Although they started out as geometric abstractionists, the most important among them—notably, Rafael Soriano—evolved into a very personal style of organic, sensual, veiled forms with true mastery of color.

The next generation, the very young students of San Alejandro in the late 1930s and 1940s—Roberto Estopiñán, Agustín Fernández, Jorge Camacho, Gina Pellón—became the first generation of Cuban artists to go into exile, leaving the island with scholarships to Paris or New York or simply escaping the impending choking regime to cities in Europe or the United States.

So the exodus began—in the 1960s, 1970s, 1980s, 1990s, and

continuing to the present day. The date of leaving defines the content of the cultural and historical memory and experience of each artist, with the artists who are now in their eighties, or those who have died true products of four hundred years of accumulated Cuban experience. Curiously, they have lived the longest in exile, and they are true Parisians, New Yorkers, or Miamians.

II: FAVORITES

The art made by Cubans after the 1950s—like the art of Jackson Pollock, Robert Motherwell, Jean Dubuffet, and Joan Miró—has broken with the canons of academia and, contrary to what the *Vanguardia* painters did, helped define a Cuban identity; these artists let loose the ropes tying their souls to their native land. They create art with joy or with angst, with different techniques and media, different palettes and styles, with an underlying obsession with the human figure. There is a universal flight of fancy, no longer bound by rules or materials in the creations of the post-*Vanguardia* generation. Gina Pellón, Agustín Fernández, Roberto Estopiñán, and Jorge Camacho, now in their eighties—Fernández died in 2006—paint ideas, feelings—often, a yearning of the exile for his or her native land—and their own interpretation of reality, at times phantasmagoric, at times erotic, sometimes strangely beautiful, but always very strong creations of line and color.

The younger group, although now in their sixties and beyond, following these masters are Lydia Rubio, Ramón Alejandro, Hernán García, and Luis Cruz Azaceta. Their creation is truly not merely Cuban—they are universal paintings about the human condition, gorgeous or brutal, erotic or shocking. Alejandro's seductive fruits are highly sensual in a tropical sort of way; Azaceta's brutal themes of loneliness, uprootedness, or violence are caustic comments on the experience of man alone and the social ills that haunt him. García's "magisterial balance between monstrosity and platonic beauty" creates a tension that is perhaps the central definition of contemporary art.[4] Lydia Rubio is perceived as the most challenging and intellectual of these four artists, drawing concepts and materials from gorgeously drawn notebooks which reflect her restless thoughts, unafraid to search for answers—everywhere. All four are postmodern masters, really contemporary artists, painting whatever moves them.

Also of importance is María Martínez-Cañas, a phenomenal photographer and installation artist unbound by categories, coolly cerebral, and a consummate craftswoman with the head of a philosopher. Having left Cuba as a toddler, acknowledging her roots, Martínez-Cañas is unbound by any definitions: witness her eerie mural installation on nature with haunting branches sticking out from painted forests, at the Frost Museum in Miami, the phenomenal installation at the Miami Airport, the *Años Continuos,* or her early series of the *Cuban Stamps*—a gorgeous rendering of iconic Cuban stamps of *Vanguardia* paintings into photographic masterpieces.

The last artist to consider is Gustavo Acosta, born in Cuba, educated like the famous Cuban painters long gone or now in their eighties in San Alejandro in Havana, and exiled in the 1990s. Acosta, born in the 1950s, exiled in 1990, shows the immense longing for his native habitat in his particular memories of Cuba: a painter's painter, he makes the ruins of Havana come to life in the *Malecón* series, or in the beautifully haunting and fantastic barely discerned coat of arms in his Castilian-inspired *Objects* series—inspiration, in turn, for a recent historical fantasy novel.

Other artists to consider are José Bedia, Mario Bencomo, Leonel Matheu, Arturo Cuenca, and Humberto Castro. Bedia has reached international fame with his stunning installations and strange paintings; he depicts the images and the feelings of the *Palo* religion, or *santería*, or even—in his neo-primitive style—the lost images of the Taínos, like the late Jesús González de Armas. Bedia's work shows an undeniable affinity with De Armas's work, linking both in the forms of the only Cuban native tribes before 1492.[5] Bedia's installations are gigantic, a bit scary—they are very foreign to most viewers, whether Cuban or not—and absolutely awesome. Of great impact is also the work of Mario Bencomo, at his core a surrealist, an abstract painter committed to an interpretation of ancient myths defined only by line and color. In Carlos Luis' words,

> *For some time, Mario Bencomo slowly approached the works of the poets touching his imagination. His affinity with poets such as Milton, Cavafy, Rimbaud or Lezama became tracings in his workbooks or actual strokes in his canvases, with titles linking Bencomo's works with the works of the poets. Thus, his paintings began to show new elements that had nothing or very little to do with the abstract compositions of his early career as a painter. In these new paintings, one sees the beginning of a tendency trying to relate his early abstractionism with a series of very sensual forms, now taking an important place in the new compositions.*[6]

Arturo Cuenca's gift starts to unveil urban landscapes to suddenly hide them mysteriously, illuminating portions of perceived realities through the mastery of his craft—and his enormous creativity. Facing Leonel Matheu's "random objects with an absurdist bent" in the words of critic Omar Sommereyns, one can't decide if the feeling evoked is one of fear or hilarity. An accomplished painter, Matheu describes his work as being that of a storyteller, often creating urban tough symbols that oscillate between simplicity and mystery. Humberto Castro's haunting, blurred, dream-like images are the result of a fierce imagination and a consummate skill: he works in painting, drawing, printmaking, ceramics, and installations. In his early years, he also delved into performance art, especially using it as a vehicle for social criticism in his country. He is one of the most active members of the group widely recognized as the "Generation of the 80s" in Cuba, which created changes in the aesthetic and conceptual art scene of the island. Castro left Cuba and settled in Paris, where he lived for ten years, coming to the U.S., where he lives and works now, in 1999.

In conclusion, the art made by these Cuban artists may fit or not a classification as CoBrA, surrealist, abstract expressionist, conceptual, pop, or whatever else; the styles are as varied as the artists and their sources, their media, and their techniques. Experiences in the country of their birth and personal experiences of exile may tie them together—or they may not.

III: POLITICS AND PATRIMONY

The four Chartrand paintings, commissioned by the Matanzas family probably between 1840 and 1860, were in the family's possession from the time they were painted until the last member of the family left Cuba as exiles—not immigrants—in 1961. Where are the paintings? In a Cuban aparatchik's collection? In a museum? In the salon of a French politician in Paris? In the apartment of a Mexican, Italian, Canadian, or Spaniard, bought from the repositories where the paintings, objects d'art, priceless china, flatware, laces, photographs, and jewels of the ones who left the island were placed for personal use of the dictator and his intimates, or for gifting or selling to foreign sycophants?

In the debacle, a whole nation—if we understand nation as the community of individual citizens sharing a space and linked by generations—lost the objects they had loved and collected and received from their forebears; worse, a whole nation lost its patrimony as the National Archives and the National Library have been sacked by small and big Communist Party members and government bureaucrats to sell abroad: letters of Varela, Maceo, Aldama, Aguilera, Carlos Manuel de Céspedes; copies of the 1901 Constitution; books from Cuba's National Library or the *Sociedad de Amigos del Pais* . . . the loss of the historical and cultural objects which help define a nation is part of the tragedy of the dismemberment of the Cuban nation—and the loss of its historical memory.

We do know that Egyptian obelisks were carted off to Rome and the Parthenon marbles taken to England by Lord Elgin. But the Cuban pilfering has been slightly, but crucially, different: an all-powerful abusive regime has stolen the *private property* of exiles and political prisoners and sold it off as if it were its own. The commerce between Havana and European capitals is scandalous, but so is the trade between Havana and Miami. The only fine line has been drawn by those with a developed ethical sense, or with a good notion of historic sensitivity, the proverbial line drawn in the sand by the Cuban exiles that fit this description. Excluded from this rather demanding definition are purchases from artists who live in Cuba and are still painting; after all, they may be exiles soon. Also excluded are goods found in auction houses throughout the world—the objects have already been stolen from Cuba and, if returned there, they would go back into the hands of the thieves.

The art and the antiques and the furnishings of those who followed the road of exile belong to those same people, not to the current regime to do with them as it pleases. As artist F. Lennox Campello writes in his blog, *ARTistic*:

> *. . . worldwide courts have consistently recognized the right of original owners to the return of artwork which has been looted by governments and dictatorships, confiscated, sold and re-sold.*
>
> *It has taken in some cases several decades for the artwork to return to the familial descendants of the original and rightful owners, but essentially international law is pretty clear on the subject that generally no government can confiscate private property.*
>
> *When the abomination known as the Soviet Union collapsed in the 1990s and Cuba's sugar daddy stopped sending billions of dollars in subsidy to the Castro brothers, the Cuban economy collapsed, and one of the results of that collapse was the mass selling, by the Cuban government, of those*

confiscated masterpieces, most of which found their way to European museums and European and Asian private collections via French auction houses. Thus many masterpieces once owned by the Fanjul family, or the Bacardí family, or by sugar magnate Julio Lobo (whose interest in Napoleonic memorabilia led to him amassing one of the world's largest collections of Bonaparte memorabilia such as weapons, furniture, paintings, letters, etc.) were sold to European museums and collectors.[7]

The issues confronting this universe of art made by Cubans is as political as it is aesthetic. Nothing escapes this truism. Like personal morality and integrity, the artist's behavior towards the brutal government of Cuba and the ruins of a nation marks him or her forever. At least in Miami it does.[8] Why? Because every family of Cuban ancestry or every Cuban-born Miamian knows *at least* a person who has been tortured, killed, or robbed in Cuba. In Miami, "dictatorship" is not a political science phrase but an existential reality. The paintings of a great-great-great grandfather's may be found in a private collection in one's own neighborhood, purchased in Havana by a trader, sold in the United States by private agents and dealers. Quandaries of political exile transported to the world of art.

The different definitions of what constitutes moral behavior vis à vis the dictatorship create dissension and even acrimony between those who casually travel to Cuba to look at art and perhaps buy it, and those who consider such behavior a clear nod to the Castro regime. However, in the last twenty-five years, Miami has evolved into a sophisticated and open city as Cubans—and non-Cubans—of all persuasions interact.

No one is above politics, certainly not above being ethical, even moral, in the use of power; being an artist does not explain, much less excuse, support and subservience to a horrific, brutal government. But it casts a light on creating art in a dictatorship, within circles of obeisance; this narrow existence is anathema to true creative expression, and creative expression needs to be particularly bold, persistent, and brave in order to survive first, and perhaps someday, in freedom, to come forth in its full power.

Whether anyone likes it or not, with a diaspora of artists as strong and as large as the Cuban exile—in Paris, in New York, in Caracas, in Madrid, in Miami—and the artists who remained in Cuba, there is a commonality brought about by, this time, contemporary art and the plight of the artist—to express, to paint, to create despite the tragic displacement of not belonging in a land of oppression or belonging in the eternal—even if submerged—angst of exile.

IV: ON LOOKING

Why do we love a particular piece to the point that we must have it? What makes this work of art a masterpiece, and this other—perhaps by the same artist—a boring piece? There is a combination of a soaring idea with great passion and great craft, even if hidden, behind great art. "Great art" to some is junk to others, or, in the best of cases, an "interesting" piece. Leo Steinberg wrote about the "plight of the public" in his book *Criteria*: avant-garde critics were shocked by Matisse's *Joy of Life* (1906), "with heavy black lines around the figures," as Matisse was horrified on seeing Picassos's *Demoiselles d'Avignon* (1907). The critics were Matisse's public in the first case, and Matisse was Picasso's public in the second. It is important to remember that both Matisse and Picasso had been rather academic, proficient craftsmen in Drawing and Painting 101 before they broke free with *Joy* and *Demoiselles* over a century ago, breaking all the rules of academic painting and opening the door to modern art.

The freshness of the eye when first faced with a work of art is the ultimate arbiter of "good" art. The eye is a muscle, a physical reality. Like marathon runners who train their muscles a bit at a time before a run, to look at art, one has to . . . look at art. What one could see when one first looked, perhaps had to be unthreatening, beautiful, and peaceful. As the eye takes in more and more, it seeks hidden beauty in all kinds of things. That is the ideal point at which reading art criticism or art history may be helpful. Reading, and its natural result —information and knowledge—will build a superstructure on what the eye discerned. Creating an intellectual superstructure ("This is a very good investment," "I must have works by all the Cuban painters," "The blues have to match," "Everyone has a painting by Mr. X among my friends," "All the *Vanguardia* painters are superb because they broke the barriers to Modern and Postmodern art in Cuba") before you are face-to-face with a work of art is actually boring and very banal: it takes away the passion—and the shock—of the new. Agustín Fernández, the great Cuban painter, like Chinese nobles and mandarins of the T'ang Dynasty, believed that paintings should not be hung and shown to anyone, that the soul and strength of the art was lost in exposure; art was not for the public. An extreme view—definitely not shared by the hordes of museum-goers or collectors of today—is actually explained when the heart misses a beat when confronted with a "new work" of art, whether it is a Greek disc thrower from antiquity in the Louvre, or a painting by Gustavo Acosta.

But when looking first, thinking second, the ten artists selected as the focus for this chapter do not conform to any kind of classification, except that their art was created by someone born in Cuba and exiled fifty years ago, or born in Cuba having lived in the revolution and exiled twenty years ago—or less.

There are beautiful paintings and installations, terrifying drawings— Jorge Camacho's and Azaceta's, for example—magnificent constructions, Renaissance-like *sanguines* by Lydia Rubio, powerful images, exquisite calligraphies, bold color, weird sculptures, sad pieces, very funny pieces—like a Buñuel film is funny. The suicide quote by Cabrera Infante refers to that abandon of Cubans to throw everything away—and go into exile. Or to say *"De mejores lugares me han botado"* and quit—whatever. It refers to not being afraid. Not being afraid is something these artists share. They push the limits, they question, and they make powerful art.

Of the hundreds of Cuban artists and of the art created by Cubans in the last fifty years, the ten artists in this selection are selected because their work is filled with passion resting on evident or hidden craft and, frankly, because it is superb. A different eye, a different "public," would and does choose others. There is plenty more where these came from. It's all about how and what we *see*. In that sense, we bring to the art piece our complex web of knowledge, biases, proclivities, emotions, and preferences.

Great mentors on looking at art—from Leo Stein on, when writing about Delacroix, to Carlos Franqui, when looking at a Miró or Henry Moore—stress "getting intimate with the piece first" by approaching it to within inches, then moving back to take a look from the distance, always keeping a fresh eye to keep discovering those who find new ways of making art. There will always be those who look and see with a fresh eye, and those who obey trends or seek to create them in making, selling, or collecting art.

V: THE TEN

Here they are, ten world-class artists chosen not by fame, price, or success but by the strength of the works they create; they were born in Cuba. Nine are exiles, and the tenth, also an exile, died in 2006.

The Older Generation:

Gina Pellón

Passionate bursts of color with a riotous joy, a complete freedom of color and form, a sense that inspiration for her paintings could be found in children's drawings, mark Gina Pellón's work as a close relative of the early European Abstract Expressionists and certainly, of her fellow painters from the brief but enormously significant CoBrA movement (1948-1952). Her depiction of women and small animals "are called forth from the blank canvas to become real by means of gestures, [my] brushstrokes . . ."[9] she likes to explain. Continues Pellón when asked to explain her work: "Each painting is a different history, with the main character hiding his identity and intentions behind the canvas; I move the brush vigorously, left and right, right and left, and pull forth the character. . . . My painting is gestural. . . ."[10] uncovering hidden grief and doubts, her expressionistic paintings rest on consummate skill and technique hidden under a pretension of ease. Critic Carlos Luis describes her paintings as truly exceptional paintings; he believes that "if the figure were taken away from one of her paintings, one could see a clear tendency towards abstraction."[11]

Pellón left Havana in 1959 and has resided in Paris since then. There, she paints in a luminous loft, accompanied by her little dog, Tenso, and every afternoon takes walks near the Eiffel Tower, the Champ de Mars, or the lovely streets of her neighborhood. Her collectors are in Holland, Norway, Sweden, France, Denmark, and the United States. A recipient of France's Legion of Honor, she is without doubt the *grand-doyenne* of Cuban artists, still exhibiting with the son of her original dealer, one of the main dealers of CoBrA artists in Silkeborg, Denmark, north of Copenhagen.

Jorge Camacho

Also living in Paris since the 1940s under the mentorship of none other than the surrealist master philosopher Andre Breton, Camacho is probably, in Zoé Valdés' phrase, "*the last of the great Latin American surrealists.*"[12] Carlos Luis, then the youngest member of the *Orígenes* group in Havana, a lifelong friend, introduced Camacho to Lezama Lima. Of surrealists—applicable to Camacho's work—he notes: ". . . The teratology used by both [alchemists and surrealists] in some cases show that the alchemic imagination, as well as the surrealist, are in the service of the quete, whose ultimate destiny is the revelation of the secret."[13] Carlos Luis believes that the Swiss and German *graveurs* of the sixteenth century had a great influence in the works of important surrealist artists and in Camacho's case, in his series *The Dance of Death* (*La Danse de la Mort, 1976*).[14]

He has been equally honored by the French government and the art world. Like Pellón's, Camacho's art shows a consummate technique and know-how, always hidden under his creations, be them nightmarish dreams or bursts of very controlled color. His palette now filled with greens, reds, yellows, and rich browns and in the past filled with grays, blues, reds, taupes, and ochres form solitary and surreal landscapes. Carlos Luis again traces Camacho's development from the impact of Breton to inspiration from the surrealist/alchemist universe, especially to the desolate deserts of native tribes and their shamantic Kachina dolls, filled with an almost incantatory character.

His deformed, demonic creatures—beasts and men alike—jump out or crouch as lines in the paper, superb craft of a superb draftsman, saved from technical perfection by his humanity and the haunting menace of the emerging creatures. His works, about shamans, and solitary landscapes are truly magnificent. Camacho likes to work with limited or no information at all to be able to develop the creative impulse to the limit.[15] Reinaldo Arenas, in an essay on Camacho's work called "The Insular Challenge of Jorge Camacho" in 1984 writes: ". . . the works of Camacho, like all truly original creation, is the result of an obsession, of a restlessness: the conscience of the lack of equilibrium between our thirst for eternity and that ephemeral piece of reality which we are. . . . An artist is always, despite himself, the voice of a transcendent and exclusive fear; the voice of his landscape and his people. . . . Here is Jorge Camacho's insular challenge."[16]

In the fall of 2009 Camacho was working on a series of "transparent" drawings and crystal sculptures to be premiered in December 2009 in *ARS Atelier*, the Paris gallery of Zoé Valdés, Ricardo Vega, and Gustavo Valdés.

Roberto Estopiñán

Estopiñán entered San Alejandro at fourteen years of age and later became an apprentice of sculptor Juan José Sicre, known for his public monuments. His early works have the beauty and organic shapes of the works of Carl Milles, but he was saved from this sweet and predictable art by his passion to draw. In drawings from forty or fifty years ago, particularly *The Prisoner* series, Estopiñán can perhaps be compared to the greats—Grünewald and Goya. *The Prisoners* depict the horrors of prisoners of conscience. Detroit critic Judith Weiner comments in the catalog of his 1983 retrospective at the Schweyer-Galdo Galleries:

> *Compassionate without seeming sentimental, Estopiñán depicts the harsh treatment of the prisoners with their hollow eyes, haunting faces, bound hands. . . . Like Goya before him, [he] creates expressive human postures filled with despair and pain.*[17]

The anguish of his drawings, and even of the sculptures, is linked, in the opinion of critic and art historian Giulio Blanc (*cf. "Artists in Exile" video by Ray Blanco*), to his exile from Cuba. His sculptures at that time (late 1960s, early 1970s) began to evolve, from rounded Milles-like female torsos to stylized bones, like prehistoric relics of the human form, invaded by chains or nails. Poet and writer Carlos Franqui describes his *Torsos* series thus:

> *Sensual, suggestive, dark, feminine harmony: love. Prehistoric bone that is reborn as a living modern sculpture.*[18]

First prize in sculpture in the famous Florentine *Maggio Miro* exhibition of 1981, Estopiñán establishes then a unique vision poured in bronze, marking him as a master sculptor. After four decades in New York, Estopiñán moved to Miami where he now resides.

Agustín Fernández

Aristocratic, refined, masterful, Fernández lived in Paris, Puerto Rico, and then New York during all his life in exile. His vertical, unchanging, anti-Castro stance of forty some years was not followed by his artistic exploration, which was bold unexpected and endlessly creative, inventing new forms with evident ease. Early works were clearly modernist, slowly transforming into harsh, tough paintings and later assemblages. His canvases may seem wild and passionate, but, by Fernandez' own definition, they are actually engineered creations of awesome beauty. According to a review of critic and art historian Carol Damian, ". . . his art is fraught with the tensions that exist between the real and the surreal, the organic and the inorganic, and the figurative and the objective . . . [he] enjoys breaking physical boundaries in painting and sculpture to emphasize their psychological context."[19]

As the critical comments in his webpage state:

Today, his work is most recognizable for its ambiguous and precariously balanced forms, erotic overtones, surreal juxtapositions, and metallic palette. Inspired by the demands of survival in an urban environment and the mundane objects that clutter its alleys and streets, Fernández is a collector on a quest for the substance of creativity, complete with the armor of protection necessary to maneuver through time and place that becomes such an important source of his imagery. Paintings and objects are related and complementary and further complicate the identification of organic versus inorganic forms; human and machine; real and imagined; obsessive and cerebral. Throughout his long and prolific years as an artist, Agustín Fernández was respected as a dedicated professional able to distinguish himself with a unique style and masterful techniques.[20]

Although Fernández liked to think of himself as a metaphysical painter, "like Morandi" (*cf. Artists in Exile* video by Ray Blanco) critic Giulio Blanc described him as a painter with "a very strong erotic component in his art . . ." while art historian and academic Alejandro Anreus says in the same video that "his art is profoundly erotic..." underpinned by his extraordinary technique and discipline, and his ever-present search for new creative outlets.

Despite the changes, Fernández always acknowledged his discipline in painting, following a *"basic structure . . . whatever you do, you need structure . . . I have great structure in my work"* (*cf. Artists in Exile* video by Ray Blanco). Besides his changing style and palette over forty some years, Blanc thought there was "great anger, a lot of angst, in Fernández' work ... caused by exile."

> *In my work there are certain erotic references*
> *which have images compelling to me.*
> *There are things one sees subconsciously*
> *that conjure up specific images.*
> *But my work is not erotic. My esthetic preoccupation*
> *has been with volume. And with the oscillation between*
> *the exact and the inexact. I have always painted*
> *the same theme, but in different ways. Even so,*
> *my paintings were more Cuban, more romantic*
> *before 1960; in exile they have become*
> *more metaphysical. I don't know if exile*
> *influences my work, but it has influenced me.*
> *It is not that I left Cuba, it is not being able to return.*[21]

As these conversations developed, a rare consensus between collectors, critics, and the artists themselves seemed to form, acknowledging the pre-eminence and mastery of Fernández' work.

Fernández died in New York in 2006 without having returned to Cuba.

The Slightly Younger Generation:

Lydia Rubio

The notable literary and art critic, Enrico M. Santi, writes in the catalog for Rubio's fall 2010 exhibition at Cremata Gallery in Miami: "It would be difficult, I think, to find in the present art horizon any meriting equivalent, in either canvas or paper, to Rubio's masterful balance of formal elegance, technical flair and conceptual daring." Trained as an architect at Harvard, Rubio has an exquisite eye for form and design, but it is her conceptual flights, her unlikely visions of connections between ideas, concepts, and territories, that make her works a delight of discovery for the viewer. The visual and cognitive impact of her works, and the profound presence of Cuba in what she does, was beautifully expressed by Elena Tamargo in a conference at Cremata Gallery:

> *The Island is a very important character in Lydia's work, appearing since 1993 . . . "that mountain I call island," as a sculpture encased in a cage, encased in a suitcase, a suitcase to carry with her always, a past, an integrative power, a space compressed in time and space, dreams. The Island is a beautiful fossil living in the subconscious, the island holds the unmovable childhood, the island is maternal.*[22]

But it is Marijean Miyar's framing of Rubio's work in the manner of the great artists of the Renaissance through her craft, and with the semiotics of Umberto Eco, that best describes Lydia's work—from her exquisite drawings-studies to her playful handling of lost letters, to hidden meanings and word symbols, Miyar, a noted art historian, concludes that Lydia Rubio is an artist for all times, from roots in classical technique to challenging constructions for a cutting-edge contemporary world.[23]

> *Lydia Rubio's multidisciplinary works are distinguished by the use of words and images in multi-paneled pieces and integrated installations. Her multimedia*

works suggest discontinuous narratives, riddles in spatial sequences; paintings are often accompanied by artist journals. Ms. Rubio has completed important public art commissions. In 2008 The Gate of Earth, a large scale sculpture and terrazzo design for the Raleigh Durham Airport, and in 2009 The Women's Park Art Gates, for Miami Dade County Art in Public Places. The Gate of Air, a second RDU commission, will be completed in December 2010. She is a recipient of the Creative Capital Professional Development Fellowship in 2010 and 2007, Pollock Krasner Fellowship in 2006, the State of Florida Individual Artist Fellowship in Painting 1994 the Cintas Fellowship 1982 and a Graham Foundation Award in 1975. Rubio has traveled extensively and lived in Italy, Puerto Rico, Boston and New York. She is now based in Miami, Florida and currently represented by Beaux Arts Des Ameriques in Montreal QB and Cremata Gallery in Miami.[24]

Ramón Alejandro

Belonging to a transitional generation, after the San Alejandro-trained older four, Alejandro left Cuba in 1961 and was a wanderer of the world until he settled in Paris. A man of immense culture, fascinated by calligraphy and Eastern philosophies, Alejandro befriended Roland Barthes, drawn by the great French intellectual's exploration of Semiotics and Structuralism. He traveled to Morocco and other exotic locations, a bit in the footsteps of Delacroix, and created a stunning collection of notebooks, which he continues to use, to this day, with his everyday musings, writings, drawings, and *croquis* in black and white or full color, filled with exquisite calligraphy and gorgeous erotic paintings and strange drawings. Back in Paris, Alejandro created a series of oil paintings depicting forbidding cliffs, rock formations, and stone towers; later, he began to play with tropical fruits as a hidden symbol of a sexual world. Alejandro's work resembles the compositions of Renaissance masters in eerie terms; extraordinary perspectives, laborious and painstaking details, references to figures, myths or themes hidden in his paintings to surprise, delight or shock the eye.

A brief sojourn in Miami intensifies the tropical fruits series, followed by a disastrous and very brief move to Havana and then back to his home in Paris. His painting-drawing *Palmarito*, a huge black and white charcoal and pencil work, is truly a Renaissance-like tableau with subtle and unexpected, almost hidden, pokes of humor, a bit like a *trompetilla* in the midst of a solemn speech. Currently Alejandro, who can see *Sacré Coeur* from his window in a great Montmartre apartment, is working in a series of shells and mollusks and solitary beaches, again in the manner of a Renaissance painter.

Luis Cruz Azaceta

Alejandro Anreus brilliantly describes Azaceta's creative habitat and his art:

> *His art stubbornly resists and questions the world and its official histories. Even though the solid concrete building literally keeps out the sounds and furies of uptown New Orleans, Cruz Azaceta's work, piled up and hanging all over the edifice, contains the wounds and screams of this outside world.*[25]

The experience of displacement, of not belonging—which could be everyman's plight—is a particularly Cuban exile experience, even despite perfect English or French and true affection and loyalty to one's adoptive land.

The works of Azaceta reflect all of these feelings, and more: New York City was his first home outside of Cuba and that experience, "of a very aggressive city," marks much of his work. He describes his passage from geometric art "like everybody else's" to expressionistic art after a trip to Europe "where [he] did not know anybody," spent his time in museums, and was faced with Goya and Bosch—who changed forever how he created art. In a video interview at the Gertrude Herbert Art Center in Augusta, Georgia, in 2008, Azaceta said that "when I saw the black paintings of Goya I had to ask myself: what kind of painter do I want to be? And Goya gave me the answer: I want to deal with social issues that affect us individually and collectively . . ." in an aesthetic manner.

An artist of tremendous creative force and output, Azaceta's Cuban motif—*Balsero* images, for instance, seem to populate his paintings, but we don't know if these are Cuban *balseros* or modern man floating in a sea of loneliness—is present in a large portion of his works. Azaceta works with oils on canvas, mixed media on paper, on sculptures, and installations. From his website:

> *Luis Cruz Azaceta is an artist whose work carries the indelible imprint of displacement. The solitude, cultural and linguistic isolation, and the certainty of no longer belonging anywhere has marked his view of the world since he immigrated to the United States from Cuba at the beginning of the sixties. Throughout his career, his works have continually exuded that feeling, whether veiledly or explicitly. His perspective is that of a displaced individual attempting to find a personal route in the midst of that strange labyrinth that is identity.*[26]

Although the pain of exile seems to be present in different degrees of intensity in the works of these nine masters, Azaceta, perhaps better than anybody else, is the painter of Exile.

Hernán García

García, a traditional painter of oil on canvas, without the enrichment or the distraction of other media, is a truly surrealist explorer of the human condition. His creatures show the full range of abandonment, not just of exile, and together with a sense of the tragic, there is a certain sadness and pathos in them, without losing the possibility of goodness—of redemption. Critic Manuel Alvarez Lezama writes in García's catalog for his 2010 exhibition at Cremata Gallery in Miami:

> *Hernán García belongs to the artistic generation that followed the Cuban artists*

. . . who defined Modernism in Cuba: Ponce, Lam, Victor Manuel . . . to mention a few. (García) returns as one of the most consequent voices among Cuban artists (after a necessary rest imposed by what César Vallejo called "the black messengers" (los heraldos negros), those brutal blows that life bestows on us).

Together with monster-like beings with sad faces, García paints chairs which seem to tell stories of their human users, marked by the colors and the positions of the chairs. Greens and blues, a falling tower of chairs, a single chair, tell a story of passion and of solitude with great parsimony in his canvases. A consummate and experienced painter, García is capable of eliciting emotion from a simple painting of one red chair among ten blue ones, crying to be heard, to be understood, as the leftover relics of human passage.

Many viewers are moved by the revelation that Hernán García's characters and his ubiquitous chairs are revelations of our internal struggles between good and evil, beauty and ugliness. It is indeed in the tension of his works that we find the true artist.

Even Younger Artists:

María Martínez-Cañas

Superb imagination encased in extraordinary discipline and craftsmanship describes María Martínez-Cañas' work. In twenty-plus years she has not stopped for a minute in creating fierce beauty, in exploring the limits of identity, photography, installation, space, volume . . . Olga Viso, curator for Contemporary Art at the Hirshhorn Museum in Washington, D.C., describes Martínez-Cañas' early trajectory well:

When Martínez-Cañas came to the mainland United States in 1978 to study art in Philadelphia, and later Chicago, her feelings of dislocation intensified as she found herself in a primarily English-speaking setting with a climate and attitude quite different from her Caribbean background. The resulting

> *tensions began to express themselves in her art of the early 1980s. Although Martínez-Cañas' primary medium has always been photography, an important early video from 1984 considered (as the title of the work suggests)* Un Problema de Identidad/A Problem of Identity. *The video, [. . .], featured the artist wearing a series of masks. This exploration inaugurated a search that became a central focus of her art throughout most of the late 1990s. Many pieces from this time were also inspired by music. In* The Concert Book, *1981, she translated a violin concerto into photography by printing a sparse, syncopated arrangement of graphic design elements and fragments of spliced photo-negatives across the surface of photographic paper. . . .*[27]

Travelers in Miami Airport stand transfixed at her sand-blasted, forty-by-forty-foot mural, *Años Continuos*, a powerful, truly beautiful entity. Martínez-Cañas, urbane, cultured, sensitive, and highly intelligent, is an extraordinary artist not afraid of exploring beyond the frontiers of philosophical and artistic lines.

Martínez-Cañas' powerful 2009 exhibition at the Freedom Tower space in Miami showcases an absolutely dazzling "Tetralogy," the title of the show. Her artworks—photographs—from old José Gómez Sicre negatives are stunning photos printed on canvas and traced with delicate gestures to emphasize some figures and relegate others to the background. Her exploration of identity and duplicity, again, takes her fearlessly into profound psychological and visual realms, creating an extraordinary series of artworks.

In the introduction to the gorgeous catalog of this exhibition, Miami Dade College Gallery Art System Curator Jorge Luis Gutiérrez says:

> *With photography there is always a mystery, a veil which does not allow us to have the clarity we desire. Photography is the most painful reiteration of what we are and what we don't want to be; its veil permeates every aspect of contemporary culture. / With its four series of works* TETRALOGY . . . *places us in territories of identity, truth and fiction, memory and time, representation*

and meaning. [The] exhibition highlights the gradual transitions between a real world and an imaginary one, with many images straddling both worlds.[28]

María Martínez-Cañas has come of age: the mastery of her medium is complete. The slight anxiety produced by not knowing "what we are and what we are not" when faced with her works is an encomium to her immense creativity and skill.

Gustavo Acosta

In the text to an Acosta catalog exhibition at Elite Fine Arts in 2002, Donald Cesspit writes: "Like a true Old Master, he [Acosta] wants to enlist perspective in the service of internal truth—to use the movement of the lines that build perspective to build mood."[29] **And** mood is exactly what the viewer gets when faced with an Acosta painting! Empty cities, as if seen from above in a Google Earth map, people absent but imagined. From the enchanting and somewhat scary objects—a cork, a part of a land tiller, a segment of a suit of armor—of his early 1990s paintings, to his profoundly beautiful and eerie new series—"Hypothesis of Madness," "The Great Systems," "Adult Games"—Acosta makes the viewer enter into feelings of nostalgia, elation, awe, sadness, surprise, sometimes even joy, with each of his paintings.

Recent paintings (from *Great Systems*) delve into all kinds of greens to soothe, mesmerize, and enchant: his rendition of strong waves and rough seas is truly magnificent, his depiction of a piece of the reality portrayed, a masterful technique. The sad, moody, beautiful greenish paintings of an abandoned city—Havana—evoke a great deal of emotion. *The Big Splash*, *The Glass Shield*, and *The Mirror and the East View* painted for an exhibition this year, are truly magical paintings. Acosta is a painter—not a sculptor or an assemblage artist or an installation artist. His utter cutting-edge impact using a very old medium shows the level of his craft.

Carol Damian, director & chief curator of the Frost Museum at Florida International University writes: ". . . Undoubtedly the sense of loss relates to his homeland of Cuba, which he left in 1991 . . . Cuba is the place on his maps. . . . It is Cuba that he painted to capture and preserve its history and memory."[30]

Actually, the paintings of Gustavo Acosta make the viewer think of Borges' texts, both in the absolute solitude of his landscapes, and in the concentration of the artist on basic ego questions—that are not answered.

VI: A CATALOG OF CUBAN ARTISTS

An invitation to look at the works of these artists:

Born in the 1920s and Before
Cundo Bermúdez
S. Cabrera Moreno
Jorge Camacho
Agustín Cárdenas
Mario Carreño
Hugo Consuegra
Antonia Eiriz
Roberto Estopiñán
Agustín Fernández
Joaquín Ferrer
Gay García
Carmen Herrera
Raquel Lázaro
Guido Llinás
R. López-Dirube
Tomás Oliva
Felipe Orlando

Gina Pellón
Emilio Sánchez
Rafael Soriano

Born in the 1930s
Jesús G. de Armas
Margarita Cano
Ramón Carulla
Hernán García
Mickey Jorge
Carlos M. Luis
Baruj Salinas

Born in the 1940s
Ramón Alejandro
María Brito Avellana
Luis Cruz Azaceta
Humberto Calzada

Víctor Gómez
Ana Mendieta
Lydia Rubio
Tomás Sánchez

Born in the 1950s
Gustavo Acosta
Carlos Alfonzo
José Bedia
Mario Bencomo
Humberto Castro
Arturo Cuenca
Demi
María Martínez-Cañas
Ernesto Pujol
Arturo Rodríguez
Rubén Torres Llorca

Born in the 1960s	*Born in the 1980s*	Victor Manuel García
Pablo Cano	César Santos	Antonio Gattorno
Ismael Gómez Peralta		Wifredo Lam
Leonel Matheu	*The Vanguardia Painters*	Amelia Peláez
Juan Martín Oliva	Jorge Arche	Marcelo Pogolotti
	Cundo Bermúdez	Fidelio Ponce de León
Born in the 1970s	Servando Cabrera Moreno	René Portocarrero
Cristina Lei Rodríguez	Carlos Enríquez	Mariano Rodríguez

VII: SOURCES, REFERENCES, AND NOTES

Personal Conversations

The "conversations" of the title took place largely over a four-month period in the fall of 2009 and during most of 2010 with major figures in Cuban art: dealers, collectors, critics, academics, art historians, and of course, some of the artists themselves, and in some cases their families. Alejandro Anreus, Carlos Luis, Zoë Valdés, Marijean Miyar, and Juan Martínez; Raúl and Lourdes Cremata, José Raúl Alonso, Dora Valdés Fauli, Ramón Berrnuda, Marta Gutiérrez, and José Manuel Martínez-Cañas; Rafael and, again, Marijean Miyar, in her role as a collector, and two more important collectors who wished to remain unnamed; Clear Fernández, Margarita and Jorge Camacho, Leonel Matheu, Mario Bencomo, Lydia Rubio, Ramón Alejandro, María Martínez-Cañas, and Gustavo Acosta. To all, the author's appreciation for sharing their perspectives, knowledge, biases, humor, and passion for art.

NOTES

It should be noted that since its foundation FACE (*Facts About Cuban Exiles*), has bestowed an art award to notable Cuban exiled painters and sculptors, among them: Cundo Bermúdez, Manuel Carbonell, Guy García, Julio Larraz, Gina Pellón, and Andrés Valerio.

1. The San Alejandro Academy, a cradle for painting and drawing in Cuba, is the oldest of its type in Latin America. It was founded in January 11, 1818, at San Agustín, in the Old Havana convent of that name. In 1832, it was named San Alejandro to honor Don Alejandro Ramírez, general superintendent and director of the Real Sociedad Económica Amigos del País.
2. Juan Martínez, *Cuban Art & National Identity: The Vanguardia Painters 1927-1950* (Gainesville: University Press of Florida, 2004).
3. Carlos Franqui, *Jorge Camacho* (Barcelona: Ediciones Polígrafa, 1979).
4. Manuel Alvarez Lezama, *Hernán García and His Enigmatic Realities* (Hernán: Landscapes, exhibition catalog at Cremata Gallery, February 2010).
5. Noted by Zoé Valdés in her article *La Vastedad Sosegada: Pintores Cubanos* (Ecodiario.es, September 23, 2009).
6. Carlos Luis, *Mario Bencomo* (exhibition catalog for Bencomo's exhibition in 2010 at Gallerie Beaux Arts des Ameriques, in Quebec, Canada).
7. F. Lennox Campello, *On the Return of Stolen Cuban Artwork* (ARTistic.com, February 2009).
8. Miami has the largest concentration of exiles, followed by Union City, N.J., New York City, and Los Angeles. These experiences of exile also apply outside of Miami.
9. Author conversations with Gina Pellón.
10. Ibid.
11. Author conversations with Carlos Luis.
12. Valdés, *La Vastedad Sosegada*.
13. Carlos M. Luis unpublished manuscript, 2009, 5. Courtesy of the author. Translation by this author from the Spanish original.
14. Author conversations with Carlos Luis.
15. Author conversations with Margarita Camacho.
16. Translation by this author from the French edition of the Arenas' letters to the Camachos.
17. Judith Weiner, "The Quest for Self-Knowledge," in *Roberto Estopiñán: A Retrospective* (Birmingham: Schweyer-Galdo Editions, 1983).
18. Carlos Franqui, "The European Presence of Roberto Estopiñán," in *Roberto Estopiñán: A Retrospective* (Birmingham: Schweyer-Galdo Editions, 1983).
19. Carol Damian, "Agustín Fernández: Galería Aroca," *ARTNexus*, no. 40, May-June 2001.
20. www.agustinfernandez.net.
21. Ibid.
22. Elena Tamargo notes from conference at Cremata Gallery, October 15, 2010.
23. Marijean Miyar notes from a conference on Lydia Rubio at Cremata Gallery, September 30, 2010.
24. From the Cremata Gallery web page notes on Lydia Rubio.
25. Alejandro Anreus, unpublished manuscript, 2009, 1. Courtesy of the author.
26. www.luiscruzacaceta.com.
27. Olga Viso, *Texts*, in www.mariamartinezcanas.com.
28. Jorge Luis Gutiérrez. *Introduction* (Miami: Tetralogy exhibition catalog, Miami Dade College, 2009).
29. Donald Kuspit, *The Past as Space,* Gustavo Acosta's *Book of Hours* exhibition (Coral Gables, Fla.: Elite Fine Arts, 2002).
30. Carol Damian, *Gustavo Acosta: Questions to the Mirror* (Panama, Fla.: Contemporary Art Museum exhibition catalog, 2009).

23

THEATER

BY FRANCISCO RODRIGUEZ

During the Republic period (1902-1958), Cubans were forced into exile, either fleeing the dictatorships of Gerardo Machado or Fulgencio Batista. With the Castro takeover, history repeated itself. For example, the late scholar Dr. Carlos Ripoll, noted expert on José Martí, was a triple exile in New York in each of these dictatorships. Castro's policy of persecution, imprisonment, and harassment resulted in the exile of thousands of writers and artists. This policy divided Cuban intellectuals in two distinct groups: those who remained in Cuba supporting the system following Fidel Castro's infamous phrase "Within the Revolution, everything; against the Revolution, nothing,"[1] and those who went into exile after paying the high price of cutting themselves off from their culture while allowing themselves to continue their lives without the fear of being censored by Castro, as evidenced by the closing of the cultural weekly publication *Lunes de Revolución* on his direct orders.[2]

And so, Cubans in exile faced two immediate realities: struggling for their livelihoods and keeping their culture alive. The former they achieved through hard work and personal effort. The latter—although more complex, but not impossible—consisted of defending their identity as a people. Already during the early years of the exile experience, cultural expressions began to take shape. Music became the most viable way to maintain the national identity, while theater came to be viewed more as entertainment and a means of expressing nostalgia for the enslaved island while reflecting the new reality in which the exiles now found themselves. The 1962 play *Hamberguers y Sirenazos* by Pedro Román is regarded as the first play written in this early phase of exile. It made its debut in 1969 during the *Añorada Cuba* festival. This work has been staged more than sixteen times by different casts, and it has been seen by several generations of exiles.

The theater as nostalgia and entertainment helped mitigate some of the pain of exile. Major figures such as comedian Leopoldo Fernández, "Tres Patines," together with other legendary figures such as Alberto Garrido, Federico Piñero, and Rosendo Rosell played a leading role in entertaining Miami. Over the years, especially in the 1970s and 1980s, and perhaps even into the 1990s, several theaters served as venues for this genre. The now-demolished Teatro Martí, in the heart of Little Havana, founded by impresario Ernesto Capote, was for a long time the main magnet for nostalgic comedies. It immediately became the cultural meeting point for these first exiles, later to be called "historic exiles." Alberto González and Armando Roblán also performed there for many years. The latter's parody of Fidel Castro is still greeted with laughter. Some of his more memorable comedies were *Se Le Fue Por el Mariel Hasta la Vaca a Fidel* and *En el Noventa Fidel Revienta*.

In Las Máscaras theater, Salvador Ugarte and Alfonso Cremata were active in this genre until Ugarte's passing in 2006 (Cremata continued his career as a comedian). At Bellas Artes theater, comedian Néstor Cabell also remains active with continuous and renewed musical revues and comedy shows. However, at present this kind of Cuban theater shows signs of weakness, in part because many of its comedians have either died or are retired, and the new generations have followed different paths. But in the words of Cabell himself, "The theater called vernacular (or popular) will never disappear because it is the mirror of the people, of ordinary people . . . although it has been changing."[3]

For his part, comedian and character actor Mario Martín, a multifaceted stage figure, had his comedy *Me Voy Para Cuba* in theaters for more than a year. Another thespian worth mentioning is Raúl de Cárdenas, who combines local customs, history, and everyday life into his plays. Currently, one of the few signs of life of this genre has the encouragement of businessman, actor, and director Juan Roca and his company Havanafama.

Alongside this vernacular theater, a different style of dramatic writing was also developing. In the 1960s and 1970s, playwrights like Matías Montes Huidobro and Julio Matas went into exile. While exiled, they continued to work, providing a guiding influence on the development of the Cuban theater as playwrights as well as scholars of the genre. No one has studied the Cuban theater on the island and in exile more than Montes Huidobro, first with his book *Persona, Vida y Máscara en el Teatro Cubano*, and then in the series *Cuba Detrás del Telón*, now in its fourth volume.

Directors such as Francisco Morín and María Julia Casanova were pivotal in the development of the theater on the island and in exile. Miami and New York stand out as the most significant forums for the performance and development of Cuban exile drama. Some of the playwrights who have excelled in this art are Herberto Dumé, José Corrales, Héctor Santiago, René Alomá, and Pedro Monge Rafuls. The latter created the *Revista Ollantay* and the Ollantay Center for the Arts, an important venue for the dissemination of the Hispanic theater in the U.S.

A look at the development of the Cuban theater in Miami shows that between the 1960s and the 1980s, numerous theater groups were formed and theater halls opened. In the course of time some survived, others were altered, while some disappeared. The Teatro Radio Centro on Flagler Street, where Garrido, Piñero, and Leopoldo Fernández worked, was the starting point for the Cuban theater in exile in Miami in the early 1960s. Then came Teatro 66, created by Miguel Ponce in 1966, and other venues where Cabell, Ugarte, and Cremata performed. Next came *Los Comediantes* with Norma Zúñiga and Oswaldo Calvo, and others such as *Lecuona* and *La Comparsa* opened in Hialeah, where Orlando Lima, Armando Navarro, and Pedro Román would perform.

After these early efforts and with the continued arrival of more Cubans in Miami, a dramatic spurt in drama took place with the addition of *zarzuelas* (Spanish operettas) and large-scale musicals in 1967 by Sociedad Pro Arte Grateli, featuring the great diva of Cuba, Marta Pérez, and the work by Pili de la Rosa and Miguel de Grandy, among others. It quickly became one of the great pillars of the city of Miami and an example of perseverance and hard work. Two other lyrical groups appeared during this same period, Sociedad Hispano-Americana de Arte and the Sociedad Lírica Euterpe, are now long gone.

A defining moment in the cultural development of Cuban exile drama began in 1969 with the transformation of a boxing arena into a theater: Teatro Martí. Many Miami celebrities performed there, among them Martha Flores, Aleida Leal, Mario Martín, and Martha Picanes, as well as legends of the stage like Rolando Ochoa, Pepa Berrios, Sergio Doré (father and son), Norma Zúñiga, Oswaldo Calvo, and Manolo Villaverde. The late entrepreneur and director María Julia Casanova stated in her biography that "Ernesto Capote was opening more rooms in his theater [Martí] to have four operating simultaneously to present the most successful work of the time: *Mi hijo no es lo que parece*, with Pedro de Paul heading the cast."[4]

A limited list of theatrical venues in the first twenty years of the Cuban exile experience include: Teatrila—Mario Martín and Norma Zúñiga; Arlequín—José Vicente Quiroga; Círculo—Cecilio Noble; Teatro Amateur—Paul Díaz; Studio 3—Griselda Nogueras and Teresa María Rojas; Prometeo—Teresa María Rojas, sponsored by Miami Dade College; Los Juglares—Sergio Doré; Taller de Arte y Drama—Patricia Parra; CDMI and Repertorio VII—Eduardo Corbé; Teatro 80—Griselda Nogueras and Rosa Felipe; RAS—Mario Ernesto Sánchez, Teresa María Rojas, and Alina Interián; Grupo Teatral de FUI—sponsored by Florida

International University; ARCO—Manolo Coego and Aurora Collazo; and La Ronda Teatro Bar—Lourdes and Ernesto Montaner, among others.

During the 1980s, 1990s, and into the new millennium emerged a number of art centers managed by Cubans or places where Cuban themes were developed. Worth mentioning are the Teatro Avante, founded by Mario Ernesto Sánchez. Teatro Avante has hosted the International Hispanic Theatre Festival of Miami for almost thirty years, and it has been the site where some of the most outstanding national and international theater groups, as well as dance groups, have performed.

John Rodaz, who was born in Matanzas, Cuba, founded the Area Stage Company in 1989. In collaboration with young up-and-coming Cuban-American playwrights, Rodaz developed scripts that expressed the core of the Cuban exile in the country such as *Passage* and *Sleepwalkers*. His production of *Rum and Coke* was the inspiration for the June 12, 1998, edition of *Nightline* with Ted Kopel; it was the only theatre company to be featured on the program. In 2008, the Area Stage Company moved into the Riviera Theatre in Coral Gables, a venue that permits the organization to function as an art center. Rodaz trained at New York University's Tisch School of the Arts Professional Theatre Program.

Other important and active venues include the Teatro 8, Teatro de Bellas Artes, Teatro en Miami Studio, Havanafama Teatro Estudio, Teatro Abanico, ArtSpoken Performing Art, and the recently opened Akuara Teatro and the Black Box Stage at Miami-Dade County Auditorium.

Some of these venues placed more emphasis on works by Cuban authors, but in general a remarkable scenic variety has been achieved. There has always been a lively theatrical environment in exile, with top-ranking actors, directors with wide interests, and authors with solid works.

Although the exile activity should be viewed as a whole, some individual efforts excel. Perhaps one that contributed the most to the theater in Miami was María Julia Casanova, founder of the Sala de Teatro La Danza, where dozens of works that had a very positive impact on the local dramatic scene premiered. Among them was *Corona de Amor* by Alejandro Casona, with Aurora Collazo and Evelio Taillacq in the leading roles. This work played for a year and was quite the cultural event in Miami. María Julia created a very diverse theater, with attractive scenery, lush costumes, and ambitious presentations such as *Mujeres*, with a cast of big names including Pilar Arenas, Martha Picanes, Julia Menéndez, Glenda Díaz-Rigaud, Julie de Grandy, Margarita Prieto, Alina Interián, Lourdes Menci, Liliana Gibrán, Cristina Coego, Cary Roque, Patricia Jiménez Rojo, Maribel González, Cristina Martí, and July Ortega. It was staged in the Teatro de Bellas Artes. Other memorable performances include *Rosa de Otoño* with Amparo Rivelles; *The Diary of Anne Frank, Un Amante de 3 a 5,* and *Las Mariposas son Libres*, all in the now-extinct Teatro Carrusel, with performances by Mario Ernesto Sánchez and Alina Interián; and *La Reina Enamorada* in the Teatro de Bellas Artes with Griselda Nogueras, Manolo Villaverde, and Sergio Doré, among others. With the premiere of *Rivales*, María Julia opened her own room, the Casanova Theater, home of many future theatrical hits. The extraordinary cast of *Rivales* included Pilar Arenas, Manolo Villaverde, Martha Picanes, Evelio Taillacq, Rosa Felipe, Jorge Ovies, Ileana Quirch, and Humberto Rossenfeld. The theater has been renamed twice: first as Teatro Zayón, and now Teatro 8.[5]

Francisco Morín, the founding figure of the Cuban theater on the island and in exile, made first-class theater. He is an institution—the great living legend of the Cuban theater. In the 1940s, he created *Prometeo* and launched a long and successful career in the island and later in exile. Morín was always controversial and innovative, bringing to Cuban theaters the works of renowned international playwrights while also encouraging the works of local authors—a task he continued in exile for many years. He once said:

> *When I read a work that I liked I just did it. It's that simple. There was Cocteau, among other major European playwrights, and I brought him to the*

stage. I read *Calígula* by Camus and I made it known, just like when a work by Bjørnstjerne Bjomson, a contemporary of Ibsen, fell into my hands. I liked it and I staged it in Cuba. I made a different theater to what we were accustomed to and they called this a revolutionary theater. I say again that one must do what one considers to be the best—doing his best regardless of criticism. I premiered Virgilio Piñera in Cuba with the presentation of *Electra Garrigó*. That was his first work to be staged. I also premiered Antón Arrufat, Jorge del Busto and José Triana. I did it for the simple reason that I had a feeling for these works.[6]

At the age of ninety, Morín is still revered and his presence at gatherings or representations constitute a significant event.

The theme of exile and of the Cuban and Cuban-American reality has been an almost permanent presence in Cuban plays written outside the island. Professor José A. Escarpanter, one of the most notable scholars of the Cuban theater, reaffirms this reality when he says, "Exile, and the motif of the exile are a constant in the Cuban theater."[7] In 1999, Escarpanter counted that in the U.S. alone (primarily in Miami, New York, and California), forty-six Cuban playwrights had been involved in the theater while exiled, reflecting the strength of exile dramatic writing.

Among the works by Cuban authors that have premiered in the U.S. (some as dramatic readings) are those by the most important Cuban playwright of all time, Virgilio Piñera: *Electra Garrigó, Falsa Alarma, Jesús, Aire Frío, Los Siervos, El No*, and *Una Caja de Zapatos Vacía* (world premier, Teatro Avante). Another Cuban playwright is Matías Montes Huidobro, one of the island's most prolific dramatists. Huidobro wrote *La Navaja de Olofé, La Madre y la Guillotina, Ojos Para no Ver, Gas en los Poros, Exilio, Funeral en Teruel, Los Acosados, Un Objeto de Deseo*, and *Oscuro Total*. Another figure prominent in exile is Julio Matas, author of *El extravío, Los Parientes Lejanos, Juego de Damas*, and *El Rapto de La Habana*. Pedro Monge Rafuls wrote *Las Lágrimas del Alma, Las Vidas del Gato, Recordando a Mamá*, and *Soldados Somos y a la Guerra Vamos*. Héctor Santiago, winner of the Letras de Oro Award in 1995, penned *Vida y Pasión de la Peregrina*, about the life of Gertrudis Gómez de Avellaneda (also staged at Teatro Avante), and *Balada Para un Verano en La Habana, En Busca del Paraíso, Madame Camille, Escuela de Danza, El Día que se Robaron los Colores, Un Dulce Cafecito, Rosalba la Lluvia, La Diva en la Octava Casa,* and *El Milagro de Madame Kirovska*. Raúl de Cárdenas wrote *Recuerdos de Familia, Las Carbonell de la Calle Obispo, Las Pepillas del Vedado, Luz Divina, Santera, Espiritista, Se van las Capote, La Muerte de Rosendo, Juventud Divino Tesoro,* and *Sucedió en La Habana*. In addition, Cárdenas wrote a monogram in two acts, *Un Hombre al Amanecer*, based on the life of José Martí and winner of the 1988-1989 Letras de Oro Award. Other works by Cárdenas include *Los Hijos de Ochún, En el Barrio de Colón, Las Sombras no se Olvidan, Amapola Indómita, Suite Miami, La Ceci, El Pasatiempo Nacional,* and *Dile a Fragancia que yo la Quiero*.[8]

If the playwrights have been central to the projection of the Cuban theater in the U.S., no less important is the work of the directors, some of them with solid track records, such as Herberto Dumé, Eduardo Corbé, Rolando Moreno, María Julia Casanova, Mario Ernesto Sánchez, Mario Martín, Juan Roca, Pedro Monge Rafuls, Teresa María Rojas, Ernesto García, Eddy Díaz Souza, Lilliam Vega, Yoshvani Medina, and Alberto Sarraín. These are names that make up a comprehensive list of directors, some actors turned directors, and even writers who have dabbled in directing and acting.

The works of Cuban writers on American billboards have been quite successful. One of the most important playwrights is José Triana, now living in France, where he has developed an important part of his work. *La Noche de los Asesinos* is considered his most important work, alongside *El Parque de la Fraternidad, El Mayor General Hablará de Teogonía, Revolico en el Campo de Martes,* and *La Muerte del ñeque*.

The work of Nilo Cruz is worth mentioning. A playwright whose work is mostly in English, just as Eduardo Manet's is in French, Cruz won a Pulitzer Prize. He explores a very variable repertoire of dramatic issues. Some of his works include *A Park in Our House, Two Sisters and a*

Piano, Anna in the Tropics (Pulitzer Prize), and *Lorca in a Green Dress*. It is remarkable that a playwright educated in the U.S. carries out his work in the language learned in exile. The same is the case of Iván Acosta, author of *El Súper*, a classic of the Cuban theater in exile; and Manuel Martín, whose work includes such pieces as *Swallows* and *Union City Thanksgiving*. To the list of authors who have done their dramatic work in English one must add Dolores Prida, author of *Coser y Cantar* and *Beautiful Señoritas*. These are just a few names of writers who have written in English.

For a long time groups of Cuban playwrights and directors in New York represented the vanguard, with institutions such as Intar of Max Ferrá; the Teatro Repertorio Español of René Buch and Gilberto Zaldívar; the Teatro Dúo of Manuel Martín and Magaly Alabau; the Centro Cultural Cubano, with Ileana Fuentes, Iván Acosta, and Omar Torres; the Thalia Spanish Theater of Silvia Brito; El Portón of Mario Peña; and Ollantay of Pedro Monge Rafuls. By comparison, in Miami the vernacular or popular theater took greater hold. However, over the years there has been a shift, and Miami is now the source for a renewal in the serious theater.

The first decade of twenty-first century has evidenced a great boost in Cuban exile theater. During this phase Miami has become the capital of Cuban exile dramatic theater. Some authors, like Matías Montes Huidobro and Julio Matas—who lived and worked in Hawaii and Pennsylvania, respectively—have now settled in Miami. Yvonne López Arenal, Roberto Antinoo, and Juan Roca left Los Angeles, where they worked for decades, to begin anew in Miami. Max Ferrá left New York and also settled in Miami. Miguel Ponce crossed the Atlantic and returned to Miami from Spain. To all this must be added a steady stream of authors and directors from the island who have joined the artistic exile community. Among them are Víctor Varela, Ernesto García, José González, Raúl Martín, and Yoshvani Medina. There still are Cuban playwrights writing and staging works in France, such as José Triana and Eduardo Manet. Others work in Spain and Brazil, among other places around the world. Pedro Monge Rafuls is currently working in Honduras, and Miguel Ponce, after many years in Spain, returned to Miami and then went on to Colombia. Additionally, works by the exiled writer Julie de Grandy have been performed in Buenos Aires, and by Maricel Mayor Marsán in Santiago, Chile.

The work done in Miami has brought forth fruits. The durability of Miami's *Festival Internacional de Teatro Hispano* (International Hispanic Theatre Festival of Miami), with an international profile, and the consolidation of the Havanafama Teatro Studio as a venue for surprising productions from *El Pene Crudo*, a comedy by Raúl de Cárdenas, to *Bernarda*—a renewed production of *La Casa de Bernarda Alba* by Federico García Lorca, under the direction of Juan Roca—evidence the strength of exile theater.

Teatro Avante is the headquarters for the *Festival Internacional de Teatro Hispano* in Miami. Teatro Avante was founded by Mario Ernesto Sánchez in 1979, delaring its goal to be the preservation of the Hispanic heritage. His group has represented the U.S. at international festivals in Mexico, Costa Rica, Spain, Japan, France, Colombia, the Dominican Republic, Guatemala, Portugal, Venezuela, Argentina, Puerto Rico, Los Angeles, California, and New York. Under the auspices of the Teatro Avante, works have been produced by important Cuban playwrights, among them Eduardo Manet, Julio Matas, René Alomá, René Ariza, Rolando Ferrer, Virgilio Piñera, Manuel Reguera Saumell, José Triana, and Héctor Santiago. In recent years, Avante has staged pieces by Shakespeare, including *La Tempestad* (*The Tempest*), adapted by Raquel Carrió as *Otra Tempestad*, directed by Lilliam Vega; and *Aire Frío* by Virgilio Piñera, successfully directed by Sánchez himself.[9]

Teatro Avante's contribution to Miami's artistic development has been considerable. Sánchez received the 2007 Special Recognition Award from the Arts and Business Council of Miami to honor and celebrate the artistic achievements of Miami's *Festival Internacional de Teatro Hispano* since its inception in 1986.

Mention must be made of Prometeo, the cradle of many actors in Miami created by Teresa María Rojas in 1985. Rojas headed the Miami-Dade College School of Drama for more than three decades until her retirement. Under her guidance, more than ninety works were put on stage, many of them from the international repertoire, as well as around twenty-five works by Cuban authors. Under the current director, Colombian Joann María Yarrow, the school continues its educational work with more than five hundred acting students every year.

Also enjoying a solid reputation is Teatro en Miami Studio, an institution created by Ernesto García and his wife, actress and teacher Sandra García. In just five years at its headquarters, they have introduced a variety of works, including several texts by Ernesto García, which offer a stimulating theater with a psychological profile. Among his works are *Aromas de un Viaje, Sangre, El Reloj Dodecafónico, El Celador del Desierto, Enema, Fifty fifty, Al Horizonte se Llega en una Barca de Papel*, and *Oda a la Tortura*. The Teatro en Miami has also created TEMFest (Teatro en Miami Festival), now in its second edition, mostly with works by Cuban authors. This festival created the Premios Baco (Baco Awards), awarded to Mario Ernesto Sánchez, Teresa María Rojas, Marcos Casanova, Rolando Moreno, and Daniel Fernández.

The work of Ernesto García merits special mention. In addition to being a writer, he serves also as director, set designer, lighting expert, and musician. He is also the documentary filmmaker of *Raíces Aéreas*, a major work that tries to compile the works of exiled playwrights and researchers through interviews with Matías Montes Huidobro, José A. Escarpanter, Julio Matas, José Abreu Felippe, Pedro Monge Rafuls, and Yvonne López Arenal.

Also prominent in recent years is the creation of the Instituto Cultural René Ariza (ICRA), founded with the purpose of promoting Cuban exile theater. The institution also established the Premio René Ariza, awarded annually to those persons who have contributed to the propagation and promotion of the Cuban theater in exile. Among the winners are José A. Escarpanter, Matías Montes Huidobro, Julio Matas, Pedro Monge Rafuls, Nena Acevedo, Mario Martín, Francisco Morín, Teresa María Rojas, Raúl de Cárdenas, Héctor Santiago, and Magaly Boix.

The ICRA, led in its first phase by Yvonne López Arenal, was the venue for several dramatized readings: *Si de Verdad uno Muriera* by José Abreu Felippe; *Gaviotas Habaneras*, Yvonne López Arenal; *Los Acosados*, Matías Montes Huidobro; *El Plan de las Aguas*, Maricel Mayor Marsán; *Reencuentro con Doble E*, Jorge Trigoura; *Dile a Fragancia que yo la Quiero*, Raúl de Cárdenas; *La Diva en la Octava Casa*, Héctor Santiago; *La Visita*, Orlando Rossardi; *Los Siervos* and *Ser Escritor*, Virgilio Piñera; *Rezando con el Enemigo*, Luis Santeiro; *El Mayor General Hablará de Teogonía*, José Triana; *El Vestido Rojo*, José Corrales; *Flores no me Pongan*, Rita Martín; *Siempre Tuvimos Miedo*, Leopoldo Hernández; *Lina*, Marcos Miranda; *Triángulos Obtusos*, Julie de Grandy; *Las Monjas*, EduardoManet; *Las Vidas del Gato*, Pedro Monge Rafuls; *Fuerte Como la Muerte*, Daniel Fernández; *Una Rosa para Catalina Laza*, Rosa Ileana Boudet; *El Hueco en la Pared*, Jorge Carrigan; *El Príncipe y el Mar*, Eddy Díaz Souza; *Gas en los Poros* and *La Madre y la Guillotina*, Matías Montes Huidobro; and *Los Días del Milagro*, Mario Martín.

The ICRA entered a second phase under the leadership of Matías Montes Huidobro. It has continued the Premio René Ariza awards, with the 2011 recipients being Manuel Reguera Saumell, Iván Acosta, and Miriam Lezcano.

The theatrical renewal of the exile theater continues with new playwrights, actors, directors, and even new venues, such as the Akuara Teatro or the reopening of the Teatro Trail, now under Colombian ownership. The publication of *Teatro Cubano de Miami*, published by Luis de la Paz, includes seven works by Cuban exiles of different generations, and it is a reflection of the changes that have taken place in this genre. In the foreword to his book *Teatro Cubano de Miami*, De la Paz writes that the book's purpose is to attempt:

to publicize the work of some of the playwrights of Cuban origin residing in the capital of the exiles. Moreover, the selected material also seeks to serve as liaison between the authors and those who might be interested in staging their works. . . . Teatro Cubano de Miami makes an effort to fill the lack of plays published in a book format. I emphasize the words "in a book format" because for years I have had such a project in mind. The online magazine El Ateje (now defunct) published 23 plays by Cuban exiles between 2001 and 2008.[10]

To all this must be added the very recent rise of two new theater groups, El Ingenio Teatro, created by Lilliam Vega, and Hybrid Scene by José Manuel Domínguez. Thus, the legacy of Cuban exiles' contribution to the theater remains a work in progress that will entertain and educate both Cubans and Americans for years to come.

BIBLIOGRAPHY

Domínguez, Carlos Espinosa. *Una Dramaturgia Escindida, Teatro Cubano Contemporáneo* (Madrid: Centro de Documentación Teatral, 1992).

Escarpanter, José A. "El teatro cubano fuera de la isla." In *Escenarios de dos Mundos: Inventario Teatral de Iberoamérica*, vol. 2 (Madrid: Centro de Documentación Teatral/Ministry of Culture, 1988), 333-41.

------. "Veinticinco años de teatro cubano en el exilio." Latin American Theater Review. Spring, 1986.

Huidobro, Matías Montes.

http://cvc.cervantes.es/lengua/anuario/anuario_08/pdf/espectaculos02.pdf.

------. *Cuba detrás del telón*, four volumes, Ediciones Universal. *Mi vida en el Teatro*, María Julia Casanova.

Morín, Francisco. *Por Amor al Arte: Memorias de un Teatrista Cubano, 1940-1970* (Miami: Ediciones Universal, 1998).

NOTES

1. Statement by Fidel Castro on June 30, 1961, in the auditorium of José Martí National Library in Havana.
2. Weekly literary supplement of the newspaper *Revolución*. The magazine was directed by Guillermo Cabrera Infante and major artistic figures from Cuba and foreign nations collaborated with it. It was closed on orders of Castro on November 6, 1961.
3. Néstor Cabell, interview in *Diario Las Americas*, September 28, 2008.
4. María Julia Casanova, *Mi Vida en el Teatro* (Miami: Ediciones Universal, 2001), 96.
5. Unlike the Teatro Casanova and Teatro Zayón, the current Teatro 8 operates as part of the Hispanic Theater Guild, an organization created in 1989.
6. Francisco Morín, interview in *Diario Las Americas*, June 27, 2004.
7. Jorge Febles, Cuba, Exile and Culture Congress, October 1999, at Dadeland Marriot Hotel, sponsored by the Asociación Nacional de Educadores Cubano-Americanos and Herencia Cultural Cubana.
8. Carlos Felipe, José Triana, Virgilio Piñera, Julio Matas, René Ariza, Matías Montes Huidobro, Raúl de Cárdenas, Cristina Rebull, Héctor Santiago, Pedro Monge Rafuls, Mario Ernesto Sánchez, José Abreu Felippe, Manuel Reguera Saumell, René Alomá, Nilo Cruz, Reinaldo Arenas, Orlando González Esteva, Orlando Rossardi, Dolores Prida, Carmen Duarte, Ivonne López Arenal, Luis Santeiro, Mario Martín, Ernesto García, Leopoldo Hernández, Fermín Blanco, Eddy Díaz Souza, Rolando Moreno, José Sánchez Boudy, Maricel Mayor Marsán, José Corrales, Marcos Miranda, Manuel Martín, Iván Acosta, Andrés Nóbregas, Manuel Pereira, Rosa Ileana Boudet, Eduardo Manet, Yoshavani Medina, Pedro Román, Julie de Grandy, Daniel Fernández, Jorge Carrigan, Evelio Taillacq, Rita Martin, Abilio Estévez, Jorge Trigoura, and Frank Quintana.
9. Interview with Mario Ernesto Sánchez, August 26, 2011.
10. Luis de la Paz, *Teatro Cubano de Miami* (Miami: Editorial Silueta, 2010), 7-8.

24

MOVIES AND DOCUMENTARIES

BY ALEJANDRO RIOS

Blanquita Amaro enters a crowded market in Miami taking care of an old woman whom I assume is a close relative. That memorable *Bella la Salvaje* (The Beautiful Wild One), just like any neighbor's daughter, is busy with the everyday things of this country.

I talk on the phone with old Manolo Alonso, who is somewhere in Manhattan stringing together his memoirs: "Do not forget to send copies of that book made in Cuba in which my name appears."

That scholar of the republican cinema era, Joaquín Eguillor, spends his time drinking coffee at Café Versailles, trying to convince us that all times gone by were better.

These are the witnesses and foolish ghosts of a motion picture industry that has been ruined, forgotten, and misunderstood by two irreconcilable points of views: "nostalgia," which puts it on the edge of unreality, and "politics," which doesn't even give it the benefit of the doubt.

The Cuban passion for the cinema goes back to the nineteenth century, specifically to the Havana of 1897 when Frenchman Gabriel Veyre, envoy of the Lumiere House, traveled from Mexico with the invention of the cinema in his luggage. He arrived in Havana, a cosmopolitan city open to all forms of modernity and entertainment, a place in the Caribbean that was already burning on all sides, as it was—at the time—in the midst of a grueling war of independence.

Havana, that fascinating city, continued on its way at times indifferent to what was happening in the *Manigua,* the rebel countryside, just like it would be a century later when the "bearded men of the mountains" announced a second redemption to cleanse the island of inequity and corruption. Meanwhile, life went on unperturbed in the city.

Miraculously, cinema coexisted in both times. Through its passions and crises, the country did not arrest the driving pace dictated by a group of enterprising citizens living in the midst of an imperfect market economy that nonetheless pointed to a promising future.

When it was still merely a hope-filled toy, a gadget capable of reproducing on a canvas or a wall silent passages of life—real or imagined—the people of Havana were among the first in the Americas to endorse what was later called the Seventh Art.

The motion picture industry's fascinating Cuban adventure is divided into three periods outlined by historians: republican-era silent movies and talkies, revolutionary cinema, and exile cinema, although this way of categorizing an uneven, gradual, and organic experience does not usually do justice to the most persistent and stubborn creators of the craft.

On the other hand, the motion picture industry's relationship with governmental paternalism—whether erroneously yearned for or applied for the wrong reasons—resulted in works influenced by interests that went beyond the artistic. In a letter dated 1917, President Menocal wrote to distributors Santos and Artigas about the first screening at Cuba's Presidential Palace of the film *El Rescate del Brigadier Sanguily por el Mayor General Ignacio Agramonte* (Rescue of Brigadier Sanguily by Major General Ignacio Agramonte): "I take this opportunity to congratulate you on the high degree of development which—as this film shows—the cinematic art has reached in Cuba, as well as the correct nature of the theme that has served you as the story line and one that surely must stir in our youth a feeling of nationality, which is the key foundation on which rests the future of the Republic."

It is interesting to note that the president directed his letter to the business promoters of the film and not to its director and photographer, Enrique Díaz Quesada. The letter was worded in a rhetorical style that could well have been written by Fidel Castro to the directors of the *Instituto Cubano del Arte e Industria Cinematográficos* (Cuban Institute of Cinematographic Art and Industry, ICAIC) during the early 1960s. Those years saw the full honeymoon between the state and its cultural representatives long before the dictator took drastic actions even against the late Tomás Gutiérrez Alea, whom Castro could not forgive for his last film, *Guantanamera*.

The cinematic industry that began in 1959 under the protective umbrella of the government-controlled ICAIC wanted to break with the narrative mold of the immediate past. The successful formula of U.S. movies was to be discarded for the sake of adopting the experiments of European avant-garde. To be sure, the national legacy and tradition was rapidly ignored. No rumba or Lady of the Charity (*Virgen de la Caridad*, Cuba's patron saint); it was to be a clean slate.

The story was re-told, but in a different way, and always to prove a preconceived thesis. The directors were pristine artists, untouched by the "dirty" work of the producers, and they were well-off subordinates on a state budget. They were shaped on the fly, like so many guerrillas, with cameras on their shoulders. Many of them were products of the documentary genre.

After the initial epic and experimental enthusiasm came institutionalized sanity. Early on, the ideological tide began to be a burden difficult to bear. The first case of censorship, the banning of a documentary about Havana's vanishing nightlife, put an end to the perfect marriage between arrogant artists, untouchable producers from Olympus, and the power that granted them shelter and story lines.

Since then, Cuban cinema played out in a sort of costume party with strange dance partners, full of double entendres, metaphors, and other ruses to be able to "speak" and deliberate without actually violating the principles of dogma.

The film institute, however, continued to be an exclusive club within a society of masses akin to sublime minstrels on a utopian dirt road full of potholes.

When the Berlin Wall fell in 1989, these filmmakers could not imagine that part of the debris would fall on their heads, but soon they had to learn to sell themselves in the marketplace. This resulted in terrible co-productions erected on top of the ruins of the once egalitarian illusion in which mediocre sitcoms abounded with local and foreign rogues trying to survive without any major philosophical or aesthetic desires.

Certainly, the formative years of Cuban cinema are the object of the most imaginative speculation. Only two complete films remain of the silent era, among them *La Virgen de la Caridad* by Ramón Peón, as well as many contemporary press reviews and commentaries that inform us of a very particular love by Cubans for film. These works reflected a constant search for an artistic profile in the midst of commercial demands.

The flames that devoured the unstable material used by photographers of the time easily consumed whatever was lost along the way.

These first filmmakers, men like Enrique Díaz Quesada and Ramón Peón, faced many ups and downs as they worked to rid the art form of the traditions of the era and start a career completely unknown in the country, one with no tradition and very little infrastructure.

It does no good to mourn over the problems that stalled the establishment of a film industry in Cuba, an industry that was to be so successful years later, as radio and television would be in the future.

Those who, despite numerous obstacles, did not give up in their efforts merit not our disdain but our admiration. A review, especially for the titles and themes of this lost cinema, assumes the existence of an affluence of topics, plots, and variety. Examples include *El Amante Enmascarado, La Leyenda del Charco de Güije, La Hija del Policía, Las Cosas de mi Mujer* (respectively, The Masked Lover, The Legend of the Güije Pond, The Policeman's Daughter, and My Wife's Things).

Both documentaries and fictional movies were promoted. What today seems ridiculous, naïve, or improbable delighted our ancestors, who were fascinated by the unpretentious imagery of the domestic film industry. Aesthetic standards change and grow—as do tastes. No film industry anywhere, not even the most developed of the world, is nurtured solely by masterpieces.

Why punish so harshly the cinematic inconsistencies of the republic—their stereotypes, their näiveté, and their vernacular ravings—while ignoring the strong emphasis on the kitsch or tasteless, the pretentious, dogmatic, paternalistic, and didactic approaches of many films produced by the ICAIC?

Comparing, on the one hand, *La Mesera del Café del Puerto* (The Waitress of the Harbor Café, 1955), *La Única* (The Only One, 1952), and *Mi Tía de América* (My Aunt from America—1939) with *No Hay Sábado Sin Sol* (There Are No Saturdays Without Sun, 1979), *Los Refugiados de la Cueva del Muerto* (The Refugees of Deadman's Cave, 1983), and *En el Aire* (On the Air, 1988), on the other, one can see that the first group depicts a realistic sense of casualness in these early attempts at filmmaking, combined with a sense of adventure. This contrasts to the fleeting idea of ICAIC's directors of designing a "work" for posterity, "inspiring" examples of the new Cuban culture.

Future generations of the island will be amazed at the passion plays of "good and evil"—morality plays in black and white—made under the guidance of the so-called revolution. Perhaps even attempts to be cutting edge or avant-garde will remain as memories, not only of underdevelopment but also of a time of drastic changes during which daily life was hijacked by an aberrant political zeal.

Max Tosquella's short fiction film *Maracas y Bongo* (1932) signaled the arrival of the talkies in the Cuban movie industry, which had witnessed a less-than-perfect previous example, the brief documentary *Un Rollo Movietone* (A Movietone Reel), also produced that same year by Tosquella.

However, the feature-length sound film had to wait until 1937 with the release of the motion picture *La Serpiente Roja* (The Red Snake) by Ernesto Caparrós. The movie was based on a successful radio serial written by Felix B. Cagnet, starring what has since become a personality in Cuba's popular culture, the Chinese detective Chan Li Po. The film's commercial success was noteworthy, as it brought in $50,000 at the box office in just three weeks.

The book *La Tienda Negra* (The Black Store) by María Eulalia Douglas is full of facts and information about the kind of cinematography preferred by ICAIC. Between 1897 and 1960, as many as 714 fiction films and 357 documentaries were produced in Cuba.

The same book notes that during the silent-film era the capital invested in film production reached $448,000, while during the sound or talkie era—prior to 1959—it came to $973,000 and included the work of the many production companies that flourished in the island: Santos y Artigas, the Hermanos Díaz Quesada Laboratory, Películas Cubanas S.A., Juan Orol, Gómez Castro, and Cinegrafistas Unidos.

In truth, Cuban filmmakers of that bygone era never wavered in their commitment to consolidating the elusive motion picture industry. With the gradual growth of the Republic, a number of entities were created or put in place. They included groups, associations, labor unions, and entities at the service of left- or right-wing ideologies. They also included quasi-governmental institutions, firms, corporations, commissions, distributors, producers, legislative projects, and film studios. They were all components of a demanding living and breathing social network that had a voice, a vote, and a competitive spirit.

That democratic structure collapsed with the creation of ICAIC early in 1959, when all properties were seized from their rightful owners under the guise that "ill-gotten" assets needed to be nationalized.

Special mention should be made of the many co-productions that were made primarily with Mexican artists and funding, taking advantage of the musical and other cultural links shared by Cuba and Mexico. This collaboration was responded to in kind by Cubans who worked in the Mexican film industry.

Another curious fact of the times is the outstanding films left for posterity by amateur filmmakers as early as 1938. Among those movie rookies, so to speak, were artists who later became film professionals: Néstor Almendros, Tomás Gutiérrez Alea, and Ramón Suárez.

Any intimation of artistic independence was quickly snuffed out with the creation of ICAIC in March 1959. All the staples of Cuban drama—such as popular jokes, partying, passion-filled melodramas, a broad range of popular music, the *negrito* (the black man) and the *gallego* (Galician), show biz stars, nightlife, the clubs, the drunkard, the bar and the corner café, magazines and newspapers, political humor, Cuban native wit, the middle-class values—they all packed their bags in search of a better life.

Like Stendahl's mirror, the camera wandered through the streets full of euphoria for the revolution. The nation became serious and responsible, artistic, intellectual, deep, a brother of Eastern Europe, which had for years tried to walk down the same failed path toward a classless future without inequalities.

In the words of the symbolic folk song, "*Llegó el Comandante y Mandó a Parar*" (the commander arrived and put a stop to it). No more tales of rich and poor, no passionate dramas or songs under the palm trees. No longer did the humble hero triumph over adversity, nor would any more adventures of the *Villalobos* (a popular radio show) be required or allowed. Guidelines were carefully drawn and the inspiration whispered into the ears of the creator, who pretended to have freedom in this closed game reserve.

A notable saying served as the official tag line: The redeeming revolution versus the wretched Republic.

Problems such as social exclusion and racism were "officially" ended in 1959 by decree. Blacks had been slaves, maroons, and *mambises* (freedom fighters against Spain), and now discrimination would no longer exist in the contemporary scene.

"*Asere*" (Cuban slang for "buddy," "homie," or "pimp") is now a hindrance from the past and is finally relegated to the memory of a disgraceful era. There are no nightclubs, no prostitutes, no pimps, no peanut vendors, and no *bolero* singers of sad songs, no thieves, no pot-smoking balladeers, no rich folks or con men, no store owners, no bus drivers. They have all been changed into avant-garde workers, committed intellectuals, soldiers, literacy teachers, security agents, and Soviet-style "makarenko" teachers—among many other versions of the "new man" and his contradictions. (Antón Makarenko [1888-1939], Soviet educator who promoted combining study with work.)

The nation could finally begin the longed-for national cinematography under the sign of an unshakable ideology.

Ernesto Caparrós, the set designer for *La Virgen de la Caridad*, died in 1992 in the United States. Max Tosquella, to whom we owe the first short sound film of the Cuban cinema, *Maracas y Bongo*, photographed by Caparrós, also died in the U.S. Manolo Alonso still lives in New York. Ramón Peón died in Puerto Rico in 1970. Other actors, technicians, entrepreneurs, producers, and artists also abandoned, as if plague-infested, the society in which they learned and developed their skills.

ICAIC's film industry barely made room for actors considered "remnants of the past" that had remained in Cuba but were unable to show any kind of political activism in favor of the revolution. Thus, cabaret star Rosita Fornés returned to cinema in 1983 with the movie *Se Permute* (*The Swap*), while Maritza Rosales complains in the documentary *Divas*, directed by Adolfo Llauradó, that she is still waiting for that opportunity. The same thing happened to Gina Cabrera.

The turbulent events of 1959 divided the island's society, and many filmmakers, actors, and other technicians of the cinema world were forced to start all over again in an uncertain exile, with a foreign language and where the first priority was, to be sure, not so much art but where to get the next meal. Freedom once again turned Cuban cinema into an orphan who was left to his fate to seek truth on a barely explored path—at a total disadvantage because of a variety of circumstances.

Filmmakers who went into exile and who were educated outside of Cuba might well have dispensed with the idea of creating a Cuban motion picture industry outside of the island. But all of them, even the most experimental and strange, ventured in some way into the issue of the nationality that obsessed them.

One of the most outstanding actors of contemporary Cuban cinema, Reynaldo Miravalles, upon arriving in exile declared that those same Latin American directors and producers who had previously employed him in co-productions in which he was paid less than a mediocre Spanish or French performer while he was a "revolutionary" actor, left him out of their casts altogether when he broke with the Castroite dream by taking up residence in the vilified Miami.

We owe a debt to producer Manuel de la Pedrosa, who already had a cinematic career in pre-Castro Cuba, and to his hard-working producer, Eduardo Palmer, for the first attempts to put on the record Cuban filmmakers openly opposed to the totalitarian and Communist direction taken by the Cuban regime with documentaries such as *La Verdad de Cuba* (The Truth about Cuba, 1962) and *Cuba Satélite 13* (Cuba Satellite 13, 1963). To this we must add one of the forerunners of this trend, Manolo Alonso, who had a proven track record in the motion picture industry of the republican era. He produced *La Cuba de Ayer* (Yesterday's Cuba, 1963), which included much of the material rescued from his legendary newscasts.

In the movie *El Super* (The Super, 1979), by filmmakers León Ichaso and Orlando Jiménez-Leal, the inadequately studied exile cinema has a production that has not since been matched in conceptual and aesthetic terms. Based on a theater play by Iván Acosta, in this small, warm, and unpretentious masterpiece there comes together a unique fragment of the Cubans' foreign experience in terms of exile and alienation.

That group of founders has set the guidelines—in one way or another—in Cuba's culture. Acosta carried on his successful career as a playwright and filmmaker, especially documentaries that rescued for posterity areas of Cuban popular music passed over by the political situation. Jiménez Leal has also made documentaries strongly charged with the emotional and the political. There is also Jorge Ulla, who made his foray into fiction film with *Guaguasí* (1978); he also made important contributions to the testimonial genre with *En Sus Propias Palabras* (In His Own Words, 1980), his incomparable documentary about the Mariel Boatlift. Ichaso, meanwhile, can boast of the most consistent cinematography in the field of fiction with movies for Hollywood and others done independently in which he outlined his concerns about the contemporary Cuban drama with such works as *Azúcar Amarga* (Bitter Sugar, 1996) and *Paraíso* (Paradise, 2009).

This preliminary group also includes Camilo Vila, who only once approached his native culture with the film *Los Gusanos* (The Worms, 1977). This movie has a singular introspective quality and brings together a group of anti-Castro fighters who have been captured and tortured in a country house while their fate is being decided. There is also Miñuca Villaverde, with her own experimental and provocative films such as *A Mi Padre* (To My Father, 1974) and *Tent City* (1984).

Thanks to the close teamwork of Jorge Ulla and Orlando Jiménez Leal with the great Cuban-Spanish photographer Néstor Almendros, the motion picture industry by Cuban exile boasts two key productions in workmanship and social scope. They are *Nadie Escuchaba* (Nobody Was Listening, 1988) and *Conducta Impropia* (Improper Behavior, 1984). They capture in the early stages of the Cuban exile cinema the outrages suffered by the people of Cuba—outrages that are practically ignored or silenced by international public opinion.

Jiménez Leal, moreover, attempted in the docudrama *8A* (1992) to unravel the legal farce that ultimately led to putting General Arnaldo Ochoa and several of his collaborators before a firing squad on charges of drug trafficking and other acts of treason to the fatherland. He also produced what amounted to a comprehensive look at the history of the Republic in *La otra Cuba* (The Other Cuba, 1985). Ulla, meanwhile, made his own foray into the fictional film genre with *Guaguasí* (1978), the frantic story of a modest Sierra Maestra fighter who falls in love with a chorus girl when he arrives triumphantly in 1959 in Havana, a city where everything seemed possible.

Iván Acosta directed *Amigos* (Friends, 1985) and some years later *Rosa y el Ajusticiador del Canalla* (Rosa and the Scoundrel's Executioner, 2009). Both are based on his own playwritings. The first is sort of a comedy dealing with local customs and using characters based on people who arrived with the Mariel Boatlift. The second is about a powerful dialogue between a Jewish woman from New York who escaped from Nazi concentration camps and a young man who attempts to execute the scoundrel who is responsible for Cuba's fifty-year disaster.

León Ichaso has had a noteworthy career in Hollywood, and he has made use of the independent nature of his work to take on a trilogy about the Cuban tragedy as told by its protagonists. *Azúcar Amarga* (Bitter Sugar) and *Paraíso* (Paradise) are two non-indulgent films that try to explain the damage done to the psyche of the nation by the breakup of the family and the supremacy of ideology in everyday life, a life in which the native person becomes a second-class citizen within his own country. The first film shows the "factory" of so-called "new men" and Ichaso's disagreements with that process; the second shows what happens when this new, everyday life is exported with all its corresponding throwbacks.

There is another aspect of the Cuban exile cinema, and that has to do with local or popular humor that borrows, as it were, from the humor of television and theater. Examples are works by the great comedian Guillermo Alvarez Guedes, such as *Dios Te Salve* (God Save You) and *Psiquiatra* (Psychiatrist, 1966) and *BLA, BLA, BLA* (1978). It also includes the works of other directors, including Javier Durán's *¡Qué Caliente Está Miami!* (Miami Is Hot!, 1980) and Modesto Reyes' *Dos Agentes a la Cañona* (Two Agents Against Their Will, 1989).

In terms of a group with organic conceptual and artistic interests, we should await the appearance of filmmakers born in exile and members of the so-called Generación Ñ, which produced magazines, books, television, and radio programs as well as valuable documentaries explaining their circumstances and several fiction films. Joe Cardona, Mario de Varona, Alex Antón, and Bill Teck are among the most persevering and hardworking filmmakers in this group.

At times, Cardona has the most extensive and consistent cinematography, such as his collaboration with Mario de Varona in such documentaries as *Café con Leche* (Coffee with Milk, 1997), *Havana, Portrait of Yesteryear* (1998), *Celia: The Queen* (2008), and *Adiós Patria* (Goodbye Fatherland), together with Alex Antón in 1999. This is in addition to fiction films such as *Honey Girl* (1998), *Water, Mud and Factory* (2000), and *Bro* (2001). Bill Teck made *El Florida* (The Florida) in 1998 and later renamed it *Cuba on My Back*. He has always been one of the most consistent cultural leaders of the group. Unlike previous generations troubled by the fact that they felt culturally alienated, the philosophy of these artists boasts of enjoying the better of two worlds: their Cuban ancestry and the overwhelming might of American modernity.

There is another group that works with similar persistence in the exile environment, and that is the *Instituto de la Memoria Histórica Cubana Contra el Totalitarismo* (the Institute of Cuban Historical Remembrance Against Totalitarianism). It has managed to produce nearly a dozen documentary testimonials about the neglected and distorted aspects of the enormous struggle of anti-Castro fighters on various fronts and at various times throughout the half century of dictatorship. Leading this admirable project is the tireless work of producer Pedro Corzo and of directors such as Luis Guardia and Daniel Urdanivia. Noteworthy among their cinema productions are works such as *Boitel, Muriendo a Plazos* (Dying by Installments), *Yo lo he Visto Partir* (I Have Seen Him Leave), and *Un Presidio Plantado* (A Jail of the Most Stubborn Political Prisoners).

Another producer of motion pictures with political themes is Mari

Rodríguez Ichaso, sister of León Ichaso. She has produced very interesting themes in her documentaries about the Cuban dictatorial hell and its impact on women and children in *Marcadas por el Paraíso* (Branded by Paradise, 1998) and *Hecho en Cuba: Niños del Paraíso* (Made in Cuba: Children of the Paradise, 2000).

All these anxieties bring in a unique characteristic of the Cuban film industry outside Cuba, something that has continued after more than fifty years. It is an ennobling of the enduring value of Cuban national identity by means of story lines and statements that take precedence, in some cases, or offer an alternative, in others, to the social model imposed since 1959.

Directors, who were once mainstays at ICAIC and are now outside their country, have continued trying new ideas, such as Sergio Giral in *La Imagen Rota* (The Broken Image, 1995), which features statements about filmmakers who made their careers in Cuba but had to go into exile. There is also *Dos Veces Ana* (Ana Twice, 2010), the story of two Cuban women performed by the same actress, Elvira Valdés, who are struggling to find a place in the multifaceted city of Miami. Rolando Díaz's *Cercanía* (Nearness, 2008) uses a stellar cast to tell of the generational conflict among the various exile groups. *Bailarina Sola Busca Compañía* (Dancer in Search of Companionship, 2009), by Orlando Rojas, shows us lying in state while the great prima donna of Cuban ballet, Rosario Suárez, finds both triumph and tribulation in a new life away from her natural environment.

The same group could include Emilio Oscar Alcalde, who did not belong to ICAIC but was famous in Cuba as the writer of the motion picture *El Encanto del Regreso* (The Enjoyment of Return), censored with premeditated malice. In his exile homes—in Colombia and Miami—Alcalde has refined the arts of the documentary and fiction in such works as *Puerta Cerrada* (Closed Door, 1997), and *René Cabell: El Tenor de Las Antillas* (René Cabell: The Tenor of the Antilles, 2005). Both contained themes linked to the island of his birth.

In Paris, meanwhile, Ricardo Vega, one of the pioneers of the young cinema in Cuba during the 1980s, has produced valuable cinema records about Cuban painters as well as an essential documentary for understanding the contradictory and mean nature of a dictator: *Cuba la Bella* (Cuba the Beautiful, 2004). In this production, historical cuts of newsreels showing Fidel Castro's speeches and other appearances are edited in an unusual sequence to depict the whims and contradictions that brought the nation to tragedy.

The Cuban diaspora has grown so much that it will be the task of determined historians to trace the films made by Cubans outside their native land about issues that concern the country. This task becomes even more complex when considering the kind of cinema made by Cuban filmmakers working for other motion picture industries around the world—and there already are quite a number of them.

The Cuban exile cinema is currently shaped by the guidance of independent productions, and that has generated some odd paradoxes. The successful actor Andy García ventured into the documentary field with *Como su Ritmo no Hay Dos* (His Unique Rhythm, 1993) about the great musician Israel López Cachao. A few years later, García debuted in the fictional film *La Ciudad Perdida* (The Lost City, 2005), the story of a traditional Cuban family cruelly split apart by politics. Meanwhile, Magdiel Aspillaga, recently arrived from Cuba and now a resident of Miami, produced his first major work, *Neuralgia* (2010). Another young man who was formed in Cuba but now lives in New York, Miguel Coyula, premiered his *Memorias del Desarrollo* (Memoirs of Development, 2010), in theory the sequel to the classic film *Memorias del Subdesarrollo* (Memories of Underdevelopment) by Gutiérrez Alea.

CUBAN EXILES IN HOLLYWOOD

Andy García's first break as an actor came as a gang member in the first episode of *Hill Street Blues* (1981). He eventually was cast in *The Untouchables* (1987) and in *The Godfather III* (1990). García starred and directed the movie *For Love or Country: The Arturo Sandoval Story*. It was based on the true story of Sandoval's career, his eventual flight to the United States with his family, and the unexpected roadblocks that nearly prevented him from becoming a naturalized American citizen. García, the most recognized Cuban film actor in the world, is active in Cuba's plight. He organized a march in Los Angeles in 2011 in support of the Ladies in White, who were being victimized in Cuba for demanding the freedom of their political prisoners.

Steven Bauer's name was Esteban Echevarría Samson when he was born in Havana. His break came in PBS's bilingual sitcom *¿Qué Pasa USA?* (1977-79) when he went by the name Rocky Echevarría. He was married to actress Melanie Griffith and starred opposite Al Pacino in *Scarface* (1983), earning a Golden Globe nomination for Supporting Actor.

The daughter of Cuban-American Emilio Díaz, Cameron Díaz was born in San Diego and is the most recognized Cuban-American actress in the world. She has been nominated for four Golden Globes and starred in movies such as *There's Something About Mary* (1998), *Gangs of New York* (2002), *Charlie's Angels* (2000), and *Knight and Day* (2010).

Another famous Cuban actor, Mel Ferrer, was born in New Jersey, the son of a Cuban surgeon. He was a leading actor, director, and producer for most of the second half of the twentieth century. He produced the film *Wait Until Dark* (1967) that featured his then-wife Audrey Hepburn.

Eva Mendes was born in Miami and raised in Los Angeles. Though taking many smaller roles in movies, she was little known until playing the girlfriend of Denzel Washington's character in *Training Day* (2001). In addition to playing leading Hollywood roles with stars like Will Smith

(*Hitch*, 2005), she is a spokesperson for Revlon.

Tony Plana was born José Antonio Plana in Havana. His family fled to Culver City, California. He has played leading and supporting roles in over seventy films, from *An Officer and a Gentleman* (1982) to *Picking Up the Pieces* (2000) with Woody Allen. He also played the role of Rudy in the *Zoot Suit* (1981) in L.A., and he plays the patriarch Ignacio Suarez on *Ugly Betty* (2006)

Born to Cuban immigrants, Laz Alonso was raised in the Washington, D.C., area. After appearances in various commercials and on *CSI*, he has starred in many movies, including *Avatar* (2009), *Jumping the Broom* (2011), and *Miracle at St. Anna* (2008).

María Conchita Alonso was born in Cuba and raised in Caracas. She was crowned Miss Teenager of the World in 1971 and Miss Venezuela in 1975. Alonso became a popular actress in Latin America, working in ten soap operas, and in Venezuelan films. She is also a popular singer with three Grammy nominations. In 1982, she emigrated to the U.S. and made her Hollywood film debut in 1984 in *Moscow on the Hudson*, opposite Robin Williams. In 1995, she starred in the Broadway production of *Kiss of the Spider Woman*, making her the first South American woman to star on Broadway. She is an ardent opponent of the dictatorships of the Castro brothers and of Hugo Chávez.

Mercedes Ruehl is an actress born in Queens, New York, of Cuban and Irish descent, the daughter of FBI agents who moved frequently before settling in Silver Spring, Maryland. She won two Obie Awards and a Tony for Best Actress for *Lost in Yonkers*. Her critical success was an Oscar-winning supporting performance in *The Fisher King* in 1991. She then took a recurring guest role on the sitcom *Frasier*, and most recently she joined the cast of HBO's *Entourage*.

Bobby Cannavale was born in Union City, New Jersey, in 1971 to an Italian father and Cuban mother. The actor has appeared in many movies, among them *The Station Agent* (2003), *Shall We Dance?* (2004), and *The Other Guys* (2010). He had recurring roles in leading TV shows such as

Six Feet Under and *Will & Grace*, and he earned a Tony Award nomination in 2007 for his Broadway debut in "Mauritius."

Another descendent, of a Cuban mother, David Lee Gallagher was born in College Point, New York. He had a lead role in the movies *Look Who's Talking Now* (1993) and *Phenomenon* (1996).

DOCUMENTARIES

Ernesto Fundora is an exceptional celebrity established in Mexico. He has been an influential image-shaper and thinker who blazed a trail with his music videos, among which the most notable are those devoted to Celia Cruz and Willy Chirino. Fundora has also successfully dabbled in the genre of fiction and documentary motion picture.

Other makers of images of experimental expression include Dinorah de Jesús Rodríguez and Tony Labat, as well as directors who produced some outstanding work in this type of disjointed filmography. They include:

Rubén Lavernia with his documentary *Retrato Inconcluso de René Ariza* (Unfinished Portrait of René Ariza, 1983).

Lisandro Pérez, who filmed the current victims of Mariel in *Más Allá del Mar* (Beyond the Sea, 2003), as well as a documentary about rappers in Cuba, *La Fabri-K* (2004).

Juan Carlos Zaldívar and his treatise about the two seashores (Cuba and Florida) in *90 Millas* (90 Miles, 2000).

Javier Echeverría, with a documentary in which he links the ordeal of the Cuban mother with the island's patron saint in *Caridad, Madre Mía* (Caridad, My Mother, 2006).

Carlos Carcas, a Cuban-American living in Spain, who has portrayed many events involving Cuban music throughout the world and to whom we owe *Old Man Bebo* (2008), the well-deserved tribute to a timeless and masterful musician, Bebo Valdés.

Carlos Gutiérrez with his story of whether it's possible to reach the longed-for freedom after escaping from the island on a raft in *Pies Secos, Pies Mojados* (Wet Foot/Dry Foot, 2006).

Juan Gerard, whose *Cuba Libre* (Free Cuba, 2003) portrays the sentimental education of a child in eastern Cuba when life changes dramatically in 1959.

Lillian Rosado's *La Mala* (The Evil One), jointly directed with her husband Pedro Pérez Rosado, turns the singer Lena Burke—granddaughter of Elena Burke—into an actress in a drama in which the ghost of another legend, the singer La Lupe, depicts the sorrows and joys of a small-town girl who aspires to become a star.

MIAMI INTERNATIONAL FILM FESTIVAL

The Miami International Film Festival began in 1983 when Nora Swan, commissioner of film for the city of Miami, asked help from Dr. Steven Bowles, head of the film department at the University of Miami, and Nat Chediak, a Cuban exile active in the world of film with many international contacts and owner of the Cinematheque and the Arcadia art theaters. Chediak took over the film selection with the aid of Jerry Winters and Hank Kaufman. Together, they identified international films for consideration. Ms. Swan then put together an executive board and volunteered to manage the festival.

The festival, known as the premier Ibero-American film festival in the United States, has succeeded in presenting for nearly thirty years works by Martin Scorsese, Pedro Almódovar, Fernando Trueba, and others. The festival introduced many films, such as Academy Award nominee *Gatica-el Mono,* as well as *Bitter Sugar, Rafters/Balseros, El Benny, Mambo Kings, For Love or Country,* and others.[1]

The Miami International Film Festival is now produced and directed by Miami-Dade College, attracting more than seventy thousand film enthusiasts and four hundred filmmakers and stars.[2] The legacy of Cuba's influence on the world of film endures.

NOTES

1. www.miamifilmfestival.com
2. www.miamifilmfestival.com/press/pr011211MIFF.

25

POPULAR MUSIC

BY ELOY CEPERO AND SONIA FRÍAS

The origins of what was to become Cuba's popular music—one of the most prodigious in the world, being comprised of engendered thirty-three musical genres—go back to the middle of the eighteenth century.

In 1763, the pianist and violinist Esteban Salas Baroque composed the first works of baroque music in the Americas, including liturgical and sacred music and carols. This was the opening salvo of what was to become an ever-expanding musical explosion.

By 1830, pianist Manuel Saumell, forerunner of the Cuban *contradanza*, took a major step in music composition. He would become known as the "Father of Cuban Musical Nationalism."

In the 1850s, two major Cuban violinists, Claudio Brindis de Salas and José White, were among the most important international musicians of their time. Brindis de Salas was called the "black Paganini" (after Italian composer and violinist Niccolo Paganini, one of the greatest violinists of all time). He became a chamber musician in the Court of Kaiser Wilhelm II of Germany and won the First Prize of the Paris Conservatory. His virtuosity took him to all cities of Europe, and he was named as knight and baron of the Legion of Honor.

José White, the creator of *La Bella Cubana*, was also awarded First Prize by the Paris Conservatory. White was called specifically to compose for and conduct the orchestra of the Imperial Conservatory of Emperor Pedro I of Brazil.

The 1870s were of real importance because of the presence of pianist Ignacio Cervantes. The most important Cuban musician of the nineteenth century, he was influenced by the European classical and romantic music of his time when he composed his famous dances.

Two great Cuban musicians emerged at the end of the nineteenth century: Failde Miguel Pérez, creator of the first *danzón*, "Las Alturas de Simpson," with his representative brass orchestra, and Antonio María Romeu, who changed the format of the *danzón* to include violin and flute.

By 1883, José "Pepe" Sánchez had composed his first *bolero* entitled *Tristezas* (Sadness), which is the first *bolero* about which we have a precise reference. By this time in Santiago de Cuba, *bolero* singers and minstrels accompanied by guitars sang their songs as serenades, or the so-called *penas* (sorrows) performing as duos, trios and even quintets, including musicians and artists such as Sindo Garay, María Teresa Vera, Manuel Corona, Rosendo Ruiz, and Sánchez himself, among others. The *bolero* can be considered the most widely disseminated Cuban musical genre around the world and one whose relevancy has been maintained throughout the ages. The *bolero* has been—and continues to be—performed by the world's most famous singers.

The *son* was born probably by the late nineteenth century in the mountainous southeastern Cuban province of Oriente. In 1920, it arrived in Havana and produced a musical shock wave: the rhythmic accents of the silent *danzón*, were now performed with a brass band, adding new instruments and voices.

THE INFLUENCE OF CUBAN MUSIC IN THE UNITED STATES:

THE NINETEENTH AND TWENTIETH CENTURIES

In 1850, the American pianist Louis Gottchalk from New Orleans visited Havana, thus beginning the strong influence of Cuban music on American music.

After that visit, Gottchalk composed *Creole Eyes* and *Tropical Nights*, with what he called "a Latin tinge" (e*l toque latino*). Both songs were very successful from the moment they were first introduced at Boston Hall in the late 1800s.

In the 1890s, several Cuban musicians, including the brothers Tió, the brothers Núñez, Manuel Pérez, and Jimmy Palacios, introduced the Cuban *contradanza* to New Orleans, which—along with ragtime and blues—is one of the precursors of American jazz.

In the first decades of the twentieth century, Catalan violinist Xavier Cougat and flutist Alberto Socarrás travel from Cuba to the United States. Cougat successfully helped spread Cuban music in the country, while Socarrás played the first jazz flute solo.

In the 1930s, three Cuban musicians brought their art to the United States: composer and pianist Ernesto Lecuona, who performed in major theaters across the nation; and Justo Aspiazu who—together with Antonio Machín—performed the song *El Manisero* (The Peanut Vendor) in New York, which became an instant success.

Another representative figure of that era was Desiderio "Desi" Arnaz, who along with Miguelito Valdés introduced the "Rumba Craze" and the "Conga Craze" to the United States in the late 1930s and the 1940s.

Other major musical figures of that time were Mario Bauzá, his sister-in-law Graciela Pérez, and his brother-in-law "Machito," and his Afro Cubans. In the middle of that decade, Mario Bauzá composed *Tanga*, and Luciano "Chano" Pozo and Dizzy Gillespie, in turn, composed *Manteca*.

These were the first two tunes of what became known as Afro-Cuban Jazz. Gillespie is famous as one of the originators of "Be-Bop," and Bauzá created "Cu-Bop"—the two genres that led to the renewal of jazz in the U.S.

In the 1950s, Dámaso Pérez Prado introduced the "Mambo Craze" in the United States, which, along with the "Cha-Cha Craze," became a boon for dance studios such as those franchised by Fred Astaire and Arthur Murray, where Americans could learn to dance to these Cuban rhythms. Two songs, "Cherry Pink and Apple Blossom White" and "Tequila," became international hits. Other major figures of this decade were Pupi Campos, musical director of the *Jack Paar Show*, the forerunner of NBC's *Tonight Show*, and Marco Rizzo, a concert pianist, composer, and creator of the theme of the *I Love Lucy* show.

Also in the 1950s, Arsenio Rodríguez, known as the "Father of Salsa," introduced the *guaguancó*, *guaracha*, and *son montuno* in the United States with his All Stars (Todos Estrellas) band. Other Cuban musicians of the 1950s who had great influence in the United States were Marcelino and Juan Guerra, René Hernández, Chocolate Armenteros, José and Fausto Curbelo, Lou Pérez, Mongo Santamaría, Cándido Camero, Justi Barreto, Alfredito Valdés, and many others.

THE CUBAN REVOLUTION—BIG CHANGES IN MUSIC

The Cuban Revolution led to very important developments in the popular music of the Caribbean and United States. On the one hand, the U.S. trade embargo closed the doors to the island that had been the ideal junction of all musical trends. On the other hand, Cuban artists and musicians faced many obstacles, including not being able to travel freely and perform abroad.

As tensions between Cuba and the United States grew, fewer and fewer tourists visited the island to enjoy its music and nightlife. Similarly,

Cubans began to leave the country for an exile that would not end. The result was that many nightclubs closed their doors, and others were seized by the government; thus began the diaspora of great artists and musicians. From that moment on, Cuban music followed two paths: that of the island, and that in exile.

Miami replaced Havana and became part of the Miami-New York-San Juan axis as the center of Cuban music for years to come.

1959—CUBAN MUSIC IN EXILE

THE MIAMI SOUND

The Miami Sound begins with the arrival of the first Cuban exiles to South Florida, particularly Miami. This first wave of political refugees included many singers and musicians already successful in Cuba; others who had recently begun their musical careers; and, finally, teenage boys who already had inclination and talent for music and who had studied and later developed their talents in Miami.

The artists and musicians best-known in Cuba soon began to perform wherever they found an opportunity, especially in area clubs and restaurants like the Toledo, Café de Artistas, Los Violines, and others. Among them were pianists Pepe Delgado and Paquito Hechevarría; violinists Manuel Godínez, Sr. and Jr.; and trumpet player César Godínez.[1]

Younger Cuban artists like Pedro Román, who had started early in Cuba and had already acted in Las Vegas and New York (on *The Ed Sullivan Show*), was the first to sing in the Latin Village Club, located across from the Freedom Tower on Miami's Biscayne Boulevard. He at once got jobs for other Cubans such as Martica Rams, Alberto Piñero, and his partner Maritza. One of the first singers to find work in Miami was Gilberto Díaz, who sang at the Barbarán Club, accompanied by pianist Eddie Lester.

Soon they were followed by some of Cuba's most popular singers, including Ñico Membiela, Rolando Laserie, Roberto Ledesma, Orlando Vallejo, Leo Castañeda, Rodolfo Hoyos, Xiomara Alfaro, Felo Bohr, Wilfredo Mendi, Chucho Alvarez, Oscar de Fontana, the duo of Jesús Cabrisas and Irene Farach, and *Los Rufinos* (The Rufinos Quartet: Mother, Father, Carlos, and Julie Rufino).

Many of the most popular Cuban musicians went directly to New York. Celia Cruz was the lead singer of *La Sonora Matancera* who first went to Mexico and then moved to New York. She was known as "*La Guarachera de Cuba*," and soon she was recording in exile many of the hits that made her famous in Cuba, like "*Yerbero Moderno and Burundanga*." Still, most of her best work would be done as an exile. She produced a never-ending number of hits and became a popular attraction in Miami, Puerto Rico, and Latin America. Among her best known songs were: "*La Vida es un Carnaval*" (Life is a Carnival); "*El Guabá*"; "*La Candela*"; and "*La Negra Tiene Tumbao*." Celia Cruz died in Miami in July 2003, and after thousands attended funerals for her in Miami and New York, she was buried in New York, where she had lived for decades, next to her beloved husband and fellow musician Pedro Knight.

José Antonio Fajardo of *La Orquesta Fajardo* first went to Japan and then formed a new orchestra in New York with Roberto Ledesma as soloist. Many Cuban musicians already lived and performed in New York: Frank Grillo "Machito" and his Afro Cubans; Arsenio Rodríguez; Tito Puente; Mongo Santamaría; and trumpeter Alfredo "Chocolate" Armenteros.[2]

Victoria Yolí Raymond-La Lupe, whose popularity led to a film about her eventful life, is considered by many to be one of the leading singers in the salsa music genre. She died in the Bronx, New York, in 1992.

Also meeting and getting together in New York were Vicentico Valdés, known as *La Voz Elástica de Cuba* (Cuba's Elastic Voice), and one of the most prominent *bolero* singers at that time. His singing voice made famous such songs as *Los Aretes de la Luna* and *Envidia*. Another

Valdés, Miguelito Valdés, "Mr. Babalú," was one of the first great Cuban artists to arrive in the United States. At that time, others who came to the U.S. were Rolando Valdés (*Sensación Orchestra*), Monguito, Mario Muñoz "Papaíto," Chano Monte, Angelo Vaillant, Virgilio Martí, and the *India de Oriente*, among others.

The list grows and multiplies during these years as more musicians and performers continued to join the exile.

While the great Latin bands—such as Machito, Tito Rodríguez, Tito Puente, and others—were at their peak during this decade, a new sound was coming from Cuba. It was called *pachanga*, and it was the last of Cuba's musical styles created on the island before the revolution. It was brought to the United States by its originator, Eduardo Davidson, and it was skillfully assimilated by a lot of New York musicians between 1960 and 1963. Among them were the Broadway Orchestra, a Cuban *charanga* big band founded in 1962 by the brothers Eddy, Rudy, and Kevin Zervigon and Roberto Torres. (*charanga*—in effect, a brass band—is a term that comes from the name given to traditional ensembles of Cuban dance music).

These bands, or *charangas*, now saw the horizon wide open to them; before this time, they had merely been small combos with not many major requirements of sound and space. This rhythm of the *charangas*, brought from Cuba by Fajardo, is incorporated into the repertoires of Lou Peréz and his Charanga, of Mongo Santamaria and his Charanga, Felipe Ramos' *Charanga Casino*, Roberto Torres' *Charanga de la Cuatro*, Mike Peréz's *La Típica de New York*, Joseíto Valdés' *La Charanga Ideal*, and charanga violinists Pupi Legarreta and Alfredito de la Fe.

In 1964, the Beatles arrived in New York and music in general took a significant turn. Since 1966, music embarked on an evolution, with new sounds giving way to *salsa* in 1967 and thus creating jobs for newly arrived Cuban musicians who settled in New York. Many of them have remained in the city to this day.

Puerto Rico has been an important enclave of Cuban music before and after the revolution. This is mainly because of the great reception that Puerto Ricans have always given to the musical styles from Cuba, and they have always gave Cuban musicians a warm welcome.

Equally important, many of the songs that had impacted greatly on Cuban musical styles during the 1930s, 1940s, and 1950s were the work of great Puerto Rican composers such as Rafael Hernández, composer of *El Jibarito (Lamento Borincano), Silencio*, and *Preciosa*; Pedro Flores, composer of *Perdón*; Plácido Acevedo, composer of *Boda Gris*; and Bobby Capó, who wrote *Piel Canela*. These songs resonated widely in Cuba to the point that many Cubans mistakenly thought they were works of Cuban composers.

Cuban musicians and musical groups such as the *Trio Matamoros*, Sindo Garay, Ñico Saquito (trova singer and guitarist Benito Antonio Fernández Ortiz), *Los Guaracheros de Oriente*, and Ernesto Lecuona and his musical revue were already famous and cherished in Puerto Rico before the revolution of 1959. All but Saquito, who remained in Cuba, sought refuge in the neighboring island-nation that had always welcome Cuban musicians with open arms.

They were followed later by Guillermo Portabales, Manolo Fernández, Olga Chorens and Tony Alvarez and their daughters Lissette and Olguita, who then followed in the career path of their famous parents. Others who settled in Puerto Rico were Elizabeth del Río, Blanca Rosa Gil, Flor de Loto, Titi Soto, Marisela Verena, and Servando Díaz. There were more, listed in the notes.[3]

Other exiles who were active in the field of music were historian and writer Cristóbal Díaz Ayala, the host and radio and television actor Fernando Hidalgo, and businessman Tony Trelles.

One must not forget the founding of La Casa Cuba during the 1940s, which later—beginning in the 1960s—would become the place at which many Cuban musicians have performed while visiting Puerto Rico.

California became the home for the great composer and pianist René Touzet, composer of *No te Importe Saber* and *La Noche de Anoche*.

Others who settled in California were folk music percussionist Francisco Aguabella, singer "Peter Pan" Candy Sosa, and percussionist Miguel Cruz and his group *Skins*. Others who arrived later include Tata Ramos, Francisco Céspedes and his Orchestra, his wife Bobbi Céspedes, and many others.

Percussionist Armando Sánchez, founder of the charanga *Nuevo Ritmo de Cuba*, moved to Chicago and later founded the group *Son de la Loma* in New York. Singer Luis Bravo lived in Chicago successfully for a long time until his return and subsequent death in Miami.

One of the first to arrive in Tampa was the composer, pianist, and internationally renowned director Ernesto Lecuona, who lived there for about three years before moving on to Spain, where he lived until his death in 1963. Lecuona, the most important Cuba composer of the twentieth century, wrote great classics like *Siboney, Siempre en mi Corazón (With a Song in My Heart), Como el Arrullo de Palmas,* and *Damisela Encantadora*. Many of these songs were featured in Hollywood movies. Tampa was also the home of pianist Antonio Curbelo.[4]

The young engineer and businessman Enrique Chía settled in Atlanta, where he became a renowned international pianist with large worldwide sales of his recorded music.

Singer Olga Guillot—*Olga de Cuba*—arrived in Mexico very early in exile. She was one the most prominent Cuban *bolero* singer of all time. Her inimitable voice made famous big hits such as *¿Qué Sabes Tú? La Noche de Anoche, Miénteme,* and *Tú Me Acostumbraste*. Guillot was known for her uncompromising anti-Castro stance, making her views known in many markets were governments had good relations with Cuba.

Already living in México was the "king of mambo" Dámaso Pérez Prado; the composer and pianist Juan Bruno Tarraza, composer of *Palabras Calladas* and *La Novia de Todos*; and pianist Everardo Ordaz, singer Kike Mendive, Orlando Guerra "Cascarita," Francisco Fellove, the versatile Silvestre Méndez, songwriter and entrepreneur Mario Alvarez, and singer and revolutionary Orlando de Cárdenas. There were also dancers:

María Antonieta Pons, Amalia Aguilar, Ninón Sevilla, and Rosa Carmina. Later arrivals included pianists Everardo Ordaz, Jesús (Chuchito) Valdés, Frank Domíguez (composer of such hits as *Tú Me Acostumbraste* and *Imágenes*), and the composer and guitarist Ela O'Farrill.

Venezuela welcomed singers Fernando Albuerne, Rolando Laserie, and Vicky Roig. The young singer and actress María Conchita Alonso began her musical career in Venezuela where she arrived at age five. Later, she continued her career starring in a number of television shows and films in Hollywood.

Among the artists who arrived in Colombia were singers René Cabell and Orlando Contreras, who made Colombia their permanent home for many years. For singer Roberto Ledesma—even though he didn't live there—Colombia was his most important venue, and he was the most beloved of the Cuban singers there.

Cabaret star Blanquita Amaro, who already lived and worked in Buenos Aires, provided great support to Cubans who came through Argentina in search of a better life. She later moved to Miami with her daughter Idania, where they resided and staged successful musicals.

In Spain, the first exiles were welcomed by the legendary Antonio Machín, who had lived in that country since 1939. The music impresario and comedian Guillermo Alvarez Guedes also settled in Spain, as did the pianist Ernesto Duarte with his full orchestra, including the great Israel López (Cachao), one of the world's most important bass players. Others were singer Tata Ramos; the trio *Los Rivero*; the famous pianist and composer Armando Orefiche, who composed the *Rumba Blanca* and *Messie Julian*; director of orchestras *Lecuona* and *Havana Cuban Boys*; and composer José Dolores Quiñones, who later moved to France where he died.

Over the years, Spain became the home to composer and arranger Juanito Márquez, singers Luisa María Guell and Barbarito Diez, Jr., and composer and pianist Memé Solís. All of them eventually settled in the United States. Sometime later, singers Farah María and Lucrecia went to live in Spain, too.

Singer and reciter Bobby Jiménez moved to Belgium, where he has lived since 1974. In the 1980s, pianist Alfredo Rodríguez settled in Paris, where he died, after living in New York for about twenty years.

Sweden became the home of pianist, composer, and arranger Bebo Valdés, who lives part of the year in Madrid. He was the director of orchestras *Sabor de Cuba*, *Tropicana*, and many others, and he is considered one of the most important Cuban musicians. Valdés became famous in the 1990s with the recording of *Lágrimas Negras* with the flamenco singer El Cigala.

Chucho Valdés, son of Bebo, an equally renowned pianist, frequently plays in the U.S., although he lives in Cuba. But Cuban exile musicians are not allowed to play in Cuba to this day, and their works and personas are routinely silenced and erased from all mention in the government-controlled media. However, Cuban artists are allowed to come to the United States in a clearly one-sided "cultural exchange."

A second group of exiles was made up of teenagers who started learning to play music in schools in the Miami area and who organized the first rock and roll groups of young Cubans. These groups played at private parties and open houses that they organized and for which they sold their own tickets. The first of these musicians was the singer and composer Gustavo Rojas, who in 1962 founded the group *Los Ideales* and then *The Brotherhood* in 1971. At first these groups only sang in English, but in 1964 they became greatly influenced by the Mexican guitarist Carlos Santana with his crossover hits like "*Oye Cómo Va*" and "Evil Ways," performed with a catchy tropical beat.

Then there were other local groups such as Antiques, Coke, Opus, Mantrap, Wild Wind, Pearly Queen, Clockwork, Adam's Apple, Ray & His Court, Los Sobrinos del Juez, Willy Chirino, Alma and Clouds, Hansel y Raúl, and brothers Carlos and Javier Oliva, forerunners of the "Miami Sound." They all recorded and left their musical legacy in Miami.

Finally came The Miami Sound Machine, featuring Gloria Estefan and her husband Emilio. In time, Gloria became the first important exile crossover success. Guided by her husband, who founded Estefan Enterprises, Gloria was an indisputable star in both English and Spanish. Her music traveled the world with her. Some of her greatest hits included: "Conga," "Renacer," "*Oye Mi Canto*," "Rhythm is Gonna Get You," and "*Mi Tierra*."

Estefan Enterprises has recorded many important singers. Among them were fellow exiles Jon Secada and Carlos Ponce, as well as Mexican idols such as Alejandro Fernández, Ana Gabriel, and Thalía. Emilio Estefan is one of the most successful impresarios in exile, venturing into many other businesses such as the Miami Dolphins football team, Lario's on the Beach Restaurant, and Bongo's in Orlando and in Miami.[5]

Many of these musicians are still active in their profession, among them Willy Chirino, whose famous song "*Ya viene llegando*" became an anthem for freedom in Cuba in the early 1990s with the fall of Communism in Europe. Among those who must be mentioned are drummer Elio Rodríguez (Chiko and the Man), who had great impact in Miami. He now has his own radio show with his wife, Eunice Ricard, and hostess and singer Susy Leman.[6]

While Miami was growing in population and in the number of Cuban exiles, other traditional groups were being formed and creating their own songs: *Los Caminantes, Casinos de Miami, Conjunto Cristal, Conjunto Colonial, Los Profesionales, Conjunto Impacto, La Suprema,* and the group *Universal*. All of these reigned over Miami's musical scene for a long time.

Among the typical Charanga orchestras are *Jóvenes del Hierro*, directed by José Dono and Agustín Jauma, and their singers Arnaldo Valiente, Armando Miranda, German Pérez, Frank Herman, and *Típica Tropical* with its director Eduardo Aguirre and its singers Felo Barrios, Frank Pérez, Pepe Cordo, Oscar Peña, Mario Toledo, and the orchestras *Ritmos de Estrellas* and *Aragón de Miami*, both of which continued to delight Miami audiences while achieving success.[7]

A new wave of great musicians arrived in Miami in the 1980s, while saxophonist Paquito D'Rivera, considered one of the world's best jazz musicians, arrived in New Jersey/New York.

Others who arrived in those years were the saxophone players Carlos Averhoff, Enrique Varela and Fofi Gómez; the flautist René Lorente; drummer Ignacio Berroa, Jr.; trombonist Juan Pablo Torres; percussionists Daniel Ponce and Lacho Rivera; *trecero* (*tres* is a three-string guitar) Jorge Cabrera; the late singer and musician Israel Kantor; the versatile El Niño Jesús; arranger and conductor Germán Piferrer; and musicologist and drummer Omar Reyes, among others.

This was a period that saw the arrival as exiles of many artists, most of them young and shaped by the Castroite system, as were many musicians of international stature, such as trumpet player Arturo Sandoval. Sandoval's history, including his flight from Cuba, was the subject of a movie by Andy García, *For Love or Country: The Arturo Sandoval Story*. Andy García played the role of Sandoval. The biographical drama was produced for the HBO premium cable network and first aired on October 18, 2000. The made-for-TV movie also features two other Cuban-American stars: Gloria Estefan and Steven Bauer (Esteban Ernesto Echevarría). All three—García, Estefan, and Bauer—were born in Havana.

The exodus continued with Maggie Carles, Albita Rodríguez, Malena and Lena Burke, and Manolín (*El Médico de la Salsa*). Others who reached the U.S. shores after leaving their Cuban homeland are listed in the notes.[8]

A special mention must be made of the music from Cuba's countryside or *música guajira,* which also saw many of its interpreters flee the island, among them Ramoncito Veloz.[9]

From the very beginning of the exile, it included important performers of "*la nueva trova,*" which has its roots in the traditional *trova* (or ballad) and describes a movement in Cuban music that emerged in the late 1960s in Cuba. Among the youngest came Sergio Fiallo, Pedro Tamayo, Jean Paul Cole, and others who arrived later such as Mike Purcell.[10]

Along with the artists, a number of great composers whose songs were already known internationally started arriving in the exile.

Among the first to arrive was José Carbó Menéndez, composer of the first exile song, *Flagler Street*, which was performed by Carlos Montiel and recorded with the group *Panchito Calimano*. Another prominent figure who went into exile early on was the percussionist Eduardo Davidson.

Also leaving Cuba were prominent artists of the 1940s generation such as Pepe Delgado, Bobby Collazo, Mario Fernández Porta, Nico Cevedo, Fernando Mulens, Facundo Rivero, Rosendo Rosell, Juan Bruno Tarraza, Julio Gutiérrez, Osvaldo Farrés, Rene Touzet and Humberto Suárez. After them came Rubén Rios, Arty Valdés, Ricardo García Perdomo, Nazario López, Rodríguez Fife, Espigul del Valle, José "Pepe" Longarela, Hiran Díaz, Juan Valdés Terán, and from the ladies composers Lilly Batet, Cristina Saladrigas, Concha Valdés-Miranda, Yolanda del Castillo Cobelo and Odilia Moreno. Among the last to arrive was Armando Larrinaga.

The arrival as exiles of artists, musicians, and singers resulted in the creation of record companies and record distributors that already existed in Cuba, such labels as Gema, of the brothers Alvarez Guedes and Ernesto Duarte; Panart Records, of Galo and Ramón Sabat and Julia Riera; Velvet Records, of Roberto and José Pagés; Puchito, of Jesús Gorís; Kubaney, of Mateo San Martín; Modiner, of Nilo Gómez; Maype Records of Arthur Machado and Eugenio "Tito" Garrote. In Miami, Musart Records was founded by Eliseo Valdés; Acapulco Records by Lázaro Fernández; Teca Records by Luis Iglesias; and the distributors M & M Records by Manolo Matos. In New York, Antonio López created Suarito Records.

Later, the following record labels were established in Miami: Reyes Records by Enrique Reyes; Lily Records by Lily Reyes; Casino Records by Pedro Alvarez Cepero; Ultra Records by Miguel Angel Palmero, Ricky Records by Jorge, Ricky and Manolo Díaz; El Palacio de la Música by Eddy Martínez; Do Re Mi Music Center by Rolando and Zoraida Rivero; Santana Records Shop by Humberto Santana; and El Museo del Disco by Insul Lazo.

The huge demand triggered by the arrival of many thousands of exiles—including musicians, singers, restaurant staff, and entertainment and show business entrepreneurs—gave rise to the opening of a number of night clubs and restaurants that would provide employment to all these people who had been displaced by the Communist government when it took over or closed these types of business establishments in Cuba.

Miami became home to many nightclubs after 1959. Prevalent among them were, among others:

El Club Raúl 21 (Raúl González Jerez)
Café de Artistas (Martin Fox and Oscar Echemendía)
El Toledo Restaurant (Miguel Angel Cano)
Los Violines Nightclub (Manuel Godínez, José Currais and Gustavo Cachaldora)
El Club at the Everglades Hotel (Juvenal Piña)
El Flamenco Nightclub (Wenceslao "Laito" Castro and Albino Currais)
El Montmartre Nightclub (Jesús Navarro and Mario Cabrisas)
El Prila's Nightclub (Rubén Pérez and associates)
El Centro Vasco (Juan and Juanito Zaizarbitoria)
El Bodegón de Castilla (Jaime Bajo and Associates)

Others that opened in those years included:

El Scaramouge (Rubén Pérez)
El Maxim's Restaurant (Enrique Fernández)
La Cascada Restaurant (Enrique Fernández)
El Swiss Chalet (Enrique Fernández)
El Centro Español (Ardón Grau)
El Chateau Seville (Ardón Grau, Pedro Márquez and Miguel Herrero)
Los Marinos Restaurant (Humberto Méndez and Pedro Márquez)
El Horóscopo Restaurant (Pedro Márquez and Jorge Nasco)
El Vizcaya Restaurant (Tomás Arrezabálaga, Justo Zubimendi, Aramis

Piñon and Oscar Vilas)

El Bilbao Restaurant (Tomas Arrezabálaga, Justo Zubimendi, Aramis Piñon and Oscar Vilas)

Club Johnny 88 (Emilio Saumat)

El Minerva Club (Wenceslao "Laito" Castro)

El Lion's Club (Pedro Milián)

El Kasbah (Pedro Márquez)

El Matador (Pedro Márquez, Jorge Novo and Isidro Villota)

El Miamian (Pedro Márquez, Jorge Novo and Isidro Villota)

El Concord Club (Normando Campos)

El Greco Club (Rogelio Novo)

The Office Club (Rogelio Novo)

Rogers on the Green (Rogelio Novo)

Los Amantes (Néstor Fernández)

Mon Petit (The brothers Fernández and associates)

El Casino (Ñico Membiela)

El Club 47 (Ñico Membiela)

Desiree Club (Roberto Coello and Alina García)

El Barbaran (Sergio Niebla)

El Trojan Lounge (Arty Valdés).

El Don Quijote (Manuel Balado, Orlndo Hidalgo, Eddy González and Sergio Vidal Cairo)

Cubans now live all over the world, separated by an ideology. Their music is still a strong unifying force.

NOTES

1. Others included Panchito Calimano, Eddie Lester, Homero Balboa, Luis García, Eugenio de la Osa, Carlos Barnett, Baserva Soler, César Morales, Raúl Ferrer, Facundo Rivero, Raúl Azpiazu (son of Don Azpiazu), Estebita, Rey Formoso, Juanito Ayala, and Olguita Díaz; the guitarists Pablo Cano and his brother Luis,

and Eddie Romero; the saxophone players Pedro Chao, Tata Palau, Gerardo Levatar, Armando Mena, and Rafael Sorí; and the percussionist Nelson "El Loco" Padrón.
2. Others who lived in New York were: Composer Marcelino Guerra, pianist Armando Valdespí, flutist Belisario López, René Hernández "El Látigo," and pianist and arranger René Hernández (no relation to "El Látigo"), who was the arranger for the orchestras of "Machito," Tito Puente, Tito Rodríguez and many others. Also in that city were: percussionists Cándido Camero and Armando Peraza, Armando Sánchez (of the group *Son de la Loma*), "Chihuahua" Martínez, saxophonist Chombo Silva and the young pianist Alfredito Valdés, Jr.
3. Humberto Suárez, René Barrios, and Ana del Pilar Pérez; Saxophone player Jesús Caunedo; base player Mandy Vizoso and violinst Lorenzo Pego also arrived in Puerto Rico in the 1960s.
4. Others who settled there were Panchito Calimano and later the brothers Gabriel "Puly" and Armando Zequeira; also, Roberto Ferrer and Pepe Urquiaga. Gaby Gabriel and Margarita García arrived in Tampa at a young age and forged a major musical career with their band The Gabriels. Gabriel later moved to Miami while Margarita remained in Tampa.
5. The 20th Anniversary Billboard Tribute by John Lannert for *Billboard Magazine*, September 1998
6. Others still active and successful included: Roberto Losano, Peter Fernández, Joe Rubio, Frank Batista, Luis Serrano, Manny Salas, Frankie Marcos, Alberto Guerra, Miguel Martín, and the architect Ramón Arronte.
7. There were also other musicians among them: Jaime García, Joe Coello, Roberto Gómez, Jesús Argaín, Rubén Otero, Candito Camps, Fausto Dorado, Jorge Cabrera, Felipe Villaraus and singers like Eddie Gual, Aquiles Santiago, Manuel Santayana, Monchi Estévez, and Mario San Pedro.
8. Other musicians among them: Raúl Gómez and wife Leonor Zamora, Annia Linares, Mirtha Medina, Xiomara Lougart, the sisters Nubiola, Argelia Fragoso, Delia Díaz de Villegas, Luis Bofill, Osvaldo Rodríguez, Isaac Delgado, Carlos Manuel, the duo of Las Diego and Los Tres de La Habana. Among musicians, trumpeter Leonardo Timor, saxophone player José "Pepe" Vera, percussionist Wikly Nogueras, bassist Omar Hernández, and physician and pianist Arturo Ramos, among others.
9. The first poets-improvisers to arrive in Miami were Neida Revuelta, Isidro Cárdenas, Carlos Alas del Casino, El Cacique Jaruqueño, Arturito Baldomero, Evaristo Quintanales, and Berto Acevedo. Others who followed them in time were Pablo León, Manuel Soriano, Asael Díaz "Candelita," Juan Antonio Díaz, Jesusito Cruz, Binicio, Robertico García, Jorge Vergel, Chano Isidrón, and the poets Dionisio Gil and Roberto N. Morales, "El Guajiro."
10. They were followed by Alberto Menéndez, a member of the *movimiento del feeling* (the feeling movement) and the traditional *trova*. And from the group *Loquibambia* there was Benito González, who replaced Miguel Matamoros in the second period of the *Trío Matamoros* (1971-1986), the duos *Carlos y Marta* and *Norberto y Marisela* and the *Duo Contraste*, the trios *Voces de Oro*, *Voces del Trópico*, *Trio Pinareño*, *Trio Garay*, and *Mi Son Cubano* of Chichi Caney.

26

CLASSICAL MUSIC AND BALLET

BY ELOY CEPERO AND SONIA FRÍAS

Long before the founding of the Republic, cultured or classical music—also called concert music—was well represented among composers, performers, and singers in Cuba.

When the Castros came to power in 1959, all provinces—and especially Havana—had important institutions such as Pro Arte Musical and theaters like the Nacional, the Martí, and the Auditorium that promoted the development of that musical genre featuring internationally known artists—Cubans as well as from other countries. Operas, operettas, *zarzuelas* (traditional Spanish operettas), choral music, and concerts were always presented before enthusiastic audiences.

Classical singers, musicians, composers, and a combination of performers of these musical genres began to go into exile after the revolution, as thousands of other Cubans had.

The first Cuban performers of classical music went into exile very early. Many of them had triumphed on international stages, among them Ernesto Lecuona, a pianist, composer, and orchestra leader who went into exile in 1960. Endowed with exceptional qualities, Lecuona made great contributions to Cuban piano music in a variety of musical genres and composed more than six hundred works, among them about seventy dances for piano, the *zarzuelas Niña Rita, María la O,* and *El Cafetal*. Among Lecuona's best-known international compositions are *Siboney,*

Andalucía, La Malagueña, and *La Comparsa.* He is the most important Cuban musician and composer of all times. His work has transcended eras and countries. Lecuona took up residence in the Canary Islands, where he died in 1963.

The violinist and composer Julián Orbon arrived in exile in Miami in 1960. Born in Spain but raised and educated in Cuba since he was seven years old, Orbon was one of the founders of the *Renovación Musical* (Musical Renewal) movement and of the *Orígenes* group. Orbon is credited with the fusion of elements of Cuban and Spanish folk music in a symphonic composition. Among his innovations are that he added José Martí's *Versos Sencillos* (Simple Verses) to the chorus of *La Guantanamera.* They later achieved international fame when performed by American singer Peter Seeger. Orbon died in Miami in 1991, following a continued successful international career.

Jorge Bolet is one of the most significant Cuban classical pianists of the twentieth century. Bolet is considered the most important interpreter of Hungarian composer and piano virtuoso Franz Liszt and performed Liszt's piano works in the 1960 film about the composer's life titled *Canción Sin Final* (Song Without End). He was a professor and chief lecturer head at the Curtis Musical Institute in Philadelphia. He lived in New York but never again wanted to return to Cuba and died in California in 1990.

Aurelio de la Vega is one of the best known and innovative of Cuban pianists in the twentieth century. In 1959, he settled down in Los Angeles. Even though he proclaimed his opposition to nationalism in music, he utilized Cuban melodies and typical features in his first compositions and was the first Cuban composer to use atonality. Beginning in the decade of the 1960s, he gradually abandoned the method of musical composition known as serialism and began to make use of electronic media in open forms. His musical career continued to rise once he was in exile.

Natalio Galán is a great pianist, composer, writer, and musicologist from Camagüey. He collaborated with the writer Alejo Carpentier in researching for his book *La Música en Cuba*. He composed various chamber works, including the opera for small orchestra *Los Días Llenos* and *El Paseo*, with a version for two pianos called *Intermedio*, filled with expressionistic lines and drawn from the basic rhythmic shapes of the *son*. He was a composer of great sensitivity, creative power, and strength. He settled in New Orleans since 1947 and died there in 1985 without returning to Cuba.

René Touzet, classical pianist and composer, also wrote popular musical styles, among them one hundred boleros, and jazz. His eight sets of *contradanzas* (contredanse), including *Saumeliana* and dances (forty in all), enrich the concept of the dance as a musical form that comes close to contemporary and original styles. His works can be seen as a continuation of that by Manuel Saumell, Ignacio Cervantes, and Ernesto Lecuona. In 1984, Touzet composed *Caperucita Roja* (Little Red Riding Hood) with a text by Carlos Irigoyen, music related to the theater. He lived in Los Angeles for many years and finally in Miami where he died in 2003 without ever returning to Cuba.

The pianist, composer, and conductor Marco Rizo created a fascinating mixture of popular and classical music, inseparably linked to the historical context of the Cuban nation. He was successful with dances and *habaneras*, among which we can mention *La Edad de Oro, Junto a las Cascadas, La Avellaneda, Ecue Yamba-O,* and *Tocata*. He was the author of the theme soundtrack of TV's *I Love Lucy*, renowned throughout the world. Among his countless achievements was conducting the *101 Strings* orchestra, in Hamburg, Germany. He died in New York in 2000.

With the passing of time, other musicians and singers left Cuba to enrich the musical life not only of Miami but also that of other cities of the United States.

Many of the best classical musicians who sought exile were pianists. Among those were pianist, composer and conductor Alfredo Munar; pianist and composer Luis Carballo, who wrote *La Gentil*, the first *zarzuela* composed in exile. There were also the outstanding pianists Zenaida

Manfugás, César Morales, Jesús "Raspuli" García, Olga Díaz Pancier, Lourdes Salvador, Bertha Zimmerman, Velia Yedra, and Mercy Ferrer, among others. Young artists who were formed here include Gustavo and Eyda Ponzoa, Horacio Gutiérrez, Elier Suárez, Hector García, José Ignacio Díaz-Gravier, Sergio Alejandro, Javier Ruiz, Conchita Betancourt Leyla Torres, Darleen Trujillo, and José Ruiz Elcoro, all outstanding concert performers.

Among the violinists who arrived in exile were Alberto Fajardo, Jorge Orbon, Andrés Trujillo, Gerardo Aguillón, José Aron Martínez, M. Montoto, Orlando Forte, and José Haza. The young Lisbeth Martínez made history when she played the U.S. national anthem from a refugee tent in the Guantánamo Naval Base during the Cuban Balsero (Rafter) Crisis of 1994. Lisbeth continued her violin studies once she arrived in the land of freedom and graduated with honors. Dairién Santamaría went to Tampa, Florida, and now lives in Hollywood, California.

Among the first performers of classical guitar who arrived in exile was Juan Mercadal of Guanabacoa. He became a professor at the University of Miami. Later came Carlos Molina, Jesús Fuertes, Rey Guerra, and Rafael Padrón, among others.

Outstanding internationally known singers also left. Among the first to arrive were Manolo Alvarez Mera, José LeMatt, Miguel De Grandy I and II, Manolo Torrente, Armando Terrón, Pedro Román, Orlando González Esteva, Armando Pico, Alberto Piñero, Manny Pérez and Luis Serrano. Among the women were Zoraida Marrero, Hortensia Coalla, Caridad Suárez, America Crespo, Zoraida Beato, Estelita Santaló, Georgina Granados, Maruja Gonzalez, María Cervide, Elizabeth del Rio, Blanca Varela, Teresa Pons, Esperanza Chediak, Angelita Castany, Ada Luque, Tania Martí, Mara González, Martha Ruiz, Natacha Amador, and Lola Peña.

Two singers who especially distinguished themselves were the mezzo-soprano Marta Pérez, who sang several times at La Scala in Milan, and Virginia Alonso, the only Cuban singer who has performed major roles alongside Luciano Pavarotti and Plácido Domingo. Also formed in exile and joining this stellar group were Ana María Munar, Elizabeth Caballero, and Eglisse Gutiérrez, among other young people who have been honored on both national and international stages.

LYRICAL THEATER: GRATELI

In 1969, in view of the demand generated by the growing exile community eager to preserve while in exile its tradition of a people fond of all kinds of music, the mezzo-soprano Marta Pérez, Pili de la Rosa, Miguel de Grandy II, and Demetrius Menéndez—all members of the artistic community—joined to create the *Gran Teatro Lírico* (Great Lyrical Theater), which they called Grateli, an acronym made up of the first letter of the theater's name in Spanish. From the beginning they had the unconditional support of Dr. Horacio Aguirre, editor-in-chief of *Diario Las Americas* and of his wife, Helen. Aguirre was one of the group's mainstays. This was also the case with the Rev. Max Salvador and his wife. Gaspar and Paquita Aldrich as well as the businessman Diego Suárez deserve a special mention for their constant support.

The first presentation of Grateli was the staging of the *Verbena de la Paloma* at the Dade County Auditorium. Despite the tiny budget, the work was staged with an enviable cast: Marta Pérez, Marta Salas, Mario Martín, Miguel de Grandy II, René Pérez, Julita Muñoz, Norma Zuñiga, Mary Munné, Lupe Suárez, José San Marty, Oswaldo Calvo, Bertha Sandoval, and Marta Castellanos, all top singers and actors from Cuba's republican era. It was a standing-room only performance.

From that date onwards, important *zarzuelas* and musical comedies—all sponsored by Grateli—have been staged, including *Las Leandras, María La O, Doña Francisquita, La Viuda Alegre, Cecilia Valdés, Los Gavilanes, Luisa Fernanda, The Sound of Music, Gigi,* among many others. The list is endless. The cast has included local artists as well as singers and actors of international fame. No one can speak about Grateli without mentioning the Carmen Riera choral that for years has supported the staged productions.

It is important to emphasize the presence of orchestra leaders who with great tenacity managed to unite their efforts to establish such institutions in the musical exile. Ernesto Lecuona, Manuel Ochoa, Antonio Hernández Lisazo, Alfredo Munnar, Omar Reyes, José and Marlene Urbay, and the young New York-born Cuban-American Oscar Bustillo, Jr., whose parents were Cuban and who was the assistant director of the Florida West Coast Symphony.

MIAMI SYMPHONY ORCHESTRA (MISO)

In 1989, the talented maestro Manuel Ochoa founded the Miami Symphony Orchestra with eighty musicians selected from among leading professionals from all over the world, thus creating an institution that reflects the international and multicultural diversity of the city. Beginning in 1997, MISO successfully presented musical and artistic education programs in Miami-Dade County public primary schools. In 2000, the orchestra traveled to New York City for an appearance at Carnegie Hall. Years of perseverance have yielded results that have been highly recognized and in March 2003 the flag of Cuba flew over the National Capitol in Washington, D.C., in honor of the Miami Symphony Orchestra and its founder and director maestro Manuel Ochoa for their love and dedication to classical music, and for Ochoa being the first Latino director and founder of a symphony orchestra in the United States. Ochoa died in 2006 but MISO continued.

FLORIDA CHAMBER ORCHESTRA

The Florida Chamber Orchestra (FCO) was founded in 1995 by the prominent conductor Marlene Urbay, descendant of a family of musicians. Their repertoire ranged from the baroque and classical to Gershwin, Lecuona, and most representative composers of Europe and Latin America. Since its founding the FCO has successfully toured countless concert halls, and has participated in music festivals and ballet performances.

MIAMI POP ORCHESTRA

The Miami Pop Orchestra, a small symphony orchestra of twenty-four teachers, was established at the end of the 1980s by Omar Reyes, who was interested in salvaging—in his own words—"the role that had been usurped from Cuban music." In addition to participating in radio and television programs and musical shows, Reyes organized several gala concerts of Cuban music. In those concerts, international performers and soloists have performed with Reyes' orchestra. Among them are the following musicians of international stature: Tania Martí, Martica Ruiz, Reynaldo Rey, and many others. The Miami Pop Orchestra is officially known as the *Gran Orquesta de La Pequeña Habana* (the Great Orchestra of Little Havana).

THE BALLET

There is no doubt that the ballet has a deeply rooted tradition in Cuba. It began in 1948 when Fernando Alonso and Alicia Martínez (who later adopted the Alonso surname of her husband, the dancer Fernando) and her brother-in-law Alberto—a dancer and internationally renowned choreographer—founded the Alicia Alonso Ballet Company under the auspices Pro Arte Musical. This was later renamed as the Ballet Nacional de Cuba, the cradle of the renowned Cuban School of Ballet, directed by prima ballerina Alicia Alonso.

Once Communism took power in Cuba, very important Cuban ballet figures decided to take the road of exile, a road on which others have traveled over the years—quite in contrast to the pro-regime political attitude assumed by Alicia Alonso, the director of the National Ballet.

From that school one must mention the Feijoo sisters: Lorena, a leading performer with the San Francisco Ballet and Lorna, prima ballerina of the Boston Ballet. Others are Dagmar Moradillo, Rosario "Charín" Suárez, José Manuel Carreño, Taras Domitro, Carlos Guerra, Joan Boada, Carlos Acosta, Adiaris Almeida, Hayna Gutiérrez, and Alihaydee Carreño. These are performers who stand out in their presentations with various ballet groups, both locally and internationally.

Charín Suárez, also a product of that ballet academy, founded her own ballet company in Miami where this prima ballerina is a teacher.

Fernando Bujones, Jr., was born in Miami of Cuban parents, Fernando Bujones, Sr., and the ballerina Mary Calleiro. His mother was visiting and soon thereafter both returned to Cuba. According to Notable Biographies, Bujones, Jr., started ballet as a child when he was five years old. Among his ballet teachers were Alicia Alonso and Zaida Cecilia Méndez. Bujones, Jr., and his mother moved to Miami permanently in 1964. He was considered one of the best dancers of classical ballet during the 1970s and the 1980s, until his death in 2005. Notable Biographies said he was as good if not better than the more famous Russian dancer Mikhail Baryshnikov. Bujones was the first American dancer to win a gold medal at the International Ballet Olympics in 1974.

In 1960, the Sylvia Medina de Gaudie Studio had three branches: Coral Way, Westchester, and Hialeah, with more than 350 students. Some of the outstanding graduates of these studios are dancers such as Cecilio A. Gaudie, Jr., and Susana Prieto. The schools closed in 1975 and Mrs.

Gaudie died in 1997.

The Compañía Ballet Concerto (the Concerto Ballet Company) was founded in 1968 by Sonia Díaz, Marta del Pino, and Eduardo Recalt. The group has participated in dozens of occasions with its choreography in Grateli presentations during more than forty years, in addition to being a school for ballet.

In February 2006, Pedro Pablo Peña, founder and director of the prestigious International Ballet Festival of Miami, founded the Cuban Classical Ballet of Miami. The company's main purpose is to preserve the repertoire of the legendary tradition of classical Cuban ballet and outstanding exiled artists—who were trained at the Cuban School of Ballet—performed at many of its shows.

27

CUBAN SPORTS BEFORE AND AFTER THE REVOLUTION

BY ROLY MARTIN

The Island of Cuba has produced top athletes from the early twentieth century until the present. No matter the system of government, Cubans have been successful on the baseball diamond, in the boxing ring, in track and field, and many other athletic endeavors. The great achievements of Cuban athletes began with fencer Ramón Fonst, "Second to None," the first Latin American Olympic gold medalist at the 1900 Games in Paris and the 1904 Olympics in St. Louis. Fonst was only seventeen years old when he earned his first Olympic gold medal in Paris. But the achievements of Cuban athletes continue to this day, inside and outside the island, as many left their homeland after the triumph of Castro's dictatorship to make history on foreign soil.

CUBA: A COUNTRY OF GREAT BASEBALL PLAYERS

Baseball and boxing are Cuba's favorite sports and the ones where Cuban athletes have excelled. Baseball began to be played at Palmar del Junco field in the city of Matanzas in 1874. It was a game in which "the team from Havana demolished Matanzas by a score of 51-9. Havana was led by the pitching of Ricardo Mora and the hitting of catcher Esteban Bellán of New York's Mutual Club." During that game, Bellán was the first Latin American to hit three homers in one game, and in 1871 he was the first Latin American to play in the U.S. professional leagues. He played in the National Association of Professional Baseball Leagues, the forerunner of the National League.[1]

The first Cuban professional baseball league began in the 1878-79 season, with Habana winning the championship. Since then—and until the 1960-61 season—professional baseball was played in ballparks throughout Cuba. In 1961, the Communist government abolished professional sports. The Habana club also won the last championship that year. Infielder Octavio "Cookie" Rojas was the Most Valuable Player, with a .322 batting average. Rojas later became a star in the U.S. Major Leagues, where he played on several teams, including the Kansas City Royals.

In the Cuban League, played in the winter, the four teams were Almendares, Cienfuegos, Habana, and Marianao. The "Leones" (Lions) of Habana were the top winners in Cuban baseball with a total of thirty championships, while the "Alacranes" (Scorpions) of Almendares were second with twenty-five titles.

The first Cuban ballplayers to play in the U.S. Major Leagues (according to most record books and historians) were Armando Marsans and Rafael Almeida in 1911—both for the Cincinnati Reds.

Since then, and until professional baseball was banned in Cuba in 1961, tens of Cuban ballplayers wore the uniforms of the Big Show. Among them, Adolfo Luque, who in 1923 had a record of 27-8, with an ERA of 1.93, becoming the leader in both categories in the National League that season as well as the Latin American with the most wins in a season in the history of the Major Leagues. Other outstanding players include Orestes "Minnie" Miñoso, who had his debut in 1949 with the Cleveland Indians and also had an outstanding career with the Chicago White Sox, with a lifetime batting average of .298 over seventeen years. Pitcher Camilo Pascual played with several teams, including the Washington Senators and the Minnesota Twins from 1954 to 1971. He had 174 wins and 170 losses. But there were many others who also stood out in those fifty years (1911-61) when around ninety Cubans played in the Major Leagues. In the 1950s, Orioles shortstop Willie Miranda was also a standout, as was pitcher Pedro Ramos. In recent years, the most outstanding Cuban players have included Hall of Famer Tony Pérez, of the famed Big Red Machine; Tony Oliva, batting champion of the American League; Luis Tiant, a pitcher with a very unique delivery to the plate; and sluggers Rafael Palmeiro and José Canseco (these last two are under the cloud of steroid use).

Cubans not only excelled on the field, but also as managers and team leaders. Miguel Angel González was the first Latin American to lead a team in the Majors when he took the reins of the St. Louis Cardinals on an interim basis in 1938. In 1969, Cuban-American Preston Gómez became the first Latin American to take permanent charge of a team when he was appointed manager of the San Diego Padres.

Four more Cubans have been Major League managers (in all, a total of six—more than from any other Latin American country). Tony "Tany" Pérez (Cincinnati Reds and Florida Marlins), Cookie Rojas (Los Angeles Angels, Florida Marlins, and Toronto Blue Jays), Carlos Tosca (Toronto Blue Jays), and Fredi González (Florida Marlins and Atlanta Braves).

Cuban ballplayers not only left their imprints on the U.S. Major Leagues, but also starred in other baseball leagues during the first sixty years of the twentieth century. Many black players played in the Cuban League while at the end of the season in Cuba they would transfer over to the Negro Leagues in the U.S. To this day, fans talk of the exploits on the diamond of pitcher José de la Caridad Méndez, known as "The Black Diamond." There was also the multitalented Martín Dihigo, the "Super Versatile," regarded by many as the most complete baseball player of all time—in and out of Cuba. And then there was outfielder Cristóbal Torriente. If it had not been for the color barrier all would have played in the Major Leagues.

José de la Caridad Méndez starred in the Negro Leagues with a record of 44-2 in 1909 with the Cuban Stars. In the Cuban League, he had a lifetime record of 72-26. Dihigo—a member of the Halls of Fame of Cuba, Mexico, the U.S., and the Latin America—started with the Havana team in the 1922-23 season when he was only seventeen. He played there for twenty-one years, until 1947, achieving a record of 106-50 as pitcher with a batting average of .293. During twelve seasons between 1923 and 1947, Dihigo played and competed with such Negro League stars as Satchel Paige, Oscar Charleston, and James "Cool Papa" Bell, batting .299 with 69 homers and a 25-18 record as pitcher.

Torriente, a left-handed hitter, was considered the best center fielder in the Negro Leagues. In a career spanning from 1913 to 1932, his batting average was .329. Others who excelled in the Cuban League and the U.S. Negro Leagues were outfielder Alejandro Oms, pitcher Eustaquio "Bombín" Pedroso, and shortstop Luis "Anguilla" Bustamante.

Two Cuban baseball teams also joined the U.S. professional Minor Leagues. First came the Havana Cubans, who played in the Florida International League from 1946 to 1953; initially their games were played at Havana's Tropical Stadium. Bobby Maduro purchased the club, and its name was changed in 1954 to Cuban Sugar Kings. The club also changed affiliation when it joined the International AAA League (baseball's second highest-ranked professional league). The Cuban Sugar Kings played their games in La Habana's *Estadio del Cerro* (renamed Estadio Latinoamericano), but the franchise left Cuba and moved to Jersey City after Fidel Castro nationalized all American companies by decree in July 1960. This happened even before the Cuban government banned professional baseball in Cuba in 1961. The Sugar Kings won the Minor Leagues World Series in 1959 against the Minneapolis Millers. Several of their players went to the Major Leagues, such as catcher René Friol. They did not play in Cuba again.

SIX IN THE HALL OF FAME

A total of six Cubans have been inducted into the Baseball Hall of Fame in Cooperstown; except for the U.S., that is more than all other countries combined.

Three players have been chosen for their play and one executive for his activities in the Negro Leagues, in an era where black players were not allowed in the Major Leagues, despite their indisputable talent: José de la Caridad Méndez, Martín Dihigo, and Cristóbal Torriente. Alejandro Pómpez was chosen as a Negro Leagues executive.

The only Cuban baseball player of the modern era to have been voted into the Hall has been Tony Pérez. Many baseball writers believe others, like pitcher Luis Tiant and outfielder Tony Oliva, also deserve to be included.

In 2001, Felo Ramírez, a legendary radio and television broadcaster in Cuba, Puerto Rico, Venezuela, and the U.S. won the National Baseball Hall of Fame's Ford C. Frick Award given to an outstanding broadcaster each year. Well past his eightieth birthday, Ramírez is the Spanish radio voice of the Florida Marlins as of this writing.

THE AMATEUR LEAGUES

Many of those who played professional baseball in the Cuban League, the Negro Leagues, the Minor Leagues, and the Major Leagues had started in amateur or semi-pro leagues. In Cuba, there were several amateur and semi-professional leagues from the early twentieth century until 1960. But the National Amateurs League is considered the most important one. Its first championship was held in 1914, and it was won by the Vedado Tennis Club. This league was a "super birthplace for players who went on to play professional ball." The following ballplayers—among many others—rose from the amateur leagues to the ranks of professional baseball: Andrés and Angel Fleitas, Roberto Ortiz, Pedro "Pudding" Jiménez, Vicente López, Conrado Marrero, Agapito Mayor, Sandalio "Potrerillo" Consuegra, Julio "Jiquí" Moreno, and Rogelio "Limonar" Martínez. "Conrado Marrero was Cuba's most successful pitcher, having won 123 games in the Cuban Amateurs League." Antonio "Quilla" Valdés, shortstop at Hershey, never played professional baseball, but many believe he was one of the best Cuban shortstops of all time.[2]

IT ALL BEGAN WITH CHOCOLATE AND GAVILAN

Boxing is the other sport in which Cubans have greatly excelled. In 1915, the fight for the world's heavyweight title between defending champion Jack Johnson and challenger Jess Willard took place in the Oriental Park in Marianao, a municipality adjacent to La Habana. It can be said that boxing in Cuba started that year, even though it was not until 1921 when it officially began with the creation of the National Boxing Commission. Cuba's first professional world champion was Eligio Sardiñas (1910-88). He was better known as Kid Chocolate. This great Cuban boxer (known in boxing circles as the Cuban *Bon Bon*) learned from watching old boxing films about fights in Cuba and won his first world title in 1931 when he defeated Benny Bass in a seventh-round KO, earning the junior lightweight crown. In 1932, he added the featherweight title by defeating Lew Feldman. This showman of the boxing ring finished his brilliant career in 1938 with 131 wins, 9 losses, and 6 draws.

But Kid Chocolate was not the only Cuban "Kid" who reigned in the boxing ring. Gerardo González (Kid Gavilán), who shared Kid Chocolate's birthday (January 6, 1926) was another "Kid" who brought many victories to Cuba from boxing rings around the world. Kid Gavilán never lost a fight by knockout. His record was 108 victories, 30 losses, and 5 draws—28 of those wins were by knockouts. He won the welterweight crown in 1951 when he beat Johnny Bratton in fifteen rounds at New York City's Madison Square Garden. He lost two close fights to Sugar Ray Robinson in 1948 and 1949, and he lost his welterweight crown to Johnny Saxton in 1954.

Many other Cuban boxers excelled from the 1930s through the 1950s. Among them are Kid Tunero, who won 97 fights while suffering 32 defeats and 16 draws as a middleweight fighter in a career spanning twenty years and Eladio Valdés, known as Black Bill. He began his career as a flyweight and won 107 fights, with only 19 defeats and 11 draws. He was still winning fights at the age of twenty-five when he was half-blind, syphilitic, and a heavy drinker. His end was a sad one, like that of many other boxers. In 1933, at the age of twenty-eight, he committed suicide in New York City.

GREAT MANAGERS AND TRAINERS

Cuban boxers have traveled triumphantly all over the world, and they have shared that success with a talented group of managers, promoters, and trainers. Among them were Pincho Gutiérrez and Fernando Valido, who managed the careers of boxers Kid Chocolate and Kid Gavilán. Félix "Tuto" Zabala was the promoter and manager who guided the careers of several champions, including Puerto Rican Wilfredo Vázquez, world champion in three divisions, and the former bantamweight champion Miguel "Happy" Lora from Colombia. Zabala's son, Tuto Zabala, Jr., a promoter and manager in Miami, guided Wilfredo Vázquez, Jr., to become the featherweight champion. There are also Antolín "Chino" Govín, trainer of another world champion, Colombian Rodrigo Valdés, and Félix Masud and Luis Sarria, the latter recognized as one of the best in his field (he worked many years for Muhammad Ali). Managers Luis de Cubas and Tony González both handled the career of four-time world champion Roberto Durán and several Cuban fighters, including Yuriorkis Gamboa and Guillermo Rigondeaux. Also, Caron González, brothers Manolo and Marzo Fernández, Ismael. Salas, and Pedro Luis Díaz, were professional-level trainers of Gamboa and Odlanier Solis, respectively; and Enrique Encinosa, manager, matchmaker, and journalist in charge of the career of former cruiserweight (junior heavyweight) champion, Robert Daniels. Also in Miami, banker-by-profession Ramiro Ortiz is a great boxing fan who promotes boxing in Miami and is a member of the Boxing Hall of Fame of the State of Florida.

CAPABLANCA CHESS CHAMPION

José Raúl Capablanca has been the only Hispanic world chess champion. He was born in La Habana in 1888 and was already familiar with the rules of chess at the age of four, dubbed "The Mozart of Chess." He earned the world title in 1921 defeating Emanuel Lasker, and he retained that title until 1927.

STARS OF TRACK AND FIELD

Cuban athletes were not only successful with their bats and fists. In track and field, the first major Cuban athlete was Félix "El Andarín" (The Hiker) Carvajal, who finished fourth in the marathon despite an attack of colitis on the day of the competition during the St. Louis Olympic Games of 1904. Others were 100-meter sprinters José "Pepe" Barrientos, who participated in the 1948 Olympics in London before being eliminated in the second round, and Rafael Fortún, who was a semifinalist in the 100-meter and 200-meter races, in the London Games and in the 1952 Olympics in Helsinki. Fortún also won gold medals in the 100-meter and 200-meter races in the First Pan American Games held in Buenos Aires in 1951.

The first Cuban woman to participate in an Olympiad was Berta Díaz, who reached the semifinals in the 80-meter hurdles in the Melbourne Games in 1956. Díaz was also a gold medalist for the same distance in the Pan American Games in Mexico in 1955 and in Chicago in 1959.

ROWING REGATTAS AND FORMULA 1 CAR RACING IN HAVANA

Since the mid-1930s, the sport of rowing became popular in Cuba. In those years, rowing was practiced at several private clubs on the island such as the Vedado Tennis Club, the Habana Yacht Club, the Habana Biltmore Yacht & Country Club, the Cienfuegos Yacht Club, the Naval and Military Club, the Varadero Nautical Club, and the Ciudamar Club in Santiago de Cuba. For the first time in its history Cuba took part in the rowing competitions of the 1948 London Olympics and again in the 1956 Melbourne Olympics.

Speed lovers also enjoyed themselves in Cuba's Republican era. The first auto race took place in 1903 and was sponsored by the Habana Auto Club. In the 1950s most of the auto races took place on highways such as Pinar del Río-Habana and Sagua-Habana. Among the best-known local racecar drivers were Alfonso Gómez Mena, Santiago González, José Salazar, Rafael Cabrera, Diego Febles, and many more. The Grand Prix of Cuba—with the participation of world-renowned drivers—took place in a circuit on Havana's Malecón in February 1957. It was won by Formula One world champion Juan Manuel Fangio of Argentina.

In the second Grand Prix of Cuba in 1958, Fangio—five-times world champion—was kidnapped by members of the July 26 Movement led by Fidel Castro. Their goal was to undermine the government. Fangio was held hostage for about twenty-six hours before being freed, but he was not able to drive in the Grand Prix. This race had to be stopped around the sixth lap because of a terrible accident that resulted in a large number of deaths and injuries.

CUBA BANS PROFESSIONAL SPORTS

In 1961, revolutionary-turned-prime-minister Fidel Castro outlawed professional sports in Cuba. Sports became a political instrument of government propaganda. Sports schools were established and staffed by first-class coaches, and Cuban sports—especially those that were not the most popular before 1959—became very successful at the Central American Games, the Pan American Games, and the Olympics. But at the same time, those Cuban sports figures who wanted a better future for themselves and their families left the island if they could.

INVASION OF CUBAN ATHLETES

A veritable invasion of the U.S. by Cuban athletes began in the late 1950s and intensified throughout the decade of the 1960s when professional sports—particularly baseball and boxing—were outlawed in Cuba. During the 1960s, dozens of Cuban ballplayers joined the U.S. Major Leagues. Among them were:

- The infielders Tony Taylor, Cookie Rojas, Leo Cárdenas, Zoilo Versalles, Dagoberto "Bert" Campaneris, Anastasio "Tany" Pérez (Tony Pérez), Jackie Hernández, Mike de la Hoz, Chico Ruiz, and Tito Fuentes.
- Outfielders José Cardenal, Edmundo "Sandy" Amorós (who began his career in 1952), José Tartabull, Tony González, Sandy Valdespino, and Tony Oliva.
- Pitchers Luis Tiant, Marcelino López, Pedro Ramos (who began his

career in 1955), Camilo Pascual (who started in 1954), Orlando Peña, Miguel "Mike" Cuellar, and Diego Seguí.

Oliva, from Pinar del Rio, was the rookie of the year and the leading hitter in the American League while playing for the Minnesota Twins in 1964, with a batting average of .323. He won the batting title again in 1965 with an average of .321. During his fifteen-year career in the Major Leagues, Oliva won three batting titles and finished with a lifetime batting average of .304.

Pérez, known in the United States as Tony, played in the Major Leagues for twenty-three years. This native of Ciego de Avila drove in 1,652 runs, number two among Cubans in the history of baseball. He began his career with the Cincinnati Reds in 1964 and played with this team in four World Series and eight All-Star games. He finished his career with a batting average of .279 with 379 home runs. He managed the Reds and the Florida Marlins.

During the 1960s, three Cuban pitchers excelled in the Major Leagues: Camilo Pascual, Mike Cuellar, and Luis Tiant. In 18 Major League seasons, Pascual had a 174-170 record with 36 shutouts and a 3.63 ERA. He struck out 2,167 hitters and walked 1,069 in 2,930 innings. Cuellar shared the Cy Young Award of the American League in 1969 when he played for the Baltimore Orioles, winning twenty-three games. He finished his career with a 185-130 record. Tiant, who had a successful career with the Cleveland Indians and the Boston Red Sox, had a nineteen-year career in the Major Leagues—from 1964 to 1982—finishing with a record of 229 wins and 172 losses with an ERA of 3.30.

CUBAN-AMERICANS IN THE MAJOR LEAGUES

In the decades from the 1970s to the 2000s, the Cuban-American era of Major League Baseball started with the young Cubans who were born in Cuba but had arrived in the United States at an early age, and others who were born of Cuban parents in the U.S. and other countries. The first of this group was the pitcher Oscar Zamora (1974-78). He was followed, among others, by Orlando González (1976-80); Danny Tartabull (the son of José Tartabull), born in Puerto Rico in 1962; José Canseco and Rafael Palmeiro, both born in Cuba; catcher Nelson Santovenia (1987-93); Orestes Destrade (1987-94); infielder Fernando Viña, born in Sacramento, California; Antonio "Tony" Fossas; Alex Fernández (winner of 107 games from 1990 to 2000); Raúl Ibañez; catcher Elieser Marrero; Mike Lowell, Jorge Posada, and Eduardo Pérez (son of Tony Pérez), all born in Puerto Rico; and David Seguí (son of Diego Seguí) and catcher Jorge Fábregas.

Canseco, Palmeiro, and Tartabull became great hitters in the Major Leagues. Canseco, who played in the Major Leagues from 1985 to 2001, was the American League's 1986 Rookie of the Year while playing for the Oakland Athletics and the American League's MVP in 1988. He was the first player who hit at least forty home runs and stole at least forty bases (40-40) in the same year, hitting forty-two home runs and stealing forty bases in 1988. He finished his career with an average of .262, with 1,407 RBIs and 462 home runs. In 2005, many of his fans were bitterly disappointed when he admitted in a book that he had used steroids during his career and implicated several other players.

Palmeiro, infielder-outfielder, started his career in 1986 with the Chicago Cubs. He retired in 2005. He finished his brilliant career with 3,020 hits, a .288 average, and 569 home runs, number twelve on the all-time list for homers. He also drove in 1,835 runs, fifteenth on the all-time list and number one among Latin American ballplayers. He tested positive for steroids in 2005, but he has never admitted to using illegal substances.

Tartabull began playing in 1984 with the Seattle Mariners. He hit 262 homers and had a career total of 925 RBIs.

Lowell played for the New York Yankees, the Florida Marlins, and the Boston Red Sox for thirteen seasons, ending his career in 2010 with a .279 lifetime average, 223 homers, and 952 RBIs. He won two World Series: with the Marlins in 2003, and with the Red Sox in 2007. In the latter, he won the Most Valuable Player Award when he hit .400 as the Red Sox swept the Colorado Rockies.

Posada, born in Santurce, Puerto Rico, has played sixteen seasons—all with the New York Yankees. As of 2010, his career average was .275 with 261 homers and 1,021 RBIs. He is a five-time American League All-Star. He has also won the Silver Slugger Award five times and played in four World Series.

Fernández, born in Miami Beach, has a record of 107-87 in a career that began with the Chicago White Sox and ended with the Florida Marlins. He retired in 2000 with an ERA of 3.74.

As of 2010, Raúl Ibáñez had played for three Major League teams: the Seattle Mariners, the Kansas City Royals, and—since 2009—the Philadelphia Phillies. The outfielder has a career average of .284 with 232 homers and 970 RBIs. He also has connected 1,660 hits.

CUBA'S SPORTS CRISIS:

A NEW GENERATION OF CUBAN ATHLETES

Shortly after 1989, Cuban sports went through a crisis following the downfall of the Soviet Empire that worsened the economic situation of the government of the Castro brothers. Several of the athletes who had excelled in Cuban sports began to abandon Cuba.

Bárbaro Garbey, from Santiago de Cuba, who would in 1994 be part of the World Series-winning Detroit Tigers, was the first of the new generation of Cuban ballplayers to leave the island to seek a better future in the United States. He arrived at Florida's shores as part of the "Freedom Flotilla" of the 1980 Mariel Boatlift. That same year, weightlifting world champion Roberto Urrutia became the first high-performance athlete to say farewell to the Castros.

Another athlete who did the same was pitcher René Arocha in 1991. From then on, hundreds of Cuban athletes left for good. They were, in fact, the world's lowest-paid professional athletes, and they were leaving in search of freedom and better conditions. In Cuba, high-performance athletes practice sports full-time. Arocha pitched in the Major Leagues beginning in 1993.

Arocha was followed by shortstop Rey Ordóñez, who played for the New York Mets; pitchers Eddie Oropesa, Liván Hernández, Orlando "El Duque" Hernández (Liván's brother), Osvaldo Fernández, Ariel Prieto, Rolando Arrojo, Vladimir Núñez, Danny Baez, Michael Tejera, and José Ariel Contreras. There were also infielders—Yuniesky Betancourt, Alexei Ramírez, Yunel Escobar, Juan Miranda, and Kendry Morales.

Ramírez, Contreras, and Morales established themselves as top-level players in the Major Leagues. El Duque won four World Series titles, three of them with the New York Yankees, and had a record of 90-65 from 1998 to 2007. As of 2010, brother Liván had a record of 166-163, and he was the MVP of the 1997 World Series, won that year by the Florida Marlins. Shortstop Yunel Escobar has a .289 average as of 2010 over four seasons with the Atlanta Braves and the Toronto Blue Jays. Another shortstop, Yuniesky Betancourt, who began his Major League career in 2005 with Seattle, has hit forty-seven homers and has a .272 average in six seasons. Chicago White Sox shortstop Alexei Ramírez began his career in 2008 and in three seasons has hit fifty-four homers with an average of .283. José Ariel Contreras has won seventy-seven games since 2003 when he started with the New York Yankees, while first baseman Kendry Morales, who started in 2006 with the Los Angeles Angels, had by 2009 connected thirty-four home runs with a batting average of

.306 and 108 RBIs, making him one of the best offensive players in the American League.

In 2010, another group of Cuban ballplayers who had been top stars of Cuban baseball joined the U.S. Major Leagues. Among them was the talented southpaw pitcher Chapman Aroldis, who in September 2010—while pitching for the Cincinnati Reds in a game against the San Diego Padres—threw a ball at a speed of 105.1 miles per hour, the fastest throw in the history of the Major Leagues. Another talented pitcher is right-handed Yuniesky Maya, who began playing with the Washington Nationals as the 2010 season was nearing its end. Another Cuban who joined the Major Leagues in 2010 is Dayan Viciedo, a young infielder who plays for the Chicago White Sox.

WITTELS' FEAT

At the university level, a young second baseman from Miami, son of a Cuban-Jewish mother and grandson of banker Bernardo Benes, made history in college baseball during the 2010 season while wearing the uniform of Florida International University (FIU), located in Miami. Garrett Wittels achieved the second-best record in history when he hit in fifty-six consecutive games, only two less than the college record set by Robin Ventura and tying the Major League record set by Joe DiMaggio in 1941.

FIVE WORLD TITLES IN THE 1960S

In the 1960s, Cuban boxers who had left the island after professional sports were banned began to gain world recognition with the power of their fists. In September 1961, Benny "Kid" Paret won the welterweight title, beating Emile Griffith at Madison Square Garden in New

York in the second of the three fights between the two boxers. Paret died tragically during the third fight against Griffith in March 1962.

In March 1963, two Cuban boxers won world titles on the same night in Los Angeles, California. Luis Manuel Rodríguez defeated Emile Griffith in fifteen rounds to win the welterweight crown, while Ultiminio "Sugar" Ramos won the featherweight crown, defeating Davey Moore. But tragedy continued to pursue the Cuban boxers, as Moore died several days after the fight with Ramos. José Legra, a Cuban boxer living in Spain and trained by Kid Tunero, also won the featherweight title, beating Winston Howard of Wales in 1968. One year later, in 1969, José Angel "Mantequilla" Nápoles, who lives in Mexico, won the welterweight crown, knocking out Curtis Cokes in Inglewood, California. Nápoles is recognized as one of the best welterweights in history, with a record of 79 victories and only seven defeats. Luis Manuel Rodríguez, on the other hand, fought 120 professional bouts with a record of 107 victories and only 13 setbacks.

Another giant of the ring who was triumphant in the 1960s—but who was never able to win a world title—was middleweight Florentino Fernández, "El Foro." He had a tremendous punch, but he lost a split decision against Gene Fullmer while seeking the middleweight title in 1961.

OTHER CHAMPIONS LEAVE CUBA BEGINNING IN 1998

Cuba was not finished yet in producing champions. Cuban boxers who had great success at the amateur level after the revolution began to abandon the powerful Cuban boxing teams in search of freedom, glory, and greenbacks. In 1998, Juan Carlos Gómez, who remained in Germany, won the cruiserweight (or junior heavyweight) crown of the World Boxing Council, beating Marcelo Fabián Domínguez in Buenos Aires. Gómez defended his title successfully on ten occasions, and he now has a career record of forty-seven wins, two defeats, and one no-contest, with twenty-six knockouts.

José "El Cepillo" Casamayor, an Olympic champion at the 1992 Barcelona Games, arrived in the United States in 1996 and in 2002 became the junior lightweight champion defeating Korean Jon-Kwon Baek. Casamayor also beat Diego Corrales in 2006 to become the WBC's lightweight champion. His record: thirty-seven wins, five losses and one draw, with twenty-two knockouts.

Diosbelys Hurtado became junior welterweight champion of the World Boxing Association in 2002 when he defeated Randall Bailey by knockout. Yuriorkis Gamboa, former 1992 Barcelona Olympic champion, reached the Land of the Free in 2007 and won the WBA featherweight crown in 2009, beating José Rojas by knockout. In 2010, Gamboa also won the featherweight crown of the International Boxing Federation, defeating Orlando Salido.

Guillermo Rigondeaux, one of the greatest amateur boxers in history, and twice Olympic and world champion, reached the U.S. in 2009 after a second attempt to flee. In just his seventh professional fight, Rigondeaux won the WBA's super bantamweight crown with a split decision victory over Panamanian Ricardo Córdoba.

Other fighters who have left Cuba since 2006 include the heavyweight Odlanier Solís and the junior middleweight Erislandy Lara. Both now have a chance to win world boxing titles in their categories.

OTHER ATHLETES BID FAREWELL TO CUBA

Many other Cuban sports figures have left the island since the mid-1980s in search of freedom, among other things. Central American Games champion gymnast Ana Portuondo, of Santiago de Cuba, joined the U.S. Olympic Team for the 2004 Games in Athens, Greece. Now known as Ana Harris, she won a team gold medal and an individual silver medal.

Niurka Montalvo, long jumper and triple jumper, won the world track and field championship in Seville in 1999. She is now a Spanish citizen by marriage.

Several star players left Cuba's powerful men's and women's volleyball teams. Among them were such stars as Regla Bell, Magali Carvajal, Taimiris Aguero, and Ihosvany Hernández. The latter is considered the best striker in the history of Cuban men's volleyball.

In cycling, Ahmed López, Yesmani Pol, and Odaimis Alvarez left the Cuban team that competed in Mexico in 2009. There was also a group of powerful soccer players, including Maykel Galindo, Lester More, Reynier Alcantara, Pedro Faife, and many more. In 2008 alone, nine soccer players left the Cuban national team looking for new horizons in the U.S. Another one was judo martial arts star Héctor Lombard, who as national Cuban champion excelled in mixed martial arts as he did as a champion in the Bellator Fighting Championships, a mixed martial arts promotion based in the United States.

GREAT CUBAN-AMERICAN ATHLETES

The achievements of the Cuban-American athletes (those born in Cuba and raised in the United States or of Cuban ancestry, but born outside the island) have not been confined to baseball only. Ice skater Jennifer Rodríguez, marathon runner Alberto Salazar, tennis player Mary Joe Fernández, judo martial art practitioner René Capó, basketball players—and twin brothers—Brook and Robin López, football players Carlos Alvarez, Rafael Ortega, Luis Sharpe, and Mario Cristóbal, and swimmer Pablo Morales are among those who have triumphed on U.S. soil.

- Rodríguez was born in Miami and began her sports career as a figure skater, but she also became well known as a speed skater. She won the bronze medals in the 1,000-meter and the 1,500-meter competitions at the 2002 Winter Olympics in Salt Lake City, Utah. She won the gold medal in the sprint competition at the 2005 World Championships, also in Salt Lake City. She won the silver medal in the 1,000 meters at the 2002 World Championship in Berlin.
- Salazar, born in Cuba in 1958, won three consecutive marathon titles at the New York City Marathon from 1980 to 1982. He also won the Boston Marathon in 1982. During the same year, he also became the U.S. record holder in the 5,000 and the 10,000 meters.
- Fernández was born in the Dominican Republic of a Cuban mother and a Spanish father. She was selected to represent the United States at the 1992 Olympic Games in Barcelona, winning a gold medal in women's doubles (with Gigi Fernández) and a bronze medal in singles. Her individual World Tennis Association career record includes seven singles titles and seventeen doubles titles. She was also a singles finalist at the 1990 and 1992 Australian Open, and the French Open in 1993.
- Capó, born in Cuba in 1961, emigrated to the United States a year later and became the judo champion of the United States. He was a member of the U.S. Olympic Team in two Olympics. In the 1988 Games he finished in nineteenth place in the heavyweight division.
- Twin brothers Brook and Robin López, sons of a Cuban father, are seven feet tall and currently top players in the NBA. Both are center forwards who were picked in the first draft round by the New Jersey Nets and the Phoenix Suns, respectively.
- Alvarez, known as "The Cuban Comet," was the first Cuban-American to become a U.S. college football star when he played for the University of Florida Gators, from 1969 to 1971. Alvarez, a receiver, caught eighty-eight passes for the Gators in 1969 and was chosen an All-American.

- Ortega, a linebacker who also played for the Gators, played for six seasons in the NFL with the Atlanta Falcons and the Miami Dolphins.
- Sharpe played as an offensive tackle in the NFL with St. Louis and Phoenix for thirteen seasons, and he was selected three times to the NFL's All-Pro Team.
- Cristóbal was an offensive tackle for the University of Miami Hurricanes and later became the Hurricanes' assistant coach and he held the same position with Rutgers University. In December 2006, Florida International University (FIU) hired him as head coach.
- Morales was born in Chicago in 1964 and—as Olympic swimmer—won a gold medal in the relay and two silver medals in butterfly as member of the U.S. Team at the 1988 Olympic Games in Seoul, South Korea. He returned to the Olympics for the 1992 Games in Barcelona as captain of Team USA and won a gold medal in the 100-meter butterfly.

Cubans also have had important roles as referees in professional sports in the United States. Alberto Riverón, born in Cuba, was until 2010 the only Hispanic referee in the NFL. Angel Hernández, Lázaro Rodríguez, and Armando Díaz are current umpires in the Major Leagues. Rodríguez, a native of Matanzas, was the first Hispanic umpire in the Major Leagues, starting in the American League in 1974.

As a promoter, Rafael "Ralph" Sánchez is the pioneer of modern car racing in Miami where he created the IMSA racing circuit from 1983 until 1993 on the grounds of Bicentennial Park in Downtown Miami. He was also the key driving force in promoting the construction of the Homestead Race Track, where the first race (a CART race circuit) was held in 1996.

As for youth basketball, Marcos "Shakey" Rodríguez guided the team of the Miami Senior High School to five Florida state titles from 1987 to 1993. Later, he was the coach at Florida International University (FIU) in Miami.

Frank Martín, born in Miami of Cuban parents, currently works as basketball coach at Kansas State University, generally rated among the best college hoop teams in the United States. Martín also led the Miami Senior High School team that won three state titles from 1996 to 1998.

MIAMI ROWING CLUB: HOME OF CHAMPIONS

From its inception in 1974, the Miami Rowing Club was regarded as the home for rowing enthusiasts in South Florida. A large number of Cuban and Cuban-American rowers emerged from that rowing club. The club's youth program is recognized worldwide, and it has been awarded numerous state, regional, national, and world titles. On a worldwide basis, the club's under-twenty-three team won a silver medal at the World Championships in the Men's 4X category. In 1987, the team won a gold medal in the Men's 8+ category at the Junior World Championships. The Miami International Regatta is held every year on March 21. In 2011, it was the event's thirty-eighth edition.

PROMINENT CUBAN SPORTSCASTERS AND SPORTSWRITERS

Cuba enjoyed the talents of many excellent sportswriters in the days of the Republic. They included people like Eladio Secades, Jess Lozada, Pedro Galiana, Manolo de la Reguera, Fausto Lavilla, René Cubas, Fausto Miranda, and many more who were able to ply their trade in freedom after becoming exiles.

Secades "achieved with his articles (*Estampas de la Época* [*Scenes of an Era*]) the Justo de Lara Award, a cherished journalistic award in the profession."[3]

Broadcast journalism also had excellent sportscasters and commentators, including René Cañizares, Felo Ramírez (Cooperstown Hall of Famer), Orlando Sánchez Diago, Jess Lozada (who came from CMQ TV in Cuba), Pedro Galiana, Cuco Conde, René Molina, and many more. Worthy of note in Miami are Cuban-American Will Manso, sports director at WPLG, and Raúl Striker, whose mother is Cuban and who is currently narrating the Marlins games on television as well becoming the Spanish voice of the Miami Dolphins on radio station WQBA.

Many Cuban sports reporters emigrated to the United States and to other countries in Latin America during the 1960s and were able to start anew.

Fausto Miranda was a columnist for *El Nuevo Herald* in Miami and analyst at radio station WQBA for many years. Felo Ramírez and Manuel Alvarez were the first broadcasters of the Florida Marlins when the team was founded in 1993. For several years, Jess Losada was an analyst for Miami's Channel 23 while René Molina settled in Puerto Rico and Luis Pérez López joined Miranda as a sports columnist for the *El Nuevo Herald* in Miami.

Others joined the profession while in exile. The late Sarvelio del Valle, a former amateur boxer and sports analyst on *Radio Mambí* in Miami, was recently replaced upon his death by Jerry del Castillo. Héctor Salazar worked for Channel 23, Emilio Cabrera on Miami radio station "*La Fabulosa*," and Minito Navarro—former mayor of the Cuban town of San José de las Lajas who worked with former boxing champion Roberto Durán—became a well-known sports broadcaster for radio station WRHC in Miami.

Others arrived in exile as children or were born in the United States and made their careers in this country. René Giraldo is a sports reporter for television's Channel 23, Channel 51, the Telemundo Network, and he is a sportscaster for the Miami Dolphins and the University of Miami; Jess Losada, Jr., worked as a sports analyst for both Univisión and Telemundo networks and broadcasts American football games; Dan

LeBatard is a sportswriter for the *Miami Herald*, a radio host, and a television reporter. LeBatard began his career with the *Herald* in 1990 and also works as a radio sportscaster for AM-790 (The Ticket, in Miami) and nationally for the ESPN Sports Network; Leo Suárez was a sportswriter for the *Miami News* and later the sports editor of the *Miami Herald*; Armando Salguero started his career in sports journalism in 1982 and since 1990 has been a sports columnist for the *Miami Herald*, covering the Miami Dolphins; Marino Martínez, a sportswriter for the *El Nuevo Herald;* and Roly Martín has been a sports commentator for radio stations WQBA, WCMQ and WSUA Radio Caracol. He also worked for Channels 23, 51, and now for América TV, Channel 41 in Miami. In addition, Martín is an analyst and sportscaster of American football games for the Miami Dolphins and the University of Miami.

There are also several Cuban sportswriters, sportscasters, and commentators who worked for Cuba's government-controlled press but left their country in search of, among other things, the freedom of the press they were never able to enjoy at home. Among them are Luis Yiky Quintana, who works at América TV in Miami and is the Spanish voice of the Florida Marlins, together with Felo Ramírez; Angel "Tito" Rodríguez, a former broadcaster for the Marlins; Armando Fernández Lima, sports reporter for radio station WQBA in Miami; Omar Claro, who works at Mega TV in Miami and TV Martí (broadcasts to Cuba); José Luis Nápoles; sports analyst for Channel 23; Edemio Nava, sports analyst for Radio Martí; and Jorge Ebro and Bobby Salamanca, Jr., sportswriters for Miami's *El Nuevo Herald*.

A FANTASTIC SPORTS HISTORY

When the experts review the sports record books, one thing becomes very clear. Cuba, an island of just over six million inhabitants in 1958 and a present population of eleven million, has been a veritable factory of champions—from the days of Fonst, Dihigo, and Capablanca to the stars of the twenty-first century such as Gamboa, Rigondeaux, and Morales. Cubans, having excelled at the highest levels, are recognized as giants in worldwide sports, and Cubans have had to continually leave Cuba to practice their sports in order to be individuals and not cogs in Castro's propaganda sports machine.

NOTES

1. Angel Torres, *La Leyenda del Béisbol Cubano* (Miami: Review Printers, 1996).
2. Roberto González Echevarría, *The Pride of Havana, A History of Cuban Baseball* (New York: Oxford University Press, 1999).
3. Bernardo Jiménez Perdomo and Willy del Pino, *Enciclopedia del Boxeo Cuban* (Miami: Continental Printing Co. Inc., 1988).

28

RELIGION

BY MARCOS ANTONIO RAMOS

Since events and trends don't happen in a vacuum it would be necessary to turn to a great reality that, among many others, is linked to the Cuban exile. One can logically resort to political and economic factors to explain what prompted the massive exodus of hundreds of thousands of Cubans to the United States, as well as of significant numbers of Cubans to other parts of the world. The religious climate in Cuba after the triumph of Fidel Castro's revolution on January 1, 1959, also has important links to the experience of the Cuban exile and to the history of contemporary Cuba.

The Republic of Cuba was born in 1902 through a special relationship with the United States that lasted until 1934 (the famous Platt Amendment). One of its features was an absolute freedom of religion together with a reasonable—but never overstated—separation of church and state. When Cuba began its life as an independent nation, the traditional Catholic Church, as well as several Protestant denominations, had already been established. Among the latter were the Episcopal, Baptist, Methodist, Presbyterian, Disciples of Christ, and Congregationalist churches. Already in 1917, these last two denominations joined the Presbyterian Church; but this decision, taken by their boards of directors in the United States, was an event unique to Cuba and, to be sure, an interesting project of integration. Shortly after 1902, the Pentecostal and the Seventh-Day Adventist churches were established in Cuba. And from times immemorial, there began to spread an Afro-Cuban religion that combined elements of African faiths with the Catholicism brought from Spain. This happened at about the same time that the last traces of the country's original religious beliefs—based on the indigenous gods Atabex and Mabuya—were disappearing.

Religious pluralism had increased by the dawn of the 1950s. There was a significant Catholic majority—between 72 and 80 percent, based on several different studies. However, regular attendance at religious services was rather low. In fact, church attendance was especially low in the interior of the country, particularly in rural areas. This was largely due to the shortage of priests, which began in the nineteenth century. But Catholicism was renewing itself beginning in the 1930s. Hundreds of Catholic schools had contributed through Catholic teachings to give religious education and upbringing to a small but significant number of Cubans.

The number of Protestants reached at most 6 percent. However, most of them were not only regular churchgoers but also contributed generously to their churches. This was despite the fact that the bulk of the Protestant community came from lower economic classes, especially the lower middle class, with a growing number of professionals in some cities due to a network of more than one hundred Protestant parochial schools, also attended by persons from other religious denominations.

The religious Afro-Cuban syncretism or symbiosis attracted a large number of people. But these generally preferred to publicly identify themselves differently because of conventional social customs, a situation that changed after 1959. Other minority denominations, such as Jehovah's Witnesses and the Spiritualists, were also active in the country. The Jehovah's Witnesses grew considerably, especially in small villages and rural areas, while the Spiritualists were active throughout the entire country—in small numbers, but with a clear presence in cities such as Manzanillo and others.

Looking at religion through a sociological prism, an academic subject that became acceptable at the higher education level in large parts of the twentieth-century world, it can be affirmed that the percentage of practicing Catholics grew among the upper classes while non-Catholic Christian religions were more common in the small towns and in the countryside.

At the time of the March 1952 coup d'état, there followed an interesting development in that a number of people identified with religious groups and denominations had a more visible and more active role in political activities. Until that time, both Catholics and Protestants had been part of political parties, but in the 1950s a large number of persons with strong religious beliefs—coming from organizations such as the *Acción Católica* (Catholic Action) and the Protestant-based *Concilio de Iglesias Evangélicas* (Council of Evangelical Churches)—became involved in activities considered as subversive by the new regime headed by Gen. Fulgencio Batista. This development is not in contradiction to the reality that other religious Cubans were active both in official (pro-government) groups and in nonviolent opposition groups.

The opposition by many to the Batista regime was not related in any way to religious persecution, discrimination or restrictions. In fact, complete freedom of religion was in effect throughout all of Cuba. But many young Catholics figured prominently in the struggle against the Batista government, among them José Antonio Echeverría, president of the *Federación Estudiantil Universitaria* or FEU (University Students Federation), which played a key role in the attack on the presidential palace in March 1957. Several young evangelical Christians, among them most notably Frank País, also figured prominently in the struggle. País was the son of a Baptist minister and leader of the *Movimiento 26 de Julio* (26th of July Movement) in the eastern Cuban province of Oriente. País was also a Baptist Church teacher. Some consider that after Fidel Castro, País was the most important leader of the 26th of July Movement. Echeverría and País were leaders not under the control of Castro. As did many others, these two historical figures died during the struggle against Batista.

In 1958, the Catholic Church hierarchy voiced its opposition to the government and called for the establishment of a national unity cabinet as the first step prior to a political transition toward a solution of the civil war that began in late 1956 with Castro's landing near the Sierra Maestra in Oriente Province. The starting point of that civil war was the July 1953 attack on the Moncada Barracks in Santiago de Cuba. Several influential members of the religious community were among the signers of the declaration of the *Conjunto de Instituciones Cívicas de Cuba* (United Cuban Civic Institutions), which called for an end to the Batista government. This group included a large part of Cuba's civil society and the country's main institutions. The *Acción Católica Cubana* as well as the Protestant-based *Concilio Cubano de Iglesias Evangélicas* signed the document and the person who acted as secretary of the *Conjunto de Instituciones Cívicas de Cuba*, the Rev. Raúl Fernández Ceballos, was also the executive secretary of the Protestant *Concilio*. The Rev. Fernández Ceballos was linked by close bonds to fellow Protestant Faustino Pérez, leader of the urban-based underground resistance movement of the 26th of July.

But the rise to power of the Fidel Castro government after the ouster of Batista on January 1, 1959, did not—either in the medium or long terms—represent a situation of normality for the country's churches and other religions. The first months of Castro's government saw the elation of a people who overwhelmingly supported the new regime. From all the speeches and promises it was not easy to sort out the details of what would complicate the relations between state and church, and the space religion would occupy under the new system. Among other reasons, there was the fact that a number of practicing Catholics were initially appointed as cabinet members or as vice ministers (deputy secretaries), while others joined high-level positions in government departments or agencies.

During the 1959-1960 period, three Cuban Protestants held the positions of government ministers. At least one Catholic priest and one

Baptist minister were chaplains of the Rebel Army with the official rank of officers. However, some tensions surfaced in 1959 and in November of that year the Catholic Church held a national assembly in Havana attended by an estimated hundreds of thousands. At that assembly, many voiced their rejection of what was seen as the government edging toward the Soviet Union and the international Communist movement. Several months later, in February 1960, the visit to Cuba of Anastas Mikoyan, vice president of the Council of Ministers of the Soviet Union, convinced the people that a change toward a new system was underway. It also convinced the country's established churches of the coming confrontation between religion and the Communist ideology, which the Castro government was imposing as the country's official ideology.

Lay leaders and some Catholic priests joined the resistance against the new regime. Some well-known Protestants joined in those activities, but initially most of the participants were leaders of *Acción Católica* and other practicing Catholics because the Castro government's first target was the religion of the majority of Cubans—Catholicism. Almost immediately after the failed April 1961 invasion of Playa Girón by the Brigade 2506, the government took much more radical measures, especially expropriations—officially called "nationalization"—of private schools. These included hundreds of Catholic schools and more than one hundred Protestant schools as well as others belonging to different religious denominations, including the Jewish community. But even before these dramatic measures were taken there had already been problems in some individual cases. Now, however, the situation was reaching massive proportions. It went so far that on September 8, 1961, there were clashes between the forces of repression and people who were taking part in religious marches to celebrate the *Virgen de la Caridad del Cobre* (Virgin of the Caridad del Cobre). The largest of these confrontations took place in the capital city. Several days later, more than three hundred priests and religious persons were forced to leave the country aboard the ship *Covadonga*, which sailed for Spain. Among those deported from Cuba were the auxiliary bishop of Havana, Eduardo Boza Masvidal, the dean of the Catholic University Santo Tomás de Villanueva, and the future auxiliary bishop of Miami, Agustín A. Román.

The Catholic Church, faced with a declining number of priests and religious persons, met with great difficulties in taking care of its parishes. Government pressures against people of faith resulted in a reduction in the number of persons who openly attended religious services. Those pressures included limits on employment and study opportunity given the obvious differences with official policies, especially the teachings of Marxist-Leninism, and historical and dialectical materialism. Because of those pressures, a large number of persons of faith decided to leave the country in search of a better climate for the practice of religion for the family, especially the young ones. The latter were now subjected to a system of education totally controlled by the Communist state that Cuba had become, ever since it was officially announced as such when Fidel Castro proclaimed its Marxist-Leninist ideology in a December 1961 speech.

By 1962, these restrictions were also apparent to other religious communities. An exodus of hundreds of foreign missionaries had begun in 1960; most of these were from the United States who had gone to live in Cuba and were sponsored by Protestant denominations. Hundreds of them left Cuba beginning in January 1961 when the United States broke diplomatic relations with Cuba. That same year, all religious radio and television broadcasts were ended. Beginning in 1962, restrictions were imposed on the activities of churches, including the closing of several Protestant chapels in rural areas and a ban on religious services in public places, restricting the ceremonies to the interior of churches and chapels. At that time, the only Christian schools allowed to operate were theological seminaries. The government prohibited the importation of religious materials, except for very special cases. One significant event was the destruction of thousands of bibles sent to Cuba by the *Sociedades Bíblicas Unidas* (United Biblical Societies) for use in Protestant churches.

Attendance at religious services declined considerably. In fact, by 1965 only 80,000 persons went to Catholic mass on Sundays while the total for all the other churches was about 100,000—at most. That same year, 54 Baptist ministers were jailed on charges of, among other things, *diversionismo ideológico* (roughly translated as "ideological deviation") and of having links with the CIA (the U.S. Central Intelligence Agency). Almost everyone was sentenced to jail terms ranging from two to 30 years. Among them was one of the few American missionaries who had stayed in Cuba, including Dr. Herbert Caudill, the superintendent of all Baptist churches in the western region of the country.

The *Unidades Militares de Ayuda a la Producción* (Military Units to Aid Production—or UMAP, for its Spanish initials) were active during the same decade of the 1960s. Tens of thousands of young people were sent to these types of concentration camps. A large number of practicing Catholics and Protestants were among those drafted for the camps. Catholic and Protestant seminarians were sent to perform forced labor with these units. In addition to Catholics and Baptists from the traditional churches, others sent to UMAP camps for agricultural labor included thousands of Jehovah's Witnesses, members of the Seventh-Day Adventist Church, Pentecostals and members of the *Bando Gedeón* (an evangelical group organized in Cuba in the 1920s by an American missionary). The Jehovah's Witnesses showed a great strength of resistance to the government's policies and refused to cooperate with all kinds of activities advocated by the regime. But neither the official pressures nor the persistent repression in any way stopped the growth of this religious movement. This is an interesting development that merits its own special history. No one should be surprised at the vast number of religious persons who left Cuba during the 1960s. Many of them felt threatened because of their religious beliefs or they were—literally—discriminated against by a Cuban society that the regime was attempting to change completely as part of a process that, like other similar experiments, was called "the creation of socialism."

It must be noted that Afro-Cuban religious fervor has grown considerably in Cuba as far as supporters and activists are concerned. The regime has attempted to leave the impression that Afro-Cuban religions enjoy a large degree of freedom and some have even compared this situation to that of other religious groups. However, that has just been a smoke screen to reflect an image—not necessarily a truthful one—of racial integration in Cuba. In many cases, this has served in some activities to attract foreign visitors. This type of religion does not have the kind of institutional or structural organization associated with the more established and traditional churches, Catholic or Protestant, and thus did not necessarily represent the same kind of threat to the regime. However, it's necessary to point out the strength of the Afro-Cuban religious experience in trying to maintain its identity, traditions, and beliefs.

The roots of the religious influence on the contemporary Cuban exile (1959-2009) are directly linked to the religious experience in Cuba and the United States. If we look at the United States, we see a fundamental fact and that is the proven ability of the American nation to absorb and make the best of all kinds of immigrations. In the specific case of religion, the United States has assimilated an almost endless variety of religions from the outside. These diverse types of religions range from the Pilgrims' Calvinism to the Anglicanism of the colonial era born under the direct patronage of the British Crown in places like Virginia, Georgia, and many other regions. And this religious diversity during the colonial era came in many forms of religious cults—from the English Baptists and Quakers to the Scotch-Irish Presbyterianism to German Lutheranism, and so forth.

A fundamental aspect in the development of religion among immigrants was the Roman Catholicism of some—not that many, to be sure—of the first settlers of Maryland, followed by a never-ending Catholic immigration after the U.S. achieved its independence, especially during the nineteenth century with the massive immigration of Irish, Italians, Poles, and Germans from the southern regions of that country.

This trend continues today, especially with the arrival of Hispanics in the United States.

Among the different features of the United States' religious experience there is a tradition one might describe as "ethnic religiousness," using the old name referring to those who were neither Anglo-Saxon Protestants nor African-American or "Native Americans" (the descendants of the country's indigenous population). In some circles, Hispanics were not classified as "ethnic," simply as Hispanics, Latinos, and so on. The people considered as white have over time been identified as "Anglos" and, curiously enough, include such diverse groups as Anglo-Saxons, Irish Celts, Germans, Dutch, Italians, Slavs, and even Jews. Even so, it is important that we be able to distinguish some details that can help us understand how a particular group of people can exert influence over a religious community. Traditionally, there has been an Irish influence in the Catholic hierarchy of the United States and Catholics have, by and large, been classified as "Ethnics" or "Hispanics," even though there are millions of Anglo-Saxons who consider themselves Catholic.

Among Protestants, there are cultural differences between whites and persons of color. Anglo-Saxons are the largest group of whites within the Protestant community, followed by Germans and Scandinavians. However, at this time very many "Ethnics" attend Protestant churches. Persons of color are not only those considered African-Americans, but also Haitians and other persons from the English-speaking Caribbean. But the differences based on national origins have been diluted in an unusual and visible manner. Many Lutheran churches founded by Germans or Scandinavians now have Anglo-Saxon pastors and leaders. Among the white Southern Protestants—especially in Virginia and the states of the so-called "Deep South"—there are many descendants of the Scotch-Irish, so called because they came from Northern Ireland. By now, as in many other instances, an Anglo mentality has taken over, one that goes beyond any differences based on national origins. This can be applied in one form or another to all the other religious communities.

The Cuban exile community has not merged, so to speak, with the larger Hispanic community, even though it is a part of that community. This is especially the case in certain cities and communities where the Cubans are not a clear majority among the Hispanics. But even so, the Cuban community has preserved its own characteristics, which are easily apparent in the religious lifestyle. Thus, it would be a mistake to assume that the Cubans as a group have been totally integrated within parishes, churches, synagogues and other types of religious congregations. Many younger Cuban-Americans have lived through such experiences for a variety of reasons—social and cultural preferences, marriage to persons from other ethnic groups, residents of places where the Cuban presence is less visible or evident. However, whether due to larger or lesser influence, the Cuban presence can be easily recognized.

Despite the differences between the various studies that have been published on this issue, it can be stated with certainty that at least 70 percent (maybe a bit higher) of Cuban exiles identified themselves as Roman Catholics. But it is more difficult to determine the number or percentage of Protestants or Evangelicals because of the division between many faiths or denominations, including those independent churches that have a substantial membership of Cuban parishioners. A number of statistics have been suggested ranging from a low of 10 percent to as high as 22 percent; this latter percentage represents "preference" rather than formal "affiliation." Marcos Antonio Ramos, a PhD in theology, does not accept any precise percentage, but he believes that it could be that between 10 and 15 percent of Cubans are dedicated Protestants, and that many others have expressed a preference for the Protestant or the conservative Evangelical movement. An estimated 2 percent include Jehovah's Witnesses (who already had a significant presence inside Cuba), Mormons (who did not have much of a presence in Cuba before 1959, but who are present among Cuban exiles), and other Christian groups who do not profess a Trinity theology (as do Catholics, Protestants, and Orthodox Christians). The Cuban Jewish community probably represents comparable statistics. However, the Afro-Cuban religious syncretism continues to defy precise statistics because its followers and supporters don't always clearly identify themselves, but nobody can question their numerical and social importance. There are millions of them in Cuba and tens of thousands—maybe even more—in the exile community.

To properly analyze the influence of religion on the Cuban exile community one must travel the roads of the exiles' geography. Miami is logically the starting point, but the journey soon would take the exiles to other parts of the South Florida county once known as Dade (now Miami-Dade). And then to other regions of the United States such as New York, New Jersey, California, Texas, Puerto Rico, and many others of the fifty states. While this was happening in the United States, Cubans also settled down in other nations such as Mexico and Spain. Eventually, Cubans went to many parts of the world because of the situation in Cuba itself.

The majority religions in the Miami of 1959 were the traditional Protestant churches: Baptists, Methodists, Presbyterians, Episcopalians, Lutherans, Congregationalists, and so on. They were always considered one large group of denominations. Judaism was especially influential in Miami Beach. Meanwhile, Catholicism was becoming stronger and the city of Miami was elevated to the category of diocese in 1958. The arrival of Cubans increased the Catholic presence, which grew even considerably more with the arrival of other Hispanic (Latin American) nationalities.

A Hispanic community made up of Cubans and non-Cubans already existed in 1959, but that year marked the beginning of an uninterrupted and sustained Hispanic growth. The religious makeup would change along with the new demographic changes. Soon, more and more Spanish-language signs appeared announcing *Misa en español* and *Servicios en español* (Mass in Spanish and [Religious] Service in Spanish). The Southern Baptists owned buildings all over the cities and soon other signs appeared on them announcing the presence of a *Departamento Hispano* (Hispanic Section). In fact, the word *hispano* (Hispanic) began to appear on other buildings—not always necessarily churches or temples—announcing a *Centro Hispano* (Hispanic Center). These were places where exiles were offered help by and at Catholic, Baptist, Methodist, Episcopal, Reformed Christians (Dutch Calvinists from Michigan), Lutheran, Assembly of God, and Church of God churches.

As soon as the *Centro de Refugiados Cubanos* (Cuban Refugee Center), located near downtown Miami, began its operations, the religious aid agencies became very popular. Among them were the National Catholic Welfare Conference, the Church World Service (Protestant) and the Hebrew Immigrant Aid Society (Jewish). These were later joined by the aid agency World Relief, affiliated with the Church World Service; however, it dealt mainly with the more conservative churches. The task of resettling Cuban exiles to other cities and states was mainly carried out by these agencies. Catholic parishes, Protestant congregations, Jewish synagogues, and the relatives of some of these denominations were in charge of taking care of most of those Cubans searching for greener pastures, as it were, in other regions of the United States.

The biggest impact on Catholicism was the Cuban influence. The Miami Diocese became an archdiocese over time. Bishop Coleman Carroll was an important presence in the community and among the Hispanics he delegated many tasks to Monsignor Bryan Walsh. Walsh, in fact, was in charge of the program known as Pedro Pan that brought to the United States more than 14,000 young Cubans whose parents did not leave Cuba early on, although many did so later. With the passage of time, a large number of Pedro Pan boys and girls rose to become prominent members of the nation's business and professional communities—they are, indeed, the members of an endless list. Others became well-known political figures, among them former Sen. Mel Martínez (R-Fla.), who was also national chairman of the Republican Party and Secretary of Housing and Urban Development (HUD) during the administration of former President George W. Bush. And yet others were active in religious affairs as is the case of the Rev. Luis León, who became the minister of St. John's Episcopal Church in Washington, D.C. Known as "The Church of the Presidents," this church is located just a block north of the White House. The Rev. León was in charge of the religious service component of the second Bush inauguration in 2004.

Cuban exiles have risen to important positions within the Roman Catholic Church, but none has been named to become a diocesan bishop or archbishop in the Diocese (now Archdiocese) of Miami. Monsignors Agustín Alcido Román, Gilberto Fernández, and Felipe de Jesús Estévez all have been named, at one time or another, as auxiliary bishops of Miami. Other Cubans have served in other ecclesiastic jurisdictions in the United States as auxiliary bishops or diocesan bishops, among them Jesuit Monsignor Enrique San Pedro. In 2009, Havana-born Father Fernando Isern was named bishop of the diocese of Puebla in Colorado. And of special importance are the works of Cuban priests and prelates in the northeastern and southwestern regions of the United States. Cuban-American theologians and professors of religious studies are now to be found in many universities and seminaries across the United States. Some have become famous, such as Roberto Goizueta, Jr., Fernando Segovia, Ada María Isasi Díaz, Justo L. González, Sixto García, and many more.

Roman Catholic theologian Miguel H. Díaz, born in Cuba and raised in Miami, was named by President Barack Obama as the United States ambassador to the Holy See (the Vatican).

The impact of the Cuban presence became evident in the Archdiocese of Miami in 1985 when the then-Archbishop Edward McCarthy stated that 50 percent of Miami was Catholic and the area covered by the archdiocese was at least 30 percent Catholic. In 1958, there were 185,000 Catholics—served by sixty-five diocesan priests and twenty-one religious orders—in the sixteen counties that make up South Florida. There were a total of fifty-one parishes in that region. At that time there were two dioceses in the entire state of Florida—one in St. Augustine in the north and the other in Miami in the south. In 1968, Florida became an ecclesiastical province and Miami a metropolitan area.

By 1990, the Catholic population in the Archdiocese of Miami—which included the counties of Miami-Dade, Broward, and Monroe—had grown to 1.1 million parishioners. Most of them, about 800,000, lived in Miami-Dade and 52 percent of them were Cubans or the children of Cubans. In 1990, there were in the Archdiocese of Miami a total of 105 parishes, three missions, two Marian sanctuaries, 437 priests, 47 deacons, 432 nuns, and 61 religious men. In 2008, the archdiocese included 1.3 million Catholics, 118 parishes and missions, 428 priests, 300 nuns, and 50 religious men.

In addition there were sixty elementary schools, thirteen secondary or high schools, two universities, and two theological seminaries. Those, plus a very extensive network of social and charity services, one hospital, and a number of other programs made the Archdiocese of Miami the most influential religious organization in South Florida. A high percentage of priests, deacons, nuns, and religious persons in the parishes and sanctuaries (such as the *Ermita de la Caridad del Cobre* [the Shrine of the Virgin of the Caridad del Cobre] in Miami) were Cuban-born Cubans or the sons and daughters of Cubans. The shrine was built with financial contributions, many of them from some of the poorest parishioners who parted with the few cents they had. It has been declared a National Church Sanctuary in the United States.

The number of parishioners has grown by 2008 while the percentage of Cubans had shrunk due to the arrival of other Hispanics (Latin Americans), most of them also Catholics. Nevertheless, Cubans are still the group with the largest number of Catholics in South Florida. It's most likely that one in five Catholic Cuban-Americans regularly practices his or her religion through regular church attendance. Be that as it may, it is higher than the average church attendance inside Cuba. This is largely due to the pastoral work in the region, but also because contributions by the parochial and religious schools that attract a large percentage of the children of middle class and upper class families. It's also a reflection of the social classes due to the high percentage of Cubans from the middle and upper classes who arrived in the United States during the 1960s and 1970s.

Catholic Cubans in the island and in South Florida lived a few short days of religious fervor when in January of 1998 Pope John Paul II visited Cuba and was received by enormous crowds anywhere he went to celebrate masses. For a few days people held out hope that the Pope could soften the grip that the Cuban government has on its people. "May Cuba open to the world, and may the world open to Cuba," Pope John Paul told Cubans and a worldwide television audience. Cuban President Castro, who had attended a Jesuit high school, sat through one of the Pope's masses and at the end he even gave a friendly pat on the back to the Pontiff.

But outside the joy of the three days the Pope was in Cuba, little changed. For a brief period of time Cubans were given more leeway to attend church and the United States increased the number of licenses it granted to church related organizations to send food and medicines to the island. But as months turned to years, little changed in Cuba or in Cuba-U.S. relations.

The second group among the institutional religions practiced by Cubans was comprised by the Protestant churches. They were considered as one group, but many of them were also identified as Evangelical churches, especially those with a more conservative theology. The arrival in the United States of a substantial number of Protestants during the exodus of 1961-62—and in particular also those aboard the "Freedom Flights" that started in 1965—strengthened the Hispanic presence at churches in several Miami-Dade neighborhoods.

Two groups were particularly favored during the first years. The Baptists as well as the Methodists, especially the former, had a larger number of churches in the neighborhoods settled by Cubans and the Anglos allowed for religious services the use of chapels inside the main church buildings or in nearby structures. As time went by, many of these Anglo churches and temples were turned over to Hispanics, most of them Cubans. The Baptists have the largest number of places of worship among the Hispanics in Miami. But with the arrival of the 1980s, and especially during the 1990s, there was a growing influence of independent churches. Some of these were regarded as mega churches established by congregations leaning toward the Charismatic movement or the more conservative branch of the Evangelicals. It's difficult to estimate the number of Cubans who belong to these churches since Central Americans and other immigrants from Latin America have also joined these churches, sometimes in larger number, thus becoming the majorities.

Several hundred Hispanic Protestant congregations are active in Miami-Dade, most of them led by Cuban-Americans and a growing number of Central Americans. This trend is taking place, up to a certain point, in the one state with the very large number of these types of churches and where the Cuban-Americans—even though they are not a majority in the state—make up the largest number of Spanish-speaking ministers. Among them were the Rev. Martin Añorga, a Presbyterian, and the Rev. Max Salvador, an Episcopal.

In 1989, the largest Protestant church, the Southern Baptists, chose Marcos Antonio Ramos as its moderator (or president). Ramos had also been the academic dean of the Florida Center for Theological Studies, a learning institution that in 1994 elected an Irish-American as the first Catholic priest—anywhere—who served as the president of a Protestant theological seminary. And the current bishop of the Episcopal Church in southeastern Florida, based in Miami, is another Cuban-American, the Right Reverend Leopoldo Frade, the highest-ranking Anglican official in that region. Across the United States, several Cubans have held ecclesiastical positions such as auxiliary bishop in Anglican dioceses, moderators (or presidents) in officially authorized Baptist organizations, elders in the Presbyterian Church and superintendents in Methodist districts. Among the nation's scholarly religious personalities are Cubans well known in the religious community, including Dr. Justo González, former professor of the Candler School of Theology of Atlanta's Emory University in Georgia, and many others. Cuban-American ministers and pastors conduct religious services in Protestant churches in most U.S. states.

At the international level, Cuban exiles have also been considerably influential. Monsignor Eduardo Boza Masvidal, the former auxiliary bishop of Havana and rector of Havana's University of Villanueva, was a bishop in Venezuela. A number of Cuban Catholic priests have been parish priests and missionaries in many Latin American and Caribbean nations and regions, including Costa Rica, Honduras, Puerto Rico, and the Dominican Republic. The Episcopal (or Anglican) Church has particularly felt the influence of Cuban Episcopal clergymen who have been bishops with a nation-wide jurisdiction in the following countries: Honduras, Guatemala, Venezuela, and Uruguay. Cuban Protestant missionaries have worked in Europe, Latin America, and Africa. Two of them have been rectors of important Protestant seminaries with international student bodies in Guatemala and Costa Rica. Cuban-Americans have also held important positions in Protestant publishing houses in the United States and Latin America.

The religious influence is not limited to Catholics and Protestants. The presence among Cubans of a large number of Jehovah's Witnesses has been felt in South Florida and other regions since about 1960. The Witnesses as well as the Seventh-Day Adventists arrived by the thousands during the Mariel Exodus of 1980. Many Cubans have held important positions in both religious denominations. And the Cuban-Americans affiliated with the Mormon Church have also began to make their religious presence felt somewhat.

The Cuban-American Jewish community has become a very influential sector in South Florida, especially as it regards community, professional, and economic issues. There is little doubt that Jewish Cuban-Americans have held top-level positions in Miami-Dade. A substantial number of Cuban-Americans belong to several synagogues in this region.

According to Ruth Behar—anthropologist and author of *An Island Come Home: Returning to Cuba* published by Rutgers University Press, about 16,500 Jews lived in Cuba before the revolution—most left Cuba to settle in South Florida. Only 1,000 to 1,500 remained in the island.

The exiles and other Cuban immigrants—and their children—have become an especially important factor in the spread of religious syncretism. Such is the case with *Santería* and other Afro-Cuban and Afro-Caribbean cults whose influence has also been noted in other regions such as Puerto Rico and within Hispanics communities in the United States. Notable books about Afro-Cuban religiousness have been written by Cuban-Americans like Dr. Mercedes Cros Sandoval (herself a member of the Episcopal Church) and the Catholic priest Juan Sosa. Dr. Cros Sandoval is regarded as one of the outstanding specialists in this area, along with other Cubans who are either deceased or live in Cuba, such as Fernando Ortiz, Lydia Cabrera, and Professor Natalia Bolívar.

Even though Cubans and Cuban-Americans are not a nationality or ethnic group as notably active in religious issues as other Hispanic-Americans, the influence of the Cuban exile community is considered as substantial by the Spanish-speaking religious leadership in the United States. Just to think of the hundreds who have been educated and continue to be educated at Catholic and Protestant theological seminaries and college-level divinity schools in the United States and Europe is evidence that the influence endures.

MEDIA AND ADVERTISING

29

PRINT MEDIA

BY ARMANDO GONZALEZ

Cuba had a long and distinguished newspaper tradition dating back to the end of the eighteenth century. During the nineteenth century, in the final decades of Spain's domination of the island, *Diario de la Marina, El Comercio, La Lucha, La Discusión,* and *El Nuevo País* constituted the foundation of the Cuban press.

These newspapers continued publication after May 20, 1902, when the new Republic of Cuba was officially established and they were joined by newly founded *El Mundo, Patria,* and *La República Cubana*. During the four-year period in which the United States governed Cuba, 1898-1902, the *Havana Post* was founded (1900). It was the first newspaper published in English in Cuba and operated until shortly after the Cuban revolution took over the island's government. There were also two newspapers in the Chinese language in 1913 and 1921.[1]

It was *Diario de la Marina,* founded in 1832, that became the main journalistic force by the last quarter of the nineteenth century. Under the direction of Nicolás Rivero, the newspaper survived and thrived during the most difficult period at the end of the century when Spaniards wanted to hold on to Cuba, one of their last two colonies in the Western Hemisphere.

In the new Republic, the press continued to grow. *El Mundo* was founded by José Manuel Govín in 1901, and later it was sold to a group headed by entrepreneur Amadeo Barletta that included a young attorney, Luis J. Botifoll. Botifoll would, years later, play a distinguished civic role in exile.

Información was founded in 1937 by Santiago Claret and, along with *Diario de la Marina*, *El Mundo*, and *Excelsior*, were the leading morning papers. *El País* was the sister paper of *Excelsior* and was the leading evening paper. Both were owned by Alfredo Hornedo and Cristóbal Díaz. *Mañana* was founded and directed by José López Vilaboy in 1939.

El País was joined in the evening by *Avance* (1934) and *Prensa Libre* (1941). And then there were afternoon papers sold by street vendors or *voceadores*: *Alerta*, founded in 1936; *El Crisol* in 1934, owned by Alfredo Izaguirre Hornedo and Julio César González Rebull; and *Ataja*, founded in 1951 and converted to daily in 1952 by editor Alberto Salas Amaro.

In 1938, Carlos Robreño founded *Zig-Zag*, a tabloid devoted to political satire. Years later, José M. Roseñada and Castor Vispo took over the paper. However, by 1959, *Zig-Zag* had gone into exile in Miami.

Noticias de Hoy, founded in 1938, was the organ of the Partido Socialista Popular (Communist) and was the Cuban voice of international Communism under editor Anibal Escalante. *Tiempo en Cuba*, a daily since 1950, was controlled by Rolando Masferrer, a man with a long and controversial history as an international revolutionary who became part of the Batista regime in the 1950s.

There were also a large number of newspapers in the provinces that reached the local markets. In 1902, *El Camagueyano*, in the city of Camaguey, and *El Comercio*, in Cienfuegos, began circulating. Other such newspapers were:

- *El Fénix* in Sancti Spíritus (1904)
- *El Pueblo* in Ciego de Avila (1905)
- *El Sol* in Marianao (1908)
- *El Diario de Cuba* in Santiago de Cuba (1917)
- *Oriente* in Santiago (1924)

- *El Criterio Libre* in Morón (1932)
- *El Villareño* in Santa Clara (1938)
- *Adelante* and *El Imparcial* in Matanzas (1938).

On January 1, 1959, a new era in Cuban history began when Fidel Castro took over the reins of the country. At the time of Castro's takeover, there were 58 newspapers circulating in the country with a combined circulation of 796,000 copies. Given Cuba's population at the time, newspaper circulation was 129 copies per 1,000 population, thus placing Cuba as the No. 3 country in newspaper readership in Latin America, behind Uruguay and Argentina with 180 copies per 1,000 population.[2]

Many of these papers had a distinguished history of opposition to the Batista regime. They suffered the persecution of reporters, economic pressures, and general harassment, but they kept their opposition until the regime came to an end on January 1, 1959. Then a new nightmare began. One of Castro's early steps was the confiscation of every newspaper in the country. It began on January 23, 1960, with *Avance*, followed by the creation of a new government-controlled news agency, Prensa Latina, that was forced upon every newspaper in the country. More confiscations followed in 1960: *El Mundo* on February 23, *Excelsior* and *El País* on February 24, *Diario de la Marina* on May 11, and later *Información* and *Prensa Libre* on December 23.[3]

One of the early government actions was known as *la coletilla*. This was the first form of coercion that the new dictatorship used against journalists who did not follow the government's line. This dreaded practice lasted about two years, 1959 and 1960. The journalists or columnists expressed his/her opinions and, immediately, the government's monitors would attach a version saying the workers of the newspaper disagreed with the articles' contents. As soon as all press was confiscated, the *coletillas* disappeared.

While they lasted, the *coletilla* read: "This article has been published out of respect for press freedom. However, the workers of this newspaper warn that this information neither follows the truth nor complies, even at minimum, with the most elementary journalism standards."[4]

Following the tumultuous early years of exile and the disaster of the Bay of Pigs action, Cuban exiles started looking seriously at a future outside their country. Greater Miami, with the largest exile population, started to flourish as the exile enclave. It was the obvious choice to restart a truncated newspaper experience.

The market already had a six-day-a-week evening newspaper, *Diario Las Américas,* founded in July 4, 1953, by Dr. Horacio Aguirre, a Nicaraguan exile. Dr. Aguirre and his staff correctly identified the market. From the start of the exile period, Dr. Aguirre sensed the needs and wants of this large mass of exiles, and—under his enlightened guidance—*Diario* reflected the feelings of the new community and became the journalistic reference for Cuban exiles. Over the years, *Diario* became the home of a number of Cuban exile journalists: Ariel Remos, for example, established himself as one of the most respected voices in exile journalism. *Diario* quickly picked daily and weekly columns by some of Cuba's most respected journalists, including José Ignacio Rivero, Humberto Medrano, Sergio Carbó, and Guillermo Martínez Márquez. Years later, Ariel Martínez took over the commercial reins of the company as general manager of Central American Printing, the business arm of *Diario Las Américas,* with Víctor Vega as business manager of America's Publishing Co.

The next generation of the Aguirre family, Alejandro, Helen, and Carmen María, followed in their father's footsteps, and the paper continued to be one of the main sources of news and opinion for South Florida's Hispanic community.

Ironically, *Diario*'s success became the main commercial obstacle to the creation of a local Cuban newspaper. Starting a daily newspaper is a difficult task in any U.S. market. Miami was no exception. It was a daunting, very expensive challenge.

Weekly tabloids proved to be the affordable choice. They were referred to as *los periodiquitos* (the little papers) probably because of their tabloid format. The Cuban Heritage Collection at the University of Miami lists 665 titles over the years. Titles such as *Patria* (Armando García Sifredo), *Avance* (Jorge Zayas), *El Sol de Hialeah* (Raúl Martínez), *El Matancero Libre*, later re-titled *Libre* (Demetrio Pérez), and *La Voz de la Calle* (Vicente Rodríguez) achieved a measure of success.

Ernesto Montaner, who co-founded *Patria*, was a journalist and an epigram writer. He was considered by many the "poet of the exiles."

Just as Greater Miami was the obvious choice for a rebirth of Cuba's printed press, other areas with large Cuban exile presences followed suit. This was the case with New Jersey and Puerto Rico. In New Jersey as in Miami, the *periodiquitos* proved to be the practical choice. "They devoted most of their space to anti-Castro news and opinions and, as some New Jersey Cuban journalists have said, they were created to convey to Cubans and other Hispanics in the area the truth about Cuba's present slavery conditions."[5]

Exiled Cuban journalists such as Don Galaor, Yiyo Jiménez, Rodolfo Rodríguez Zaldívar, and others restarted their careers in publications such as *El Heraldo de la Semana* (Weekly Herald), *La Tribuna* (The Forum), *El Clarín, Información, Guerra, Nuestra Cuba, Reportaje Gráfico, Avance, Última Hora, El Independiente, La Voz,* and *La Razón y El Especial.* For many years, the *Hudson Dispatch,* the main English newspaper in Union City, published a Spanish supplement which was directed by Cuban journalist Aleida Durán.[6]

In Puerto Rico, the experience was somewhat different. In their book *Cubans in Puerto Rico*, José A. Cobas and Jorge Duany write about the media in the island nation:

> *Cuban exile publications in Puerto Rico have a common purpose, the preservation of traditional Cuban culture. La Crónica does it by promoting conservative political ideology, Casa de Cuba by celebrating the life style of the middle and upper classes, and Anuario de Familias Cubanas and Anuario*

de la Caridad by espousing family codes and religious traditions. All of these publications tend to present an idealized version of the Cuban past.[7]

A number of Cuban exile journalists achieved prominent positions in local newspapers. Such was the case with Carlos Castañeda, José Luis Díaz de Villegas, Gloria Leal, Humberto Castelló, "Chú" García, and others.

As Cuban exile journalists searched for opportunities in their new environment, it did not take long for them to get organized. In 1962, the Colegio Nacional de Periodistas en el Exilio was founded in Miami by a group headed, among others, by Mario Barrera, its first chairman; Carlos Romero; Fausto Lavilla; and Roberto Fernández. Since 2000 it has been led by Vicente P. Rodríguez. It is headquartered in Miami. In its early stages it was a source of assistance to newly arrived journalists.

Decades later, in 1994, the Círculo Nacional de Periodistas was founded in Miami by, among others, Luis David Rodríguez, Laurentino Rodríguez, Salvador Romaní, and Hiram Rodríguez Sigler.

The two local papers in English, the morning *Miami Herald* and the afternoon *Miami News*, produced some early efforts in the 1960s to reach the growing Cuban population. Each paper published columns in Spanish. The *Herald*'s appeared five times a week, written by Carlos Martínez Barraqué, while the *News* was written by Tony Solar, both Cuban exiles.

Given the growing Cuban exile presence in Dade County, it was natural that some of them would join the existing newspapers in the administration and commercial departments. Such was the case with Roberto Suarez and Ariel Martínez, who started working in the mailroom of the *Miami Herald* in the early 1960s. Suárez eventually became president of the paper, while Martínez went to *Diario Las Américas* as a top executive. Later came others: Sam Verdeja in 1967 and Armando González in 1973. Verdeja would become vice president and González a director.

As the Cuban exile population continued to grow, The Miami Herald Publishing Company, a Knight-Ridder subsidiary, decided to test the waters with a standard-size daily that would reach the market as a free insert into the main English paper. Named *El Miami Herald*, it first published in March 29, 1976. *El Miami Herald* published, on average, twenty-four pages with a newsroom staff of about thirty people. It carried local, national, and international news, with special emphasis on local stories of the Hispanic community of South Florida, Cuba, and Latin America.

The decision to launch *El Miami Herald* was a business decision. The ethnic composition of the community had changed and the newspaper had to change to reach its new readers. The *Miami Herald* set up a task force to study and implement the project. It was co-chaired by Sam Verdeja, at that time circulation manager and the highest ranking Cuban-American executive at the *Miami Herald*.

Frank Soler, who followed Martínez Barraqué as a Spanish-language columnist in the *Miami Herald*, became editor of the opinion pages of *El Miami Herald* and then executive editor after Hal Simmonds—a longtime news editor at the *Miami Herald* who had run *El Herald* for the first few months—returned to the English language newspaper. When Soler resigned in 1980, he was replaced by Roberto Fabricio, a longtime reporter for the *Miami Herald*.

El Herald, as it became known, had its own local reporters. Guillermo Martínez was its first city editor, and he later became a reporter with the *Miami Herald* City Desk and, eventually, a member of the *Miami Herald* editorial board.

El Herald also had sports, arts, and entertainment sections, and it published two daily opinion pages. It injected new vitality into the careers of exile journalists such as photographer Eduardo Hernandez (Guayo) and sportswriter Fausto Miranda. Guayo and Miranda had a long and distinguished journalism career in Cuba and in the United States before joining *El Miami Herald*. It also opened doors for young newcomers such as Cristina Saralegui, whose career later flourished in Spanish television.

When Soler left he was replaced by Araceli Perdomo and Olga Connor on the opinion pages of *El Herald*.

El Herald circulated as a supplement of the *Miami Herald* for eleven years. After a decade, it became clear to *Herald* management and that of its parent company that further growth would require a significant upgrade of *El Miami Herald*.

As a result, Knight-Ridder management "drafted" the highest-ranking Cuban-American in the organization, Roberto Suárez, then president of the *Charlotte News* and *Observer* in Charlotte, N.C., to become the first publisher of the new *El Nuevo Herald*. The new paper would still be a supplement of the English paper and have no editorial opinion, but it would have a staff that almost tripled that of *El Miami Herald*.

On November 21, 1987, *El Nuevo Herald* was first published. Its new, enhanced format, vastly improved content, and colorful appearance got the paper off to a good start. *El Nuevo Herald* started with Gustavo Pupo Mayo as editor. He was followed by Carlos Verdecia and Bárbara Gutiérrez. Carlos Alberto Montaner was opinion page editor for *El Nuevo Herald*. They helped establish the new publication as the leading Spanish newspaper in the market. César Pizarro, an advertising executive for the *Miami Herald*, became business manager of *El Nuevo Herald* and then vice president of the *Miami Herald*. Another vice president of the *Miami Herald* was Alexandra Villoch, who headed the advertising division.

In 1996, after Suárez retired, Alberto Ibarguen replaced him as publisher of *El Nuevo Herald*. Knight-Ridder management gave Ibarguen the go-ahead to separate *El Nuevo Herald* from the English paper and function as an independent entity within the organization.

Ibarguen, an attorney and the son of a Puerto Rican mother and Cuban father, began his newspaper career at the *Hartford Courant* in Connecticut and *Newsday* in New York before joining *El Nuevo Herald* as its publisher in 1996. In 1998 he became chairman and publisher of The Miami Herald Publishing Company and in July 2005 became president and CEO of the John S. and James L. Knight Foundation in

Miami, which is dedicated to promoting journalism and community development. Ibarguen has also served as chairman of the board of the Newseum in Washington, D.C., and a member of the board of directors of Pepsico, Inc. and AMR, the parent company of American Airlines.

Ibarguen also hired Carlos Castañeda, a well-known Cuban journalist, as editor of *El Nuevo Herald*. Castañeda started his journalistic career with *Bohemia* magazine in Havana. Later, in exile, he joined Henry Luce's publishing empire with *Time* and *Life* magazines. In the late 1970s he was hired by *El Día*, in Ponce, P.R., redesigned the paper—graphically and in format—renamed it *El Nuevo Día*, and relocated it to the capital, San Juan, where *El Nuevo Día* became the newspaper with the largest circulation on the island. Castañeda's right-hand man was another Cuban exile, graphic artist José Luis Díaz de Villegas.

After Castañeda passed away, Humberto Castelló succeeded him at the helm of *El Nuevo Herald* for several years. He was, in turn, succeeded by Manny García, a younger generation Cuban-American with a distinguished journalistic career at the *Miami Herald*.

Jesús Díaz, another younger generation Cuban-American, joined The Miami Herald Publishing Co. as its chief financial officer in 1993. He progressed through the ranks to the general manager position and then to publisher of the company in July of 2005, until he resigned in October of 2006.

Cuban-Americans also occupied important positions in the *Miami Herald*'s English-language newsroom. The first to become assistant managing editor news was Angel Castillo, a lawyer who had worked at the *New York Times*. Others followed: among them Ileana Oroza was an assistant managing editor; Bea García, executive business editor; Jay Ducassi, metro editor; Jorge Rojas, sports editor; María García, associate editor personnel; and Eddie Alvarez, graphics.

By the new century, two Cuban-American women occupied the two top editorial positions at the *Miami Herald*. Aminda Marques González was executive editor; and Myriam Márquez was editorial page editor.

Ronnie Ramos worked for thirteen years at the *Miami Herald* and was also senior editor sports and features at the *Atlanta Journal Constitution* and executive editor at the *Shreveport Times*. In 2009 he was hired by the National Collegiate Athletic Association (NCAA) as managing director of digital communications.

George de Lama, worked for the *Chicago Tribune* for thirty years, and as managing editor of the newspaper, he helped oversee a team of reporters and editors that won the 2008 Pulitzer Prize for Investigative Reporting and the George Polk Award. Antonio Finns was the first Cuban-American appointed editorial page editor of a South Florida newspaper when he was appointed at the *Sun-Sentinel*.

One other *Miami Herald* alum was Nuri Ducassi, who has been design director of several newspapers in the United States and Canada, most recently at the *South Florida Sun-Sentinel*.

Many other Cuban exiles have excelled in their journalistic careers. Among the first generation of exiles, Guillermo Martínez Márquez, the former editor *El País*, was one who stood out. In Cuba he had been a newspaper editor for almost twenty years and a founding member and president of the Inter American Press Association (IAPA)—also known in Spanish as *Sociedad Interamericana de Prensa* (SIP).

When Martínez Márquez left Cuba in April 1960, he was sixty years old. He was a syndicated columnist in many of the top newspapers in Latin America for twenty-seven years. From September 1963 Martínez Márquez published a weekly newspaper in New York called *Ahora* with some of the most important writers from Cuba and Latin America. It ceased publication in April of 1964.

Martínez Márquez used to say he was no more than a journalist, but nothing less than a journalist. Martínez Márquez was an active practicing journalist for over sixty-seven years. He wrote a daily column until past his eighty-seventh birthday.

But Mártinez Márquez was more. He was a founding member in the 1940s and president, in 1956, of the Inter-American Press Association

(IAPA). He was passionate about journalism and about freedom of the press. When Cuban dictator Fulgencio Batista censored the press, Mártinez Márquez automatically resigned his job as editor of *El País*, only to take it back when the censorship was lifted.

In May of 1959, Castro accused Martínez Márquez, on national television, of being on Batista's secret payroll. A week later, Martínez Márquez went on the same program—*Ante la Prensa*—and refuted Castro's allegations. The comments went back and forth for several weeks, until the Cuban dictator dropped the subject. Márquez resigned as editor of *El País* in February of 1960 after Castro imposed the infamous *coletillas* on articles it disliked. Two months later, in April, he left Cuba.

Humberto Medrano's career in exile took a turn from *Diario Las Américas* to the cause of human rights when he pioneered the efforts of Cuban exiles before the UN Human Rights Commission in Geneva, Switzerland. He was also one of the early contributors to Radio Martí.

Antonio Prohías was an established political cartoonist in Cuba where he created a famous strip titled "El Hombre Siniestro" (The Sinister Man). Later, after he went into exile, this strip was picked up by *MAD Magazine*, retitled "Spy vs Spy." It was one of the most popular features of the magazine.

Carlos Alberto Montaner is, arguably, one of the most widely read political columnists in the Spanish language, based in Madrid, Spain, and Miami. He is also a prolific writer of history, politics, and even novels.

The second generation of exiles produced Eduardo Ulibarri, whose career flourished in Costa Rica where he reached the executive editor position at *La Nación*, the leading newspaper in Central America.

Dr. Mario García developed his career as a graphic newspaper designer and as a teacher of his specialty. From Syracuse University to the University of South Florida and the Poynter Institute, in St. Petersburg, Florida, Dr. García performed major newspapers graphic redesigns for the *Wall Street Journal-Asia Edition*, a number of Scandinavian papers, *Diario de Navarra* (Pamplona, Spain), the *Miami Herald*, and many others.

Since their inception in 1917, Pulitzer Prizes became the highest honor for practicing journalists. A number of Cuban exile journalists have been honored over the years.

In 1991, in the category of Spot News Reporting, the *Miami Herald* was awarded the Pulitzer Prize for reporting on the Yaweh religious cult. Cuban exile journalists Fabiola Santiago, Liz Balmaseda, and Nery Inclán were part of the reporting team.

In 1993, *Herald* writer Liz Balmaseda became the first and, thus far only, Cuban exile to receive an individual Pulitzer in journalism in the category of Commentary. Also in 1993, the *Miami Herald* organization received the Pulitzer for Public Service for its reporting and actions during Hurricane Andrew and its aftermath. A number of Cuban exiles in the news and commercial sides of the company participated in the activities that merited the honor.

In 1999, the Pulitzer for News Reporting was awarded to the *Miami Herald* staff for its reporting on a tainted mayoral election in the city of Miami. Cuban exile journalist Manuel (Manny) García was the lead reporter on this major story.

In 2000, in the category of National Reporting, a team of *New York Times* reporters received the Pulitzer for the series "How Race Is Lived in America." Cuban exile journalist Mirta Ojito was part of the team.

And in 2001, the Pulitzer for Investigative Reporting went to the *Miami Herald* staff for its reporting on the Elián González saga. A number of Cuban exile journalists were part of that team, such as Juan Tamayo, Ana Acle-Menéndez, Liz Balmaseda, and Manny García.

Another aspect of Cuban exiles' involvement in the newspaper business is their participation in the non-journalistic side of the industry. As newspapers adopted computerized technology and United States firms established themselves as the technical leaders, it opened great opportunities for a number of Cuban exiles based in the United States, particularly in the Latin American markets. Cuban exiles with engineering and other technical training found a new niche in the newspaper industry as Latin

American newspapers jumped at the opportunity to modernize their installations. Names such as Otto Lanz, with Harris Corporation and Atex Publishing Systems (Electronic Editing Systems), Felipe Ordoño and Reynaldo Vergara with nuArc Co. (Photomechanics), Jorge Arellano and Otto de Córdoba with Abitibi Price Sales Corp. (newsprint), and others developed successful careers serving the Latin American markets for the newspaper industry.

Magazines in Cuba also had a long tradition in the general interest as well as political, cultural, fashion, and entertainment categories. In the 1950s the leading general interest magazines were *Bohemia* and *Carteles*. *Bohemia* was directed by Miguel A. Quevedo, while *Carteles* was owned by Alfredo T. Quilez. The best-known entertainment magazine was *Vanidades*, owned by Francisco Saralegui, whose daughter, Cristina, later became a very popular television personality in the United States.

On the production side of magazines, Litografía Omega rates a special mention. Founded in Havana by Francisco Lagueruela and operated with his sons, Benito and Frank, Omega printed in Havana, for distribution in Latin America, such titles as *Selecciones del Reader's Digest* (monthly circulation of 1,500,000), *Cosmopolitan*, *Buen Hogar* (*Good Housekeeping*), *Mecánica Popular* (*Popular Mechanics*), *Geomundo*, and others. As the company grew, they incorporated Henry Luce's *Time* and *Life* magazines, as well as the leading titles in the Cuba market such as *Bohemia, Romances, Vanidades, Ellas*, and the phone books for the Cuban Telephone Company.

Unfortunately, magazines followed the path of newspapers under Castro's regime. *Litografía Omega* was confiscated on September 5, 1960, and the Lagueruelas went into exile in the United States. Entrepreneurship overcame the shock of confiscation. Benito and Frank joined Arthur D. Weiss Co, to re-create, in Miami, the business that they had created and developed in Havana, and they did so successfully. Benito died in 1977, and Frank kept the business which was eventually sold to a British company.[8]

Miguel Angel Quevedo started *Bohemia Libre* in exile; he published it until his death in 1969. Saralegui started *Editorial America* in Miami in 1961. Guillermo Bermello, an attorney and public accountant in Cuba, joined the magazine in 1961 to work as an accountant. Bermello, who later directed the operations for years, recalled the rapid growth of the company, and *Vanidades*, in particular, becoming one of the most successful magazines in Latin America. In 1963, Saralegui sold the company to Venezuelan entrepreneurs Miguel Angel Capriles and Armando de Armas.[9] Bermello retired in 1985. After a couple of ownership changes, the company ended up as part of Televisa, the Mexican media giant.

A prominent Cuban journalist was instrumental in the success of *Vanidades* both in Cuba and in early exile. Herminia del Portal was editor of the magazine in Cuba from 1954 until she went into exile, and then she served as its editor until the mid-1960s.

Irene Carol was the editorial vice president of Editorial Televisa's magazines.

There were others:

In 1985, Fred Estrada, an engineer by profession, joined forces with Arturo Villar to publish *Vista* magazine, distributed as an insert in American newspapers. Estrada then founded the magazine *Hispanic* with his son, Alfredo, in 1987 with a monthly circulation of 300,000. Then in 2003, he added *Hispanic Trends*, a bi-monthly publication with the U.S. Hispanic Chamber of Commerce.

In 2003, a group headed by Sam Verdeja purchased *Hispanic Magazine* and *Hispanic Trends*. Three years later, the two magazines were sold to Editorial Televisa of Mexico. Later, Estrada sold *Vista* to Impremedia.

Réplica, a Miami-based political magazine, was founded by Max Lesnick in 1968. *Miami Mensual*, a general interest magazine, was founded by Frank Soler in December 1980. Selecta, founded in the early 1980s by Nora Bulnes, covered society and high-end fashion. By 1991, *Cristina—the Magazine*—a monthly founded by Cristina Saralegui in 1991—covered the world of celebrity news.

When Cuban newspaper owners, managers, and employees saw their world crumble, they picked up and marched into exile, never accepting the end of an era.

NOTES

1. Octavio Costa, *Imagen y Trayectoria del Cubano en la Historia* (Miami: Ediciones Universal, 1998).
2. José Alvarez Díaz, *Un Estudio Sobre Cuba* (Grupo Cubano de Investigaciones Económicas, University of Miami Press, 1963), Table 334.
3. Leovigildo Cruz, *Diario de una Traición—Cuba 1960* (University of Miami, InterAmerican Press Association, The Indian Printing, October 1970).
4. Ibid.
5. Yolanda Prieto, *The Cubans of Union City* (Philadelphia: Temple University Press, 2009).
6. Ibid.
7. José a Cobas and Jorge Duany, *Cubans in Puerto Rico* (Gainesville: University Press of Florida, 1997).
8. Author interview with Mary Polles Lagueruela, August 27, 2010.
9. Author interview with Guillermo R. Bermello, June 10, 2008.

30

ELECTRONIC MEDIA

BY ALBERTO VILAR, JOSE CANCELA, AND GUILLERMO MARTINEZ

Fidel Castro's revolution didn't just change Cuba, it impacted television and radio in the Western Hemisphere. By the time Castro came to power in 1959 Americans were already familiar with one of Cuba's most famous exiles. They knew him as Ricky Ricardo, the heavily accented Cuban crooner who played (and was) Lucy's husband on the phenomenally popular television series *I Love Lucy*. The show made Desi Arnaz one of the most recognizable men in America, but it was his behind-the-scenes skills that helped him make a lasting impact on the world of television production.

Desi Arnaz was born in Santiago de Cuba in 1917. But his family was forced into exile in 1933 after Fulgencio Batista, the man Castro would later depose, seized power. Desi graduated from a Catholic high school in Miami Beach and was on Broadway a few short years later. He met Lucille Ball on the set of his first Hollywood movie, in 1940.

Ten years later, Desi and Lucy founded Desilu Productions, and in 1951, they produced and starred in the first episode of the show that would make them household names across the country. Most television programs were broadcast live, and since the largest markets were in the Northeast, the rest of the country received only kinescope images, which were not always of the highest quality. Desi was not happy with this, so he set out to find solutions.

First he introduced the use of film to shoot *I Love Lucy*, which enabled every station around the country to broadcast high-quality images of the show. Network executives considered the use of film an unnecessary extravagance. Desi convinced them to allow Desilu Productions to cover all additional costs associated with the filming process, under the stipulation that Desilu owned and controlled all rights to the film. This unprecedented arrangement is widely considered to be one of the shrewdest deals in television history. As a result of his foresight, Desilu reaped the profits from all reruns of the series.

Second, after being told that it would be impossible to allow a live audience onto a sound stage, he worked with his team to design a set that would accommodate one. This allowed him to capture the reactions of a live audience, thus enriching the television experience for those watching at home.

Desilu Productions went on to produce many of the shows now considered classics: the original *Star Trek*, *The Andy Griffith Show*, *Mission: Impossible*, *The Dick Van Dyke Show*, *Make Room for Daddy*, *The Untouchables*, and *I Spy*.

Desi Arnaz may have been a giant among his Cuban peers in the television industry, and certainly the most well known to the American public, but he was far from the only exile from the island to make a lasting mark in broadcasting.

The reason that Cubans would go on to play such important roles in the areas of radio and television outside of Cuba can be traced to the origins of those media in their native homeland. Cuba played a pioneering role in the development of commercial radio and television throughout the Caribbean and Latin America.

During the 1950s, two fiercely competitive men are credited with laying the foundation that would put Cuba at the forefront of the broadcasting industry, second only to the United States anywhere south of the border.

Goar Mestre and Gaspar Pumarejo came from very distinct

professional backgrounds into the broadcasting industry. Pumarejo, a broadcaster at heart, came up through the ranks. The founder of Union Radio/Television enjoyed the business behind the microphone or the camera, but not as much as he loved to be in front of them. Mestre, however, who was Yale educated, was much more comfortable in the board room. He enjoyed finding ways for his radio and television empire—known to millions as CMQ Radio/Television—to be technologically advanced.

Pumarejo's CMUR-TV won the race to be first, beaming television images from Havana on October 24, 1950. On December 18 of that same year, Mestre's CMQ-TV went on the air. The station quickly rose to dominance with its slate of popular music shows and soap operas, and within a year had expanded to eight stations across the island.

This race of the airwaves would mean the hiring of hundreds of individuals who were needed as the radio and television industry exploded in Cuba. What had started out as a two man race in Havana would spawn a very competitive Cuban broadcasting industry that was the beneficiary of the close ties between Cuba and the United States when it came time to access the latest in U.S. broadcasting technology.

Cubans took to the new medium with a passion. In 1952, they bought more than 100,000 television sets, and by 1954, Havana was home to five TV stations. By 1957, Cubans owned more television sets per capita than any other country in Latin America, and it was fifth in the world.[1]

Once in exile in 1959, Mestre would turn to Latin America, where he would go on to make his mark once again. His activities included involvement with TV stations in Puerto Rico, Buenos Aires, Lima, and a TV network in Venezuela, plus production and distribution companies in Argentina and Peru. His legacy of excellence in broadcasting is still in place today throughout the Americas.

Pumarejo would turn his sights to Puerto Rico where he would become a household name doing what he loved most, hosting his own television and radio shows. In Puerto Rico he would come to be known as "El Maestro," or in English "The Master," in recognition of the respect and admiration they had for him and his knowledge of the broadcasting business.

Little did Mestre and Pumarejo know then that the hundreds of employees who had worked with them and for them would soon be exiled and serve as the basis for a legion of broadcasting industry personnel that would populate radio and television stations everywhere, including, of course, the capital of the exile community, Miami.

As the Castro revolution took hold of Cuba, Miami became the epicenter for all things Cuban, including what would later be termed "Cuban Radio." The same could not be said about television, although by the 1980s, Miami would become the capital of Spanish-language television for the U.S. Hispanic market.

But the Cuban exile experience was not limited to Miami. Its impact would be felt in the broadcasting industry throughout the United States and Latin America.

In the early 1960s, the streets of Miami were buzzing with thousands of new Cuban arrivals, desperate for information in the language they understood. Among them were many familiar faces and voices from broadcast media on the island.

A handful of individuals recognized the need, and the opportunity, in the market created by the new Spanish-speaking arrivals. With much knowledge, but limited financial resources, they began buying blocks of time from local Miami radio stations, and launching information, talk, and music programs in Spanish. Then, these entrepreneurs went out into the fledgling local Cuban-owned business community—furniture stores, grocers, and other merchants—and sold advertising spots within their time slots.

The "Time Brokers," as they are known in the broadcast industry, included former station owners, politicians, and broadcasting personalities from Cuba. Norman Díaz, among the first to hit the airwaves in Spanish in Miami, had owned a station on the island. He ran a newscast called

Panamericano. Others included Juan Amador Rodríguez, a well-known boxing champion and politician in Cuba; and Salvador Lew, who eventually came to be co-owner of WRHC with Jorge Rodríguez. Later Lew became the head of the Office of Cuba Broadcasting and Radio and TV Martí. For the first time, brokers bought time slots on WMIE, the first station to broadcast Spanish-language programs directed at the Cuban exiles. Most of the programs were broadcast at night.

WFAB, La Fabulosa, was the first station to broadcast all its programs in Spanish with Sergio Vidal Cairo as program director and sales manager. Its on-air personalities included two forceful and dynamic Cuban exile newscasters, Tomás García Fusté and Tomás Regalado, who proved his popularity and the power of the platform provided by the station even forty years later when he was elected Miami's mayor in 2009.

In 1966, the English-language radio network Susquehanna Broadcasting bought WMIE in Miami and sent Herb Levin to do market research and help decide the best programming format for the station. Based in York, Penn., Susquehanna ran mostly pop and rock stations around the country, but Levin quickly decided that two warring stations dominated that format in the Miami market. Something else caught his attention, however.

"Literally everywhere we went we ran into Spanish-speaking people in stores," he said, recalling the trip nearly four decades later, in 2011. "This is late 1966, probably in November. We'd see *farmacias, bodegas, mueblerías* and *supermercados* and we just were, I would say, shocked by that. We had no concept of what was going on."[2]

It was a revelation that would help shape the future of Spanish-language radio. Levin's team recommended the station go Spanish. They renamed the station Radio Continental, converted most of the Cuban time brokers into station employees, and sent salespeople to sell commercial time. The problem (which, surprisingly, still exists in much of the country) was convincing national accounts and non-Hispanic companies that the Spanish speakers provided a strong, viable, and profitable market.

In 1967, WMIE, now re-named Radio Continental began another all-Spanish station in Miami as the Cuban exodus was at its peak back then. Hundreds of new exiles arrived every week from the island, or from other places where they had been relocated in the United States. But the census data, gathered in 1959 and published a year later, was nearly a decade old. It calculated the "Latino" population at approximately 119,000. Levin thought there were more and contracted an independent researcher to determine the Hispanic population in the area. The result put the number at around 305,000 Spanish-speaking people in the area.

The real turning point, however, came when the new station used Susquehanna's clout to force one of the rating services to conduct their surveys in Spanish and English, and to include the Spanish-language stations (there were now two in the area) in their listings. "We went from nowhere and not booked to like number three in the market," Levin said. "So both La Fabulosa and (WQBA) ourselves, looked great in our ratings as soon as the methodology allowed Hispanics to be counted."

At the time, though, the arrival of Radio Continental sparked an immediate and intense war—on-air, and off. Levin could never prove his suspicions, but he blamed La Fabulosa for what happened next.

"We bought billboards and bus benches around town and they sprayed 'CIA' on all our benches," he said. "We had lost the Bay of Pigs. It was a bad thing. The CIA was not looked at favorably."

The effect was devastating. "It didn't go well. It couldn't get traction. And in the late fall of 1967, maybe early 1968, we were going to give up on Radio Continental. We gave away a Lincoln Continental, and we tried a contest—all the typical things that American pop stations do. And we said, 'We're going to reformat.'"

The result, however, was the opposite of what La Fabulosa's management could have hoped for. In a brainstorming session with the station's top Cuban personalities—Norman Díaz, Salvador Lew, and Juan Amador Rodríguez—Levin laid out the situation and debated possibilities. To distance themselves from the negative "CIA" label, they needed to change format, and change the station's call letters. They considered renaming it after Cuba's most famous stations, CMQ and RHC.

It was Díaz who came up with the call letters that define the station and help make it a leader in the market. It was WQBA, which, repeated on air hundreds of times during the course of the day brought to mind exactly the image they wanted to project—"Cu-ba." The promotion campaign included a new logo, which included the Cuban flag. And, while WFAB continued to be known as La Fabulosa, WQBA became "*La Cubanísima*"—the "most Cuban."

The format change reinforced that image with a blast of nostalgia from the island's radio history. The morning news show adopted the "*Radio Reloj*" (Clock Radio) style that had been a staple of one of Cuba's dominant news programs, including the distinctive ticking metronome that played throughout the newscast. It came at regular intervals throughout the broadcast, and was a reminder of its Cuban roots.

"That was the turning point," Levin said. "The flag-waving and the imagery was so powerful at Cubanísima that we couldn't be CIA if we were Cubanísima. It just didn't go together."

Rather than killing Susquehanna's Spanish-language experiment in Miami, the radio war gave birth to a powerful new entry into the market and sparked the growth of "Cuban Radio." WRHC came on the air in the early 1970s. By the 1980s, La Fabulosa was gone, but ten Spanish-language stations were crowding the airwaves in Miami, including four predominantly news and commentary stations: WAQI, WOCN, WQBA, and WRHC and saw the birth of FM Cuban and Latin American music stations, which began broadcasting in FM.[3]

Among the pioneers of the early days of Cuban Radio in South Florida, two personalities have remained as key figures in the community for more than fifty years. They are Martha Flores and Tomás García Fusté. Flores began broadcasting on WMIE in a thirty-minute program called *La Voz de la Mujer* in mid-1959. Fusté began as one of the early broadcasters on the same station in 1960. Over the years they changed stations often as the market grew and provided bigger and better opportunities.

Both Flores and Fusté remained active well into 2011. Many called Flores the *Reina de la Noche* (the queen of the night) because of her large and loyal listeners. She has been at either WQBA or Radio Mambí for the last twenty years. She once interrupted an on-air interview with then Gov. Jeb Bush because a caller had lost her dog. Flores loved dogs almost as much as politics. She was the "godmother" of many young Cuban-American politicians who considered her program a frequent must-stop in their campaigns.

Fusté switched to a local South Florida television station, TeleMiami, where he broadcasts a live radio-style interview, news, and commentary program.[4]

There have been others. Eduardo González Rubio has been a broadcast voice for five decades. He started in the days of the time brokers in the early 1960s and was still working in WQBA in 2011.

Among the many who distinguished themselves during the last fifty-two years in South Florida Spanish radio one has to include Alexis Farís, Ricardo Vila, Pedro de Pol, Agustín Acosta, Fernando Peñabaz, Maucha Gutiérrez, and Aleida Leal. Also Raquel Regalado, who was married to broadcaster politician Tomás Regalado, and Lourdes Montaner, who covered entertainment news at WQBA and Radio Mambí for twenty-five years.[5]

During the 1970s Emilio Milián was one of the most important voices of Spanish-language radio. In 1976, he lost his legs when a bomb blew up his car in the parking lot of WQBA. He went back on the air, but never regained the stature he had before the incident. Milián died in 2001.

Armando Pérez Roura started his career in Miami in 1970 in WOCN. From there he went to WQBA and WRHC, where he built a huge audience despite the lower power of the station. By 1985 he became Amancio Suárez and Jorge Rodríguez's partner and news director at WAQI, Radio

Mambí. This had been Perez Roura's dream, because the 710 frequency on the AM dial that they broadcasted on had 50,000 watts of power, day and night. His broadcasts could now be heard all over South Florida and in Cuba. Since then, Pérez Roura has been one of the most influential radio personalities in South Florida. With him at different points in his career were Agustín Tamargo and Ninoska Pérez-Castellón, two prominent Cuban journalists. Tamargo had a distinguished career in print before becoming a commentator on Radio Mambí, and Pérez-Castellón became an important source of information for the American news media covering the exile community.

In the 1970s, music in radio began the steady march from AM to FM. It was a revolution. The AM stations could not compete playing music, so the Latin music stations joined the migration. The first in Miami was WCMQ-FM, better known as FM 92, which benefitted both from being first and from being blessed with a brilliant program director, Ecuadorean Betty Pino. Eventually that station became *Clásica 92* when it was purchased by Raúl Alarcón, Sr.

Susquehanna soon followed with WQBA-FM in 1979, known to its listeners as Super Q. FM 92 introduced new Spanish-language music during the day and nostalgic Cuban melodies at night. Super Q, on the other hand, bridged the bicultural gap with a bilingual mix of disco and salsa.

Alarcón, Sr., who had owned fourteen stations in his homeland, vowed to rebuild his radio empire in the United States. Beginning as an announcer at a Spanish-language station in New York, he eventually worked his way up to station manager. In 1983, he borrowed $3.5 million and bought WSKQ (Super 1380) in New York City. Shortly thereafter, his son joined him. They formed the Spanish Broadcasting System and began acquiring stations around the country, including WCMQ-FM in Miami, and by 2010 were the largest Hispanic-controlled radio group in the country, with twenty FM stations.

Other Spanish-language stations soon followed with the transition of music stations to the FM dial. In Miami it was Radio Ritmo, purchased by Amancio Suárez and his partners in 1987.

Marcos Rodríguez and his father owned and operated radio stations in Dallas. Marcos has enjoyed great success in buying, reformatting, developing, operating, and selling radio and television stations.

Claudia Puig, the daughter of Ramón "Ñongo" Puig who was executed by a Castro firing squad in 1961 is one of the most important radio executives in the nation. Puig began her career as a sales rep for the Bell South Yellow Pages in Miami. By 1984 she began her sales career in radio at WCMQ and eventually became sales manager. Her meteoric rise in radio saw her become senior vice president Eastern Regional for Univisión Radio in 2004 in charge of all of the company's radio stations in Miami, New York, and Puerto Rico.

By the twenty-first century, Tomás Martínez had become general manager of WSUA, Caracol, a station that targeted the Latino market in South Florida, particularly a growing Colombian population.

Four men and one woman distinguished themselves. In sales they were: Herb Espino, Julito Méndez, and Enrique Landín. In marketing it was Jorge Plasencia and Monica Rabassa, vice president of marketing, corporate communications, and public affairs at Univisión Radio.

Comedy also played a role in radio, both in Cuba and in exile. One name in particular stands out—Leopoldo Fernández, better known for his on-air personality *Tres Patines*. More than fifty years after *La Tremenda Corte* with Mimi Cal, Anibal de Mar, and Leopoldo Fernández was recorded in Cuba, re-runs of the classic episodes of the series were still being broadcast in the United States and in many countries of Latin America.

Also important in this genre were Guillermo Alvarez Guedes, a marvelous stand-up comedian; and Rosendo Rossell, a comedy writer and comedian.

THE BIRTH OF TELEVISION IN SPANISH

The very first Spanish-language TV station in the United States began broadcasting in San Antonio, Texas, in 1955. KCOR-TV, Channel 41, originally went on the air from 5 P.M. to midnight, with a slate of live variety and entertainment shows featuring talent from Mexico. It didn't last. The station went broke and owner Raoul A. Cortez was forced to sell.

In 1961, Mexican media mogul Emilio Azcárraga Milmo changed the call letters to KWEX. It would become the cornerstone of the Spanish International Network (SIN), the first and largest Spanish-language network in the United States. It was operated by Azcárraga and René Anselmo. Today it is known as Univisión.

Then, in 1971, SIN bought Channel 23 in Miami and rechristened it WLTV. It would prove to be a fateful purchase. The network's base of operations shifted to the station in South Florida, putting a cadre of Cuban exiles in charge of creating programming and information aimed at what they recognized as a newly emerging Latino demographic: U.S. Hispanics.

Cubans at the Network Level

At the time, most of the programming consisted of imports from Mexico, including telenovelas produced by Azcárraga's Mexican production company, Televisa. Surrounded by Cubans in South Florida, Joaquin Blaya, a Chilean rising through the ranks at SIN, had a different vision. Blaya, who would eventually become the head of Univisión and, later, Telemundo, says now that the idea of producing programming for Hispanics living in the United States sparked great battles with the heads of the corporation.

His argument was based on something that was difficult to recognize in Mexico, but which would dramatically alter the evolution of the network. Blaya has spoken frequently and eloquently on his vision of Spanish-language television in the United States. He reiterated those views in a telephone interview October 10, 2011.

"I realized that a Spanish-language television network in the United States was not going to have any relevance if it wasn't a U.S. television network that produces for the interests of the Hispanics in the United States," he says. "In reality, the word Hispanic doesn't exist in our language. We are Chilean or Cuban or Argentine. We become Hispanics when we cross the border. And everything changes radically. We enjoy seeing shows from our own country of origin. But there are things that happen in this country that don't get reported on the channels from our home countries. If you speak English you don't find out about these things."[6]

"I wasn't going to invent television," Blaya says. "Television had already been invented. But I wanted to do it in Spanish because I understood that doing the right thing was also good business."

Eventually the original programming produced in the United States would include *El Show de Cristina* with Cristina Saralegui, the Oprah Winfrey of Spanish-language television, which after close to two decades at Univisión went to Telemundo in 2011. María Laria at Telemundo had an earlier network show—the first—of this genre in Spanish-language television. She began producing *Cara a Cara* in 1989 in Los Angeles. By 2011 Laria was working for Channel 41, América TV, in Miami producing and hosting an interview program called *Arrebatados*.

The National Newscasts

One of the first and most crucial steps Blaya took was to create a national Spanish-language newscast, under the direction of Gustavo Godoy, a Cuban exile working in Miami as a producer with a CBS affiliate television station. Blaya brought him on board to develop the local news show for Channel 23, and then asked him to construct the first nationwide Spanish-language program, *Noticiero SIN*, which would later become *Noticiero Univisión*. One of the engineers hired by Godoy in 1984 was still at the network in 2011. José Boveda was vice president of engineering and broadcast technology.

In its early days, Godoy produced the national newscast from the television studios at the school of communication at Howard University in Washington, D.C. In 1982, it transferred to Miami, with news bureaus in Washington, New York, El Salvador, Argentina, Mexico, Puerto Rico, Israel, and London.

The network established a programming schedule that would provide a full hour of news designed specifically for U.S. Hispanics, with a half-hour of local news from 6:00 to 6:30 P.M., followed by the half-hour-long national program. Working with Blaya, Godoy, and two other Cuban exiles, Gustavo Pupo Mayo and Guillermo Martínez, built the local and national news programs into serious and dynamic institutions noted for their credibility, influence, and dedication to the audience they served.

Under Blaya then WLTV station manager Alfredo Durán produced the first political candidate debates in Spanish, beginning in 1981 with the Miami mayoral elections. The effort established a model for the network, which continued to expand its coverage of elections, campaign issues, and candidates. In 1984, SIN rolled out its national coverage of the presidential elections under the banner "Destino '84," and promoted Hispanic voter registration. Four years later the network was renamed Univisión with Blaya as its president.

Carlos Barba, who had been a leading actor in Cuban telenovelas before the revolution, went into the business side of the industry when he arrived in the United States. In 1969 Barba was director of programming for WAPA-TV in Puerto Rico. A year later he was president and general manager of WNJU-TV in the New York–New Jersey market. Barba said that "WNJU became the highest rated Spanish-language television station in its market. While I was there, nobody beat us."[7]

Barba was also a part of the early days of Telemundo, the second-largest Spanish-language network. Through 1985 there was no network; just a series of stations in different markets. It included KVEA, Channel 52, in Los Angeles; WSCV, Channel 51 in Miami; and WKAQ, Channel 2, in San Juan. Julio Rumbaut, a pioneer of Spanish-language radio, became general manager of Channel 51 in Miami in 1983. By 1986, with the addition of WNJU in New York, Telemundo became the second Spanish-language network in the country. One of the pioneers of the early Telemundo days, even before it became a network was María Cristina Barros, who joined WSCV—Channel 51 in January of 1985 and by 2011 was director of marketing and community relations. Barros was active in many community affairs, including chairman of FACE.

Late in 1986 an internal fight at SIN over control of its newscast had an impact on the two Spanish-language television networks. Godoy quit, and thirty-six of the SIN staffers of newscast left with him to create a new newscast for the Telemundo network. The new newscast would be produced by HBC for Telemundo. Amancio Suárez was the owner of HBC. The newscast was Telemundo's first locally produced national program.

Some of the best reporters and producers at SIN back then left with Godoy. They included correspondent/anchor María Elvira Salazar, reporters Ricardo Brown, José Díaz Balart, Pedro Sevcec, a native Uruguayan, and producers Josie Goytisolo, Marlene May, and Raoúl Alfonso.

At the same time, other important on-air personalities remained at SIN; most prominent among them was Cuban-born anchor Teresa Rodríguez. She helped keep SIN afloat during the difficult transition in 1986-87. Rodríguez was also a local and national anchor in English and in 2011 was co-anchoring Univisión news magazine show *Aquí y Ahora*.

By 1988, Blaya was president of Univisión. Around him, many Cubans played predominant roles. He appointed Tony Oquendo as vice president of operations, Omar Marchant, was vice president of special projects and promotions, and Guillermo Martínez as vice president of news. Raúl Toraño became senior vice president of sales; all at the network level. José Cancela was appointed general manager of WLTV in Miami. In 1990 Blaya brought Ray Rodríguez to Univisión as vice president. Until then Rodríguez had been worldwide manager and CEO for Julio Iglesias, one of the top Spanish-language entertainers in the world.

Meanwhile at Telemundo, Barba had a prominent role in programming the new network. He canceled the HBC newscast and hired CNN en Español to do its newscast.

Four years later, in 1992, Barba put together a conglomerate that included California film and television producer Jerry Perenchio, and two Latin American media moguls, Mexican Emilio Azcarraga Milmo of Televisa, and Venezuelan Gustavo Cisneros of Venevisión to purchase Univisión. Blaya left and was replaced by Ray Rodríguez in 1992. Blaya then went to become president of Telemundo and took with him many of those he had hired at Univisión. Among them were Cancela and Marchant. He also re-hired Pupo Mayo as vice president of news. Pupo Mayo put together TeleNoticias, a twenty-four-hour news service for Hispanics in the United States and Latin America.

Other Cuban-Americans, however, remained with Rodríguez at Univisión. They included: Toraño, Oquendo, Martínez, and Boveda. Rodríguez went on to run Univisión Communications as president and COO for the next seventeen years. During his tenure he helped transform Univisión into a Hispanic media empire including three television networks, an Internet portal and a mayor radio company.

Barba came in with the new Univisión owners and became president and chief operating office of Univisión Television Group in 1993. By 1996 he too had left Univisión and was president and general manager of WAPA-TV in San Juan, Puerto Rico.

For Cuban exiles in television, Blaya opened the doors to scores of them as men and women with a vision that helped the industry in its infancy. Rodríguez then took that rapidly growing industry and helped it become one of the most powerful broadcast companies in the nation. He also kept and hired many Cuban-Americans, not for their nationality, but for their talent.

In 1993, Miami-born Alina Falcón, long-time executive news director of WLTV, became executive vice president and operations manager of the Univisión Network. Falcón had begun her career at WLTV in 1984. At the network, she promoted colleagues and like her, former University of Miami (UM) alums, Sylvia Rosabal as vice president, director of news at Univisión. Rosabal, of Cuban parents, was born in Puerto Rico. María López Alvarez, born in New Jersey, also of Cuban parents became vice president, director of news—splitting responsibilities with Rosabal. Miami-born Elizabeth Valdés was re-hired as assignment manager, Univisión News.

When new owners bought Univisión in 2007, the group was slowly disbanded. Rodríguez left in 2009 and was replaced as Univisión president by César Conde, whose father was Peruvian and his mother Cuban. By 2011, all but Falcón had left the company. Falcón remained as a consultant to Conde.

A fifth UM colleague, Cynthia Hudson worked for both Univisión and Telemundo until she left for several emerging cable companies broadcasting to Latin America. Hudson in 2011 was senior vice president and general manager of CNN/Español and Hispanic strategy for CNN/US.

Another journalist who made an impact was Helga Silva, a print reporter at the *Miami News*, before becoming news director at three Spanish-language network affiliates. She headed the news departments at WNJU-41 (Univisión) in New York, at WLTV-23 (Univisión) in Miami, and WSCV-51 (Telemundo) in Miami.

Several Cuban-Americans held important positions at Univisión. Otto Padrón was senior vice president of programming and promotions at Univisión Network until 2009, Bert Medina, was senior vice president and operating manager of TeleFutura through 2011, Sebastián Trujillo, senior vice president at Galavisión and Cisco Suárez was vice president of special events.

Others left Univisión to join Telemundo. Prominent among them were Jorge Hidalgo senior vice president sports, became president of sports at Telemundo, and Guillermo Santa Cruz, vice president of special projects. Santa Cruz then went on to work as a top executive at Radio and TV Martí.

Cuban exiles have also been prominent as general manager of television stations in Miami, New York, Phoenix, San Francisco, San Antonio, and Los Angeles—both at Telemundo and at Univisión. Prominent among them is José Cancela, who held the job at several stations and in 2011 was hired by Telemundo to run KVEA-34, in Los Angeles, the network's largest station.

Others in Univisión include Mara Rankin at WNJU-41 in the New York; Tomás Johansen in WLTV in Miami; and Luis Fernández Rocha, who first was GM at the Telemundo station in Miami and then became general manager of the Univisión station in the same city.

Telemundo Miami has also had many exiles as general manager of its South Florida affiliate. Among them were Julio Rumbaut, Alfredo Durán, Mike Rodríguez, and Manuel Martínez. Martínez previously had held the same job at WNJU Channel 47, the New York-New Jersey station. Mike Rodríguez, who is former Univisión president Ray Rodríguez's younger brother, went on to become a vice president for NBC/Universal and by 2011 was back in Miami as vice president of multi-media development and distribution for the Telemundo Network.

Because they are in front of the camera, the history of on-air talent is better known to Hispanics across the nation—in the case of those who made a name for themselves in network television, English or Spanish.

One cannot write the history of Spanish-language television news without talking about Manolo Reyes, Lucy Pereda, and Leticia Callava, a pioneer anchor at WLTV, Channel 23 and later at WSCV Channel 51, both in Miami. Callava was not only a pioneer of Spanish-language local newscasts, but she was also a much loved personality in the local Hispanic community. Reyes had a late-night Spanish-language newscast on WTVJ at the end of the station's daily programming. His program, though broadcast past midnight, always was a prized source of information for those exiles living in South Florida that in the 1960s did not have any other television news in Spanish available to them. Pereda was the host of many Univisión programs, starting with *Mundo Latino* in 1987.

Two others who must be mentioned were Esteban Lamela, at WLTV; and Rafael Orizondo, who worked at both the Telemundo and Univisión affiliates. Both were the "essence" of being Cuban and covered stories that touched the community's heart.

Other anchors come to mind. Alina Mayo Azze has been an anchor at both Miami stations for decades—for the last two decades the lead female anchor at WLTV-Channel 23. Meanwhile, WSCV-Channel 51 also has been very stable in the last two decades with Ambrosio Hernández who came to Miami from Chicago, and María Montoya, an actress in Cuba who came on the Mariel Boatlift. Myrka de Llanos, a former Queen of the Orange Bowl Parade, anchored shows for both the South Florida affiliate and for the Univisión network.

Recently, new stations have opened in the South Florida area, creating opportunities for Cubans who have continued arriving in the United States. Among them were Juan Manuel Cao, who after years at WSCV became an anchor-reporter at Channel 41, América TV. Also in that station were news and on air personalities such as Josie Galindo, Félix Guillermo, Alejandra Molina, and Carlos Otero. Alexis Valdés worked for Alarcón in Mega TV, Channel 22. For many years, María Elvira Salazar hosted a program in this network.

Earlier, Salazar would be a correspondent and anchor at HBC, CNN en Español, and Noticiero Telemundo. Later, José Díaz Balart would become the main figure at Noticiero Telemundo.

Several Cuban-American anchors made the crossover and worked for English-language networks. Among them were Jackie Nespral and

Maggie Rodríguez, who after brief careers at Univisión went on to the national networks. Nespral went on to the weekend *Today Show* for NBC before returning to the NBC affiliate in Miami. Rodríguez worked for the ABC affiliate in Los Angeles, anchored for the CBS affiliate in Miami and spent several years doing the *CBS Early Show*, and occasionally anchoring the CBS Evening News.

Others like Michelle Caruso-Cabrera went on to careers on cable television networks. Caruso-Cabrera became an anchor/reporter for CNBC; Soledad O'Brien, whose mother is Cuban and her father Australian, and Rick Sánchez worked for CNN; Sánchez after stints in South Florida and Texas. Bertha Coombs and Bonnie Anderson, whose father was executed in Cuba by the Castro regime, were correspondents; Coombs at CNBC and Anderson at NBC and CNN.

At the local level, getting English-language stations to hire Cuban-Americans was not easy. The first to become anchor reporter was Ana Azcuy at then the CBS affiliate, WTVJ. That was in the mid-1980s. She eventually went to WPLG-Channel 10; worked at a San Antonio, Texas, station and was the host of Univisión's news magazine *Portada* in the early 1990s. Anderson, Ileana Bravo, and Ileana Varela were some of the Cuban-American pioneers on local television in South Florida.

With time their numbers have grown. Many Cuban-Americans are now working in English as anchors. Among them are Elliott Rodríguez at WPLG-Channel 10; and Antonio Mora at WFOR-Channel 4; both of them in South Florida.

Other Cubans have had important acting or correspondent roles in American television networks. They include: Dr. Manny Alvarez has been a medical contributor for the Fox News Channel. Alvarez has worked in both Spanish and English. He began his career as a health and science reporter for Telemundo. Since 1996 he has been the chairman of the Deparment of Obstetrics and Gynecology and Reproductive Science at Hachensack University Medical Center in New Jersey.

Néstor Carbonell is the son of a Bay of Pigs veteran who became a

Pepsi executive. He has won two Alma Awards for Outstanding Actor in a Comedy Series (1998, 1999) for his role as Luis Rivera on the Brooke Shields sitcom *Suddenly Susan* (1996-2000). He made his primetime TV debut in 1991 in an episode of the series *Law & Order*.

Daisy Fuentes, who was born in Havana, was successful in making the crossover into English and working the Latin market almost seamlessly. She worked for both MTV US and MTV Latino. She has been a model, a model/spokesperson, and an entrepreneur in her own right.

Another Havana-born actor, David Fumero was raised in Miami, joined the U.S. Marine Corps, and by the 1990s he appeared in soap operas such as *One Life to Live* between 1998 and 2005.

Julie Stav was truly a crossover story, who managed to have a successful career in both English and Spanish. Born in Vertientes, a sugar mill in Camagüey, Julieta Alfonso came to the United States as a teenager. In California she became a teacher and financial planner. Soon she had a Spanish-language radio program on Univisión and a series of programs in English and Spanish on PBS. She is also a frequent speaker, a magazine columnist, and has written several personal finance books.

And two real-life judges became judges in nationally syndicated television shows—Marilyn Milián of *The People's Court*, Alex Ferrer of *Judge Alex*. In their programs they preside over real cases and decide them on the air.

In Spanish-language television Ana María Polo has done much the same in her top-rated program *Caso Cerrado* on Telemundo. Polo, whose inimitable style has her ending each show by announcing her decision and then banging the bench with her gavel as she says in a loud, authoritative voice—"*Caso Cerrado*" (Case Closed).

One cannot write about Cuban exiles in the electronic media without mentioning *¿Qué Pasa? USA*. This was the first truly bilingual situation comedy produced in the United States, written in a way that even those who only spoke either English or Spanish could understand it. It chronicled the trials and tribulations of the Peña family as it adapted to life in the United States. Produced by WPBT, the South Florida public television network, it ran for the first time from May 1, 1977, through January 1, 1980. Thirty years later its episodes are seen frequently as the plots of the shows are timeless.

Many of the actors and actresses on the program were already famous in Cuba. Others began their careers in this country. The show depicts three generations, each with its own vision of life in their new country. The grandparents, who speak in Spanish and understand almost no English, are played by Luis Oquendo and Velia Martínez. The parents, who are caught between the two worlds and two generations, speak Spanish and English—this last one with difficulty. They are played by Ana Margarita Martínez Casado and Manolo Villaverde. And the two teenage children who speak English and Spanglish are played by Ana Margarita Méndez and Rocky Echevarría, who later changed his name to Steven Bauer and has acted in several Hollywood movies. This American classic was created by Luis Santeiro.

NOTES

1. U.S. Department of State, *Zenith and Eclipse: A Comparative Look at Socio-Economic Conditions in Pre-Castro and Present Day Cuba* (Released by the Bureau of Inter-American Affairs, February 9, 1998. Revised June 2002), 4, Table 4.
2. Author interviews with Herb Levin—February 28, 2011, and August 24, 2011.
3. Santiago, Fabiola, "Pennsylvania Company Owns Top-Rated Spanish Stations," *Miami Herald,* June 22, 1986.
4. Author telephone interviews with Martha Flores, August 23, 2011, and Tomás García Fusté, August 19, 2011.
5. Author interview with Loretta Amaya, August 25, 2011.
6. Author interview with Joaquín Blaya, October 10, 2011.
7. Author interview with Carlos Barba, September 14, 2011.

ADVERTISING AND PUBLIC RELATIONS

BY AIDA LEVITAN

In 2006 Carl Kravetz, a Mexican American advertising agency CEO who was then president of the Association of Hispanic Advertising Agencies (AHAA), stated: "It was the Cuban revolution that kicked off U.S. Hispanic advertising. In 1959 and 1960, a number of Havana advertising men exiled to the United States wanted to continue practicing their craft and began the long arduous process of convincing American advertisers that there was a vast, untapped market hidden here."[1]

In an essay called "The Latin Side of Madison Avenue: Marketing and the Language that Makes Us 'Hispanics,'" Arlene Dávila states that "it was Cuban executives who were behind the development of the first and largest advertising agencies targeting populations of Latin American background not only in New York but in the United States." Historians have pointed out that U.S. advertising had a presence in Cuba as early as September 1898, when an "advertising contractor," George Benson, established an advertising agency in Havana, soliciting contracts from U.S. companies. According to Louis Pérez, "Franklin Matthews was astonished by the prevalence of U.S. advertising during a visit to Havana in 1899: 'Everywhere . . . there were brilliant lithographs advertising various brands of American beer. It was a wonder that some enterprising agent had not plastered the sides of Morro Castle with these signs.'"

U.S. companies continued to open advertising firms in the early twentieth century in Havana, and in 1907 the Liga Cubana de Publicidad (the Advertising League) was formed. In addition, numerous Cubans were employed as representatives and employees of U.S. corporations. American culture had a strong presence in the early development of the Cuban Republic.[2]

During the first half of the twentieth century, and especially in the 1950s, American culture and businesses continued to have a strong influence over the Cuban economy and culture. Cuban advertising executives became very familiar with the American advertising systems and agencies. A review of just a couple of pages of the 1958 Cuban Yellow Pages reveals more than twenty advertising agencies, including Publicitaria Siboney and Mestre Conill & Co. This professional experience would become the solid foundation for the beginning of U.S. Hispanic advertising.

THE 1960S PIONEERS IN NEW YORK AND MIAMI

The story of U.S. Hispanic advertising agencies begins in the 1960s and 1970s with Cuban exiles who had run advertising agencies in Cuba and had a valuable knowledge of American corporate culture. Cuban-American writer and film director Ivan Acosta gives credit to New York Hispanic advertising pioneers Luis Díaz Albertini, Rafael and Alicia Conill, and Castor Fernández. Other important Cuban advertising leaders were Bill Munder, Pupi Hurtado, Sara Sunshine, Don Pasante, Rafael Llerena, and Silvia Rodríguez.

Cuban advertising experts such as José Manuel Cubas, Tere Zubizarreta, and Ricardo Arregui; Sara Sunshine (in the creative field); Pedro Font; and Jorge Reynardus, all made major contribution during the 1960s and 1970s. Prominent media leaders Eduardo Caballero, Raúl Alarcon, Sr., Raúl Toraño, and Omar Marchant also made pioneering contributions to Hispanic marketing.

Luis Díaz Albertini

In 1962 Luis Díaz-Albertini, a New York Cuban executive who had owned an advertising agency in Cuba, founded SAMS (Spanish Advertising and Marketing Services), which was billing $7.5 million by 1979, according to George San José, CEO of San José Advertising. SAMS clients included Banco de Ponce, Bulova, Colgate Palmolive, Newport and True cigarettes, Mazola Corn Oil, Libby's Nectars, and Royal Gelatins & Breyers Ice Cream. SAMS had offices in Miami (for Latin America), Chicago, and Los Angeles.

Díaz-Albertini was so successful that he was able to close New York's *Liborio* club one night in order to hear Celia Cruz sing exclusively for him and his guests. Among early SAMS employees were other Cubans who would achieve significant success in the industry: George San José; Raúl Toraño, later a top Univisión executive; and Sara Sunshine. "We traveled 56 times in one particular year," says George San José, who considers Díaz Albertini the father of Hispanic advertising in the U.S. In 1979 DeGarmo, later bought by D'Arcy MacMannus, bought SAMS. Díaz-Albertini, now deceased, retired in the early 1980s. Years after, SAMS was bankrupt.

Ricardo Arregui

In Miami, Ricardo Arregui, who had also owned the fourth largest advertising agency in Cuba in 1959, started Arregui Advertising in 1962. "Ours was the first Hispanic ad agency established in South Florida . . . and possibly in the U.S.," says Arregui.

With a bachelor's degree in marketing and advertising and a master's degree in diplomacy from the University of Havana, Arregui had been an innovator in Cuba, sponsoring demographic research studies. The Arregui brothers arrived in Miami as exiles and had to start from scratch. During Arregui Advertising's forty-three years, it served clients such as Café Bustelo, Café Pilón, Diana Foods, Goya Foods, Kirby Foods,

Sedano's Supermarket, El Dorado Furniture, Citco Petroleum, Colonial Bank, Ballantine Scotch Whiskey, Polar Beer, and Materva.

Sara Sunshine

Advertising executive Rochelle Newman wrote that Sara Sunshine "may have been the first woman to hold a creative position, or in fact, any influential position in the world of U.S. Hispanic Advertising." Originally, Sunshine worked at Publicidad Siboney in Cuba, interviewing consumers—a job that she hated, but one which provided an excellent foundation for her creative work later on.

In 1962 she joined SAMS. According to Sunshine, "The industry didn't exist so it wasn't like I could have a calling to it. But, by the second week working with clients like Goya and with movie chains—there were two movie chains and over thirty Spanish movie houses in the New York area—I could feel something. I could feel the potential."[3]

She bravely resisted dubbing English-language ads because she understood the need for cultural relevance and authenticity. Some of her groundbreaking work included campaigns for Palmolive Dishwashing Liquid, using Madge the manicurist and then Charytin as spokespersons. Sunshine got Madge to speak Spanish by "recording and starting with syllables like Pal-mo-li-ve. Then I moved on to words and then sentences. First everything would be said slowly and then in regular speed."

Sunshine helped co-found Siboney Advertising in New York and then joined Bravo Advertising in 1997 as director of advertising resources, with a voice in Strategic Planning and Consumers Insights. Her great creative work earned her the first Hispanic Clio in 1986, for a Pepsi commercial entitled *Drummer*. Another innovation was her use of Chayanne for Pepsi in the 1980s commercials, singing in Spanish in the English Grammy TV ceremonies.

Rafael and Alicia Conill

In 1968 Cuban advertising executives Rafael and Alicia Conill founded Conill Advertising in New York. Rafael Conill had owned Mestre Conill Publicidad in Havana in the 1950s. New York's Hispanic population at that time was primarily Puerto Rican and, as Alicia Conill noted, "Hispanic marketing was a very tough sell in the early days."[4] Banco Popular of Puerto Rico was their first client. Three years later they attracted their first blue-chip client, Campbell Soup Co. According to Alicia Conill, they were successful because "[w]e had a broad base of knowledge about Hispanics in this country. We were indefatigable in pursuing our own independent research about the products we were targeting. We were careful, consistent and honest in handling all budgets assigned to us."

The Conills brought significant skills from Cuba, where they had been associated with major U.S. advertising agencies. Alicia Conill, whom Jorge Reynardus calls "the perfect lady," also worked for ten years at J. Walter Thompson and William Esty Company in the U.S. "Those links were invaluable to me when I became part of Conill Advertising," says Conill.

Conill Advertising faced the challenge of attracting major advertisers at a time when Hispanics were not yet a significant percentage of the U.S. population. According to Reynardus, Rafael Conill gained his respect because he focused on today's market in a singularly effective way with national accounts instead of acting as consultants to general market agencies.

Alicia Conill explains that they had to educate American marketers about the fact that a literal translation from English to Spanish "would make no sense to an audience with a Hispanic perspective." Conill believes that their greatest contribution was "to gain the respect of many important domestic clients. . . . By doing this, we paved the way for many other . . . agencies. We were . . . the first to negotiate with AFTRA and SAG for special rates for the Hispanic market, assuring that Hispanic talent would receive fair (union) rates thus eliminating buyouts."

The Conills also contributed to the development of other Hispanic professionals. Says Alicia Conill, "I am proud and honored that many of my former employees and trainees are now in leadership positions at Hispanic agencies."

Castor Fernández

Castor Fernández started Castor Advertising in New York in 1968, after obtaining an MBA from CCNY. Unlike other Cuban advertising pioneers, Fernández did not have advertising experience from Cuba. He first held various positions at the Foreign Advertising and Service Bureau, for the Palmer family. According to Fernández, "There was an absolute lack of interest from most advertisers in Hispanic advertising. Only those who had had some international experience showed some modest interest."

One of his first clients was Heublein Inc., then the largest liquor company in the world, with brands such as Don Q Rum, Smirnoff Vodka, and Lancer's Wine. About this period, Fernández says, "I was blessed to be able to operate at a time when agencies were able to convince new clients to enter the market. My greatest contribution was . . . convincing many important clients, known the world over, that the U.S. Hispanic was a viable business too."

Castor Advertising attracted major clients, e.g., Anheuser-Busch, Bacardí, Burger King, Coca-Cola, General Motors, McDonald's, K-Mart, Procter & Gamble, Pizza Hut, Ralston Purina, S. S. Johnson, Southland Corp., the U.S. Army, the U.S. Census, and Warner Lambert. Jorge Reynardus, who also worked with Fernández, respects his creativity and for teaching both clients and agency executives the difference between the different Hispanic segments. *Advertising Age* pointed out that "[h]e [Fernández] introduced the philosophy that while all Hispanics speak the same language, there are real differences in their customs, food, music and holidays."

In 1989 Castor merged with Miami-based García-Serra & Blanco, thus projecting billings of sixty million dollars. The merger was later dissolved.

When asked how he was able to succeed, Fernández points out that fear of not being able to make a living and having no other choice but to succeed were major motivators: "When you have no other alternatives; when you cannot return to your country or ask your father for money, there is no going back. Somehow, you will manage to achieve your goals."

THE PIONEERS OF THE 1970S—MIAMI AND NEW YORK

Tere Zubizarreta

Advertising experts admire the achievements of Tere Zubizarreta (known as Tere Zubi) who founded Zubi Advertising in 1976 in Miami. Zubi was number six in the 2009 *Advertising Age* Hispanic agency ranking.

Like many Cuban-American entrepreneurs, Zubi's story begins in 1960, when she and her husband fled from Cuba, arriving in Miami with a baby and no money. Two years later, she used her secretarial skills for the McCann/Marschalk Advertising Agency, later becoming an account executive. After McCann/Marschalk closed the agency's Miami office, their condo real estate client asked Zubi to open an agency. Zubi then won the *El Miami Herald* account, which gave her credibility and prestige.

Her first big national account was Ryder Systems, which gave her local firm a presence in the Texas and Los Angeles markets. Then came Pizza Hut; then S. C. Johnson (makers of Raid bug spray), and, finally, in 1986, the largest national account—Ford Motor Company.

Zubi Advertising's national clients have also included Chase Bank, American Airlines, and Olive Garden.

According to Tere Zubi's son, Joe Zubizarreta, who now serves as the agency's CEO, his mother's traits of honesty and hard work have been key aspects of her legacy, as well as her commitment to giving clients good value for their money. To illustrate her respect for the industry, Joe tells an anecdote about a national brand that was "not sold about Hispanics." Tere Zubi rejected the business because the potential client wanted to focus only on one market and a short test, and she did not believe this was the right approach.

The agency succeeded thanks to dedication to teamwork—and an understanding that no one can do it alone. Joe Zubi says, "Mom had a way of making people feel that they were part of a team. She gave everyone responsibility and accountability." He commented on the challenges that they faced: "Continuity was definitely one—keeping clients engaged and growing. Also, in the current times, the challenge of bilingualism and acculturation. . . . Should we reach them in Spanish or in English? Are they acculturated to the point where we can reach them in English? Spanish language is a strong marketing tool to communicate."

An amusing anecdote illustrates the challenges that Tere Zubi and her children have faced. According to Joe Zubi, "We had a relatively new client and we presented an ad with a dog in it. The client asked if the dog was Hispanic." The client really wanted to know whether the dog was one that Hispanics would own. In other words, was it the appropriate dog, since it was not a Chihuahua? Tere Zubi understood that Hispanic advertising sometimes requires sensitivity and cultural training.

Tere Zubi was also honorable in her way of dealing with competitors. When Sánchez & Levitán won the Florida Lottery account, in a close competition with Zubi, Tere Zubi sent Aida Levitán a huge flower arrangement. "She always believed," says Joe Zubi, "that there should be enough business for everyone and that we would all have a chance to win accounts. We should celebrate when the competitor wins a piece of business instead of being envious."

Her legacy also includes her commitment to giving back to the community that had given her much success. She co-founded and chaired

FACE (Facts About Cuban Exiles). She was the first Hispanic woman to serve as a committee chair for the United Way of America and also served on the boards of the Orange Bowl Committee and the Beacon Council.

Even as she was dying from cancer, Tere Zubi showed her sense of humor. "It's in my glands," she told *Hispanic Business* magazine one year before she died. "I've been a fighter all my life, and I call the cancer my Talibans—it has sneaked into my caves. But my treatment is the entire U.S. military, the Army, the Navy and the Marines."

The fact that Zubi remained stubbornly independent set an example for other Hispanic advertising agencies and businesses. Joe adds, "This has been difficult but it shows the others: Yes we can." He adds:

> *As people think about Tere, she should be remembered as much for what she was as a mother and a wife as she is remembered for her success in business. She should be an inspiration for others—there has to be a balance in one's life—everyone should learn from this. . . . My mother was my teacher, adviser and my greatest inspiration. Her goodwill, passion and perseverance have left a wonderful impression on all of the fortunate people that have crossed her path.*[5]

Pedro Font

Cuban-American executive Pedro Font opened the doors of his advertising agency in 1979 in New York. Rochelle Newman, who worked for this agency, wrote that Font later partnered with Joséph Vaamonde, a Y&R executive from Puerto Rico. Thus began Font & Vaamonde Associates, Inc. The partnership did not last, but Font kept the name, and the agency would become one of the leading U.S. Hispanic advertising firms.

Font's clients included Times Supermarket, Magoo Pizza, Mennen, Marcal, Glenbrook Laboratories (Bayer Aspirin, Panadol, and Mejoral), Procter & Gamble (Crisco Corn Oil and Shortening, Jif Peanut Butter,

Downy, Joy, Pantene, Cover Girl), and some General Foods' accounts (Jello and Kool Aid). Font & Vaamonde was the first U.S. Hispanic agency to be Agency of Record for P&G media buying.

Newman explains that Font "was able to go beyond the traditional role of advertising agency and become a business partner where the Hispanic market opportunity was concerned. He emphasized what today might be called an integrated marketing approach, in that he took a leadership position by offering clients advertising and merchandising and promotions under one roof."

According to Newman, Font & Vaamonde was a pioneer in the area of branded programming for P&G with the creation of two programs—*Cocina Crisco,* a cooking show, and *Hablando,* a talk show with product integration as the main focus of conversation. He developed the first U.S. produced *novela, Angelica mi Vida,* which was shot in partnership with Telemundo and used locations in New York City, San Antonio, and Los Angeles. Font also opened offices in Miami, Los Angeles, San Antonio, and Chicago.

Font achieved all this in spite of what Newman describes as his "colorful" behavior, his heavy English accent, and the fact that he frequently smoked torpedo-like Cuban cigars. He only dealt with top people on the client side and treated them like royalty. One source told the story of his sending an "advance" person to *La Cote Basque* before arriving with clients to ensure that they would treat him like a celebrity. Most important, he created a team that was very results-oriented.

Advertising Age pointed out in February 2007, "Pedro Font . . . understood that much of Hispanic brand loyalty is based on what's now called buzz marketing or word-of-mouth marketing, and he worked to put promotions in stores where employees would recommend the products with prominent displays."

By 1993 Grey Advertising had bought 100 percent of the agency. Font left the advertising business in the early 1990s.

Ana María Fernández-Haar

In 1978 Ana María Fernández-Haar founded Inter-American Communications in Miami, later known as The IAC Group, focusing on affluent Latin Americans driving bilateral international trade and finance through the Miami gateway. Because of her financial and business acumen, she developed her agency into a full-service, multicultural marketing and advertising firm, with forty employees and billings exceeding $25 million by September 1998.

During her tenure at IAC, Fernández-Haar served clients such as Barnett Banks, Procter & Gamble, BellSouth, Publix Super Markets, Coca-Cola, Hyundai Motor America, Anheuser-Busch, Johnnie Walker Black Label, and Blue Cross & Blue Shield. Under her leadership, IAC earned more than 150 local, regional, and national awards, including the Hispanic Business Roundtable's Circle of Excellence Award, the American Red Cross's Spectrum Award for Entrepreneurship in 2000, and the Brillante Award from the Association of Hispanic MBAs. In 2004 she sold the agency to Manuel Machado.

Fernández-Haar also wrote and produced documentaries for both English- and Spanish-language television; hosted *Viva*, a PBS program focusing on the achievements of Latinos in the United States; and created *Comercio Sin Fronteras* (Commerce Without Borders), the first pan-regional weekly international business program, broadcast in CBS Telenoticias.

An active professional and civic leader, Fernández-Haar chaired the Hispanic Heritage Council and the New America Alliance, where she provided Congressional testimony at hearings relating to minorities' access to capital and participation in the financial services sector. She chaired the World Trade Center Miami and was a presidential appointee to the Florida District Export Council. She was listed in *Who's Who in the World*, included among *Hispanic Business* magazine's Top 100 Hispanics, and won *Inc Magazine*'s Minority Entrepreneur of the Year for Florida. She also served as president of AHAA.

Fernández-Haar sold the agency to MGS COMM and retired from the advertising industry. She continues to be an active philanthropist.

THE 1980S—MIAMI, NEW YORK, AND CHICAGO

George San José

A Chicago success story, Cuban-American George San José founded The San José Group in 1981, which is the first and only national independent Hispanic advertising agency in Chicago and is number nineteen in the 2009 *Advertising Age* Hispanic agency ranking. San José is also the "longest running president of any U.S. Hispanic agency," as he calls himself. His clients include Ace Hardware, Hormel, MGM Grand, Exelon, the Chicago White Sox, and Abbot Laboratories.

In a *Smart Business* 2007 article, Nank John writes that San José "is not impressed by the flash-in-the-pans of the world and prefers to liken his company . . . to a well-conditioned marathoner. . . . San José has stressed persistence and consistency since founding the Hispanic-focused marketing agency."

In the early days, like other pioneers, San José worked with some corporate clients who did not understand the market at all. He tells the anecdote of one *Fortune 500* client with whom he had to tour the country in order to do store checks in U.S. Hispanic markets. When they arrived at Miami International Airport, the young client exclaimed, "Wow! Everybody here speaks Spanish, but they don't look Hispanic." San José upbraided the client: "What were you expecting: Indians with bows and arrows? What the heck is the Hispanic look?"

A committed professional, George San José has served on the board of the Association of Hispanic Advertising Agencies, in the Economic Club of Chicago, and is a director in the Membership Committee for Advertising, Marketing and Public Relations Professionals. As a presidential appointee, he served as chairman of the Regional District Board of Selected Services.

San José is proud of the "fusion of bringing two needs together: the need for corporate America to reach consumers and educating those consumers about products and services that will make their life easier." He recommends the following in order to lead effectively:

Personify your vision and build buy-in. If you're expecting people to follow you and to follow your example, then you have to live your example. You have to be a living testament as to what they can achieve. . . . To achieve excellence, it's something that you have to constantly work on. Excellence is in the details. To get people to see your vision and to capture the fact that if we do work at a higher level of excellence, we don't have to do as much.[6]

Julio Blanco and Alberto García-Serra

García Serra & Blanco (GS&B) opened its doors in Miami in 1982. Alberto García-Serra, son of the owner of Radio García-Serra in Cuba, had studied advertising and worked in the industry for several years. Julio Blanco had owned Blanco, Blanco & Blank, a design firm. The agency served clients such as Falls Home Furnishing, Government Securities Corporation, Publix, Butcher & Singer Securities, and Jefferson Ward Television.

In 1989 *Hispanic Business* magazine named GS&B the fastest-growing Hispanic advertising agency in the U.S. After merging with Castor that year, they worked on major national brands and later, after separating from Castor, they merged with Lintas. Among the clients served were Continental Airlines, McDonald's, Hanes, Lipton, Maybelline, Budweiser, Lysol, and Michelob. They sold the agency to Del Rivero Messianu in 1994.

José Manuel Cubas

José Manuel Cubas, an experienced advertising executive whose family had founded Publicitaria Siboney in 1953 in Cuba, started Siboney Advertising in the U.S. in 1983. Siboney ranks among the leading forty U.S. Hispanic advertising agencies, according to *Advertising Age* (2009). Among the clients it has served are: Colgate-Palmolive, Sedano's Supermarkets, MilkPEP, Red Lobster, Kellogg Co., and Blue Cross Blue Shield of Florida.

After leaving Cuba in the 1960s, José Manuel and Gustavo Cubas opened Publicidad Siboney in San Juan, Puerto Rico, in 1963, with partners Manuel de la Vega and Antonio López Graña. In 1967 Siboney expanded to Latin America, starting with Venezuela. In the late 1980s José Manuel Cubas sold the Latin American agencies to Foote, Cone & Belding. Thus, they became one of the first Hispanic advertising agencies to sell to a major American agency.

After opening the agency in New York at the request of a major client, Siboney acquired other U.S. national accounts. In the 1990s the agency opened Siboney Dallas and produced major campaigns for Pepsi-Cola featuring Gloria Estefan, Chayanne, and Juan Luis Guerra. The Pepsi campaign, *La sed de la nueva generación*, created by Sara Sunshine, won the first Clio Award ever given to Hispanic agencies. After Cubas acquired the Nestlé account, he opened Siboney Advertising in California. He also opened a Latin American office in Miami, which is now the Siboney corporate headquarters. In 2001 he sold Siboney Dallas and Los Angeles to Publicis.

Cubas met many challenges along the way. "The main challenge," he says, "was to convince these corporations of the importance of the market. We presented research and case studies involving major U.S. brands and this helped us persuade them." Cubas' sense of humor also helped him face any kind of conflict. Siboney was able to become a partner with its clients, at the highest level, and some invited Cubas to sit at their high-level meetings.

"We grew and became successful," says Cubas, "because we had great dedication to the consumer and to results. *Back to street* is a rule at Siboney. I insisted on not becoming isolated from the consumer but to return to the street to observe him/her and to get to know him/her." He understood that what the agency staff liked was not necessarily what the consumer would like or relate to. Cubas says that "Creativity at Siboney is the realm of anyone who has a good idea."

Cubas has always made an effort to be very sincere with the client in explaining how the agency would communicate the benefit and competitive difference of the brand to consumers. He has never been afraid to ask the right questions and to point out truths about the market. His sincere interest in human beings was a definite competitive advantage of the agency.

Cubas believes that Cuban exiles were the pioneers of Hispanic advertising because of their natural tendency to expressiveness and creativity in addition to the education, entrepreneurial spirit, and professional experience that they brought to the U.S. "These Cubans had the gift of communication," says Cubas, "and they did not feel like strangers in the U.S."

Aida Levitán, PhD, and Fausto Sánchez

In 1983 Aida Levitán, PhD, a well-known director of government information agencies and the Hispanic Heritage Festival, founded a public relations firm in Miami. Fausto Sánchez, a Cuban-American film and advertising expert from Los Angeles, joined the firm in 1986; thus was born Sánchez & Levitán, Inc., a Miami-based marketing communications agency.

In 1995 they defined the agency's mission: "To become the number one Hispanic advertising agency in the U.S." By 2004 they sold Sánchez & Levitán to Publicis. Publicis Sánchez & Levitán soon had offices in Miami, New York, Dallas, and Los Angeles. Co-chaired by Levitán

(CEO) and Sánchez (executive vice president), it ranked number eight among U.S. Hispanic advertising agencies, according to *Advertising Age* in 2003, and it served clients such as Nestlé (several brands), BMW, and Zales. In 2004 Sánchez & Levitán merged with Publicis-owned Bromley. As vice chairperson and president of Bromley Communications Aida Levitán became a top leader of the number one Hispanic advertising agency in the U.S., as ranked by *Advertising Age*.

Sánchez & Levitán's focus on integrated marketing communications was a compelling selling point, since it connected the clients' brands with consumers not only through advertising but also through public relations, promotions, events, and direct mail.

In the late 1980s and early 1990s, Sánchez & Levitán won major accounts such as the Florida Lottery, NCNB National Bank, BellSouth, Coors Brewing Company, Seagram Americas, and Coca-Cola USA. The agency then acquired national advertising clients such as Chivas Regal, Crown Royal, the Money Store, and TJX Cos. and won creative awards such as the Clio, the Addy, the Beverage World Ethnic Advertising Award, and the first Radio Mercury Award.

In 1992 the partners directed the *Cachao Mambo & Descarga* concert series in Miami and New York's Radio City Music Hall, in collaboration with actor Andy García. The campaign won them national recognition and the PRSA National Multicultural Excellence Award. They also co-produced a film on Cachao with García. In the 1990s they produced the Fair of Spain in Miami and the Fair of Spain, attracting thousands of consumers.

"I strongly believe that we have to give back to the community as much or more than we have received," says Dr. Levitán. The agency produced the Alex Rodríguez Boys and Girls Club of Florida campaign and the branding for Brothers to the Rescue. A winner of the PRSA Royal Palm Award and the *Hispanic Magazine* Award for Entrepreneurship, Dr. Levitán has served on many boards, including the Miami Art Museum, the Latin Chamber of Commerce, the Greater Miami Chamber of Commerce, and the Spanish Cultural Center. She was president of the

Association of Hispanic Advertising Agencies in 2004.

Dr. Levitán left Bromley in early 2005 and retired from advertising in 2007. She is president of The Levitán Group, Inc., a consulting firm, and chairs the Aetna National Latino Advisory Council and the Public Communications Committee of the National Museum of the American Latino Commission.

Richard Marañón

After arriving in the U.S. from Cuba at the age of seventeen, Richard Marañón had to wash dishes at María Julia restaurant in New York in exchange for food. He soon learned English and started working in sales at Reingold Beer and later at a liquor company, followed by sales work at WQBA, with Eduardo Gonzalez Rubio and Tomas de San Julián. After founding Vica—a radio station in Honduras in 1983—Richard Marañón opened the doors of Marañón & Associates in 1985 in Miami. His clients have included Estrella Insurance, Revlon, Gillette, and Coors. By the end of the 1980s his billings had increased to $30 million. Marañón, who proudly speaks about his family (he now has eight grandchildren), was also able to attract his daughters to the business. Lissette began working with him in 1990, and Ligia, who is now the president of Marañón & Associates, joined the agency in 1996.

As of 2010, Marañón serves clients such as SBS; US Century Bank, Jack National; Toyota of South Florida, Ocean Mazda, and Preferred Medical Plan. As a leading political agency, Marañón has also developed advertising for more than a hundred political campaigns in the last few years, including the George W. Bush presidential and the Manny Díaz city of Miami mayoral campaign. Marañón believes that his success and staying power in the advertising industry is due to his commitment to integrity, his strong relationships with media executives and his serious approach to Hispanic advertising. He once faced a financial crisis in the 1990s, but, instead of going into bankruptcy, he decided to sacrifice and pay all of his creditors. His commitment is to "resolving" his clients' problems and not stopping until he does.

Alicia Martínez-Fonts and María Madruga

The founders of MASS Hispanic, started in 1986, were Alicia Martínez-Fonts and María Madruga (who is now president of the agency). They were one of the pioneers in the area of Hispanic promotions, serving clients such as Unilever/Bestfoods (since 1989), Kimberly Clark, Unilever, Clorox, Wrigley's, Procter & Gamble, General Mills, and Quaker, among others.

A winner of the 2010 PMA Reggies Silver and Bronze Awards for its Kleenex art contest, MASS prides itself in focusing on client satisfaction and producing two-fold results. The agency is ranked among the top fifty Hispanic agencies, according to *Advertising Age* (2009).

Steve Blanco

In 1986 Steve Blanco founded an agency in Miami; the firm became Accentmarketing in 1994. Ranked number twelve among U.S. Hispanic advertising agencies by *Advertising Age* in 2009, Accentmarketing has offices in Miami and Los Angeles. The agency has served major national clients such as General Motors, Chevrolet, the U.S. Navy, Nextel, Valvoline, Unilever/Snuggle, Buick, Kaiser Permanente, and GMAC Financial Services. Blanco also sold part of the agency to Interpublic Group. The agency's current president is Lisette Hoyo. Current clients include Dunkin' Donuts, Farmers Insurance, and Jack Daniels.

NEW AGENCIES STARTED BY CUBAN-AMERICANS IN THE 1990S

Manny Vidal, Antonio Ruiz, and Carlos Hernández

In 1991 Manolo "Manny" Vidal co-founded a New York-based agency with Jorge Reynardus and Jorge Moya: Vidal, Reynardus & Moya, which later became The Vidal Partnership after Vidal acquired it in December 1999. It is considered the second Hispanic advertising agency in the U.S. by the 2009 *Advertising Age* ranking.

As the president/CEO of The Vidal Partnership (TVP) in 2000, Manny's goal was to build the most effective multicultural marketing communications firm, raise the bar, and make a difference in the marketplace. The vision to create a best-in-class agency has led him on a thrilling journey. More than nine years later, TVP is the largest independent multicultural marketing communications agency in the U.S., with a hundred employees. The agency's client roster includes Nestlé, Heineken, Johnson & Johnson, Sprint, and Kraft.

Under Vidal's leadership and with partners such as Cuban/Dominican-American Antonio Ruiz (chief strategic officer) and Cuban Carlos Hernández (chief financial officer), the agency has grown to $35 million in revenues, as reported by *Advertising Age* in 2008.

Named one of the Most Influential Hispanics by *People Magazine*, *Poder Magazine*, and *Urban Latino Magazine*, Vidal is a founding member of the Association of Hispanic Advertising Agencies, an executive board member of the Ad Council, and a member of the American Association of Advertising Agencies.

Antonio Ruiz, Vidal partner and chief strategic officer, has been in marketing communications since 1983, specializing in the U.S. Hispanic market. After working as managing partner of Conill Advertising (then Saatchi's Hispanic affiliate) and as regional marketing manager for McDonald's, Ruiz joined The Vidal Partnership as partner. Antonio currently serves on the Board of Directors of the New York Ad Club.

Carlos Hernández, also a partner and CFO at Vidal, was CFO of

McCann-Erickson USA and Lintas. An entrepreneurial CPA with diversified "Big 5" experience and an innovative approach to solving problems, he is certified in the state of New York and is a member of the AICPA and the New York State Society of CPAs.

Daisy Expósito-Ulla

A pioneer in the New York Hispanic advertising industry, Daisy Expósito-Ulla led d'expósito & Partners, an agency with clients such as Anheuser-Busch, Census 2010, Conagra Foods, McDonald's, and Amway Global. Expósito became nationally renowned as president and CEO of The Bravo Group, the number one Hispanic agency during nine consecutive years under her leadership.

Expósito's advertising career began at Conill Advertising, where Alicia Conill charged her with production and creative duties on the McDonald's account. Expósito became CEO of The Bravo Group in 1990 and later the chairperson of several multicultural companies under Bravo's umbrella. Soon after London's WPP acquired Y&R, Expósito was overseeing billings of nearly half a billion dollars. Expósito left the agency in November 2004 and founded d'expósito & Partners, alongside her life partner, Jorge Ulla, in 2007.

Among the major clients that Expósito served was Mazola Corn Oil, which Bravo won on its own, without Y&R participation. Another very significant client was AT&T, a brand that signified another new phase for Bravo and a turning point for the U.S. Hispanic Market itself. Never before had the market seen the level of activity brought by AT&T's clear vision of our market's potential. Then came the great story of Bravo's acquisition of the Sears account.

Like other Hispanic executives, she lived the struggle of the pioneers "selling" the market, as she points out: "We all had to preach this gospel and push against a wall of silence and incomprehension. These were tough days in which we were creating and building a new market, struggling with its many ethnic complexities, and beginning to create scientific approaches to this market and methodologies that could operate with coherence and reliability."

Expósito also faced the challenge of educating and converting "non- and dis-believers." Expósito says, "When the Census 2000 figures validated our presence here, my mind threw a party! We had arrived—years before, though."

A tireless professional and civic leader, Expósito has served as chairman of Latino Initiatives and of the National Campaign to Prevent Pregnancy. She is also on the board of the Advertising Council, the board of the American Education Foundation, and she is a founder of the New America Alliance. She co-founded and was president of AHAA. In addition, she was instrumental in helping institute the Hispanic Clio.

When asked why she was successful, Expósito answers: "I guess because I was—and remain—a fighter. I work hard because I believe in what I do—strongly. I apply a 'can do' spirit in the face of what other people may see as an enormous impossibility. I know I can be an agent of change but if I am going to do something, I'll do it right and I'll do it with passion. But don't let the 'I' outshine the 'We.'"

One of her greatest contributions was her "unwavering conviction, while at Bravo, that media should remain under our roof—not only because we correctly viewed it as a science that required a cultural connection to our consumer, but also because doing the opposite would weaken our industry as a whole and the potential of brands in our market."

Another major contribution, in her opinion, is:

> *Knowing that young, key leaders of today have a place in your past life is incredibly rewarding to know that you contributed in creating the basic blueprint of how agencies in our milieu work today is something rewarding too. Looking back and seeing that perhaps you were an instrument of social involvement and that inspiration and a collective commitment can be contagious are forever energizing.*

Jorge Ulla—Expósito's partner, husband, and head of creative services—is a seasoned professional who ensures excellence in ideation and innovation at d'Expósito & Partners. His world-renowned documentary *Nobody Listened* (1987) is, according to the *New York Times*, a collection of "the extremely persuasive testimony of many Cubans who regard themselves as victims of Castro."

Jorge Reynardus and Jorge Moya

Reynardus & Moya Advertising, born in New York in 1999, was led by Jorge Reynardus and Jorge Moya. Reynardus & Moya served clients such as the ITT Technical Institute, Heineken, La Salle Bank, Schering Plough Claritin, Time Warner Cable, Wyeth, and The Hispanic Federation. In 2009 they merged with MGS COMM. Reynardus is chief strategy officer and Moya is chief creative officer.

Reynardus and Moya had also co-founded Vidal, Reynardus & Moya in New York in 1991. Reynardus has an MBA from the Harvard Graduate School of Business Administration, where his mentor was Dr. Theodor Levitt, considered the father of what we now know as marketing. At Vidal, Reynardus & Moya, Reynardus spearheaded the agency's strategic thinking and oversaw the planning function for clients such as Avon Products, Brown Forman, Buick Division of GM, Chase Manhattan Bank, HBO en Español, Heineken USA, McDonalds Co-op, and Schering-Plough.

From 1984 to 1988 Reynardus worked as vice president and general manager at Castor Advertising, whose founder he considers one of his most inspiring mentors. Reynardus is the author of *The Spanish Market in the United States* (1974) and *Advertising in Latin America* (1973). He serves on the board of the Hispanic Federation of New York.

Jorge Moya has years of advertising experience and the entrepreneurial spirit of his family, owners of Moya Tobacco in Cuba. From 1991 to 1999 he served as the co-founder and creative director of

Vidal, Reynardus & Moya, developing campaigns for HBO en Español, Heineken USA, ITT Technical Institute, and McDonald's. Previously he had worked as creative director at Sosa & Associates in San Antonio, developing advertising for Burger King, Coca-Cola USA, Head & Shoulders, and SC Johnson. Moya has won Best of New York Addy Awards and Clio Awards.

Other Cuban Advertising Leaders

Anthony Baradat founded Anthony Baradat and Associates (AB&A) in Miami in 1994. The agency has served clients such as the University of Miami, Florida Power & Light, Premier American Bank, and the Beacon Council.

Also in 1994 Hermán Echevarría founded BVK/MEKA in Miami. The agency, a Miami branch of a national agency, has served regional and international clients such as: Adorno & Yoss, Aeromexico Vacations, Miami-Dade Water and Sewer, Samsonite, Shaw Ross Importers, Citgo, and other clients. A former Hialeah Councilman, Echevarría serves on the boards of the Beacon Council and Mount Sinai Medical Center.

CUBAN-AMERICAN AGENCIES IN THE TWENTY-FIRST CENTURY

Manuel Machado and Alberto García-Serra

Manny Machado and Hispanic advertising pioneer Alberto García-Serra founded Machado García Serra (MGSCOMM) in 2004 and merged it with IAC, thus creating a national full-service advertising and marketing communications agency, number seventeen among the Hispanic Agencies in the 2009 *Advertising Age* ranking. In 2009 they merged the agency with Reynardus & Moya.

Machado began his career at Sánchez & Levitán at the age of twenty-one and later worked at Univisión. Eventually, he created his own agency and partnered with Alberto García-Serra, one of Miami's Hispanic advertising pioneers, with forty years of advertising expertise.

The company's client roster has included the Florida Lottery, Southeast Toyota, Scion, Tiffany & Co., FPL, Pfizer, BB&T, and Bird's Eye.

Machado also served as president of the Association of Hispanic Advertising Agencies. He is on the board of SBS and past chairman and current board member of AHAA.

In 2008 García-Serra won the Hispanic Business Entrepreneur of the Year Award. He has served on the boards of the American Red Cross and MADD.

Jorge Plasencia and Luis Casamayor

A former top Univisión Radio executive, Jorge A. Plasencia, chairman and CEO of República, started a national agency in Miami in 2006 with partner Luis Casamayor. Between 2006 and 2009, República has served accounts such as Pernod Ricard (Absolut Vodka, Chivas Regal, Kahlúa, Jameson, and Malibu), Goya, Burger King Corporation, Universal Studios, Nielsen, Sedano's Supermarkets, National Council of La Raza, the Miami Dolphins, and the National Museum of the American Latino Commission. República is ranked as one of the top fifty Hispanic agencies by *Advertising Age* (2009).

Prior to joining Univisión, Plasencia served as vice president of Estefan Enterprises, Inc., owned by superstar Gloria and Emilio Estefan, Jr., and he was the director of Hispanic marketing for the Florida Marlins Baseball Club.

A nationally renowned community leader, Plasencia serves as vice chair of the National Council of La Raza (NCLR) and on the advisory boards of the Congressional Hispanic Leadership Institute (CHLI) and the Broadcasting Board of Governors' OCB. He is chairman and co-founder of Amigos For Kids, and he serves on the boards of the

Adrienne Arsht Center, Miami-Dade College Foundation, and others. Among his many accolades, Plasencia received the UNICEF For the Love of Children Award, Big Brothers Big Sisters Miracle Maker Award, and the PRSA Royal Palm Award.

Before joining forces with Plasencia, Luis Casamayor, República's president and chief creative officer, founded Cosmyk Group, a creative marketing agency, in 1994. Casamayor is an expert in broadcast, print, social media, advertising, and web design. Casamayor has received national and international recognition and awards for his creativity, including National Addys.

THE SIGNIFICANCE OF THE CUBAN-AMERICAN

Contribution to U.S. Hispanic Advertising

At a time when the Hispanic market was a small percentage of the U.S. population, the visionary work of Cuban-American advertising and media pioneers inspired others to start Hispanic advertising agencies throughout the U.S. "The Cubans who arrived in the '60s included many advertising professionals with experience and with excellent contacts with American companies," says Jorge Reynardus. Combined with the innovative work of Cuban media leaders such as Eduardo Caballero, who created the first Hispanic radio media network in the U.S., and Raúl Alarcon, Sr., founder of SBS Radio Network, these advertising pioneers were instrumental in creating the Hispanic marketing and media industries.

As Carl Kravetz told *Advertising Age* in 2007: "These passionate trail-blazers battled misperceptions, small budgets and prejudice at times to achieve the impossible. . . . Overcoming seemingly insurmountable problems, they established themselves in the U.S. marketing and media industry and, in the process, created what is today a $5 billion-plus industry segment."

According to Daisy Expósito-Ulla, the reason for these pioneers' success was that they "came from a place where there was an advanced communications infrastructure: a great radio and print tradition, a creatively fertile television industry that shared pioneering of the medium with the USA before most countries in the region."

Richard Marañón attributes the accomplishments of Cubans in advertising to their work ethic. "My father was a Spaniard who worked very hard in his business," says Marañón. "Cuban-Americans advertising agency owners are similar to the Spanish immigrants who were hard-working entrepreneurs in Cuba during the first half of the twentieth century. Their motto was: *Trabajar y no mirar atrás* (Work and don't look back)."

Also crucial was their ability to think big, to dream of owning their own business, to believe that they could succeed, even as they were working cleaning the floors.

During the 1980s, 1990s, and in the first few years of the twenty-first century, Cuban-Americans continued to make a significant contribution to the development of the U.S. Hispanic marketing communications industry. It is they who will most probably offer an important foundation for the rebirth of the advertising industry once Cuba is free.

NOTES

1. Association of Hispanic Advertising Agencies (AHAA), 2006 News Release to Media.
2. Louis A. Pérez, *On Becoming Cuban: Identity, Nationality and Culture* (New York: HarperCollins, 2001), 132.
3. *AHAA* interview with Rochelle Newman.
4. *Advertising Age*, February 19, 2007.
5. Author interview with Joe Zubizarreta in August 2008 and *HispanicBusiness.com* 2007.
6. John Nank (*Smart Business,* 2007).

PROFESSIONALS

32

MEDICINE

BY RENE F. RODRIGUEZ

Ever since Christopher Columbus discovered Cuba during his first voyage in 1492, the Caribbean island nation has been an important crossroads and stopping point between Europe and the new American continents. This privileged geographic location made the port of Havana the beneficiary of great ideas and different cultures, but also made it the target of diseases brought over from the Old World.

During the nineteenth century, the Caribbean and other tropical regions experienced a terrible and devastating yellow fever epidemic. This epidemic killed more soldiers than the *"machetes"* wielded by our freedom-seeking and heroic *"Mambises"* (Cuban guerrilla fighters during the Ten Years' War [1868-78] and the Independence War of 1895) against Spain. It also halted construction in the region of the Panama Canal. Scientists from different countries traveled to Cuba and became involved in research to discover the etiology and control of this epidemic.

During the Spanish Colonial era, Cuba's medical profession was influenced by scientists from Europe (especially France and Germany) and North America. This fact gave special character to the faculty of the Havana University Medical School. Because of this foreign influence in medicine and medical teaching, some Cuban physicians became known the world over. Among them were Drs. Pedro Castillo, José Centurión, Vicente Pardo Castelló, José Lastra, Fernando Milanés, Sr.,

Héctor Rocamora, Agustín Castellanos, Angel Aballí, Manuel Viamonte, Sr., Angel Vieta Barahona, Francisco Barrera, Antonio Rodríguez Díaz, and many others.

During a meeting of the Pan American Health Organization Association in Havana in 1891, Cuban-born and Philadelphia-educated physician Dr. Carlos J. Finlay unveiled his theory that a specific type of mosquito was the carrier of yellow fever, thus earning the nickname of "Mosquito Man." However, his theory and speeches about yellow fever fell on deaf ears. During the U.S. occupation of Cuba in 1899—and after two unsuccessful U.S. commissions had been sent to Havana to investigate the cause of yellow fever—a third U.S. Army commission arrived and sought the advice and knowledge of Dr. Finlay, who was a renowned and respected acquaintance of an American governor. This time, Dr. Finlay's theory that the mosquito was the carrier of yellow fever was validated, and General Leonard Wood, a physician who was U.S. military governor of Cuba between 1900 and 1902, publicly recognized Dr. Finlay's discovery during a luncheon celebrating this important medical and scientific breakthrough.

Dr. Finlay's recommendations were accepted and put into practice, and in a short period, yellow fever was eradicated from Havana and the tropics. Also, the building of the Panama Canal was resumed and successfully completed in 1914, thus opening the interoceanic waterway between the Atlantic and the Pacific oceans to merchant and passenger shipping.

But even though Dr. Finlay's historic medical discovery has been well documented, the discovery that led to the eradication of yellow fever has been attributed to Major Walter Reed, a physician who headed the third U.S. Army commission and who was its main researcher. To this day, Dr. Reed is recognized as the person who discovered that mosquitoes transmit the disease. But, for the record, Reed himself credited Finlay with the discovery of the yellow fever vector and how it might be controlled. It must also be noted that Dr. Finlay was nominated for the Nobel Prize for his study of the mosquito and yellow fever.

Following this important medical discovery, more Cuban scientists became interested in "tropical medicine." During the research period on yellow fever, a young American nurse, Clara Maas, lost her life as a volunteer on the study, and her sacrifice and efforts were ignored for more than fifty years.

One of the most enduring myths surrounding Cuba's Marxist Revolution is that prior to Fidel Castro's rise to power in 1959, Cuba was a poor and backward Third World nation. But international statistics about health, education, and Cuba's socioeconomic development belie that myth. In fact, a paper released by the U.S. State Department in 1998 and later revised and expanded by its authors, Kirby Smith and Hugo Llorens, showed—among others things—the following:

- *Readily available data show that Cuba was already a relatively well-advanced country by 1958, certainly by Latin American standards, and in some cases by world standards.*

- *The data show that Cuba has at best maintained what were already high levels of development in health and education, but that in other areas, Cubans have borne extraordinary costs as a result of Castro-style totalitarianism and misguided economic policies.*

- *With the possible exception of health and education, Cuba's relative position among Latin American countries is lower today [in the late 1990s] than it was in 1958 for virtually every socio-economic measure for which reliable data are available.*

- *The health care system is often touted by many observers as one of the Castro government's greatest achievements. . . . (but) what (many analyses and analysts ignore) is that the revolutionary government inherited an already advanced health sector when it took power in 1959.*

- *In terms of physicians and dentists per capita, Cuba ranked third in Latin America in 1957, behind only Uruguay and Argentina—both of which were more advanced than the United States in this measure. . . . Unfortunately, the UN Statistical Yearbook no longer publishes these statistics, so more recent comparisons are not possible.*

Cuban physicians have earned deserved great professional reputations and have set up private medical practices all over the USA.

Dr. Fernando "Cuco" López Fernández was the director of Las Animas Hospital, an infectious disease hospital in Havana, and later became deputy secretary of Public Health in Cuba. In 1951, during the presidency of Dr. Carlos Prío Socarrás, Dr. López Fernández spearheaded the issuance of a Cuban postage stamp honoring Clara Maas. When the U.S.-bound exodus of Cuban physicians began in 1959, Dr. López Fernández moved to Chicago, where he became the chief of staff of the North Washington Hospital. Because of his tenacity, he was instrumental in the issuance of the U.S. postage stamp honoring Clara Maas. Unfortunately, he was not able to celebrate this achievement, but his widow and family received the recognition on his behalf at the Clara Maas Hospital in Newark, N.J.

Dr. Joaquín Albarrán, born in Sagua La Grande, Cuba, traveled to Barcelona, Spain, to study medicine after completing his elementary education, and then went on to Paris, France, where he graduated. He worked under Dr. Félix Guyón, a famous educator dedicated to the study of the urinary tract. While in Paris, Dr. Albarrán designed a small instrument that allowed the passage of a catheter through the urethra to the kidneys.

This instrument is known as the "Albarrán Nail." Since that time, urology has become a specialty separate from surgery. Dr. Albarrán also described a third lobe in the prostate known as the "Albarrán Lobe."

Among prominent Cuban urologists are Dr. Félix Rodríguez-Molina, a pioneer and the first president of the Cuban Urology Society; and Drs.

Gonzalo Pedroso, Angel Calderón, and Ramón Guiteras. The last was born in Bristol, R.I., the son of Cuban immigrant Ramón Guiteras, and he became the first president of the American Urology Society. Another Cuban urologist, Dr. José Iglesias de la Torre, introduced the transurethral resection, a procedure that at the beginning was not fully accepted in Cuba due to early failures and complications. After he left Cuba and settled in the United States, Dr. de la Torres' resectorscope was improved. The instrument used carries his name and is successfully used around the world by thousands of urologists.

The Cuban medical profession made great contributions to society. It created a public and private health system that allowed even less-affluent people to receive treatment in hospitals and clinics from well-known private-sector physicians.

These hospitals and clinics, known as *Centros Regionales* (Regional Centers) and other private clinics and hospitals, were established on the principle of prepaid affordable medical care. Some, like La Covadonga, Las Hijas de Galicia, and La Asociación de Dependientes de Comercio de La Habana, had ties to organizations whose members came from different regions of Spain. Other medical facilities—like the Centro Médico Quirúrgico—were open to members who paid monthly dues. This system was widely accepted in Cuba. Regional medical care centers became known as "Cuban clinics." The clinics were later introduced in Miami at the beginning of the Cuban exile, mainly because immigrant Cuban doctors were well known to their fellow Cuban immigrant patients. These types of clinics are similar to what is now known as Health Maintenance Organizations (HMOs). The bulk of these clinics' services were mainly oriented to preventive medicine. These clinics have saved millions of dollars to the state of Florida.

Industrialist Henry J. Kaiser and Dr. Sidney R. Garfield co-founded Kaiser Permanente, a prepaid medical plan system in the United States in 1945, similar to the system that had existed in Cuba for many decades.

In 1960 the chairman of the Department of Medicine of the

University of Miami School of Medicine, Dr. Ralph Jones, encouraged and helped create the University of Havana, Medical School in exile. Its purpose was to offer a twelve-week course to help Cuban physicians newly arrived in the U.S. pass the examination of the Educational Council for Foreign Medical Graduates (ECFMG), as well as to credential those arriving without their identifying documents. The professors were Vicente Pardo Castelló (dermatology), José Centurión (medicine), Fernando R. Milanés (medicine), José Lastra (surgery), Héctor Rocamora (obstetrics and gynecology), and later on Angel Vieta Barahona (who had been the dean of the Medical School in Havana), Agustín Castellanos (cardiology), and Rafael Peñalver, who directed these courses for many years.

Dr. Rafael Peñalver offered these courses not only to Cuban physicians, but also to physicians of all nations who wanted to prepare for the exam. More than ten thousand physicians from sixty different countries benefited from these courses and were able to restore their medical career in the United States. In addition, these courses served as a good networking forum to help spread the message all over the world about the political situation inside Cuba. They also helped establish better relations and understanding between Cuban exiles and different countries.

In 1960, a series of events took place—centered in a small town in south-central Georgia—that became a crucial and pivotal chapter in the history of Cuban medical in exile. The pioneers were two Cuban psychiatrists: Drs. José Balbona and Julián Gómez. The setting for this development was the Central State Hospital (CSH), located in Milledgeville, Georgia, the state's largest facility for treatment of mental illness and developmental disabilities. Milledgeville, the former state capital, is a city of about eighteen thousand inhabitants located about a hundred miles southeast of Atlanta.

Balbona and Gómez were best friends who studied together at the same Jesuit high school in Cuba and arrived in the United States in 1960 within two or three weeks of each other. "From Miami, we sent letters to all the psychiatric hospitals (throughout the United States) and the only response came from Milledgeville," said Berta Gómez, the wife of the late Dr. Gómez, who—after Balbona—became the second Cuban psychiatrist to go to work at the Milledgeville hospital.

At the time, the Milledgeville hospital had about twelve thousand patients, but not enough staff to take care of them. The problem, as Mrs. Gómez explained in an interview from her home in Charlottesville, Virginia, was that few physicians wanted to work there. By autumn 1960, a retired New York psychoanalyst was appointed to head the hospital. Dr. Balbona went to see him, and soon the new administrator began hiring Cuban doctors, who were not allowed to practice medicine on their own, but who could work at the hospital under his medical supervision.

Shortly after the new administrator's arrival on the scene, close to eighty Cuban doctors were working at the hospital. "I think that about 90 percent of the hospital's medical staff was Cuban, in addition to several Colombians and one Peruvian," Mrs. Gómez remembered.

Some ten years later, in 1971, Cuban doctors still made up 68 percent (and five of the ten directors) of the 113 doctors on staff at the Milledgeville facility, according to a document published by The Heritage Foundation in July 1980.

"This hospital would not be open today were it not for the services of Cuban physicians. I dread to think of the many hundreds of citizens who would be without medical attention in that situation," said Howard Palmatier, Cuban Refugee Program director under the Nixon Administration.[1]

Other Cuban doctors who worked at Milledgeville included: Drs. José (Joe) García Mendoza, Emilio Soto Pradera, Joaquín Piedra, Ronaldo Nodal, José Miguel Portuondo y de Castro, Carlos Maruri, Manuel Antón, and his wife, Blanca Menéndez de Antón.

Later the Milledgeville hospital made arrangements with Atlanta's Emory University for the Cuban doctors to enroll in a three-year psychiatric residency program, working three and one-half days a week at the Milledgeville hospital and another three and one-half days a week at Emory.

Between 1960 and 1964, the Miami Veterans Administration (VA) Hospital helped the Cuban physicians who had to take and pass the ECFGM. The VA, through the leadership of its chief of staff, Dr. Edward C. White, with the support of the VA director Dr. Earl G. Gluckman, also helped the exile Cuban physicians relocate to different parts of the U.S.

By 1961 there were more than seven hundred Cuban physicians in exile who were not working in their profession and were awaiting their return to Cuba. After the unsuccessful 1961 Bay of Pigs invasion, Cuban physicians already in the United States began to realize that there was little hope of an early return to their homeland, and so they began to settle down in the United States and practice medicine there.

Cuban physicians made extraordinary medical contributions to their new host country that had welcomed them in exile. This is how the Nixon Administration's director of Cuban Refugee Program, Howard Palmatier, put it:

It is of general knowledge the scientific capacity of Cuban physicians. This fact is known throughout the American territory. A day does not go by without our offices in Washington receiving a telephone call or a letter by a Senator, a member of the House of Representatives or a private citizen asking information as to how to employ a Cuban physician so as to give them the opportunity to practice his profession. Generally, the request is preceded by numerous praises on the professional capacity of the Cuban physician whom they have met or of whom they have reference.

The Cuban Medical Association in Exile (*Colegio Médico Cubano Libre*, or CMA in Exile) was established in October 1960 with eighty-seven founding members headed by Dr. Enrique Huertas. In August 1962, the American Medical Association (AMA) recognized the new Cuban professional organization, which later was also recognized by other Latin American medical associations. The CMA in Exile worked closely with the Cuban Refugee Program, the state of Florida, the U.S. Health, Education & Welfare Department (HEW), and other recognized medical groups throughout the world. In 1961, the CMA in exile brought the atrocities and wrongdoings of the Fidel Castro regime to international attention at the World Medical Association's (WMA) General Assembly in Rio de Janeiro. It did the same at subsequent international meetings in Chicago, London, Chile, and Germany.

In October 1963, during WMA's 17th General Assembly, a committee comprised of Drs. Héctor Rodríguez of Chile, Ernest Fromm of Germany, and Edward R. Annis from the United States was named to lead the investigations into the concerns raised by the CMA in Exile. The group's evaluation and report was approved by the Pan American Medical Confederation and the WMA, and led to the repudiation and expulsion of the Cuban Medical National Association and its Communist medical delegates. This was a great victory for the CMA in Exile. Dr. Enrique Huertas became a delegate to the General Assembly of the WMA, and he later was elected president of the WMA.

Another Cuban medical group born in exile was the League Against Cancer (*La Liga Contra el Cáncer*), a Miami-based non-profit organization. The League was founded in Miami in 1975 as a community-based organization that provided free medical care to needy cancer patients. Today, more than 350 Florida physicians volunteer their services for the League.

According to the group's own publication, "The League Against Cancer is the last resort for cancer victims who have no financial resources or health insurance." Since 1975, more than fifty thousand low-income, uninsured men, women, and children have received treatment from the League. The group's General Coordinator was Lourdes Aguila, who served in that position from 1975 until her death in 1999.

Not many Cuban physicians went to the United States before

Castro's 1959 revolution. However, those who did, established a good and reputable practice, opening the doorway to the many physicians who immigrated to the United States after 1959.

In South Florida, Dr. Modesto Mora and his brothers founded the Pan American Hospital in 1963—the first hospital in Miami adapted to the Cuban culture. Later, Dr. Mora became co-owner of the American Hospital (now Kendall Regional) and North Ridge Hospital in Ft. Lauderdale. He also became involved in medical-related politics and was a member of the Florida Board of Medical Examiners. Dr. Mora and the Pan American Hospital sponsored the Cuban Medical Convention, and—together with Dr. Enrique Huertas' CMA in Exile—offered alternate annual medical congresses that were very successful in the Cuban medical community throughout the USA.

The Penrose Cancer Hospital in Colorado Springs, Colorado, enlisted the services of Dr. Juan del Regato, a Cuban-born physician trained at the Curie Institute in Paris. Dr. del Regato was the director of Radiation Therapy at the Colorado Springs hospital, and he co-authored, with Dr. Lauren Ackerman, a world-renowned textbook on cancer. He organized annual cancer seminars at the hospital, which were well attended and provided outstanding scientific information. He moved to Tampa, where he continued to teach radiation oncology at the University of South Florida, and where he was named "Teacher of the Year" by the student body on several occasions.

The Florida Medical Association was one of the first institutions to recognize the outstanding contributions of Cuban physicians in South Florida. Dr. Luis Pérez Samper, a physician born and trained in Cuba, established his practice in Central Florida, became president of the Florida Medical Association, and was a leading force behind the fight against the rising costs of medical malpractice.

It should be mentioned that the actual president of the Florida Medical Association is a Cuban-born physician, Dr. Madelyn Butler, and the president-elect is another Cuban-born physician, Dr. Miguel Machado.

The University of Miami (UM) School of Medicine also welcomed many of the Cuban physicians who left their homeland for South Florida. Among them was Dr. Agustín Castellanos, Jr., a well-known international authority on cardiac electrophysiology. He is a professor of medicine at UM and co-director of the cardiology meeting sponsored annually by the Division of Cardiology of the Department of Medicine of UM's School of Medicine. He is one of the world's best-known Cuban-born physicians.

Dr. Agustín Castellanos, Sr., considered the "Father of Angiocardiography" of the right heart chamber, was nominated for the Nobel Prize in recognition of his contributions to the field of cardiac diagnosis and his angiocardiography work in Cuba. He practiced medicine in Miami and worked at Children's Hospital. He was a national and international lecturer at medical conventions and published extensively.

Dr. Frank Hernández, also born in Cuba, had established his medical practice in Miami in 1940, and he was the director of National Children's Cardiac Hospital, which subsequently became the University of Miami Hospital. He organized the first cardiac catheterization unit for children at this institution. In the early history of this facility, children with rheumatic heart disease were Dr. Hernández's primary medical concern. He died in late 1970, debilitated by diffused pulmonary emphysema but remembered as a well-known pediatric cardiologist in the world.

Dr. Fernando Milanés, Jr., also Cuban born, became head of the Department of Psychiatry of the VA Medical Center and held the position until his retirement. During his time at the VA, Dr. Milanés trained many psychiatrists and was a superb administrator.

Dr. Horacio Ferrer established a famous school of ophthalmology in Cuba. His daughter, Dr. Olga Ferrer, also an ophthalmologist, followed in his footsteps and was director of the Ophthalmology Institute in Miami. Dr. Ferrer also made significant contributions to the field of ophthalmology.

In northern Florida, Cuban physician Dr. Angel de la Torre was the director of Cardiology at St. Vincent's Hospital in Jacksonville. He was affiliated with the University of Florida in Gainesville, and later he created a very prestigious invasive and non-invasive cardiac laboratory. He helped develop a cardiac program which, to date, is one of the most respected in the nation.

Many Cuban physicians have made great contributions to South Florida and to the country in general. In 1984 Dr. Pedro José Greer, Jr., founded the Camillus Health Concerns, which provides health care to the poor and the homeless. He was awarded a McArthur "genius grant" in 1993 as well as the Presidential Medal of Freedom in 2009. He is now the assistant dean of Academic Affairs at Florida International University's School of Medicine.

Dr. Ramón Rodríguez Torres, a Cuban-born physician, worked in New York at Downstate Medical Center; later he was chairman of Pediatrics in Dayton, Ohio. He became chief of staff of the Miami Children's Hospital, previously known as the Variety Children's Hospital, where he designed an educational program that in turn made this hospital a renowned pediatric institution throughout the United States.

The Miami Medical Team has had a unique contribution made possible by the Cuban physicians in exile. Spearheaded by orthopedic surgeon Dr. Manuel Alzugaray, this organization has undertaken numerous missions to difficult and problematic areas in Latin America with humanitarian medical care and supplies. It has also performed life-saving surgeries on the poor and people in need. Dr. Mario Soler, another orthopedic surgeon, and Dr. Alexis Abril, a general surgeon, also have contributed their time and efforts to this organization.

Dr. Eneida O. Roldán is the personification of the American Dream. Born in the Vedado neighborhood of Havana, she came to Miami at age two. Since June 2009, she was president and chief executive officer (CEO) of the Jackson Health System (JHS)—the leading public health system of the Miami-Dade County area in South Florida. Prior to joining JHS, she was president and CEO of the Metropolitan Hospital of Miami, previously known as the Pan American Hospital. Dr. Roldán took charge of the hospital in 2005 when it was in Chapter 11 and facing a myriad of troubles. She resigned in 2011 and was replaced by Carlos Migoya, a banker who also helped straighten out the finances of the city of Miami as its city manager.

Dr. Roldán has impressive educational and professional credentials. She attended the University of Miami as an undergraduate and Ross University School of Medicine. She completed her residency in anatomic and clinical pathology and fellowship training in pediatric pathology at Jackson Memorial Hospital. She also has degrees from the University of South Florida and an MBA from the University of Tennessee with the highest honors and distinctions. Dr. Roldán is a member of the Harvard Business School Executive Education program.

Also in South Florida, Dr. Eduardo C. Alfonso—born in Cuba and raised in Puerto Rico before moving to the United States to attend college—is the chairman of the Bascom Palmer Eye Institute, which serves as the Department of Ophthalmology for the University of Miami Miller School of Medicine. It is considered one of the world's finest and most progressive centers for ophthalmic care, research, and education.

In May 2010, Dr. Manuel Antón III became president and CEO of Miami's Mercy Hospital. He had joined the Catholic hospital in Miami in 2001. Prior to Mercy Hospital, Dr. Antón served ten years at Orlando Regional Healthcare System (Orlando Health) in various capacities.

Dr. Rafael A. Peñalver already practiced medicine in his native Cuba as member of a medical family before he came to the United States. Once in the states, he had a dream about a facility that would provide high-quality, affordable, preventive medicine, education, and personalized treatment for all. That dream became a reality in 1996 after his passing, when his family founded the Dr. Rafael A. Peñalver Clinic, which now serves more than thirty-five thousand patients annually. Located in the heart of Miami's Little Havana, the Dr. Peñalver Clinic has become more than just the health care facility of choice for residents in Little Havana;

the clinic's range of services now covers the entire Miami-Dade County community.

In Tampa, Florida, for example, Dr. José Mijares developed a good practice and became a medical leader and publisher in different journals. Dr. Ortelio Rodríguez established a well-known orthopedic practice in the same city.

In New Orleans, Cuban orthopedic surgeon Dr. Raoul Rodríguez was a member of the faculty of Tulane University Medical School. He followed in the footsteps of his father, Dr. Raoul M. Rodríguez, who was the director of the Orthopedic Hospital in Cuba.

Many physicians were members of Florida's Board of Medical Licensing. Among them were Drs. Modesto Mora, Alberto Hernández, Gustavo León, Luis Serentil, Gastón Acosta, and Manuel Coto.

In California, Dr. José Manuel de los Reyes established an outstanding medical practice and became the chairman of surgery at the University of California as well as a member of the California Board of Medicine. Dr. Tirso del Junco also became a member of the same Board of Medicine while practicing general surgery. He became active in politics during the Reagan Administration, when he was elected chairman of the Republican Party of California. Dr. Gladys Hoed and many other Cuban-born physicians have made significant contributions to medicine and to their communities in California.

Many other Cuban physicians also settled in Texas. In San Antonio, Dr. Virgilio Beato reopened a prominent practice of internal medicine just as he had done in Cuba. He served the San Antonio community for many years before relocating to Miami, Florida. He has been clinical professor of medicine at the University of Texas, San Antonio, and the University of Miami. He is very well known for his brilliant oratory and his vast knowledge of culture, being invited frequently to participate not only in medical meetings but also in non-medical panels. He is editor of *40 Años de Revolución (Colección Cuba y sus Jueces* (1999) and co-author of *50 Años de Revolución en Cuba/ 50 Years of Cuba's Revolution: El Legado de los*

Castro/The Legacy of the Castros (2009).

Dr. Pedro Ruiz, a first-rate clinical psychiatrist, was the chairman of psychiatry of Baylor Medical Center and became the first Cuban-born physician to be elected president of the American Psychiatric Association. Currently, Dr. Ruiz is the cochairman of the Department of Psychiatry at the Miller School of Medicine at the University of Miami. Dr. David Almeida founded the Hispanic Medical Society in Houston, Texas.

Chicago was also the destination for many Cuban physicians who will be remembered for generations to come. Among them are Drs. Domingo O'Cherony and Frank Yánez. Both are pediatricians who practiced in Hispanic neighborhoods of Chicago and were honored with numerous awards from their communities for their dedication. Dr. Fernando López Fernández, an outstanding internist and clinician, was deeply loved by his patients because of his kind and gentle bedside manners as well as the excellent care he gave to his patients. Unfortunately, he died very young and is greatly missed in the Chicago community where he practiced medicine. Dr. López Fernández was co-founder of the Inter-American College of Physicians and Surgeons and of *MÉDICO Interamericano*, a Spanish medical journal. Also in Chicago was a very prominent physician, Dr. Aldo Pedroso, who was the delegate of the Cuban Medical Association in Exile in that city. Another Cuban-born physician who became chairman of the Department of Ophthalmology of the Illinois Masonic Medical Center in Chicago is Dr Osvaldo López-Fernández.

During the early years of the Cuban exile, New Jersey became the home of Dr. Juan B. Pulido, a past president of the Student Council of the Havana Medical School. His wife, Zoraida Calderón, practiced pediatrics. Unfortunately, Dr. Pulido died young of a heart attack. In the New York/New Jersey area, Dr. Julio Rodríguez-Fariñas set up a very successful practice while also helping other physicians to start their practice in this area. Dr. Rodríguez Fariñas was a very committed physician and surgeon who practiced in Cuba for many years. He retrained at New York Polyclinic Hospital.

In New York, Dr. Elsa M. Echemendía, an endocrinologist, was the delegate of the CMA in Exile. On every December 3, the association held a celebration in honor of Dr. Carlos J. Finlay—it was one of the main events of the association. Dr. Echemendía practiced in New York City along with her husband, Dr. Juan de Dios Pérez. Dr. Orlando Cañizares, a renowned dermatologist in New York City, was also professor at New York University and helped many of the Cuban doctors newly arrived in New York to set up their medical practices. Also in New York were Drs. Armando Núñez and Dr. Armando de Cárdenas. The former was an excellent surgeon and the latter a first-rate clinician who helped and guided Cuban physicians arriving in the area. Prior to their arrival as exiles in the United States, these Cuban physicians had made their reputation practicing medicine, whether within their own specialty or in general practice. Among these early pioneers were Drs. Rogelio Enríquez, Adrian Van Canagham, Eulogio Cantillo, Orlando Cartaya, and Roberto Sánchez.

The Spanish American Medical Society had been in existence in New York since 1929. Dr. Orlando Cañizares became the first Cuban-born president of the society in 1959 and worked intensely to promote membership among the physicians of the Hispanic-Latino community in the New York metropolitan area. In 1972, Dr. René Rodríguez Pouget became the second Cuban-born president of the Spanish American Medical Society. He was succeeded in that position by Dr. Francisco Grau in 1976; Dr. René F. Rodríguez, elected for two periods from 1977 to 1979; and Dr. Armando Fernández Fox, in 1987. The period covered by these Cuban-led presidencies is considered the society's golden age. The Inter-American Medical Congress was created during the 1977-79 period and still holds an annual medical congress in New York City every October.

Dr. Reinaldo Muñiz-Cano is a distinguished internist who developed a great reputation in Caracas, Venezuela. He is also a sought-after speaker in the subjects of the history of medicine and medical ethics.

Meanwhile, Cuba bragged about its own medical system, but in truth it is a fraud, as columnist Myriam Márquez described in the *Miami Herald* on October 4, 2009: "The communist island's much-lauded health-care system is an evil hoax."

And what's more, the "export" of Cuban doctors—like, for example, to oil-rich socialist Venezuela—has become a cash-for-doctors program, according to the *Wall Street Journal* in an article published August 16, 2010:

> *For decades, Cuba has "exported" doctors, nurses and health technicians to earn diplomatic influence in poor countries and hard cash for its floundering economy. According to Cuba's official media, an estimated 38,544 Cuban health professionals were serving abroad in 2008, 17,697 of them doctors. (Cuba reports having 70,000 doctors in all.)*
>
> *These "missionaries of the revolution" are well-received in host countries from Algeria to South Africa to Venezuela. Yet those who hail Cuba's generosity overlook the uglier aspects of Cuba's health diplomacy. The regime stands accused of violating various international agreements such as the Trafficking in Persons Protocol and ILO Convention on the Protection of Wages because of the way these health-care providers are treated.*

NOTES

1. "The Cuban Refugee Problem in Perspective, 1959 -1980," July 18, 1980, the Heritage Foundation.

33

ENGINEERING AND SCIENCE

BY JOSE C. IRASTORZA

Engineering has been a favored occupation of Cuban professionals since before the Republic. Among the most significant Cuban-Spanish early accomplishments in the technological world are:

- First railroad in Latin America (Havana-Guines), 1837, which by the way was eleven years before Spain had its first railroad.
- Cuba inaugurated its first public lighting system in 1889, covering some streets then called *"Parque Isabel II"* and *"Paseo de Isabel la Catolica."*
- The first street car in Cuba traveled four kilometers from the city of Regla to Guanabacoa in March 1900.
- Cuba was one of the first countries in the world with TV transmission starting with Union Radio, Canal 4 on October 1950.
- Cuba was the second country in the world to broadcast a color television signal and the third, in 1958, to have a color television station.

The University of Havana started producing engineering graduates that distinguished themselves in all disciplines, including sugar production, civil engineering, mining (Moa Mining Co.), and oil refineries with their contributions to the Shell, Esso, and Texaco refining facilities and electric power generation.

The University of Havana was by far the largest producer of Cuban engineers, but not the only one. A small but significant number of Cuban engineers began coming to the U.S. for their education early in the twentieth century.

Beginning around 1960, Cuban graduates of the University of Havana, Santo Tomas de Villanueva, and those who graduated from American universities became the Cuban engineering exiles that made significant contributions outside Cuba.

Engineers by the nature of their profession, except for the civil engineers, made the bulk of their contributions within large corporations or in academia. The civil engineers, in a significant number of cases, tend to create professional firms, relatively small firms, much like the architects do. Mechanical and electrical engineers, if they are in the construction business also create relatively small firms and quite a few Cubans have made significant contributions in creating such firms.

It is a challenge to tell the stories of these engineers and scientists. How to provide a unifying structure to this plethora of individual accomplishments? We could do so by when they arrived, by discipline, or by achievement.

Regardless of how you classify them, there was a group of remarkable individuals that must be mentioned before all others.

There are several common themes, and one of them is the challenges faced by these waves of immigrants.

The first wave which came from late 1959 escaping Castro (and some from the mid-1950s escaping Batista) and who were already practicing engineers but came with nothing except their knowledge to start a new life, a second group which faced the challenge of completing their education mostly in the U.S. in the 1960s and 1970s, but sharing all of them, a passion for getting ahead in their chosen profession.

In fact, the LSU Chemical Engineer Newsletter of spring 2002 is dedicated to these individuals with its main article titled "From Cuba to Louisiana: 1961-1975." Another school with a major Cuban representation in the late 1950s and early 1960s was Georgia Tech.[1]

One of the best ways to organize these individuals is by looking at their achievements and where they were made. The list of engineering and science distinguished academics is very extensive and some appear in other chapters of this book.

Dr. Jorge I. Aunón received his BS in electrical engineering (1967) MA, and PhD (1972) degrees from George Washington University. Aunón then taught at Purdue University, was a professor and head of the Department of Electrical Engineering at Colorado State University, where he was the interim dean of engineering until 1994. From there he was appointed dean, College of Engineering at Texas Tech University in 1995, and in 1999 he accepted the position of dean, College of Engineering at the University of Alabama, in Huntsville.

Aunón is a cofounder of ECG Analyzer, Inc. a hardware and software company that manufactures EKG machines for canines and felines.

Dr. Ruben G. Carbonell is the Kenan distinguished professor of chemical and biomolecular engineering at North Carolina State University. He joined NC State in 1984, after ten years in the Chemical Engineering Department at the University of California, Davis. He was department head of Chemical Engineering at NC State from 1994 to 1999. He is currently director of the Kenan Institute for Engineering, Technology & Science, and director of the Golden Leaf Biomanufacturing Training and Education Center.

Carbonell's research has led to the design of improved trickle bed reactors in petroleum processing and the creation of two new corporate entities, Ligamar, Inc., and Pathogen Removal and Diagnostic Technologies, Inc. (PRDT). Professor Carbonell was born in Cuba, moved to the U.S. in 1958 and earned his BS degree in chemical engineering from Manhattan College in 1969 and MA and PhD (1973) degrees in chemical engineering from Princeton University.

Dr. Rodrigo Rodríguez-Kabana is a distinguished university professor at the College of Agriculture, Auburn University. He has been a member of the Auburn research staff and faculty since 1965.

Rodríguez-Kabana received a BS in agronomy from Louisiana State University in 1961, then an MS in soil microbiology (1962) and a PhD in plant pathology in 1965. His professional association activities include president, Organization of Nematologists of Tropical America (ONTA) 2001-2002; Methyl Bromide Technical Options Committee (MBTOC), co-chairman 1993-1999. Rodríguez-Kabana has also written more than four hundred articles in referred research publications.

Dr. Carlos A Smith received his PhD in chemical engineering from Louisiana State University in 1972. He started at the University of South Florida (USF) in 1972, became a full professor in 1983 and was chairman of the Department of Chemical Engineering from 1988 to 1992. He has written two textbooks. He has recently been named as the interim director for the institute for the study of Latin America and the Caribbean (ISLAC).

Dr. Annie I. Antón, a professor of software engineering in the College of Engineering at North Carolina State University. She received a BS in information and computer science in 1990, an MS in 1992 and a PhD in Computer Science in 1997, all from Georgia Tech. She was awarded an NSF Career Award in 2000, named a CRA Digital Government fellow in 2002, selected for the 2004-2005 IDA/DARPA Defense Science Study Group and received the *CSO Magazine* Woman of Influence in the Public Sector Award at the 2005 Executive Women's Forum. She is associate editor of the IEEE Transactions on Software Engineering.

Antón currently serves on several boards, including the NSF Computer and Information Science & Engineering Directorate Advisory Council; Advisory Board of the Department of Homeland Security Data Privacy and Integrity, Georgia.

The classification of distinguished engineers and scientists into enterprise categories is extremely difficult because many of these accomplished individuals have multiple careers and easily move between business, technical careers, academia, and government service; in fact, often they are simultaneously involved in several of these fields. This is especially true when major government boards or appointments are involved.

José Abreú was born in Cuba in 1954; he holds a BS degree in civil engineering from the University of Miami. Abreú is the director of Miami-Dade Aviation Department and directs the operations at Miami International Airport (MIA) and four general aviation airports in the Miami area. Abreú oversees one of the largest airport expansion programs in the U.S., a $6.2 billion capital improvement program that is adding new terminals, roadways, and other infrastructure to MIA and the county's general aviation airports. Prior to his July 2005 appointment as aviation director, Abreu served two and half years as secretary of the Florida Department of Transportation (FDOT).

Dr. José Amador was born in Cuba. He attended the University of Havana and then transferred to Louisiana State University where he earned a BS in agronomy (1960) and MS and PhD (1965) degrees in plant pathology.

He worked as the extension plant pathologist with the Texas Agricultural Research Extension Service. In 1991, Amador was promoted to center director of the Texas A&M University Kingsville Citrus Center. In 1994, he was appointed assistant secretary of agriculture for science and education by President Bill Clinton. He returned to his center director position after his stay in Washington.

Dr. Serena María Aunón is an engineer, surgeon, and NASA astronaut candidate. She is a second-generation Cuban-American, born in Indianapolis, Indiana, the daughter of Dr. Jorge Aunón. She holds a BS in electrical engineering from George Washington University, and a master of public health and a doctorate of medicine from the University of Texas.

Aunón was hired by NASA as a flight surgeon and spent over nine months in Russia supporting medical operations for International Space Stations (ISS) astronauts. She is currently the deputy crew surgeon for

STS-127 and expedition 22. She also serves as deputy lead for Orion Medical Operations. Aunón was selected as an astronaut candidate in June 2009.

Manuel Delgado, Jr., was born in Havana in 1958 and came to the U.S. in 1964. He received his BS in electrical engineering in 1983 from the University of Miami. He was the chief of the Electrical Division of the Engineering Directorate at NASA's John F. Kennedy Space Center in Florida when he passed away in 2009.

Prior to his last assignment, he was deputy director of the Independent Technical Authority and Systems Management Office at Kennedy where he provided leadership to the interface between center management, NASA headquarters, and other NASA centers. Delgado was previously the engineering division chief in the Spaceport Engineering and Technology Directorate, where he managed an organization that developed spaceport and range technologies. He served as the chief engineer for Advanced Development and Shuttle Upgrades from September 1996 to 2000. In 1990, Delgado was selected as Kennedy's project engineer for the space shuttle *Endeavour*.

Dr. Nils J. Díaz has BS in mechanical engineering from the University of Villanova in Havana and MS and PhD degrees in nuclear engineering from the University of Florida.

Díaz was named by President Clinton in 1996 to serve as a member of the Nuclear Regulatory Commission (NRC). At the time, he was a professor of nuclear engineering sciences at the University of Florida and director of the Innovative Nuclear Space Power and Propulsion Institute (INSPI) for the Ballistic Missile Defense Initiative. After serving two terms on the NRC, Díaz was appointed as chairman of the commission by President Bush.

As the story goes, the young émigré had left Cuba with nothing to prove that he had earned a degree in mechanical engineering in his native country. He had only his motivation, ambition, and intelligence to recommend him.

Díaz also served as the director of the Nuclear Space Power Institute (INSPI). As director of INSPI, Dr. Díaz exercises prime contractor management responsibility for a diverse group of industries (including Aerojet, Pratt & Whitney, Hughes Electronics, and SRI), national laboratories (including LANL, SNL and LLNL), and seven universities under contract with the Air Force, DNA, NASA, and DOE. He also spent two years as associate dean for research at the California State University, Long Beach and one year as principal advisor to Spain's Nuclear Regulatory Commission. He has also co-owned and managed six small corporations serving the nuclear industry and government, and conducting high technology development.

Dr. Pedro Sánchez is the director of Tropical Agriculture and senior research scholar at the Earth Institute of Columbia University. Sánchez spent much of his childhood at his family's farm outside Havana, where he was born in 1940. He received his BS, MS, and PhD (1968) degrees from Cornell University. With his family he left for the United States in the early 1960s. He received the 2002 World Food Prize and serves as coordinator of the Hunger Task Force of the United Nations Millennium Development Project.

Sánchez served as director general of the World Agroforestry Center (ICRAF) headquartered in Nairobi, Kenya, from 1991 to 2001. He is also professor emeritus of soil science and forestry at North Carolina State University, and was a visiting professor at the University of California, Berkeley.

Sánchez and his wife, Dr. Cheryl Palm, established the Sánchez Tropical Agriculture Foundation to directly fund and support the scientists and farmers working to end hunger in the world poorest regions. In 2004, he won the MacArthur Foundation's "Genius Award" in honor of his numerous achievements in expanding food supplies and improving ecological conditions in developing countries around the world.

José P. Bared came to Miami in the early 1960s via New York City and used to park his old Buick in a Miami cemetery because he had no other place to sleep. Today he co-owns the fourth largest engineering corporation in Florida. In addition to his engineering Company, Bared, from 1992 to 2001, was CEO and chairman of Farm Stores Grocery, Inc. the nation's largest drive-through grocery. He is a board member of Jackson/United Petroleum Corp., Air Ops, and La Vaquita Properties.

Víctor M. Benítez started Metric Engineering in 1976. With Benítez as president, Metric is one of the leading professional civil engineering firm in Florida with about three hundred people. Victor studied Civil Engineering at Rensselaer Polytechnic Institute in Troy, N.Y., graduating in 1961.

In 1976 decided to start his own firm, partnering with a surveyor, LeRoy C. Van Wyk. The company landed its first FDOT major interchange job in 1977, and its first major transit project, the Metro Rail Line Section 6 in 1978.

Miguel A. Hernández earned a bachelor's degree in engineering and master's degree in system management from the University of Florida. He is the founder and CEO of Hernández Engineering, Inc., established in 1982.

The company provides engineering services, scientific support and risk assessment for the aerospace industry. As of 2007, the company had more than four hundred employees and provides services and products to NASA and its contractors in six states.

Jorge Hernández is the president and founder of Bastion Technologies. Building on a family legacy that started during the Apollo program with Hernández Engineering, Jorge embraces science and the aerospace industry. Jorge graduated from Texas A&M with a BS in civil engineering, he was honored with a National Science Foundation Scholarship to attend Stanford University where he received an MS degree in mechanical engineering. He founded Bastion Engineering in 1998 and in only ten years, it grew from three employees to 650 nationwide. In 2001, Bastion expanded its business base to include the oil, gas, and energy markets. Today the company supports seven NASA centers from coast to coast and major oil, gas, and energy providers in the Houston area.

Dr. Federico Poey received his BS in agronomy from the University of Missouri in 1954. He then received an MS and PhD in vegetal genetics (1974) from the postgraduate school at the University of Chapingo, Mexico. He is a specialist in the improvement of corn and sorghum and on the production of seeds. He started working in 1954 as a research and seed producer with Semillas Poey in Cuba. Then he became the drector of research and production for Semillas Mejoradas de Mexico, S.A. (1963-1976).

Next Poey went with North King and Co as coordinator of research for Mexico and Central America and then went as genetist with the *"Centro Internacional para el Mejoramiento de Maiz y Trigo"* (CIMMYT) in Mexico (1976-1989). He is the president of Agricultural Development Consultants, Inc. (Agridec) in Miami.

Francisco H. Recio moved with his family to New York in the 1960s. He attended Rensselaer Polytechnic Institute (RPI) in Troy, N.Y., where he earned an engineering degree and also an MS in business administration. Recio started working in the consulting division of KPMG in 1976. He was elected partner in 1997 and shortly thereafter he was placed in charge of Florida and Latin America consulting operations. He was elected chairman of the Worldwide Operations Management Practice Committee and member of the Management Consulting Practice Committee.

Recio joined SabiaMed in 2004 as chairman of the board and CEO. SabiaMed was founded in 1997 and is a software company specializing in hospital systems products, both on the clinical side and the business side. The company has about one hundred technical personnel and has expanded into Latin America.

Ysrael Seinuk graduated as a civil engineer in 1954 from the University of Havana. He went into private practice shortly thereafter, designed several tall buildings in Havana, left Cuba in 1960 and settled in

New York where he joined the firm of Abrahams, Hertzberg & Cantor. By 1976 the Cantor/Seinuk Group was formed with offices in New York, Miami and London. He was chief executive of the firm. Seinuk was internationally recognized as one of the foremost structural engineers and pioneers in the field of tall buildings and special structures.

You can't walk the streets of Manhattan without seeing a building that Ysrael Seinuk hasn't touched. His firm engineered over fifty high-rise office buildings, numerous major hotels, and hundreds of apartment structures within New York alone.[2]

Worlwide, Cantor/Seinuk has completed billions of dollars worth of construction in the United States, Latin America, Europe, the Philippines, South America, the Middle East, and Far East. Other notable buildings include the Met Complex in Miami; the 014 Tower in Dubai and the Chapultepec Tower in Mexico City. The 014 Tower is a twenty-two-story concrete structure which received the 2009 out of the country award of merit from the New York Concrete Institute and which features the building's skin as its structure.

Professor Seinuk began teaching structural courses at the Irwin S. Chanin School of Architecture, where he headed the structural department, served as the chairman of the Academic Standards Committee, and was past acting dean of the School of Architecture. His firm received multiple awards, was named by *Time* magazine as one of the twenty-five most influential Hispanics in America in 2005. He died in 2010.

With some corporations, due to their headquarters location such as Florida Power and Light, or due to a significant presence in Cuba, such as Coca Cola, one could expect Cuban engineers to migrate to them in the United States or other parts of the Americas.

For example, Florida Power & Light has as its president and CEO Armando H.Olivera. António Rodríguez is the senior vice president of the Power Generation Division and is currently a member of FPL's Board of Directors. Adalberto Alfonso is the vice president of distribution, Manuel Rodríguez-Pérez is a senior technical lead in the Advanced

Metering Infrastructure Group, Gonzalo J. Sánchez, and Jorge G. Valdés had senior engineering responsibilities, and there are many others.

Armando J. Olivera was president and chief executive officer of Florida Power & Light Company. He was appointed in June 2003.

Olivera joined FPL in 1972. Prior to becoming president and CEO, he was senior vice president of FPL's power system business unit. Under Olivera's leadership FPL has become a clean energy leader and is moving forward to bring three state of the art solar power plants to Florida as well as additional emission-free nuclear power.

Olivera holds a BS in electrical engineering from Cornell University and an MBA from the University of Miami. He also is a graduate of the professional management development program of the Harvard Business School.

António Rodríguez is executive vice president of the power generation division for Florida Power & Light (FPL). He directs power production activities for FPL's fossil fueled plants and FPL energy's independent generating plants. He is currently on the FPL's Board and has been an officer since 1999.

He began his career in 1971 as plant engineer, plant general manager, vice president of power delivery, and then senior vice president power generation division in 1999. Rodríguez received a BS in electrical engineering from the University of Miami. He is also a graduate of the program for management development at Harvard University.

There are other companies that for more subtle reasons employed a large number of Cuban engineers and where many of them made major contributions. Some of these are IBM and AT&T/Bell Labs/Lucent. But the foremost example is Dow Chemical Company. In a book published in 1997 by the Michigan University Press titled *Growth Company—Dow Chemical's First Century,* there is a chapter dedicated to the Cubans at Dow, mostly engineers, some business managers, a couple of them lawyers.

Some of the engineers are profiled later, but as a group, the president and/or the chairman of Dow at the time of publishing this book was being written credited the Cubans for being the "creators of Dow Latin America" and state that the Cubans are smart, hard working, they were "hungry" and were loyal and honest. Ben Branch, the Dow CEO stated "Dow really ought to erect a statue to Fidel Castro in the center of Midland (Texas)" just to recognize his help to the company. At one point of about thirty directors at Dow, four were Cubans.

The Dow chapter on Cubans tells the story of Manuel Maza who was the marketing manager of Dow's distributor's in Cuba. Sometime after he left Cuba, Maza was installed as general manager of the Dow office in Bogota, Colombia. Maza outlined in a detailed letter the opportunities for Dow in South America which was instrumental in moving the company in that direction. Maza was the creator of Dow Latin America. Eighty percent of the initial investment of Dow in Latin America was his idea.

Another of the first wave was German Alvarez Fuentes, who became an assistant to William R. Dixon, then in the process of developing a world-class Dow Pharmaceutical Organization.

Enrique Sosa held top-level positions at Dow Chemical, Amoco, and BP Amoco. He holds BS, MS, and PhD degrees in agriculture from the University of Florida.

Sosa joined Dow in Midland, Texas, in 1964 in bioproducts research. In 1970, he was named district sales manager for agricultural products in Colombia, and became general manager for the Venezuela region in 1974 and the Mexico region in 1977. In 1984, he became president of Dow Brazil and was selected senior vice president in 1991. At this time Sosa was also director of Dow Corporation's product department, a member of the corporate executive committee and of the corporate management board.

In December 1992 he was appointed president of the newly expanded Dow North America which combined Dow Canada, Dow USA, and the Mexican Region of Dow Latin America.

In the mid-1990s, Sosa went to Amoco Corporation as executive vice president, where he oversaw worldwide chemical and marketing operations which in 1997 reported product revenues of over $5 billion. Amoco and BP merged in 1999, and Sosa became president of BP Amoco Chemicals after the merger. He resigned shortly thereafter.

Enrique Falla had a brilliant career with the company becoming an executive vice president and until 1996 chief financial officer. Pablo Valdez-Pagés became Dow's general manager in Argentina and then president of Dow Brazil. Pedro Martínez-Fonts was Dow's general manager in Costa Rica and Mexico and then went on to become North America commercial director for epoxy products. Rafael Mugarte became Dow International's representative in Washington, D.C.; Hugo Andricaín became a major manager in Dow's Louisiana Division.

The next group was led by the legendary Roberto Goizueta who became CEO of Coca Cola. He started his career a young chemical engineer in Cuba.

Another Coca Cola executive was Miguel Macías who graduated from Miami University in 1950 with a degree in mechanical engineering. He started in the Engineering Department in Cuba, with responsibility for the Caribbean and eventually Latin America. In 1963, he moved to Venezuela in charge of company owned plant operations and eventually moved to New York as vice president of engineering of the Coca-Cola Export Corporation with responsibility for the engineering function outside of North America. Mike moved to Atlanta until his retirement in the 1980s.

Dr. Manuel Jorge Cutillas was recognized internationally for transforming the Bacardí Company into the fifth-largest spirits company in the world. He received a BS in chemical engineering from Rensselaer Polytechnic Institute. He is a member of the Bacardí family and began his career as assistant distillery superintendent of Ron Bacardí S.A. in 1955. He left Cuba in 1960 and was promoted to plant superintendent in 1961. He eventually became chairman of the board of Bacardí Limited in 1997.

Cutillas also was responsible for breathing a new spirit of social responsibility into the company, from global environmental preservation and a strong campaign of moderation to an unyielding commitment to quality.

Enrique Chía received an MS and PhD (1975) in metallurgy from Georgia Tech. He started his career as director of research at Southwire Corporation, where he authored or co-authored forty published papers and patents. He moved to the Georgia Tech Research Institute and in 1990 became executive vice president of American Fine Wire. He retired in 1995 but continued to work as a consultant, teaching seminars on wire technology and dedicating more time to music, his first love. Chía has produced forty-two CDs, several DVDs, and was nomination for a Grammy Award in 2002 for his recording of *The Music of Ernesto Lecuona*.

Manuel A. Fernández is a classic American success story. A teenage refugee from Cuba in 1959, he learned English and engineering at the same time, and built a career capped by running a billion-dollar business which he was instrumental in getting to that level.

Fernández received his BS in engineering in 1963 and began a fast-moving career working in succession for ITT, Harris Corporation, and Fairchild. While at Fairchild he made the switch to management and in 1968 became the CEO of the Zilog Company, at one time Intel's main competitor.

In 1982, Fernández founded the Gavilan Computer Corporation, which made the first truly portable laptop. In 1985, Fernández became the CEO of the Dataquest Company, which under his leadership grew to be a preeminent IT Research Company. In 1991, Fernández took over as Gartner's CEO and took it from a relatively small niche company with revenues of $40 million to a multinational billion-dollar company that reached a market capitalization over $4 billion. He retired form Gartner in 2003 and served as chairman emeritus; since then, he has focused on SI Ventures, a venture capital company based in Ft. Myers, Florida.

Raúl Fernández is an American entrepreneur. He is currently

chairman and CEO of Object Video and co-owner of the National Hockey League Washington Capitals, the NBA Washington Wizards, and the Women's National Basketball Association, the Washington Mystics.

He grew up in Maryland, the son of a Cuban father and Ecuadorian mother. He graduated from the University of Maryland in 1991. He left his job at Digicon and founded Proxicom. The company became a top global provider of e-business services for *Fortune 500* companies and the ultimate success was signing two big clients in the mid-1990s, MCI and AOL. Proxicom had a $58.5 million IPO in 1999 and generated more than $200 million in revenue in 2000. Later in 2000, Proxicom was bought by Dimension Data.

In 2001, Fernández was appointed to the President's Council of Advisors on Science and Technology. He also led the Information Technology Analysis Team for Virginia Governor Mark Warner's Commission on Efficiency and Effectiveness.

George W. Foyo earned his BS in engineering from the University of Illinois in Chicago and an MS in engineering from Purdue University in Indiana. He started his career with AT&T; was managing director and CEO of AT&T Microelectrónica de España, later he became managing director and CEO of AT&T Microelectronics Europe, leading a regional marketing and sales organization operating in six countries. From 1992 through 1994, he was executive vice president of AT&T International.

Upon his return from Europe, Foyo was named vice president of Sales for AT&T largest business customers in the Mid-Atlantic and South East Regions of the U.S., a position he held for two years.

In January 2000, Foyo became president of Direct TV Latin America, and in 2006 he took over as market president for Blue Cross and Blue Shield of Florida.

The stories of Nelson González and Alex Aguiler belong together. They started their company in 1996 with $10,000, operating from a home garage in Miami. Alienware produced high end desktops and laptops to support graphically intense applications and high performance gaming.

The company grew quickly and at the end of 2005 fiscal year brought over $170 million in annual sales. Dell bought Alienware in 2006. The new subsidiary maintained its autonomy in term of design and marketing. In the Spring of 2008 Alienware became Dell's premier gaming brand.

Pablo Lancella received an agronomical engineer degree in 1942 and a chemical engineer (sugar) degree in 1946; both at the Universidad de la Habana.

Lancella first worked with the U.S. War Department (1942-1943) during World War II as a surveyor. He joined *"Compañia Azucarera Atlantica del Golfo"* (1943-1959), becoming general manager of the Hershey Division in Cuba. He then moved to manager of Sugar Refinery with Godchaux Sugar Refining (1962-1965) in Louisiana and then to WR Grace in Peru (1965-1970) as manager of the Chemical Division.

Lancella worked with Riviana Foods (1973-1980) as general manager of Central American, Mexican and Spanish Operations. Then he went with a division of the World Bank (1981-1984) and after retirement went to Spain as general manager of the Cattle Division of UNIASA which had more than eleven thousand cows.

Jesús León received BS and MA degrees in electrical engineering from the University of Florida and completed all but the dissertation for a PhD from Georgia Tech. He also has an MBA from the executive program at Georgia State University.

He started his professional career with Scientific Atlanta as an engineer and then moved on to become director of programs. León went to Alcatel in Europe as vice president of engineering. León led the design and installation of the first fiber-to-the-curb system installed in Europe. In this project he led twelve hundred engineers in seven countries over three continents: Australia, South Africa, and five European countries.

He moved to Ciena (in Maryland) as senior vice president of engineering and chief development officer (1996-2008). At Ciena, he led the development of state of the art fiber optics transmission systems that increased band width capacity by eighty-fold helping enable the telecom revolution that permits instant worldwide communication of voice, data, and pictures.

Ricardo Lima received a BS in chemical engineering in 1970 from Louisiana State University. Lima was the vice president and general manager of Okeelanta Corp., part of Florida Crystals Corporation. Okeelanta includes 65,000 acres of cane field plus a sugar mill, processing plant, and distribution center. In 2011, Lima was vice president of Capital Projects in Florida and International Operations.

Dr. Alfredo M. López, vice president of research and development at Exxon Mobile Research and Engineering received his BS from LSU in 1963, MS in 1965, and PhD in 1967, all in chemical engineering. He joined Esso Research and Engineering and a series of promotions took him into senior management.

In 1977, he became manager of Exxon research and engineering's gas and heavy oils process division; in 1984 he became director of process development in the Baton Rouge laboratories of Exxon; in 1987 he joined the staff of the president of Exxon research and engineering as quality manager. In 1993, he was promoted to vice president corporate research, and later assumed the position of vice president of research and development.

Reinaldo B. Moré came to the United States as a refugee at the age of seven and for a short time lived with a foster family. He went on to receive a BS in electrical engineering from Tulane University and an MS from Florida Atlantic University.

He has served at Motorola locations all over the world and built a broad background in product and systems design and development, marketing, business management, high-volume manufacturing, and physical distribution. Moré became the vice president and general manager, Worldwide Systems Development Division of Motorola. He led an organization of sixteen hundred engineers and computer systems people in the U.S., Europe, and Asia.

Ernesto J. Rodríguez has worked at the cutting edge of the

telecommunications industry since he began at AT&T Bell Labs in 1967. In 1987, he took a leave of absence to create a world-class research and development center for Telefonica de Espana. Later, Rodríguez was named the first CEO of Telefónica ISD (Investigación y Desarollo).

He joined Lucent, where he had full accountability for research, development, manufacturing, and customer support for the company global switching systems. He led an organization of 11,000 employees with an annual budget of $1.5 billion.

René L. Sagebién graduated as a chemical engineer from LSU in 1963. After graduating, Sagebién began working for the Dupont Company in Chattanooga, Tennessee, as a research engineer. He then worked for Ethyl Corporation, Hess Oil Virgin Islands HOVENSA (a joint venture between Amerada Hess and Petroleos de Venezuela). Sagebién then moved to St. Croix, Virgin Islands, and became the president and CEO of Hovensa.

Robert E. Sánchez received a BS in electrical engineering with a minor in computer science from the University of Miami and a MBA from the Wharton School at the University of Pennsylvania. Sánchez worked two years with Florida Power and Light and then went to Pratt and Whitney Aircraft in 1987.

He joined Ryder in 1993 and served as regional finance director for Supply Chain Solutions (SCS), and other senior manager positions.

Sánchez then became senior vice president and chief information officer of Ryder where he was responsible for all technology related functions of US. Fleet Management Solutions (FMS), where he was responsible for all U.S. operations. This included responsibility for a fleet of more than 145,000 vehicles and more than eight hundred maintenance facilities. In 2007, Sánchez was named executive vice president and chief financial officer for Ryder Systems.

José Ricardo Tarajano received his engineering degree from Rensselaer Polytechnic Institute (RPI) in 1956. He worked for Owens-Illinois for a number of years and then started Pala, Inc. in 1973.

The Pala Group, LLC, a contractor in the heavy construction business, headquartered in Baton Rouge, Louisiana, with revenues of over $100 million and eight hundred employees, was founded by Tarajano in 1973 as a general industrial contractor for the sugar industry. In 1974, it expanded its service offerings to include refineries and petrochemical plants in the Baton Rouge area.

In 1980, Pala Inc. management formed Interstate Industrial Contracting. The next generation of Tarajanos, such as Jorge Tarajano, have assumed major responsibilities in the business.

Al Trujillo received a BS in aerospace engineering from Georgia Tech (1977-1981) where he finished at the top of his class. He also received an MS in mechanical engineering (1985) and a MBA (1988) from Stanford University.

After graduation Trujillo went into the waste management business with American Nukern in New Jersey. He then took an ailing CyanoKem (1982) in Detroit, at that time he was responsible for the largest treatment facility of cyanide-bearing waste in the United States. After financially turning the company around, it was sold (1995). Trujillo was a vice president and general manager at that point.

The next stop was with the giant multinational, multidivisional Australian Company Brambles Industries where he worked eleven years. Initially it was back in the waste business with the Atlantic Waste Management Division as vice president and general manager (1996-2000).

He then moved to Recall Corp., another Brambles division where he was promoted to president and CEO in 2002. Recall employs more than three thousand people in more than two hundred facilities around the world. Trujillo retired from Recall in 2007.

Dr. Irving Wladawsky-Berger was born in Cuba and immigrated to the United States at the age of fifteen and settled in Chicago with his family. He earned BS, MS, and PhD degrees in physics from the University of Chicago.

He has been a visionary leader throughout his more than thirty years at the IBM Corporation. As vice president of technology and strategy, he is responsible for key IBM initiatives critical to the future of the IT industry. Beginning in 1970, he spent his early years at IBM's Thomas J. Watson Research Center, where his technical and managerial contributions to IBM's initial research in large-scale numerically intensive computing earned him a promotion to vice president of systems, IBM Research.

In 1985, he joined the company's product development groups, where he led IBM to a preeminent position in supercomputing and parallel computing. It was this kind of innovative leadership which led IBM in 1996 to name him the general manager of its Internet Division. He was the first executive to head this IBM division.

He and his team succeeded in positioning IBM at the forefront of e-business. He then led IBM's company-wide e-business "On Demand" initiative which helped customers fuse business processes with advanced IT capabilities to achieve whole new dimensions in productivity and innovation. He also led IBM's overall initiatives to develop leadership technology, products, and policies for the Next Generation Internet (NGI). Because engineering and science are the same in any language, Cubans were able to transfer their expertise with greater ease than those of most other professions. This means there were more of them establishing a name for themselves in the United States.

NOTES

1. Among them were Dr. Nils Díaz, Dr. Pedro Sánchez, Dr. Modesto Maidique, Dr. Elsa Murano, Dr. Jorge Aunón, Dr. Ruben Carbonell, Ysrael Seinuk, Roberto Goizueta, Armando Olivera, Manuel Jorge Cutillas, Manuel A. Fernández, George Foyo, Ralph de la Vega, Enrique Sosa, Raúl Fernández, Ernesto J. Rodríguez, and Robert E. Sánchez; all giants in their fields. Of course, there are many others.
2. Among the firm most notable New York projects are the Trump World Tower; the Trump International Hotel and Tower; the 42nd Street redevelopment project at Times Square; the New York Mercantile Exchange, Four Times Square; the "Lipstick" Building; Trump Tower on Fifth Avenue, the award-winning Arthur Ashe Tennis Stadium in Flushing Meadows; Morgan Bank Headquarters, 7 World Trade Center, and hotels for Grand Hyatt, Crowne Plaza, and Marriott.

34

ARCHITECTURE

BY RAUL L. RODRIGUEZ

Postwar prosperity in Cuba found its architectural expression in the language of modernism. Prior to this time, the neo-classical representation of the aspirations of the Republic, founded in 1902, had slowed after the market crash of 1929 and come to almost a complete halt after the 1933 revolution. As a result of the political and economic transformations that occurred in Cuba during and after World War II, architecture responded to new ideals.

The first generation of Cuban architects was trained either at the Universidad de La Habana Escuela de Ingenieros, Arquitectos y Electricistas founded during the First U.S. Intervention (1898-1902), at the Ecole des Beaux Arts in Paris where they had been influenced by the 1900 Exhibition Universalle, or at U.S. schools of architecture where they had been influenced by Daniel Burnham's White City at the Chicago 1893 Columbian Exposition. During the early twentieth century, Leonardo Morales Pedroso (1887-1965), a graduate from Columbia University in 1909, became one of the most influential first-generation Cuban architects due to his traditional designs for, among others, Vedado Tennis Club in 1912; Banco Mendoza y Cía in 1913, Colegio de Belén in 1925, and Compañía Cubana de Teléfonos in 1927.

However, due to the rise of totalitarianism during the 1930s in Europe and the resulting flight of its vanguard architects to universities in the United States, students from all of Latin America, including Cuba, came under their influence. These exiled European architects rejected traditional historic ornamentation and instead embraced a machine aesthetic that emphasized the use of technology as well as the simplification of form.

The Austrian Richard Neutra (1892-1970) was the first to arrive in the United States; he had become an American citizen by 1929. Between 1927 and 1969 Neutra designed some of the most important modernist houses in California, including the Lovell House in Los Angeles (1929) and the Schultess House in a suburb of La Habana (1956). The German Walter Gropius (1883-1965), founder of the Bauhaus School of Design in Weimar in 1917, went into exile in Cambridge, Massachusetts, in 1937 and taught at the Harvard Graduate School of Design. Only one year later, Ludwig Mies Van der Rohe (1886-1969), director of the Bauhaus in 1930, went into exile in Chicago, where he accepted a position as chairman of the Department of Architecture at the Illinois Institute of Technology and designed its new campus. Catalán Josep Lluis Sert (1902-83) went into exile in 1939 in New York City, where he joined Town Planning Associates. In 1953 he moved to Cambridge Massachusetts, becoming dean of the Harvard Graduate School of Design. In 1956 Sert, with Town Planning Associates, developed an urban plan for La Habana. Neutra, Mies Van der Rohe, Gropius, and Sert were invited to visit Cuba in the early 1950s to meet with Eugenio Batista, the father of modern architecture in Cuba.

Eugenio Batista (1900-1992), educated both at the Ecole des Beaux Arts and at Princeton University and therefore conversant in traditional as well as modern architectural design theories, became the principal transition figure and elder statesman for younger Cuban architects. He structured the curriculum at the new architectural school of the Universidad Santo Tomás de Villanueva, combining the Bellas Artes system inherited from the Spanish Colonial era with the method practiced by Jean Labatute, the chairman of architecture at Princeton and winner of the international competition in 1940 for the design of the Plaza Cívica project in Havana.

Cuban students schooled in the United States returned home to practice their profession along with their colleagues from La Universidad de La Habana, resolute in their desire to have the Cuban people reap the benefits made possible by modernism, such as affordable housing. Modernism applied design simplicity and the promise of economy through technological advancements in mass production to methods of construction. Cuban architects quickly took it upon themselves to *acriollar* (regionalize) modernism with traditional elements suggested by Eugenio Batista such as *patios* (courtyards), *portales* (porches), and *persianas* (sun-shading louvers).

Mario Romañach (1917-1984) was the chief proponent of modernism among a remarkable second generation of Cuban architects that included Humberto Alonso, principal architect for the Centro Universitario José Antonio Echeverría (CUJAE); Max Borges Recio (1925-2010), a graduate of Georgia Tech and Harvard Graduate School of Design and the architect for Salón Arcos de Cristal at the world-famous Cabaret Tropicana, awarded the 1953 Gold Medal from the Colegio Nacional de Arquitectos de Cuba; Manuel Copado, the architect in 1944 for the Edificio Solimar with its sensuously curved balconies, one of the earliest examples of modernism in Cuba; Manolo Gutiérrez, the architect for the Engineering Laboratory Building of the Universidad Católica Santo Tomás de Villanueva; Frank Martínez, the architect in 1954 for Edificio Farfante and many single-family houses, among them two in 1959—one for Eloísa Lezama Lima and one for Stanley Wax; Ricardo Porro (1925-), principal architect for Las Escuelas Nacionales de Arte; Nicolás Quintana, director of the Urban and Regional Master Plans for the tourist center of Varadero and the historic city of Trinidad; and Ernesto Gómez Sampera (1912-2004) the lead architect for Edificio FOCSA which inaugurated the high-rise era in La Habana.

The Edificio FOCSA, an acronym for its developer, Fomento de

Obras y Construcciones, S.A., is a thirty-nine-story reinforced concrete structure which, when completed in 1956, was the second tallest of its type in the world. Its mixed-uses included 373 residential units, offices, retail stores, movie theatre, television studio, restaurant, nightclub, and 500-car underground parking garage.

Romañach found an early patron in José Noval Cueto, who commissioned him to design a house for his parents, José Noval Medio and Julia Cueto. The design of this house earned Romañach the 1950 Gold Medal from the Colegio Nacional de Arquitectos de Cuba. One year later, Romañach designed what many consider his most important house, one for Noval Cueto and his wife María Teresa Rodríguez. The house Romañach designed for Evangelina Aristigueta de Vidana earned him the Gold Medal for the best house in Cuba from 1953 to 1955.

By September 1959, only nine months after Fidel Castro had assumed power, Cuba's premier modernist architect had to leave for exile in the United States, unbeknownst to him, never to return. Romañach first taught at the Harvard Graduate School of Design, later Cornell University, and finally at the University of Pennsylvania Graduate School of Fine Arts, until his death. Romañach was among the first Cuban architects to go into exile. Hundreds and eventually thousands of architects of his generation and the next, mostly still students, followed.

If one believes that architecture reflects society, exile for Cuban architects meant radical change.

Left behind was an island society with a rich, centuries-old tradition of architectural high design and exceptional quality construction. Left behind were established professional practices with clients who functioned more like patrons; they built to keep rather than to speculate. Left behind, inaccessible to them even to photograph, were their buildings.

Ahead lay, for those exiled in the United States, a continent spanning between two oceans, demanding multiple climatic design responses and building methods, where time is money and the market determines quality. Ahead lay the need to intern, regardless of university degree origin or years in practice, to become licensed to practice their profession. Ahead lay the need to become proficient in other than their native language and building methods.

Guillermo Carreras (1934-), an architecture student at Cornell University during the 1950s, had interned with Romañach during summer vacations in Havana. After graduation in 1958, he returned to Cuba eager to contribute his talent and energy to the practice. Instead, due to the political situation in 1960, he followed Romañach into exile. In New York Carreras joined Skidmore, Owings and Merrill, working on projects such as the Hunts Point Terminal Market in the Bronx, New York, and the Pittsburgh Center for the Performing Arts with Gordon Bunshaft and the Albright Gallery in Buffalo, New York. Carreras, in 1961, joined Marcel Breuer and Associates, working on St. Francis de Sales Church in Muskegon, Michigan, and a ski resort in Flaine, near Chamonix in the French Alps. Carreras opened the firm's office in Paris, France, where he worked on Z.U.P. de Bayonne, an urbanization zone of priority and satellite to the city of Bayonne.

Carreras then re-joined Romañach at the office of Kelly and Gruzen in New York City, where Romañach was serving as chief designer at a time when the firm was working with Javier Carvajal on the Spanish Pavilion for the New York World's Fair. Romañach and Carreras collaborated on the American Express Pavilion.

Carreras, in 1967, joined Welton Becket and Associates in New York City, where he collaborated with Antonio Quiroga on the U.S. Military Academy in West Point, New York. Carreras also participated in the design of the New Queens High School, Mutual Benefit Life Insurance in Newark, N.J., the Pittsburgh National Bank Headquarters, and the Nassau County Coliseum in Long Island.

Carreras divided his time during the 1970s and early 1980s between Puerto Rico and Venezuela, where he taught at Universidad Simón Bolívar in Caracas before moving to Miami in 1984. There he joined Spillis Candela and designed Concourse A at Miami International Airport

(MIA) and a new terminal for the Fort Myers International Airport before being named MIA director of design for Dade Aviation Consultants (DAC).

Antonio Quiroga (1937-), after working for Alfred Easton Poor on the Communications Relay Stations linking Manhattan's East and West Sides, joined Guillermo Carreras at Welton Becket and Associates, working on the U.S. Military Academy Cadet Union in West Point, N.Y. Quiroga collaborated on The Home Insurance Building in NYC, the Aetna Building in San Francisco, the Xerox Center in Rochester New York, and the Moscow World Trade Center for Bechtel Corporation. In 1983 he founded his own firm, Rodríguez and Quiroga, in Coral Gables, Florida.

Raúl de Armas Rayneri (1941-), after graduating from Cornell, joined Skidmore Owings and Merrill in New York, designing buildings in the United States, Canada, Europe, and the Middle East until he founded his practice Moed, de Armas & Shannon, in 1991.

Orlando Díaz-Azcuy (1939-) began studying architecture in Havana, transferred to Catholic University of America in 1961, and later earned master's degrees in landscape architecture and city and regional planning from the University of California at Berkeley. He worked for Gensler from 1976 to 1987, when he founded his own firm, ODA Design Associates. Diane Dorrans Saeks, founding editor of *Metropolitan Magazine* who writes for many publications, including the *New York Times* and *House Beautiful*, wrote about Díaz-Azcuy, "Orlando Díaz-Azcuy's mastery of interior design has made him one of America's most renowned designers. Regarded by his peers as a 'dean of interior design' and a pioneer of minimal design since the early 1980s, Díaz-Azcuy has been an epic if under-recognized influence to interior architecture and design professionals and enthusiasts."

Ricardo Porro (1925-), exiled in Paris during the Batista regime, had returned to Cuba upon Castro's assuming power to design the acclaimed Escuelas Nacionales de Arte. In 1965 he chose exile in Paris once again.

In exile, Porro designed the Centro de Arte of Vaduz, Lichstenstein (1976) the Ecole Elsa Triolet in St. Denis, Paris (1990).

The Cuban appreciation for modernism was shared by Bacardí, the premier rum company founded in 1862 by Facundo Bacardí in Santiago de Cuba. In 1958, Pepín Bosch, its chairman, had commissioned Ludwig Mies van der Rohe to design Bacardí's corporate headquarters in Santiago de Cuba. The project was abandoned in 1960 after the Castro government nationalized all industries. After the erection of the Berlin Wall in 1961, Mies reinterpreted the reinforced-concrete design in structural steel for the Neuenationalgalerie, which opened in West Berlin in 1968.

It did not take long for Cuban exiled architects to leave their mark on Miami, their adopted city. Bacardí, again under the leadership of Pepín Bosch, erected a modernist building in 1963 on Biscayne Boulevard. The design is by Enrique Gutiérrez, a partner in the firm SACMAG Internacional de Puerto Rico. The murals, of blue and white ceramic tiles, are the works of Francísco Brennand; from Recife Brazil came the veneer north and south facades, which constitute the first collaboration between an artist and a modernist architect in Miami.

Bacardí, in 1976, commissioned Ignacio Carrera-Jústiz to design its second building in Miami. The architect integrated a design from the German artist Johannes M. Dietz to each one of the four-color glass facades. The superstructure of the building rests over a pedestal and appears to float over the plaza. Both buildings, in 2008, were designated historic by the city of Miami.

The firm of Pancoast, Ferendino, Skeels and Burnham in Miami's Coconut Grove welcomed, throughout the 1960s, several Cuban architects, among them Adolfo Albaisa, Hilario Candela, José Corbato, Jorge Delgado, Andrés Fabregas, José Feito, Gilberto Martínez, Efraím Oliver, Ramón Pacheco, David Pérez, José Pérez Benitoa, Jaime Sallés, and José Luis Sierra, among others. A majority of these architects collaborated in one way or another in the planning and design of the newly founded Miami Dade College. Inspired by their modernist education, these young architects—all in their thirties—help create a college campus which expresses its concrete structure and responds to Miami's climate using design elements learned back home in Cuba, such as the aforementioned courtyards, porches, and sun-shading louvers. In 1971, Hilario Candela became a named partner in the firm.

Hervin A. R. Romney arrived in Miami midway through the decade of the 1970s to establish his own architectural practice after seventeen years of architectural studies which began at Universidad Católica Santo Tomás de Villanueva in Havana and continued at Cooper Union in New York, Catholic University in Washington, D.C., Ècole Speciale D'Architecture de París, and concluded in 1975 at Yale University in New Haven, Connecticut. Romney, at the suggestion of his wife, Ana María Miyares, named his firm, Arquitectónica.

Andrés Duany, born in New York of Cuban parents, and the Peruvian Bernardo Fort-Brescia, both recent graduates, joined Arquitectónica in 1976. Shortly thereafter, in 1976, Elizabeth Plater-Zyberk and, in 1977, Laurinda Spear joined the firm. Together, they designed on Brickell Avenue four of the most recognized condominiums in Miami: the Babylon (1977), the Atlantis and the Palace (1978), and the Imperial (1980). Of these, the Atlantis, with its facade perforated by a courtyard on the eleventh floor with a pool and a coconut tree, became a symbol of Miami through the international broadcast of the TV series *Miami Vice*.

Romney, in 1984, left the firm he founded and in 1985 won a design competition celebrating the centenary of Dade County Public Schools with his bold design for Jane Roberts Elementary. Romney returned to Brickell Avenue in 1988 to design The Acropolis. In 1990, Romney designed Terminals 8 and 9 at the Port of Miami for the firm Post, Buckley, Shuh & Jernigan. Romney's recent work in Florida includes Villa Lapidus in Pinecrest and Chediak House in Key Biscayne.

Andrés Duany and Elizabeth Plater-Zyberk decided to separate from Arquitectónica in 1980, "disenchanted with the creation of architectural forms without relation to the principles of urbanism." Married since 1976, Andrés and Elizabeth founded a new firm which bears their name, also known by its acronym, DPZ. Among its first projects was the master plan for the town of Seaside, Florida, described in *Time* magazine in January 1990 as "The most amazing design achievement of its era." This eighty-acre town was the first of more than a hundred projects for neighborhoods, towns, and cities planned by Andrés and his firm in America, the Caribbean, Europe, Asia, and Australia. The contribution of Andrés to architectural education began at the University of Miami in 1975, where today Elizabeth is the dean of the School of Architecture. During more than three decades, Andrés and Elizabeth have attracted to UM nationally and internationally recognized practitioners and lecturers and educated a first generation of Cuban-American architects who, after completing post-graduate courses at universities such as Harvard, Yale, Columbia, Princeton, and Cornell, returned to Miami and joined the school faculty.

More than fifty years after Cuban architects began to arrive in exile, their imprint on the United States in particular and the world in general has been significant. The question of whether their condition as exiles ultimately facilitated or partially obstructed the magnitude of this imprint is debatable. What is a matter of record is that these architects left their country of birth for political, not economic reasons. They were born in a country where, for five centuries, three major cultural streams—the African, the European, and the North American—had been syncretized into one national identity and where, overcoming almost continuous political unrest, a middle class had emerged and flourished.

The more important question is whether the people of Cuba may soon or ever benefit from the experience gained abroad by these exiles.

35

ACCOUNTANTS IN EXILE

BY ENRIQUE VICIANA AND LEONARDO RODRIGUEZ

At the beginning of 1959, when the Castro government initiated its "revolution" in Cuba, there were three public universities, plus eight private institutions that had been functioning prior to 1958.[1] Most of these academic institutions of higher learning offered programs to students aspiring to graduate as public accountants. Upon completion of their degrees as majors in accounting, the graduates received their diploma as public accountants (*contadores públicos*), thus becoming an important segment of the professionals graduating from Cuban universities.

The curricula of the universities followed those of the United States, whereby textbooks were translated into Spanish resembling closely the changes demanded by the nascent economies of the free world after the end of World War II. It should be added that the quality of the various faculties responsible for the instruction imparted to the future graduates helped undoubtedly to create a highly marketable number of professionals. It must be stressed that the quality of this education was later proven when many of the former graduates were forced to go into exile and had to practice their profession in foreign countries. Cuban public accountants could be found in Central America, Puerto Rico, Venezuela, and the United States. Most were highly regarded due to their professional skills, ethics, and integrity.

The last two presidential periods (1944 to 1952) of constitutional democratic government in Cuba brought to the island the establishment of laws seeking to improve the governance of its institutions. Among them, the most important perhaps, was the creation of a general accounting office (*tribunal de cuentas*) on December 20, 1950 (Law No. 14), to which applicants were to be admitted after passing proficiency tests in accounting and auditing matters as well as background checks.[2]

Cuba's 1940 Constitution in its Article 280 stated that the national government should organize a banking system and called for the creation of a National Bank. The Cuban National Bank (*Banco Nacional de Cuba*) was officially established by President Carlos Prío Socarrás in 1948. However, it did not begin operations until April 1950. Soon afterwards on December 20, 1950, the Bank of Agriculture and Industrial Development (*Banco de Fomento Agrícola e Industrial*) (BANFAIC) was founded.[3]

In the following years a series of other governmental banks were established. The National Finance Agency (*Financiera Nacional de Cuba*) in 1953, the Cuban Bank of Foreign Trade (*Banco de Comercio Exterior*) (BANCEX) on May 12, 1954, Bank for Social and Economic Development (*Banco de Desarrollo Económico y Social*) (BANDES) on January 22, 1955, the Mortgage Insurance Institute (*Fondo de Hipotecas Aseguradas*) (FHA), originally created as a division of BANFAIC in 1953 but as an autonomous institution in 1955.[4]

Parallel to the creation of the above official or governmental banks (*La Banca Oficial*) there was in the period from 1945 to 1960 the return of Cuban-owned banks. In 1959, there were 49 commercial banks (foreign and domestic) with at least 204 branch offices operating throughout Cuba.[5]

Logically, the many banking institutions of the period, both the privates as well as the government ones, were staffed by the new breed of economists and public accountants who worked side by side at all levels of operations.

POLITICAL TURMOIL BROUGHT ABOUT BY THE CASTRO GOVERNMENT

Political changes came about in the year 1959, when the new government, by decision of its Council of Ministers, separated from their positions all the magistrates of the General Accounting Office. They were Fernández Camus, José R, Mestre Benavides, Carlos Bustamante Sánchez, Ramón Miyar, Jorge Vailláns, and Germán San Miguel Pagés.

During the month of January 1959 and as a reflection of the enmity of the "revolution" against the Catholic Church, all diplomas issued, as well as the grades of the students of the University of Villanueva were annulled by Law No. 11 of January 11, 1959, enacted by the provisional government.[6]

Following the attacks on all free institutions, the "revolution" started its attacks on all professional associations, accusing them of harboring "counter-revolutionaries." The "intervention" of the Association of Public Accountants' offices in Havana in August 1960 is directly linked to the role the association and its directors took in the defense of the faculty of the School of Accounting (Escuela de Ciencias Comerciales) of the University of Havana.

On July 15, 1960, a group of students and faculty members ignoring the authority of the University Council "appointed" a new board of governors to direct the university. The board then dismissed the council and faculty boards related to the different schools. Four university faculties opposed this takeover, among them the School of Public Accounting. Outside of the university, the Association of Public Accountants—whose membership was mostly made up of graduates from the University of Havana—supported the stand taken by their former professors and faculty members at the School of Public Accountants. The result was that the offices of the association were "intervened" by supporters of the

Castro government on August 2, 1960.[7]

After this, it was evident that the activities of a profession such as public accountancy was not considered necessary to the new government plans to convert the economy into a Communist model, where goods are exchanged under a barter system, and most economic activities regulated by government bureaucrats without accounting or economic training.

THE CUBAN ACCOUNTING PROFESSIONALS AS PART OF THE DIASPORA

Among the many different professionals arriving in the United States, Puerto Rico, and other countries in Latin America, the accountants were perhaps the ones with more possibilities of employment. Most of the arrivals in the early stages of the exile spoke some English, while those that did not were able to obtain employment with entities where their "abilities with numbers" were deciding factors for their hiring.

To accommodate the influx of refugees from Cuba, the U.S. government initially created on December 2, 1960, the Cuban Refugee Emergency Center whose purpose was to provide help and guidance to the new arrivals. This was followed on February 3, 1961, with the U.S. Refugee Program under the Department of Health, Education and Welfare.[8]

As the number of refugees continued to increase over the years these included a substantial number of professionals, among which there were a large number of public and private accountants (the latter not university graduates). Since many of these professionals wanted to attend college-level education, the federal government proceeded to institute a federal loan assistance program to cover the educational costs of those professionals. This was known as the "Cuban Loan Program," and the funds received by the applicants were to be repaid after graduation at a very low interest rate.[9]

A substantial wave of immigrants from Cuba during the 1970s (known as the Freedom Flights) brought more professional accountants to the United States. By then, with the opening of the new public university in the Miami area (Florida International University) and the cooperation of the Florida State Board of Accountancy, a program to qualify the newly arrived public accountants was put in place.

The state of Florida promulgated in 1974 Public Law Chapters 74-195 that allowed for the first time in the United States a group of public accountants graduated and licensed in a foreign country to sit for the Certified Public Accounting (CPA) exam in the Spanish language. The purpose of this unique program was three fold: 1) to familiarize the students with the ethics and practices of the public accounting profession in the United States; 2) return to the accounting profession a great number of former Cuban professionals that since their arrival to the U.S. had drifted away from their profession; and 3) make the students that participated in the program eligible to sit for the CPA exam in the state of Florida.[10]

In later years refresher courses were offered by various institutions for those students who, in their first attempts, had only passed portions of the CPA exam. Of a total of 114 Cuban exiles taking advantage of the aforementioned program, 110 finished the program. While not all took the state's examination, 25 of them were finally able to obtain the required certification.[11]

After this attempt to bring the exiled professionals into the mainstream of their respective interests within the accounting profession, the program was no longer offered. A new generation of exiles was by then finishing their studies throughout various institutions of higher learning in Florida and elsewhere.

Quite a number of the exiled professionals were hired by international accounting firms, which by taking advantage of their bilingual proficiency in addition to their accounting skills, offered them positions in their foreign offices to better serve their extended clientele. In the offices of many of these international firms in Central America, South America, and Spain you could find Cuban accountants. Globalism was not yet a word of the business world, but the Cuban exiled community of well-trained accountants certainly played an important role in its development.

CUBAN ACCOUNTING ASSOCIATIONS IN EXILE

In 1961, those accountants graduated from the Cuban universities, and those from other commercial schools incorporated an association called La Asociación de Contadores Públicos y Privados de Cuba en el Exilio (Association of Public and Private Accountants in Exile) under the laws of the state of Florida. Later in 1962 the name was changed to Asociación de Contadores de Cuba en el Exilio (Association of Cuban Accountants in Exile). By 1962, the association had more than seventy chapters worldwide with more than one thousand members.[12]

The Asociación de Contadores de Contadores de Cuba en el Exilio was admitted as an "oficial delegation," representing Cuba to the VI Interamerican Accounting Conference meeting of the "Interamerican Accounting Association" (IAA) in 1962 in New York City.[13] The admission of the exiled association by the IAA brought additional recognition to the Cuban exiled accountants both public and private. To be part of an international organization (in representation of Cuba) where thirty-two other accounting organizations of the Western Hemisphere were represented with over 1.5 million members was an enormous success and a sign of continental acknowledgement not only to the individual Cuban accountants in exile but to the exiled organization that represented them.

Every two years the IAA celebrates its main event, the Inter American

Accounting Conference. The responsibility of holding the event is rotated among the organizations represented within the IAA. In 1985 the Asociación de Contadores de Cuba en el Exilio requested and was granted the responsibility of planning, organizing and carrying out the event. The XVI Interamerican Accounting Conference was held in Miami with more than two thousand participants from all of the Americas. The president of the conference was Eugenio Sansón CPA, and the technical director was Fernando Fernandez CPA, both Cuban exiles. All the technical seminars and presentations were performed by Cuban CPAs.

Years later another Cuban, Dr. Leonardo Rodríguez, was elected first vice president of the IAA in Punta del Este, Uruguay, in 1991 during the XXIV Interamerican Accounting Conference and president of the IAA in Panama in 1993 during the XXV Interamerican Accounting Conference. It was during Rodríguez two-year tenure as president of the IAA that the Cuban-American CPA Association based in Miami was also admitted as representing Cuba.

Currently two Cuban exiled accounting associations, the Cuban-American CPA Association and the Asociación de Contadores de Cuba en el Exilio, share joint representation of Cuba within the IAA. At the time of writing this history Cuba in Exile is represented within the executive committee with the position of vice president in the person of Fernando Fernández CPA.

Over the years the new generation of Cuban-American accountants educated in this country and graduates of American universities, after becoming CPAs have joined the Cuban-American CPA Association. This very active and fast-moving association represents the future rather than the sentimental past which was embodied in the original two Cuban accounting associations in exile created back in 1961 and 1962. In a way the torch is being passed from the generation of Cuban accountants that left Cuba fifty years ago and came to the United States, to their sons and grandsons now professionally involved in the new accounting organization.

CUBAN CPA FIRMS IN THE UNITED STATES

During the 1970s, the first accounting firms, established by certified public accountants of Cuban ancestry, began to emerge to serve not only the general business community, but a breed of Cuban-owned businesses and later Latin and Hispanic firms of various nationalities. Individually other new certified public accountants of Cuban background established their position with international and/or local firms and some were appointed to various Florida Boards including the Florida Board of Accountancy. Among them we recognize the following ones:

Antonio L. Argiz was a graduate of Florida International University and of Virginia's National AICPA Banking School. Argiz holds CPA certificates from Florida, New York, Colorado, and Pennsylvania. Currently chief executive officer and managing partner of Morrison, Brown, Argiz and Farra, LLP, the largest auditing firm in Miami and one of the fifty nationally, Argiz is a former chairman of the Board of Accountancy of the state of Florida.

Frank Paredes CPA, an audit and risk regional managing partner of Deloitte Latin America/Caribbean, was the leader of Deloitte Caribbean Bermuda, whose purpose was the development of the right teams to match client's needs.

Ralph Morera CPA would not have been able to accomplish what he did without the help of a Good Samaritan in his first job. At age seventeen, Ralph found himself alone in the U.S. as part of the Pedro Pan program. After a short while in Miami he ended up in New York City living with other Cuban youth and working, along with about several dozens other countrymen, at Saks Fifth Avenue department store. One day, about a year after he began working for the store, he found a check made out to him for $10,000 from a store executive.

Shocked, he went to see her, only to find out that she had been observing how hard and dedicated he worked and how hard he wanted to study. She wanted him to have money to go to college. Later on she even paid his tuition to the prestigious Rhodes High School, where the Rockefeller children went to school.

The lady also paid for his education at Pace College as well as the college costs of five others, including two in medical school. Thanks to her, Morera's parents were able to obtain visas first to Spain and later to the U.S., bringing them to him in New York and paying their expenses for a year and a half.

His initial part-time job was with Cooper and Lybrand while attending Pace, his first full-time job was with Arthur Andersen in 1969 first in New York and later in Puerto Rico. He returned to Cooper and Lybrand from 1976 to 2000 when he retired as partner. In May 2000, Morera joined Bacardí Limited as executive vice president and chief financial officer until his retirement in July 2009.[14]

Carlos Fernández CPA, an audit partner with KPMG, elected early retirement in 1991 but returned in 1994 until his retirement in 2004. During this period, he was a managing director involved in mergers and acquisitions, forensic accounting, litigation support, and other advisory services. On January 23, 2007, Fernández became chair of Audit Committee and member of the Government and Nominating Committee and Capital Committee of Elandia Inc. He is a graduate of the University of Florida in 1963 and obtained his CPA in 1965.

Other Cuban CPAs who distinguished themselves at the international and national level were: Alberto Krieger who led Arthur Andersen; Carlos Morales at Arthur Young in Venezuela. Ernest and Whitney managing partner was Luis Pérez Mena, who became the partner in charge of Latin America at Ernst and Young World Council; Tony Vidal Larrauri as head of Peat, Marwick and Mitchell for Latin America also based in Caracas. Finally, Aurelio Fernández Díaz not only was the managing partner of Deloitte and Touche in Guatemala but his book was the classic text for CPAs all over Latin America.[15]

Many other names come to the list of professionals who have contributed to the prestige of the Cuban exile community. Without trying to be all inclusive, we would recognize those pioneers for their professional activity in this country: Carlos Arazoza, Emilio Alvarez, Leonardo Gravier, Mirtha Guerra, Marcos A. Guerra, Andres Iriondo, Antonio Jacomino, Octavio Mestre, Luis San Miguel, Carlos Salcines, Eugenio Sansón, Fernando Fernández, José Urréchega, Octavio Verdeja, and Enrique Viciana.

Finally, this brief resumé of the history of the Cuban accountants in exile since 1959 cannot be concluded without mentioning those who paid the ultimate sacrifice in the pursuit of liberty. It is fitting to remember three public accountants who gave all for the freedom of Cuba. Their names will be always remembered as they were executed by firing squads: Porfirio Ramírez, Jorge Fundora, and Manolín Guillot.

NOTES

1. José R. Alvarez Díaz, *Un Estudio Sobre Cuba* (Miami: Grupo Cubano de Investigaciones Económicas de University of Miami, 1963), 1525.
2. Ibid., 1194.
3. Cuban Banking Study Group, Inc. "CUBA Past, Present and Future of its Banking and Financial System," 1995, 35-39.
4. Ibid., 39-42.
5. Ibid., 43-47.
6. Díaz, *Un Estudio Sobre Cuba*, 1526.
7. Aurelio Fernández Díaz, *Nacimiento, Desarrollo y Muerte del Contador Público Cubano* (Delgado Impresos & Cia. Ltda. September 1992), 52-63.
8. A study for the Department of Health, Education and Welfare, United States Government Contract: HEW WA-66-05, "The Cuban Immigration 1959-1966 and Its Impact on Miami-Dade County, Florida," the Research Institute for Cuba and the Caribbean Center for Advanced International Studies University of Miami, Coral Gables, July 10, 1967, 4, 24.
9. Ibid., 106-109.
10. Leonardo Rodríguez and Leandro Núñez. "Algo Nuevo en la Enseñanza de la Contabilidad Un Programa para CPAs en Lengua Española," (Revista del Colegio de Comercio School of Business Review, Centro de Investigaciones Facultad de Administración Comercial Universidad de Puerto Rico. Julio-Diciembre 1980), 1-5.
11. Ibid., 4.
12. Díaz, *Nacimiento, Desarrollo y Muerte del Contador Público Cubano*, IV.
13. Ibid.
14. Author interview with Ralph Morera, July 9, 2011.
15. Oscar A. Echevarría, "Cuba's Builders of Wealth Prior to 1959 A Wide Brush Review," Arlington, Virginia, January 11, 2006, 9.

36

EDUCATION

BY FEDERICO R. JUSTINIANI, ROGELIO DE LA TORRE, AND EDUARDO ZAYAS-BAZAN

For the past fifty years, the Castro brothers and their government have been committed to trying to demonstrate not only that the Cuban educational system was deplorable at the time they took over in 1959 but also that the educational level of the Cuban people at that time was one of the worst in the Western Hemisphere. These assertions could not be further from reality.

It is patently evident that at the beginning of the socialist revolution in 1959, the educational system in Cuba was fairly well developed, although certain improvements were desirable. The primary level needed to be organized more effectively, and more schools and teachers were required in the rural areas. This last change would have lowered the percentage of illiteracy in the country. Nevertheless, the level of education in Cuba was one of the highest in Latin America, and the rate of illiteracy was one of the lowest in the Western Hemisphere. Furthermore, in 1959 Cuba boasted a well-developed professional middle class, which included lawyers, engineers, medical doctors, scientists, poets, authors, essayists, businessmen, and entrepreneurs. There is no doubt then that in 1959, the general Cuban population was perfectly well equipped to face the challenge of starting a new life in any other country, and to make positive and significant contributions in the field of education, as will be noted in this chapter.

EDUCATION BEFORE THE REVOLUTION (1902-1958)

In 1958 UNESCO stated that Cuba was the Latin American country that apportioned the highest percentage of its budget to education. Unfortunately, much of this money was either diverted from its intended use by pilfering and misuse, or it was not adequately applied to solving educational problems. The state of education was further hampered by the concentration of schools in cities, and the lack thereof in the rural areas.

During almost the entire era of the Republic, secondary education was provided by the Institutos de Segunda Enseñanza, together with private schools established later. This produced a laudable educational system during the course of the Republic.

There were also numerous specialized schools. The first of these institutions was the Escuela de Dibujo y Pintura de San Alejandro (Saint Alexander School of Design and Painting) founded in 1818 in Havana by the Sociedad Económica de Amigos del País (Society of Economics of Friends of the Nation). In 1902, the Escuela Normal de Kindergarten (Teachers' College for Kindergarten) was founded in Havana. In 1915 two Escuelas Normales para Maestros (Teachers' Colleges) were established in Havana, and later on, they were established in the capital city of each province as well. The Escuela Normal para Maestras del Hogar (Teachers' College for Home Economics) was established in Havana in 1918, and by the end of this period before the revolution, they increased in numbers to fourteen.

Among other specialized schools, the Escuelas Profesionales de Comercio (Professional Schools of Commerce) were of particular note. There were eleven by the end of the Republic.

Also established were the Escuelas de Artes y Oficios (Schools of Arts and Crafts), where civil engineers, industrial mechanics, industrial chemists, and industrial electricians were formed. Until 1928 there was only one such school in Havana, but later a second was founded in

Santiago de Cuba. Eventually, there were twelve Schools of Arts and Crafts. Six Escuelas de Bellas Artes (Schools of Fine Arts) were established in addition to the San Alejandro School previously mentioned. These schools produced the future teachers of plastic arts, but above all, instructed painters and sculptors in the most modern techniques of their art.

There were several specialized schools in Cuba that functioned as boarding schools. Worthy of mention are the *Escuelas Técnicas Industriales* (industrial technical schools) in Havana, Santa Clara, and Bayamo, the *Escuelas Politécnicas* (polytechnic schools), and several *Escuelas Tecnológicas* (technical schools).

A few other specialized schools deserve to be referenced, particularly the *Escuelas de Periodismo* (schools of journalism). The first of these, named "Manuel Márquez Sterling," was founded in Havana in 1942 and awarded degrees in journalism, as well as in *Periodista Técnico Gráfico* (technical graphic journalism). Toward the latter years of the Republic, there were four schools of journalism, the new ones having been established in Matanzas, Santa Clara, and Santiago de Cuba. Finally, the Instituto Nacional de Educación Física (National Institute of Physical Education), existing in Havana since 1941, should be considered among the specialized schools of Cuba, although in reality this school was a professional institute because its graduates were academically qualified to teach physical education in secondary schools.

University Education

The university level of education in Cuba throughout most of the Republic era was solely the responsibility of the public Universidad de La Habana (University of Havana) since for much of that time it was the only institution at that level in Cuba. This university was accessible to all socio-economic classes due to its minimal tuition fee. In spite of the lack of competition, the University of Havana always upheld the highest intellectual standards, and it was widely regarded for its academic and cultural excellence on the island and abroad.

Due to the population growth the need to create other public universities was met by the founding of new institutions. The first was the Universidad de Oriente, established in Santiago de Cuba in the year 1947. In 1949, the Universidad Central Marta Abreu (Central University Marta Abreu) was founded in the city of Santa Clara.

In the final years of the Republic, several private universities were established. The first was the Universidad Católica de Santo Tomás de Villanueva (The Catholic University of Saint Thomas of Villanova) instituted by the Augustinian Order in 1946. This university quickly acquired prestige within the island. Toward the end of the 1950s, other private universities were also inaugurated. These were the Universidad Nacional José Martí, the Universidad de San Juan Bautista de La Salle, the Universidad Masónica, and the Universidad del Candler.

EXILES IN EDUCATION—THE EARLY YEARS

As Cuban exiles began to arrive in the United States and other countries, many of those who had been teachers and professors in Cuba tried to revalidate their pedagogy degrees to pursue their careers. The Cuban Refugee Assistant Program in the United States played a significant role in relocating refugees with an interest in education to many parts of the country. In the early sixties there was a need in the United States for Spanish teachers and librarians. Thus colleges and universities such as Indiana State and Kansas State Teachers College began to offer scholarships to former lawyers and Cuban pedagogues to obtain teaching certificates which would enable them to become elementary, middle and high school teachers. More than one hundred lawyers and other Cubans with doctorates in pedagogy and other graduate degrees took advantage of these scholarships and relocated. Other universities such as the University of Miami developed their own programs to certify Cuban exiles.

In addition, well-known religious schools in Cuba were started in Miami, as La Salle High School, Belén Preparatory School and Champagnat Catholic School, founded by Reinaldo Alonso and his wife María Isabel, and a number of lay private academies began to sprout in the Miami area such as the one started by Conchita Espinosa and La Progresiva. Worthy of particular mention are the Lincoln-Martí schools located in Little Havana and other areas of Miami.

Bilingual Education

The role of Cuban exiles in bilingual education in Miami began with the 1962-1963 implementation of a Ford Foundation grant. This grant established a project to facilitate the integration of arriving Cuban children into the Miami-Dade County Public Schools System. The project had two dimensions: one, to directly appropriate curricular support materials and two, to establish a bilingual instructional setting for the implementation of those materials. Among the staff of the project were three Cuban exile educators, Rosa Inclán, Herminia Cantero, and Olga Miyar, whose educational background in Cuba helped shape both the curricular and instructional dimensions of the program to be offered to Cubans at the elementary school level.

In the beginning, many of the Cuban teachers were needed to implement the developing bilingual programs, although well-qualified in Cuba, they lacked certain legal requirements set forth in order to teach in the state of Florida. Thus an accelerated teacher education program had to be implemented in order to have legally qualified personnel available. As new generations of Cuban youth graduated with the required background, Cubans moved from a support to a leadership role in bilingual education as the program spread to other levels and school systems. Prominent among such who led this movement were Mercedes Toural and Lourdes Rovira.

First Cuban Principals

In Miami-Dade County, Elvira Dopico was the first Cuban exile who became an elementary school principal, and Piedad Placencia the first one to become a high school principal. Frank de Varona was the first one to be named junior high and adult education principal.

Presidents of Colleges and Universities

Six Cuban-Americans have reached the top of their educational professions as administrators by becoming presidents of colleges and universities:

Rolando Bonachea became the eleventh president of Salem State College in 1988 and held that position until he resigned in 1989. Previously he had served as vice president and acting president of Duquesne University. Bonachea later was director of Radio Martí.

Piedad Ferrer Robertson is since February 2005 president of the Education Commission of the States, an interstate compact created to improve public education. She previously served as president of Santa Monica College, secretary of education for the Commonwealth of Massachusetts, and president of Bunker Hill Community College.

José López-Isa became in 1982 the third president of Bergen Community College and served until 1995. In October 2009, the college celebrated the architect of its international identity by renaming the Center of Intercultural Studies in his honor.

Modesto A. Maidique most recently was the Alvah H. Chapman, Jr., Eminent Scholar Chair in Leadership, and professor of management in the College of Business Administration at Florida International University (FIU). Maidique was president of FIU from 1986 to 2009 and led its transformation from a comprehensive university to a major research institution classified in the highest ranking awarded by the Carnegie Foundation. Under his leadership, FIU tripled in physical size, grew to nearly 40,000 students, and now ranks among the twenty largest universities in the United States. During his tenure FIU established accredited Colleges of Law, Engineering, Architecture, and Public Health; and most recently, Dr. Maidique spearheaded the historic opening of the new FIU College of Medicine, one of only three U.S. medical schools established in the last twenty-five years. In June 2009 Dr. Maidique was named president emeritus of FIU and the main university campus was named after him by the FIU Board of Trustees in recognition of his leadership, dedication, and transformational accomplishments during his twenty-three-year tenure as university president.

Elsa Murano became president of Texas A&M in January 2008 and resigned in June of 2009. She was the first female, and the first Hispanic American to serve in this position. In 2001 she was appointed undersecretary of agriculture for food safety for the U. S. Department of Agriculture. Murano resigned in November 2004 and returned to Texas A&M in January 2005, becoming the vice chancellor of agriculture and life sciences of the university.

Eduardo J. Padrón has served since 1995 as president of Miami-Dade College (MDC), the largest institution of higher education in America with more than 170,000 students. Padron's pace-setting work at MDC has been hailed as a model of innovation in higher education. He is credited with engineering a culture of success that has produced impressive results in student access, retention, graduation, and overall achievement. In 2009, *Time* magazine included him on the list of "The ten best college presidents."

Administration of Educational Systems

Eduardo Aguirre Reyes was appointed by then Governor George W. Bush to the Board of Regents of the University of Houston System for a six-year term. He served as its chairman from 1996 to 1998.

Rogelio "Roger" Cuevas started his career as an educator in the

Miami-Dade County School system in 1969. He was superintendent from 1996 to 2002.

Pedro Enrique García was director of Nashville Metro Schools from 2001 to 2008.

Demetrio Pérez, Jr., in 1968, together with his father Demetrio Pérez Arencibia, founded the Lincoln-Martí private school system in Miami. He was elected twice to the Miami-Dade School Board, serving as its vice president during his first two years in the position.

Domingo J. Trujillo was chief instructional officer (2002-2005) at the Chicago Public Schools, the third largest public school system in the country, where he started as a classroom teacher in 1973.

Octavio J. Visiedo was superintendent of schools in Miami-Dade County, Florida, the country's fourth largest school district. After serving six years in that position, he resigned and founded Chancellor Academies, Inc., a leading developer and manager of high-quality public charter schools and independent private schools serving students from pre-kindergarten through grade 12. Chancellor Academies is the No. 2 charter company in the country, with seventy-plus schools in eight states.

ACHIEVEMENTS OF CUBAN EXILE EDUCATORS BY DISCIPLINES

What follows is a compilation of the achievements by disciplines of Cuban exile professors in the United States and other countries. The selection was made by identifying candidates and evaluating their accomplishments and their publications. We sincerely apologize for any inadvertent omission of worthy educators who fit these criteria.

Accounting

Elisa S. Moncarz, in 1992, was appointed professor of accounting and finance, School of Hospitality and Tourism Management, Florida International University, Biscayne Bay Campus. She has co-authored several books, including *Accounting for the Hospitality Industry* (2004, Canadian Edition 2005, Chinese Edition 2006).

Agriculture

Rodrigo Rodríguez Kábana is distinguished university professor at the College of Agriculture, Auburn University. He is a world-renowned expert in entomology and plant pathology. He is the author of more than one hundred scientific articles and has nine patents to his name.[1]

Anthropology

Ruth Behar is professor of anthropology at the University of Michigan. In 1988 she was given a MacArthur Foundation (genius) Award. In 1999 *Latina* magazine named her one of the fifty Latina who made history in the twentieth century. Among others, she is the author of *The Vulnerable Observer: Anthropology that Breaks Your Heart*.[2]

Architecture

Juan Antonio Bueno has served as dean of the School of Architecture at Florida International University. He is professor of landscape architecture, and has served as director of the School of Design and director of the Graduate Program in Landscape. He has received numerous awards from the American Society of Landscape Architecture for design projects, visionary work, teaching, and research.

Felipe J. Préstamo, died in 2007. He was professor emeritus at University of Miami's School of Architecture and the author of many works on architecture and urban planning.[3]

Arts

Ricardo Viera is professor of Art at Lehigh University, Bethlehem, Pennsylvania, and director and curator of the Lehigh University Art Galleries at the Zoellner Arts Center. Among others, he is the author of *Light in Bethlehem: A 250th Photography Celebration* (1992).[4]

Biology

René J. Herrera is professor of genetics and molecular biology at Florida International University. He is FIU's director of the Human Genetic Diversity Research Group and co-author of *DNA Fingerprinting* (1997).[5]

Business

José de la Torre is dean of the Alvah H. Chapman Graduate School of Business at Florida International University, where he also holds the James Batten Eminent Scholar Chair in Management. He is the author of *Clothing-Industry Adjustments in Developed Countries* (1987) and the co-author of *The Activities of IT Multinationals in the European Community* (1985) and *Managing the Global Corporation* (2000).

Chemistry

Juana (Jennie) Vivó Acrivos is professor of chemistry emerita at San José State University in California, where she has been very active in research, publishing more than one hundred articles in American, British, German, Scandinavian, and French scientific journals. In 1984 she was director of NATO Advanced Study Institute: Physics and Chemistry of Electrons and Ions in Condensed Matter, Cambridge University, England. She has been one of the recognized leaders in the field or intercalation chemistry with an international reputation, and a pioneer in the study of condensed matter.[6]

Economics

George J. Borjas is the Robert W. Scrivner Professor of Economics and Social Policy at the Harvard Kennedy School. Borjas has been called "America's leading immigration economist" by *Business Week* and the *Wall Street Journal*. His books include, among others, *Labor Economics* (1996, 2000, 2005).

Antonio Jorge is professor emeritus of political economy at Florida International University, College of Arts and Sciences. He is the author or editor of twenty books, among them *Competition, Cooperation, Efficiency, and Social Organization* (1978).

Carmelo Mesa-Lago is distinguished service professor emeritus of economics and Latin America at the University of Pittsburgh. He has authored fifty-eight books including *Market, Socialist and Mixed Economies: Comparative Policy and Performance—Chile, Cuba and Costa Rica*, published in 2000.

Jorge Salazar-Carrillo is a professor of economics at Florida International University, and director of its Center of Economic Research. He has edited or authored over one hundred articles, a hundred book chapters, and over sixty books. Among his publications is *The Future of the Cuban Economy*.[7]

Engineering

Armando Corripio is the Jay Affolter Professor at the Department of Chemical Engineering at Louisiana State University. He is the co-author of *Principles and Practice of Automatic Process Control* (1997), *Tuning Industrial Control Systems* (2000), and *Design and Applications of Process Control Systems* (1998)

Miguel A. Medina is director of the International Honors Program of the Pratt School of Engineering at Duke University. He is associate editor of the *Journal of Hydrologic Engineering*.[8]

Geosciences

Oswaldo García is chair of the Department of Geosciences at the College of Science and Engineering at San Francisco State University. His areas of expertise are meteorology, atmospheric effects of past El Niño patterns in the Pacific, and air-sea interactions. He is the author of *Atlas of Highly Reflective Clouds for the Global Tropics: 1971-1983* (1985).

History

Jorge Castellanos Taquechel is professor emeritus of history at Marygrove College in Detroit, Michigan. Among others, he is the author of *Encuentro en 1898: Tres Pueblos y Cuatro Hombres* (2006).

José B. Fernández is dean of the College of Arts and Humanities at the University of Central Florida since 2006. Among other titles, he is the author of *Los Abuelos: Historial Oral Cubana* (1987), and co-author of the first edition of the textbook *¡Arriba!* (1993).

María Cristina García is a professor of history at Cornell University, and Acting Chair of the American Studies Program. Among other titles, she is the author of *Havana USA: Cuban Exiles and Cuban Americans in South Florida, 1959-1994* (1996).

Manuel Márquez-Sterling is professor emeritus of history at Plymouth State University, N.H. Among other titles, he is the author of *The True Story of Castro's Rise to Power* (2009).

Leví Marrero died in Puerto Rico in 1995. When he left Cuba he became professor of the Experimental Pedagogic Institute in Barquisimeto, Venezuela. Later on he was a professor of geography at the University of Puerto Rico. His most important books are: *La Tierra y sus Recursos: Una Nueva Geografía General Visualizada* (1980), *Venezuela y sus Recursos* (1964), and his fifteen-volume *Cuba: Economía y Sociedad*.

María Rosa Menocal is a scholar of medieval culture and history at Yale University since 1986. She is currently director of the Yale Whitney Humanities Center and the author of *The Ornament of the World: How Muslims, Jews, and Christians Created a Culture of Tolerance in Medieval Spain* (2002).

Augusto Montenegro González died in 2010. He was a professor at the Facultad de Ciencias Sociales of the Universidad Pontificia Javeriana, Bogotá, Colombia. Among other titles he is the author of *Colombia en la última Guerra de Independencia Cubana 1895-1898* (1998).

Louis A. Pérez, Jr., is the J. Carlyle Sitterson professor of history in the College of Arts and Sciences of the University of North Carolina. His most recent books include *Cuba: Between Reform and Revolution*; *Cuba and the United States: Ties of Singular Intimacy*, and *The War of 1898: The United States and Cuba in History and Historiography*.

Rafael Rojas is professor of the Centro de Investigación y Docencia Económica in México City. Among other titles, he is the author of *Cuba Mexicana. Historia de una Anexión Imposible* (2001), which received the Matías Romero Award for Diplomatic History; *Tumbas sin Sosiego. Revolución, Disidencia y Exilio del Intelectual Cubano* (2006), won the Anagrama Essay Award; and *Las Repúblicas de Aire. Utopía y Desencanto en la Revolución de Hispanoamérica* (2009), received the Isabel de Polanco Essay Award.

Jaime Suchlicki is the Emilio Bacardí Moreau's chair of Cuban Studies and director of the Institute for Cuban and Cuban-American

Studies, University of Miami. He is the author of *Cuba: From Columbus to Castro* (2002), among other titles.[9]

International Studies

Jorge I. Domínguez is the Antonio Madero Professor of Mexican and Latin American politics and economics and vice provost for International Affairs at Harvard University. He is the author or co-author of several books, among them: *The Cuban Economy at the Start of the Twenty-First Century*, and *Cuba Hoy: Analizando su Pasado, Imaginando su Futuro*.

Damián Fernández is professor of international relations at Florida International University and director of its Cuban Research Institute. He is the author of *Cuba and the Politics of Passion* and *Cuba's Foreign Policy in the Middle East*.

Andy S. Gómez is assistant provost for accreditation and assessment at Miami University and a senior fellow at the Institute for Cuban and Cuban-American Studies. He is the author of *The Role of Education in Promoting Cuba's Integration Into the International Society* (2003).

Journalism

Luis Mario is professor of journalism at the University of Miami and an editor-in-chief of *Diario Las Américas*. He is the author of twelve poetry and prose books, among them *Ciencia y Arte del Verso Castellano* and *Inspiradores* (2006)

Carlos Márquez Sterling died in Miami in 1981. He taught in exile at Colombia University and C.W. Post College. In 1979 he moved to Miami and taught at Biscayne College (now St. Thomas University) and was a lecturer at Florida International University. He was the author of more than twenty books, including biographies of José Martí and Ignacio Agramonte, and *Historia de Cuba* (1969).[10]

Law

Beatriz Bernal is a retired professor of Roman law at Universidad Nacional Autónoma de México and former professor at the School of Law of the Universidad Complutense de Madrid. She is the author of *Constituciones Iberoamericanas Cuba* (2008).

Efrén Córdova has been a professor of law in Puerto Rico and Florida International Universities. He is the author of nine books, among them *Apuntes Para una Historia de la Dictadura Castrista* (2007).

Jorge L. Esquirol is professor of law and director of International and Comparative Law Programs at Florida International University's College of Law. He is the author of *Writing the Law of Latin America*.

Alfredo P. García is dean and professor of law at St. Thomas University's School of Law. Among other titles he is the author of *The Sixth Amendment in Modern American Jurisprudence: A Critical Perspective* (2002).

Miguel Zaldívar Zaydín was professor of labor law at Universidad Católica Andrés Bello, Caracas, Venezuela from 1985 to 2005. He is co-author of *Comentarios a la Reforma de la Ley del Trabajo de Venezuela* (1998).[11]

Library Sciences

Rosa Abella died in 2007. She was professor emerita at the University of Miami. She is one of the pioneer librarians that started the Cuban Heritage Collection. She is the author of *Index to the SALALM progress reports, 1956-1970* (1975).

Jorge Aguayo in 1962 became branch librarian of the Pan American Union (PAU), and from 1968 to 1973 Head Librarian of the PAU's Central Columbus Library. In 1967 he co-authored a compilation of the PAU-sponsored *Lista de Encabezamientos de Material Para Bibliotecas*.

Ana Rosa Núñez died in 1999. At the Otto G. Richter Library of the University of Miami, she was one of the pioneer librarians who started the Cuban Heritage Collection. She is the author of several books of poetry, among them *Crisantemos* (1990).

Esperanza B. de Varona is director of the Cuban Heritage Collection of the University of Miami Otto G. Richter Library. The Cuban Heritage Collection is housed at the 10,000-square-foot Roberto C. Goizueta Pavilion, and consists of thousands of books, periodicals, and archival materials that span more than four hundred years. De Varona is the author of *Cuban Exile Periodicals at the University of Miami Library: An Annotated Bibliography* (1987).[12]

Linguistics

Humberto López Morales is professor emeritus of linguistics at the University of Puerto Rico, Río Piedras. He is the author of fifty-two books, among them *Sociolingüística* (1989, 1993, 2004).

Beatriz Varela is professor emerita of Spanish at New Orleans University. She is the author of *Lo Chino en el Habla Cubana* (1980).

Juan Clemente Zamora Munné died in 2007. He was professor of linguistics at the University of Massachusetts, Amherst from 1971 to 2006. He was chair of the Department of Spanish and Portuguese from 1987 to 1993. He is the author of *Historiografía lingüística: Edad Media y Renacimiento* (1993).[13]

Literature

Elio Alba Buffill is professor emeritus of the City University of New York, Kingsborough College. He is national executive secretary of Círculo de Cultura Panamericano and the editor of *Círculo: Revista de Cultura*. He is the author of seven books, among them, *Cuba: Agonía y Deber. De Letras e Historia* (2009).

Isabel Alvarez Borland is professor of Spanish and the Monsignor Edward G. Murray Professor in the Arts and Humanities at the College of the Holy Cross, Worcester, Mass. Among other titles, she is the author of *Cuban-American Narrative of Exile: From Person to Persona* (2000).

Uva de Aragón is retired professor of humanities at Florida International University. She is the author, among others, of *Memorias del Silencio* (2002).

Andrea B. Bermúdez is professor emerita at the University of Houston System. She has been dean of academic affairs at Miami-Dade College, associate provost at the University of Houston-Clear Lake, and vice president for Academic and Student Affairs at Santa Fe Community College. Among other titles, she is the author of *Influence of the Institution of Free Learning on Spanish Education* (1978).

Jorge M. Febles is chair, Department of World Languages at University of North Florida. He is professor emeritus of Spanish at Western Michigan University. Among his books are *Into the Mainstream: Essays on Spanish American and Latino Literature and Culture* (2008).

Gastón Fernández de Cárdenas is professor emeritus of Spanish at Clemson University, South Carolina. He is the author of *Temas e imágenes en los Versos Sencillos de José Martí* (1977), and co-author of *Así somos* (1983).

Gastón Fernández de la Torriente died in 2007. He was professor emeritus of foreign languages and Hispanic literature at the University of Arkansas in Fayetteville. His last publication was a book of poems *Impresiones de Tiempo* (2007).

Eugenio Florit was professor emeritus of Latin American literature at Barnard College. He died in Miami in 1999. Among other titles, he was the author of *Hispanic-American Literature* (1960) and *Hispanic-American Poetry Since Modernism* (1968).

Arturo Fox is the William W. Edel professor of humanities, emeritus, at Dickinson College. Among other titles, he is the author of *Latinoamérica: Presente y Pasado* (1998, 2003, 20006).

Mercedes García Tudurí died in 1997. She was professor of Spanish literature and philosophy at Biscayne College (later Saint Thomas University), Miami. Among other titles, she was the author of *Ausencia* (1968).

Rita Geada is professor emerita at Southern Connecticut State University. Her poetry collection includes among others *Espejo de la Tierra* (2001).

Luis González del Valle is professor at the University of Colorado-Boulder. He has written and edited twenty-two scholarly books. He is editor of the six-volume book *Eugenio Florit Complete Works*.

Roberto González Echevarría is the Sterling Professor of Hispanic and Comparative Literature at Yale University. He is the author of *Myth and Archive: A Theory of Latin American Narrative* (1990, 1998) awarded the Katherine Singer Kovacs Prize and the Latin American Studies Association's 1992 Bryce Wood Award; *The Pride of Havana: A History of Cuban Baseball* (1999) earned the Dave Moore Award for the Best Baseball Book of 2002.

Mariela A. Gutiérrez is professor of Spanish at the University of Waterloo, Ontario, Canada. Among other titles, she is the author of *An Ethnological Interpretation of the Afro-Cuban World of Lydia Cabrera*.

Julio E. Hernández Miyares is professor emeritus of Kingsboro Community College of the City University of New York. Among others, he is the author of *Narrativa y Libertad: Cuentos Cubanos de la diáspora* (1996).

Magali R. Jerez is professor and chairwoman of world languages and cultures discipline at Bergen Community College, Paramus, New Jersey. She is the author of *Empecemos* (first edition 1997, now preparing the sixth edition).

Onilda A. Jiménez is professor emerita of New Jersey City University. Among her publications are *La Crítica Literaria en la Obra de Gabriela Mistral*, and the novel *De Vuelta al Génesis*.

Robert F. Lima, Jr., is professor emeritus of Spanish and contemporary literature at the Pennsylvania State University. Among his twenty books are *The Theater of García Lorca, Valle Inclán*, and *Dark Prisms: Occultism in Hispanic Drama*.

Ellen Lismore Leeder is professor emerita of Spanish, in the department of English and foreign languages at Barry University, Miami. Among other titles, she is the author of *Dimensión Existencial en la Narrativa de Lera (1992)*.

Jacobo Machover has been exiled in France since 1963. He teaches at the University of Paris XII and is a lecturer at the University of Avignon. Among other titles, he is the author of *La Dinastía Castro. Los Misterios y Secretos de su Poder* (2007).

José A. Madrigal is professor emeritus at Auburn University, Alabama, where he was the chair of the Department of Foreign Languages and Literature. Among other titles, he is the author of *New Historicism and the Comedia: Poetics, Politics, and Praxis* (1997). He co-founded the National Association of Cuban-American Educators.

Lillian Manzor is professor of comparative literature, Department of Foreign Languages and Literature, at the University of Miami, where she is also the director of Latin American Studies. She is the author of *Borges/Escher, Sarduy/CoBrA: Un Encuentro Posmoderno*.

Ofelia Martin Hudson is professor emerita of Spanish at the Interamerican Campus, Miami-Dade College. Among others, she is the author of *Cantar Otras Hazañas* (1996).

Matías Montes Huidobro is professor emeritus of the University of Hawaii. He is the author of *La Narrativa Cubana Entre la Memoria y el Olvido* (2005). His dramas include among others *Exilio* (1999). In 2000 he founded *Pro Teatro Cubano*.

Rolando D. H. Morelli is professor at Villanova University. Among other titles, he is the author of the bilingual book *Algo Está Pasando/Something Is Brewing* (2006).

Andrea O'Reilly Herrera is professor of literature and director of Ethnic Studies at the University of Colorado at Colorado Springs. Her work includes a novel *The Pearl of the Antilles* (2001) chronicling the lives of four generations of Cuban women, awarded the Golden Quill Book Award in 2005.

Carlos Ripoll was professor of Romance Languages at Queens

College of the City University of New York. He is the author of a bilingual anthology of José Martí's thoughts. He is co-author of a web page that contains the work of José Martí (www.eldosrios.com).

Eliana Rivero is professor of Spanish in the Department of Spanish and Portuguese of the University of Arizona. She is co-author and co-editor of *Infinite Divisions: An Anthology of Chicana Literature* (1993) and *Telling to Live: Latina Feminist Testimonios* (2002), recipient of the Myers Award for Diversity.

José Sánchez-Boudy is professor emeritus of North Carolina University at Greensboro. His book *Diccionario de Cubanismos Más Usuales* in six volumes is an extensive study of the peculiarities of Cubans' language and idioms.

Enrico Mario Santí is the first William T. Bryan Professor of Hispanic Studies at the University of Kentucky. His book *Sobre Cultura Cubana* (2002) gathers thirty years' worth of his essays on Cuban topics.

José I. Suárez is professor of Hispanic studies at the University of Northern Colorado. From 1999 to 2005 he chaired the department. Among other titles, he is the author of *The Carnival Stage: Vicentine Comedy within the Serio-Comic Mode* (1993).

Laurentino Suárez was from 1993 to 1995 vice president for administration at Florida National College, prior to that, from 1984 to 1986 he was dean of the College of Arts and Sciences at Saint Thomas University. He is co-author of *De Aquí de Allá* (1981).

Andrés Valdespino died in 1974. He was professor of Spanish at Hunter College of the City University of New York. In 1975, the Andrés Valdespino Memorial Award was established at the Department of Romance Languages at Hunter College. He is co-author of *Teatro Hispanoamericano: Antología Crítica, Tomo I: Época Colonial (1972),* and *Tomo II: Siglo XIX (1973).*[14]

Mathematics

Celestino G. Méndez is professor of Mathematical Sciences at the Metropolitan State College in Denver, Colorado. He was chairman of the Department of Mathematical Sciences (1980-1983), and assistant to the vice president for academic affairs and provost (1989-1990).

Jorge Luis Romeu is a research professor in statistics and operations research with the Department of Mechanical and Aerospace Engineering, Syracuse University. He is involved in international education, and created and directs the Juárez-Lincoln-Martí International Education Project. He is the author of *A Practical Guide to Statistical Analysis of Material Data* (1999), and more than thirty scientific publications.

Medicine

Agustín Castellanos, Jr., is professor of medicine, Department of Cardiology at the University of Miami, School of Medicine. He has made major contributions in the subjects of electrophysiology, arrhythmias, and the use of artificial pacemakers. He is the co-author of *A Programmed Introduction to the Electrical Axis and Action Potential (Tampa Papers)* (1974).

Julio E. Ferreiro is professor emeritus at the University of Miami, School of Medicine. The Florida Chapter of the American College of Physicians presented him with the Internist of the Year Award in 2000, and in 2004 he was granted the prestigious designation of Master of the American College of Physicians, being one of only three Cuban-exile internists to ever receive this distinction.

Francisco García-Bengochea was professor of neurological surgery at the University of Florida. He was one of two faculty members when the Division of Neurosurgery was created in 1958. He was the author of important scientific articles published in many peer-reviewed medical journals.

Roberto C. Heros is professor, co-chairman, and program director, Department of Neurological Surgery, University of Miami, School of Medicine. He is the co-author of *Surgical Management of Cerebrovascular Disease* (1989) and *Kempe's Operative Neurosurgery. Volumes One and Two: Cranial, Cerebral and Intracranial Vascular Disease (Posterior Fossa, Spinal, and Peripheral Nerve)* (2003).

Eduardo de Marchena is professor of medicine and surgery, director of Interventional Cardiology, and associate dean for International Medicine, all at the University of Miami, School of Medicine. His research in the areas of interventional cardiology, coronary artery disease, atherosclerosis, and congestive heart failure has been widely published in more than two hundred articles. He is co-author of *Secrets in Interventional Cardiology*.

Luis O. Martínez-Fariñas died in 2004. He was professor of radiology at the University of Miami School of Medicine and associate chairman and residency program director at the Department of Radiology of Mount Sinai Medical Center. He was the author of numerous scientific articles, and editor of the journal of the Sociedad Interamericana de Radiología.

Fernando J. Milanés is retired professor and was vice chairman of the Department of Psychiatry at the University of Miami. He was also assistant chief of Miami's Veterans Administration Hospital Mental Health Department.

Azórides Morales is professor of pathology at the University of Miami, School of Medicine. He was acting chairman of the department from 1972 to 1974 and has published extensively.

Victoriano Pardo is professor of pathology and director of the Electromicroscopy Laboratory at the University of Miami, School of Medicine. He is co-author of numerous scientific papers in the field of nephropathology, and in 1984 he co-authored an article credited to be the first description of HIV-associated nephropathy

Manuel Peñalver is professor and chairman of the Department

of Obstetrics and Gynecology of the recently established College of Medicine at Florida International University. Previously he was chair of the Department of Obstetrics and Gynecology at the University of Miami, School of Medicine. He was honored with the Distinguished Alumnus Award by the University of Miami Alumni Association

Guido Pérez is professor emeritus of Medicine at the University of Miami, School of Medicine. He was a member of the Nephrology Section and chief of the Dialysis Unit at the Miami Veterans Administration Hospital. He was the first Cuban-American graduate of the University of Miami, School of Medicine, and has received the Distinguished Alumnus Award of the Alumni Association. He is the author of *Beyond the Science/Religion Debate: A Naturalistic World View* (2008).

Eliseo Pérez-Stable was professor emeritus, University of Miami, School of Medicine at the Veterans Administration Hospital. He became chief of Medical Services, chief of staff and associate dean for Veterans Affairs. He is one of the only three Cuban-exile internists to be awarded the prestigious designation of Master of the American College of Physicians.

Eliseo Pérez-Stable, Jr., is professor of medicine at the University of California, San Francisco, School of Medicine. His research has focused on health and health-care disparities by race and ethnicity in the areas of tobacco use and cessation, cancer prevention, and aging. He is the co-author of more than twenty scientific publications.

Ileana L. Piña is professor of medicine in the Division of Cardiology at Case Western Reserve University in Cleveland. At the present time she is the VA Quality Scholar at the Lewis Stokes VA Medical Center in Cleveland. She is chairperson for the American Heart Association in the capacity of Heart Failure and Transplantation of the Council on Clinical Cardiology. She is the editor of *An AARP Guide: Living with Heart Disease: Everything You Need to Know to Safeguard your Health and Take Control of Your Life* (2007).

Armando Ruiz-Leiro died in 2004. He was professor emeritus of medicine at the School of Medicine, Tulane University, New Orleans. In 1980 Tulane honored him with the Gloria P. Walsh Award. In 1995 the National Association of Cuban-American Educators gave him the Educator of the Year Award, and in 1998 he received the Dr. Joaquín Albarrán Award from the Cuban Medical Convention in Miami. He was a role model for several generations of young Cuban and American students.

Rubén Darío Rumbaut was professor emeritus of psychiatry at Baylor College of Medicine, Houston, Texas. He was director of the Veterans Administration Hospital's Mental Hygiene Clinic in Albuquerque, New Mexico, and in Topeka, Kansas. He is the author of *John of God: His Place in the History of Psychiatry* and of a poetry book, *Esa Palabra* (1981).

Charles Santos-Buch is professor emeritus of pathology at the Joan and Sandford E. Weill Medical College of Cornell University, where he served as associate dean. He is well known for his research on the immunology of Chagas disease, conducted in Brazil as part of the Cornell's Bahia Program of International Education.

Emil R. Unanue is the Paul & Ellen Lacy Professor at Washington University, St. Louis, Missouri. In 1970 Unanue joined the Department of Pathology at Harvard Medical School, and became the Mallinckrodt Professor of Immunology in 1974. He has made a series of important contributions to the field of renal pathophysiology by examining the immune basis of glomerulonephritis, and has made seminal observations in the field of antigen processing and presentation.

Manuel Viamonte, Jr., is retired professor of radiology at the University of Miami, School of Medicine. He was the chairman and director of the Department of Radiology at Mount Sinai Medical Center in Miami Beach, Florida. He is the author or co-author of more than 240 scientific papers and seventeen books, among them *Errors in Uroradiology* (1992), and *Geriatric Radiology* (1991), and co-editor of *Clinical Uses of Radionuclides: Critical Comparison with Other Techniques* (1972).[15]

Music

Teresa Escandón died in 2001. She was professor of piano at the Frost School of Music of the University of Miami. She wrote a multiple volume set called *Jorge Bolet Memorial Editions*, which details Bolet's playing of Liszt and Chopin. She recorded a CD of Granados' *Goyescas o Los Majos Enamorados*.

Raúl A. Fernández is professor at the School of Social Sciences, at University of California, Irvine. He is the author of six books, among them *From Afro-Cuban Rhythms to Latin Jazz* (2006).

Tania León is distinguished professor of music at Brooklyn College, of the City University of New York. Among her compositions are an opera *Scourge of Hyacinths*, that won the BMW Prize as best new work at the 1994 Munich Biennale; also the ballets *The Beloved*, *Haiku*, *Dougla*, and *Tones*; the orchestra pieces *Batá*, *Carabalí*, *Concerto Criollo*, *Kabiosile Para Viola and Orchestra*, and *Seven Spirituals*.

Rosalina G. Sackstein is professor emerita of piano at the Frost School of Music of the University of Miami. She has appeared as a soloist with orchestras in the United States and abroad, conducts master classes and piano workshops, and serves as an adjudicator in piano competitions.

Aurelio de la Vega is a distinguished emeritus professor at the California State University, Northridge, and was its professor of music and director of the Electronic Music Studio (1959-1993). His list of compositions includes symphonic pieces, chamber music works, solo instrumental pieces, vocal works, piano, guitar, and ballet music, and electronic composition. In 2002 he was honored by the Library of Congress when his graphic score *The Magic Labyrinth* was included in the library's 733-page volume *Music History from Primary Sources*. In 2009 he received the William B. Warren Lifetime Achievement Award in Music Composition, by the Cintas Foundation.[16]

Philosophy

Jorge J.E. Gracia is distinguished professor and the Samuel P. Chapman Chair of the Department of Philosophy and Department of Comparative Literature at State University of New York at Buffalo. He is the author of sixteen books, among them *Introduction to the Problem of Individuation in the Early Middle Ages* (1984, 1988, translated to Spanish 1987), *Philosophy and Its History: Issues in Philosophical Historiography* (1992, translated into Serbo-Croatian and Chinese).

Physics

Marcelo Alonso died in 2005. He was a nuclear physicist and former professor of physics at Georgetown University Graduate School. He was the author of *Quantum and Statistical Physics (Fundamental University Physics)* (1968) and *Física Volumen 2—Campos y Ondas* (1999). And among other titles, he was co-author of *Physics* (1992) and *Física* (2002, translated into eighteen languages).

Vivian Incera is the chairperson of the Physics Department at Western Illinois University where she teaches mathematical physics. She has collaborated on nearly sixty professional publications, and some forty conferences and invited seminars worldwide. Her main research interest at the present time is the phenomenon of color superconductivity, aimed at understanding the effects of large magnetic fields in a color superconductor.[17]

Political Sciences

Alfred G. Cuzán is chairman and professor of political science at the Department of Government, the University of West Florida, Pensacola. Among others, he is the author of *A Tale of Two Cities: Political Structure and Policy Performance in Costa Rica and El Salvador* (1977).

Darío Moreno is professor of political science and director of the Metropolitan Center at Florida International University. He conducts research on Cuban-American politics, Miami and Florida politics. Among others, he is the author of *The Struggle for Peace in Central America* (1994).

Eusebio Mujal León is professor and former chair of the Department of Government at Georgetown University. Among other titles, he is the author of *Communism and Political Change in Spain* (1983).

Mauriclo Solaún is a professor of Latin American Social and Political Institutions at the University of Illinois. Among others, he is co-author of *U.S. Intervention and Regiment Change in Nicaragua.*[18]

Psychology

Oliva M. Espín is professor emerita of Women's Studies at San Diego University. She is the author and co-author of six books, among them *Latina Healers: Lives of Power and Tradition* (1996).

José Szapocznik is professor and chair of the Department of Epidemiology and Public Health, associate dean for Community Development, and director of the Center for Family Studies all at the University of Miami. He is the co-author of numerous scientific publications, among them *Cuban Americans: Acculturation, Adjustment, and the Family* (1978).

Sociology

Guillermo Grenier is professor of sociology at Florida International University. Among others, he is the author of *Inhumane Relations: Quality Circles and Anti-Unionism* (1988).

Silvia Pedraza is professor of sociology and American culture at the Department of Sociology, University of Michigan, Ann Arbor. Among others, she is the author of *Political Disaffection in Cuba's Revolution and Exodus* (2007).

Lisandro Pérez is professor of sociology at Florida International University. In 1991 he founded a Cuban Research Institute at FIU and served as its director until 2003. He is co-author of *The Legacy of Exile: Cubans in the United States* (2003).

Marifeli Pérez-Stable is professor of sociology and anthropology at Florida International University. She is the author of *Cuban Revolution: Origins, Course, and Legacy* (1993, 1999, Spanish translation 1998), and *Cuba en el Siglo XXI: Ensayos Sobre la Transición.*

Alejandro Portes is professor of sociology at Princeton University. He was president of the American Sociological Association (1998-1999). He is the author and co-author of ten books, among them *City on the Edge: The Transformation of Miami* (1994), for which he received the Anthony Leeds Award for best book in urban anthropology by the Society for Urban Anthropology of the American Anthropological Association, and the Robert B. Park Award for the best book in urban sociology by the Community and Urban Sociology Section of the American Sociological Association.

Rubén G. Rumbaut is professor of sociology in the School of Social Sciences at the University of California–Irvine. He is the author of more than one hundred scientific papers on immigrants and refugees in the U.S. and co-author or coeditor of a dozen books, including *Immigrant America: A Portrait* (2006), and *Legacies: The Story of the Immigrant Second Generation,* which won the 2002 Distinguished Book Award of the American Sociological Association, and the 2002 Thomas and Znaniecki Award for best book in the immigration field.[19]

Theology

Ada María Isasi-Díaz is professor of ethics and theology at Drew University Theological School, Graduate Division of Religion, in Madison, New Jersey. She is a member of the Order of St. Ursula. For many years she has worked in the women's movement focusing on women's oppression in churches, religion and theology, as well as in the interconnections of sexism, ethnic prejudice-racism, and economic oppression-classism. She is an activist-theologian and has elaborated the Mujerista Theology. Among other titles, she is the author of *Mujerista Theology—A Theology for the 21st Century* (1996).[20]

NOTES

1. Other professors of agriculture worth mentioning are José Alvarez, University of Florida, and Pedro A. Sánchez, Columbia University.
2. Also a professor of anthropology was Julio Sánchez de Cárdenas, Universidad Interamericana, Bayamón, Puerto Rico.
3. Other professors of architecture worth mentioning are Jaime Canavés, FIU, José Gelabert Navia, University of Miami (UM), Miriam Gusevich, Catholic University, Washington, D.C., Jorge Hernández, UM, and Tomás Luis López-Gottardi, UM.
4. Other professors of arts are Luis Garzón, Autonomous University of Baja California, Tijuana, Mexico, and Derby L. Ulloa, Florida Community College, Jacksonville.
5. Also a professor of biology is León Cuervo, FIU.
6. Also a professor of chemistry is Héctor Novoa de Armas, Katholieke Universiteit Leuven, Belgium.
7. Other professors of economy worth mentioning are Alberto Martínez Piedra, Institute of World Politics, and Raúl Moncarz, FIU.
8. Other professors of engineering are Manuel Cereijo, FIU, and Jorge Marbán, Palm Beach Community College.
9. Other professors of history: Arnhilda Badía, FIU, Graciella Cruz-Taura, Florida Atlantic University, Boca Ratón, Félix Masud-Piloto, De Paul University, Chicago, and Frank de Varona, FIU.
10. Other professors of journalism are Fernando Figueredo, FIU, Mirta Ojito, Columbia University, and José Ignacio Rasco, Miami-Dade College and FIU.
11. Other professors of law: José Gabilondo, FIU, and José Miró Cardona, University of Puerto Rico.
12. Other librarians: María Rosa Estorino, UM, Rosa Q. Mesa, University of Florida, María Luisa Pérez Ruíz, Miami-Dade College, Sara M. Sánchez, UM, Celia C. Suárez, Miami-Dade College, and Lesbia de Varona, UM.
13. Other professors of linguistics are Jorge Guitart, SUNY at Buffalo, Ricardo L. Ortiz, George Washington University, and Ana Roca, FIU.
14. Other professors of literature: Nicolás Emilio Alvarez, Auburn University, Florinda Alzaga Loret de Mola, Barry University, Rubén C. Arango, Saint Thomas University (Biscayne College), Jesús J. Barquet, New Mexico State University, Las Cruces, N.M., Emilio Bejel, University of Colorado at Boulder, Antonio Benítez-Rojo, Amherst College, Massachusetts, Matilde O. Castells, University of California, Los Angeles, Miguel Correa, Hostos Community College, New York,

Ivo Domínguez, University of Delaware, José A. Escarpenter, Auburn University, Alabama, Roberto G. Fernández, Florida State University, Leonardo Fernández Marcané, SUNY at Albany, Lourdes Gil, Baruch College, N.Y., Jorge Giró, Townson University, Maryland, Olimpia B. González, Loyola University, Chicago, Luis González Cruz, Penn State University, Yara González Montes, University of Hawaii, Alberto Gutiérrez de la Solana, New York University, Alberto Hernández-Chiroldes, Davidson College, N.C., Olga Karman, D'Youville College, Buffalo, N.Y., José Kozer, Queens College, SUNY, Raúl A. Laborde, Franklin Pierce University, N.H., Pablo La Rosa, Baker University, Kansas, Sara Lequerica de la Vega, Los Angeles Valley College, Eduardo Lolo, Kingsboro Community College, CUNY, Ramón Magrans, Arkansas Tech University, Jorge A. Marbán, College of Charleston, SC, Pablo Medina, Warren Wilson College, Ashville, NC, Andrea O'Reilly Herrera, University of Colorado, Tomás G. Oria, University of Michigan, Augusto Portuondo, University of Virginia at Wise, Carlos M. Raggi Ageo, Russell Sage College, Troy, N.Y., Rosario Rexach, Hunter College, SUNY, Héctor Romero, University of Texas-Pan American, Georgina Sabat de Rivers, SUNY, Stony Brook, Esther Sánchez-Grey Alba, Tombrock College, Drew University, Rafael Saumell-Muñoz, Sam Houston State University, Huntsville, Texas, Arístides Sosa de Quesada, Dana College, Blair, Nebraska, Arístides Sosa de Quesada, Jr., University of Nebraska at Kearny, Rafael Sosa de Quesada, Wayne State College, Nebraska, Virgil Suárez, Lousiana State University, Amalia Varela de la Torre, Saint Mary's College, Notre Dame, and Rosa Leonor Whitmarsh, Miami-Dade College.

15. Other medicine professors: Raúl Blanco Quintana, Northwestern University, Chicago, Alejandro Chediak, UM, Rafael Peñalver, who directed courses at the UM to help exile physicians pass the examinations of the Educational Council for Foreign Medical Graduates (ECFMG), and Roger de la Torre, University of Missouri-Columbia.
16. Other professors of music: Mario Abril, University of Tennessee at Chatanooga, Kevin Miguel Delgado, San Diego State University, Aldo Rafael Forte, Christopher Newport University, Newportnews, V.A., Orlando Jacinto García, FIU, Jacobo Lateiner, Mannes College The New School for Music, Martha Marchena, Kean University, Union City, N.J., Solomon Mikowsky, Columbia University, Julián Orbón, National Conservatory of Music, Mexico, Keyla Orozco Alemán, Amsterdam Conservatory, The Netherlands, Rafael Padrón, UM, Ileana Pérez Velázquez, Williams College, Williamstown, Mass., and Armando Tranquilino, University of Arizona.
17. Also a professor of physics: Efraín J. Ferrer, Western Illinois University.
18. Other professors of political sciences: Juan M. del Aguila, Emory University, Atlanta, Juan Carlos Espinosa, FIU, and Laura Ymayo Tartakoff, Case Western Reserve University, Cleveland.
19. Also a professor of sociology: Roberto D. Agramonte, University of Puerto Rico.
20. Other professors of theology: Juan M. Navia, Spring Hill College, Mobile, Alabama, Manuel H. Díaz, St. John's University, Minnesota, and Miguel de la Torre, Iliff School of Theology, Denver.

37

LAWYERS AND JUDGES

BY RENE V. MURAI

INTRODUCTION

Cuba's most famous and infamous lawyer is Fidel Castro, who attended the University of Havana law school in the 1940s. Its student organization, la Federación Estudiantil Universitaria (the University Student Federation), was a hotbed of political activity, going back to the 1920s and the uprisings that led to the end of the government of President Gerardo Machado in 1933. It was during his university years that Castro participated in an attempt to overthrow the government of Rafael Trujillo in the Dominican Republic, and, as one of the organizers of a student congress in Bogotá, Colombia, in a violent uprising that became known as the *Bogotazo*.

As in many countries, Cuban lawyers were prominent in public life. A number of its presidents were lawyers: Mario García Menocal (1913-1921), Alfredo Zayas (1921-1925), Miguel Mariano Gómez (1936), and Carlos Prío Socarrás (1948-1952). Many others held important positions in government, including Carlos Márquez Sterling, who served as president of Cuba's House of Representatives, secretary of education, and president of the Constitutional Assembly that authored the much-praised 1940 Constitution; José Miró Cardona, a professor and dean of the University of Havana Law School, who was the first prime minister under Castro's government for a brief period (replaced by Castro himself) and later a leader in exile of the forces opposing Castro; Alberto Inocente Alvarez, who held various appointed and elected positions in Cuba, served as Cuba's representative to the United Nations and president of the UN Security Council in 1949; Miguel Angel de la Campa, who served as Cuba's ambassador to the United States as well as being foreign minister, attorney general, and defense minister; Rafael Díaz Balart, who was elected to Congress and served as majority leader of Cuba's House of Representatives. He is the father of U.S. Congressman Mario Díaz Balart and former U.S. Congressman Lincoln Díaz Balart. In 1955, Rafael Díaz Balart made an impassioned speech in Congress opposing a law proposed by President Fulgencio Batista, and passed by the Congress, which granted amnesty to political prisoners, including Castro and the men who were involved in the 1953 attack on the Moncada garrison in Santiago de Cuba. Díaz Balart warned of dire consequences for the country if Castro and the others were freed. Díaz Balart knew Castro well as a fellow law student and as his brother-in-law. Unfortunately for Cuba, his words were not heeded.

THE EARLY EXILE YEARS

The legal profession is not easily transportable from country to country. The basics of many other professions are not country dependent. The law is. Cuba's legal system was a civil law system, premised on the Roman and Napoleonic codes, which also formed the basis for the legal systems of Latin American and many European countries. In contrast, the United States adopted the English common law system (except in Louisiana where the legal system continues to have roots in the Roman and Napoleonic codes). The civil law system relies almost exclusively on codified law. The common law system relies heavily on the development and interpretation of the law by courts.

In Florida, as in many (if not all) states, foreign educated lawyers were required to pass a college equivalency exam and be graduates of U.S. law schools before being eligible for admission to the practice. This meant that an exiled Cuban lawyer, who may have practiced law in Cuba for many years, was required to "start all over" and graduate from a U.S. law school in order to continue in the legal profession. The barriers were high. Law school was not a welcoming place for exiles with less than a good command of the English language. Money for tuition was scarce. And last but not least, Florida and all states required United States citizenship as a condition to admission to the bar. Citizenship in turn was conditioned on five years of legal residence. In the early years, almost all Cuban exiles were admitted to the U.S. as parolees and did not have a green card as a result. To obtain residency, one had to travel to a U.S. consulate abroad. Due to the numbers requesting them, appointments at these consulates were difficult to obtain. The Cuban-American Bar Association's (CABA) first elected president and later Judge Mario Goderich, who graduated from the University of Miami in 1966, had to work as a librarian at the University of Miami Law School for several years until he became eligible for citizenship.

Organizations came to the aid of the exile lawyers. Following a meeting with a group of exile lawyers headed by Miró Cardona, the University of Miami organized a program for Cuban lawyers, which ran from 1961 to 1963, supported by grants from the U.S. Department of Health, Education and Welfare. The program covered the basics of United States law and was designed to improve employment opportunities. One hundred and fifty exile lawyers completed the first courses in 1961. A university report showed that the program helped its graduates to obtain employment, whether law related or otherwise. For example, lawyer José Cuervo reported that the program was invaluable in his securing a position as research assistant at the Miami law firm of Walton Lantaff. The American Bar Association set up a "Special Committee to Cooperate with Cuban Lawyers in Exile." In a letter dated October 10, 1961, New

York lawyer John Burton, chairman of the committee, reported that a "number of insurance companies and industrial corporations have hired one or more Cuban lawyers or have indicated that it is their intention to do so."

Not surprisingly then, the decade of the 1960s would see few practicing Cuban-American lawyers. There may have been fewer than twenty Cuban-born lawyers practicing in Florida by the end of the 1960s. A federal agency reviewing the work of the Miami legal services program for the poor noted in 1972 the absence of any program office in the Spanish-speaking areas of Miami. The young Cubans who were attending high school or college in this country had not yet come of age for law school. Those who had practiced law in Cuba had to find other ways to earn a living and support their families. Eduardo Le Riverend, a justice of Cuba's Supreme Court, became the international law librarian at the University of Miami. Luis Botifoll, a well-known international lawyer and the editor in chief of one of Havana's most important dailies, *El Mundo*, became a banker. He chaired the loan committee and for seventeen years the Board of Directors of Republic National Bank, then the biggest Cuban-American led bank in the U.S.

One of the first Cuban-American lawyers in Miami was Carlos Fernández, father of State Attorney Katherine Fernández Rundle. Carlos Fernández graduated as a lawyer from the University of Havana in 1943, then went to the University of Miami Law School and was licensed as a Florida lawyer in 1949. He served as a municipal judge (municipal courts have since been abolished in Florida) from 1961 to 1972. He became involved with the exile community, was a founder of CABA, a political commentator, and writer.

Exiled lawyers also relocated to other states or countries in search of employment. Tomás and Olga Gamba, both lawyers in Cuba and parents of former CABA Tomás Gamba, along with many others, attended Indiana State University to study education and become high school teachers. After completing those courses, these lawyers taught

Spanish in different states. Because of the similarity of the legal systems, some Cuban lawyers settled and became lawyers in Spain. Among them, the best-known one was Manolo Vega Penichet, who founded the Bufete (law firm) of M. Vega Penichet in 1962. The firm today has approximately seventeen lawyers.

Two significant events accelerated the entry of Cuban-born lawyers into the American legal profession. The first was the Cuban Adjustment Act of 1966, passed during Lyndon Johnson's presidency, which, among other things, allowed Cuban exiles to obtain immediate legal residency and receive credit for up to half (but no more than two and one half years) of their stay in this country toward the five-year residency requirement. This law made Cuban exiles eligible for citizenship much sooner than would have been possible otherwise. Had it not been for this act, the Cuban-born law students of the late 1960s and early 1970s would have been unable to practice law in most states upon graduation.

The second important event occurred in July of 1973, when the Florida Supreme Court sanctioned law school programs at the University of Miami and the University of Florida for exiles who had obtained law degrees in Cuba prior to 1961. The National Association of Cuban Lawyers (in exile) had petitioned the Supreme Court for such a program, and the Florida Bar had supported the petition. After a twenty months course, the program graduates became eligible to take the Florida Bar exam. Classes were conducted nights and weekends, allowing lawyers to continue to support their families while obtaining their law degree. A federal loan program made tuition monies available to the students. Approximately 330 Cuban lawyers registered for these courses. The program opened the Florida Bar doors to many Cuban educated lawyers. Similar programs were approved in California and Illinois.

THE CUBAN-AMERICAN BAR ASSOCIATION

By 1974, there were approximately sixty Cuban-Americans practicing law in Florida. That year, a number of Cuban-American lawyers attending a continuing legal education course met for lunch. As Luis Figueroa recalls it, the conversation focused on the need for an association of Cuban-American lawyers. They felt that such an association would allow Cuban-American lawyers, with little history or contacts in this country, to gain prominence, to become better known to the judiciary and government officials, to help the community and to socialize with each other. CABA was not organized to replace any other bar association. It was formed as an association that brought together individuals who shared a profession, roots, and a common interest in matters affecting the Cuban community.

In August of 1974, Irma Hernández filed CABA's Articles of Incorporation. Its initial directors were Guillermo Fernández Mascaró, Mario Goderich, Irma Hernández, Manuel Vázquez, and Antonio Zamora, with Manuel Vázquez designated as the initial president until elections could be held. In the first election, Goderich (in a friendly contested election) was elected president. He was followed by Fernández Mascaró and Vázquez.

Monthly dinner meetings were held at the Centro Vasco restaurant and quickly became a forum for Cuban-American lawyers to meet. Elections were also held at the Centro Vasco Restaurant, and, in the best CABA tradition, they were held in December at the same time as CABA's annual Christmas party. Soon elections were attended by judges, elected officials, and other friends of CABA. When the ballot box closed at 9:00 P.M., lawyers and their spouses would have dinner while awaiting the result of the elections. In 1980, the late Judge Manuel Crespo and Francisco Angones ran for president. In a Bush-Gore-type finish, after several recounts, the vote was tied. Angones yielded to Crespo and the office of president-elect was born, with Angones as the first president-elect. The annual installation dinner quickly became the best lawyers' party in Miami. These parties were sold out events, attended by senators, governors, a vice president of the United States, members of the federal and state judiciary, and many government officials. In time, many "Anglo" lawyers joined the party. By the late 1980s, CABA had removed the requirement that one had to be of Cuban extraction to join its membership.

Today, CABA is one of the largest voluntary bar associations in the country with approximately two thousand dues-paying members, and none more supportive than Osvaldo Soto, an early president who served on its board of directors for many years and whom many regard as the heart and soul of CABA.

CABA ACTIVITIES

In 1984, under the leadership of José A. Garrido, Jr., later a CABA president, CABA began a pro bono project to provide civil legal assistance to Spanish-speaking individuals without the means to afford a lawyer. The project's first office was at the Gesu church in downtown Miami, and the lawyers providing the legal assistance came from the CABA ranks. The project continues to this day. But already in the mid-1980s, Cuban-American lawyers, such as Leopoldo Ochoa, Alina Antonetti, and Isabel McCormack, were representing, without charge, Cubans who had come through the port of Mariel and who were at risk of deportation.

The next year, during the presidency of this writer, CABA organized the Cuban-American Bar Foundation, with the objective of raising funds for loans and scholarships for Cuban law students. Its initial funds came from the profits made by CABA and the University of Miami from the biennial summer Conferences for Lawyers of the Americas. By 1987, CABA had created a $50,000 loan fund for University of Miami Law

School students. The foundation continues to date to award scholarships and provide loans to Cuban-American law students in various law schools.

More recently, CABA has initiated a mentoring program for law students and has submitted from time to time amicus briefs in important cases of interest to the CABA membership. In addition, CABA's lawyers have participated in the drafting of a transitional law intended to govern the period between the end of a Communist state in Cuba and the adoption of a new democratic constitution.

THE GUANTANAMO CASE

In 1994, there was once again a mass exodus from Cuba, except that this time the United States Coast Guard intercepted the boats and rafts and sent all that were fleeing to the U.S. military base in Guantánamo, Cuba. By November 1994, approximately 33,000 Cubans had been taken to Guantánamo. A group of Cuban-American lawyers led by Angones began meeting to determine a legal strategy for ending the detention. Harold Koh, a Korean American, then a Yale Law School professor, subsequently dean of Yale Law School, and today the legal advisor to the U.S. Department of State, had experience in similar cases for Haitians and agreed to join the Cuban-American legal team. Dozens of Cuban-American lawyers participated in the effort. All lawyers worked without compensation. After an unsuccessful trip to the White House to attempt to work out a solution, twenty-four Cuban-American lawyers filed a lawsuit in federal court challenging the detention.

The lawsuit sought to make new law by establishing rights for refugees, temporarily provided safe haven at the naval base, under the Immigration and Naturalization Act, the 1951 United Nations Convention relating to the Status of Refugees, the Cuban Adjustment Act, the Cuban Democracy Act, and the U.S. Constitution. The lawsuit also sought to establish that legal organizations had a First Amendment right of freedom of speech and association with these refugees. Roberto Martínez, Marc Jiménez, Manuel Kadre, and Professor Koh acted as principal trial counsel. The district court entered preliminary injunctions granting the attorneys for the Cuban refugees access to all Cuban refugees in Guantánamo, thereby insuring that these refugees would be able to consult an American lawyer prior to agreeing to voluntary repatriation, and barring the government from forcefully repatriating any Cuban refugee prior to the refugee's consultation with a lawyer.

Soon the lawyers began traveling to Guantánamo to obtain evidence and inform the detainees of the pending legal proceedings. For most lawyers, it was the first time that they had touched Cuban soil since they had left as exiles. Some had never touched Cuban soil, having been born in the United States. Brothers to the Rescue pilots including its founders, José Basulto and William "Billy" Schuss, flew Orlando Cabrera, José García-Pedrosa, Ramón Rasco, and former Miami Mayor Xavier Suárez on the first trip. A number of other trips followed in a plane provided by Joe Klock, then managing partner of the Miami law firm of Steel, Hector and Davis. The U.S. government appealed the grant of these injunctions to the 11th Circuit Court of Appeals, which ruled against the Cubans in *Cuban American Bar Association v. Cristopher* (43 F. 3d 1412 (11th Cir. 1995). Nevertheless, ultimately, the wide publicity given to the case may have contributed to the subsequent decision of President Clinton to allow most of the Guantánamo detainees to obtain legal entry into the United States. For their efforts on this case, the lawyers received the Florida Bar's highest honor for group *pro bono* work—the Voluntary Bar Association Pro Bono Service Award of 1996 from the Florida Supreme Court.

THE BAR

All lawyers in Florida are required to be members of the Florida Bar. The position of president of the Florida Bar is the ultimate achievement for a Florida lawyer, is often highly-contested, and requires almost a full-time commitment for two years, the first year as president-elect and the second as president. In 1989, Steve Zack became the first Cuban-American to serve as president of the Florida Bar. Zack in addition began in 2011 a one-year term as president of the American Bar Association, a voluntary association of more than 400,000 lawyers. Zack was the first Cuban-American lawyer elected to the most important bar association position in this country. Zack is a partner in the Miami office of the firm of Boies, Schiller & Flexner LLP.

Angones, who came to the United States at age thirteen in Operation Pedro Pan, is the only other Cuban-American lawyer who has served as president of the Florida Bar. Angones previously served also as president of the Dade County Bar and of CABA and is the founder of the firm of Angones, McClure & García, P.A. A number of other Cuban-American lawyers have served on the Board of Governors of the Florida Bar, including the late Judge Manuel Crespo, Manuel Morales, and Ramon Abadín, who is a current member, and all three of whom are past presidents of CABA, Erwin González and Raquel Matas.

The Florida Bar Foundation is a statewide organization and the charitable arm of the Florida Bar. It makes grants annually of approximately $20 million, mostly for programs throughout the state that provide legal assistance to those who cannot otherwise afford a lawyer. René V. Murai served as president of the foundation in 2000 and is the only Cuban-American lawyer to have served in that position.

THE JUDICIARY

The Federal Judiciary

Three Cuban-Americans have been appointed United States District judges. The first to be appointed was Eduardo Robreño, appointed by President George H. W. Bush in 1992 to the District Court for the Eastern District of Pennsylvania. Judge Robreño had previously been a lawyer with the Antitrust Division of the U.S. Justice Department and had also been in private practice. Adalberto Jordán and Cecilia Altonaga were appointed to the District Court for the Southern District of Florida by President Bill Clinton in 1999 and President George W. Bush in 2003, respectively. Judge Jordán had served as an assistant United States attorney and chief of the Appellate Division in the Southern District of Florida, and Judge Altonaga as a County Court and Circuit Court judge in Miami-Dade County.

All federal judges have "clerks," usually recent graduates who assist judges with the research and writing of opinions. These clerkships are highly sought after, and the most coveted ones are those with the Supreme Court justices. Supreme Court clerks numbered approximately thirty-six during the 2010-11 term. Cuban-Americans who have clerked at the Supreme Court include the following (the justices for whom they have served are shown in parenthesis): Judge Adalberto Jordán (O'Connor); Judge Denise Posse-Blanco Lindberg (O'Connor), today a state of Utah trial judge; Eduardo Peñalver (Stevens), now a law professor at Cornell Law School; and Román Martínez (Roberts), a 2008 graduate of Yale Law School and currently at the law firm of Latham Watkins in New York City.

The State Judiciary

Goderich, CABA's first elected president, was also the first Cuban-American appointed to a constitutional state court, when he was appointed by Governor Reubin Askew to the Circuit Court in Miami-Dade County. Circuit courts are courts of general jurisdiction. Judge Goderich was soon followed in the Circuit Court bench by Judges María Korvick and Margarita Esquiroz. In 2011, thirty-one Cuban-American lawyers were serving as judges in the Circuit and County Courts of Miami-Dade County. Judge Goderich was also the first Cuban-American to be appointed to the Third District Court of Appeals, where he served from 1990 until he retired as a judge in 2005. Judge Goderich is now in private practice. Cuban-Americans currently serving on the Third District Court of Appeals are Juan Ramírez (chief judge), Angel Cortiñas, and Bárbara Lagoa. Rudy Sorondo, a partner at the Miami office of the firm of Holland & Knight, served on the Third District Court of Appeals from 1997 to 2002.

In 2002, Raoúl García Cantero, a Harvard law graduate and Fulbright scholar, became the first Cuban-American to be appointed to the Florida Supreme Court. He served with distinction until his retirement in 2008 in order to return to Miami. García Cantero is a partner in the Miami office of the firm of White and Case. In January 2009, Jorge Labarga was appointed to the Florida Supreme Court by Governor Charlie Christ. Justice Labarga had been appointed a month earlier to the Fourth District Court of Appeals and had served as a Circuit Court judge since his appointment in 1996.

LAWYERS IN GOVERNMENT

U.S. Attorneys and State Attorney

The U.S. Attorney's Office Southern District of Florida is one of the largest in the country with approximately 265 assistant U.S. attorneys. The first Cuban-American lawyer appointed U.S. attorney for the Southern District of Florida was Roberto Martínez, now a partner with the firm of Colson Hicks Eidson. Subsequently, Marcos Jiménez, currently a partner in the Miami office of the firm of Kasowitz, Benson, Torres and Friedman LLP; Alex Acosta, currently dean of the Law School at Florida International University; and Wilfredo "Willy" Ferrer have served as U.S. attorneys. Cuban-American lawyer Paul Pérez served from 2002 to 2007 as U.S. attorney for the Middle District of Florida, which includes the cities of Jacksonville, Orlando, Tampa, and Fort Myers.

Katherine Fernández Rundle was the first and only Cuban-American who has served as a state attorney in Miami-Dade County, a position to which she was appointed in 1993 by Governor Chiles. She was re-elected without opposition to a fifth term as state attorney in 2008. The Miami-Dade County State Attorney's Office is the largest prosecutors' office in the state and fourth largest in the nation.

LAW FIRMS AND INDIVIDUALS

Law Firms

Cuban-American lawyers can be found in national law firms, regional firms, *boutique* firms, and as solo practitioners. By 2011, there were many prominent Cuban-American lawyers throughout the country and a listing of them would be impossible. Greenberg Traurig is the only top twenty law firm in the country with a Hispanic as its chairman, Cuban-American lawyer César Alvarez. Greenberg Traurig ranks as the number one firm in the country with the most minority partners and the most Hispanic-American attorneys. A number of firms in Miami have had Cuban-American lawyers serve as managing partners, including Akerman Senterfitt, where Luis Pérez served as managing partner of the Miami office; Holland & Knight, where José Sirvén and Peter Prieto have managed the Miami office; and Richman Greer, currently managed by Manuel García-Linares, a president of CABA in 2008.

A listing of the top South Florida firms in the 2010 edition of the South Florida Legal Guide includes a number of firms with Cuban-Americans as name partners.

Individuals

Without this writer intending to slight anyone, the achievements of a number of lawyers, who may not otherwise have been singled out in this chapter and who are representatives of all Cuban-American lawyers, are noted below. These individuals are listed in alphabetical order.

César Alvarez was the first Cuban-American lawyer hired by the law firm of Greenberg Traurig (at a time when he was known as the brother of Carlos, a star receiver for the University of Florida football team!). In 1997, Alvarez became the CEO of Greenberg Traurig, which then had approximately 340 lawyers in four states and one international office. During the thirteen years of his stewardship, Greenberg Traurig became an international powerhouse, with approximately 1,800 lawyers and thirty-three offices worldwide.

Armando Bucelo, a past president of CABA and a member of the Board of Trustees of Miami Dade College, served as chairman of the Securities Investor Protection Corporation, after being nominated by President George W. Bush in 2002. He was appointed by President George H.W. Bush to the Board of Directors of the federal Home Loan Mortgage Corporation (Freddie Mac).

Alberto Cárdenas, a name partner in the Miami law firm of Tew & Cardenas, has held a number of important public posts, including two terms as chairman of the Florida Republican Party and membership in the Board of Directors of the Federal National Mortgage Association (Fannie Mae).

Alfredo Durán, a veteran of the Bay of Pigs invasion and today a solo practitioner, was the first Hispanic to serve on the Dade County School Board and was chairman of the Florida Democratic Party from 1976 to 1980.

Simón Ferro, served as ambassador to the Republic of Pánama during the Clinton presidency and led the U.S. diplomatic mission to Panama during the turn-over of the Panama Canal. He was appointed by President Clinton, and confirmed by the Senate, to the Overseas Private Investment Corporation. Ferro also served as chairman of the Florida and Miami-Dade County Democratic Party, and today practices with the Miami law firm of Genovese, Joblove & Batista.

Frank Jiménez has held a number of senior posts in the Florida State and the federal governments. He served as general counsel of the U.S. Department of the Navy from 2006 to 2009 and general counsel to ITT Corporation.

Alberto Mora was general counsel to the U.S. Information Agency during the administration of George H.W. Bush and was appointed general counsel to the U.S. Department of the Navy in 2001. During his tenure, Mora, risking his career, argued repeatedly that the coercive interrogation of prisoners in the Guantánamo Naval Base was illegal. For his courageous stand, Mora was awarded in 2006 the Profiles in Courage Award by the John F. Kennedy Library Foundation, the pre-eminent award for public servants. The award honors those who defy personal risk and public opinion and follow their conscience. Mora currently serves as vice president, secretary, and general counsel of the Mars Corporation (manufacturer of well-known brands such as M & M, Snickersm and Spearmint gum).

José Luis Pelleyá (deceased), a Cuban-educated lawyer, arrived in the United States in 1970 after spending most of the preceding ten years in Castro's jails for "counter-revolutionary activities." He immediately enrolled at the University of Miami Law School and by 1974 was practicing law in Florida.

Rafael Peñalver, who practices with his sister Aurora in the Miami law firm of Peñalver and Peñalver, has devoted much of his life to public service. Peñalver has led the restoration and almost single-handedly has maintained open the San Carlos Institute in Key West, a Cuban heritage center founded by Cuban exiles in 1871. His civic activities are too numerous to mention.

Sofia Powell-Cosío, a solo practitioner in Miami, has been involved in a number of Cuban causes. She served, for free, as counsel to Brothers to the Rescue, and its co-founder, José Basulto, and in that capacity was often embroiled in confrontation with federal authorities. She was also part of a group of young professionals, born outside of Cuba, called Alianza de Jóvenes Cubanos (Young Cuban Alliance). Alianza conducted a billboard campaign in Canada, with slogans like "As you pay to go, they die to leave" and "Your paradise, their hell," with pictures of rafters on inner tubes.

María Elena Prío, daughter of the last elected president of Cuba, was for many years the volunteer president and driving force of the East Little Havana Community Development Corporation ELHCDC, a not-for-profit corporation. During her tenure, ELHCDC built over 500 housing units for low-income families in the Little Havana area of Miami.

A LEGAL SYSTEM

Alejandre et al. v. The Republic of Cuba; The Cuban Air Force, Case No. 96-10126-Civ-King; Case No. 96-10127-Civ-King; Case No. 96-10128-Civ-King

In 1997, Cuban-American attorneys Frank Angones, Victor Díaz, later a CABA president, and Roberto Martínez, working with attorneys Ronald Kleinman and Aaron Podhurst, obtained the first judgment ever against a foreign state under the Anti-Terrorism and Effective Death Penalty Act of 1996. The district court ruled against the Republic of Cuba and the Cuban Air Force, awarding compensatory damages of $49,927,911 and punitive damages of $137,000,000 arising out of the murder by the Cuban government of three United States nationals who were shot down by Cuban MiGs while they were flying unarmed civilian aircrafts in international waters as part of Brothers to the Rescue organization. Brothers to the Rescue had been flying missions since 1991, spotting Cuban rafters in the Florida Straits. This was a novel case. After the conclusion of the trial proceedings, the lawyers were instrumental in obtaining a change in the federal statutes to permit satisfaction of an Anti-Terrorism judgment from the frozen assets of the Cuban government located in the United States. Ultimately, the families of the victims were able to collect $96 million from the frozen assets.

Fuentes v. Shevin, 407 U.S. 67 (1972)

Margarita Fuentes, a Cuban living in the section of Miami known as Little Havana, purchased in installments a stove and a record player from the Firestone Tire and Rubber Company's store at Flagler Street and Twelfth Avenue. When the stove broke down, Mrs. Fuentes made a lump sum payment which she thought would pay for the record player and stopped her monthly payments.

Pursuant to Florida's replevin law, Firestone went to court and obtained an order directing the sheriff to repossess both items. Three recent law graduates, who then worked for the Legal Services Program of Miami, including this writer, sued Firestone in federal court, claiming that the repossession of these goods without a prior hearing at which Mrs. Fuentes could have contested Firestone's default allegations violated the due process clause of the 14th Amendment of the U.S. Constitution. In a two to one decision, the District Court rejected her claim. The case was appealed to the U.S. Supreme Court, and, on June 12, 1972, the Supreme Court, in a landmark decision, ruled in favor of Mrs. Fuentes, holding unconstitutional on due process grounds the replevin law of Florida and similar laws in forty-seven other states. The Supreme Court remanded the case to the state county court for ultimate resolution. The case was settled when Firestone agreed to pay Mrs. Fuentes three hundred dollars so that she could purchase a new record player. Fuentes, a Cuban exile, had become part of the annals of American jurisprudence. Her case was widely reported in the press and made Walter Cronkite's CBS Evening News.

FINAL OBSERVATIONS

What a country! This the most generous country in the world. Much has been given to Cuban-American lawyers: entry into this country, intensive courses in English, programs to permit Cuban educated lawyers to pursue other careers in the U.S., an accelerated law school course for those who had already graduated from law school in Cuba, the Cuban Adjustment Act of 1966 which shortened the wait for citizenship, the Cuban Loan Program without which many would not have been able to attend college or law school, and a lot more. In turn, much has been given back by Cuban-American lawyers, consistent with the best traditions of the United States and Cuba.

POLITICAL, CIVIC, AND SOCIAL LIFE

38

EXILES IN U.S. POLITICS

BY CARLOS CURBELO

When Cubans first arrived in the United States, most believed their stay would be temporary. It is important to recall that Cubans—especially those that came to America shortly after the revolution—are exiles and not typical immigrants seeking a better life. That is why early on their interest in American politics was limited to the U.S. federal government and its handling of Cuba's new government. Their top, and in most cases only, priority was regime change in Havana.

While these early exiles were staunchly anticommunist or conservative in their foreign policy views, as far as social policies were concerned they were more moderate. In fact, Cuba's last constitution before the revolution, the Constitution of 1940, was a progressive document when considered on the U.S. political spectrum. That is why at the beginning many Cubans identified with the Democratic Party and President Kennedy. This remained the case until the failed Bay of Pigs Invasion. The exile community considered Kennedy had betrayed their cause and began rejecting the young president. Kennedy regained some goodwill with the Cuban government's release of members of the Brigade 2506 and his historic visit to Miami's Orange Bowl where he promised to return the Brigade's flag in a free Havana.

However the revelation of the Kennedy-Khrushchev Pact that ended the October 1962 Missile Crisis and President Johnson's suspension of CIA financial support for anti-Castro efforts added to the disappointment of many Cubans with the national Democratic Party.

Despite President Johnson's commitment to Cuban family reunification by way of the freedom flights, many exiles were disappointed that the United States was fighting communism in Vietnam and not ninety miles away from its shore.

Beyond their obvious significance in the histories of the United States and Cuba, the failure of the 1961 Bay of Pigs Invasion and the missile crisis were also extremely significant to the emerging Cuban nation in exile. Cuban refugees began realizing that their stay in America would be longer than expected and that perhaps it was time to settle in. This led many to begin naturalizing in the 1970s. The Cuban Adjustment Act passed by Congress in 1966 facilitated this process by giving Cubans special privileges that others that came to the United States did not have. Still today, Cubans are eligible for a "green card" just one year after arriving to the United States. Most other émigrés have to wait at least five years. Naturalization meant Cubans would now have access to the American political system, and it would not take them long to put their newfound rights in America to use.

In a nod to exiles' growing influence, in 1972 Manolo Reboso was appointed to the city of Miami Commission becoming the first Cuban to hold public office. In 1981, Raúl Martínez became the first Cuban elected to be mayor of Hialeah, and a few years later, in the landmark election of 1985, Xavier Suárez became the first Cuban elected to serve as mayor of Miami, South Florida's signature city. The election of Suárez was a sign that Cubans had become a political force to reckon with, in Miami-Dade County politics.

Simultaneously Cubans began getting elected to the state legislature. The first three elected to the Florida House of Representatives were Roberto Casas, Humberto Cortina, and Ileana Ros-Lehtinen in 1982. They were followed by Javier Souto in 1984 and Lincoln Díaz-Balart in 1985. All were Republicans.

The only Cuban-American Democrat elected to county-wide office in that era was Paul Cejas, elected to the Miami-Dade School Board in 1980. In 1973 Alfredo Durán, also a Democrat had been appointed to the school board by Gov. Reubin Askew.

The power, influence, and sheer numbers of the Cuban exile community did not go unnoticed by national politicians. President Reagan was the first American president to politically engage Cuban exiles in a significant way. In 1980, Reagan was heavily supported by Cuban-Americans throughout the country, but especially in the state of Florida—for many years a key piece of the electoral puzzle for Republican presidential candidates.

For many Cubans, President Carter was too soft on Communism, having opened an Interests Section in Havana and allowing the Castro regime to open one in Washington, D.C. Moreover, while most exiles welcomed those fleeing Cuba vis-à-vis the Mariel Boatlift, many considered the incident itself as evidence of weakness in Washington. Reagan's tough anticommunist rhetoric was the final piece. Cuban-Americans supported him solidly. Since then, Cuban-Americans have predominantly voted for Republican candidates for president.

Reagan was quick to express his gratitude. "For the first time in many years, Americans had elected a president whose views on communism (and Cuba) were compatible with those of the emigrés."[1]

Carlos Salmán became a key supporter of Reagan's presidential bid in 1980. Another Cuban exile working on Reagan's campaign was Mario Elgarresta, who was appointed to the Reagan presidential transition team. There Elgarresta met Richard V. Allen, one of Reagan's top national security advisors. Allen met with Elgarresta, Salmán, Miami banker Raúl Masvidal, and Jorge Mas Canosa, who had been active in a Cuban exile organization Representación Cubana en el Exilio (RECE), the acronym for the organization's name in Spanish.

The group believed that it was important that Cuban exiles be assertive; not to expect Washington to come up with a plan to fight the

Cuban regime. Instead they wanted it to be proactive and to come up with its own ideas; practical things that Washington could consider and carry out.

They discussed the need for Cuban exiles to become involved in Congressional campaign races throughout the United States and organize themselves as the Jewish community had done. Subsequently the Cuban exile group met with Jewish lobbying groups that suggested the way they should organize themselves. As a result two organizations were created in 1981; the National Coalition for a Free Cuba (a Political Action Committee—PAC) and the Cuban American National Foundation (CANF). President Reagan and his administration immediately became the groups' chief ally. Reagan and Jorge Mas Canosa, the chairman of the new organization, developed a relationship, and Reagan visited Miami to address what quickly became the foremost Cuban-American political organization. Wearing a guayabera tailor-made by Ramón Puig, a Cuban exile known as the "king of the guayabera," Reagan commended the group and vowed to work for a free Cuba. His support brought great prominence and legitimacy to the cause of Cuban exiles.

Among the group's founding members—in addition to Masvidal, Mas Canosa, and Salman—were other business and civic leaders that contributed to its establishment.[2]

To Mas Canosa, a very important item on his agenda was to create a radio station to broadcast news to Cuba. The model was that of Radio Free Europe and Radio Liberty that had been doing the same thing to nations behind the Iron Curtain. In order to accomplish this, CANF members and its PAC began making political contributions and establishing personal relationships to help Republican and Democratic candidates in congressional campaigns throughout the United States.

This took time. Getting bills approved by Congress is never easy and the fight to approve Radio Martí, named after the Cuban patriot, was particularly long and difficult. Four years after the CANF and its PAC were created; the group obtained an important victory in Congress; the approval of Radio Martí, which began its broadcasts to Cuba on May 20, 1985.[3]

By then, CANF had become, and was for many years, the most influential Cuban exile organization with Mas Canosa as its leader.

Years later after Mas Canosa died, his son Jorge Mas Santos, who had become chairman of CANF reflected on the political accomplishments of the organizations. Santos told the author in an interview in July 2011:

> *In historical terms the most important achievement and enduring legacy of the Cuban American National Foundation has been to bring the cause of a free and democratic Cuba into the American political mainstream, thereby giving it legitimacy in national political circles and public opinion. This of course, has been the central issue in our community and the original reason for our exile. When our foundation was created the Castro regime had a monopoly on access to American political power circles in Washington, and holding meetings right on Capitol Hill while Cuban exiles were shunned in the halls of Congress.*

Reagan's presence and participation in Cuban-American politics rallied the community and encouraged exiles to register and to vote in big numbers. The result was that being Republican arguably became a part of Cuban exile culture. Not so much because exiles were traditional American conservatives but more due to the strong anticommunist credentials projected by Reagan and other Republicans in the latter part of the twentieth century. The contrast with the likes of President Carter and Senator Chris Dodd, perceived to be "soft on Communism," also contributed to the mass migration to the GOP.

Reagan also made a strong effort to include Cuban-Americans in his administration. The president's friend, Dr. Tirso del Junco, served as chairman of the Republican Party of California in the 1980s and was appointed to the U.S. Postal Service Board of Governors. Del Junco recalls that, "Reagan adopted very strong positions with regards to communism in Cuba and in other places such as Nicaragua against the Sandinistas. The contrast with Carter was significant. Del Junco also served as chairman of the University of California Board of Regents."[4]

José Sorzano served as ambassador and deputy to the U.S. ambassador to the United Nations from 1981 to 1985. He later became special assistant to President Reagan for National Security Affairs from 1987 to 1988. Otto Reich was named ambassador to Venezuela in 1986. José Manuel Casanova was appointed by the president to serve as executive director of the Inter-American Development Bank.

After the Reagan presidency, the Cuban-American community helped elect President George Herbert Walker Bush and three new members of Congress, Ileana Ros-Lehtinen and Lincoln Díaz-Balart—Miami Republicans—and Bob Menéndez, a Democrat from New Jersey. In the case of Ros-Lehtinen, she filled the seat vacated when Congressman Claude Pepper passed away in 1989, and became the first Hispanic woman ever elected to the U.S. Congress. In 1992, Díaz-Balart decisively won the seat formerly held by Dante Fascell. Shortly thereafter he was appointed by Speaker Newt Gingrich to serve on the powerful House Rules Committee. Ros-Lehtinen, Díaz-Balart, and Menéndez had been supported by Cuban-American voters for many years.

The elections of these three products of the exiled community were landmark events in Cuban-American history. For the first time exiles had their own representatives in Congress, and these three Members would use their political capital to fight the battle against the Castro dictatorship from the Hill.

President Bush (41) followed his predecessor's practice of appointing Cuban-Americans to prominent posts in the federal government. José Antonio Villamil was named U.S. undersecretary of commerce for economic affairs. Aquiles Suárez served as an attorney in the White House Counsel's Office.

After the strong wave of Republicanism brought on by President Reagan, Cuban-American political homogeneity first showed fissures in

1992, when President George H. W. Bush was defeated by a youthful Arkansas governor, William Jefferson Clinton. While Bush decisively won the Cuban-American vote, Clinton was able to siphon off support from prominent community leaders. Just weeks before the election Jorge Mas Canosa and other Cuban-American National Foundation leaders made remarks favorable to Clinton after having met with him privately.

Clinton's first major test with regards to Cuba was the mass exodus of 1994 when over 38,000 rafters (*balseros*) fled the island by raft and other makeshift sea vessels. The three Cuban-American Members of Congress aggressively advocated for the new Cuban refugees. When the Clinton Administration began interdicting them at sea and housing them in tent cities in the U.S. Naval Base in Guantánamo Bay, Cuba, the three members of Congress pressured the government to eventually grant them entry to the United States. They were greeted as heroes when they visited the refugees in Guantánamo.

"It was very moving. I remember approaching the tent cities that had been set up and learning that the refugees had elected leaders from their own ranks. Those were the first free elections in Cuba since the Castro dictatorship came to power," the now Sen. Bob Menéndez (D.-N.J.) told the author on September 25, 2011. "They knew our names (Lincoln, Ileana, and Bob), and when they talked to us I was amazed by what I heard. I fully expected they would ask us when they would be able to leave. Instead I remember them asking me why we could not get the Spanish, Canadians, and others to support the embargo and other sanctions against the regime. It was special to observe that they were more concerned about their country than about their difficult personal situation."

The exodus of 1994 was the catalyst for the controversial "Wet Foot, Dry Foot" policy, still in effect today, which dictates that Cuban migrants intercepted by U.S. authorities at sea are repatriated to Cuba and those reaching land can remain in the United States legally.

In 1996, Clinton again impressed some political observers when he won approximately 35 percent of the Cuban-American vote in his bid for reelection. Clinton's relative success might be attributed to his signing into law the Helms-Burton legislation (Cuban Liberty and Democratic Solidarity Act of 1996) in response to the Castro government's shoot down of two Brothers to the Rescue aircrafts flown by American citizens over international waters near Cuba. This legislation, authored in large part by Representatives Lincoln Díaz-Balart, Bob Menendez, and Ileana Ros-Lehtinen, was significant due to its codification of the U.S. economic embargo against Cuba and the ban on U.S. tourism to the island. Prior to the law, sanctions against Cuba were for the most part based on an Executive Order signed by President Kennedy. Lincoln Díaz-Balart, the author of the codification of the U.S. embargo within the Helms-Burton Law, has stated that, "The reason why Cuba policy continues to be debated in Washington and the Cuban internal opposition is known—in contrast to the dictatorships in China and many other countries—is because we codified the U.S. embargo in the Helms-Burton Law in 1996."[5]

Clinton won favor from Cuban-Americans for agreeing to sign the law which he had previously opposed and cruised to reelection with significant support from a solidly Republican constituency in Florida. Incidentally, in 1996, Miami-Dade County elected its first executive mayor, Democrat Alex Penelas. The young Cuban-American attorney won with the strong support of his community despite his political affiliation. In South Florida, Democratic candidates winning substantial Cuban-American support have typically done so in non-partisan elections.

President Clinton also made a number of important Cuban-American appointments to key positions. Paul Cejas was named ambassador to Belgium and served from 1998 to 2001. In 1994, Florida Governor Lawton Chiles appointed him to the State of Florida University System's Board of Regents. In 2000, Luis Lauredo was named by the president to serve as U.S. ambassador to the Organization of American States. Simón Ferro was appointed ambassador to Panama, where he served during the last three years of the Clinton Administration. Lino Gutiérrez, a career diplomat, was named by Clinton to serve as ambassador to Nicaragua in 1996. He later served as ambassador to Argentina under President George W. Bush. Pedro Pablo Permuy served as deputy assistant secretary of defense for Latin America.

The next seminal event in the political history of exiled Cubans was the seizing of little Elián González by President Clinton's Justice Department under the leadership of then Attorney General Janet Reno. The predawn raid in the wee hours of April 22, 2000, generated extreme emotions of anger and outrage in Cuban Miami that spilled into that year's political season. Opposition to the government's actions was nearly unanimous among Cuban-Americans. Mayor Penelas denied the federal government any assistance in conducting the operation, and even prominent non-Hispanic Democrats like attorney Aaron Podhurst expressed their disapproval. In November of that year, Cuban-Americans still had the Elián González case fresh on their minds and punished Vice President Al Gore by giving Governor George W. Bush approximately 80 percent of the community's votes. The intensity of Cuban-American support for the Bush-Cheney ticket ended up being crucial to the result of the presidential election, considering only 537 votes separated the two candidates in Florida.

The Cuban-American community had flexed its political muscle and did so again in 2002, by electing another Cuban-American to Congress. This time it was Mario Díaz-Balart, who joined his brother Lincoln in Congress after fourteen years serving in the state legislature. The Elián drama also propelled attorney Manny Díaz to public office. The Democrat-turned-Independent, who represented Elián González and his Miami family, was elected mayor of the city of Miami in 2001.

Also in 2001, twenty years after its founding and just four years after the death of its chairman, the Cuban-American National Foundation (CANF) experienced a major rift. Some of its directors split with the organization and created another group named the Cuban Liberty Council. Among the founders of the new group were Diego Suárez, Ninoska

Pérez-Castellón, and Alberto Hernández. "Many of those who were directors saw that the Foundation was taking a different course and we did not want to be a part of it," said Pérez-Castellón.[6] Many of these longtime leaders of CANF opposed decisions taken by Jorge Mas Santos, the new chairman and son of the late Mas Canosa.

Cuban-Americans had great hopes for President George W. Bush with regards to Cuba. The new president increased aide to Cuban opposition leaders inside the island and tightened restrictions on Cuban-American travel to Cuba and on cash remittances in an effort to limit the proceeds the Castro regime receives from such activities. He also forcefully defended the sanctions policy pledging to veto any bill from Congress that weakened the economic embargo or the ban on U.S. tourist travel.

In 2004, Bush did not receive the same level of support from Cuban-Americans as he had in the wake of the Elián González affair in 2000, but still was reelected with great support from the community. The year 2004 was also significant because Florida elected the first Cuban-American to the U.S. Senate, Mel Martínez, who had served as chairman of Orange County (Greater Orlando) in Central Florida and on President Bush's cabinet, as secretary of the Department of Housing and Urban Development. Martínez resigned from the Senate in the summer of 2009 before his term expired.

Another Cuban-American made it to the U.S. Senate in 2006 when New Jersey elected Democratic Congressman Bob Menéndez to what some refer to as the world's most exclusive club. Menéndez was appointed senator in January of that year and elected to a full-six year term in November. That same year Albio Sires, a former speaker of the New Jersey State House, was elected to fill Menéndez's seat in Congress' lower chamber. Now there were six Cuban-Americans in Congress—four Republicans and two Democrats.

Adding to the Cuban-American numbers in Washington, were President George W. Bush's appointees. Carlos Gutiérrez, former CEO of Kellogg's became the second Cuban-American to earn a cabinet position when he was named U.S. Secretary of Commerce. Eduardo Aguirre, Jr., became the first director of the newly created U.S. Citizenship and Immigration Services (USCIS), an undersecretary position in the Department of Homeland Security. He later was appointed ambassador to Spain. Col. Emilio González was appointed to serve on the National Security Council early in the administration and later replaced Aguirre as director of USCIS. Ambassador Otto Reich was named assistant secretary of state for the Western Hemisphere in January 2002, and served under a recess appointment. In 2003, Bush appointed him U.S. special envoy to the Western Hemisphere. Josefina Carbonell became the highest ranking Hispanic-American appointee in the Department of Health and Human Services. In 2001, she was named to head the Administration on Aging. Another Cuban-American woman, Dr. Cristina Beato served as deputy director of the Pan American Health Organization. Hugo Lloréns was named Ambassador to Honduras under President Bush and remained there after President Obama took office. He was the U.S. ambassador during the leadership crisis in Honduras that featured the dramatic ousting of President Manuel Zelaya.

While George W. Bush served in the White House, his brother Jeb was governor of the state of Florida. During this time Florida's Republican Party was chaired by a Cuban-American for the first time, Al Cárdenas. Governor Bush also made numerous Cuban-American appointments including José Abreu, Florida's first Cuban-American secretary of transportation. Abreu now serves as director of Miami International Airport, one of the most important airports in the world.

The 2008 presidential election demonstrated a similar degree of support for Republican candidate John McCain as President Bush had received four years earlier. The Arizona senator had a special affinity with Cuban-Americans given the time he served as a prisoner of war in Vietnam. His opponent, Senator Barack Obama garnered significant support from younger Cuban-Americans but only won roughly 30 percent of votes cast by the community. However, Cuban-American intensity for McCain was not enough to deliver Florida for Republicans. Obama won Florida by over 200,000 votes.

The year 2008 also featured the first serious challenge to South Florida's three Republican Cuban-American members of Congress. Democrats fielded well-funded opponents against Ileana Ros-Lehtinen, Lincoln Díaz-Balart, and Mario Díaz-Balart. The campaigns were intense and drew the attention of national and international media. However, Ros-Lehtinen and the elder Díaz-Balart easily defeated their opponents while Mario won by seven points despite a national political climate that heavily favored Democrats. The Democratic challengers sought to divide Cuban exiles by asking that travel and remittance restrictions on Cuban-Americans imposed by President Bush be lifted. Still, in 2008, he Cuban-American community reaffirmed its support of candidates that take a hard line stance against the Castro dictatorship.

Like his predecessors, President Obama also made significant Cuban-American appointments to his administration. Miguel H. Díaz was appointed ambassador to the Vatican. Until his appointment, he was a professor of theology at the College of Saint Benedict in St. Joseph, Minnesota, and Saint John's University in Collegeville, Minnesota (State Department Bio). His deputy is Julietta Valls-Noyes, a Bush appointee retained by the Obama Administration. Carlos Pascual, a career diplomat, served as ambassador to Mexico until his resignation in March of 2011 as a result of the Wikileaks diplomatic crisis. Secretary of State Hillary Clinton accepted his resignation with reluctance calling him the "'architect and advocate' of U.S.-Mexico relations in Washington."[7] Frank Mora, another Cuban-American, was appointed by the president, deputy asstistant secretary of defense for Latin America.

Two years after President Obama's historic election, Cuban-American Republicans again celebrated electoral success. Marco Rubio, a Miami Cuban-American from Miami was elected to represent Florida in the United States Senate. Rubio would replace Republican George LeMieux who had been appointed to serve out Senator Mel Martínez's term.

Rubio defeated Democratic and Independent challengers and rode a Republican wave to Capitol Hill with enthusiastic support from the Cuban-American community. In the same elections, Republican David Rivera was elected to represent South Florida in the U.S. House. The opportunity to elect another Cuban-American was the result of Congressman Lincoln Díaz-Balart's retirement after serving eighteen years in Congress and six years in the state legislature.

Perhaps the most significant political event for Cuban-Americans that year was Congresswoman Ileana Ros-Lehtinen's selection to serve as chairwoman of the U.S. House Committee on Foreign Affairs. After Republicans won control of the lower chamber in the elections of November 2010, Ros-Lehtinen was selected by her colleagues for this important post.

Another powerful manifestation of Cuban-American political influence emerged in 2003, the U.S.-Cuba Democracy PAC. The group filled a void left by the death of exile leader Jorge Mas Canosa in 1997, who had become the most recognizable advocate for the cause of a free Cuba in the corridors of Congress. At the turn of the millennium, both Houses of Congress voted in favor of relaxing sanctions against the Castro regime on several occasions. This alarmed many in the Cuban-American community including members of Congress.

As a result, Remedios Díaz-Oliver, Gus Machado, and other prominent Cuban-American business and civic leaders banded together to form one of the strongest political action committees dedicated to foreign policy matters in recent American history. As of this publication, the PAC has raised millions of dollars in political contributions mostly from Cuban-Americans of all income levels. The group has been successful in educating and informing members of Congress regarding the repressive and rogue nature of the Castro regime, the internal opposition movement in Cuba, and U.S.-Cuba policy. Through the PAC, the Cuban-American community has supported hundreds of members of

Congress from both political parties that vote in favor of the current sanctions policy denying Cuba's dictatorship the unilateral concessions it has sought over the years.

Within a matter of months, the PAC, under the leadership of Mauricio Claver-Carone, an attorney based in Washington, D.C., reversed the trend in Congress favoring unilateral concessions and helped build a solid bipartisan coalition in support of the current sanctions regime. The coalition has proved to be durable, remaining intact despite shifts in the balance of power in Congress. "Our goal was to make Cuba policy akin to Israel policy—a bipartisan foreign policy issue—not simply a Florida Republican issue. Today, a majority of Congress stands in unison against providing unilateral concessions to the brutal Castro dictatorship. And tomorrow, it will ensure that a free and democratic Cuba has all of the tools and resources necessary for its economic reconstruction and development," said Claver-Carone.[8]

Cuban-Americans have also made their mark as administrators in local governments and military officers. Miami-Dade County, one of the largest local governments in the country has been run by three Cuban-born exiles, Sergio Pereira, Joaquín Aviñó, and Armando Vidal. Other Cuban-Americans have served as department directors, superintendents, police chiefs, city managers, and in other key leadership positions throughout the United States. In the military some have even achieved the rank of general.

Once Cuban refugees realized that exile would be a more permanent condition, they began participating in American politics by voting, contributing to campaigns, running for political office, advising American officials, and competing for key positions. At first, these efforts were concentrated almost exclusively on influencing U.S.-Cuba policy, and they have proved to be quite successful. In fact, it is clear that at least since the Reagan presidency, U.S. policy towards the Castro dictatorship has been dominated by powerful Cuban exile organizations and their leaders. These groups have benefitted from the participation of hundreds of thousands of Cuban-Americans in the political process and from the serendipity of having settled mostly in Florida, a pivotal swing state in presidential elections.

Today Cuban-Americans are using their power and influence not only to frame U.S.-Cuba policy. Cuban-Americans are making critical decisions every day that impact domestic and international policies and that shape world events. What has not changed is that these individuals continue reaping the benefits of a community that participates actively in American politics.

One of the more common criticisms of those that inhabited Cuba during the years of the Republic (1902-1958) was their lack of involvement in the political process. Some claim that for Cuban society, politics was somewhat of a nuisance and political matters were considered to have little relevance. If this criticism is accurate, then it is fair to say that in exile, Cubans learned their lesson and have left an indelible mark on American politics that will continue benefiting Cuban-Americans for generations to come.

NOTES

1. María Cristina García, *Havana, USA* (Berkley: University of California Press, 1996), 146.
2. They included: Francisco (Pepe) Hernández, a businessman; Alberto Hernández, a medical doctor; Tony Zamora, an attorney; Domingo Moreira, a businessman; José Luis Rodíguez, a Palm Beach entrepreneur active in agricultural products; Miguel Angel Martínez, a businessman in Puerto Rico; Luis Botifoll, a Miami banker; and Manny Medina, a developer. Mas Canosa was elected chairman of CANF. Frank Calzón, a human rights activist, was named executive director of the group's Washington, D.C., office, and Elgarresta was chosen to head the Miami office.
3. Author interviews with Raúl Masvidal, October 2010, and with Masvidal and Mario Elgarresta, December 2010.
4. Author telephone interview with Tirso del Junco, May 6, 2011.
5. Author telephone interview with Lincoln Díaz-Balart, June 27, 2011.
6. Author telephone interview with Ninoska Pérez-Castellón, June 25, 2011.
7. José de Córdoba, *U.S. Ambassador to Mexico Resigns Following WikiLeak Flap,* WSJ March 19, 2011.
8. Author telephone interview with Mauricio Claver-Carone—June 25, 2011.

39

EXILE CIVIC AND SOCIAL ORGANIZATIONS

BY JOSE R. GARRIGO

Cubans are gregarious by nature, with a strong tendency to socialize and participate in group activities. It may be that living under the tropical sun warms the heart and one needs to communicate that warmth. It may be that by virtue of living in a small island people tend to share life with others, whether they are relatives, friends, or, at times, even strangers. Participating in civic, religious, social, or professional organizations was a way of life for many in republican Cuba prior to the 1959 Communist takeover. It was only natural that, upon arriving to the United States, they tried to replicate the traditional Cuban lifestyle and customs in their adopted country. They had left a life in which hard work and some luck got one through into prosperity and a comfortable middle-class status.

Community associations have been an important and helpful bridge in the immigrant experience in the United States. Ethnic organizations in the past century have helped the Italians, Irish, Jewish, and other groups to adjust and find a new life in this country. The Cubans' experience has not been any different. Life was not easy during the first couple of decades of the Cuban Exile. They all had to survive and many relied on other Cubans to make the transition easier.

Business ownership and work opportunities were scarce, if not absent. Joining peer groups, whether professional or social, helped in the process. The first to organize were business people, followed by professionals.

Initial barriers have been overcome, and today Cuban-Americans are part of all major civic, social, and professional groups in the communities where they live. Many second-generation Cuban-Americans attribute their work ethic as well as community involvement to their parents.

This chapter gives you a very brief overview of the most important civic and professional organizations established by Cuban-Americans in exile.

ASOCIACION INTERAMERICANA DE HOMBRES DE EMPRESA (AIHE)

INTERAMERICAN BUSINESSMEN ASSOCIATION (IBA)

The association had an organizational meeting in Miami, Florida, on November 1960 and their first formal members' meeting in January 1961. It was initially integrated by former members of the *Asociación de Ejecutivos de Cuba* (Cuban Executives Association) and conducted monthly dinner meetings in which its members kept up to date of their respective activities and mutually referred business. Among its founders were Leslie P. Pantín (insurance executive), José R. Garrigó (banker), Orlando de la Gándara (pharmaceutical laboratory owner), Nicolás Pons (airline executive), and Javier Caballero (funeral home owner). The organization expanded and established sister chapters in San Juan, Puerto Rico (1961); Santo Domingo, Dominican Republic (1975); Port-au-Prince, Haiti (1979); Nordeste, Dominican Republic (1975); Cibao, Dominican Republic (1986); Area Oeste, Puerto Rico (1991); Asunción, Paraguay (1998); and Mendoza, Argentina (1998), all under the guidance of an International Board of Directors whose first president was Jerónimo Esteve. Its objectives were "to work diligently for the advancement of all Interamerican businessmen, to support and defend the interests of said businessmen, to work diligently for the improvement and development of the economic and social relationships between the members of the association and their community, as well as to promote the economic and social interests of said community," all within the framework of the free enterprise system.

CAMARA DE COMERCIO LATINA DE LOS ESTADOS UNIDOS (CAMACOL)

LATIN CHAMBER OF COMMERCE

The *Cámara de Comercio Latina de los Estados Unidos (Camacol)* was founded in 1961 by a group of Cuban-American businesspersons, among which were Eliseo Riera-Gómez, its first president, Gilberto Almeida, Manuel Balado, and Román Campa. Due to their activities and membership it has become the largest Hispanic chamber of commerce in the United States. It strongly promotes free enterprise and has various local, national, and international projects promoting business, exports, and investments throughout the hemisphere. The late Luis Sabines, Camacol's charismatic president for two decades, led the organization through a period of great activity and healthy growth. Among other past presidents were Gilberto Ameida, Manuel Balado, Eloy González, and Rogelio Barrios. In 1979, under the leadership of William Alexander, its president today, it organized the First Hemispheric Congress of Latin American Chambers of Commerce and formed a Permanent Secretariat including the presidents of the chambers of commerce in Latin America. Camacol is actively involved in a number of activities which benefit not only its members but also the community at large, such as the Façade Program, which has secured government and private funding to improve the fronts of small businesses in the city of Miami. Camacol Tower houses the chamber's offices as well as one hundred apartments for low-income senior citizens.

LATIN BUILDERS ASSOCIATION (LBA)

The Latin Builders Association (LBA) was founded on September 14, 1971, by a number of Cuban-Americans associated with the building industry, among which were Mike Ortega (its first president), Julio Viyella, Alberto Santos, and Mario Fernández. In February 1974, the association had eighty-five members growing now to more than one thousand corporate memberships. Presently they are working on an expansion to neighboring Broward and Palm Beach counties. Their *Proyecto* magazine, recognized as one of the best in the trade, started to be published that same year. In 1975, they opened an office to manage the association's business and members' needs. One of their most important goals is to provide assistance to its members in their needs and relations with the various city and county departments as well as lobbying, through the LBA Political Action Committee (PAC), regarding regulations that affect the building and construction industries. They organize programs to help members find new contracts and projects as well as plan workshops to keep them informed on issues affecting the building industry and help obtain certification as minority builders and contractors. Some of their more recent presidents have been Erelio Peña, Jesús Portela, Lorenzo Luaces, Sergio Pino, Alberto Pérez, Carlos Herrera, Eloy Cepero, and Noelia Moreno, the latter being LBA's first woman president.

HISPANIC AMERICAN BANKERS ASSOCIATION

FORMERLY CUBAN AMERICAN BANKERS ASSOCIATION (CABAI)

Although many Cuban-American bankers had been meeting informally since the mid-1960s, on March 14, 2000, they formally incorporated Cuban American Bankers Association, Inc. (CABAI). The group's purpose was to "unite the local Cuban-American commercial, mortgage and investment bankers, help them through educational and social programs and participate as a group in community affairs." Antonio S. Caula served as its first president, jointly with Silvio Santana, José H. Muzaurrieta, Laureano Fernández, José Sánchez Villalba, Amadeo López Castro, Pablo Bravo, and José R. Garrigó as Charter Board members. The group meets periodically with prominent national and international bankers, bank regulators, and economists to hear their views and discuss banking and financial issues and trends. The Miami Branch of the Federal Reserve Bank often hosts such meetings in their offices. In 2010 the association changed its name to Hispanic American Bankers Association.

CUBAN BANKING STUDY GROUP (CBSG)

The Cuban Banking Study Group (CBSG) was established on December 15, 1992, by a group of Cuban-American bankers and professionals. Its first executive board was comprised by Fernando A. Capablanca, president; José R. Garrigó, vice president; George Harper, secretary; and Carlos J. Fernández, treasurer. Its objective was to "make a historical analysis of the Cuban banking and financial system from 1832 to 1992, and prepare and disseminate recommendations for the establishment of a modern banking system under a free market and pluralistic society in Cuba." In 1995, with the cooperation of dozens of bankers of Cuban descent and the advice of highly experienced and well-known figures such as Felipe Pazos, former president of *Banco Nacional de Cuba* (the island's Central Bank), and Justo Carrillo, president of *Banco de Fomento Agrícola e Industrial de Cuba* (a government development bank), the association published its findings and recommendations in a book titled *Cuba—Past, Present and Future of its Banking and Financial System,* which was distributed without cost to the major national and global banks, universities, academics, and various organizations in the U.S. In doing so, it enlisted the support of the Federal Reserve Bank of Atlanta and other organizations that would play pivotal roles in the growth and development of the banking system in a free Cuba. An agreement was reached with the Federal Reserve Bank for the expedited clearing and payment of checks in U.S. dollars and Cuban pesos between both countries. An agreement was also reached with former owners of private Banks in Cuba as to compensation and future development.

CUBAN-AMERICAN NATIONAL COUNCIL (CNC)

This organization was established in 1972 to "provide human services to needed persons without distinction of race or ethnic group, to help those persons to succeed through their own efforts and to encourage a better understanding among the different communities in the U.S." CNC has provided services to more than 100,000 individuals of many races and national groups, mainly Hispanics from more than fifteen Latin American countries or born in the U.S. Its national conferences play an important role as a networking opportunity and as a forum where relevant policy issues are discussed. Their biennial conferences draw Hispanic leaders, policy makers, direct service providers, advocates, and corporate leaders from all over the United States for discussion, analysis, and agenda settings on critical issues affecting the U.S. Hispanic community.

Among the CNC main accomplishments are two alternative schools where a large number of high school students have graduated. Under the leadership of Guarioné M. Díaz, president and chief executive officer, they have constructed and presently administer seventeen hundred housing units for low-income families. Its founding Board of Directors was chaired by Father Mario Vizcaíno with a group of community oriented persons among which were Luis H. Vidaña, Luis P. Sala, Nelson A. Benedico, Sister Armantina Peláez, and Sergio Pereira.

BIG FIVE CLUB

As soon as their family incomes improved, Cuban-Americans organized social and country clubs where they could meet their old friends in a relaxed atmosphere and their children could play, practice sports, and meet other children. The Big Five Club was established in remembrance of the five most important social clubs in Havana prior to the Communist takeover. Starting on February 1967 individuals interested in participating deposited $100 in a Trust Account which would be disbursed to the club's first Board of Directors if and when the idea came to fruition. On October 10, 1967, Big Five Club was officially chartered with Manuel R. Morales Gómez serving as president, Leslie P. Pantín as vice president, Eduardo S. Sardiña as secretary, Manuel Domínguez as assistant secretary, José R. Garrigó as treasurer, and José Manuel Casanova as assistant treasurer.

The Big Five Club's objectives were "to always preserve the Love of God, the Fatherland, the Family, the Cuban Traditions and the Principles of Freedom and Democracy among its members." It is the only Cuban social club in Miami that has survived forty-four years. Under the present leadership of Fernando Martínez, Jr., its membership now includes 765 families who participate actively in the various club activities. Its attractive clubhouse, gymnasium, large swimming pool, children playgrounds and various sports fields for base ball, soccer, tennis, volley ball and front tennis are located in the western section of Miami-Dade County.

MUNICIPIOS DE CUBA EN EL EXILIO
CUBAN MUNICIPALITIES IN EXILE

In the early 1960s, groups from each of the 126 municipalities in their country of origin started to organize in order to help those who continued arriving and to work towards the return of democracy in their captive island. The first such group was the municipality of San José de las Lajas, which was organized in 1960. On June 29, 1965, an executive board was formed to unite and coordinate the efforts of the 126 different groups, adopting the name *Municipios de Cuba en el Exilio* (Cuban Municipalities in Exile). They legally incorporated the organization and defined its objectives and the responsibilities of each associated group. Some of the initial board members were José Cabrera Riesgo, Rogelio del Pino, Julio Estorino, Mario Franqui, Mario Goderich, Sr., Nicomedes Hernández, Demetrio Pérez, Sr., Roberto Rodríguez Aragón, Miguel Angel Tudela, and others.

In 1978, they celebrated the First National Congress of the Municipios, to analyze the situation in Cuba and of Cubans in the United States. Its Second National Congress was held in 1986, in which prominent Cubans from its republican era participated. Among them was Carlos Márquez Sterling, president of the 1940 Cuban Constitutional Assembly; Guillermo Martínez Márquez, former president of the Interamerican Press Association; and Santiago Rey Pernas and Andrés Rivero Aguero, both of which held ministerial positions in republican Cuba.

Each Municipio holds its internal election every year and designates its representatives to the National Assembly. The organization meets individually (each group) and nationally to foster and celebrate Cuban holy days and traditions and to strengthen the ties among its members. It transmits evening programs (*Radio Esperanza*—Radio Hope and *La Voz de los Municipios*—The Voice of the Municipios) through Miami commercial radio stations with signals that can be heard in Cuba.

COALITION OF HISPANIC-AMERICAN WOMEN (CHAW)

In 1979, a small group of Cuban-American women led by María Elena Toraño and Aida Levitán, formed the Coalition of Hispanic-American Women (CHAW). Alma Guerra, María Cristina Barros, and Irela Díaz were part of that initial group. The organization's purpose was "to provide a platform from which Hispanic-American women can address issues that impact their educational, socio-economic and political empowerment at the local, state and national levels." To accomplish those objectives they proposed "to promote Hispanic-American women to leadership positions in the work place and the community." They held monthly membership meetings which provided networking opportunities and in which nationally renowned guest speakers discussed topics of interest.

From its start, CHAW fought discrimination in education, employment, social services, housing and the judicial system. That was accomplished through participation in ad-hoc committees and task forces, preparation of position papers and cooperation with other women organizations, all tending to create public awareness of the presence and concerns of Hispanic-American women.

KIWANIS CLUB OF LITTLE HAVANA

The Kiwanis Club of Little Havana was founded to serve the Greater Miami community; especially its over 500,000 citizens of Latin American origin. Its main goal is to reach and help the Latin youth. The charter meeting was held on November 1, 1975. Leslie Pantín, Jr., served as its first president, jointly with José L. Castro as vice president, Oscar Rodríguez as secretary, and Ray Rodríguez as treasurer, all joined by a number of young and energetic directors. The Kiwanis' main events are *Carnaval* Miami and *Calle Ocho*. First held in 1978, *Calle Ocho* is the largest Hispanic celebration of its kind in the U.S. Over one million people gather one Sunday in March to hear music, dance, eat, and celebrate their Hispanic traditions. It is the culmination of *Carnaval* Miami, two weeks of events in March of every year, that begin with an 8-K (eight-kilometer) footrace, a full weekend of jazz concerts and art pavilions, a cooking contest, golf and domino tournaments, and a soccer challenge for the children. The funds raised by the Kiwanis Club of Little Havana allow the organization to conduct projects and programs of great impact to the underserved children of South Florida.

The club's basketball league has trained more than four thousand leaguers and has provided a summer full of activities for more than one thousand children at the annual sports camp where campers receive uniforms, free lunch, attend weekly field trips, and practice sports including swimming and rowing. School supplies have been distributed to nearly sixty thousand students in low-income elementary schools with an average of six thousand schools every year. The students receive bags with books, notebooks, paper, and other essentials to last a full year. Their scholarship program has graduated two hundred scholars over the years and currently has fifty-five students in full four-year scholarships in state of Florida universities and colleges. During the Christmas holidays they have distributed toys and bicycles to over 75,000 children.

SPANISH-AMERICAN LEAGUE AGAINST DISCRIMINATION (SALAD)

SALAD was founded in 1974, as a response to an emerging and evolving Hispanic population in South Florida, during a time of great hardships. Among the founding members were Osvaldo Soto, Eduardo Padron, Paul Cejas, Mario Goderich, Javier Bray, and Luisa García-Toledo. In its almost forty years, SALAD has been active in challenging all forms of bigotry and discrimination, seeking equal access and opportunity for Hispanics and other minorities. Its development has been focused on education, employment, social services, housing, and the judicial system.

In 2011, SALAD elected a new leadership integrating diverse nationalities, professions, generations and cultures. Today SALAD has reaffirmed its commitment to the vibrant South Florida community, dedicated to its traditional efforts and to other topics such as diversity and inclusion advocacy; support to victims of discrimination; Foreclosure Defense Program; business development and networking; Diversity and Inclusion Advancement Model; voter registration drives and citizenship guidance; fair immigration reform legislation.

INSTITUTO SAN CARLOS

Instituto San Carlos, a civic and cultural center was founded in *Cayo Hueso* (Key West), Florida, by Cuban exiles in 1871 "to promote Cuban cultural and patriotic ideals." It was named after *Seminario San Carlos* (San Carlos Catholic Seminary in Havana), a place of religious and higher learning renowned in Spain and Spanish America for its academic excellence. Initially it was maintained with the contributions made by the employees of the local cigar making factories, who donated a portion of their modest wages. Among prominent patriots of the Cuban independence from Spain, the revered Father Félix Varela taught classes in the Institute, instilling in its students the seeds for Cuba's independence and the need for the state to promote moral and humanistic values. Varela is considered by many historians as "the one who taught Cubans how to think." Classes were taught in English and Spanish to children of all races, becoming one of the nation's first bilingual schools. In 1890, following the city's great fire of 1886, the San Carlos was transferred to its present location on Duval Street, in the heart of Key West downtown. Many Cuban patriots, including José Martí, who also called the San Carlos *La Casa Cuba*, made speeches at the Institute promoting their ideas for a free and independent Cuba.

On May 20, 1902, the Cuban exiles and residents in Key West celebrated the creation of the new Republic of Cuba at the San Carlos. In 1919, a hurricane devastated Key West, the southernmost point of the U.S. and the San Carlos was severely damaged. José M. Renedo, the

Institute's then president, traveled to Havana to secure $80,000 for the reconstruction of the building. Francisco Centurión, one of Cuba's most prominent architects of that time, designed the new two-story building in a typical Cuban-style, which earned it being called *"La Joya de Key West"* (Key West's Jewell). The Institute reopened its doors and renewed activities October 10, 1924.

In 1959, the small financial assistance provided by the Cuban government was suspended when the Communist dictatorship seized power. In spite of local efforts to upkeep the building and activities, the San Carlos fell unto disrepair and a few locals proposed to commercially develop the property. In 1985, a group led by Rafael A. Peñalver, including Bishop Agustín A. Román from the Catholic Archdiocese of Miami, Luis Botifoll, Feliciano Foyo, Jorge Más Canosa, and others contacted the Florida State Hispanic Commission and funds were obtained for the restoration of the building, carefully doing it according to its original plans and making handmade replicas of missing tiles and other parts of the original structure. Various artists donated paintings and sculptures of prominent Cuba patriots, including José Martí and Father Félix Varela. The "new" San Carlos opened its doors on January 4, 1992, exactly one hundred years after Cuban patriot José Martí delivered his first speech to the employees of cigar-making factories and *cayohueseros* (Key Westers).

Instituto San Carlos is a Cuban Heritage center and one of the institutions and buildings most revered by Cuban-Americans.

CUBAN WOMEN'S CLUB

In October 1968 a group of Cuban women, among them were Elvira Dopico, Julieta O'Farrill de Secades (its first elected president), Mignon Pérez, Ofelia Tabares Fernández, Asela Abascal, and others, founded an organization whose main purpose would be to make available to Cuban and women in general the means to provide orientation within the community, social help services, cultural activities, and work together with other similar organizations.

Another stated objective was "to stimulate, promote and make known the truth about Cuba while reaffirming our efforts to obtain the liberation of our Fatherland."

According to Wilma G. Tuñón and Ellen Leedor, the organization's actual president and treasurer respectively, among their main accomplishments are: organize Spanish grammar and literature competitions, grant scholarships to deserving students from Miami-Dade College, Florida International University, and the Public School System, conduct periodic meetings to debate about cultural issues and current events, fund the publication of a book about the experiences of a former Cuban political prisoner, and grant the *Premios Floridana*s (Floridiana Awards) to prominent women who have distinguished themselves.

CÍRCULO CUBANO HEBREO DE MIAMI

CUBAN HEBREW CONGREGATION

The Cuban Jewish community in Miami began with the 1959 Communist takeover of Cuba, when most Jews fled and started new lives in the United States. According to some estimates, about ten thousand Jews have left Cuba after Fidel Castro's assumption of power. The Cuban-Hebrew Social Circle of Miami, Inc., also known in Spanish as *El Círculo Cubano Hebreo de Miami*, was founded in Miami Beach on September 22, 1961. Its founders were Enrique Kalusin, Félix H. Reyler, Bernardo Benes, and Oscar White. In 1965, its name was changed to Cuban Hebrew Congregation. It quickly became a force, contributing both to local Jewish community needs and to ongoing efforts to help the people of the State of Israel.

The congregation worshipped in various rented facilities in South

Miami Beach until its first permanent synagogue, Temple Beth Shmuel, opened in August 1975, at 1700 Michigan Avenue, Miami Beach. Next door, at 1701 Lenox Avenue, the much larger synagogue and social hall was dedicated on January 27, 1985. That building includes award-winning designs of the structure and the sanctuary. Both the sanctuary and the Olemberg Ballroom have hosted numerous Jewish, Cuban, American, and general community programs and celebrations. Temple Beth Shmuel's Estrella and Elías Pasternak Montessori School opened in 2004 and currently enrolls more than fifty children from a variety of countries and cultures.

The Cuban Hebrew Congregation presently has over 450 active families and will celebrate its fiftieth anniversary in 2011. Since its inception, their mission was bringing together the arriving Cuban-Jewish families and to develop, promote, and provide a permanent place of worship as well as educational, traditional, social, cultural, recreational, and philanthropic services. The congregation also intended to be a center for information and history about the Cuban Jews in Cuba and the United States, and to be a gathering and learning center for Cuban and Latin American Jews, their descendants, and those of the community at large who are interested in their history and culture. The *"Jewbans,"* as they are fondly called, are examples of the diversity within the Miami cultural landscape. It makes them very Cuban while, in some ways, different from other Jews and different from other Cubans.

COLEGIO NACIONAL DE INGENIEROS AGRÓNOMOS Y AZUCAREROS DE CUBA EN EL EXILIO

NATIONAL ASSOCIATION OF AGRONOMIC AND SUGAR ENGINEERS OF CUBA IN EXILE

The first informal meetings of *Colegio Nacional de Ingenieros Agrónomos y Azucareros de Cuba en el Exilio* (CNIAA) were held in 1961 at the home of Viriato Gutiérrez. On December 15, 1972, the organization was formally incorporated in the state of Florida. Héctor Andreu served as its first president, Raquel Cabal as treasurer, and Alberto Ros as secretary. According to Carlos Balerdi, its actual president, the main purpose is "to promote democracy in Cuba based on the principles stated in the 1940 Cuban Constitution and the Constitution of the United States." Another objective is "to give advice and support to the newly arrived agronomists, help them to find work and to obtain a revalidation of related university courses in U.S. colleges." One of its accomplishments was the recognition by state universities of the doctor in agronomy diploma as an equivalent to their doctor of science. Annual dinners are held in January of every year. Yearly meetings are also held with the civil engineers as well as the various groups formed by the mechanical, electrical, and chemical engineers.

Agroindustry was an important segment of Cuba's economy, although only about 25 percent of the island's total land area was cultivated in the 1950s. Cuba was the largest sugar producer and exporter (12.8 percent of the world production in 1957) and considered to be the best organized for that purpose. By the mid-1950s, cattle and beef were the second-largest industry. Cuban tobacco and cigars have always been the finest and most sought-after in the world. Other important crops were coffee, rice, produce, and citric fruits.

FUNDACION PADRE FELIX VARELA

FATHER FELIX VARELA FOUNDATION

On May 1, 1989, the foundation was incorporated in the state of Florida. It was preceded by a committee created to commemorate the bicentennial of Father Félix Varela's birth on November 20, 1788. Subsequently the group decided to create the foundation to continue educating the public about the personal characteristics, teachings, life, and work of Father Varela, a Cuban patriot considered by many historians as "the one who taught Cubans how to think" and one of the first to write promoting Cuba's independence from Spain, for which he was exiled from his native country by the Spanish government. He came to the U.S. and in 1837 was named vicar general of the Catholic Diocese of New York, where he played a major role with the way the American Church dealt with the influx of Irish refugees. Varela wrote many articles about human rights, religious tolerance, and the importance of education, which were published in the local newspapers. With his heart and mind always in Cuba, for Varela the idea of exile was the most painful punishment.

Among the foundation's initial members were Father Rafael Escala, Mercedes García Tudurí, Luisa García Toledo, José Ignacio Lasaga, Marcelino Alvarez Pí, Bishop Felipe Estévez, Alberto Muller, José Ignacio Rasco, Miguel A. Tudela, Javier Souto, and Rafael Abislaimán. Among those who have served as president are Amalia Varela de la Torre, Rogelio de la Torre, Armando Cobelo, Germán Miret, and Pedro Guerra.

To reach those goals the foundation publishes books and writes newspaper articles, appear in radio and television programs, and hold events such as concerts and conferences. The *Peña Vareliana* (Varelian Circle) has been meeting monthly for more than twenty years to discuss Cuban issues and try to offer solutions within the framework of Varela's thinking and philosophy. They also organize annual pilgrimages to Saint Augustine, where Father Varela lived as a child (1794-1801). The pilgrimages were started in 1978 by Bishop Agustín A. Román and Mercedes García Tudurí with the main purpose of visiting the place where Varela was previously interred.

The foundation raised funds for a monument erected in front of the Westchester Regional Library in Miami. As part of their work statues of Varela have been placed in the Instituto San Carlos, Key West; the Ermita de la Caridad (Our Lady of Charity National Shrine, located in Miami); and the Catholic Cathedral atrium in Saint Augustine, Florida. On March 1999, the Miami-Dade County School Board approved the naming of Félix Varela Senior High School. Partly due to the foundation's efforts, in 1997 the U.S. Postal Service honored Father Varela with a first-class stamp "for his humanitarian work with the poor, the sick, youth, immigrants, women, and his thirty years of community service in the U.S."

CAMARA DE COMERCIO HISPANA DE HIALEAH

HIALEAH HISPANIC CHAMBER OF COMMERCE

This chamber was established on January 28, 1985. Its organizing committee was integrated by Vicente Rodríguez as president, who still holds that position. Also included Pedro Acosta as vice president, Dr. Ramiro Marrero, Julián Miel, Jr., Miguel Piñeiro, and Benigno Galnares. Its objectives were to help its members in obtaining loans for their businesses, assist in the creation of new business corporations, create an employment bureau, organize workshops to promote business contacts, and seminars with subjects geared to improve the members' businesses. The chamber presently has more than one thousand members.

LA CASA CUBA (SAN JUAN, PUERTO RICO)

CIRCULO CUBANO DE PUERTO RICO

On February 24, 1949, forty-five Cuban emigrés in San Juan formed the *Círculo Cubano de Puerto Rico* to "attain the spiritual unity and to foster the fraternal relations between all Cubans residing in Puerto Rico and the friends of Cuba who may deserve that distinction." Most of the founders were not political exiles. They were living in Puerto Rico for personal and professional reasons. As a matter of fact, before 1959 (the year of the Communist takeover in Cuba) the club had more Puerto Rican than Cuban members. Most of the Círculo's initial activities were geared to raise funds to build a clubhouse. A newsletter was published and meetings were held at a Cuban restaurant. In 1956 a clubhouse was inaugurated at a cost of over $100,000 and the organization had only 152 members. With the massive influx of anti-Castro exiles, the club took on a new life. In 1965 the *Círculo Cubano* merged with the *Lyceum Cubano*, an organization comprised by Cuban exiles. Although the merger would ensure the institution's viability, it led many of the old members of the *Círculo Cubano* to leave the organization. The club's facilities were expanded between 1967 and 1974 to accommodate a booming membership.

The 1960s witnessed extraordinary physical growth and social effervescence in *La Casa Cuba*. Sport competitions (rowing teams were introduced by Cubans to Puerto Rico), squash courts (the first in the island), debutante balls, and other events marked those days. The club also organized national and international athletic tournaments, promoted Cuban music and dances. A magazine to cover the intense social life of the members was published. At that time, additional land was acquired to expand their facilities as well as adding a second floor to the clubhouse.

In the late 1970s and early 1980s many Cuban families emigrated to Miami and other parts of the world although new families came and joined. Cobas and Duany's book offers a documented profile of the Cubans arriving in Puerto Rico from the early 1960s to the late 1980s.[1]

The 1979 "*Reglamento*" states that the *Círculo's* main objective is "to promote the rapprochement, mutual understanding, and friendship among all democratic Cubans who live outside their Fatherland and especially between Cubans and Puerto Ricans." Emphasis was on "keeping the image of the distant Fatherland alive at all times and makes it known to the new generations." The club retained its initial middle-class orientation, although many of its members belonged to the upper levels of managements, commerce, and the professions, who joined through a strict mechanism of member sponsorship with the club reserving the right of admission. It also served as a place to network and as a gathering venue for events held by the various Cuban organizations in the island.

In an interesting comment, Cobas and Duany wrote that "Cubans reaffirm their ethnic identity through an elaborate ritual of integration and intensification. Every Sunday club members separate themselves physically and socially from the outside world. Once they enter the club, members extinguish their other social statuses: they are no longer managers or housewives, teachers of students, but Cubans among Cubans."

In 1997 Cobas and Duany wrote that "*Casa Cuba* still serves the interests of Cubans as a middleman group. First, it offers a place where its members, principally Cuban businessmen and professional, may mingle with coethnics who share their social status. Second, Casa Cuba strengthens the bonds between Cubans in Puerto Rico and Cubans in [continental] United States. Third, through linkages between Casa Cuba and elite Puerto Rican institutions, such as Caparra Country Club and *Casa de España*, members of the Cuban community can establish bonds with the Puerto Rican upper crust."

LICEO CUBANO (UNION CITY, N.J.)

Cubans began settling in Union City, N.J., and surrounding towns in the early 1960s. Employment opportunities in Miami were not aplenty and many exiles migrated to other cities in the U.S. to find jobs and survive. Eventually, the most entrepreneurial ones started small businesses to cater to the newcomers. Many professionals revalidated their diplomas and opened offices to help their countrymen. Younger and second generation Cuban-Americans wanted to maintain their Cuban customs and roots and opened businesses to preserve their elders' traditions.[2]

As it happened in most places where Cubans established themselves, they started meeting and organizing themselves. The main objectives were to meet old friends, make new ones, and discuss issues related to Cuba. Also important was helping each other to adapt to the new circumstances and let them know about employment opportunities. Their first informal meetings were held at various restaurants. They soon decided to formalize the gatherings and established the Liceo Cubano, "a social club that served the community in various ways." A building was purchased to house the organization and which was rented for social and community events at a reasonable price. As Prieto indicates in her book, "they held benefit concerts and other functions for specific purposes, especially political causes." Money was collected for efforts to free Cuba from Castro. As the various immigrant waves arrived, the Liceo provided social and community services. The organization raised funds for a telemarathon to help the Mariel immigrants establish themselves in the area and adjusted to the new life.

As Cubans migrated from the area to other parts of the United States, the importance of the Liceo Cubano diminished and the building was eventually sold. Other Cuban social clubs were started and met in various places. One of those groups was *Tertulias de Antaño* (Gatherings of Yesterday), which met at Saint Joseph of the Palisades Church social hall.

LATIN AMERICAN BUSINESS ASSOCIATION (LABA)

As the Cuban exile evolves, its business and professional organizations change composition but the objectives are always the same: network and promote their businesses and professions. The Hispanic population of Miami-Dade County has also changed in the past couple of decades, and, although Cubans are still the majority, it is estimated that about one third came from other countries in Latin America. Due to the economic and political turmoil in some of those countries, many of their entrepreneurs and business class migrated to Miami trying to find a more stable environment where to conduct their business.

Acknowledging that reality, a group of local businesspersons organized Latin American Business Association (LABA) to try to unite those efforts and benefit from their common synergy. LABA was officially incorporated on April 1, 2008, after various meetings of its steering committee led by William Delgado, who had experience as executive director of other similar groups. Delgado was elected its first president and still serves in that capacity, leading a board of thirty-five directors. LABA presently has about 220 members.

Its main purpose is "to promote and encourage meetings between Miami-Dade and Broward County businesspersons in order to find ways to increase the sale of their products or services." At the same time, the group also tries to help and provide assistance to low-income families in the two counties.

SOUTH FLORIDA HISPANIC CHAMBER OF COMMERCE

The South Florida Hispanic Chamber of Commerce (SFLHCC) was incorporated in July 1994 by Liliam M. López, who now serves as its executive president. In those sixteen years, the group has been recognized as one of the three most influential Hispanic chambers of commerce in the United States and has more than one thousand members, mostly from Miami-Dade and Broward counties. Its membership includes a number of American corporations interested in doing business with the Hispanic community. The organization's objectives are to support and promote the growth of the South Florida businesses, to help procure contracts, and to include more Hispanics in corporate boards in the country.

The SFLHCC organizes an annual golf tournament as a fund-raiser to help Hispanic youth by means of scholarships to those with limited financial resources, having granted, according to López, over $200,000 in scholarships.

THE ATLANTA CUBAN CLUB

CLUB CUBANO DE ATLANTA

As with other cities where one finds a Cuban community, those residing in Atlanta felt a need to gather and preserve some of the Old Country's customs and traditions. Orlando Rojas was elected its first president. The Atlanta Cuban Club (*Club Cubano de Atlanta*) was created by a group of eight couples and incorporated on November 1977.

The club was founded "as a social and cultural venue with the objectives of promoting and preserving Cuban traditions and culture, but also welcoming citizens from other countries who wanted to share in those objectives."

Initially the Atlanta Cuban Club held quarterly parties for its members at various venues. In 1982, the club leased space at a convenient location, which was remodeled to accommodate their needs. It includes a spacious ballroom which seats 250 people. During its most active period, the club had 240 family members although its present membership is composed of 105 families. It continues its mission of having not only social events but also meetings and seminars on Cuban patriotic dates and themes.

OTHER ORGANIZATIONS

Other Cuban-American organizations not previously mentioned here are *Museo Cubano de Arte* (Cuban Art Museum) as well as local chapters affiliated with national and international organizations, such as Lions Club *(Club de Leones)*, Rotary Club *(Club Rotario)*, Sertoma (Service to Mankind), and others.

Other organizations for Accountants, Lawyers, Doctors, etc. are included in the chapters covering those areas.

This book was written and published under the auspices of Facts About Cuban Exiles (FACE). An abbreviated history of the organization is in the next page.

NOTES

1. Much of the information was taken from the book: José A. Cobas and Jorge Duany, *Cubans in Puerto Rico, Ethnic Economy and Clutural Identity* (Gainesville: University Press of Florida, 1997), 77-90.
2. Much of the information was taken from the book: Yolanda Prieto, *The Cubans of Union City* (Philadelphia: Temple University Press, 2009), 53-56.

1982 FOUNDING BOARD EXECUTIVE COMMITTEE
Sam Verdeja, Chair
Luis Botifoll, Co-Chair
Frank Paredes, Treasurer
Frank Angones, Secretary
Carlos Arboleya
Edgardo Caturla Pérez
Armando Codina
José Feito
Willy Gort
Ariel Remos
Luis Sabines
Octavio Verdeja
Tere Zubizarreta

PAST CHAIRS
Sam Verdeja
Luis J. Botifoll
Tere A. Zubizarreta
Carlos Arboleya
Francisco J. Paredes
René V. Murai
Armando L. González
Raúl L. Rodríguez
María Cristina Barros
Rafael Peñalver
José C. Cancela
Sandra González-Levy
Pedro A. Freyre
Gustavo Alfonso
Raúl Masvidal

PRESENT EXECUTIVE COMMITTEE
César Pizarro, Chair
Vera Dubson, Secretary
Irela Díaz, Treasurer
Fausto Gómez
María Domínguez
Gustavo Godoy
Jorge Plasencia
Siro del Castillo
Sofía Powell-Cosio
Manuel Rodríguez

FACTS ABOUT CUBAN EXILES

Facts about Cuban Exiles (FACE)

In August 1982, Facts about Cuban Exiles (FACE) was founded "to defend the image of the Cuban Exiles." The incorporating group was active in many other civic and community organizations and represented a cross section of the Cuban diaspora in Miami.

FACE's mission is "to promote, foster and improve the goodwill, reputation and image of those persons of Cuban origin, and their descendants, in the United States and the world, who have sought refuge outside of Cuba due to existing political conditions" and works toward the development of mutual understanding and cooperation with other groups in the community. FACE has encouraged fair and balanced media coverage and has responded to biased or erroneous reports. It periodically publishes information concerning Cuban exiles. Since 1984, has presented Excellence Awards to deserving individuals and institutions for their contributions to a better and more just society.

EPILOGUE
THE CUBAN NATION

BY RAUL CHAO

The Stranger within my gate,
He may be true or kind,
But he does not talk my talk—
I cannot feel his mind,
I see the face and the eyes and the mouth,
But not the soul behind.

The men of my own stock
They may do ill or well,
But they tell the lies I am accustomed to
They are used to the lies I tell;
And we do not need interpreters
When we go to buy and sell.

The Stranger within my gates,
He may be evil or good,
But I cannot tell what powers control—
What reasons sway his mood;
Nor when the Gods of his far-off land
May repossess his blood.

RUDYARD KIPLING *(1865-1936)*

Starting in 1959, one fifth of the Cuban nation began to leave the island of Cuba in the largest population migration in the history of the Americas. They were induced and motivated by diverse reasons: fear of persecution, rejection of a totalitarian rule imposed on them, economic uncertainty, apprehension about the future of their children, uncertainty about the life quality prospects under a Marxist regime, and concerns about the free exercise of their religion and values, among others. Those Cubans that stayed in the island were either of the same mind as the ruling government or were not able to leave for a variety of personal reasons. A good number were uncertain, more tolerant, shortsighted, or unenthusiastic to follow the path of some of the great exiles of history like José Martí (Spain, 1871), Felix Varela (New York, 1823), José María Heredia (México, 1823), José Antonio Saco (Madrid, 1835), and, why not, Petrarch (Arezzo, 1304), Dante (Rome, 1289), Victor Hugo (Guernsey Island, 1851), and Rousseau (Paris, 1742).

Most of those who left their native island went to the United States; they saw their beliefs reinforced in exile by a society based in freedom and the autonomy of the individual. They became conscious of the greatness of democracy and the primacy of the citizen over the state. Most of them never shed aside their Cubanness, however, and never ceased to build and complement their character with nostalgic memories of the land they had left behind. In a feat seldom found in mankind's history, they overcame the passage of half a century and never ceased to feel Cuban, even if over the years the possibility of returning to Cuba looked more and more like a chimera.

In the meantime, things in Cuba went from bad to worse after 1959. Years and years of an imposed educational monopoly by a totalitarian government, and half a century of an absolute control of the normal sources of information—together with a merciless treatment of dissent—increasingly suppressed in Cuba the will, the power, and the hope to recover its sovereignty. The absolute restraint of personal initiatives in the realms of political ideas, religion, human rights, and the manipulation of social behavior by controlling survival basic wants and needs, gave rise to a society where only a few individuals could share and participate in the human goals of personal happiness, peace, security, and comfort.

For a long time fate has provided many different and contrasting experiences for the Cuban exiles and those Cubans who stayed behind in Cuba. It is certainly reflected in the spiritual inheritance and character both groups have gifted to their descendants during the last fifty years.

Is it unreasonable to ask if both groups do still belong to the same nation?

Don't nations evolve in their values and interests according to the historical environment in which they find themselves?

Didn't these two groups, the Cubans in Cuba and the Cubans in exile, have most of the time been completely devoid of even the minimal levels of contact?

Have they evolved separately into two distinct nations, like *criollos* in America differentiated themselves from Spanish peninsulars, or like North Americans became a separate nation from the British?

WHAT IS A NATION?

A nation is a very elusive entity to characterize and, in the final analysis, there has never been a consensus on how to define it. Before we attempt to describe what it is, it may be a good idea to jump to conclusions and accept that it is, first and foremost, a *collective state of mind*, an *act of free and voluntary group-consciousness* which, since the American and the French Revolutions, has become increasingly prevalent among citizens of the world.

Nationhood is what gives people *a certain sense of belonging to a community* of larger dimensions, more durability but similar commitments to what they have for the family, the clan, the village, or the church. It is certainly a *feeling* of lasting loyalty, deliberate or unconscious, professed to a group of *important others*, much more powerful than what one feels about the hardiness of belonging to a sports team or among the subscribers to an opera season.

Ever since the end of the nineteenth century there have been hundreds of philosophers, sociologists, psychologists, politicians, anthropologists, and even totalitarian dictators that have attempted to define the concept of nation. In *Marxism and the National Question* (1913), none other than Joseph Stalin defined a nation as *"A historically evolved, stable community of language, territory, economic life and psychological make-up manifested by a commonality of culture. It is sufficient for a single one of these characteristics to be absent and the nation ceases to be a nation."* It is left to the reader to decide if the Soviet Union ever fulfilled all the conditions prescribed by its leader.

It is probably necessary to sharpen this definition into more understandable and familiar terms.

A nation is a body of individuals who realize they share a real or fantasized common history, culture, values, literature, traditions, ethnicity, territory, and language. As more ingredients are introduced in this definition, more exceptions are found in real life; this phenomenon is at the root of the elusiveness of the concept of nation.

There are other elements that help to define a nation, but they are even more susceptible to objections and exclusions. Some writers feel for instance, that members of a nation must have a common ancestry, a clear sovereignty, shared myths, common heroes and enemies, and must have lived together over time on the same land. Others have suggested that no nation can exist if most or all its members cannot trace their ancestors along an uninterrupted path of historical narrative or if they do not feel some communal bond among themselves. Regardless of the precision of these definitions, the concept of nation escapes every attempt to wrap it up in a tidy and comprehensible package.

An additional issue is that for most of the time the term *nation* has been around, it has been treated as a synonym of the word *state*.

Evidently nation is a psychological, sociological, and/or anthropological reality, while *state* is a political and/or legal reality. Both can coexist, and the proper term when that happens is what we call the *nation-state*. The inexcusable and unforgivable confusion nation-state has produced such incoherent terms as the *League of Nations*, the *United Nations*, the *National Anthem*, etc., all incongruities that should have been baptized as the *League of Sovereign States*, the *United Countries,* the *Country Anthem,* and so on.

The concept of *nation* emanates from natural law, totally independent of the existence of a state. A *state*, in the socio-economic sense that the Abbot Sieyès used the term in 1789 when referring to the third state (What is the third state? The third state is us!), is a political construct that results when a nation has been invested with powers to control the life of its citizens. The *nation* is the source of sovereignty, which can only be exercised through the organization and universal recognition of the *state*. Nations have a *latent right* to statehood and self-determination but because of pragmatic or political concerns they are not always accepted as such. Witness the many efforts of alleged nations within Spain that have claimed for centuries their rights to statehood: the Basques, the Catalonians, the Galicians, among others.

The nation *per se* has no power until it is invested with powers and territory after becoming a state. The *Cuban nation* already existed in December of 1898 but it had no power whatsoever; on May 20, 1902, the *Cuban state* was born, declared, organized, and recognized by others with powers to assume control of its citizens. A *nation* is impervious to treaties or international laws, but a *state* is expected to follow laws and respect treaties.

Given this to be the case, it is certain we can assign to the term *nation* two distinctive meanings: the *political nation*, which is the use of the term nation in the context of describing a *nation-state*, and the *cultural nation*, which is the elusive hard-to-define term to which we are referring to. The French, one of the first people who tried to define the difference between *nation* and *state*, refer to the nation as the *pouvoir constituent* (the power in potency), and the state as the *pouvoir constitué* (the power in reality), a difference that no one needs to speak French to appreciate.

THE *SEMAS* OF THE WORD NATION

In linguistic semantics a *sema* (from the Greek *sign, meaning*) or *semantic trait*, is any of the small, indivisible, and most constricted specific characteristics that contribute to the definition of a word or an idea. A classical illustration offered by linguistic experts is the case of the *semas* of what defines a chair. For a chair to be a chair and nothing else it has to have *four legs* and a *backrest*; it has to be an object used by people *to sit*; and it must be intended to be used by only *one person* at a time. If any of these *semas* is not present, the object is no longer a chair. It could be a *stool* if it has no back support, a *table* if it is not used to sit, a *bench* if it is intended for more than one person, and so on, but it would no longer be a chair.

What are then the possible *semas* of the word nation? Herein lays the problem; for every *sema* that seems to be appropriate one can find a variety of real life exceptions. In spite of that, it may be fruitful to register them, perhaps under the pretense of *defining the cultural and behavioral features* of a nation.

A cultural nation is a body of people who share a common language. Here we have to recognize exceptions in instances like the Chinese, the Indians and Pakistanis, the Belgians, the Swiss, the Canadians, and many others: all of these nations where a variety of languages are spoken. Worthy of notice is also the failed effort of the *English Only* movement in the United States, which has not found track among the American population. To the American nation, language does not seem to be a *sine qua non* condition. Americans are reluctant to exclude from their nation individuals who speak languages other than English.

A nation would at times be defined as consisting of individuals who populate a defined territory. There are many exceptions to this rule in history; in contemporary times the Jewish nation, the Kurds, the descendants of the Mayans, and other nations that have kept their identities, values, and cultural traits while living in a diaspora. The sparkle and zeal of the Jewish nation over hundreds of years is overwhelming evidence of the small role of *territory* in defining a nation, in spite of its apparent importance. On the other extreme there are territories that are shared by different nations such as Chinese descendants and island natives in the state of Indonesia and the peoples of British descent and the native Aboriginals in continental Australia.

The cultural trait of common religion needs no longer to be included, given the spread of such phenomena as secularization, agnosticism, syncretism, ecumenism, religious tolerance, etc. The English nation was transformed overnight from *Catholicism* to *Anglicanism* with no discernible permanent national changes. Thousands of Indonesians left the *Dutch Reformed Church* and *Calvinism* after the 1949 military and diplomatic defeats of the Dutch colonial government after World War II in the Pacific, without having an impact on the national fervor. In both instances there were radical metaphysical conceptual changes, but the national ideals remained unscathed. The importance of religion, however, cannot be carelessly minimized. The British, for instance, created two nation-states in their ancient colony of India by separating the Moslems (Pakistan) from the Hindus (India); the conflicts in the partition of the old Yugoslavia have been the result of separating in distinct nation-states the Catholic Croats from the Orthodox Serbs; the worst disasters in Ireland have occurred after counties of Protestant Ulster opted out of the Catholic Irish Free State in 1922.

The traits of shared origin, ethnicity, and common ancestry have long been discarded as essential to the definition of nationhood, even though as recently as the 1990s these notions gave rise to eugenics and ethnic cleansing in Europe, the Balkans, Asia, and Africa. Ever since the great divide of the Industrial Revolution (1750-1910), technology has provided the means for easier mobility across seas and land and stimulated the blending of many individuals into formerly homogeneous national entities. The forging of the American nation is the best example of this phenomenon. The fifty-year-long assimilation of island-born Cubans and their descendants into the American nation is perhaps evidence of an ongoing process in this category.

The concepts of common behaviors and attitudes have been widely regarded as national traits, particularly since they seem the tightest bond in the intuitive opinion of the masses. All Cubans are presumed to know how to dance a rumba, all Mexicans like jalapeños, and all British have bad teeth. Yet behaviors and attitudes are learned attributes, and national culture is an evolving process, not a destination. Some specific patterns of thought and behavior persist through generations, but many others evolve with time. Today's Spain is quite different from Spain during the Napoleonic times, yet travelers in the nineteenth century, as well as observers in the twenty-first century, could and can easily recognize a Spaniard when they ran or run across one. They are looking to the same nationality over a span of a century and a half; behaviors and attitudes have evolved but the national identification has endured.

What is left after language, territory, religion, common origin, ethnicity and ancestry, behavior, and attitudes are discarded as the *semas* that define the concept of *nation*? To answer this question one should look at the methodology of successful instances of *nation-building* and/or *nation-reforming*.

Nations can be created, developed, or changed by the concerted efforts of a few nation-builders or nation-reformers. They do it by bringing to light or inventing *real, bogus, or imaginary traditions*, by *reconstructing and revising history*, and by *validating actual or pseudo historical memories and accounts*. For nation-builders and nation-reformers a nation is simply "*A group of individuals that embrace and share a common fantasy about their origin and heritage, created mostly by one or several charismatic individuals who forever earn the title of Founding Fathers.*"

THE BIRTH OF THE CUBAN NATION, 1800 TO 1902

Originally the Cuban nation was created out of existing ethnographic and political realities when a new emotion began to be experienced by *criollos*[1] that until then had been immune to separatist feelings for several centuries. During the first half of the nineteenth century, a distinguished group of Cuban-born intellectuals began to profess sentiments of intense national perspective. At the call of men like Felix Varela (1787-1853), José de la Luz y Caballero (1800-1862), José Antonio Saco (1797-1879), Francisco de Arango y Parreño (1765-1837), Rafael María de Mendive (1821-1886), and others, island *criollos* were first induced to form a community of common interests. A community characterized by autonomous creative cultural endeavors, capable of providing for the self-supporting economic well-being of its members.

These initial nation-builders were unable to convince but a small number of their contemporaries. National feelings in the mid-1800s were only experienced by a few young lawyers, liberal priests, students, and poets. They sought support in those times from a community of believers growing within the secularized University of Havana, which at the time was already a hothouse of national fervor and was almost exclusively staffed by Cuban-feeling faculty.

Their arguments were powerful and straightforward: Spain was ruling Cuba only for its own benefit. Its ruling masters in Cuba were self-serving and corrupt. The metropolis had turned Cuba into a training ground for the hardening of its military forces, the enrichment of its decadent nobility, and the source of rewards for its debauched aristocracy. Numerous promises of reform were always discarded by a central government that exploited the colony and had no regard for the dignity of the Cuban-born.

Those sentiments were spread and reinforced by a generation of men who decided to take arms in order to seek a functioning autonomy or total independence from Spain: Carlos Manuel de Céspedes (1819-1874), Francisco Vicente Aguilera (1821-1877), Gaspar Betancourt Cisneros (1803-1866), Domingo del Monte (1804-1853), Salvador Cisneros Betancourt (1828-1914), Vicente García (1833-1886), Miguel de Aldama (1821-1888), and many others. Unfortunately these feelings were deeply rooted but limited to a few leaders and their followers and not yet to the general population of Cuba. Regionalism or indifference and unconcern prevailed over a national mindset.

A national, all-encompassing sentiment was not even aroused during the war of 1868-1878. It was difficult to launch the war in the prosperous provinces in western Cuba. The wealthier *criollos* of Havana, Pinar del Rio, and Matanzas, whether they believed in annexionism, reformism, autonomism, or independentism[2] were, above all, fearful of the economic perils of a Cuba ruled by Cubans. Santiagueros, on one hand, never wanted to fight in Camagüey; residents of Las Tunas did not see themselves fighting under anyone else but Vicente García. The Spaniards even engaged *criollos* to fight alongside them; they did not realize the fratricidal nature of these endeavors. The war and confrontation sponsored and fought by the self-proclaimed Cuban nationals were nevertheless expressions of a renewed sense of national identity; they became evidence of an indignant sentiment against Spain; the answer of a budding nation to a declining imperial exploiter; an impending birth of a nation that had so far proven loyal to the empire long after her mainland possessions had shaken their shackles.

After the stalemate that ended the Ten Year War (1868-1878) and the Guerra Chiquita (1879-1880), the subjugation of the Cuban population to the Spanish became more and more precarious as a stronger shift in loyalty began to occur from the respect or fear of Spain to the notion of Cuba as a nation. With the inspiration of José Martí, new thoughts and sentiments began to absorb the minds and hearts of Cubans, and the idea of Cuba as a sovereign state began to look not only possible but desirable. The national sentiment, of course, demanded the creation of a nation-state, which in turn stimulated and strengthened the national dream. The Cubans again undertook to fight Spain for the sovereignty of their native territory in 1895.

Knowing that the *criollos* had no great enthusiasm for revolting and that previous exhortations had led to indifference and failure, Martí smartly pushed the independence war agenda as the natural claim of a mystical nation that was seeking justice, humanity, and the happiness of all and for the good of all. In fact, the undersized nation of Cuba, limited in size by its coastal frontiers, lacking industrial impetus, subjected for the first—and not the last—time to the indifference of its sister republics, launched a gallant struggle for its independence and its conversion into a nation-state. The reality soon overcame the dreams of the Apostle, however. Martí died early in the war; the armed conflict dragged for three indecisive years; Cubans were victorious in battles as important as *Bunker Hill* (the 1775 battle won at great expense by the British against the Americans on the outskirts of Boston); *Maipú* (the 1818 battle of the Chileans against the Spaniards that made possible the independence of Chile), *Carabobo* (the 1821 battle that decided the independence of Venezuela), and *Pichincha* (the 1822 battle that led to the independence of Ecuador). Yet at the end, a long-feared U.S. intervention eroded the victories of the Cuban arms; the state that was intended to be a nation-state was occupied by a condescending but not necessarily welcomed army.

Regardless of the best intentions of its patriots, many Cubans remained indifferent to the occupation for several years. They even remained somewhat content with the generous improvements that the American treasure undertook in the severely ruined island. Soon the future citizens of Cuba realized that they had little time to either claim their sovereignty or submerge themselves forever in the comforts of the American Dream. It was the hardest and most assertive push for the definition of the Cuban nation, and it finally yielded the desired dividend.

With the advent and reality of their independence, the Cubans were no longer loyal second-class members of a faraway foreign state, nor the newest and poorest state in a formidable but alien national entity; Cubans realized they were citizens of their own *nation-state*. They were elated and felt that no insurmountable obstacles could get on their way. Witnesses attested to the intensity of the glorious joy that filled the hearts of all Cubans on May 20, 1902, the day the Cuban flag flew over the city of Havana for the first time.

As it will be seen later, this magical nation that Martí created in his mind, presumably ready to assume the control of its destiny, had finally reached its destiny but was soon demystified by the reality of conflicts, divisions, and ambitions.

THE GROWTH OF THE NATION-STATE DURING 1902-1959

During the first fifty years of Cuba as a nation-state, its development was filled with countless examples of national fervor. The state sustained a rapid growth of its economy and its population worked hard under the guiding counsel of illustrious men like Enrique José Varona (1849-1933), Manuel Sanguily (1849-1925), Juan Gualberto Gómez (1854-1933), Fernando Ortiz (1881-1969), Manuel Márquez Sterling (1872-1934), Gonzalo de Quesada (1868-1915), Jorge Mañach (1898-1961), Juan J. Remos (1896-1969), José María Chacón y Calvo (1892-1969), Agustín Acosta (1886-1979), and many others; a swelling of educated masses became a success history thanks to the enthusiastic zeal of hundreds of teachers; the industrious efforts of dedicated technical men and jurists like Antonio Sánchez de Bustamante (1865-1951), Ramiro Guerra (1880-1970), José Ramón Villalón (1864-1923), Manuel F. Gran (1893-1962), and Marcelo Alonso (1921-2005), among others, placed the young republic among the most advanced in the concert of nation-states.

The middle class grew significantly in the fifty-year Cuban Republican period. Cuban-born entrepreneurs, boosted by an unprecedented growth of a sugar business that was more and more in their hands, capitalized on an incessant wave of modernization that took Cuba by storm. Both the middle class (highly educated professionals, small businessmen, merchants, skilled technicians, administrators, etc.) and the high bourgeoisie (sugar barons, real estate tycoons, industrialists, and old-moneyed families that remained in Cuba) developed an outstanding social and cultural life that rivaled those found in any nation in the new and old continent. The working classes, however, (staff employees, clerks, blue collar workers, the agricultural workforce) found few occasions to participate in the economic and cultural booms, less so the further they were from the main urban centers. The Cuban nation, nevertheless, acquired a peculiar brilliance and grandeur with the contributions not only of intellectuals, musicians, and artists—Humberto Piñera (1912-1986), Pablo Lavín (1905-1992), Miguel de Marcos (1894-1954), Aurelio de la Vega (1925-), Ernesto Lecuona (1895-1963), Armando Menocal (1863-1942), Leopoldo Romañach (1862-1961), Victor Manuel García (1897-1969), Amelia Peláez (1895-1968), and others mentioned elsewhere—but also of popular participants in the characterization of the Cuban temperament and the definition of the Cuban nation; Eduardo Abela (1891-1965), Sindo Garay (1867-1968), Miguel Matamoros (1894-1971), Celia Cruz (1926-2003), Benny Moré (1919-1963), Dalia Iñiguez (1911-1995), Luis Carbonell (1923-), Olga Guillot (1922-), Enrique Jorrín (1926-1987), Arturo Sandoval (1949-), Gloria Estefan (1957-), Willy Chirino (1947-), and many others.

Not everything went well, however. The idea of a progressive nation that would accommodate and turn into a reality all the dreams of a hundred years of struggle in the *manigua*, proved from the very beginning to be an effort of unprecedented difficulty. Greed, conflicts of interest, corruption and self-indulgence made progress very difficult. The persistence of dishonesty, which at first was merely an inconvenience and an obstacle for the development of the nation, began to undermine the resilience of the Cuban nation and to erode the belief that Cubans could govern themselves. The forward thrusts of good and patriotic Cubans to move their nation ahead began to be insufficient to carry the dead weight of the dishonest activities of many of its persistently corrupt politicians and leaders.

Many devoted Cubans suffered in silence the dishonesty and duplicity of the political life during practically every national government, with the possible exception of Tomás Estrada Palma's. Cuba was a nation with a large number of educated and cultivated spirits, men and women; they could not stem the tide of deceit and of dishonesty that asphyxiated the young nation. Individual liberties had almost completely eradicated class barriers; religious tolerance had become prevalent; race discrimination had almost disappeared in spite of several centuries of Spanish tradition. The dream that Cuba could become a great nation because its geographical location, the fertility of its soil and the ingenuity, character, and audacity of its citizens, however, became nothing but a chimera. The fabric of the nation was eventually torn in a thousand pieces and the young republic gave way with unimaginable ease; the disintegrating nation-state soon fell prey in 1959 to an opportunistic gang of bogus and sinister Samaritans led by a well-known charismatic and demagogical leader.

THE FORCED TRANSFORMATION IN THE ISLAND OF THE TRADITIONAL CUBAN NATION

In spite of the errors, the false starts, the deceptions, and the betrayals, most Cubans believed in 1959 that nothing was more worthy of their love, nothing so sacred and deserving of their sacrifice as was their nation. For the majority of citizens, the Cuban nation, in spite of its misadventures with corrupt politicians, was superior to religion, party affiliation, and practically any sort of loyalty or conviction. Catholics, Masons, Protestants, Jews, the irreligious, the wealthy, and the indigent, young and old, all had a deep sense of love and loyalty for the Cuban nation. The sense of Cubanness transcended all sentiments and interests; it meant to think and feel in Cuban and to dream a common illusion. No grammarians, linguistic experts, politicians, or philosophers could define the love most Cubans felt for their nation, but it was there; Cubans felt proud that they were part of a nation with common thoughts, feelings and intentions. They were sure it could be improved if they only had the time.

It was for these reasons many Cubans embraced in 1959 the dubious and seemingly romantic unknowns who descended from the mountains of Oriente Province promising to renew and set straight the political life of the nation; their credibility was vouched by some prominent and exalted figures of political and intellectual Cuba; both reluctant and partisan observers spoke of the rebels as providential liberators that were ready to carry on the unrealized dreams that José Martí had so clearly defined for the Cuban nation.

With an evident lack of political maturity and culture, and with little or no understanding or familiarity with the Marxist strategies to seize popular movements, the Cuban people trusted the rosary-clad insurgents who paraded across the island and reached Havana in the midst of a popular frenzy. They felt reassured when they witnessed trusted men joining a provisional revolutionary government: José Miró Cardona (appointed prime minister), Manuel Urrutia (president), Roberto Agramonte (state and health), Andrés Valdespino and Rufo López Fresquet (treasury), Felipe Pazos (National Bank), Justo Carrillo (BANFAIC), Elena Mederos (social welfare), and others. Most of them would not remain in their positions by the end of 1959.

The dispensation with the laws and the constitution of the nation did not take long. New penal laws were imposed retroactively. Private property began to be confiscated at the whim of Fidel Castro, the self-proclaimed leader. The death penalty was sanctioned and the right to *habeas corpus* abandoned. The maximum leader began to visit communities across Cuba with a checkbook, drawing funds at his pleasure from the national treasury. The studies and credentials of students from private universities were voided. A new *Ley Fundamental* replaced the Constitution of 1940, and in the process, the word *God* disappeared from its preamble. Ministers and career public servants were replaced without cause; the Cuban citizenship was granted to Ernesto Guevara, alias *el Ché*, a foreign adventurer that knew nothing and felt nothing for the Cuban nation; court decisions were revoked; newspapers were shut down; TV and radio stations were confiscated; the University of Havana was deprived of its autonomy; two new slogans surfaced from the mouths of the men that had seized the destinies of the Cuban nation: «*Armas, ¿Para Qué?*» and «*¡Cuba no está lista para elecciones!*» (*No need for weapons* and *No need for elections*).

On December 2, 1961, the supreme leader declared himself a *Marxist-Leninist*. In rapid succession all private schools were forced to close (from kindergarten to graduate university studies) and a new government-run system of schools took their place; most priests in Cuba were taken by force to a ship that happened to be in the port of Havana, the *Covadonga,* and exiled to Spain; all business large and small, foreign or Cuban-owned, were confiscated; the workers unions were seized by government partisans; hundreds of Cubans in disaccord with the new definition of the nation were incarcerated, deported, incorporated to the arm forces, tortured, or shot; the free transit of Cubans in and out of their country was forbidden; books disappeared from the libraries and bookstores and were replaced with the writings of followers of the dominating regime; intellectuals were admonished of their duty to think in terms attuned to the revolution; artists were told to produce plastic creations with social value; scientists were forced to confine their research in terms of their export value.

The entire cultural life of Cuba was kidnapped and recast in Marxist terms; all civil organizations ceased to exist and community life in Cuba became the media to indoctrinate the population into a new sort of nation forged along Marxist lines; the traditional ethics and morality of the Cuban people were considered an obstacle to the advance of the revolution; promiscuity, deception, prevarication, and mendacity became the means of destroying all remembrances of the Cuban past.

Many Cubans watched these events in disbelief. How was it possible that those transformations could occur ninety miles from the coast of the most powerful and democratic nation in the world? What fundamental flaw was present in the Cuban character that tolerated the breakdown of the Republic with the blessings of the majority of the population? How could it happen so early after a gallant and painful thirty-year period of independence wars? How could the Cuban people fall for and support men who were unremittingly imposing such a foreign doctrine? What had happened to the university students, those nationalistic leaders of the upheavals from 1927 to 1933, who had before shown the resolve to be the strongest watchdogs for democracy in Cuba? Where were the courageous civic resistance men and women that so heroically had resisted and ousted the man who had disrupted the democratic rhythm of the nation in 1952?

For the next fifty long years Cubans were subjected to a deliberate agenda of the government in Cuba that sought to erase its historical patrimony; a scheme designed to tear away and rip off the roots of the Cuban nation and leave the nation-state without principles, traditions, and culture. Cuba became a blank slate in which they would carve a different religion, a new set of mores, a falsified history, and a rejection of elegance and good manners. Fifty years on indoctrination followed; the worst historical flaws that had been so painfully eradicated from the Cuban character were deliberately re-doubled and re-injected in the bloodstream of the nation: political ignorance, indifference, vagrancy, dependency, submission, betrayal, delinquency, snitching, envy, larceny, and acquiescence. The transformation was so thorough and so relentlessly inculcated that the behavior of many Cubans in the island at the turn of the twenty-first century became practically indistinguishable with the manners and demeanor of the Cuban plantation slaves of the nineteenth century.

THE TRADITIONAL CUBAN NATION SOUGHT REFUGE ABROAD

While this was happening in Cuba, one fifth of its population sought refuge abroad; mostly in the United States but also in Spain, several Latin American countries, and various nations in Europe. They integrated—first momentarily and later definitively—into countries with similar degrees of development and comparable systems of values than the ones they had left behind.

Cubans going into exile knew—or learned rapidly—that they had to face lonesomeness, uncertainty, insecurity, and perhaps lack of basic sustenance in countries where they had no families, friends or mechanisms of support. Whether they were professionals, students, or salaried employees, regardless of their age and credentials, their knowledge of languages, their experiences living abroad, the economic conditions when they left Cuba, the people they knew in the countries and cities where they arrived, they showed a remarkable zest for life, an amazing power of adaptation, and a resolve to succeed.

With time, Cuban exiles created in the places where they settled supporting communities that reminded them of Cuba and collectively preserved their traditions. Recovering the integrity of the extended family was the first order of business. Food, the last sanctuary of a threatened culture, was the second, followed by the quest of a logical and ascending continuation of their professions, businesses, trades, and dreams. While at first this was a defensive posture, over the years it became a way of life that would irrevocably integrate them to the societies they had chosen.

In the process, Cubans maintained their traditional national traits and enriched them with many of the cultural traits of their host countries. Memories of old Cuba were never forgotten. Their language remained dotted with *cubanismos*, such as *ser un bárbaro, te la comiste, perder la tabla, arroz con mango, caer pesado,* etc. But the cultural traits they brought from Cuba were enriched with the best qualities of the nations where they settled to start a new life, particularly in the United Sates.

They acquired a new respect for free enterprise and self-sufficiency. They valued the right to vote more than they had ever cherished it in Cuba. They took advantage of institutions of higher learning where discipline, erudition, and honesty prevailed over meaningless values and goals that had injured the Cuban universities like autonomy, co-government, and political militancy. They affirmed or began to believe in principles that were dear to the American culture like justice, equal opportunity, civilized discourse, profound respect for the rights of others, deference to opponents and their ideas, and thoughtful reverence to the rights to speak freely, to move everywhere without conditions, to associate without restrictions, and to unreservedly respect the property of others.

WHAT HAPPENED TO THE CUBAN NATION

AFTER FIFTY YEARS OF DISCONNECTIONS

The Cuban nation inevitably unfolded into two nations along a cleavage imposed and distended by fifty years of very dissimilar experiences in the island and abroad.

One reduced segment of the Cuban society had emigrated and, keeping its traditions, values and idiosyncrasy, continued to grow and develop in distant lands. One could call it the remains of the *Traditional* Cuban nation. It tried hard to keep intact the remembrance of its origins, its heroes, its traditions, its folklore, and its legends. It never discarded anything Cuban and incessantly tried to place each memory in its proper context and perspective. It first hoped to return to the island and rejoin in time the rest of the Cuban nation; eventually it realized that historical, political, and generational realities precluded such reunion. Today that reduced segment has evolved into an improved version of itself and constitutes the closest thing that any anthropologist would have anticipated for half a century of growth of the original Cuba of the first half of the twentieth century.

The largest segment of Cuban society remained imprisoned in the national territory. One could call it the *Captive* Cuban nation. It was subject to fifty years of a strenuous effort to change its values, to reinvent its history, and to reject its traditional quirks, foibles, and habits. So many things were discarded of its past that after fifty years it had no resemblance whatsoever to the traditional Cuban nation that was dreamed by Martí; it had no continuous lifeline with the men of *Baraguá, Montecristi*, las *Guásimas,* or *Jimaguayú*; it was no longer attached to the original roots that were planted by Carlos Manuel de Céspedes, Perucho Figueredo, Calixto García, Ignacio Agramonte, or Flor Crombet; it became a grafted foreign-inspired entity that has been stabbed on a national trunk forced to dry up, perish and fritter away. This segment of the Cuban nation was forced to trash its past and its character; it is now wasting its present; it is also letting its future careen like a rudderless log with no control of its destiny. It is most probably condemned to continue to drift aimlessly in the challenging modern world of the twenty-first century.

There is unfortunately no likely mitigation to the misfortune of both Cuban nations.

Except for a reduced number of men and women that have kept faith with their forefathers and even from inside Cuba continue to be members of traditional Cuba, the *Captive* nation in Cuban soil is no longer a community that could reasonably claim heritage to the efforts of Father Félix Varela, José Antonio Saco, Miguel de Aldama, the Carlos Manuel de Céspedes, José Martí, and Antonio and José Maceo.

On the other hand, the *Traditional* nation in the diaspora, even as it has often been infiltrated by some temporary or permanent visitors from the Captive nation, will find itself with an uncertain Cuban outlook; it is destined to disappear. A good number of the captive visitors from Cuba—the strangers within our gate—will probably return to their more familiar grounds. Some of the original exiles from the 1960s to the 1990s will probably depart in their senior years to spend time in the place of their youth and their dreams. Many will inevitably stay in their adopted countries and reach in exile the end of their life journey. Their children will feel, as they should, that they belong to the nation where they were born and not to the intangible and never seen paradise described by their parents and grandparents.

It is very unlikely that the gallant and courageous men and women that have kept the faith inside Cuba, joining with a returning contingent of the best men and women in exile, could heal and reverse the injuries that have overwhelmed the original Cuban nation. It is highly improbable that the two Cuban nations, the *Traditional* and the *Captive*, could surmount the myriad of differences of the general population in character, dreams, moral fiber, and disposition, to join in a common project and peacefully share the same territory. As it is asked during many human tragedies and after many ruined dreams, the persistent unanswerable question is: Why did it have to happen to us?

NOTES

1. Cuban-born descendants of Spanish residents in Cuba. A term sometimes translated as *creoles* in other latitudes.
2. Political movements and beliefs of residents favoring changes in the status of the island of Cuba: *Annexionists* favored integration into the American republic; *Reformists* believed that some changes in the Cuban-Spain relations would bring about peace and prosperity. *Autonomists* felt the Spaniards should legislate an autonomous status for Cuba with an abundance of local decision-making; *Independentistas* felt that nothing but a total political separation was the desired status.

APPENDIX I

TIMELINE OF THE HISTORY OF CUBA
A CHRONOLOGY OF KEY EVENTS, 1940-2011

BY LEONARDO RODRIGUEZ

1940 – July 14: Fulgencio Batista won presidency in a free election. October 10: Constitution of 1940 became effective.

1941 – December 8, Cuba declared war against Japan and on the 11th on Germany.

1944 – October 10: Dr. Ramón Grau San Martín replaced Batista as president.

1948 – October 10: Carlos Prío Socarrás became president.

1952 – March 10: Batista overthrew Prío and seized power in a *coup d'etat*.

1953 – July 26: Fidel Castro attacked an army garrison (Moncada barracks) in an unsuccessful revolt against Batista. Castro was sentenced to fifteen years in prison. Others in the group received lighter sentences; none greater than ten years.

1955 – May 15: Batista declared an amnesty. Castro, his brother Raúl, and their accomplices were freed. They served twenty-one months and fifteen days.

1956 – April 29: Another groups of anti-Batista fighters attacked the Goicuría Army Barracks in Matanzas. The attack failed.

December 2: Fidel and Raúl Castro, Ernesto "Ché" Guevara, and a group of eighty-two men aboard the yacht *Gramma* reached Cuba: several were killed in clashes with the Cuban Army. The remaining group reached the Sierra Maestra Mountains.

1957 – March 13: A group led by Menelao Mora unsuccessfully attacked the presidential palace in Havana in an attempt to kill Batista. Mora died in the attack. José Antonio Echeverria, a student leader at the University of Havana, died after announcing the attack on a radio station. Pelayo Cuervo Navarro, a respected opposition leader who was not involved in the attack was assassinated by the police.

September 5: Cuban Navy units in the port of Cienfuegos rebelled and were crushed.

1958 – March 27: U.S. suspended the sale of arms to Batista's government.

April 9: A call for a national strike to bring down Batista's regime failed. Several were killed.

In December, guerrilla warfare was intense in Cuba's central and eastern provinces.

1959 – January 1: Batista fled Cuba with family and close friends.

January 2: Guevara occupied La Cabaña fortress and Camilo Cienfuegos occupied Columbia military garrison, both in Havana.

January 8: Fidel arrived in Havana.

Revolutionary government began to use firing squads after quick conviction by "kangaroo courts."

January 12: Seventy-one persons were killed by firing squads in Santiago de Cuba. It was the largest mass execution in Cuban history.

The new Cuban government requested the withdrawal of the U.S. Military Mission.

February 13: José Miró Cardona resigned as prime minister.

February 16: Fidel Castro replaced Miró Cardona.

March 2: Revolutionary tribunal acquits former Batista Air Force pilots of charges of bombing innocent civilians. Castro demanded they be tried again.

March 9: Batista pilots convicted in a second trial and sentenced to twenty to thirty years in jail.

April 23: Raúl Castro asked for Soviet military assistance. The Soviet Union agreed to provide it.

May 17: Agrarian Reform Law signed, which for all practical purposes gave the government control of agriculture in Cuba.

July 17: Castro forced President Manuel Urrutia Lleó to resign. He was replaced by Osvaldo Dorticós, a Communist.

October 21: Major Húber Matos, military commander in Camagüey, resigned and was arrested.

October 28: After arresting Matos, Major Camilo Cienfuegos, disappeared on a flight from Camagüey to Havana. Neither Cienfuegos nor his plane were ever found.

1960 – Cuban government confiscated U.S. businesses and branches of American banks on the island without compensation.

In October the government confiscated hundreds of Cuban-owned businesses, industries and banks. No compensation was paid.

October 14: Government approved Urban Reform Law that affected ownership of rented property.

October 24: Resolution No. 3 resulted in the expropriation without compensation of the remaining foreign and privately owned commercial, industrial, and service enterprises in the country.

By the end of the year, all media companies had been confiscated and taken over by the government.

December: Cuban parents began sending their unaccompanied children to the United States in an operation that became known as Pedro Pan. Over fourteen thousand children were part of this program.

1961 – January 2: Castro demanded the U.S. to reduce its embassy personnel to eleven employees.

January 3: U.S. President Dwight Eisenhower retaliated by breaking diplomatic relations with Cuba.

April 16: Castro for the first time referred to the Cuban revolution as Socialist.

April 17: U.S. sponsored Cuban exiles Brigade 2506 invaded Cuba at the Bay of Pigs. Without adequate air coverage, after three days the invasion failed.

May 1: Castro proclaimed Cuba a Socialist state.

September 17: Government clashed with the Catholic Church and expelled more than three hundred priests and religious persons from the island.

December 2: Castro in a television speech indicated that for many years he had been a Marxist-Leninist.

1962 – October 4: Atomic missile warheads arrived in the port of Mariel. This was the start of the missile crisis that brought the world to the edge of nuclear holocaust.

October 14: U.S. confirmed the Soviet Union had installed offensive missiles in Cuba.

October 23: U.S. President John F. Kennedy ordered U.S. naval forces to quarantine Cuba.

October 28: Soviet President Nikita Khrushchev and President Kennedy reached an agreement to end the crisis. The Soviet Union would remove offensive missiles from Cuba while the United States promised not to invade Cuba and to prevent Cuban exiles from attacking the island.

November 20: The missile crisis ended. The Soviet government agreed to withdraw the Ilushin-28 bombers from Cuba.

December 23-24: Bay of Pigs Brigade 2506 prisoners in Cuba arrived in the U.S. after months of negotiations with the Cuban government. The price for their release was $53 million paid in baby food and medicine.

December 30: President Kennedy met with returning Brigade prisoners at the Orange Bowl in Miami Florida and received the Brigade's flag with a promise to return it in a free Cuba.

1965 – Cuba officially became a one-party state. It was the Cuban Communist Party.

In October, Castro opened port of Camarioca for exiles to go and pick up family and friends.

President Lyndon Johnson approved for freedom flights to replace boats to make the migration from Cuba orderly. The flights began in December.

1967 – October 9: Ché Guevara was killed in Bolivia.

1973 – Freedom Flights ended after 2,879 flights bringing more than 270,000 Cuban refugees to the U.S.

1976 – February 24: Cuban Communist government approved a new constitution.

1978 – November-December: Dialogue between a group of seventy-five exiles and the Cuban government resulted in the release of 3,600 political prisoners.

The U.S. and Cuba reach an agreement that would allow Cuban exiles to go visit their relatives on the island.

1980 – April 1-6: Peruvian Embassy incident. Over 10,800 Cubans sought asylum in the embassy.

April 15 to September 26: The Mariel Boatlift (the Exodus): more than 125,000 Cubans came to the U.S.

1985 – May 20: Radio Martí began to broadcast.

1988 – Agreement between Cuba, South Africa, and Angola on a cease-fire in Angola and Namibia. Cuba agreed to withdraw 50,000 troops from Angola. Last Cuban troops left Angola in May 1991.

1989 – July 13: Angola war veteran General Arnaldo Ochoa was executed by firing squad. Also executed that day were Colonel Antonio de la Guardia and Captains Antonio Padrón and Jorge Martínez.

November 9: The Berlin Wall fell, signaling the collapse of the Soviet Empire.

1990 – March 27: TV Martí began to broadcast.

1991 – December 1991: The Soviet Union is broken up into fifteen separate countries.

Following the collapse of the Soviet Union, Soviet military advisors left Cuba and support for the Cuban economy came to an end.

1993 – July 21: Mario Chanes de Armas, longest-held Cuban political prisoner, was released after serving his full thirty-year sentence.

1994 – July 13: Cuban tugboat named "13 de Marzo" was hijacked from the port of Havana. It was rammed by Cuban government ships and thirty-two of the sixty-three people aboard drowned.

August 5: The first massive protest against the Cuban government in more than thirty years took hundreds of Cubans to the waterfront of Havana in a protest known as the "maleconazo" in reference to the site where it happened. Castro said he would allow anyone who wanted to leave Cuba to do so. This was the start of the rafters crisis.

From August 19 to September 23, 38,000 Cuban rafters were picked up in the Gulf of Mexico and taken to U.S. bases in Guantánamo, Cuba, and Panama.

September 9: The U.S. set a quota of 20,000 immigrant visas annually for Cubans.

1995 – May 2: The Wet-Foot, Dry-Foot immigration policy applicable to Cubans was announced by the Clinton Administration. Those who made it ashore would be allowed to remain in the United States while those picked up at sea would be returned to Cuba. This was a revision of the Cuban Adjustment Act of 1966. The Clinton Administration also approved the admission of 21,000 Cuban refugees that had remained in Guantánamo.

1996 – February 24: Cuban warplanes in international waters shot down two small U.S. aircrafts piloted by Cuban-Americans of Miami-based Brothers to the Rescue. Four were killed.

March 12: As a result of the downing of the two planes, the U.S. strengthened the trade embargo against Cuba. The U.S. Congress passed the Helms Burton Act, which was signed by President Clinton.

1997 – November 23: Jorge Más Canosa died.

1998 – January 21-25: Pope John Paul II made a historical visit to Cuba asking for Cuba to open to the world and for the world to open to Cuba.

1999 – November 25: Elián González, a six-year-old Cuban boy, was rescued by fishermen along the coast of Florida floating on an inner tube, after his mother and several others accompanying him had drowned in an attempt to escape from Cuba.

2000 – April 22: After a legal battle between Elián's family in the U.S. and the U.S. government, Elián was forcibly removed from his family home in Miami by the U.S. immigration authorities. He was given to his father, who came from Cuba to return Elián to his country.

June 28: Elián and his father returned to Cuba after a long legal and political battle between his family in the U.S. and the Cuban and American governments.

2001 – Five Cuban spies known as the "*Red Avispa*" were sentenced to stiff prison terms in Miami. They were found guilty of spying for the Cuban government and for their role in tipping off Havana to the flight plans of Brothers to the Rescue that killed four of their members in 1996.

2002 – March 12-17: Former U.S. president Jimmy Carter visited Cuba. Carter was the only former or serving president to visit Cuba.

2003 – March/April: The Cuban government sentenced and jailed seventy-five dissidents up to twenty-eight years in prison in what was known as Primavera Negra (Black Spring).

April 1: The Damas de Blanco (Ladies in White) began to march every Sunday after mass to protest the arrest of the seventy-five dissidents.

April 11: Three young Cuban men tried to hijack a ferry boat in an attempt to escape to the United States. They were apprehended and executed by the Castro government.

2004 – April: The United Nations Human Rights Commission censured Cuba over its human rights violations.

2006 – July 31: Fidel Castro announced that he would be temporarily handing over the control of the Cuban government to his brother, Raúl. Fidel Castro had undergone emergency surgery, the nature of which was a closely guarded state secret.

2008 – February 24: Raúl Castro, seventy-six, officially was elected as president of Cuba, José Ramón Machado Ventura, seventy-seven, became the new No. 2 man and Gen. Julio Casas Regueiro, seventy-two, was chosen defense minister. The average age of Cuba's new leaders was seventy years old.

2010 – February 23: Orlando Zapata Tamayo a Cuban political prisoner, died after eighty-five days of a hunger strike.

July: The Cuban government began to release fifty-two political prisoners of conscience of the Primavera Negra (Black Spring) as a result of an agreement between the Cuban Catholic Church, the Spanish government, and the Cuban government.

July 13: Seven Cuban political prisoners of the Black Spring were set free and expatriated to Spain.

July: Fidel Castro reappeared publicly for the first time since 2006.

2011 – March: Dr. Oscar Elías Biscet, the last of the prisoners arrested in the Black Spring of 2003, was freed.

May: Raúl Castro promised to fire half a million state workers.

APPENDIX II

CUBA 1958: BY THE NUMBERS

BY LEONARDO RODRIGUEZ

ECONOMIC EXECUTIVE SUMMARY

In 1958, the year before Castro took over, Cuba had 24 cars per 1,000 inhabitants, far ahead of Japan 4 per 1000, Portugal 15 per 1,000, Spain 6 per 1,000, Greece 4 per1,000, as well as the rest of Latin America, except for Venezuela 27 per 1,000.[1]

In radios per capita during the 1950s Cuba ranked second only to Uruguay with 169 radio sets per 1,000 people, which placed Cuba worldwide ahead of Japan. In terms of TV sets per capita, 1950s Cuba was far ahead of the rest of Latin America and was among the world's leaders. Cuba had 45 television sets per 1,000 inhabitants in 1957, by far the most in Latin America, and fifth in the world, behind only of Monaco, the United States, Canada, and the United Kingdom.[2]

In regard to mass media, Cuba in 1957 had more TV stations—twenty-three—than any country in Latin America. It also led Latin America and ranked eight in the world in number of radio stations with 160, ahead of Austria with 83 radio stations, United Kingdom 62, and France 50, according to the UN Statistical Yearbook. Cuba, despite its small size and limited population, had fifty-eight daily newspapers during the 1950s, according to the UN Statistical Yearbook.[3]

According to the UN's Statistical Yearbook of 1960 (pp. 312-316) pre-Castro Cuba ranked third out of eleven Latin American countries in per capita daily caloric consumption at 2,730.[4]

Cuba's infant mortality rate of 32 per 1,000 live births in 1957 was the lowest in Latin America and the thirteenth lowest in the world, according to UN data. Cuba ranked ahead of France, Belgium, West Germany, Israel, Japan, Austria, Italy, Spain, and Portugal in this sensitive indicator.[5]

In terms of physicians and dentists per capita, Cuba ranked third in Latin America in 1957, behind only Uruguay and Argentina. Cuba's 128 physicians and dentists per 100,000 people in 1957 placed Cuba at the same level as the Netherlands and ahead of the United Kingdom at 122 per 100,000 and Finland 96.[6]

Regarding medical facilities, in 1958 Cuba had seventy-two large hospitals with more than 21,000 beds. This figure does not include the municipal centers, which provided emergency clinical and surgical assistance in large cities, and the 250 privately-run medical centers, most of which were structured on a "mutual aid" basis that gave patients access to medical and surgical care for less than five pesos (five U.S. dollars) per month. At least a half million Cubans were enrolled in such programs as of 1958. Including governmental, municipal, and private hospitals and clinics, Cuba had about 35,000 beds for 6.6 million inhabitants—an impressive one bed per 190 inhabitants.[7]

Additional contemporary research studies by Professors Norton Ginsburg of the University of Chicago, Dr. H. T. Ishima from Stanford University, and Donald H. Niewiaroski attests to Cuba's rapid economic advance as evidenced by the following statistical data.[8]

DETAILED STATISTICAL DATA WITH SOURCES

Geographical Size

Area: The size of the territory of Cuba is 42,804 sq. mi. or 110,861 sq. km[9] which makes it comparable to the territorial area of the state of Florida in the U.S. with 58,599 sq. mi. or 151,771 sq. km.[10]

Demography

Population: 1953 Census 5,829,029[11]
1958 Estimate 6,459,000[12]

Ethnic Composition: 1953 Census: Whites 72.8 percent, Blacks 12.4 percent, Mixed 14.5 percent, Chinese 0.3 percent[13]

Major Cities 1953: Greater Havana 1,165,096 inhabitants, Santiago de Cuba 163,237, Camagüey 110,388, Santa Clara 77,398, Guantánamo 64,671, Matanzas 63,917, Cienfuegos 57,991, Holguín 57,573, Cárdenas 43,750, Pinar del Río 38,885.[14]

Religión Affiliation: Roman Catholic 80-85 percent, Protestant 10-15 percent, Others: Jews 16,500 mostly in Havana, Santería.[15]

National Economy

Budget 1957-1958: Revenues: $387,044,000 (tax revenues 96 percent, non tax revenues 4 percent). Expenditures: $385,554,000 (Interest Public Debt 9 percent, Education 23 percent, Public Health 7 percent, Defense 13 percent, Other 48 percent)[16]

Production

Agriculture: Raw Sugar 5,613,823 metric tons[17]

Livestock (number or live animals)
Cattle 5,700,000[18]

Mining and Quarrying 1958:
Nickel	17,900 metric tons
Cooper	13,000 metric tons
Iron	15,000 metric tons[19]

Manufacturing

Cement	715,100 metric tons[20]
Beer	123.2 millions of liters
Cigarettes	10,197,000,000 units[21]
Tobacco-cigars	408,000,000 units[22]

Energy Production (consumption) 1958

Electricity	2,588,000,000 Kw-hr[23]
Natural Gas	75,000,000 cubic meters[24]

Foreign Trade

Exports	$763,000,000[25]
Imports	$808,000,000[26]

Airline Service

Domestic Airlines Serving Cuba in 1958:

Cubana de Aviación

Aerovias "Q"

Cuba Aero-Postal

Expreso Aero Postal Interamericano

Foreign Airlines Serving Cuba in 1958:

Delta-Chicago, Southern Airlines, National Airlines, Inc., Pan-American World Airways, Braniff International Airways, KLM (Royal Dutch Airlines, Aeropostal Venezolana, Compañía Mexicana de Aviación, S.A., Iberia, Aerolineas Argentinas, Transportes Aereos Nacionales (TAN), y Lineas Aereas Costarricenses, S.A. (LACSA).

Airports: Cuba had about one hundred public and private airports including four—Havana, Varadero, Santiago de Cuba, and Camagüey—that provided service for international travel.[27]

Literacy: 76.4 percent (1950-53)[28]

Annual Per Capita Income in Latin America (in U.S. Dollars)

Country	Year	Per Capita	Rank
Venezuela	1959	$857	1
Uruguay	1957	365	2
Cuba	**1958***	**356**	**3**
Costa Rica	1959	333	4
Panama	1958	320	5
Argentina	1959	296	6
Chile	1959	295	7
Mexico	1959	263	8
El Salvador	1958	254	9
Nicaragua	1958	233	10[29]

NOTES

1. U.S. Department of State, "Zenith and Eclipse: A Comparative Look at Socio-Economic Conditions in Pre-Castro and Present Day Cuba." Released by the Bureau of Inter-American Affairs, February 9, 1998. Revised June 2002, 4, Table 4.
2. Ibid., 5.
3. Ibid., 6.
4. Ibid., 3-4, Table 3.
5. Ibid., 1 2.
6. Ibid., 1.
7. Kirby Smith and Hugo Llorens, "Renaissance and Decay: A Comparison of Socioeconomic Indicators in Pre-Castro and Current-Day Cuba" (Cuba in Transition Volume 8, Papers and Proceedings of the 8th Annual Meeting of the Association for the Study of the Cuban Economy [ASCE], Miami, Florida, August 6-8, 1998), 248.
8. Levi Marrero, *Geografía de Cuba* (New York: Tercera Edició, Minerva Books, Ltd., 1966), XXVII-LVIII.
9. "Time Almanac, 2009," Encyclopedia Britannica. Inc., 2009, 209.
10. Ibid., 658.
11. Cuba 1953 National Census.
12. José R. Alvarez Díaz, *Un Estudio Sobre Cuba* (Miami: University of Miami Press, Unión Panamericana, Instituto Interamericano de Estadísticas, América en Cifras, 1960), Table No. 295, page 794.
13. Cuba 1953 National Census.

14. Marrero, *Geografía de Cuba*, 694-698.
15. Wyatt Macgaffey & Clifford R. Barnett, *Twentieth Century Cuba,* Prepared under the auspices of The American University (New York: Anchor Books Doubleday & Company Inc., 1965), 236. Ana Venciana-Suarez, "Addicted to Cuba," *Miami Herald*, November 3, 2007, 1 and 3.
16. Díaz, *Un Estudio Sobre Cuba*, Tables 352 and 353, 900-901.
17. José M. Illán, *Cuba Datos Sobre Una Economía en Ruinas* (Miami: Editorial AIP, 3rd. Edition April 1965), Table No. 19 "Cuba Producción de Azucar de Caña," 39.
18. Illán, Table No. 22 "Cuba Existencia de Ganado y Aves de Corral," 44.
19. Illán, Table No. 24 "Cuba Producción de Minerales," 49.
20. Díaz, *Un Estudio Sobre Cuba*, Table No. 463 "Cuba: Producción de Cemento 1941-1958," 1122.
21. Illán, *Cuba Datos Sobre Una Economía en Ruinas*, Table No. 26 "Cuba Volumen Físico de Algunas Producciones Industriales," 55.
22. Illán, Table 26, "Cuba Volumen Físico de Algunas Producciones Industriales," 55.
23. Illán, Table 27, "Cuba Potencia Instalada y Energía Eléctrica Producida," 67.
24. Ibid., 57.
25. *Oxford Latin America Economic History Database* (The Montevideo-Oxford Latin American Economic History Data Base for the year 1958), http://oxlad.qeh.ox.ac.uk/results.
26. Ibid.
27. Díaz, *Un Estudio Sobre Cuba*, 1157-1159.
28. Díaz, *Un Estudio Sobre Cuba*, Table No. 302, 803.
29. Díaz, *Un Estudio Sobre Cuba,* Table No. 337 "Ingreso Nacional Per Cápita de Los Países de América Latina (en U.S. Dólares)," 843.

OTHER SOURCES

Ginsburg Norton. *Atlas of Economic Development* (Chicago: The University of Chicago Press, 1961).
Donald H. Niewiaroski. "Living of Nations: Meaning and Measurement." *Journal of Inter-American Statistical Institute,* Vol. 23, No. 8, March 6, 1965.
H. T. Oshima. "Un Nuevo Estimado del Ingreso y del Producto Nacional de Cuba en 1953." *No. 3 del Volumen II de los Estudios del Instituto de Investigación Sobre Alimentación*. Universidad de Stanford, November 1961.
Statistical Yearbook of the United Nations, 1959.

APPENDIX III

CUBAN-AMERICAN COMMUNITY IN THE UNITED STATES: BY THE NUMBERS

BY LEONARDO RODRIGUEZ

Fifty-two years after the Castro revolution in Cuba took power January 1, 1959; the original Cuban exiled community in the U.S. gradually evolved into the Cuban-American minority and has become part of the Hispanic population in this country while still retaining strong cultural and emotional linkages to the home country.

The 2010 Census Briefs of the U.S. Census Bureau issued on May 2011 identifies 1,785,547 Hispanics of Cuban origin residing in the United States. They constitute the third-largest population of Hispanic origin living in the U.S., or 3.5 percent of the U.S. Hispanic population in 2010. Mexicans with 31,798,258, or 63.0 percent are first, and Puerto Ricans with 4,623,716 representing 9.2 percent are in second place.[1]

What follows is a demographic, sociological, and economic profile of Cubans in the U.S. as they compare to the Hispanic universe according to Pew Research Center-Pew Hispanic Center. Statistical Profile Hispanics of Cuban Origin in the United States, 2009. Issued on May 26, 2011.

- **Immigration status.** Six in ten Cubans (59 percent) in the U.S. are foreign born, compared with 37 percent of Hispanics and 13 percent of U.S. population overall. Most immigrants from Cuba (53 percent) arrived in the U.S. before 1990. Six in ten Cuban immigrants (58 percent) are U.S. citizens.
- **Language.** A majority of Cubans (58 percent) speak English proficiently.

Some 42 percent of Cubans ages five and older report speaking English less than very well, compared with 37 percent of all Hispanics.
- **Age.** Cubans are older than the U.S. population and Hispanics overall. The median age of Cubans is forty; the median age of the U.S. population and all Hispanics are thirty-six and twenty-seven, respectively.
- **Marital status.** Cuban-Americans are more likely than Hispanics overall to be married—49 percent versus 45 percent.
- **Fertility.** Four in ten (38 percent) of Cuban woman ages fifteen to forty-four who gave birth in the twelve months prior to the survey were unmarried. That was similar to the rate for all Hispanic women—40 percent—and the rate for U.S. women—35 percent.
- **Regional dispersion.** Cubans are the most geographically concentrated Hispanic origin group. Nearly seven in ten (68 percent) live in Florida.
- **Educational attainment.** Cubans have higher levels of education than the Hispanic population overall. Twenty-four percent of Cubans ages twenty-five and older—compared with 13 percent of all U.S. Hispanics—have obtained at least a bachelor's degree.
- **Income.** The median annual personal earnings for Cubans ages sixteen and older was $25,000 in 2009, the median earnings for all U.S. Hispanics were $20,000.
- **Poverty status.** The share of Cubans who live in poverty, 15 percent, is similar to that of the general U.S. population (14 percent) and below the 23 percent share among all Hispanics.
- **Health insurance.** Nearly one quarter of Cubans (24 percent) do not have health insurance, compared with 31 percent of all Hispanics and 15 percent of the general U.S. population. Additionally, 11 percent of Cubans younger than eighteen are uninsured.
- **Homeownership.** The rate of Cuban homeownership (59 percent) is higher than the rate for all Hispanics (48 percent) but lower than the 66 percent rate for the U.S. population as a whole.[2]

Another important characteristic of the Cuban-American community has been its propensity in the creation of firms and enterprises. According to the U.S. Census Bureau, 2007 Survey of Business Owners: Hispanics, published in October 1, 2010, the Cuban-American business community in spite of representing only 3.5 percent of the total Hispanic population in the U.S., had achieved the following in the financial and economic areas:

- **Number of firms:** 251,070 (11.1 percent of the total universe of Hispanic owned firms in the U.S. economy in 2007).
- **Sales and receipts:** $51,252,333,000 (14.8 percent of the total sales and receipts of Hispanic-owned firms in the U.S. economy in 2007).
- **Firms with employees:** 32,329 (12.97 percent of the total firms with employees of Hispanic-owned firms in the U.S. economy in 2007).
- **Employees**: 242,993 (12.79 percent of all employees of Hispanic-owned firms in the U.S. economy in 2007).
- **Annual payroll:** $8.1 billion (14.8 percent of all annual payroll of all Hispanic owned firms in the U.S. economy in 2007).[3]

The 2007 Economic Census proceeds to analyze the distribution of the 251,070 Cuban-owned firms among seven NAICS industrial sectors and has identified the following percentages within each sector: 14.6 percent in construction, 13.7 percent in repair and maintenance, and personal and laundry services, 11.5 percent in administrative and support and waste management and remediation services, 11.0 percent in health care and social assistance, 10.8 percent in transportation and warehousing, 10.6 percent professional, scientific, and technical services, and 27.7 percent in all other industries.[4]

NOTES

1. United States Census Bureau. The Hispanic Population: 2010. 2010 Census Briefs. U.S. Department of Commerce Economics and Statistics Administration. Table 1. Issued May 2011, 3.
2. Pew Research Center Pew Hispanic Center. Statistical Profile: Hispanics of Cuban. Origin in the United States, 2009. May 26, 2011.
3. http://www.census.gov/econ/sbo/get07sof.html?11. Survey of business owners of Hispanic-owned firms: 2007. Summary of fndings.
4. U.S. Census Bureau, 2007 Survey of business owners—released September 21, 2010.

APPENDIX IV

HUMAN RIGHTS VIOLATIONS IN CUBA

BY JUAN CLARK

In order to visualize in more detail the correlation between the situation of human rights and the unending exodus from the island, let's examine the operation of those rights from the perspective of Cuba's living conditions. They will be grouped under three categories: *Political and Individual Rights, Legal Rights,* and *The Economic and Social Welfare Rights*. (Chapter 15 in the book provides what Cuban exiles have done in their struggle to defend these rights on the island.)

1. POLITICAL AND INDIVIDUAL RIGHTS

The rights to freedom and equality in dignity, inherent in all humans, along with the duty of fraternal conduct (Article 1), are practically ignored as a result of the oppressive totalitarian structure that attempts to control every dimension of social life. Political and economic freedoms are obliterated and will be later examined. Great inequality is clearly present when looking at the leaders of the only political party wielding all power along with its perks but without the great shortcomings of the imposed dysfunctional system.

Likewise, the precept prohibiting discrimination against the individual (Article 2) is violated, institutionally, and in practice. In the former this occurs in an institutional basis when the prohibition of two potential forms of discrimination were left out of the Constitution: namely discrimination due to political ideas and place of birth of the person. Concerning political ideas this situation has created a sort of "apartheid," permeating all levels of society along those two lines. It prevents and/or curtails opportunities for advancement, as well as the active participation in the direction and functioning of the political, educational, and occupational dimensions of the country, to those not considered politically reliable. Cubans are also discriminated in favor of foreigners, since the former are practically forbidden to use and enjoy what the latter can, in areas such as food, health care, housing, transportation-mobility, and recreation.

It is important here to distinguish between Castro's totalitarian system and the traditional authoritarian dictatorship. In the latter, the dictator mainly controls the military-repressive apparatus, the political structure, and marginally profiting from the economic activity; but it allows the individual a wide margin of neutrality. On the contrary, the totalitarian system goes beyond those categories, attempting complete control on all dimensions (the economic, educational, health, etc.). It also, in practice, penalizes or forbids the possibility of political neutrality. This neutrality will be considered "apathy towards the system" or "ideological diversionism." It can entail various forms of a penalty such as discrimination in the economic and educational activity, in the long or short term. Among other forms of discrimination is the inability to freely participate in the country's government (Article 21), since this will be limited to those "integrated to the revolution,"[1] in other words, to those politically trustworthy by the all-powerful Communist Party.

The Security of the Individual (Article 3) is in constant danger since the individual is completely helpless and defenseless, facing the overwhelming power of what is perceived to be an omnipotent and omnipresent State. The individual who perceives that it is legally impossible to oppose such a powerful entity is left with the alternatives of joining the oppressors, feigning allegiance to it, or trying to flee at any cost.

This omnipresent repressive situation also promotes a state of distrust and constant fear that often reaches the terror level. In practice, it can be said that Cuba is a terrorist state against its own people. This reality also helps explain the prevailing high rate of alcoholism, depression, and suicide, as a form of escapism from the totalitarian repression.

The general state of coercion suggests the presence of a new form of slavery (Article 4). In order to "domesticate" or "tame" those who show some form of actual or potentially rebellious leadership, can be subjected—depending on the circumstances—to all types of abusive treatment, from the traditional physical torture to the much more frequent refined and effective psychological torture. It is designed to break down the detainee, psychologically, and also to significantly hurt his family. Those measures can range from total isolation, losing all notion of time, to a faked execution. Some label this "white terror," which practically everyone experienced.

For those that have rebelled or have tried to actively oppose the totalitarian trend, if they did not perish in the attempt or were not executed, there has been a long and harsh political imprisonment, unparalleled in the hemisphere. "Cruel, inhuman and degrading punishment" (Article 5) has been used at various levels throughout the years in the Cuban "Gulag." These range from forced labor, not used since colonial times, to confinement in the "drawers" (very small cells where several are locked in). Cuban political prisoners have suffered incredible cruelty, extensive to their families. There are some political prisoners who were imprisoned for over twenty years. Since the late 1960s political prisoners have also the aggravation of not being recognized as such by the regime, in sharp contrast with the past. They are housed with common criminals, thus making their lives more miserable.

There are basically two systems of repression in Cuba: the direct and the indirect. The first one is mostly exercised by the ministry of interior, by way of state security; the National Revolutionary Police (PNR); the Department of Technical Investigations (DTI), and the

CDRs (Committees for the Defense of the Revolution, present at the city block level), and is mostly centered on specific individuals. The indirect repression is not centered on anyone in particular, but applies like a Damocles sword to the population at-large. This is exercised by the repressive nature of the social institutions such as education, labor, the economy, and the media along with the CDRs and all of the "Mass Organizations" (MO). This type of control takes place within the totalitarian socio-economic context, bearing in mind that the government is the sole educational and health provider as well as employer, where about 90 percent has depended on the State to earn a living.

State Security takes care of controlling the political dimension, while the DTI and PNR are normally in charge of common crimes, which includes the "economic" type. These entities are, in practice, police and judge, since the detainees' sentence has been determined before trial. The CDRs constitute the long arm of those repressive organizations, both for political and common crimes dimensions; spying on citizens' lives at the city by street/block level. They can meddle in the most minute details of the neighborhood life, including the private lives of citizens, in Orwellian "Big Brother" style.

The MOs attempt to involve as many individuals as possible in an organization. Its ultimate purpose is to promote the complete control of the individual, according to some occupational categories. The MOs start with the pioneers at the elementary school level, followed by the student organizations, the labor unions, the Women's Federation, and the CDRs. Membership in these organizations constitutes a first level of "political-ideological integration," a requirement for the legal advancement within that society. Also, said organizations constitute another avenue to control even the citizens' free time. On top of this must be added the Territorial Militia Troops (MTT), which exercise further control over individuals of both sexes, who are coerced into joining his paramilitary structure which will overlap the other repressive mechanisms.

The control of the individual can be better visualized at the educational and occupational levels. The most noticeable indicator of this control effort is found in two instruments, not well known abroad: the Cumulative Academic Record (CAR) and the Labor Dossier (LD). An examination of the CAR (modified recently) shows what looks like a detailed regular academic report card (years 1-12), containing the grades for each subject. But what has made the CAR so sinister (Article 12) are the sections containing the annual evaluation of the "political-ideological integration" of the student and that of his or her parents. It uses a numerical code system as well as a written description. It also inquires on whether the family belongs to a religious group and, if so, to which one. In this evaluation the CAR also probes on whether the student belongs to any MO and his or her level of involvement, assessing this way their revolutionary militancy and ideological trustworthiness. This instrument follows the student through the twelfth grade. This degree of political supervision actually makes the teacher, *de facto,* an important instrument in the repressive apparatus.

Likewise, the LD evaluates the workers' performance, emphasizing his/her political behavior, and will follow the worker until retirement or death. This LD also contains the individual's "merits and demerits," and "special notations." Religious activity, failure to attend labor union meetings, and failure to perform "voluntary labor" are examples of "negative" behaviors or "demerits" that are recorded. In both dossiers, the political record is paramount. It may be used, in the CAR, to determine whether the person may continue to higher education and the career path. The LD has been used to determine whether the person may have the right to buy in the past an important item such as a refrigerator, at a lower price, as well as to determine the worker's career advancement.

In addition to these dossiers there are other inquiries, popularly called *"cuéntame tu vida"* ("tell me your life"), used for work applications and other purposes. A great deal of information regarding an individual's personal life, including his political views is probed here.

It can be deduced from the previously stated facts that freedom of conscience and religion (Article 18) have been severely trampled on in Cuba. At best, there is relative freedom of worship, but not religious freedom, due to the constraints imposed on the religious denominations in terms of their operation. Religious practice was confined to the churches, since public manifestations (processions) had been rigorously prohibited until recently, when this restriction was relaxed. There has been a systematic and indirect repression in which discrimination has been applied against laypersons who are publicly committed to the faith. This has been applied to priests that don't "behave properly," in terms of being critical of the system. Religious services have been undermined in many ways. No Catholic churches have been built since 1959, and the government has made difficult the repairs of the existing ones, particularly in the interior of the country. Suspiciously, theft or damage to churches used to take place with virtual impunity, and great hypocrisy. In this way temples have been deprived of vital materials, very difficult and costly to replace. These actions have also promoted great fear within the faithful.

Clergymen have been harassed in various ways. They have been defamed or harshly criticized through the media, in movies and newspapers, portraying them in the worst possible image. There has always been an effort to create internal strife among the faithful communities. Likewise, there have been efforts to entrap the priest/minister in some sexual or common crime issue, to be used for blackmailing at the right time. There have also been mass and forceful expulsions, like the 131 priests and other religious clerics in 1961, along with systematic harassment designed to coerce other clerics (male and female) into leaving the country "voluntarily." In the case of foreign ministers, according to their behavior, they could be denied a visa renewal. Governmental policy against religion can be summarized in Castro's own words of the early 1960s when he said that his strategy with religion was to "create apostates, not martyrs." Jehovah's Witnesses have been particularly singled out, suffering actual persecution, having their Halls closed, imprisoning its members, and forcibly expelling many, like in the 1980 exodus.

Castro's government has sabotaged the charitable work of the churches, preventing and making difficult the arrival of humanitarian donations from abroad. It is also known that donations in food and medications, coming mostly from Europe have been sold for hard currency stores to be used in hospitals geared to foreigners and the ruling elite.[2]

Likewise, a few years ago *Cáritas*, the catholic international humanitarian agency, not legally recognized, tried to import directly powdered milk for free distribution. Not allowed to do so, the Church tried to buy it at wholesale prices, but were not permitted, having to buy it at retail prices at the government-owned "dollar stores." Currently, they have been forced to give the government a percentage of the donations received. Churches are not allowed the free entrance of ministers and supplies, all subject to strict control by the Office of Religious Affairs of the Communist Party. The Church has had to pay double the price charged to other entities on the special stores where they have to buy items. Churches had also been forbidden to give free medication received from abroad because "the Churches are not drug stores." Some of these controls have been relaxed in recent time.

Given the nature of the totalitarian system, and what already has been presented, freedom of opinion and expression (Article 19) is nonexistent in Cuba. Article 52 of the Cuban Constitution proclaims absolute power control over the media by stating that "state or social property, can in no case, be private property, thus securing their services for the exclusive use of the working people. . . ." In practice, and with a great dose of hypocrisy, all the media is an absolute monopoly of Castro and his party.

The right of freedom of education (Article 26) is flagrantly violated. Students can only receive the instruction provided by the Castro government. That instruction is ideologically tainted with political indoctrination in practically every course, besides the special courses in Marxism-Leninism that must be taken at certain levels. Although instructional opportunities (1-12 grades) have been extended throughout the island, this instruction is qualitatively limited by the poor preparation of the instructors.

Beyond high school, education has also been highly conditioned upon the individual's "political-ideological integration." This integration has determined whether the individual will be able to pursue the university level, since it is for revolutionaries. Those who are admitted, but lack the "political integration," most likely will not be able to pursue studies with strong political or social relevance, thus hurting the vocational orientation of the individual. This restriction also occurs at lower levels due to Article 38 of the Constitution, which dogmatically establishes that the goal of education is "the communist formation of the new generations" based on the "scientific conception of the world, established and developed according to Marxism-Leninism. . . ." In practice, as indicated earlier, all children—as in the former Soviet Union—are members of the *Pioneros*, designed to further control and indoctrinate on Communist-Castroist ideas from an early age.

Furthermore, the notion of a "free" education is highly questionable since it is contradicted by the fact that students have been forced to perform agricultural work on a permanent or part-time basis. Parents do not have the right to "choose the type of education that best suits their children," as established in Article 26 of the *Human Rights Declaration*. Due to the State's complete monopoly of education, this institution has been a very effective means of indoctrination, control (physically and ideologically) of the student and his/her family.

The factual evidence already presented clearly shows that freedom of assembly (Article 20) does not exist. On the other hand, it has been virtually compulsory to join one of the government-controlled "Mass Organizations" under the unwritten penalty of experiencing discrimination in one of the aforementioned forms.

Freedom of cultural activity (Article 27) is curtailed in many ways. This starts at the institutional level with Article 38 of the Constitution, which states that "artistic expression is free as long as its content is not contrary to the Revolution." In practice, since the government controls all media and print shops, this has reached dramatic and even laughable extremes when dissidents' and exiles' books and other "dangerous" literature have been withdrawn from circulation. All independent cultural activity is considered illegal. Access to books, films, and other cultural manifestations from other countries has been extremely limited, except to top members of the government elite.

The right of internal movement (Article 13) of Cuban citizens as well as that of free entrance and departure from the country has been systematically violated since 1959. In order for a national to leave the country or re-enter after living abroad, it is necessary to obtain a visa or government permit. Changing residence requires special permission, particularly if the moving is from the eastern provinces to Havana. This measure, in turn, also violates the constitution that guarantees the right to live anywhere in the country.

Article 16 promotes the integrity of the family. These realities seriously undermine family bonds and promote their breakdown. The absence of traditional moral values by the educational system also promotes promiscuity among the young, resulting in the widespread practice of abortion. The great scarcity and poor condition of housing created by the totalitarian policies also contributes to the family crisis, promoting the current very high divorce levels.

2. LEGAL RIGHTS

In 1971 the "anti-vagrancy law" was enacted, calling for imprisonment of one to four years. This law penalized those who wanted to work on their own, and not for the State. Likewise, at the end of the 1970s, a law that allowed incarceration of those people whom the authorities considered likely to commit some type of serious crime was enacted. This is a clear violation of Article 9, which forbids arbitrary arrests.

The sentences that have been imposed for political reasons have been extremely long. The cases of political prisoners who have spent over twenty years behind bars have been common. In the "Black Spring" of March 2003, with the crackdown on dissidents, one of the seventy-five arrested received a twenty-eight-year sentence for exercising journalism and taking pictures of socialist "eye sores" in the cities. Treatment in this Cuban Gulag has been well below world standards in terms of food, medical treatment, living conditions, and discipline as well as punishment methods.

Since 1959 the Castro regime has used a variety of deportation forms (Article 9) with the disaffected, promoting or imposing their departure from the island. Massive forceful deportations were used in September 1961 (priests and religious personnel) and during the "Mariel exodus."

Forceful internal deportation has also occurred. The outstanding example took place by mid-1960s and early 1970s with hundreds of small farmers from the Escambray Mountains (in central Cuba), who were expelled from their land, losing their possessions and being mostly resettled on the westernmost end of the island with the prohibition of ever returning to their land. This measure was taken to prevent the farmers' cooperation with the peasant rebels operating in that area. In 1971, Catholic priest Armando Pérez was deported from his home parish in Camagüey Province to Santiago de Cuba in Oriente Province. The reason was a never-proved connection with Catholic anti-Castro youths from that province that allegedly were distributing by mail pro-democracy and human rights literature that was considered subversive.

According to the Cuban Constitution, the courts are not (supposed to be) impartial or independent, thus violating Article 10. Likewise, in the said Constitution Article 123, Paragraph (f) states that one of the objectives of the courts is the establishment of opportunities to educate citizens on the cause of socialism. Moreover, Article 66 of the Law of the Organization of the Cuban Judicial System of December 13, 1978, specifies that to be a court president or professional judge, the individual must have "active revolutionary integration." In reality, courts are used to provide a facade of legality to the system, since normally those indicted have already been sentenced before trial. Thus, the role of the defense lawyer is normally limited to acknowledge the accused's guilt and merely ask clemency from the court. Lawyers that go beyond these un-written limits risk expulsion from the judicial system and even imprisonment.

Contrary to what was established in the *Human Rights Declaration*, in practice, the detainee is considered guilty until proven innocent, violating Article 11.

3. ECONOMIC RIGHTS AND SOCIAL WELFARE

The first of these rights, which guarantees individual or collective property (Article 17), is violated by Article 14 of the Constitution which prohibits private ownership of the means of production, because Cuba has "the socialist property of all the people." Confiscation of private property reached incredible extremes with the 1968 "Revolutionary Offensive," where even the smallest urban businesses were "nationalized" without compensation. This legal measure was repeated in 1986, and in the late 1990s with either the confiscation or forced closing of small family and individual-run urban businesses that had been permitted, such as the "*paladares*," small private family restaurants allowing only twelve seats and only family workers. Also, the remaining small family agricultural enterprises cannot decide what to cultivate nor dispose of their production. They must sell their production to the government, at their arbitrary prices determined by the state agencies.

Castro's massive confiscation of farms since 1959 created great scarcity, forcing the imposition in March 1962 of an unprecedented rationing still in effect. Significantly, the new ruling elite do not have to endure all the drawbacks of this system, as the rest of the population, since they are fully supplied by special providers.

Even with money, the average person has not been able to buy vital household appliances such as a refrigerator. These used to be offered through the places of work, provided that he/she earned the right to buy them on the basis of accumulated "merits." With the new "dollar stores" started in 1993, the possession of that currency became the determining factor to acquire those goods, but at very high prices, imposing great hardships due to the great discrepancy between the price of goods in dollars and the personal income in devalued pesos. It must be taken into consideration that the monthly average personal income is about four hundred Cuban pesos (about U.S. $17 at 24 pesos per dollar rate).

The right to adequate housing is very negatively affected as well, due to the totalitarian control over construction and materials. This is compounded by an acute lack of maintenance, due to the lack of materials, generating a huge degree of housing deterioration nationwide. Consequently, there is a constant collapsing of dilapidated multi-story buildings, particularly in Havana. These facts have led to truly miserable living conditions, characterized by overcrowding, generating family breakdown, and the great proliferation of shantytowns inside or around cities. To make life even more difficult, in addition to the terrible condition of housing, there is also the increasingly great problem of water supply, and power blackouts. All of this constitutes a real nightmare for the average persons but again, not applicable to the leadership elite.

Medical attention is one of the areas where Castro's government claims to have had the greatest achievement after the elimination of a good private system. Undoubtedly, there has been a geographic extension of this service. But those who have experienced the system by living there, and have used it, have harsh words for the quality of the medical service, particularly with medication. This has worsened since the end of Soviet subsidies in the early 1990s. No wonder the Cuban political elite received different and separate medical attention, much superior to that of the common citizen and similar to that of foreigners. This is why exiles have been sending, since the 1960s, great amounts of medications to their relatives.

Those who have experienced the past and present Cuban medical system disagree that it was necessary to eliminate civil liberties to allegedly "achieve," in the medical field, what other countries have accomplished without resorting to any type of dictatorship. After the end of Soviet subsidies the poor quality nationwide of medical care became shocking. Essential medications and equipment were utterly lacking. Another paradox along this line has been Castro's unlimited "generosity," sending doctors, medical personnel, and medications to foreign lands. This has greatly deprived Cuban people of this service and even medication. Unfortunately, it is known that some of the medications sent by exiles and foreign donations have ended up in special pharmacies sold for dollars.

Regarding the right to work (Article 23), Cubans have been forced to do so for the government, the sole legal employer. To enforce that regulation, Castro created special legislation to achieve that goal through the "law against vagrancy" and other measures. The right to create unions and unionize is prohibited. Those who tried to do so in the 1980s were arrested, escaping the firing squad due to international pressure. This meant that working on your own has been a crime. By 2010, and due to the great economic crisis, the government of General Raúl Castro has changed this norm, allowing some self-employment (*"cuenta propismo"*) in about seventy-eight minor occupations that will be heavily taxed and regulated. No professional careers were included in this sort of economic "opening" in response to the layoff of over 500,000 persons from the inflated governmental-economic apparatus.

Furthermore, it is important to remember that the Castro government has been "selling" for many years Cuban labor to other countries, where the regime receives the lion's share of the workers' pay. Likewise, in Cuba those working for foreign companies cannot be hired directly by them but through a government agency that has the monopoly of hiring. That agency also keeps over 60 percent of what those workers are paid in hard currency. This abuse and exploitation is possible thanks to the totalitarian nature of Cuba's socioeconomic structure, with its multiple inherent controls, as tentacles, but quite invisible to the foreign visitor, with very limited or no contact with the people.

The right to rest (Article 24), supposedly "guaranteed" by Article 44 of the Constitution, has been systematically curtailed. Cubans have been forced through the aforementioned repressive mechanisms to participate in the so-called "voluntary labor" (without pay). This has included work in agricultural activities to cleanup in their neighborhoods. On top of this, citizens are compelled to participate in the many other activities starting with the labor unions and continuing with the Mass Organizations, especially the CDRs. This will include all the marches to which they are convoked, and as if that was not enough, they have to spend much of their free time procuring the essentials for their families. Some believe that this exhausting kind of life is something deliberate to keep the mind of the people geared to survival, without time to think about subversive activities.

We can now conclude that the Cuban people have witnessed the disappearance of their path to a true realization of the rights and liberties proclaimed in the *Human Rights Declaration* (Articles 28, 29, and 30). All the rights proclaimed by the UN in 1948 have been violated in various degrees by Castro's imposed totalitarian system.

Since the dawn of hope for the enjoyment of liberty with democracy and social justice that Castro heralded at his arrival to power in January 1959, the country has seen itself sunken into a dark night of unparalleled economic exploitation, destruction, repression, intolerance, and discrimination against all who try to attain those rights and liberties. It cannot be overlooked the unnecessary suffering resulting from the inherently highly inefficient economic system, destroying what took over four hundred years to build by the diligent work and entrepreneurial ability of the Cuban people.

Today, the Cuban people seem to be telling the world about the urgent need for international support and respect for human rights in their unfortunate country. On February 23, 2010, the terrible death of political prisoner Orlando Zapata Tamayo—a humble young black mason—as a result of the eighty-three-day hunger strike, who was protesting the denigrating conditions prevailing in the Cuban *Gulag*, underscores the urgent need for that support. Likewise, the subsequent international exposure of the brutal treatment endured in April 2010, in Havana's streets by the Ladies in White (female relatives of political prisoners incarcerated in 2003), while peacefully marching in the streets requesting the freedom of their relatives, dramatizes even more the dire need of that support. Ultimately, the goal of Zapata, and others who planned to follow his example, is not only the concern for the prison conditions, but also the desire to see a genuine democracy with justice and respect of human rights for all.

NOTES

1. A person "integrated" to the revolution is the one who is a member in one form or another in the vast and complex totalitarian system. Integration will vary according to the level of leadership exercised by the person.
2. Based on research conducted by this author particularly in the 1990s.

APPENDIX V

THE CUBAN DIASPORA: BY THE NUMBERS

BY LEONARDO RODRIGUEZ

Before the Castro Revolution turned Cuba into a Communist regime, Cuba was a nation of immigrants. In the fifty-two years the Castro brothers have ruled Cuba; it has become a nation of emigrants. This is the story of their exodus to all corners of the earth, strictly by the numbers—a detailed accounting of the information provided in Chapter 15 that describes the *Cuban Diaspora*.

Table I presents the gradual increase of the number of Cubans in the United States as reflected by the U.S. Census Bureau in its last five decennial censuses.

Table II describes the progressive "Cubanization" of Miami. Various local, academic, and federal sources outline the successive arrival of the exiles to their preferred geographical location in the U.S.: Miami-Dade County in Florida.

Table I
Cuban Presence in the United States
1970-2010

U.S. Census Bureau	1970[1]	1980[2]	1990[3]	2000[4]	2010[5]
Total U.S. Population	203,211,926	226,709,899	248,709,873	281,421,906	308,745,538
Hispanic Population	9,072,602	14,608,673	22,354,059	35,305,818	50,477,594[6]
Hispanic Population as % of Total Population	4.5%	6.4%	8.9%	12.5%	16.3%
Cuban Population	544,600	803,226	1,043,932	1,241,685	1,785,547
Cuban Population as % of Total Population	0.26%	0.35%	0.42%	0.44%	0.58%
Cuban Population as % of Hispanic Population	6.0%	5.5%	4.7%	3.5%	3.5%

Table II
Cuban Presence in Miami-Dade County, Florida, USA
1960-2010

U.S. Census Bureau	1960[7]	1970[9]	1980[11]	1990[12]	2000[13]	2010[14]
Miami-Dade Population	935,047	1,267,792	1,625,781	1,967,000	2,253,362	2,496,435
Hispanic Population	50,000	299,065	580,994	949,000	1,291,737	1,623,859
Hispanic Pop. as % of Total Population	5.3%	23.6%	35.7%	48.2%	57.3%	65.0%
Cuban Pop.	24,400[8]	185,411[10]	407,253	561,868	650,601	856,007
Cuban Pop. as % of Total Population	2.6%	14.6%	25.0%	28.6%	28.9%	34.3%
Cuban Pop. as % of Hispanic Pop.	48.8%	62.0%	70.0%	59.2%	50.4%	52.7%

The next three tables outline the three sites in New Jersey which originally became home to a relatively large number of Cubans during the last fifty years. They are Union City (Table III) and Hudson County (Table IV), where the number of Cubans has decreased over time, and Bergen County (Table V), where according to the 2010 U.S. Census the number of Cuban immigrants has increased.

Table III
Cuban Presence in Union City, New Jersey
1990-2010

U.S. Census Bureau	1990[15]	2000[16]	2010[17]
Union City Population	56,573	67,088	66,455
Hispanic Population	42,884	55,226	56,291
Hispanic Population as % of Total Population	75.8%	82.3%	84.7%
Cuban Population	14,709	10,296	7,510
Cuban Population as % of Total Population	26.0%	15.3%	11.3%
Cuban Population as % of Hispanic Population	34.3%	18.6%	13.3%

Table IV
Cuban Presence in Hudson County, New Jersey
1990-2010

U.S. Census Bureau	1990[18]	2000[19]	2010[20]
Hudson County Population	553,099	608,975	634,266
Hispanic Population	183,465	242,123	267,853
Hispanic Population as % of Total Population	33.17%	39.8%	42.2%
Cuban Population	44,115	33,901	28,652
Cuban Population as % of Total Population	7.98%	5.56%	4.5%
Cuban Population as % of Hispanic Population	24.0%	14.0%	10.7%

Table V
Cuban Presence in Bergen County, New Jersey
1990-2010

U.S. Census	1990[21]	2000[22]	2010[23]
Bergen County Population	825,380	884,118	905,116
Hispanic Population	49,776	91,377	145,281
Hispanic Population as % of Total Population	6.0%	10.3%	16.1%
Cuban Population	6,984	9,381	12,708
Cuban Population as % of Total Population	0.85%	1.06%	1.4%
Cuban Population as % of Hispanic Population	14.0%	10.27%	8.7%

Table VI presents the official U.S. Census Bureau's figures of Cubans living in Puerto Rico. These numbers represent a decrease from the estimated 30,410 Cubans living in the island in 1971.[24]

Table VI
Cuban Presence in Puerto Rico
2000-2010

U.S. Census	2000[25]	2010[26]
Total Population	3,808,610	3,725,789
Cuban Population	19,973	17,860
Cuban Population as % of Total Population	0.5%	0.5%

The Cuban immigration to Spain has been documented by that country's decennial census, published by el Instituto Nacional de Estadística as well as recent newspaper accounts. Table VII discloses the fluctuations in number of the Cuban population in Spain since 1981 to the present.

Table VII
Cuban Presence in Spain
1981-2006

Spain's Census: Instituto Nacional Estadística	1981[27]	2001[29]	2006
Total Population	37,683,363	40,847,371	-------
Cuban Population	21,372[28]	25,797[30]	44,739

As the reader can surmise, Cubans which had never emigrated in quantity before 1959 continue to do so fifty-two years later.

NOTES

1. U.S. Census Bureau. Table A-5. Race for the United States, Regions, Divisions, and States: 1970 (100-Percent Data) and Table D-4. Hispanic Origin (of any race), for the United States, Regions, Divisions, and States: 1940 and 1970 sample Data (5-percent sample data Spanish Origin). Internet Release: September 13, 2002.
2. U.S. Census Bureau. Table A-3. Race and Hispanic Origin, for the United States, regions, Divisions, and States: 1980 (100-Percent Data). Internet Release: September 13, 2002.
3. U.S. Census Bureau. Tables A-1 and D-1, race and Hispanic Origin for the United States, Regions, Divisions, and States: 1990 (100-Percent Data). Internet Release: September 13, 2002.
4. U.S. Census Bureau. Census 2000 PHC-T-10. Hispanic or Latino Origin for the United States, Regions, Divisions, States, and for Puerto Rico: 2000. Table 1-US. Hispanic or Latino Origin for the United States: 2000. Source: Internet Release: October 22, 2001.
5. U.S. Census Bureau. "The Hispanic Population: 2010. Census Briefs. Table 1. "Hispanic or Latin Origin Population by Type: 2000 and 2010. Issued May 2011, 3.
6. Ibid., 3.
7. Planning Research Section Department of Planning and Zoning. Stephen P. Clark Center. *Demographic Profile Miami-Dade County, Florida 1960-2000*. Table 5 Population by Race and Hispanic Origin. September 2003, p. 10.
8. The Research Institute for Cuba and the Caribbean Center for Advanced International Studies University of Miami, Coral Gables, Florida. *The Cuban Immigration 1959-1966 and Its Impact on Miami-Dade County, Florida*. A Study for the Department of Health, Education and Welfare United States Government. Contract: HEW WA-66-05. July 10, 1967. Appendix B. Table 3 Cubans in Dade County 1960-1966. Estimated Total Cubans in Dade County Beginning of Year. See footnote #3 for Table 3.
9. U.S. Census Bureau. Table 2. Persons of Spanish Origin for Selected Standard Metropolitan Statistical Areas, Central Cities and Balances. 1970 Census, 3.
10. Planning Research Section Department of Planning and Zoning. Stephen P. Clark Center. *Demographic Profile Miami-Dade County, Florida 1960-2000*. September 2003, 8.
11. U.S. Census Bureau. Table 16 Total Persons and Spanish Origin Persons by Type of Spanish Origin and Race: 1980; 11-34.
12. Planning Research Section Department of Planning and Zoning. Stephen P. Clark Center. *Demographic Profile Miami-Dade County, Florida 1960-2000*. Table 6. September 2003, 11.
13. U.S. Census Bureau. Census 2000. Table DP-1. Profile of General Demographic Characteristics: 2000 Geographic Area: Miami-Dade County, Florida; 44.

14. U.S. Census Bureau. American Fact Finder. Table DP-1 "Profile of General Population and Housing Characteristics: 2010. 2010 Demographic Profile Data." GEO Miami-Dade County, Florida.
15. U.S. Census Bureau. Poll Hispanic Origin, 1990 Summary tape File 3 (STF), Union City, New Jersey.
16. U.S. Census Bureau. Census 2000. Table DP-1. Profile of General Demographic Characteristics: 2000. Geographic Area: Union City, New Jersey. Census 2000.
17. U.S. Census Bureau. American Fact Finder. Table DP-1, "Profile of General Population and Housing Characteristics: 2010. 2010 Demographic Profile Data. GEO: Union City, New Jersey.
18. U.S. Census Bureau. Table DP-1, Profile of General Demographic Characteristics for Hudson County, New Jersey: 1990, 1990 Census of Population Characteristics (1990 CP-1), and 1990 Census of Housing, General Housing Characteristics (1990 CH-1), reports series published 1992-1993; and Summary Tape File (STF) IA, series released 1991.
19. U.S. Census Bureau. Census 2000. Table DP-1. Profile of General Demographic Characteristics for Hudson County, New Jersey: 2000.
20. U.S. Census Bureau. American Fact Finder. Table DP-1. "Profile of General Population and Housing Characteristics 2010. 2010 Demographic Profile Data." GEO: Hudson County, New Jersey.
21. New Jersey Department of Labor, Division of Labor Market Demographic Research. General Demographic Characteristics: 1990 and 2000 for New Jersey Counties; 5/23/01.
22. U.S. Census Bureau, Census 2000. Table DP-1. Profile of General Demographic Characteristics: 2000. Geographic Area: Bergen County, New Jersey.
23. U.S. Census Bureau. American Fact Finder. Table DP-1 "Profile of General Population and Housing Characteristics: 2010. 2010 Demographic Data. GEO: Bergen County, New Jersey.
24. José A. Cobas and Jorge Duany, *Cubans in Puerto Rico Ethnic Economy and Cultural Identity* (Gainesville: University Press of Florida, 1997), 41.
25. U.S. Census Bureau. DP-1. Profile of General Demographic Characteristics: 2000. Data Set: Census Summary File 1 (SF1) 100-Percent Data. Geographic Area: Puerto Rico.
26. U.S. Census Bureau. American Fact Finder. Table DP-1. "Profile of General Population and Housing Characteristics: 2010. 2010 Demographic Profile Data. GEO: Puerto Rico.
27. Instituto Nacional de Estadística. Madrid, España. Censo 1981: Población: Resultados nacionales. Características sociodemográficas. Población por Tamaño de los municipios, Población de derecho y de hecho y sexo. Total Nacional.
28. Instituto Nacional de Estadística. Madrid, España. Censo 1981: Población resultados nacionales. Lugar de nacimiento. Población de nacionalidad Española por Ppaís de nacimiento y sexo. Cuba.
29. Instituto Nacional de Estadística. Madrid, España. Censo 2001. Population Figures 1-11-2001. Census 2001 Population figures by autonomous community and Provinces. National total.
30. Censo 2001. Censo de Población y Vivienda. Resultados Definitivos. Cuba. http://www.ine.es/censo-accesible/es.
31. Instituto Nacional de Estadística. Madrid, España. Revisión del Padrón Municipal 2006. Población extranjera por sexo, país de nacionalidad y edad.

CONTRIBUTORS

EDITORS/WRITERS

Pizarro, César. BBA marketing, Florida International University. Is a pioneer Hispanic marketer instrumental in the launch of *El Nuevo Herald* and its separation from the *Miami Herald*. Conducted many conferences in the U.S. as well as South America on advertising and how to reach the U.S. Hispanic market. Mr. Pizarro was also a board member of the International Newspaper Marketing Association.

Verdeja, Sam. Former publisher and CEO of Hispanic Publishing Group, and former VP of marketing services at The Miami Herald Publishing Company. Was associate professor at the University of Navarra, Spain, for twenty-eight years. Visiting professor, the Balboa Program, Madrid. Book author and speaker on media/marketing in more than forty cities. BS mechanical engineering, Louisiana State University.

Martínez, Guillermo. BS in journalism, University of Florida. Has been a journalist for half a century. Has worked in newspapers, radio, and television. He was a member of the *Miami Herald*'s Editorial Board and a senior VP of news at Univisión, the largest Spanish-language network. He is a syndicated columnist for the *South Florida Sun-Sentinel* and has lived and worked in ten cities in our hemisphere.

Kleinberg, Howard. He was the last editor of the *Miami News*. Joining the newspaper in 1949 he rose through the ranks and, ultimately, became its editor from 1976 through 1988. His twice-weekly column on national and international affairs for Cox Newspapers was distributed worldwide by the New York Times News Service into the turn of the century. Howard has written six books on South Florida history.

Rodríguez, Francisco (Frank). MA in economics, University of Miami, thesis "Economic Development of Cuba, 1902-1958." Columnist, radio/TV commentator, and producer. Related his experiences in Operation Pedro Pan in memoir *Pancho Montana*. English and Spanish editor at Simon & Schuster and Thomson Reuters. Originator of self-teaching courses *Auto Inglés,* Firmas Press.

O'Brien, Louise. MBA, Harvard Business School and AB cum laude in international affairs, Princeton University's Woodrow Wilson School. Served on the executive committee for two *Fortune 500* companies, most recently VP for business & technology strategy at EMC, and VP and chief strategy officer at Dell. Ex-contributing editor and author at *Harvard Business Review* and partner at Bain & Company Strategy Consultancy. Was appointed to the Board of Trustees for Princeton University.

Rodríguez Leonardo. BBA, MBA, University of Miami, DBA, Florida State University. Acting dean, College of Business, VP of business and finance, and professor emeritus of accounting, Florida International University. *Fulbright Scholar*. Expert in small business management with three books. Member of the International Accounting Standards Board (IASB) Working Group for Small and Medium Entities in representation of the Interamerican Accounting Association where he served as president and recently was named *Contador Benemérito de las Américas*.

WRITERS (alphabetical order)

Cancela, José. Was appointed president and general manager of KVEA, Telemundo, and largest affiliate in Los Angeles in 2011. In the business since 1979, Cancela was GM of several Univisión and Telemundo stations and managed the station groups for both companies. From 1998 to 2004, he was COO for Radio Unica. He was president of Hispanic USA Inc. from 2004 to 2011. Author of *The Power of Business en Español*.

Cepero, Eloy. Came to the U.S. in 1962 in Operation Pedro Pan, receiving a bachelor's degree from the University of Miami in 1971 (finance, history). He co-founded and was first president of Metropolitan Federal Savings & Loan and Peninsula Mortgage Bankers. He is a Cuban music historian and collector, ex-president of the Latin Builders Association and frequent lecturer, TV host, and book author.

Chao, Raúl. PhD, started chemical engineering in Havana, continuing at the University of Puerto Rico (BS) and at Johns Hopkins University (PhD). Professor, University of Puerto Rico, heading the School of Chemical Engineering as in the University of Detroit in 1977 before founding The Systems Group. Avid Cuba historian, author of *Contramaestre*, *Baraguá*, *Jimaguayú*, and *Guáimaro*.

Clark, Juan. PhD, professor emeritus of Miami-Dade College. His doctoral dissertation at the University of Florida was on the Cuban Exodus. He has conducted research, written several research papers, and held lectures in the U.S. and abroad on the exodus as well as on critical dimensions of living conditions under Castro's totalitarian system. His most important work is the 700-page book, *Cuba: Mito y Realidad, Testimonios de un Pueblo*, now in the process of being translated to English.

Connor, Olga. PhD, University of Pennsylvania, author of stories, *Palabras de mujer/Parables of Women* and of essays *Enciclopedia del español en los Estados Unidos, Español o Espanglish, 11 años sin Paz*. Ex professor of Spanish language and literature at Swarthmore College, University of Pennsylvania, Dickinson College, and University of Miami. Arts columnist, *El Nuevo Herald/Miami Herald*.

Curbelo, Jr., Carlos. Founder Capitol Gains, public relations firm based in Miami. Serves as member Miami-Dade County School Board. BBA and masters in public administration, University of Miami. Has worked as advisor in presidential, congressional, and gubernatorial political campaigns.

de la Torre, Rogelio. PhD, professor emeritus of Spanish and was chairman of the Department of Modern Languages and associated dean of the College of Liberal Arts at the University of Indiana-South Bend. Author of *La Obra Poética de Emilio Ballagas* (1977), *Gotas de Presente* (1972), *Ausencias* (1978), and *Las Joyas del Caminante* (2008).

Frías, Sonia. As a literature student in 1980, abandoned Cuba when her "plantado" father was freed after twenty years in political prison. In Miami directed weekly *Vida Social* in *El Nuevo Herald* from 1987 to 2000, when she founded *Socialite Magazine*. Not allowed to publish in Cuba, she is currently compiling material on her years of journalistic work in Miami.

Garrigó, José R. Banker. Held positions in many banks. Senior lending officer at Espirito Santo Bank (1994-1997), VP at Citicorp North America (1990-1994), senior VP at Southeast Bank (1989-1990) and at Nationsbank (1987-1989). President, Pan American Bank of Miami (1983-1987). In 1997 created J.R. Garrigó and Associates Business and Financial Consultants.

González, Armando. BS, mechanical engineering, Louisiana State University. Director of Engineering for The Miami Herald Publishing Co., associate professor, faculty of communication, University of Navarra, Spain. Visiting professor, the Balboa Program, Madrid. International newspaper engineering consultant. *El Nuevo Herald* opinion columnist.

Irastorza, Joseph. PhD. Born in Matanzas, Cuba. BS electrical engineering and MSEE, PhD management science and faculty at Georgia Tech. He was selected the top engineering graduate of the class of 1960. At Kurt Salmon Associates (U.S., Europe, Asia), he held positions of increasing responsibility, including principal, regional, and national director of Information and Business Systems Consulting, national director of its software subsidiary, vice president, and was elected to KSA's Board of Directors in 1993.

Justiniani, Federico. MD, professor of medicine, University of Miami School of Medicine at Mount Sinai Medical Center, 1990-2010. Created and directed the annual Pan American Seminar, 1975-2005, a five-day course in Spanish for Latin American physicians. Was awarded Teacher of the Year in 1998 and Laureate Award in 2000 by the Florida Chapter of the American College of Physicians. In 2002 received designation of Master of the American College of Physicians, one of only three Cuban exiles to receive this award.

Levitán, Aida. PhD, president, The Levitan Group, Inc., (clients Aetna, the Port of Bilbao, and the non-profit ArtesMiami, Inc). A nationally recognized marketing communications expert, she presided over the number one Hispanic advertising agency in the U.S. until 2005 and was president of the Association of Hispanic Advertising Agencies. She also directed the Cachao-Andy García concerts in Miami and in Radio City Music Hall, winning the PRSA Multicultural Excellence Award.

Martín, Roly. Miami Spanish-language sports commentator at Radio Caracol-WSUA and America Teve-Channel 41. He also worked at WQBA, WCMQ, Channel 23 Univisión, and 51 Telemundo. He is also analyst and sportscaster for the Miami Dolphins and the University of Miami.

Montaner, Carlos Alberto. MA, University of Miami. CNN journalist, publisher, syndicated columnist Spain/U.S./Latin America. *Doctor honoris causa,* Francisco Marroquín University, Guatemala. Visiting professor, San Francisco de Quito; Universidad de Ciencias Aplicadas, Perú; and Francisco de Vitoria de Madrid. Active in cause of Cuban freedom. Book author, nonfiction, *El Manual del Perfecto Idiota Latinoamericano*. Fiction, *La Mujer del Coronel*.

Murai, René. BA, Brown University, cum laude, juris doctor, Columbia Law School, managing editor at Columbia Law Review. He was awarded a Reginald Heber Smith Fellowship by the federal government and served as a legal services lawyer in Miami. Founding partner Murai Wald Biondo & Moreno, ex-president Cuban American Bar Association and Florida Bar Foundation, past chairman of the Board of Directors of Miami Children's Hospital.

Nodarse, Olga. Grew up surrounded by art in Matanzas, Cuba, leaving at sixteen as a Pedro Pan. She studied history and philosophy at Trinity College and International Political Strategy at Johns Hopkins in Washington, D.C. In Michigan, she opened an art gallery. In Miami with husband Dr. Raúl Chao founded the Cuba Corps, dedicated to the reconstruction of civil society in post-Castro's Cuba.

Ramos, Rev. Marcos Antonio. ThD, Central School of Religion, London. Has been a Baptist minister for forty years. Professor of history & Latin American studies, Florida Center for Theological Studies. Member of the Royal Spanish Academy and Royal Geographical Society of London. Author of fourteen books. Recipient of the Papal Cross *Benemerenti,* given to him by Pope Benedict XVI and the Vatican's State Secretariat.

Ríos, Alejandro. Film critic and Miami TV personality hosting América TeVe's *La Mirada indiscreta*. Spanish-language media specialist for Miami Dade College; sponsor of the *Miami Film Festival* and the *Miami International Book Fair*. Frequent commentator on politics, culture, and things Cuban, widely regarded as an expert on the Cuban film industry.

Rodríguez, Raúl L. AIA, architect and founding principal of Rodriguez and Quiroga Architects Chartered. Practice includes architecture, urban design, and interior design. Graduate of the University of Miami School of Architecture.

Rodríguez, René. M.D. Orthopedic surgeon. Presently chief of orthopedics at Miami VA Medical Center and assistant professor of orthopedic surgery at University of Miami, Miller School of Medicine. Ex-U.S. Army colonel, ex-president Spanish American Medical Society. Founded *Médico Interamericano*, the only Spanish-language medical journal.

Unzueta, Silvia M. At thirteen left Cuba in Operation Pedro Pan and reunited with family at twenty-six. Harvard University, MPA '83. Lived, studied, and worked in Spain (Canary Islands) and the United States. In Miami was assistant to the city manager and acting director of Miami Dade Parks Department and headed Miami Dade County Office of Community and Economic Development. Ex-national VP YWCA and other organizations.

Viciana, Enrique. Graduate from the University of Havana with a degree in public accounting. Before leaving Cuba in 1960 he was assistant controller for the Cuban Electric Co. BBA University of Miami. He held positions with Peat Marwick, Mitchell & Co as well as Ernst & Ernst. In 1970, initiated his own accounting firm and in 1986 incorporated under Viciana & Shafer, P.A.

Vilar, Alberto. In 1954 became a TV cameraman in Cuba's first TV station, Channel 4. He held different positions and by 1959 was director of programming and vice president. After leaving Cuba worked for NBC and ABC International and was instrumental in starting TV operations in Mexico, Argentina, and managing a TV station in San Salvador. He also managed a TV station in Caracas with the Goar Mestre organization. In Miami headed distribution and sales for The Miami Herald International Edition.

Zayas-Bazán, Eduardo. Professor emeritus, foreign languages, East Tennessee State University. He was chair of the Foreign Language Department (1973-1993). Co-founder National Association of Cuban-American Educators (1990) and was the first Cuban-American president of American Association of Teachers of Spanish and Portuguese (1995). Co-author and co-editor of eighteen books. Author of textbooks *¡Arriba!, Conexiones,* and *Fusion.* He is also the co-author of a historical novel, *El Pez Volador* (2007), English version *The Flying Fish* (2009).

INDEX

13 de Marzo tugboat, 181
Abadín, Ramon, 645
Aballí, Dr. Angel, 551
Abascal, Asela, 682
Abel, Rudolf, 96
Abela, Eduardo, 357
Abella, Dr. Alicia, 328
Abella, Rosa, 339, 620
Abislaimán, Rafael, 686
Abrantes, Gen. José, 221, 229
Abreu brothers (José, Juan, and Nicolás), 342
Abreu Felippe, José, 394, 395
Abreu, José, 571, 666
Abreu, Juan, 348
Abreu, María Luisa, 244
Abril, Dr. Alexis, 561
Acevedo, Miriam, 340
Acevedo, Norma (Niurka), 340
Acevedo, Plácido, 424
Ackerman, Dr. Lauren, 559
Acosta, Agustín, 508, 706
Acosta, Alex, 648
Acosta, Carlos, 441
Acosta, Dr. Gastón, 563
Acosta, Gustavo, 361, 367, 380, 381, 382
Acosta, Iván, 342, 392, 395, 406, 408, 523
Acosta, Pedro, 687
Ada, Alma Flor, 354
Adrian, Angelina, 203
Agramonte, Ignacio, 399, 619, 714
Agramonte, Roberto, 709
Aguabella, Francisco, 425
Aguayo, Jorge, 620
Aguero, Taimiris, 460
Aguiar Reyes, Roberto, 183
Aguila Yane, Silvio, 163
Aguila Yanes, Sergio, 163, 164
Aguila, Lourdes, 558
Aguilar León, Luis, 240
Aguilar, Amalia, 426
Aguiler, Alex, 581
Aguilera, Francisco Vicente, 704
Aguillón, Gerardo, 437
Aguirre, Alejandro, 489
Aguirre, Carmen María, 489
Aguirre, Dr. Horacio, 438, 489
Aguirre, Eduardo, 428, 666
Aguirre, Helen, 286, 438, 489, 612, 666
Agusti, Filiberto, 240

Alabau, Magaly, 392
Alarcon, Raúl, 509, 523, 546
Alba Buffill, Elio, 621
Albaisa, Adolfo, 593
Albarrán, Dr. Joaquín, 553, 629
Albright, Madeleine, 189
Albuerne, Fernando, 426
Alcalde, Emilio Oscar, 410
Alcantara, Reynier, 460
Aldama, Miguel de, 356, 704, 714
Aldrich, (Gaspar y Paquita), 438
Alejandre, Jr., Armando, 188
Alejandro, Ramón, 360, 375, 381, 382
Alejandro, Sergio, 437
Alemán, José Braulio, 27, 28
Alemán, José Manuel, 26
Alfaro, Xiomara, 422
Alfonso, Adalberto, 576
Alfonso, Dr. Eduardo C., 562
Alfonso, Gustavo, 694
Alfonso, Julieta, 520
Alfonso, Raoúl, 514
Alianza de Jóvenes Cubanos, 651
Allen, Richard V., 658
Allen, Woody, 413
Allende, Salvador, 132, 134, 136
Almeida, Adiaris, 441
Almeida, Dr. David, 564
Almeida, Gilberto, 673
Almendros, Néstor, 234, 404, 407
Almódovar, Pedro, 415
Alomá, René, 386, 393
Alonso, Alicia, 441
Alonso, Angel, 302
Alonso, Diego, 302
Alonso, Fernando, 440
Alonso, Humberto, 589
Alonso, José Raúl, 382
Alonso, Laz, 413
Alonso, Luis Ricardo, 338
Alonso, Manolo, 398, 405, 406
Alonso, Marcelo, 631, 706
Alonso, María Conchita, 413, 426
Alonso, Reinaldo, 610
Alonso, Virginia, 437
Altonaga, Judge Cecilia, 646
Alvado, José, 149
Alvarado, Juan Oscar, 17
Alvarez Borland, Isabel, 621
Alvarez Cepero, Pedro, 430
Alvarez Fuentes, German, 578
Alvarez Guedes, Guillermo, 408,

426, 510
Alvarez Lezama, Manuel, 377
Alvarez Mera, Manolo, 437
Alvarez Pí, Marcelino, 686
Alvarez, Alberto Inocente, 637
Alvarez, Carlos, 207, 460, 461
Alvarez, César, 648, 649
Alvarez, Chucho, 422
Alvarez, Dr. Manny, 519
Alvarez, Eddie, 494
Alvarez, Emilio, 605
Alvarez, Jr., Santiago, 123
Alvarez, Lissette, 424
Alvarez, Mario, 425
Alvarez, Odaimis, 460
Alvarez, Ralph, 329
Alvarez, Ricky, 316
Alvarez, Sr., Santiago 123
Alvarez, Tony, 424
Alzola, Concepción, 341
Alzugaray, Dr. Manuel, 561
Amador Rodríguez, Juan, 505, 506
Amador, Natacha, 437
Amaro, Blanquita, 398, 426
Ameida, Gilberto, 673
Amnesty International, 190, 216, 226, 228, 232, 234, 236, 240
Amorós, Edmundo "Sandy," 452
Andersen, Arthur, 604
Anderson, Bonnie, 519
Anderson, Howard, 79
Andreu, Héctor, 685
Angola, 138, 721
Angones, Francisco, 641, 652, 694
Annis, Dr. Edward R., 558
Anreus, Alejandro, 372, 376, 382
Anselmo, René, 511
Antinoo, Roberto, 392
Antón, Alex, 409
Antón, Dr. Annie I., 570
Antón, Dr. Manuel, 556, 562
Antonetti, Alina, 642
Antonio Bueno, Juan, 614
Añorga, Rev. Martin
Aragón, Uva de, 240, 339, 622
Arango y Parreño, Francisco de, 703
Arazoza, Carlos, 605
Arboleya, Carlos, 172, 279, 280, 281, 694
Arche, Jorge, 357, 382
Arco, Jorge Luis, 347, 348
Arcocha, Juan, 341, 349
Arcos Bergnes, Gustavo, 228, 243

Arcos Bergnes, Sebastián, 228
Areíto, 139
Arellano, Jorge, 498
Arenas, Pilar, 389
Arenas, Reinaldo, 342, 343, 351, 370
Arencibia, Manuel, 309
Argiz, Antonio L., 603
Arias, Luis, 184
Ariza, René, 340, 342, 393, 394, 395, 414
Armand, Octavio, 343, 349
Armario, José, 329
Armas Rayneri, Raúl de, 592
Armas, Armando de, 499
Armas, Jesús G. de, 381
Armenteros, Alfredo "Chocolate," 420, 422
Arnaz, Desiderio "Desi," 419, 501, 502
Arocha, René, 456
Arregui, Ricardo, 523, 524
Arrezábalaga, Tomás, 431, 432
Arriola, Joe, 318
Arrojo, Rolando, 456
Arroyo, Anita, 341
Arrufat, Antón, 340, 342, 390
Arteaga, Manuel, 90
Artime, Manuel, 39, 54, 58, 62, 86, 92, 98, 123, 148, 258, 304
Askew, Governor Reubin, 647, 658
Asociación de Contadores de Cuba en el Exilio, 601
Asociación de Ejecutivos de Cuba, 672
Asociación Interamericana de Hombres de Empresa, 672
Aspiazu, Justo, 419
Aspillaga, Magdiel, 411
Astaire, Fred, 420
Atkinson, Carl, 322
Augusto, 91
Aunón, Dr. Jorge I., 571, 569
Aunón, Dr. Serena María, 571
Averhoff, Carlos, 429
Avila Azcuy, Federico, 132
Aviñó, Joaquín, 669
Award, Azorín, 351
Azcárraga Milmo, Emilio, 511, 515
Azqueta, Jesús, 292
Azqueta, Norberto, 292
Babun, Lincoln, 305
Babun, Omar, 305
Babun, Santiago, 305
Babun, Teófilo, 305
Bacardí Massó, Don Facundo, 292, 593

Bacardi, 292
Bacardí, Emilio, 293, 618
Badía, Azucena, 299
Badía, José, 299
Badía, Joseph, 299
Baek, Jon Kwon, 459
Baez, Danny, 456
Baeza Flores, Alberto, 339
Bahía de Cochinos, 62, 68, 83
Bailey, Randall, 459
Bajo, Jaime, 431
Balado, Manuel, 432, 673
Balbona, Dr. José, 555
Balerdi, Carlos, 685
Ball, Lucille, 501
Balmaseda, Liz, 147, 497
Banderas, Antonio, 353
Baquero, Gastón, 338, 340, 347, 348
Baradat, Anthony, 544
Barba, Carlos, 513
Barceló, Antonio, 309
Barceló, Carlos, 308
Barceló, Roberto, 309
Barceló, Rosa, 309
Bardem, Javier, 344
Bared, José P., 573
Barker, Bernardo, 134
Barletta, Amadeo, 487
Barnet, Miguel, 351
Baró, Orlando, 284
Barquet, Jesús, 346
Barquín, Ramón M., 13, 18, 32
Barr, Jr., Alfred H., 358
Barrera, Dr. Francisco, 551
Barrera, Mario, 491
Barreto de los Heros, Berta, 94, 95
Barreto, Justi, 420
Barrientos, José "Pepe," 450
Barrios, Felo, 428
Barrios, Rogelio, 673
Barrocas, Alberto, 306
Barros, María Cristina, 514, 678
Barthes, Roland, 341, 375
Baryshnikov, Mikhail, 441
Bass, Benny, 448
Basulto, José, 189, 644, 651
Batet, Lilly, 430
Batista Falla, Victor, 340, 349
Batista, Eugenio, 588, 589
Batista, Fulgencio, 10, 33, 134, 224, 256, 340, 384, 469, 496, 501, 637, 716
Bauer, Steven, 412, 429, 521
Bauzá, Mario, 419
Beato, Dr. Cristina, 666
Beato, Dr. Virgilio, 563

Beato, Zoraida, 437
Bedia, José, 361, 381
Behar, Ruth, 484, 614
Bell, James "Cool Papa," 446
Bell, Regla, 460
Bellán, Esteban, 443
Bellapart, Juan José, 308
Bencomo, Mario, 361, 362, 381, 382
Bendixen, Sergio, 199
Benedí, Claudio, 240, 245
Benedico, Nelson A., 676
Benemellis, Juan F., 206
Benes, Bernardo, 138, 457, 683
Benítez, Víctor M., 574
Benson, George, 522
Berenguer, Alfredo, 143
Berg, Mette Louise, 251, 254
Bergen, Polly, 32
Bermello, Guillermo, 499
Bermuda, Ramón, 382
Bermúdez, Andrea B., 622
Bermúdez, Cundo, 265, 358, 381, 382
Bernal, Beatriz, 620
Berrios, Pepa, 387
Berroa, Jr., Ignacio, 429
Betancourt, Amaury, 282
Betancourt, Conchita, 437
Betancourt, Rómulo, 53, 125, 252
Betancourt, Virginia, 90, 95
Betancourt, Yuniesky, 456
Big Five Club, 676
Biscet, Oscar Elías, 201, 206, 724
Bissell, Richard, 57, 59, 60, 61, 64, 66, 68, 83
Black Spring, 201, 206, 230, 723, 724, 743,
Blanc, Giulio V., 371, 343, 372
Blanco Herrera, Ramón, 296
Blanco, Julio, 534
Blanco, Ray, 371, 372, 373
Blanco, Steve, 539
Blaya, Joaquin, 511
Blumberg, Stuart, 198
Boada, Joan, 441
Bofill, Ricardo, 243, 245
Bohr, Felo, 422
Boitel, Pedro Luis, 205, 223, 246
Boix, Magaly, 395
Bolet, Jorge, 435, 630
Bolívar, Natalia, 484
Bolton, John, 200
Bonachea, Rolando, 611
Boniato Prison, 218, 219, 221
Borges, Fermín, 342
Borges, Julio, 299

Borges, Mario, 129
Borjas, George J., 616
Boruchin, Oscar, 294
Bosch, Orlando, 136
Bosh, José "Pepín," 293
Botifoll, Luis, 170, 281, 349, 487, 639, 682
Boudet, Rosa Ileana, 395
Boudy, José Sánchez, 339, 341
Boveda, José, 513
Bowles, Dr. Steven, 415
Boza Masvidal, Bishop Eduardo, 90, 240, 472, 483
Bragado Bretaña, Reinaldo, 350
Bratton, Johnny, 449
Bravo, Ileana, 519
Bravo, Luis, 425
Bravo, Pablo, 675
Bray, Javier, 680
Brennand, Francisco, 593
Breton, Andre, 369
Brigade 2506, 60, 70, 96, 656, 719, 720
Brindis de Salas Baroque, Claudio, 417
Brito Avellana, María, 381
Brito, Silvia, 392
Brothers to the Rescue, 188, 207, 243, 537, 644, 651, 652, 663, 722, 723
Brotons, Elizabet, 192
Broward, Napoleon, 21
Brown, Ricardo, 514
Bru, Abelardo E., 326
Bucelo, Armando, 649
Buch, René, 392
Buchanan, Edna, 136
Bujones, Jr., Fernando, 441
Bujones, Sr., Fernando, 441
Bulnes, Nora, 499
Bundy, McGeorge, 68, 107
Buñuel, Luis, 367
Burdine, William, 21
Burke, Admiral Arleigh, 77
Burke, Elena, 415
Burke, Lena, 415, 429
Burke, Malena, 429
Burnham, Daniel, 587
Burton, John, 639
Busch, Wiliam, 340
Bush, President George H. W., 646, 661, 662
Bush, President George W., 199, 200, 202, 269, 313, 327, 330, 479, 508, 538, 612, 649, 664, 665, 666

Bustamante Sánchez, Carlos, 598
Bustamante, Antonio Sánchez de, 706
Bustamante, Luis "Anguilla," 446
Bustelo, Gregorio, 295
Bustillo, Oscar, 282, 439
Busto Ogden, Estrella, 346
Busto, Jorge del, 390
Butler, Dr. Madelyn, 559
Cabal, Raquel, 685
Caballero, Eduardo, 523, 546
Caballero, Elizabeth, 438
Caballero, Javier, 672
Cabell, General Charles, 71
Cabell, Néstor, 385
Cabell, René, 410, 426
Cabrera Moreno, Servando, 382
Cabrera Riesgo, José, 678
Cabrera, Emilio, 464
Cabrera, Gina, 405
Cabrera, Jorge, 429
Cabrera, Lydia, 343, 484, 623
Cabrera, Marcio, 317
Cabrera, Orlando, 644
Cabrera, Rafael, 451
Cabrisas, Jesús, 422
Cachaldora, Gustavo, 431
Cagnet, Félix B., 403
Cal, Mimi, 510
Calderín, José, 74
Calderón, Dr. Angel, 554
Calderón, Dr. Zoraida, 564
Callava, Leticia, 517
Calleiro, Mary, 441
Calveiro Leon, Ramon, 163
Calveiro, Roberto, 164
Calvo Martínez, Carlitos, 74
Calvo, Oswaldo, 387, 438
Calzada, Humberto, 381
Calzón, Frank, 231, 233, 240
Camacho, Jorge, 355, 359, 360, 367, 369, 370, 381, 382
Camacho, Margarita, 382
Camacho, Simón, 294
Cámara de Comercio Latina de los Estados Unidos (CAMACOL), 673
Cámara, Madeline, 346
Camarioca, Port of, 123, 125, 127, 128, 129, 131, 133, 135, 137, 139, 141, 146, 147, 259, 720
Camero, Cándido, 420
Camilo Furniture, 280
Camp Columbia, 31, 32, 34, 35, 256, 717
Campa, Miguel Angel de la, 637

Campa, Román, 673
Campanería Angel, Virgilio, 74
Campaneris, Dagoberto "Bert," 452
Campello, F. Lennox, 364
Campins, Rolando, 340
Campo, Pupi, 32, 420
Campos, Normando, 432
Canagham, Dr. Adrian Van, 565
Cancela, José, 501, 515, 517, 759
Candela, Hilario, 593, 594
Canetti, Yanitzia, 350
Canimar, 163, 356, 357
Cannavale, Bobby, 413
Cano, Margarita, 381
Cano, Miguel Angel, 431
Cano, Pablo, 382
Canseco, José, 445, 454
Cantero, Herminia, 610
Cantillo, Dr. Eulogio, 565
Cantillo, Gen. Eulogio, 31
Cañizares, Dr. Orlando, 565
Cañizares, René, 464
Cao, Juan Manuel, 178, 350, 518
Capablanca, Fernando, 283, 675
Capablanca, Raúl, 450
Caparrós, Ernesto, 403, 405
Capó, Bobby, 424
Capó, Carlos, 309
Capó, Luis, 309
Capó, Manuel, 309
Capó, Moravia, 244
Capó, René, 460, 461
Capó, Simón, 309
Capote, Ernesto, 385, 387
Capriles, Miguel Angel, 499
Carballo, Luis, 436
Carbó Menéndez, José, 429
Carbó, Ulises, 91
Carbonell Cortina, Dr. Néstor, 325
Carbonell, Dr. Ruben G., 569
Carbonell, Josefina, 666
Carbonell, Luis, 707
Carbonell, Manuel, 382
Carbonell, Nestor, 518
Carcas, Carlos, 414
Cardenal, José, 452
Cárdenas, Agustín, 359, 381
Cárdenas, Alberto "Al," 650, 666
Cárdenas, Dr. Armando de, 565
Cárdenas, Esteban Luis, 343
Cárdenas, Leo, 452
Cárdenas, Orlando de, 425
Cárdenas, Raúl de, 342, 386, 391, 393, 395
Cardinal Cushing, Richard, 96, 97
Cardona, Joe, 409

Cardona, Miró, 36, 63, 64, 78, 638, 718
Caridad del Cobre, 90, 471, 480
Carles, Maggie, 429
Carlos, King Juan, 266
Carmina, Rosa, 426
Carol, Irene, 499
Carpentier, Alejo, 435
Carreño, Alihaydee, 441
Carreño, José Manuel, 441
Carreño, Mario, 358, 359, 381
Carrera Jústiz, Ignacio, 593
Carreras, Guillermo, 591, 592
Carretero, Julio Emilio, 129
Carricarte, Mike, 305
Carrigan, Jorge, 395
Carrillo, Justo, 54, 78, 232, 675, 709
Carrió, Raquel, 393
Carro, Laida, 244
Cartaya, Dr. Orlando, 565
Carter, President Jimmy, 137, 138, 140, 144, 146, 150, 152, 153, 156, 164, 167, 168, 169, 176, 200, 201, 658, 660, 661, 723
Carulla, Ramón, 381
Caruso Cabrera, Michelle, 519
Carvajal, Félix "El Andarín" (The Hiker), 450
Carvajal, Javier, 591
Carvajal, Magali, 460
Casal, Julián del, 133
Casamayor, José "El Cepillo," 459
Casamayor, Luis, 545, 546
Casanova, José Manuel, 286, 661, 677
Casanova, María Julia, 386, 387, 388, 389, 391
Casas Regueiro, Gen. Julio, 724
Casas, Roberto, 657
Cason, James, 201
Casona, Alejandro, 389
Castany, Angelita, 437
Castañeda, Carlos, 491, 494
Castañeda, Leo, 422
Castellanos Taquechel, Jorge, 617
Castellanos, Dr. Agustín, 551, 555, 560
Castellanos, Jr., Agustín, 626
Castellanos, Marta, 438
Castelló, Humberto, 491, 494
Castillo, Amelia del, 341
Castillo, Angel, 494
Castillo, Dr. Pedro, 550
Castillo, Jerry del, 464
Castillo, Oilda del, 240
Castillo, Siro del, 162, 235, 694
Castro, Fidel, 5, 6, 11, 12, 13, 15, 19, 27, 32, 33, 34, 35, 38, 43, 56, 63, 66, 73, 86, 93, 94, 104, 113, 116, 129, 130, 132, 136, 138, 139, 143, 171, 175, 183, 203, 213, 214, 217, 232, 234, 242, 256, 260, 265, 283, 297, 300, 327, 331, 337, 353, 384, 385, 400, 411, 446, 451, 452, 467, 469, 470, 472, 481, 488, 552, 558, 578, 590, 636, 683, 709, 716, 718, 724
Castro, Humberto, 361, 362, 381
Castro, José L., 679
Castro, Juanita, 126, 180
Castro, Raúl, 13, 17, 91, 180, 203, 208, 223, 231, 716, 717, 718, 724, 746
Castro, Wenceslao "Laito," 431, 432
Caturla Pérez, Edgardo, 694
Caudill, Dr. Herbert, 473
Caula, Antonio S., 675
Cazorla, Roberto, 347
Ceasescu, Nicolae, 177
Cejas, Dr. Antonio, 91
Cejas, Paul, 270, 317, 658, 663, 680
Center for Human Rights, 241
Centurión, Dr. José, 550, 555
Centurión, Francisco, 682
Cepero, Eloy, 674, 759
Cervantes, Ignacio, 418, 436
Cervide, María, 437
Céspedes, Bobbi, 425
Céspedes, Carlos Manuel de, 356, 363, 704, 714
Céspedes, Carlos, 317
Céspedes, Francisco, 425
Céspedes, Jorge de, 317
Cevedo, Nico, 430
Chacón y Calvo, José María, 706
Chamorro, Violeta, 177
Chanes de Armas, Mario, 260, 721
Chao, Raúl, 759
Chapman, Alvah, 313, 611
Charleston, Oscar, 446
Chartrand (Esteban, Philippe and Augusto), 356
Chaumon, Faure, 17, 35
Chavez, Hugo, 54, 252, 413
Chaviano, Daína, 351
Chediak, Esperanza, 437
Chediak, Nat, 415
Chía, Enrique, 425, 580
Chibás, Eduardo, 11, 12
Chibás, Raúl, 12
Chiles, Governor Lawton, 663
Chirino, Willy, 52, 177, 264, 414, 427, 428, 707

Chocolate, Kid, 448, 449
Chorens, Olga, 424
Christian Democratic Movement, 54, 135, 241
Christopher, Warren, 150, 151
Cid, José, 341
Cienfuegos, Camilo, 17, 34, 35, 39, 79, 232, 717, 718
Cienfuegos, Osmani, 79, 80
Cifuentes, Ramón, 293
Cisneros Betancourt, Salvador, 704
Cisneros, Gustavo, 515
Claret, Santiago, 487
Clark, Admiral John, 75
Clark, Juan, 162, 231, 240, 245, 246, 254, 734, 759
Clark, Steve, 152
Claro, Omar, 465
Claver Carone, Mauricio, 669
Clay, Gen. Lucius, 97
Clínica Cubana, 289
Clinton, President Bill, 161, 184,194, 197, 210, 261, 270, 317, 571, 572, 644, 646, 650, 662, 663, 664, 722
Clinton, Secretary of State Hillary, 667
Coalition for a Free Cuba, 169, 659
Coalition of Cuban American Women (CC-AW), 244
Coalla, Hortensia, 437
Cobas, José A., 250, 254, 490
Cobelo, Armando, 349, 686
Cobo Sausa, Manuel, 341
Cobo, Arturo, 153, 156
Coca Cola, 576
Codina, Armando, 52, 263, 274, 312, 313
Codina, Francisco, 332
Coego, Cristina, 389
Coego, Manolo, 388
Coello, Roberto, 432
Cokes, Curtis, 458
Cole, Jean Paul, 429
Collazo, Aurora, 388, 389
Collazo, Bobby, 430
Collazo, Mirto, 89
Columbié, Ena, 350
Comité Cubano Pro Derechos Humanos, 243
Comité de los 75, El, 139
Concepción, José, 284
Conde, César, 516
Conde, Cuco, 464
Confederación de Trabajadores de Cuba, 8
Congo, 57, 126,
Conill, Alicia, 523, 526, 527, 541

Conill, Rafael, 523, 526
Connor, Olga, 334, 493, 760
Constitution of 1901, 363
Constitution of 1940, 10, 12, 22, 35, 278, 597, 636
Consuegra, Hugo, 359, 381
Consuegra, Sandalio "Potrerillo," 448
Conteh, Andrew, 207
Contreras, José Ariel, 456
Contreras, Orlando, 426
Coombs, Bertha, 519
Copado, Manuel, 589
Corbato, José, 593
Corbé, Eduardo, 387, 391
Cordo, Pepe, 428
Córdoba, Otto de, 498
Córdoba, Ricardo, 459
Córdova, Efrén, 620
Coro, Ricardo, 331
Corona, Manuel, 418
Corona, Rafael, 279
Corrales, Diego, 459
Corrales, José, 386, 395
Corratgé Ferrera, Salvador, 359
Corripio, Armando, 617
Corso, Cynthia, 179
Cortázar, Mercedes, 338, 340
Cortez, Raoul A., 511
Cortina, Humberto, 657
Cortiñas, Angel, 647
Corzo, Pedro, 409
Cossio, Vicente, 296
Costa, Carlos, 188
Costa, Tony, 309
Costales Latatud, Dr., 289
Coto, Dr. Manuel, 563
Cougat, Xavier, 33, 419
Coyula, Miguel, 411
Craig, Gregory B., 194
Craig, Meg, 37
Cremata, Alfonso, 385
Cremata, Lourdes, 382
Cremata, Raúl, 382
Crespo, America, 437
Crespo, Judge Manuel, 641, 645
Cristóbal, Mario, 460, 462
Crombet, Flor, 714
Cros Sandoval, Dr. Mercedes, 484
Cruz Azaceta, Luis, 360, 376, 377, 381
Cruz Varela, Maria Elena, 346, 350
Cruz, Carlos Manuel de la, 314
Cruz, Celia, 264, 353, 414, 422, 524, 707
Cruz, Juan Felipe de la, 133
Cruz, Luís González, 346

Cruz, Miguel, 425
Cruz, Nilo, 352, 391
Cruz, Zoé, 330
Cuadra, Angel, 339, 344
Cuban Adjustment Act, 128, 188, 640, 653, 657, 722
Cuban American Bankers list, 286
Cuban American Bar Association, 644, 762
Cuban American CPA Association, CPA, 602
Cuban American National Council (CNC), 675
Cuban American National Foundation, 169, 173, 179, 190, 242, 246, 262, 304, 307, 659, 660
Cuban Art Museum, 693
Cuban Banking Study Group (CBSG), 575
Cuban diaspora, Statistics, 253
Cuban Exodus Relief Fund, 173
Cuban Hebrew Congregation, 683, 684
Cuban Liberty Council, 292, 664
Cuban Medical Association in Exile, 557
Cuban Municipalities in Exile, 243, 244, 678
Cuban Patriotic Junta, 153
Cuban Revolutionary Council, 62, 76, 125
Cuban Women's Club, 682
Cubas, Gustavo, 535
Cubas, José Manuel, 523, 535
Cubas, Luis de, 449
Cubas, René, 463
Cubela, Rolando, 17, 35
Cuellar, Miguel "Mike," 453
Cuenca, Arturo, 361, 362, 381
Cuervo Navarro, Pelayo, 16, 717
Cuervo, José, 638
Cuesta, Tony, 139
Cueto, Alfonso, 296
Cueto, Joaquín del, 79
Cueto, Juan, 350
Cueto, Julia, 590
Cuevas, Rogelio "Roger," 612
Curbelo, Antonio, 425
Curbelo, Fausto, 420
Curbelo, José, 420
Curbelo, Jr., Carlos, 656, 760
Currais, Albino, 431
Currais, José, 431
Cutillas, Dr. Manuel Jorge, 579
Cuza Malé, Belkis, 337, 349
Cuzán, Alfred G., 631

D'Rivera, Paquito, 264, 428
Daire, Alberto, 321
Dalrymple, Donato, 196, 261
Damas de Blanco, 205, 206, 262, 723
Damian, Carol, 372, 380
Daniels, Robert, 450
Darío, Rubén, 335
Dascal, Carlos, 138
Dausá, Rafael, 182
Davidson, Eduardo, 423, 430
Dávila, Arlene, 522
Davis, William, 356, 357
De Grandy, Miguel (I and II), 437
Debray, Regis, 131
Delgado, Jorge, 593
del Castillo Cobelo, Yolanda., 430
Delgado, Jr., Manuel, 572
Delgado, Pepe, 421, 430
Dennison, Admiral Robert, 66, 75, 77, 82
DePalma, Anthony, 14
DePalma, Brian, 170
Destrade, Orestes, 454
Diálogo, 123, 139, 142, 222,
Díaz (Jorge, Ricky and Manolo), 430
Díaz Albertini, Luis, 523, 524
Díaz Ayala, Cristóbal, 424
Díaz Azcuy, Orlando, 592
Díaz Balart, José, 514, 518
Díaz Balart, Lincoln, 202, 268, 637, 657, 661, 663, 667, 668
Díaz Balart, Mario, 202, 205, 268, 664, 667
Díaz Balart, Rafael, 637
Díaz de Villegas, José Luis, 491, 494
Díaz de Villegas, Néstor, 343
Díaz Gravier, José Ignacio, 437
Díaz Lanz, Pedro Luis, 39
Díaz Martínez, Manuel, 348, 349
Díaz Masvidal, Alberto, 281
Díaz Oliver, Remedio, 321, 668
Díaz Pancier, Olga, 437
Díaz Quesada, Enrique, 400, 401
Díaz Rigaud, Glenda, 389
Díaz Souza, Eddy, 391, 395
Díaz Suárez, Tulio, 72, 93
Díaz Versón, Salvador, 341
Díaz, Alan, 196, 261
Díaz, Armando, 462
Díaz, Berta, 451
Díaz, Cameron, 412
Díaz, Carlos, 349
Díaz, Carmen, 350
Díaz, Cristóbal, 424, 487
Díaz, Dr. Nils J., 572

Díaz, Emilio, 412
Díaz, Félix, 146
Díaz, Gilberto, 421
Díaz, Guarioné, 187, 676
Díaz, Hiran, 430
Díaz, Irela, 679
Díaz, Jesús, 235, 349, 494
Díaz, Manny, 538, 664
Díaz, Manuel, 309
Díaz, Miguel H., 479, 667
Díaz, Norman, 504, 506
Díaz, Paul, 387
Díaz, Pedro Luis, 450
Díaz, Rolando, 410
Díaz, Servando, 424
Díaz, Sonia, 442
Díaz, Victor, 652
Diego, "Lichy," 350
Dietz, Johannes M., 593
Diez, Jr., Barbarito, 426
Dihigo, Martín, 445, 447
Directorio Democrático Cubano, 244
Directorio Estudiantil, 35
Dixon, William R., 578
Dodd, Senator Chris, 660
Domenech, Carlos, 323
Domíguez, Frank, 426
Domingo, Plácido, 438
Domínguez, Jorge I., 619
Domínguez, José Manuel, 396
Domínguez, Manuel, 677
Domínguez, Marcelo Fabián, 458
Domitro, Taras, 441
Don Galaor, 490
Don Pasante, 523
Dono, José, 428
Donovan, James B., 96, 98, 122
Dopico, Elvira, 611, 682
Doré, Sergio, 387, 389
Dorticós, Osvaldo, 39, 718
Doster, General Reid, 60
Douglas, María Eulalia, 403
Dovelpage, Teresa, 350
Dow Chemical Company, 577
Duany, Andrés, 594
Duany, Jorge, 250, 254, 490
Duarte, Carmen, 350
Duarte, Ernesto, 426, 430
Dubson, Vera, 694
Dubuffet, Jean, 360
Ducassi, Jay, 494
Ducassi, Nuri, 495
Dumé, Herberto, 386, 391
Dunn, Marvin, 160
Durán, Alfredo, 513, 517, 650, 658
Durán, Javier, 408

Durán, Roberto, 449, 464
Easton Poor, Alfred, 592
Ebro, Jorge, 465
Echemendía, Dr. Elsa M., 565
Echemendía, Oscar, 431
Echevarría Samson, Esteban, 412
Echevarría, Hermán, 544
Echevarría, Oscar A., 291
Echevarría, Rocky, 412, 521
Echeverría, Javier, 414
Echeverría, José Antonio, 16, 469, 589
Eco, Umberto, 374
Edel, William W., 622
Editorial Cubana, 281, 349
Edwards, Jorge, 132
Egozi, David, 306
Egozi, Moisés, 289, 306
Eguillor, Joaquín, 398
Egusquiza, Raquel "Rocky," 331
Eidenberg, Eugene, 152
Fire, Carlos, 353
Eiriz, Antonia, 359, 381
Eiroa family, 294
Eisenhower, Milton, 87
Eisenhower, President Dwight, 17, 37, 38, 42, 48, 56, 57, 58, 60, 61, 65, 719
Elgarresta, Mario, 658
Encinosa, Enrique, 129, 133, 136, 137, 450
Enríquez, Carlos, 357, 358, 382
Enríquez, Dr. Rogelio, 565
Entenza, Pedro, 341
Ermita de la Caridad, 480, 687
Escala, Father Rafael, 686
Escalante, Aníbal, 487
Escalera, José Nicolás de la, 357
Escambray, 45, 58, 61, 125, 129, 130, 743
Escandón, Teresa, 630
Escarpanter, José A., 390, 394, 395
Escobar, Vicente, 357
Escobar, Yunel, 456
Espín, Olivia M., 632
Espino, Herb, 510
Espinosa Chepe, Oscar, 201
Espinosa, Conchita, 610
Espinosa, Manuel, 147
Esquirol, Jorge L., 620
Esquiroz, Judge Margarita, 165, 647
Estefan, Emilio, 264, 427, 428, 545
Estefan, Gloria, 195, 206, 264, 427, 428, 429, 535, 545, 707
Esténger, Rafael, 340
Esteve Abril, Jerónimo, 307, 308, 672

Esteve, Jerónimo Miguel, 308
Estévez, Abilio, 348
Estévez, Bishop Felipe, 479, 686
Estopiñán, Roberto, 359, 360, 371, 381
Estorino, Julio, 678
Estrada Palma, Don Tomás, 708
Estrada, Fred, 499
Expósito Ulla, Daisy, 541, 547
Fabregas, Andrés, 593
Fábregas, Jorge, 454
Fabricio, Roberto, 492
Facts About Cuban Exiles (FACE), 170, 198, 382, 530, 693
Faget, Mariano, 207
Faife, Pedro, 460
Fajardo, Alberto, 437
Fajardo, José Antonio, 422
Falcón, Alina, 516
Falcón, Antonia, 184
Falla, Enrique, 579
Fana, Angel de, 245
Fangio, Juan Manuel, 451
Fanjul, José "Pepe," 292
Fanjul, Alexander, 292
Fanjul, Alfonso "Alfy," 292
Fanjul, Andrés, 292
Fanjul, Lian, 292
Farach, Irene, 422
Farís, Alexis, 508
Farrés, Osvaldo, 430
Fascell, Dante, 151, 661
Father Felix Varela Foundation, 686
Fe, Alfredito de la, 423
Febles, Diego, 451
Febles, Jorge M., 622
Feijoo, Lorena, 441
Feito, José, 593
Feldenkreis, George, 301
Feldman, Lew, 448
Felipe, Rosa, 387, 389
Fellove, Francisco, 425
Fernández Camus, Emilio, 341, 598
Fernández Ceballos, Rev. Raúl, 470
Fernández de Cárdenas, Gastón, 622
Fernández de la Torriente, Gastón, 622
Fernández Díaz, Aurelio, 604
Fernández Ferrán, Nivaldo, 192
Fernández Fox, Dr. Armando, 565
Fernández Haar, Ana María, 532
Fernández Larrea, Ramón, 348
Fernández Lima, Armando, 465
Fernández Mascaró, Guillermo, 641
Fernández Ortiz, Benito Antonio, 424
Fernández Porta, Mario, 430
Fernández Pujals, Leopoldo, 316
Fernández Rocha, Luis, 517
Fernández Rundle, Katherine, 639, 648

Fernández Selles, Julio, 296
Fernández Travieso, José, 342
Fernandez Travieso, Tomas, 73
Fernández, Agustín, 359, 360, 367, 372, 381
Fernández, Alex, 454
Fernández, Alina, 143
Fernández, Armando, 289
Fernández, Carlos J., 675
Fernández, Carlos, 604
Fernández, Carlos, 639
Fernández, Castor, 523, 527
Fernández, Clear, 382
Fernández, Damián, 619
Fernández, Daniel, 394, 395
Fernández, Dr. Lino, 40
Fernández, Enrique, 431
Fernández, Fernando, 602, 605
Fernández, Florentino "El Foro," 458
Fernández, Gilberto, 479
Fernández, José Luis, 130
Fernández, José, 331
Fernández, Laureano, 675
Fernández, Lázaro, 430
Fernández, Leopoldo, 316, 385, 386, 510
Fernández, Manolo, 424, 450
Fernández, Manuel A., 580
Fernández, Mario, 430, 674
Fernández, Mary Joe, 461
Fernández, Marzo, 450
Fernández, Mauricio, 340
Fernández, Mike, 303, 316
Fernández, Nancy, 323
Fernández, Néstor, 323, 432
Fernández, Osvaldo, 456
Fernández, Pablo Armando, 340, 351
Fernández, Raúl A., 630
Fernández, Raúl, 580
Fernández, Roberto, 491
Ferrá, Max, 392
Ferrara, Orestes, 291
Ferré, Maurice, 144, 150, 151
Ferreira, Ramón, 338, 341
Ferreiro, Julio E., 626
Ferrer Robertson, Piedad, 611
Ferrer, Dr. Horacio, 560
Ferrer, Dr. Olga, 560
Ferrer, Joaquín, 381
Ferrer, Mel, 412
Ferrer, Mercy, 437
Ferrer, Rolando, 393
Ferrer, Wilfredo "Willy," 648
Ferro, Simón, 650, 663
Ferro, Sixto C., 297
Fiallo, Sergio, 429
Fidelity National Bank, 280

Fiedler, Tom, 198
Fife, Rodríguez, 430
Figueredo, Perucho, 714
Figueroa, Luis, 641
Finns, Antonio, 495
Fisher, Carl, 22
Flagler, Henry, 21, 25, 313
Flay, Bobby, 300
Fleitas, Andrés, 448
Fleitas, Angel, 448
Flores, Martha, 387, 507
Florida Power and Light, 584
Florit, Eugenio, 340, 622, 623
Fondevila, Orlando, 347
Font, Pedro, 523, 530, 531
Fontana, Oscar de, 422
Fornés, Rosita, 405
Fort Brescia, Bernardo, 594
Forte, Orlando, 437
Fortún, Rafael, 450
Fossas, Antonio "Tony," 454
Foundation for Human Rights in Cuba, 242
Fowler, Raoul, 341
Fox, Arturo, 341, 346, 622
Fox, Martin, 431
Foyo, Feliciano, 682
Foyo, George W., 581
Frade, Right Reverend Leopoldo, 482
Franqui, Carlos, 232, 358, 368, 371
Franqui, Mario, 678
Frayde, Martha, 243, 349
Freedom Flights, 128, 134, 248, 259, 481, 600, 657, 720
Frente Revolucionario Democratico, 59, 62
Freyre, Ernesto, 90, 94
Freyre, Pedro, 198
Frías, Sonia, 760
Friol, René, 446
Fromm, Dr. Ernest, 558
Fuentes, Carlos, 344
Fuentes, Daisy, 520
Fuentes, Ileana, 392
Fuentes, Margarita, 54, 236, 652, 653
Fuentes, Tito, 452
Fuertes, Jesús, 437
Fulbright, William, 63
Fullmer, Gene, 458
Fumero, David, 520
Fundora Fernandez, Jorge, 91
Fundora, Ernesto, 414
Fundora, Jorge, 91, 605
G.I. Bill, 24
Galán, Juan, 296

Galán, Natalio, 435
Galiana, Pedro, 463, 464
Galindo, Josie, 518
Galindo, Maykel, 460
Gallagher, David Lee, 414
Gallardo, Frank, 145, 155
Galnares, Benigno, 687
Gamba, Olga, 639
Gamba, Tomás, 639
Gamboa, Yuriorkis, 450, 459
Gándara, Orlando de la, 672
Gandolfo, Laurene, 331
Garay, Sindo, 418, 424, 707
Garbey, Bárbaro, 455
Garcia Aguilera, Carolina, 353
García Bengochea, Francisco, 626
García Brake, Bernardo, 304
García Cantero, Raoúl, 647
García Cisneros, Florencio, 343
García Fusté, Tomás, 151, 505, 507
García García, Gabriel, 131
García Hernández, César, 155
García Linares, Manuel, 649
García Lorca, Federico, 393
García Marquez, Gabriel, 37
García Mendoza, Dr. José (Joe), 556
García Menocal, Mario, 23, 399, 636
García Pedrosa, José, 644
García Perdomo, Ricardo, 430
García Pérez, Jorge Luis (Antunez), 244
García Ramos, Reinaldo, 342, 343, 350
García Serra, Alberto, 534, 544, 545
García Sifredo, Armando, 490
García Toledo, Luisa, 680, 686
García Tudurí, Mercedes, 340, 622, 686, 687
García Vega, Lorenzo, 343, 349
García, "Chú," 491
García, Alfredo P., 620
García, Alina, 432
García, Andy, 195, 265, 338, 411, 412, 429, 537, 761
García, Bea, 494
García, Calixto, 286, 714
García, Cristina, 353
García, Dr. Mario, 496
García, Ernesto, 350, 391, 392, 394
García, Gay, 359, 381, 382
García, Hector, 437
García, Hernán, 360, 377, 378, 381
García, Israel, 322
García, Jesús "Raspuli," 437
García, Manny, 494, 497
García, María Cristina, 168, 617
García, María Victoria, 182

García, María, 494
García, Orlando, 307
García, Oswaldo, 617
García, Pedro Enrique, 613
García, Raúl R., 284
García, Reynol, 13
García, Sixto, 479
García, Vicente, 704
García, Victor Manuel, 567, 382, 707
Garfield, Dr. Sidney R., 554
Garrido, Alberto, 385
Garrido, Jr., José A., 642
Garrigó, José R., 282, 671, 672, 675, 677, 760
Garrote, Eugenio "Tito," 430
Gattorno, Antonio, 358, 382
Gaudie, Jr., A., 441
Gavilán, Kid, 448, 449
Gaviña, José, 296
Geada, Rita, 340, 623
Gerard, Juan, 415
Gibrán, Liliana, 389
Gil, Blanca Rosa, 424
Gillespie, Dizzy, 266, 419
Giral, Sergio, 410
Giraldo, René, 464
Gluckman, Dr. Earl G., 557
Goderich, Judge Mario, 638, 641, 647, 678, 680
Godínez, César, 421
Godínez, Manuel, 421, 431
Godoy, Gustavo, 142, 167, 512
Goizueta, Roberto C., 262, 325, 326, 479, 579, 621
Gómez Castro, Juan Orol, 403
Gómez de Avellaneda, Gertrudis, 356, 391
Gómez Mena, Alfonso, 451
Gómez Mena, María Luisa, 358
Gómez Peralta, Ismael, 382
Gómez Sampera, Ernesto, 589
Gómez Sicre, José, 358, 379
Gomez, "Tano," 26
Gómez, Andy, 208, 429
Gómez, Berta, 556
Gómez, Dr. Julián, 555
Gómez, Fausto, 694
Gómez, Fofi, 429
Gómez, Juan Carlos, 458
Gómez, Juan Gualberto, 706
Gómez, Miguel Mariano, 636
Gómez, Nilo, 430
Gómez, Orlando A., 307
Gómez, Preston, 445
Gómez, Víctor, 381
González Corso, Rogelio, 65, 85
González de Armas, Jesús, 361

González del Valle, Luis, 623
González Echevarría, Roberto, 623
González Esteva, Orlando, 344, 437
González Jerez, Raúl, 431
Gonzalez Levy, Sandy, 128
González Montes, Yara, 340, 345
González Rebull, Julio César, 487
Gonzalez Rubio, Eduardo, 508, 538
González Yanci, Pilar, 251, 254
González, Alberto, 385
Gonzalez, Armando, 486, 491, 760
González, Caron, 450
González, Celedonio, 341
González, Col. Emilio, 666
González, Dr. Justo, 482
González, Eddy, 432
González, Elián, 192, 194 197, 199, 200, 246, 261, 497, 664, 665, 723
González, Eloy, 673
González, Erwin, 645
González, Fredi, 445
González, Isolina, 244
González, José, 392
González, Juan Miguel, 193, 194, 195
González, Julia, 225
González, Justo L., 479
González, Lázaro, 194, 195
González, Luis, 92
González, Mara, 437
González, Maribel, 389
González, Maruja, 437
González, Miguel Angel, 445
González, Nelson, 581
González, Orlando, 344, 437, 454
González, Oziel, 17, 36
González, Santiago, 451
González, Tony, 449, 452
González, Virgilio, 134
Gorbachev, Mikhail, 175, 176, 202
Gore, Al, 199, 664
Goris, Jesús, 430
Gort, Willy, 694
Gottchalk, Louis, 419
Govín, Antolín "Chino," 449
Govín, José Manuel, 486
Goytisolo, Josie, 514
Gracia, Jorge J.E., 631
Graham, Bob, 150
Gran, Manuel F., 706
Granados, Georgina, 437
Grandon, Lenor, 161
Grandy II, Miguel de, 438
Grandy, Julie de, 389, 393, 395
Grandy, Miguel de, 387
Grau San Martín, Ramón, 11, 26,

50, 716
Grau, Ardón, 431
Gran, Dr. Francisco, 565
Gravier, Leonardo, 605
Gray, General Gordon, 75
Greene, Graham, 97
Greer, Jr., Dr. Pedro José, 561
Greer, Richman, 649
Grenier, Guillermo, 632
Griffith, Emile, 457, 458
Griffith, Melanie, 412
Grillo, Frank "Machito," 422
Grinberg, Gedalio "Gerry," 303
Gropius, Walter, 588
Gross, Alan, 207
Guanabacoa Prison, 225
Guantánamo Exodus, 184, 186, 188
Guardia, Colonel Antonio de la, 721
Guardia, Luis, 409
Guedes, Alvarez, 430
Guell, Luisa María, 426
Guernica, Alberto, 283
Guerra, Alma, 678
Guerra, Armando, 299
Guerra, Carlos, 441
Guerra, German, 350
Guerra, Juan Luis, 535
Guerra, Juan, 420
Guerra, Marcelino, 420
Guerra, Marcos A., 605
Guerra, Mirtha, 605
Guerra, Orlando "Cascarita," 425
Guerra, Pedro, 686
Guerra, Ramiro, 706
Guerra, Rey, 437
Guerra, Roberto, 300
Guerrero de la Torre, Ricardo, 156
Guerrero, Ibis, 156
Guevara, Ernesto "Ché," 13, 17, 32, 34, 36, 47, 113, 125, 126, 130, 131, 132, 256, 710, 717, 720
Guillén, Nicolás, 340
Guillermo, Félix, 518
Guillot, Manolín, 605
Guillot, Olga, 265, 425, 707
Guiteras, Dr. Ramón, 554
Gutiérrez Alea, Tomás, 400, 404, 411
Gutiérrez Menoyo, Eloy, 17, 35, 58, 125, 223
Gutiérrez, Bárbara, 234, 493
Gutiérrez, Carlos, 263, 327, 415, 665
Gutiérrez, Eglisse, 438
Gutiérrez, Enrique, 593
Gutiérrez, Hayna, 441

Index 773

Gutiérrez, Horacio, 437
Gutiérrez, Jorge Luis, 379
Gutiérrez, Julio, 430
Gutiérrez, Lino, 663
Gutiérrez, Manolo, 589
Gutiérrez, Mariela A., 623
Gutiérrez, Marta, 382
Gutiérrez, Maucha, 508
Gutiérrez, Pedro Juan, 351
Gutiérrez, Pincho, 449
Gutiérrez, Viriato, 292, 685
Guyón, Dr. Félix, 553
Guzmán, Leopoldo E., 329
Hackett, Buddy, 33
Hansel y Raúl, 427
Harris, Ana, 459
Häsler, Rodolfo, 348
Haza, José, 437
Hechevarría, Paquito, 421
Helms Burton Act, 189, 663, 722
Henriques, Adolfo, 283
Hepburn, Audrey, 412
Heredia, José María, 334, 696
Herman, Frank, 428
Hernández Catá, Uva, 339
Hernández Lisazo, Antonio, 439
Hernández Miyares, Julio E., 623
Hernández, "Pepe," 71, 262
Hernández, Alberto, 665
Hernández, Ambrosio, 518
Hernández, Angel, 462
Hernández, Carlos, 540
Hernández, David, 321
Hernández, Dr. Alberto, 563
Hernández, Dr. Frank, 560
Hernández, Dr. Ismael, 304
Hernández, Ernesto, 348
Hernández, Rafael, 424
Hernández, René, 420
Hernández, Ihosvany, 460
Hernández, Irma, 641
Hernández, Jackie, 452
Hernández, Jorge Luis, 148
Hernández, Jorge, 574
Hernández, Leopoldo, 342, 395
Hernández, Liván, 456
Hernández, Miguel A., 574
Hernández, Nicomedes, 678
Hernández, Octavio 284, 286
Hernández, Orlando "El Duque," 456
Heros, Roberto C., 627
Herrán, Manuel, 284, 299
Herrera, Carlos, 674
Herrera, Carmen, 359, 381
Herrera, René J., 615
Herrero, Miguel, 431

Herring, Hubert, 5
Hevia, Carlos, 78
Hialeah Hispanic Chamber of Commerce, 687
Hicks Eidson, Colson, 648
Hidalgo, Ariel, 245
Hidalgo, Fernando, 424
Hidalgo, Jorge, 517
Hidalgo, Orlando, 432
Hispanic American Bankers Association, 674
Hoed, Dr. Gladys, 563
Holtz, Abel, 284, 306
Hooker, Jr., John, 89
Horenstein, Sofia, 302
Hornedo, Alfredo, 487
Horta, Arianne, 192
Hospital, Carolina, 352
Howard, Winston, 458
Hoyo, Lisette, 539
Hoyos, Rodolfo, 422
Hoz, León de la, 347
Hoz, Mike de la, 452
Hudson, Cynthia, 516
Hudson, Ofelia Martin, 624
Huertas, Dr. Enrique, 557, 558, 559
Hunt, E. Howard, 134
Hurtado, Diosbelys, 459
Hurtado, Pupi, 523
Ibañez, Raúl, 454, 455
Ibarguen, Alberto, 493
Ichaso, León, 406, 408, 410
Iglesias de la Torre, Dr. José, 554
Iglesias Kennedy, Daniel, 348
Iglesias, Julio, 270, 515
Iglesias, Luis, 430
Illán, José M., 6
Incera, Vivian, 631
Inclán, Nery, 497
Inclán, Rosa, 610
Infante, Anthony "Tony," 279, 283
Inguanzo, Rosi, 350
Instituto San Carlos, 681, 682, 687
Interamerican Accounting Association, 601
Interián, Alina, 387, 389
Iñiguez, Dalia, 707
Irastorza, Joseph, 761
Iriondo, Andres, 189, 605
Iriondo, Sylvia, 189
Isasi Díaz, Ada María, 479, 633
Isern, Father Fernando, 479
Izaguirre Hornedo, Alfredo, 487
Izaguirre, Alfredo, 139
Izaguirre, Rosa Rivas de, 139
J. Finlay, Dr. Carlos, 551, 565
Jackson, Everett D., 132

Jacomino, Antonio, 605
Jaime Ortega, Cardinal, 206, 223
Jarro, Miguel Angel, 127, 128
Jarro, Sandra, 127
Jauma, Agustín, 428
Javits, Jacob, 96
Jerez, Magali R., 623
Jiménez Leal, Orlando, 406
Jiménez Leal, Orlando, 407
Jiménez Rojo, Patricia, 389
Jiménez, Bobby, 427
Jiménez, Frank, 650
Jiménez, Lucila, 316
Jiménez, Marc, 644
Jiménez, Marcos, 648
Jiménez, Onilda A., 623
Jiménez, Pedro "Pudding," 448
Jiménez, Yiyo, 490
John, Nank, 533
Johnson, Jack, 448
Johnson, Lyndon, 103, 125, 248, 640, 720
Jones, Dr. Ralph, 555
Jordán, Judge Adalberto, 646
Jorge, Antonio, 616
Jorrín, Enrique, 707
Joyce, James, 266
Junco, Dr. Tirso del, 563, 660
Juster González, Félix, 152
Justiniani, Federico, 761
Kadre, Manuel, 644
Kaiser, Henry J., 554
Kalusin, Enrique, 683
Kantor, Israel, 429
Kaufman, Hank, 415
Kefauver, Sen. Estes, 25
Kellner, Leon, 171, 172
Kennedy, President John F., 25, 43, 49, 61, 62, 64, 76, 87, 97, 99, 102, 104, 106, 108, 117, 120, 123, 169, 258, 572, 650, 656, 663, 719, 729
Kennedy, Robert, 96, 97, 104, 106, 107, 108, 112, 114, 115, 116, 117, 123
Khrushchev, President Nikita, 55, 97, 102, 103, 105, 107, 108, 109, 110, 111, 112, 113, 114, 115, 116, 117, 118, 119, 120, 123, 656, 720
Kirkpatrick, Jeane, 240
Kiwanis Club of Little Havana, 679
Kleinberg, Howard, 20, 56, 70, 85, 758
Kleinman, Ronald, 652
Klock, Joe, 644
Koh, Harold, 643
Kopel, Ted, 388
Korvick, Judge María, 647

Kravetz, Carl, 522, 546
Krieger, Alberto, 604
Kugler y Sardiñas, Isabel, 356
La Casa Cuba (Puerto Rico), 424, 681, 688
La Lupe, 415, 422
Labarga, Justice Jorge, 647
Labat, Tony, 414
Labrador Ruiz, Enrique, 343
Ladies in White, 205, 206, 262, 412, 723, 748
Lage, Carlos, 204
Lago, David, 347
Lagoa, Bárbara, 647
Lagueruela, Benito, 498
Lagueruela, Francisco, 498
Lam, Wifredo, 357, 358, 382
Lama, George de, 495
Lamela, Esteban, 518
Lancella, Pablo, 582
Landa, René, 341
Landín, Enrique, 510
Lanz, Otto, 498
Lara, Erislandy, 459
Laria, María, 512
Larraz, Julio, 382
Larrinaga, Armando, 430
Lasaga, José Ignacio, 686
Laserie, Rolando, 422, 426
Lasker, Emanuel, 450
Lastra, Dr. José, 550, 555
Latin American Business Association, 691
Latin Builders Association (LBA), 674
Lauro, Alberto, 347
Lauzurica, Roberto, 132
Lavernia, Rubén, 414
Lavilla, Fausto, 463, 491
Lázaro, Felipe, 347, 349
Lázaro, Raquel, 381
Lazo, Insul, 430
Le Riverend, Eduardo, 639
Leal, Aleida, 387, 508
Leal, Gloria, 491
Leante, Caesar, 348, 348
LeBatard, Dan, 465
Lecuona, Ernesto, 419, 424, 425, 434, 436, 439, 580, 707
Ledesma, Roberto, 422, 426
Leedor, Ellen, 683
Legarreta, Pupi, 423
Legra, José, 458
Lei Rodríguez, Cristina, 382
LeMatt, José, 437
LeMieux, George, 667
Lemnitzer, Admiral, 66

León, Dr. Gustavo, 235, 563
León, Jesús, 582
León, Jr., Benjamín, 263, 282, 289, 290
León, Rev. Luis, 479
León, Tania, 630
Lesnick, Max, 499
Letelier, Orlando, 136
Levin, Herb, 148, 151, 505
Levine, Robert M., 140
Levitán, Aida, PhD, 147, 522, 529, 536, 537, 678, 761
Levitt, Dr. Theodor, 543
Lew, Salvador, 505, 506
Lewis, John, 171
Leyva, Mario, 145
Lezama Lima, Eloísa, 589
Lezama Lima, José, 343, 354, 355, 369
Lezcano, Miriam, 395
Liber, Moisés, 289
Liceo Cubano (Union City, N.J.), 690
Lima, Jr., Robert F., 623
Lima, Orlando, 387
Lima, Ricardo, 583
Lima, Roberto, 346
Linares, Manuel, 341
Lismore Leeder, Ellen, 623
Lizárraga, Félix, 350
Llanos, Myrka de, 518
Llauradó, Adolfo, 405
Llerena, Rafael, 523
Llinás, Guido, 355, 359, 381
Llorens, Hugo, 552
Lobo, Galbán, 291
Lobo, Julio, 291, 331, 365
Lombard, Héctor, 460
Longarela, José "Pepe," 430
López Alvarez, María, 516
López Arenal, Yvonne, 392, 394, 395
López Camilo, 310
López Castillo, Eddy, 243
López Castro, Amadeo, 286, 675
López Dirube, R., 381
López Fernández, Dr. Osvaldo, 564
López Fernández, Dr. Fernando "Cuco," 553, 564
López Fresquet, Rufo, 709
López Graña, Antonio, 535
López Isa, José, 611
López José, 310
López Luis, 310
López Montenegro, Omar, 242
López Morales, Humberto, 347, 621

López, Ahmed, 460
López, Antonio, 430
López, Brook, 461
López, Dr. Alfredo M., 583
López, Israel "Cachao," 411, 426
López, Liliam M., 691
López, Luis, 280
López, Marcelino, 452
López, Nazario, 430
López, Peter A., 341
López, Robin, 460, 461
López, Sergio, 133
López, Vicente, 448
Lora, Miguel "Happy," 449
Loredo, Miguel A., 241
Lorente, René, 429
Lorenzo, Father Domingo, 257
Losada, Jess, 464
Losada, Jr., Jess, 464
Loto, Flor de, 424
Lowell, Mike, 454, 455
Lozada, Jess, 463, 464
Luaces, Lorenzo, 674
Lubumba, Patrice, 126
Luis, Carlos M., 340, 359, 369, 381, 382
Luque, Ada, 437
Luque, Adolfo, 444
Luz y Caballero, José de la, 356, 703
Lyons, Thomas, 136
Macau, José Adolfo, 17
Maceo, Antonio, 78, 356, 714
Maceo, José, 714
Machado Ventura, José Ramón, 204, 724
Machado, Arthur, 430
Machado, Dr. Miguel, 559
Machado, Gerardo, 23, 224, 304, 336, 384, 636
Machado, Gus, 308, 668
Machado, Manuel, 532, 544
Machín, Antonio, 419, 426
Machito, 423
Machover, Jacobo, 130, 624
Macías González, Leonel, 183
Macías, Miguel, 579
Madrigal, José A., 624
Madrigal, Roberto, 350
Madruga, María, 539
Maduro, Bobby, 446
Maidique, Dr. Modesto, 612, 611, 267
Makarenko, Antón, 405
Maleconazo, 722,
Mancini, Vincent, 265
Manet, Eduardo, 342, 391, 392, 393, 395

Manfugás, Zenaida, 437
Manglapus, Raúl, 240
Manner, Able, 187
Manolín (El Médico de la Salsa), 429
Manrara, Luis V., 239
Manzor, Lillian, 624
Mañach, Jorge, 336, 706
Mar, Anibal de, 510
Marañón, Richard, 538, 547
Marchant, Omar, 514, 523
Marchena, Eduardo de, 627
María, Farah, 426
Mariel Boatlift, 146, 151, 165, 166, 167, 171, 178, 248, 260, 315, 322, 343, 407, 408, 456, 518, 658, 721
Marín, Manuel, 315
Mario, José, 340, 349, 350
Mario, Luis, 619
Marques González, Aminda, 494
Marquet, Jorge, 91
Márquez Sterling, Carlos, 339, 619, 636, 678
Márquez Sterling, Manuel, 618, 706
Márquez, Juanito, 426
Márquez, Myriam, 494, 566
Márquez, Pedro, 431, 432
Marrero, Conrado, 448
Marrero, Dr. Ramiro, 687
Marrero, Elieser, 454
Marrero, Leví, 618
Marrero, Zoraida, 437
Marsán, Maricel Mayor, 350, 393, 395
Marsans, Armando, 444
Martí, Cristina, 389
Martí, José, 26, 28, 33, 41, 326, 335, 336, 343, 356, 384, 391, 435, 609, 619, 622, 625, 681, 682, 696, 704, 705, 709, 714
Martí, Tania, 437, 440
Martí, Virgilio, 423
Martín Oliva, Juan, 382
Martín Pérez, Roberto, 139, 234
Martín, Frank, 463
Martín, Manuel, 392
Martín, Mario, 386, 387, 391, 395, 438
Martín, Raúl, 392
Martín, Rita, 395
Martín, Roly, 443, 465, 761
Martin, Tony, 33
Martínez Barraqué, Carlos, 492
Martínez Calzadilla, Alcides, 241
Martínez Cañas, José Manuel, 382
Martínez Cañas, María, 361, 378, 380, 381, 382
Martínez Casado, Ana Margarita, 521
Martínez Corbalán, Javier, 349
Martínez Fariñas, Luis O., 627
Martínez Fonts, Alicia, 539
Martínez Fonts, Pedro, 579
Martínez Márquez, Guillermo, 151, 460, 489, 495, 678
Martínez Martínez, Manuel, 517
Martínez Sánchez, Augusto, 81, 91
Martínez, Alicia, 440
Martínez, Ariel, 489, 491
Martínez, Captain Jorge, 721
Martínez, Carlos, 491
Martínez, Edda, 316
Martínez, Eddy, 430
Martínez, Eduardo, 62
Martínez, Frank, 589
Martínez, Gilberto, 593
Martínez, Guillermo, 5, 492, 513, 515, 757
Martínez, Jorge, 286
Martínez, José Aron, 437
Martínez, Jr., Fernando, 677
Martínez, Juan, 357, 382
Martínez, Lisbeth, 437
Martínez, Mel, 52, 269, 665
Martínez, Orlando, 166
Martínez, Raúl, 150, 490, 657
Martínez Roberto, 644, 648, 652
Martínez, Rogelio "Limonar," 448
Martínez, Rolando Eugenio, 134
Martínez, Román (Roberts), 646
Martínez, Tomás, 510
Martínez, Velia, 521
Maruri, Dr. Carlos, 556
Mas Canosa, Jorge, 169, 173, 190, 262, 304, 307, 658, 659, 682, 662, 668
Mas Santos, Jorge, 307, 660, 665
Masferrer, Rolando, 135, 487
Masó, Fausto, 341
Masud, Félix, 449
Masvidal, Raúl, 283, 658, 659
Matamoros, Miguel, 707
Matas, Julio, 342, 346, 386, 390, 392, 393, 394, 395
Matas, Raquel, 645
Matheu, Leonel, 361, 362, 382
Matisse, 366
Matos, Major Huber, 35, 39, 135, 140, 240, 718
Matos, Manolo, 430
Matthews, Franklin, 522
Matthews, Herbert, 14
May, Marlene, 514
Maya, Yuniesky, 457
Mayo Azze, Alina, 518
Mayo, Ricardo, 304
Mayor, Agapito, 448
Maza, Manuel, 578
McCain, John, 666
McCarthy, Archbishop Edward, 479
McCormack, Isabel, 642
McDuffie, Arthur, 159, 160
McKinney, E. B., 307
McNair, Angus, 79
Mederos, Elena, 239, 709
Medina de Gaudie, Sylvia, 441
Medina, Jr., Angel, 282
Medina, Manny, 314
Medina, Miguel A., 617
Medina, Yoshvani, 391, 392
Medrano, Humberto, 233, 238, 489, 496
Meese, Edwin, 172
Membiela, Ñico, 422, 432
Mena, Carlos, 305
Mena, Hilda María, 305
Menci, Lourdes, 389
Mendes, Eva, 412
Méndez, Ana Margarita, 521
Méndez, Celestino G., 626
Méndez, Humberto, 431
Méndez, José de la Caridad, 445, 446, 447
Méndez, Julito, 510
Méndez, Silvestre, 425
Méndez, Vicente, 132
Méndez, Zaida Cecilia, 441
Mendi, Wilfredo, 422
Mendieta, Ana, 381
Mendive, Kike, 425
Mendive, Rafael María de, 703
Menéndez de Antón, Dr. Blanca, 556
Menéndez, Ana Acle, 497
Menéndez, Demetrius, 438
Menéndez, Julia, 389
Menéndez, Sen.Bob, 269, 661, 662, 663, 665
Menocal, Armando, 357, 707
Menocal, María Rosa, 618
Mercadal, Juan, 437
Mesa Lago, Carmelo, 616
Meso Pérez de Corcho, Silvia, 243
Mestre Benavides, José R., 598
Mestre, Goar, 268, 275, 502, 764
Mestre, Octavio, 605
Micheline, Jack, 340
Miel, Jr., Julián, 687
Mies Van der Rohe, Ludwig, 588,

593
Migoya, Carlos, 284, 562
Mijares, Dr. José, 563
Mijares, José, 359
Mikoyan, Anastas, 41, 471
Milanés, Dr. Fernando, 550, 555
Milanés, Fernando J., 627
Milanés, Jr., Dr. Fernando, 560
Milián, Emilio, 135, 508
Milián, Marilyn, 520
Milián, Pedro, 432
Milián, Raúl, 359
Miñoso, Orestes "Minnie," 444
Miranda, Armando, 428
Miranda, Fausto, 463, 464, 492
Miranda, Jesús, 252
Miranda, Jr., Guillermo, 307
Miranda, Juan, 456
Miranda, Marcos, 395
Miranda, Sr., Guillermo, 306
Miranda, Willie, 445
Miravalles, Reynaldo, 406
Miret, Germán, 686
Miró Cardona, José, 34, 36, 62, 63, 88, 99, 636, 709, 718
Miró, Joan, 360, 368
Mistral, Gabriela, 336, 623
Mitterand, Francois, 241
Miyar, Marijean, 374, 382
Miyar, Olga, 610
Miyar, Ramón, 598
Miyares, Ana María, 594
Moffett, Ronni, 136
Molina, Alejandra, 518
Molina, Alvaro G. de, 284, 330
Molina, Carlos, 437
Molina, René, 464
Moncada, 11, 12, 32, 93, 214, 217, 224, 228, 260, 470, 637, 716
Moncarz, Elisa S., 614
Moncarz, Raúl, 272, 325
Mondale, Walter, 151
Monge Rafuls, Pedro, 386, 390, 391, 392, 393, 394, 395
Montalvo, Niurka, 460
Montalvo, Rafael, 71, 92, 330
Montaner, Carlos Alberto, 240, 310, 341, 348, 349, 493, 496, 762
Montaner, Ernesto, 388, 490
Montaner, Lourdes, 388, 508
Monte, Chano, 423
Monte, Domingo del, 356, 704
Montenegro González, Augusto, 618
Montenegro, Carlos, 343
Montes Huidobro, Matías, 338, 340, 341, 342, 345, 386, 390,

392, 394, 395, 624
Montes, Ana Belén, 207
Montiel, Carlos, 430
Montoto, M., 437
Montoya, María, 518
Moore, Davey, 458
Moore, Henry, 368
Mora Adelit, Gerardo, 240
Mora, Alberto, 650
Mora, Dr. Modesto, 559, 563
Mora, Frank, 667
Mora, Menelao, 16, 717
Mora, Ricardo, 443
Moradillo, Dagmar, 441
Morales Bermúdez, Francisco, 144
Morales del Castillo, Andrés Domingo, 12
Morales Gómez, Manuel R., 677
Morales Padrón, Francisco, 5
Morales Pedroso, Leonardo, 587
Morales, Azórides, 627
Morales, Carlos, 604
Morales, César, 437
Morales, Kendry, 456
Morales, Manuel, 645
Morales, Pablo, 189, 460, 462
Morán, Francisco, 350
Moré, Benny, 707
More, Lester, 460
Moré, Reinaldo B., 583
Moreira, Domingo A., 297
Morelli, Rolando D.H., 350, 624
Moreno, Darío, 632
Moreno, Julio "Jiquí," 448
Moreno, Noelia, 674
Moreno, Odilia, 430
Moreno, Rolando, 391
Morera, Ralph, 603, 604
Morgan, William, 35, 36, 215
Morín, Francisco, 386, 389, 395
Morse, Captain Luis, 71, 89
Mosquera, Antonio, 132
Mothers and Women Against Repression, 243
Motherwell, Robert, 360
Motta, Iván, 323
Movimiento Revolucionario del Pueblo, 62
Moya, Jorge, 540, 543
Mujal León, Eusebio, 632
Mulens, Fernando, 430
Muller, Alberto, 686
Munar, Alfredo, 436
Munar, Ana María, 438
Munder, Bill, 523
Munero García, Lázaro Rafael, 192
Muñiz Cano, Dr. Reinaldo, 565

Muñoz Marín, Luis, 53, 250
Muñoz, Mario "Papaíto," 423
Muñoz, Raúl, 180
Murai, René V., 645, 720
Murano, Elsa, 612
Murray, Edward G., 621
Murrieta, Fabio, 349
Mussolini, Benito, 14
Muzaurrieta, José H., 675
Myers, Gwendolyn Steingraber, 207
Myers, Walter Kendall, 207
Nachón, Carlos, 322
Nápoles, Angel "Mantequilla," 458
Nápoles, José Luis, 465
Naranjo, Rafael, 241
Nasco, Jorge, 431
National Association of Agronomic and Sugar Engineers of Cuba in Exile, 685
Nava, Edernio, 465
Navarrete, William, 351
Navarro, José, 303
Navarro, Antonio "Tony," 331
Navarro, Armando, 387
Navarro, Minito, 464
Nespral, Jackie, 518
Neutra, Richard, 588
Nickless, Jim, 123, 258
Nieves, Luciano, 135
Nixon, President Richard, 38, 56, 134
Noble, Cecilio, 387
Nodal, Dr. Ronaldo, 556
Nodarse, Olga, 762
Nogueras, Griselda, 387, 389
Noval Cueto, José, 590
Novás Calvo, Lino, 339
Novo, Jorge, 432
Novo, Rogelio, 432
Nuez, Iván de la, 348
Núñez Pérez, Orlando, 341
Núñez, Ana Rosa, 339, 340, 620
Núñez, Dr. Armando, 565
Núñez, Elpidio, 297
Núñez, Vladimir, 456
O'Brien, Louise, 272
O'Brien, Soledad, 519
O'Cherony, Dr. Domingo, 564
O'Farrill de Secades, Julieta, 682
O'Farrill, Ela, 426
O'Reilly Herrera, Andrea, 254, 624
Obama, Barack, 204, 479, 666
Obejas, Achy, 353
Ochoa, General Arnaldo, 228, 407, 721
Ochoa, Leopoldo, 642
Ochoa, Manuel, 439
Ochoa, Rolando, 387

Odio, Cesar, 162, 172
Ojeda, Tony, 147
Ojito, Mirta, 139, 497
Oliva, (Carlos and Javier), 427
Oliva, Erneido, 86, 92, 95, 99, 258
Oliva, Tomás, 381
Oliva, Tony, 445, 447, 452
Oliver, Efraím, 593
Olivera, Armando, 576, 577
Olivio Jiménez, José, 346
Oms, Alejandro, 446
Operation Zapata, 70
Oppenheimer, Andrés, 204
Oquendo, Luis, 521
Oquendo, Tony, 514
Orbon, Jorge, 437
Orbon, Julián, 435
Ordaz, Everardo, 425, 426
Ordóñez, Rey, 456
Ordoño, Felipe, 498
Orefiche, Armando, 426
Organización Auténtica (OA), 13, 16, 35
Organization of American States (OEA), 47, 108, 190, 229, 243, 244, 663
Orizondo, Rafael, 518
Orlando, Felipe, 381
Orol, Juan, 403
Oropesa, Eddie, 456
Oroza, Ileana, 494
Ortega, Daniel, 177
Ortega, José "Pepe," 299
Ortega, José Antonio, 299
Ortega, July, 389
Ortega, Mike, 674
Ortega, Rafael, 460, 462
Ortiz, Fernando, 484, 706
Ortiz, Ramiro, 284, 450
Ortiz, Roberto, 448
Oswald, Lee Harvey, 123
Otero, Carlos, 518
Otero, Rolando, 135
Our Lady of Charity, 90, 687
Ovies, Jorge, 389
Oyarzún, Ramón, 314
Pacheco, Ramón, 593
Pacino, Al, 170, 412
Padilla, Heberto, 132, 240, 337, 340
Padilla, Martha, 340
Padrón, Captain Antonio, 721
Padrón, Eduardo, 267, 612, 680
Padrón, Rafael, 437
Paganini, Niccolo, 417
Pagés (Roberto and José), 430
Pagés, Germán San Miguel, 598
País, Frank, 13, 469

Palacios (brothers), 419
Palacios, Héctor, 201
Palenzuela, Fernando, 349
Palm, Dr. Cheryl, 573
Palmeiro, Rafael, 445, 454
Palmer, Eduardo, 406
Palmero, Miguel Angel, 430
Palomares, Carlos, 284
Palomo, Emilio, 124, 125
Pantín, Jr., Leslie, 679
Pantín, Leslie P., 304, 305, 672, 677
Pantín, Victor, 304
Parajón, Mario, 349
Pardo Castelló, Dr. Vicente, 550, 555
Pardo, Dr. Vicente, 550
Pardo, Victoriano, 627
Paredes, Frank, 603, 694
Paret, Benny "Kid," 457
Parra, Patricia, 387
Partido Auténtico, 11
Partido del Pueblo Cubano, 11
Partido Ortodoxo, 11
Partido Revolucionario Cubano, 11
Partido Socialista Popular, 487
Pascual, Camilo, 444, 453
Pascual, Carlos, 667
Passage, David, 153
Pau Llosa, Ricardo, 352
Paul II, Pope John, 175, 176, 190, 230, 267, 481, 722
Paul Le Riverend, Paul, 340
Paul, Pedro de, 387
Pavarotti, Luciano, 438
Paz, Luis de la, 342, 350, 395
Paz, Octavio, 344
Paz, Virgilio, 136
Pazos, Felipe, 675, 709
Pedraza, Silvia, 632
Pedro Pan, 51, 52, 257, 274, 312, 313, 317, 318, 478, 603, 645, 719
Pedrosa, Manuel de la, 406
Pedroso, Dr. Aldo, 564
Pedroso, Dr. Gonzalo, 554
Pedroso, Eustaquio "Bombín," 446
Peláez, Amelia, 357, 358, 382, 707
Peláez, Sister Armantina, 676
Pelleyá, José Luis, 651
Pellón, Gina, 359, 360, 368, 381, 382
Peña, Erelio, 674
Peña, Lola, 437
Peña, Mario de la, 188
Peña, Mario, 392
Peña, Orlando, 453
Peña, Oscar, 428

Peña, Pedro Pablo, 442
Peñabaz, Fernando, 508
Peñalver, Dr. Rafael A., 555, 562, 635
Peñalver, Dr. Rafael, 555
Peñalver, Eduardo (Stevens), 646
Peñalver, Manuel, 627
Peñalver, Rafael, 172, 651, 682
Peón, Ramón, 401, 405
Pepper, Congressman Claude, 661
Perdomo, Araceli, 493
Pereda, Lucy, 517
Pereira, Sergio, 148, 163, 166, 669, 676
Perenchio, Jerry, 515
Perera, Hilda, 232, 341
Pérez Arencibia, Demetrio, 613
Pérez Benitoa, José, 593
Pérez Castellón, Ninoska, 179
Pérez Castellón, Ninoska, 509, 665
Pérez Cisneros, Guy, 94
Pérez Cisneros, Pablo, 94
Pérez Crespo, Nancy, 343, 349
Pérez de Cuellar, Javier, 242
Pérez Firmat, Gustavo, 353
Pérez López, Aida, 225
Pérez López, Luis, 464
Pérez Mena, Luis, 604
Pérez Prado, Dámaso, 420, 425
Pérez Roque, Felipe, 201, 204
Pérez Rosado, Pedro, 415
Pérez Roura, Armando, 508
Pérez Samper, Dr. Luis, 559
Pérez Sánchez, Hilda, 179, 180
Pérez Serantes, Monsignor Enrique, 12
Pérez Stable, Eliseo, 628
Pérez Stable, Marifeli, 633
Perez Tamayo, Felix, 88
Pérez, Alberto, 674
Pérez, Anastasio "Tony," 266, 445, 447, 452, 453, 454
Pérez, Carlos, 298
Pérez, David, 593
Pérez, Demetrio, 490
Pérez, Dr. Juan de Dios, 565
Pérez, Eduardo, 454
Pérez, Failde Miguel, 418
Pérez, Father Armando, 743
Pérez, Faustino, 470
Pérez, Frank, 428
Pérez, German, 428
Pérez, Graciela, 419
Pérez, Guido, 628
Pérez, Ignacio, 322
Pérez, Jorge, 314
Pérez, Jr., Demetrio, 613

Pérez, Jr., Lombardo, 322
Pérez, Jr., Louis A., 618
Pérez, Lisandro, 414, 633
Pérez, Lombardo, 322
Peréz, Lou, 420, 423
Pérez, Louis, 522
Pérez, Luis, 464, 559, 604, 649
Pérez, Lydia, 225
Pérez, Manny, 437
Pérez, Marta, 387, 437, 438
Pérez, Mignon, 682
Pérez, Mike, 423
Pérez, Paul, 648
Pérez, René, 438
Pérez, Rubén, 431
Pérez, Sr., Demetrio, 678
Permuy, Jesús, 241
Permuy, Pedro Pablo, 664
Peruvian Embassy, 142, 143, 144, 145, 146, 147, 149, 153, 155
Picanes, Martha, 387, 389
Pico, Armando, 437
Piedra, Carlos M., 31
Piedra, Dr. Joaquín, 556
Piferrer, Germán, 429
Piña, Ileana L., 628
Piña, Juvenal, 431
Piñeiro, Miguel, 687
Piñera Llera, Humberto, 346
Piñera, Virgilio, 342, 390, 393, 395
Piñero, Alberto, 421, 437
Piñero, Federico, 385
Pinko, Tom, 198
Pino, Betty, 509
Pino, Marta del, 442
Pino, Rogelio del, 678
Pino, Sergio, 284, 674
Pinochet, Augusto, 134, 136
Piñon, Aramís, 431, 432
Piñón, Jorge, 331
Pinto Basurto, Ernesto, 143, 144
Pizarro, César, 493, 757
Placencia, Piedad, 611
Plana, José Antonio "Tony," 413
Plasencia, Jorge, 510, 545
Plater Zyberk, Elizabeth, 594
Playa Girón, 66, 70, 71, 73, 75, 82, 471
Playa Larga, 71, 75
Podhurst, Aaron, 652, 664
Poey, Dr. Federico, 575
Pogolotti, Marcelo, 358, 382
Pol, Pedro de, 508
Pol, Yesmani, 460
Pollock, Jackson, 360
Polo, Ana María, 520
Pómpez, Alejandro, 447

Ponce de León, Fidelio, 358, 359, 382
Ponce, Carlos, 428
Ponce, Daniel, 429
Ponce, Miguel, 386, 392, 393
Pons, María Antonieta, 426
Pons, Teresa, 437
Ponte, Antonio José, 348, 349, 351
Ponzoa, Eyda, 437
Ponzoa, Gustavo, 437
Popular Socialist Party (PSP), 39
Porro, Ricardo, 589, 592
Portabales, Guillermo, 424
Portal, Herminia del, 499
Portela, Ena Lucía, 354
Portela, Jesús, 674
Portes, Alejandro, 160, 168, 633
Portocarrero, René, 358, 382
Portuondo y de Castro, Dr. José Miguel, 556
Portuondo, Ana, 459
Portuondo, Manuel J., 296
Posada Carriles, Luis, 137
Posada, Jorge, 454
Posse Blanco Lindberg, Judge Denise, 646
Powell Cosío, Sofía, 651
Powers, Gary Francis, 96
Pozo, Luciano "Chano," 419
Prado, Pura del, 340
Presidio Modelo, 93
Préstamo, Felipe J., 615
Prida, Dolores, 340, 392
Prieto, Ariel, 456
Prieto, Elsa, 207
Prieto, José Manuel, 350
Prieto, Margarita, 389
Prieto, Peter, 649
Prieto, Susana, 441
Prieto, Yolanda, 249, 254
Prío Socarrás, Carlos, 11, 18, 23, 35, 304, 553, 597, 636, 716
Prío, María Elena, 651
Prohías, Antonio, 496
Puente, Tito, 422, 423
Puig, Claudia, 510
Puig, Ramón "Ñongo," 302, 510, 659
Pujol, Ernesto, 381
Pulido, Dr. Juan B., 564
Pumarejo, Gaspar, 502
Pupo Mayo, Gustavo, 493, 513, 515
Quesada, Gonzalo de, 706
Quevedo, Luis, 185
Quevedo, Miguel Angel, 40, 498, 499
Quílez, Alfredo T., 498

Quinlan, Michael, 172
Quintana, Luis Yiky, 465
Quintana, Nicolás, 589
Quiñones, José Dolores, 426
Quirch, Eduardo, 297
Quirch, Guillermo, 297
Quirch, Ileana, 389
Quiroga, Antonio, 591, 592
Quiroga, José Vicente, 387
Rabassa, Mónica, 510
Radio Martí, 163, 169, 171, 243, 347, 465, 496, 611, 659, 660, 721
Radziwill, Lee, 96
Ramel Prieto, Fidencio, 180
Ramírez, Alexei, 456
Ramírez, Felo, 447, 464, 465
Ramírez, Juan, 647
Ramírez, Julio, 329
Ramírez, Porfirio, 43, 605
Ramos, Eugenio, 306
Ramos, Felipe, 423
Ramos, Pedro, 445, 452
Ramos, Rev. Marcos Antonio, 138, 467, 476, 482, 762
Ramos, Ronnie, 495
Ramos, Tata, 425, 426
Ramos, Ultiminio "Sugar," 458
Rams, Martica, 421
Rankin, Mara, 517
Rasco, José Ignacio, 54, 349, 686
Rasco, Ramón, 284, 644
Ray Robinson, Sugar, 449
Ray, Manuel, 62, 78
Reagan, President Ronald, 167, 171, 175, 176, 241, 658, 659, 661
Reboso, Manolo, 657
Recalt, Eduardo, 442
Recarey, Jr., Miguel G., 318
Recio, Francisco H., 575
Recio, Max Borges, 589
Reclusorio Nacional de Mujeres in Guanajay, 224, 225
Red Avispa, 207, 208, 723
Reed, Major Dr. Walter, 551
Regalado, Raquel, 508
Regalado, Tomás, 128, 505, 508
Regato, Dr. Juan del, 559
Reguera Saurnell, Manuel, 393, 395
Reguera, Manolo de la, 463
Regueral, Delio, 260, 265, 266
Reich, Ambassador Otto, 666
Reinke, Bill, 152
Remos, Ariel, 236, 246, 489
Remos, Juan J., 706
Renedo, José M., 681
Reno, Attorney General Janet, 188, 194, 198, 664

Revuelta, Nati, 143
Rexach, Rosario, 341
Rey Pernas, Santiago, 678
Rey, Reynaldo, 440
Reyes Benitez, Lázaro, 74
Reyes, Dr. José Manuel de los, 563
Reyes, Enrique, 430
Reyes, George, 330
Reyes, Lily, 430
Reyes, Manolo, 517
Reyes, Modesto, 408
Reyes, Omar, 429, 439, 440
Reyler, Félix H., 683
Reynardus, Jorge, 523, 526, 527, 540, 543, 546
Ricard, Eunice, 428
Ricardo, Ricky, 501
Rickles, Don, 32
Rico, Jorge, 317
Rieff, David, 197
Riera Gómez, Eliseo, 28, 673
Riera, Carmen, 439
Riera, Julia, 430
Rigondeaux, Guillermo, 450, 459
Río, Elizabeth del, 424, 437
Río, Frank del, 319
Río, Jorge del, 183
Ríos, Alejandro, 350, 351, 398, 763
Ríos, Rubén, 430
Ripoll, Carlos, 240, 245, 343, 384, 624
Rivelles, Amparo, 389
Rivera, David, 268, 668
Rivera, Lacho, 429
Riverend, Paul Le, 340
Rivero Aguero, Andrés, 678
Rivero, Eliana, 625
Rivero, Facundo, 430
Rivero, Isel, 338, 340, 347
Rivero, José Ignacio, 489
Rivero, Nicolás, 486
Rivero, Raúl, 201, 235, 348
Rivero, Zoraida, 430
Riverón, Alberto, 462
Riverón, Dr. Ramón, 26
Riverón, George, 350
Rizzo, Marco, 420, 436
Roa, Dr. Raoul, 67
Robin Hood, 15
Roblán, Armando, 385
Robreño, Carlos, 487
Robreño, Eduardo, 646
Roca, Juan, 386, 391, 392, 393
Rocamora, Dr. Héctor, 551, 555
Rodaz, John, 388
Rodríguez Aragón, Roberto, 678
Rodríguez Cabo, Carlos, 73

Rodríguez Díaz, Dr. Antonio, 551
Rodríguez Fariñas, Dr. Julio, 564
Rodríguez Ichaso, Mario, 410
Rodríguez Kábana, Rodrigo, 569, 614
Rodríguez López, Efrén, 73
Rodríguez Molina, Dr. Félix, 553
Rodríguez Pérez, José, 132
Rodríguez Pérez, Manuel, 576
Rodríguez Pouget, Dr. René, 565
Rodríguez Ravelo, Filiberto, 74
Rodríguez Saludes, Omar, 201
Rodríguez Santana, Carlos, 60
Rodríguez Sardiñas, Orlando "Rossardi," 338
Rodríguez Sigler, Hiram, 491
Rodríguez Vives, Arturo, 135
Rodríguez Zaldívar, Rodolfo, 490
Rodríguez, Albita, 429
Rodríguez, Alfredo, 427
Rodríguez, Angel "Tito," 465
Rodríguez, Antonio Orlando, 351
Rodríguez, Antonio, 576, 577
Rodríguez, Arsenio, 420, 422
Rodríguez, Arturo, 381
Rodríguez, Dagoberto, 201
Rodríguez, Dinorah de Jesús, 414
Rodríguez, Douglas, 315, 316
Rodríguez, Dr. Héctor, 558
Rodríguez, Dr. Ortelio, 563
Rodríguez, Dr. Raoul, 563
Rodríguez, Dr. René F., 565
Rodríguez, Elio, 428
Rodríguez, Elliott, 519
Rodríguez, Ernesto J., 583
Rodríguez, Felix, 130, 131
Rodríguez, Fernando, 281, 300
Rodríguez, Francisco (Frank), 278, 288, 312, 325, 384
Rodríguez, Frank (Ford), 322
Rodríguez, Isidoro, 299
Rodríguez, Jennifer, 460, 461
Rodríguez, Jorge, 505, 508
Rodríguez, José Cipriano, 257
Rodríguez, Juan Alberto, 145
Rodríguez, Laurentino, 491
Rodríguez, Lázaro, 462
Rodríguez, Leonardo, 31, 278, 288, 312, 325, 596, 602, 716, 725, 731, 749, 758
Rodríguez, Lucrecia, 244
Rodríguez, Luis David, 491
Rodríguez, Luis Manuel, 458
Rodríguez, Maggie, 519
Rodríguez, Manuel "Manny," 694
Rodríguez, Marcos "Shakey," 462
Rodríguez, Marcos, 510

Rodríguez, María Teresa, 590
Rodríguez, Mariano, 358, 382
Rodríguez, Mike, 517
Rodríguez, Omar, 315
Rodríguez, Oscar, 679
Rodríguez, Raúl L., 587, 763
Rodríguez, Ray, 270, 515, 517, 679
Rodríguez, Rene, 147, 763
Rodríguez, Silvia, 523
Rodríguez, Teresa, 514
Rodríguez, Torres, Dr. Ramón, 561
Rodríguez, Vicente P., 490, 491, 687
Roig Rodríguez, José, 132
Roig, Vicky, 426
Rojas, Gustavo, 427
Rojas, Jorge, 494
Rojas, José, 459
Rojas, Octavio "Cookie," 444, 445, 452
Rojas, Orlando, 410, 692
Rojas, Rafael, 348, 349, 618
Rojas, Teresa María, 339, 387, 391, 394, 395
Roldán, Dr. Eneida O., 561, 562
Román, Msgr. Agustín, 171, 172, 240, 267, 387, 472, 479, 682, 687
Román, Pedro, 385, 421, 437
Román, Pico, 89
Romani, Salvador, 491
Romañach, Leopoldo, 357, 707
Romañach, Mario, 589
Romero, Carlos, 491
Romeu, Antonio María, 418
Romney, Hervin A. R., 594
Roosevelt, Eleanor, 87, 88
Roque, Cary, 389
Roque, Juan Pablo, 207
Roque, Martha Beatriz, 201
Ros Lethinen, Ileana, 202, 268, 657, 661, 663, 667, 668
Ros, Alberto, 685
Ros, Enrique, 124
Rosa, Pili de la, 387
Rosabal, Sylvia, 516
Rosado, Lillian, 415
Rosales, Maritza, 405
Rosell, Rosendo, 385, 430
Roseñada, José M., 487
Ross, Alvin, 136
Ross, Stephen M., 314
Rossardi, Orlando, 395
Rossenfeld, Humberto, 389
Rostow, W. W., 7
Roth, Jeffrey R., 198
Rovira, Lourdes, 610
Rubio, Al, 28
Rubio, Lydia, 360, 361, 367, 374,

Revuelta, Nati, 143
Rexach, Rosario, 341
Rey Pernas, Santiago, 678
Rey, Reynaldo, 440
Reyes Benitez, Lázaro, 74
Reyes, Dr. José Manuel de los, 563
Reyes, Enrique, 430
Reyes, George, 330
Reyes, Lily, 430
Reyes, Manolo, 517
Reyes, Modesto, 408
Reyes, Omar, 429, 439, 440
Reyler, Félix H., 683
Reynardus, Jorge, 523, 526, 527, 540, 543, 546
Ricard, Eunice, 428
Ricardo, Ricky, 501
Rickles, Don, 32
Rico, Jorge, 317
Rieff, David, 197
Riera Gómez, Eliseo, 28, 673
Riera, Carmen, 439
Riera, Julia, 430
Rigondeaux, Guillermo, 450, 459
Río, Elizabeth del, 424, 437
Río, Frank del, 319
Río, Jorge del, 183
Ríos, Alejandro, 350, 351, 398, 763
Ríos, Rubén, 430
Ripoll, Carlos, 240, 245, 343, 384, 624
Rivelles, Amparo, 389
Rivera, David, 268, 668
Rivera, Lacho, 429
Riverend, Paul Le, 340
Rivero Aguero, Andrés, 678
Rivero, Eliana, 625
Rivero, Facundo, 430
Rivero, Isel, 338, 340, 347
Rivero, José Ignacio, 489
Rivero, Nicolás, 486
Rivero, Raúl, 201, 235, 348
Rivero, Zoraida, 430
Riverón, Alberto, 462
Riverón, Dr. Ramón, 26
Riverón, George, 350
Rizzo, Marco, 420, 436
Roa, Dr. Raoul, 67
Robin Hood, 15
Roblán, Armando, 385
Robreño, Carlos, 487
Robreño, Eduardo, 646
Roca, Juan, 386, 391, 392, 393
Rocamora, Dr. Héctor, 551, 555
Rodaz, John, 388
Rodríguez Aragón, Roberto, 678
Rodríguez Cabo, Carlos, 73

Rodríguez Díaz, Dr. Antonio, 551
Rodríguez Fariñas, Dr. Julio, 564
Rodríguez Ichaso, Mario, 410
Rodríguez Kábana, Rodrigo, 569, 614
Rodríguez López, Efrén, 73
Rodríguez Molina, Dr. Félix, 553
Rodríguez Pérez, José, 132
Rodríguez Pérez, Manuel, 576
Rodríguez Pouget, Dr. René, 565
Rodríguez Ravelo, Filiberto, 74
Rodríguez Saludes, Omar, 201
Rodríguez Santana, Carlos, 60
Rodríguez Sardiñas, Orlando "Rossardi," 338
Rodríguez Sigler, Hiram, 491
Rodríguez Vives, Arturo, 135
Rodríguez Zaldívar, Rodolfo, 490
Rodríguez, Albita, 429
Rodríguez, Alfredo, 427
Rodríguez, Angel "Tito," 465
Rodríguez, Antonio Orlando, 351
Rodríguez, Antonio, 576, 577
Rodríguez, Arsenio, 420, 422
Rodríguez, Arturo, 381
Rodríguez, Dagoberto, 201
Rodríguez, Dinorah de Jesús, 414
Rodríguez, Douglas, 315, 316
Rodríguez, Dr. Héctor, 558
Rodríguez, Dr. Ortelio, 563
Rodríguez, Dr. Raoul, 563
Rodríguez, Dr. René F., 565
Rodríguez, Elio, 428
Rodríguez, Elliott, 519
Rodríguez, Ernesto J., 583
Rodríguez, Felix, 130, 131
Rodríguez, Fernando, 281, 300
Rodríguez, Francisco (Frank), 278, 288, 312, 325, 384
Rodríguez, Frank (Ford), 322
Rodríguez, Isidoro, 299
Rodríguez, Jennifer, 460, 461
Rodríguez, Jorge, 505, 508
Rodríguez, José Cipriano, 257
Rodríguez, Juan Alberto, 145
Rodríguez, Laurentino, 491
Rodríguez, Lázaro, 462
Rodríguez, Leonardo, 31, 278, 288, 312, 325, 596, 602, 716, 725, 731, 749, 758
Rodríguez, Lucrecia, 244
Rodríguez, Luis David, 491
Rodríguez, Luis Manuel, 458
Rodríguez, Maggie, 519
Rodríguez, Manuel "Manny," 694
Rodríguez, Marcos "Shakey," 462
Rodríguez, Marcos, 510

Rodríguez, María Teresa, 590
Rodríguez, Mariano, 358, 382
Rodríguez, Mike, 517
Rodríguez, Omar, 315
Rodríguez, Oscar, 679
Rodríguez, Raúl L., 587, 763
Rodríguez, Ray, 270, 515, 517, 679
Rodríguez, Rene, 147, 763
Rodríguez, Silvia, 523
Rodríguez, Teresa, 514
Rodríguez, Torres, Dr. Ramón, 561
Rodríguez, Vicente P., 490, 491, 687
Roig Rodríguez, José, 132
Roig, Vicky, 426
Rojas, Gustavo, 427
Rojas, Jorge, 494
Rojas, José, 459
Rojas, Octavio "Cookie," 444, 445, 452
Rojas, Orlando, 410, 692
Rojas, Rafael, 348, 349, 618
Rojas, Teresa María, 339, 387, 391, 394, 395
Roldán, Dr. Eneida O., 561, 562
Román, Msgr. Agustín, 171, 172, 240, 267, 387, 472, 479, 682, 687
Román, Pedro, 385, 421, 437
Román, Pico, 89
Romani, Salvador, 491
Romañach, Leopoldo, 357, 707
Romañach, Mario, 589
Romero, Carlos, 491
Romeu, Antonio María, 418
Romney, Hervin A. R., 594
Roosevelt, Eleanor, 87, 88
Roque, Cary, 389
Roque, Juan Pablo, 207
Roque, Martha Beatriz, 201
Ros Lethinen, Ileana, 202, 268, 657, 661, 663, 667, 668
Ros, Alberto, 685
Ros, Enrique, 124
Rosa, Pili de la, 387
Rosabal, Sylvia, 516
Rosado, Lillian, 415
Rosales, Maritza, 405
Rosell, Rosendo, 385, 430
Roseñada, José M., 487
Ross, Alvin, 136
Ross, Stephen M., 314
Rossardi, Orlando, 395
Rossenfeld, Humberto, 389
Rostow, W. W., 7
Roth, Jeffrey R., 198
Rovira, Lourdes, 610
Rubio, Al, 28
Rubio, Lydia, 360, 361, 367, 374,

Soler, Dr. Mario, 561
Soler, Frank, 492, 499
Solís, Memé, 426
Solís, Odlanier, 459
Sordo, Juan, 100
Sori Marín, Humberto, 65, 85
Soriano, Rafael, 359, 381
Sorolla, Joaquín, 357
Sorondo, Rudy, 647
Sorzano, José, 661
Sosa Blanco, Jesús, 36
Sosa, Candy, 425
Sosa, Enrique, 578
Soto Pradera, Dr. Emilio, 556
Soto, Eduardo, 680
Soto, Osvaldo, 642
Soto, Titi, 424, 430
Sotolongo, Dr. Rodolfo, 289
South Florida Hispanic Chamber of Commerce, 691
Souto, Haydeé, 295
Souto, Javier, 85, 657, 686
Souto, José "Pepe," 295
Spanish American League Against Discrimination (SALAD), 680
Spear, Laurinda, 594
St. George, Andrew, 40, 41
Stav, Julie, 520
Stein, Leo, 368
Steinberg, Leo, 366
Stepick, Alex, 160, 168
Stevenson, Adlai, 67, 69, 120
Striker, Raúl, 464
Sturgis, Frank, 134
Suárez Esquivel, Eduardo, 180
Suárez, Amancio, 508, 510, 514
Suárez, Aquiles, 661
Suárez, Caridad, 437
Suárez, Charín, 441
Suárez, Cisco, 517
Suárez, Diego, 292, 438, 664
Suárez, Elier, 437
Suárez, Humberto, 430
Suarez, Ignacio, 413
Suárez, José Dionisio, 136
Suárez, José I., 625
Suárez, Karla, 350
Suárez, Laurentino, 625
Suárez, Mayor Xavier, 644, 657
Suárez, Ramón, 404
Suárez, Roberto, 493
Suárez, Rosario "Charín," 441
Suchlicki, Jaime, 618
Sueiro, Hugo, 59, 72
Sunshine, Sara, 523, 524, 525, 535
Suquet, José S., 318
Suris, Oscar, 331

Szapocznik, José, 162, 632
Szulc, Ted, 63
Tabares Fernández, Ofelia, 682
Tabernilla, Gen. Francisco (Silito), 18, 31
Taillacq, Evelio, 389
Tamargo, Agustín, 509
Tamargo, Elena, 374
Tamayo, Juan, 147, 207, 497
Tamayo, Pedro, 429
Tapia Ruano, Alberto, 74
Tarajano, José Ricardo, 584
Tarraza, Juan Bruno, 425, 430
Tartabull, Danny, 454, 455
Tartabull, José, 452, 454
Taylor, General Maxwell, 68, 104
Taylor, Tony, 452
Teck, Bill, 409
Tejera, Michael, 456
Tejera, Nivaria, 341
Terré Morell, Claribel, 350
Terrón, Armando, 437
Thatcher, Margaret, 175, 176
The Atlanta Cuban Club, 692
Thomas, Hugh, 11, 18, 240
Thomas, Jo, 144, 145, 162
Tiant, Luis, 445, 447, 452, 453
Toledo, Mario, 428
Toraño, Carlos, 294
Toraño, Don Santiago, 294
Toraño, Jaime, 294
Toraño, José, 294
Toraño, María Elena, 678
Toraño, Raúl, 515, 523, 524
Tores Llorca, Rubén, 381
Torre, Dr. Angel de la, 560
Torre, Dr. Ralph de la, 328
Torre, José de la, 615
Torre, Rogelio de la, 686, 760
Torrente, Manolo, 437
Torres Mena, Juan, 91
Torres, Arturo G., 316
Torres, Gilberto, 27
Torres, Juan Pablo, 429
Torres, Leyla, 437
Torres, Omar, 392
Torres, Roberto, 423
Torriente, Cristóbal, 445, 447
Torriente, José Elías de la, 133, 135
Tosca, Carlos, 445
Tosquella, Max, 402, 405
Toural, Mercedes, 610
Touzet, René, 424, 430, 436
Trafficante, Santo, 25
Traugh, William, 21, 35, 36, 63, 96, 111, 153, 215, 625, 673, 691
Traurig, Greenberg, 648

Treaster, Joseph, 152, 154
Trejo, Bernardo Viera, 341
Trelles, Tony, 424
Triana, José, 342, 390, 391, 392, 393, 395
Triay, Jorge, 284
Triff, Soren, 349
Trigoura, Jorge, 395
Triple A, 13, 54
Trueba, Fernando, 415
Trujillo, Andrés, 437
Trujillo, Darleen, 437
Trujillo, Domingo J., 613
Trujillo, Rafael, 636
Trujillo, Sebastián, 516
Tucker, Sophie, 32
Tudela, Rev. Miguel Angel, 244, 678, 686
Tunero, Kid, 449, 458
Tuñón, Wilma G., 683
Ugarte, Salvador, 385
Ulibarri, Eduardo, 496
Ulla, Jorge, 234, 407, 541, 543
UN Commission for Human Rights, 236, 241, 243, 244, 247
Unanue, Emil R., 629
Unidades Militares de Ayuda a la Producción (UMAP), 129, 473
Unzueta, Horacio, 149
Unzueta, Silvia, 142, 148, 153, 159, 763
Urdanivia, Daniel, 409
Urías, Roberto, 350
Uréchega, José, 605
Urrutia Lleó, President Manuel, 32, 38, 709, 718
Usátegui, Dr. Lidia, 244
Vailláns, Jorge, 598
Vaillant, Angelo, 423
Valdés Fauli, Dora, 382
Valdés Terán, Juan, 430
Valdés, Alberto, 283
Valdés, Alexis, 518
Valdés, Alfredito, 420
Valdés, Antonio "Quilla," 448
Valdés, Arty, 430, 432
Valdés, Bebo, 415, 427
Valdés, Chucho, 427
Valdés, Eladio, 449
Valdés, Eliseo, 430
Valdés, Elizabeth, 516
Valdés, Elvira, 410
Valdés, Gustavo, 370
Valdés, Jesús (Chuchito), 426
Valdés, Jorge G., 577
Valdés, Joseíto, 423
Valdés, Miguelito, 419, 423

Valdés, Rodrigo, 449
Valdés, Rolando, 423
Valdés, Vicentico, 422
Valdés, Zoe, 348, 352, 369, 370, 382
Valdes-Miranda, Concha, 430
Valdespino, Andrés, 625, 709
Valdespino, Sandy, 452
Valdez Pagés, Pablo, 579
Valerio, Andrés, 382
Valido, Fernando, 449
Valiente, Arnaldo, 428
Valladares, Armando, 219, 222, 236, 240, 241, 242
Valle, Clara María del, 179
Valle, Elaine del, 193
Valle, Espigul del, 430
Valle, Sarvelio del, 464
Vallejo, César, 378
Vallejo, Orlando, 422
Valls Noyes, Julietta, 667
Valls, Felipe, 300
Vals, Jorge, 342
Vance, Cyrus, 137, 140, 150
Varela de la Torre, Amalia, 686
Varela, Beatriz, 621
Varela, Blanca, 437
Varela, Enrique, 429
Varela, Father Félix, 335, 356, 681, 682, 686, 687, 703, 714
Varela, Ileana, 519
Varela, Víctor, 392
Vargas Gómez, Andrés, 139, 222
Vargas, Luis, 130
Varona, Enrique José, 706
Varona, Esperanza B. de, 621
Varona, Frank de, 611
Varona, Lesbia Orta de, 339
Varona, Manuel Antonio de «Tony», 88, 54, 78
Varona, Mario de, 409
Vázquez, Manuel, 687
Vázquez, Walter, 298
Vázquez, Wilfredo, 449
Vega Penichet, Manolo, 640
Vega, Aurelio de la, 435, 630, 707
Vega, Lilliam, 391, 393, 396
Vega, Manuel de la, 535
Vega, Ralph de la, 327
Vega, Ricardo, 370, 411
Vega, Víctor, 489
Vento, Osvaldo "Ovi," 321
Ventura, Robin, 457
Vera, María Teresa, 418
Verdecia, Carlos, 493
Verdeja, Octavio, 605
Verdeja, Sam, 5, 491, 492, 499, 757
Verena, Marisela, 424

Vergara, Reynaldo, 498
Versalles, Zoilo, 452
Veyre, Gabriel, 398
Viamonte, Jr., Manuel, 629
Viamonte, Sr., Dr. Manuel, 551
Viciana, Enrique, 596, 605, 763
Viciedo, Dayan, 457
Victor Manuel, 358
Victoria, Carlos, 343
Vidal Cairo, Sergio, 432, 505
Vidal Larrauri, Tony, 604
Vidal, Antonio, 359
Vidal, Armando, 669
Vidal, Manolo "Manny," 540
Vidaña, Luis H., 676
Viera, Felix Luis, 350
Viera, Ricardo, 615
Vieta Barahona, Dr. Angel, 551, 555
Vila, Camilo, 407
Vila, Ricardo, 508
Vilaboa, Napoleón, 146, 147, 148
Vilar, Alberto, 330, 501, 764
Vilariño, Antonio, 315
Vilariño, Nilda, 315
Vilas, Oscar, 431, 432
Vildóstegui, Matías, 279
Villa, Alvaro de, 341
Villafaña, Frank R., 126
Villalón, José Ramón, 706
Villamañán, Manuel, 308
Villamil, José Antonio, 661
Villar, Arturo, 499
Villaverde, Fernando, 348
Villaverde, Manolo, 387, 389, 521
Villaverde, Miñuca, 348, 407
Villiers, Mercedes de, 339
Villoch, Alexandra, 493
Villota, Isidro, 432
Viña, Fernando, 454
Visiedo, Octavio J., 613
Vispo, Castor, 487
Vitier, Cintio, 340, 359
Vivó Acrivos, Juana (Jennie), 615
Viyella, Julio, 674
Vizcaíno, Father Mario, 676
Walesa, Lech, 175, 176
Walsh, Monsignor Bryan, 257, 478
Walter, Jorge, 298
Washington, Denzel, 412
Wasp Network, 207
Watson, Jack, 150, 151
Wax, Stanley, 589
Webster, Paul, 206
Weiner, Judith, 371
Wet Foot Dry Foot, 188
Wheeler, Kent, 152
White, Dr. Edward C., 557

White, José, 417
White, Oscar, 683
Wilhelm II, Kaiser, 417
Willard, Jess, 448
Williams, Robin, 413
Winfrey, Oprah, 512
Winters, Jerry, 415
Wittels, Garrett, 457
Wladavsky Berger, Dr. Irving, 585
Wood, General Leonard, 551
Yánez, Dr. Frank, 564
Yánez, Pedro, 343
Yarrow, Joann María, 394
Ydígoras, Manuel, 60
Yedra, Velia, 437
Young, Andrew, 328
Young, Arthur, 604
Zabala, Félix "Tuto," 449
Zack, Steve, 645
Zaizarbitoria, Juan, 431
Zaldívar Zaydín, Miguel, 620
Zaldívar, Gilberto, 392
Zaldívar, Gladys, 341
Zaldívar, Juan Carlos, 414
Zamora Munné, Juan Clemente, 621
Zamora, Antonio, 641
Zamora, Oscar, 454
Zapata Tamayo, Orlando, 205, 223, 230, 724, 748
Zayas Bazán, Eduardo, 764
Zayas Bazán, Lourdes, 173
Zayas, Alfredo, 636
Zelaya, President Manuel, 666
Zenteno Anaya, Joaquín, 131
Zervigon, brothers, 423
Zimmerman, Bertha, 437
Zubi, Joe, 529
Zubimendi, Justo, 431, 432
Zubizarreta, Tere, 523, 528
Zuñiga Rey, Luis, 242
Zuñiga, Mario, 67
Zúñiga, Norma, 387